connect

SECOND EDITION

connect
College Reading

Ivan G. Dole · Leslie Taggart
North Lake College

WADSWORTH
CENGAGE Learning

Australia · Brazil · Japan · Korea · Mexico · Singapore · Spain · United Kingdom · United States

WADSWORTH
CENGAGE Learning

**Connect: College Reading,
Second Edition**
Ivan G. Dole, Leslie Taggart

Director: Annie Todd

Executive Editor: Shani Fisher

Development Editor: Marita Sermolins

Assistant Editor: Kayti Purkiss

Editorial Assistant: Erin Nixon

Media Editor: Christian Biagetti

Brand Manager: Lydia Lestar

Senior Content Project Manager:
Corinna Dibble

Art Director: Faith Brosnan

Manufacturing Planner: Betsy Donaghey

Rights Acquisition Specialist:
Alexandra Ricciardi

Production Service: Thistle Hill Publishing
Services

Composition: Cenveo Publisher
Services/Nesbitt Graphics, Inc.

Text Designer: Alisha Webber

Cover Designer: Dare Porter

Cover Image: iStockphoto.com/bubaone

For product information and technology assistance, contact us at
Cengage Learning Customer & Sales Support, 1-800-354-9706

For permission to use material from this text or product,
submit all requests online at **www.cengage.com/permissions**.
Further permissions questions can be emailed to
permissionrequest@cengage.com.

Library of Congress Control Number: 2012945950

ISBN-13: 978-1-133-60267-5
ISBN-10: 1-133-60267-3

Wadsworth
20 Channel Center Street
Boston, MA 02210
USA

Cengage Learning is a leading provider of customized learning solutions with office locations around the globe, including Singapore, the United Kingdom, Australia, Mexico, Brazil, and Japan. Locate your local office at **international.cengage.com/region**

Cengage Learning products are represented in Canada by Nelson Education, Ltd.

For your course and learning solutions, visit **www.cengage.com**.

Purchase any of our products at your local college store or at our preferred online store **www.cengagebrain.com**.

Instructors: Please visit **login.cengage.com** and log in to access instructor-specific resources.

Printed in the United States of America
1 2 3 4 5 6 7 16 15 14 13 12

Pictorial Press Ltd/Alamy

Jack Hollingsworth/Blend Images/Jupiter Images

3   Developing Your Vocabulary   113

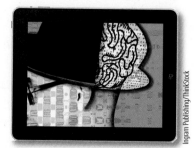

PART 2 Reading to Understand

4 Finding the Main Idea   169

James R. Martin/Shutterstock

5 Identifying Implied Main Ideas   227

Photograph by Corey Geissler

6 Recognizing Patterns of Organization   275

7 Reading and Taking Notes on Textbook Chapters   337

Shutterstock.com

Ronfromyork, Dreamstime LLC

PART 3 Reading Critically

8 Distinguishing Fact and Opinion   405

Julien Tromeur/Shutterstock.com

9 Making Inferences   451

Daniel Smith/Warner Bros/Everett Collection

10 Analyzing the Author's Tone   499

11 Evaluating the Author's Reasoning and Evidence   549

CASEBOOK   Applying Your Critical Reading Skills to Arguments   601

Red Circle Images/Fotosearch

PART 4   Resource Guides

A   A Guide to Reading Visuals   624

B   A Guide to Reading Novels   645

C   A Guide to Taking Tests   654

Connect: College Reading is the second book of a reading series designed to motivate students to read by helping them focus on their existing strengths and prior knowledge, while at the same time sharing with them new reading strategies to increase their opportunities for reading success in college. Like the other two books in the series, *Activate: College Reading* and *Engage: College Reading*, *Connect* teaches methodical approaches to common reading tasks and then provides plenty of practice to help students internalize them. All three books go beyond the typical multiple-choice format to check reading comprehension: students are asked to explain each answer with evidence from the selection. This simple step has profound implications for the way students learn to think about their reading.

The three books address three different levels of college readers and take different approaches to organizing chapters and reading selections. All three books, however, start where students start:w with a love of media.

activate *Activate* is for students at the 6th to 9th grade reading levels. *Activate*'s chapters take a one-skill-at-a-time approach. Then at the end of every major part of the book, application readings give students the opportunity to draw on all those skills in holistic reading applications from academic and real-world readings. *Activate* also includes a dedicated section of themed readings that can be used for even more practice.

connect *Connect* is for students at the 9th to 12th grade reading levels. *Connect* has a short chapter-opening reading and two chapter-end readings that are all thematically linked.

engage *Engage* is for students at the 10th to 12th grade reading levels. The chapter-opening and two chapter-end readings in *Engage* take an across-the-disciplines approach.

connect to Updates in the Second Edition

Major revisions to the second edition have focused on streamlining the approach to finding the main idea, adding a new chapter on inference, and providing more extensive vocabulary development.

▶ **NEW! Streamlined approach to finding the main idea.** *Connect* gives students an "APP" to navigate text structure. *A* stands for about (topic); the first *P* stands for point (main idea); and the second *P* stands for proof (supporting details). Just as we use apps on our smart phones to access information, readers can use their APP to comprehend the main idea and details of a reading selection.

What is the reading about?	>	**The topic.**
What is the author's point about the topic?	>	**The main idea.**
What is the proof for the main idea?	>	**The supporting details.**

▶ **NEW! A new chapter on inference.** Chapter 9, "Making Inferences," has students start off by making inferences about a series of images that are increasingly driven by a point of view, which allows them to understand how a creator's intentions affect their own interpretation of a cartoon or photo. Students then practice paying close attention to details in sentences in order to keep their inferences true to the author's intentions. Next, students learn about the importance of drawing on different kinds of prior knowledge as they read. Finally, inference making is shown within the context of the reading process, as a reader makes tentative inferences while reading and then discards or accepts them sentence by sentence. Excerpts from popular novels, poems, and nonfiction works keep the reading varied and interesting as students make this process more conscious and deliberate.

▶ **NEW! More extensive vocabulary development grounded in current research.** In addition to including the unique marginal vocabulary clues that accompanied the major readings in the first edition of *Connect*, the

---

Critical Thinking Level 6 Create

Imagine a world where no one is ever hungry, cold, or homeless. Think about yo would you see, hear, and feel?

_____

_____

Vocabulary in New Contexts

Review the vocabulary words in the margins of the reading selection and then compl activities.

EASY Note Cards

Make a note card for each of the vocabulary words that you did not know in the side, write the word. On the other side, divide the card into quarters and label ther Add a word or phrase in each area so that you wind up with an example sentence synonym, and, finally, a definition that shows you have figured out the meaning o your logic. Remember that an antonym or synonym may have appeared in the read

Relationships Between Words

Circle *yes* or *no* to answer the question. Then explain your answer.

1. If you were to implement more charitable activities and decrease your consumptio be considered a kinder person?

Yes No

Why or why not? _____

2. Do football coaches tend to distinguish between athletes who are recipients of Ol medals and athletes who have more meager talents?

Yes No

Why or why not? _____

3. Is a love affair better when both people in it are mutual recipients of the other's a

Yes No

Why or why not? _____

4. Is a sustainable future for our planet dependent only on biogas?

Yes No

Why or why not? _____

Language in Your Life

Write short answers to each question. Look at the vocabulary words closely before you answer.

1. Name one area of your life in which you want to increase (or decrease) consumption.

_____

2. Name one organization in your area that is charitable. _____

_____

3. Name one person with whom you have a mutually beneficial relationship. _____

_____

4. Name one person who has been a recipient of your love. _____

_____

5. Name one way you can distinguish friend from foe. _____

_____

Language in Use

Select the best word to complete the meaning of each sentence.

| biogas | charitable | consumption | distinguished | implement |
| meager | mutually | recipient | sustainable | |

1. Aside from a few superrich people like Bill Gates, richer Americans are less _____ than poor Americans.

2. A study conducted in 2001 _____ the donations of two groups. Americans whose incomes were more than $75,000 a year gave away, on average, 2.7% of their incomes. Americans with incomes less than $25,000 gave away 4.2% of theirs.

3. And when researchers in 2007 looked at how wealthier people _____ their charitable plans, they found they tended to give not to poor people, but to organizations they have connections with, such as the colleges they attended or the ballet or theater they go to.

4. A 2010 study found that lower-income people were more generous to and trusting of the _____ of charity, while upper-income people had _____ empathy for them.

5. Upper-income people may not be as generous because they can't imagine needing to be _____ supportive (since they have what they need already).

6. In the 2010 study, higher-income people's lack of interest in giving was not _____ once they were instructed to imagine being poor themselves.

See pages 214–215 for an example of these activities.

vocabulary practice and transfer activities have now been expanded after each of the 22 chapter-end readings, with Vocabulary in New Contexts including four different types of activities:

1. **"EASY Note Cards"** activities ask students to make note cards for vocabulary words according to the system presented in Chapter 3.
2. **"Relationships Between Words"** are sentences that include two or more vocabulary words; students have to decide if the situation in each sentence makes sense, and explain their answers.
3. **"Language in Your Life"** activities consist of brief statements in which students relate a vocabulary word to something in their own experience.
4. **"Language in Use"** activities are fill-in-the-blank sentences all related to one topic, and students are asked to insert the appropriate vocabulary words.

connect College Reading to
Students' Media Experiences

Students may not bring many formal reading strategies with them to the college reading classroom, but they do bring a wealth of life experience. And if students haven't had certain experiences themselves, they have probably lived them vicariously through the media. Because many students have enjoyed using multimedia such as television, movies, and the Internet more than they have print materials, *Connect: College Reading* draws on these experiences to help students learn reading strategies and stay engaged in reading.

► **Viewing media is linked to the reading process.** Chapter 1 shows students how they use a "before, during, and after" process when watching a television program (or movie) and then demonstrates how to apply the same process to reading.

► **REVISED! Videos bolster prior knowledge.** For readings at the beginning and end of each chapter, students can view a video on a closely related topic. They can then approach the reading with this prior knowledge, increasing the likelihood that they will comprehend the reading. In this edition, videos can be viewed by scanning the QR code on the page with a smart phone or online at the Reading CourseMate for *Connect: College Reading,* accessed via **CengageBrain.com.**

5. ⊟ **Scan to Connect!** Use your smart phone to scan this code to watch a video. (See the inside front cover for more information on how to use this.) Think about the messages in the video. Are they good examples of the future vision that Covey discusses in paragraphs 2 and 3 of "The Passion of Vision"? Why or why not?

See page 172 for an example of a QR code; the inside front cover explains how to use QR codes.

▶ **Audio makes reading more understandable.** Two kinds of audio files are available on the Reading CourseMate for *Connect: College Reading*. First, Read and Talk readings are read aloud so that students can hear the words as well as read them. Second, vocabulary words (printed in purple in the text) from Read and Talk readings and the chapter-ending readings are accompanied by a spoken audio file online. These audio files benefit ESL students and students who have auditory preferences, but they can also be used by all students who want to anchor vocabulary words in their memories.

❝ One of the reasons we choose this text is for the combination of using technology and how it integrates and involves students in the text. It's a unique approach for a reading textbook. ❞

—Cathy Hall, Indiana
University Northwest

connect College Reading and Critical Thinking

A byword of the Dole/Taggart reading series is critical thinking. Reading is only the beginning point of understanding and creating knowledge: students also need to think about authors' ideas, discover their own ideas, hear other students' ideas, and explain their responses to ideas. Then they will be able to participate fully in their college courses, make good decisions in their personal lives, and excel at work.

▶ **Critical thinking is a learning process.** Critical thinking is introduced in Chapter 2 and emphasized in every chapter. Chapter 2 teaches students to ask six levels of questions (the revised Bloom's taxonomy) as a scaffold to understand reading selections more deeply.

Level 6 **Create**	You use the information to create something new or you draw conclusions. "What other explanations or solutions are there?"
Level 5 **Evaluate**	You decide what value the information has or make choices based on it. "What factors should I consider to decide whether these ideas are worthwhile?"
Level 4 **Analyze**	You understand the parts and how they relate to one another. "How do the parts or sections fit together to make up the whole?"
Level 3 **Apply**	You can use the information in a new situation or solve problems with it. "How can I apply this knowledge or procedure to produce a certain result?"
Level 2 **Understand**	You understand the information and can explain it to someone else. "How can I retell this using my own words?"
Level 1 **Remember**	You can recall and repeat basic information. "Who? What? When? Where? How? Why?"

The Critical Thinking Questions are my favorite part of the text—certainly not the students'! I am able to quickly identify the students who are struggling, and what skills they are missing. Once the students understand the importance of these questions and being able to think critically, their understanding grows tremendously. 99

—Michelle Van de Sande, Arapahoe Community College

▶ **Six levels of questions are asked after every end-of-chapter reading.** Students are exposed to a variety of verbs so they learn to link particular verbs with particular types of thinking. These questions prepare students for essay exams in other courses that invariably ask these kinds of questions.

▶ **Students need to explain their thinking in writing.** The "Why?" question is asked after every multiple-choice comprehension question in the book. After they have selected an answer, students need to go back into the reading and find information to support their answer. By doing so, students practice analysis and learn to provide evidence for their ideas, a skill they will use in every college course. Students' answers can also provide instructors with valuable feedback about what students are noticing or ignoring as they read.

_____ **4.** Which of the following statements is true about paragraph 5?

   a. There are no supporting details.

   b. There are only supporting details.

   c. Every sentence except the first one is a supporting detail.

   d. Every sentence except the last one is a supporting detail.

Why? What information in the selection leads you to give that answer? _____

_____

_____

▶**Vocabulary in New Contexts**

Review the vocabulary words in the margins of the reading selection and then complete the following activities.

EASY Note Cards

Make a note card for each of the vocabulary words that you did not know in the reading. On one side, write the word. On the other side, divide the card into quarters and label them E, A, S, and Y. Add a word or phrase in each area so that you wind up with an example sentence, an antonym, a synonym, and, finally, a definition that shows you have figured out the meaning of the word with ur logic. Remember that an antonym or synonym may have appeared in the reading.

Relationships Between Words

Circle *yes* or *no* to answer the question. Then explain your answer.

1. If you were to **implement** more **charitable** activities and decrease your **consumption**, would you be considered a kinder person?
   Yes   No
   Why or why not? _____

2. Do football coaches tend to **distinguish** between athletes who are **recipients** of Olympic gold medals and athletes who have more **meager** talents?
   Yes   No
   Why or why not? _____

3. Is a love affair better when both people in it are **mutual recipients** of the other's affections?
   Yes   No
   Why or why not? _____

4. Is a **sustainable** future for our planet dependent only on **biogas**?
   Yes   No
   Why or why not? _____

▶ **NEW! Critical thinking underlies vocabulary questions.** Instead of providing students with a list of vocabulary words and definitions before a reading, *Connect* points to context clues and word part clues during reading so students can figure out the meanings of words. (See the margin of page 90 for an example.) This critical thinking process is true to how experienced readers figure out word meanings on the fly. New to this edition, "Relationships Between Words" questions require students to go through a process of remembering, understanding, applying, analyzing, and evaluating. After students figure out word meanings, they are asked to respond to items that link two or more new words in a relationship. (See page 97 for an example.)

connect College Reading with Students' Current Interests

By acknowledging and respecting students' current interests, *Connect* allows them to divorce content from process. After they learn the process of active reading, *Connect* changes the content to show them the many interesting ideas and experiences that more academic sources reveal.

▶ **REVISED! Readings are included on topics that students like to talk about:** their future; recent movies (based on books, of course!); inspiring figures like Oscar Pistorius and David Blaine; freedom of speech as it relates to music; fashion; health and fitness; pirates; the environment; Facebook; and how media affects body image.

▶ **REVISED! Numerous excerpts from college textbooks and other academically inclined sources are featured,** on topics as varied as poverty, food, test-taking strategies, relationships, communication, money, setting and achieving goals, and hundreds of other topics relevant to academic and everyday life.

▶ **REVISED! "Prep Readings" have become "Read and Talk"** in order to emphasize their purpose. These highly engaging readings are meant to make students feel comfortable reading and talking about their reading.

> *" This is one of my favorite parts of the Connect: College Reading text...the variety of academic content text selections here is incredible...just difficult enough and just accessible enough that students have to think about how to make sense of the selected exercise text, but not so difficult that they are never able to make connections with the text. "*
>
> —Patti Smith, Jones County Jr. College

connect College Reading with Cultural Literacy

Connect helps students build cultural literacy. Readings and paragraph-length examples introduce students to a wide range of ideas, disciplines, and current events. Many are excerpted from college textbooks from across the curriculum, including history, psychology, biology, finance, American government, sociology, mathematics, anthropology, art history, and business.

▶ **REVISED! Current events are featured.** Some of the longer readings discuss important current issues, such as the effects of globalization, the obesity epidemic, the influence of mass media, perspectives on global warming, virtual learning and socializing, and the categories of speech protected by the first amendment.

▶ ***Common Knowledge* boxes provide prior knowledge.** Where needed, a few common knowledge terms are defined for students so that they can understand the reading; they also increase cultural literacy before students reach their first-year courses.

> *" I am so happy to see the addition of various selections from other disciplines. These help students stay engaged and provide variety for our courses. The difficulty level is appropriate for our students. This is realistic to what they will encounter in courses, so they need to understand the material from that level. "*
>
> —Michelle Van de Sande, Arapahoe Community College

connect Students' Reading, Writing, and Speaking Vocabularies

Connect provides powerful vocabulary instruction for academic and life success. Students will transfer their expanding reading vocabulary over to their writing vocabulary, and the Reading CourseMate aids in the transfer of students' reading vocabulary to their speaking and listening vocabularies.

▶ **REVISED! Chapter 3 specifically focuses on vocabulary development.** It includes detailed coverage of context clues, EASY note cards, word parts, and denotation and connotation. Readings at the end of every chapter extend this lesson by including marginal vocabulary prompts that draw students' attention while reading to specific clues to understanding word meanings.

▶ **NEW! "Vocabulary in New Contexts" transfer vocabulary knowledge.** After every chapter-end reading these question sets of four different types of activities help students transfer vocabulary knowledge from the context in which they learned them to new contexts.

connect Students' Reading Skills within a Holistic Framework

In *Connect*, skills are presented individually and then integrated through practice. Each chapter includes targeted activities ("Interactions") and ends with several features that help students review and apply the main points of the chapter.

▶ **NEW! "Connect Your Skills" activities** ask students to apply all the major skills they have learned in the chapter as they read either several short selections or a longer selection.

▶ **REVISED! "Chapter Summary" activities** prompt students to remember the main points of the chapter by offering them a Cornell note-taking page with the main ideas filled in. Students must provide the major supporting details of the chapter. The result is a reading guide for the chapter skill that the student can use as a review later in the course or whenever it's needed.

▶ **Two end-of-chapter readings—22 in all— include a full reading process.** Each starts with pre-reading questions and a reminder to

86   **CHAPTER 2**   Asking Questions

Chapter Summary Activity

This chapter has discussed how asking questions can help you read and think more effectively. Fill in the Reading Guide to Asking Questions below by completing each main idea on the left with specific supporting details from the chapter on the right. You can use this guide later as you work on other reading assignments.

Reading Guide to Asking Questions

Complete this idea with...	Information from Chapter 2.
How titles can be used to aid comprehension	1. _____
Two benefits of asking questions	2. _____
	3. _____
What you do after you ask questions	4. _____
Two things to do while reading after asking questions	5. _____
	6. _____
How to avoid overmarking	7. _____
Six levels of critical thinking, organized from easiest to most difficult	8. _____
	9. _____
	10. _____
	11. _____
	12. _____
	13. _____

66 *Learning vocabulary in context is an important skill for students. This skill will help students to increase vocabulary and enhance their ability to use context to unlock word meanings. I like that students have an opportunity to immediately practice, using the newly learned words. More importantly, I like the use of the audio at the book's Web site. This procedure will greatly improve students' pronunciation of words, especially crucial for foreign-language students.* 99

—Helen Carr, San Antonio College

66 *The title for this textbook is well chosen. At key points in each lesson, students are encouraged to make connections between a particular skill being taught, readings that model the skill being used in a particular context, and their own experiences. I particularly like that after a reading, students are encouraged to take away something from the lesson and carry it into their own lives.* 99

—Jennifer Royal, Santa Rosa Junior College

annotate. While students are reading, marginal questions help them focus on important points, and vocabulary clues are pointed out. Ten multiple-choice comprehension questions that include all the major reading skills—main idea; supporting details; author's purpose; relationships; and fact, opinion, and inference—follow. Six critical thinking questions are then provided.

Chapter-by-Chapter Updates

Since the first edition, students and instructors have helped to shape this book by sharing with us their strategies, insights, and suggestions. Here are some of the major changes you will see in this edition.

REVISED! Plan for Success. Acting as a course preview to prepare students for the expectations of college courses, this brief guide introduces students to reading a syllabus; setting goals; and managing their time, including sample monthly, weekly, and daily calendars; and the importance of participating and being organized for class.

Chapter 1 Connecting to the Reading Process

▶ **NEW Interaction 1–1** What Do You Want to Do When You Get Out of School?

▶ **NEW Figures 1.1** (Average Earnings Based Upon Level of Education) **and 1.2** (Education Pays) to help students make the connection to being motivated to further and complete their educations to pursue careers

▶ **REVISED Interaction 1–2** Find Out the Income Potential of a Career You Are Interested In

▶ **REVISED Interaction 1–3** Fine-tune Your Present and Future by including a Facebook posting and asking students to make a social commitment to help them stay motivated

▶ **NEW Read and Talk** The Power of Three Little Words

▶ **REVISED "Reading Is an Interaction" section** to simply address the basic ways you can interact with a reading; includes a NEW Interaction 1–4 What Do You Do When You View?

▶ **NEW Interaction 1–6** Predict Purposes with Images and Text

▶ **REVISED Interaction 1–7** Purposes in Reading

▶ **NEW "More than One Purpose" section** to address the fact that authors can have multiple purposes in writing

▶ **REVISED discussion of prior knowledge** now includes several questions to help activate one's mind to make connections

▶ **REVISED Interaction 1–8** Connect to Your Prior Knowledge to include topics on which to discuss prior knowledge

▶ **REVISED Interaction 1–9** Practice the Reading Process has students go through the entire reading process as the chapter demonstrates on a reading of their choosing

▶ **REVISED Interaction 1–10** Common Knowledge now has students ask their other course instructors what they believe is common knowledge for that field.

Chapter 2 Asking Questions

▶ **NEW Read and Talk** Oscar Pistorius Has a Huge Carbon Footprint

▶ **NEW Interaction 2–2** Turn a Title or Heading into the Best Question

▶ **NEW Interaction 2–6** Reasons Why You Decided to Attend School

▶ **NEW section** "What Level of Critical Thinking Are You Being Asked to Use?" helps students recognize critical thinking verbs in test questions and ensure their answer demonstrates the appropriate level of thinking

- ▶ **NEW Interaction 2–9** Identify the Bloom's Taxonomy Level

- ▶ **NEW Reading 2–1** David Blaine's Feats of Will

- ▶ **NEW Reading 2–2** What Is Motivation?

Chapter 3 ▶ Developing Your Vocabulary

- ▶ **REVISED** The VAN strategy has been replaced by NEW coverage of EASY note cards to align note cards with the EASY context clues.

- ▶ **REVISED** "Word Parts" section includes more information about each word part and how to create word part note cards

- ▶ **NEW Interaction 3–9** Using Common Latin Roots to Develop Your Vocabulary

- ▶ **NEW Interaction 3–10** Using Common Greek Roots to Develop Your Vocabulary

- ▶ **NEW Interaction 3–11** Use Prefixes to Develop Your Vocabulary

- ▶ **NEW Interaction 3–12** Using Suffixes to Develop Your Vocabulary

- ▶ **NEW** expanded discussion of connotation

- ▶ **NEW Interaction 3–13** Understanding Connotation

- ▶ **NEW Reading 3–2** Alex and Me

Chapter 4 ▶ Finding the Main Idea

- ▶ **NEW** title emphasizes finding main ideas

- ▶ **REVISED discussion** for finding the main idea now focuses on the three comprehension questions: What is the reading is about? What is the author's point about the topic? What is the author's proof of the main idea?

- ▶ **REVISED Interaction 4–1** Identify the Topic of a Paragraph

- ▶ **NEW Interaction 4–2** Identify More Topics of a Paragraph

- ▶ **NEW** sample analysis of figuring out an author's point about a topic

- ▶ **REVISED Interaction 4–3** Find the Main Idea with new paragraph selections

- ▶ **REVISED Interaction 4–4** Find More Main Ideas of a Paragraph

- ▶ **REVISED Interaction 4–5** Find the Topic Sentence

- ▶ **REVISED Interaction 4–6** Find the Supporting Details

- ▶ **REVISED Interaction 4–7** Identify the Minor Details with a new reading selection

- ▶ **REVISED Interaction 4–8** Identify the Supporting Details of Paragraphs

▶ **NEW** coverage of thesis statements and Interaction 4–9 Find the Thesis Statement of a Group of Paragraphs

▶ **NEW Reading 4–1** Bringing an End to World Hunger Through Unimaginable Blessings

Chapter 5 Identifying Implied Main Ideas

▶ **NEW** placement directly after Chapter 4 addresses instructors' desires to teach implied main idea directly after main idea

▶ **NEW Read and Talk** What Is a Food? What's in a Meal?

▶ **REVISED** strategy to identify the implied main idea by focusing on the three comprehension questions covered in Chapter 4

▶ **REVISED Interaction 5–3** Decide Whether a Topic Sentence Covers the Right Amount of Information

▶ **REVISED Interaction 5–5** Identify the Implied Main Ideas of Paragraphs with new reading selections

▶ **REVISED Interaction 5–6** Identify the Implied Main Idea of a Longer Passage with new reading selections

Chapter 6 Recognizing Patterns of Organization

▶ **NEW** placement as Chapter 6

▶ **NEW Read and Talk** To Copy or NOT to Copy…

▶ **NEW** narration example paragraph

▶ **REVISED Interaction 6–6** Apply Your Knowledge of Patterns with new reading selections

▶ **REVISED Interaction 6–8** Recognize Words That Indicate Sameness with new sample sentences

▶ **NEW** chart of signal words and their associated organizational patterns

▶ **NEW Reading 6–2** Thou Shalt Covet What Thy Neighbor Covets

Chapter 7 Reading and Taking Notes on Textbook Chapters

▶ **NEW Read and Talk** Crow's-Feet and Smiles Sweet

▶ **REVISED** section on Applying the Reading Process to Textbooks to more thoroughly discuss skills learned in Chapters 1 to 6

▶ **REVISED Interaction 7–1** Refine Your Reading Strategy with a new reading selection

- ► **REVISED Interaction 7–2** Annotate Paragraphs with additional paragraphs for practice

- ► **NEW Interaction 7–3** Match Organization with a Visual Map and Interaction 7–4, Organize with Visual Maps

- ► **NEW section** "Use Cornell Notes to Record Ideas" accompanied by NEW Interaction 7–5, Apply Cornell Note Taking

Chapter 8 **Distinguishing Fact and Opinion**

- ► **NEW Read and Talk** Jammie Thomas-Rasset: The Download Martyr

- ► **REVISED Table 8.1** Highest Grossing Films Adjusted for Inflation, as of April 2012

- ► **REVISED Interaction 8–1** Identify Information That Can Be Verified

- ► **REVISED Interaction 8–2** Compare Facts and Opinions

- ► **REVISED** "Words That Can Express Opinions" with discussion of context of a word

- ► **NEW Interaction 8–5** Use Adjectives with an Image

- ► **REVISED** section on Source of Information

- ► **REVISED Interaction 8–9** Identify the Credibility of Sources with New Sentences

- ► **NEW Reading 8–2** You Are Being Lied to about Pirates

Chapter 9 **Making Inferences**

- ► **NEW** chapter to this edition

Chapter 11 **Evaluating the Author's Reasoning and Evidence**

- ► **NEW Read and Talk** Freedom of Speech in Rap Music

- ► **NEW** example paragraph and analysis of a persuasive paragraph

- ► **NEW Interaction 11–3** Annotate Issues, Claims, and Evidences

- ► **NEW** section on credibility accompanied by NEW Interaction 11–7, Evaluate Credibility

- ► **NEW** examples for expert authority, statistics, and personal experiences

- ► **REVISED Interaction 11–9** Determining Claim, Plus the Relevance and Strength of the Evidence with new reading selections

- ► **NEW Reading 11–1** What Is Free Speech?

- ► **NEW Reading 11–2** Fifth Period Is Facebook

Resource Guides

▶ **NEW Resource Guide A** A Guide to Reading Visuals

▶ **REVISED Resource Guide B** A Guide to Reading Novels

▶ **NEW Resource Guide C** A Guide to Taking Tests

connect to Supplements for Students

Reading ⚡CourseMate

Cengage Learning's Reading CourseMate brings course concepts to life with interactive learning, study, and exam preparation tools that support the printed textbook. Watch student comprehension soar as your class works with the printed textbook and the textbook-specific website. Reading CourseMate goes beyond the book to deliver what you need!

Reading CourseMate includes:

▶ An interactive eBook

▶ Interactive teaching and learning tools, including
  - Quizzes
  - Flashcards
  - Videos
  - Additional Practice Readings accompanied by Comprehension and Vocabulary Quizzes

▶ Engagement Tracker, a first-of-its-kind tool that monitors student engagement in the course.

Tailored for *Connect: College Reading*, Reading CourseMate also provides audio versions of "Read and Talk" readings with embedded videos on topics pertinent to the readings included in *Connect*. The videos give students the prior knowledge they might be lacking and increase their cultural literacy. Look for this icon 🖥 in the text, which denotes resources available within CourseMate, and access them via **login.cengage.com**.

Aplia Developmental Reading

Aplia Developmental Reading, an online reading and learning solution, uses compelling material, interactive assignments, and detailed explanations to give students the structure and motivation to become better readers. With Aplia, students practice indentifying main points and supporting details, honing critical thinking skills, reviewing vocabulary, and improving comprehension.

Each chapter assignment begins with an engagement page that features an interactive multimedia application to spark students' interest. The engagement

❝ *This text is so loaded with reading selections and work, and when combined with APLIA, it truly can change how students read and think about what they are reading.* ❞

—Julie Jackson-Coe, Genesee Community College

page also includes a quote, introduction to the chapter, and comprehension questions that correspond to the multimedia feature.

Core concepts cover the main objectives of the textbook, such as strategies to increase a student's reading comprehension, surveying and identifying the purpose, main idea and supporting details of a reading, and identifying word parts such as suffixes and prefixes. The material uses multiple choice, check box, scenario, identification, and comprehension questions.

Compelling readings provide questions of varying difficulty with detailed explanations that let students try a problem again if they get it wrong the first time. Students can also interact with the text by using built-in tools that allow them to annotate, underline, and highlight.

The in-text vocabulary review uses ten new and challenging words taken from the readings and reviews. The page also includes review of the synonyms and antonyms of each vocabulary word.

To learn more about Aplia Developmental Reading, visit www.aplia.com/devreading.

> *Aplia adds another dimension to the course, reinforces the material, and forces them to interact with university facilities (computer labs, reading lab) which integrates them into the campus. Aplia's tech support is great!*
>
> —Cathy Hall, Indiana University Northwest

connect to Supplements for Instructors

Instructor's Manual and Test Bank

Revised by Julie Jackson-Coe of Genesee Community College, this three-hole punched and perforated Instructor's Manual includes chapter summaries and various activities designed especially for every chapter of the book, offering instructors a wealth of resources from which to choose, tutoring suggestions, lab activities and discussion, and multiple test banks for each chapter.

PowerPoint Presentations

Instructor PowerPoint presentations created by Sharon Huston cover textbook topics and include interactive classroom activities. These lecture slides supply instructors with interesting ways to enrich learning and spark student interest. To access these slides and an electronic version of the Instructor's Manual with Test Bank, visit the Instructor's Companion Site at **http://login.cengage.com**.

Acknowledgments

All textbooks represent the creativity and effort of many people working together, and this one is no exception. The outstanding team at Cengage has been a pleasure to work with, especially Shani Fisher, our new sponsoring editor; Marita Sermolins, who has now been our development editor for two editions;

and Annie Todd, Director of Developmental English. Thanks also go to Katie Purkiss, Assistant Editor, who asked us many good questions, and Corinna Dibble, Content Project Manager, who swiftly and ably directed the production process.

We also enjoyed collaborating on paper with the following instructors from around the country who reviewed *Connect* and helped direct its evolution. Thank you for your careful reading, your critiques, and your honesty. We appreciate your time and your thoughts.

Margaret Bartelt, Owens Community College

Helen Carr, San Antonio College

Alicia Dominguez, St. Philip's College

Elizabeth Eggert, Genesee Community College

Janet Flores, St. Philip's College

Cathy Hall, Indiana University Northwest

Mary Harper, Broward College

Julie Jackson-Coe, Genesee Community College

Mary S. Leonard, Wytheville Community College

Deborah Maness, Wake Technical Community College

Michelle McMillen, Mid-South Community College

Laura Meyers, Hawkeye Community College

Kim Moultney, Arapahoe Community College

Yvette Myrick, Community College of Baltimore County

Brian Reeves, Lone Star College-Tomball

Helen Roland, Miami Dade College

Jennifer Royal, Santa Rosa Junior College

Valerie Schantz, Delaware County Community College

Patti Smith, Jones County Jr. College

Barbara Sussman, Miami Dade College

Michelle Van de Sande, Arapahoe Community College

In addition, Leslie would like to thank Ivan for his dedication to this project and for getting our collaboration off to a proper start by intoning those famous words of Albert-Laszlo Barabasi: "Everything is connected to everything else." Ivan's creative ideas and connection with his students have been constant sources of inspiration. I'd also like to thank Chuck, Sara, Harmony, and Phoenix—you are even more important to me than reading is! Ha!

Ivan would like to thank Leslie for another successful collaboration (is this really the second edition already?). I enjoy working with you, and I look forward to many more successful projects. Know that I respect and appreciate you, your ideas, work ethic, and creativity. To my family: that didn't hurt too much, did it? Thank you for giving me space and for eagerly awaiting our time together. I love you all: Deneé, Bella, Lilli, and baby Gia. Let's play!

ABOUT THE AUTHORS

Ivan G. Dole

North Lake Community College Developmental Reading Professor and Coordinator

Ivan G. Dole began teaching with the Dallas County Community College District in 1999 while earning an M.A. in Linguistics from the University of North Texas in Denton. Ivan has taught all levels of developmental reading, developmental writing, and English as a Second Language, including two years in South Korea. The desire to write a textbook arose very early in Ivan's career, when he realized that students needed help transferring the concepts they learned in their reading texts to the reading they have to do in other contexts. In addition, Ivan's involvement with an award-winning, innovative, multidisciplinary faculty team that focused on effective teaching and learning across academic disciplines helped him clarify the repertoire the developmental reading student needs for a strong academic foundation. Concepts such as collaborative learning, critical thinking, scaffolding of knowledge, making connections across academic disciplines, solidifying learning outcomes, and increasing student retention are all part of Ivan's andragogy.

Leslie Taggart

Leslie Taggart has developed more than one hundred college textbooks in the disciplines of college reading, developmental writing, first-year composition, linguistics, literature, and study skills, mostly as a freelance editor. She has contributed chapters to college textbooks in the fields of English as a Second Language, literature, and rhetoric, co-authored an edition of a developmental writing text, and revised several texts, including two handbooks and a five-book composition series. Leslie has taught English as a second language at the high school level, and English as a foreign language at an agricultural college in China. She has been a volunteer literacy tutor and spent two years tutoring in the Vermont Refugee Resettlement Program. Leslie earned the Master Practitioner certificate in Neuro-Linguistic Programming from the New England Institute of NLP.

PLAN FOR SUCCESS

If you want to succeed, plan for success. Don't leave your success to chance or "hope" that everything will work out somehow. The steps to being successful are not difficult, but you do need to spend some thought and time making and then following your plan. Having specific steps in your plan for success is essential. We wish you the best as you begin.

Find Out About Your Instructor

What is your instructor's name? _____

What is your instructor's e-mail address? _____

What is your instructor's office phone number? _____

What are your instructor's office hours? _____

Get to Know Your Classmates

Write down the name and contact information of at least two students in your class whom you can call or e-mail for any work you miss or have questions about. This list can be adapted as you make friends with your classmates.

1. _____

2. _____

3. _____

Read and Understand Your Class Schedule or Syllabus

What are three important goals for this course? _____

_____

_____

_____

What is the course policy on attendance? _____

How is your grade determined? _____

What is your instructor's drop policy? _____

Circle yes or no to indicate whether a certain kind of information is on your class schedule or syllabus.

1. The name of a required textbook   Yes   No
2. Student learning goals, outcomes, or objectives   Yes   No
3. The date of the midterm exam   Yes   No
4. A grading scale   Yes   No
5. The date of the final exam   Yes   No
6. Holidays   Yes   No
7. A lab requirement   Yes   No
8. A weekly reading assignment   Yes   No
9. A weekly vocabulary assignment   Yes   No
10. Information about Student Services   Yes   No

Write down dates of major assignments and tests that your class schedule or syllabus includes:

▶ _____

▶ _____

▶ _____

▶ _____

▶ _____

Ask questions about anything you are unsure of.

Write Down Your Short-Term and Long-Term Goals

Goals generally fall into one of five different categories:

1. Mental—learning, reading, studying
2. Physical—health, diet, exercise, sleep
3. Relational—family, friends
4. Financial—save, budget, make more money
5. Spiritual—grow in faith, explore your beliefs

We will define short-term goals as any goals that you can accomplish within the next year. Please write down one short-term goal you have for each category. We will help you with the first one!

1. Mental: To pass this class with an A. _____

    _____

2. Physical: _____

    _____

3. Relational: _____

    _____

4. Financial: _____

    _____

5. Spiritual: _____

    _____

We will define long-term goals as any goals that you can accomplish within the next two to five years. Please write down one long-term goal you have for each category. We will help you with the first one!

6. Mental: To graduate with a certificate or degree in [you fill in the rest] _____

    _____

7. Physical: _____

    _____

8. Relational: _____

    _____

9. Financial: _____

    _____

10. Spiritual: _____

    _____

Plan Your Time and Stick to Your Plan

Managing your time is probably the single most important skill you need to succeed in college (and at work). When you plan your time, start with the big picture—the whole semester—and then work down to smaller and smaller segments of time—month by month, then week by week, then day by day.

For each time period, refer to your goals to make sure that your activities and goals align.

- ▶ **Look over the whole semester.** At the beginning of the semester, look at your college's semester schedule, published on the college website and with the course catalog. In your planner or with a scheduling app on your smart phone, note the first day of classes, holidays when school isn't in session, and other important dates from the semester schedule. Then examine the syllabus from each of your courses, just as you did for this reading course, and write in the due dates for all major assignments and tests. Take some time to think through whether there are any time periods during which you have several major tests or assignments due, such final exams week. You'll need to make sure to start studying for finals at least several weeks in advance in order to have enough time to complete your review for each course. **Take this step now.**

- ▶ **Create a monthly schedule.** At the beginning of each month, fill out a monthly schedule. First, transfer the important dates for this month from your semester schedule. Second, write in all of your existing commitments for specific times and days, such as class times, work hours, and so on. For each class that you are taking, decide when you will do the homework and when you will need to study for tests. Space out your study as much as you can. Block out chunks of time, as in the sample schedule on the next page. If you can, allow yourself fifteen minutes before each class and a half hour after each class to review the material. **Get a monthly planner and create the first month's schedule now.**

- ▶ **Fill in your weekly schedule.** At the beginning of each week, transfer information from your monthly schedule into your weekly schedule. Then get more specific based on your current assignments. Break each day into 15-minute or half-hour chunks of time and write down what you are going to accomplish during each period. Be sure to fill in meal times, including prep time; the time it takes you to get places; and errands such as doing your laundry and going to the bank. Try to group errands to save time: If you have to go to the south end of town to go to the bank, then also get what you need at the grocery store there in the same trip. Creating a weekly schedule each Sunday can save you hours during the week. **Prepare your first week's schedule now.**

Monthly Schedule Sample

Monday	Tuesday	Wednesday	Thursday	Friday	Saturday	Sunday
				1 10–11: Writing I 1–5: Work	**2** 8–5: Work	**3** 1–3: Do writing assignment 3–4: Reading lab
4 10–11: Writing I 1–3: Do writing assignment 4–6: Reading lab	**5** 8–12: Work 2–3:30: Reading 4–5: Reading HW	**6** 10–11: Writing I 1–5: Work 7–9: Do writing assignment	**7** 8–12: Work 2–3:30: Reading 4–5: Reading HW	**8** 10–11: Writing I 1–5: Work	**9** 8–5: Work	**10** 1–3: Do writing assignment 3–4: Reading lab
11 10–11: Writing I 1–3: Do writing assignment 4–6: Reading lab	**12** 8–12: Work 2–3:30: Reading 4–5: Reading HW	**13** 10–11: Writing I 1–5: Work	**14** 8–12: Work 2–3:30: Reading 4–5: Reading HW	**15** 10–11: Writing I 1–5: Work	**16** 8–5: Work	**17** 1–3: Do writing assignment 3–4: Reading lab 7–8: Study for Reading test
18 8–5: Work 7–8: Study for Reading test *President's Day*	**19** 8–12: Work 2–3:30: Reading 4–5: Study for Reading test	**20** 10–11: Writing I 1–5: Work 6–8: Study for Reading test	**21** 8–12: Work 2–3:30: Reading TEST 4–5: Reading HW	**22** 10–11: Writing I 1–5: Work	**23** 8–5: Work	**24** 1–3: Do writing assignment 3–4: Reading lab
25 10–11: Writing I 1–3: Do writing assignment 4–6: Reading lab	**26** 8–12: Work 2–3:30: Reading 4–5: Reading HW	**27** 10–11: Writing I 1–5: Work	**28** 8–12: Work 2–3:30: Reading 4–5: Reading HW			

Sample of a Daily Plan

Monday, February 4, 2013	
07:00	Get up
07:30	Work out
08:00	↓
08:30	Shower
09:00	Eat breakfast
09:30	Catch bus to campus; review notes from last class
10:00	Go to Writing I class
10:30	↓
11:00	Review class notes at student center
11:30	Hang out with Ellie
12:00	↓
12:30	Eat lunch
01:00	Do writing assignment in library (4th floor)
01:30	
02:00	↓
02:30	
03:00	Get required novel from college library; copy reading notes for Michael
03:30	Get cash
04:00	Do Reading lab
04:30	
05:00	↓
05:30	
06:00	Catch bus for home

▶ **Prioritize your daily activities.** Look at your weekly schedule each night. Think through the next day and what you need to accomplish. Make a to-do list for the next day and order the items on your list.

1—for the most important tasks that need to be done today
2—for tasks that are important but not as urgent as the 1's
3—for tasks that are least urgent but still need to be done soon

Write down a specific plan for how you will prioritize your schoolwork.

Respect and Take Care of Yourself

▶ **Believe in yourself.** Belief in oneself is not a magic formula for automatic success. However, do not underestimate the power of belief. It affects your emotions, thoughts, assumptions, and behavior. **Write one specific way that you can believe in yourself.**

_____

▶ **Know what motivates you.** Remember why you are here. What is your goal? What are you working for? Keep your short- and long-term goals in mind. Reward yourself for jobs well done. It can be a small reward—watching your favorite TV show after completing homework. Or it can be a bigger reward—going out with your friends, or anything else that will motivate you to make a short-term sacrifice to achieve your academic goal. **Write one thing that you can use to motivate yourself to do well in this class.**

_____

▶ **Keep your health in mind.** A good night's sleep, a healthy diet, and exercise are important parts of staying healthy and powerful. All of these will help you manage stress, stay focused on your studies, and keep a positive attitude. Write down one way you can maintain or improve your health.

_____

Participate in Class and Draw on Your Community

▶ **Be active.** Participate actively in class. Ask questions and be prepared to discuss ideas with classmates. If you do not understand something, ask your instructor. Chances are someone else has the same question. Also, be present as you are studying. Do not passively read, but actively engage your mind so you do not waste your time or energy by just going through the motions. **Write one specific way you will be active in class.**

_____

▶ **Network.** Who can you use to your advantage to help you in your academic success? Are your parents a good resource? Are your friends encouraging you or distracting you from school? Are you utilizing your instructors? Have you identified the good students in your classes with whom you can form study groups? Do you know what resources your school offers, such as labs, advising, counseling, career services, and so forth? **Write down one person and one resource you can use to become a more accountable student.**

_____

Be Responsible for Your Own Learning

▶ **Take the initiative.** Read ahead. Ask questions. Make connections. If you are absent, come to the next class with any missed work done. Review your material a few minutes each day in order to be better prepared for class discussions, quizzes, and tests. Make the effort to talk to your instructor and develop a rapport with him or her. **Write down one strategy that will help you take the initiative.**

_____

▶ **Learn from your mistakes.** Making a mistake is the first half of learning. The second half is finding out more about the error and how to do things better the next time. Talk to your instructor about tasks you don't do well, and use this opportunity to learn. **Write down one way you can learn from your mistakes.**

_____

▶ **Always do your best.** If you always do your best, then you are a success, even if you do not get the highest grade. Be honest. Do not cheat, which actually leads to failure. Treat others the way you wish to be treated and chances are they will return the gesture. **Write down something that gets in the way of you doing your best. Then write down one idea for how to overcome this temptation.**

_____

Organize Your Work and Your Space

▶ **Organize your work.** Make sure you have a folder for important documents from each of your classes. Turn in your assignments in the format your instructor has requested. Take your book to class. **Write down one idea about how you will stay organized.**

_____

▶ **Organize your study space.** Have an organized place where you do your homework. The more you study in a particular place the easier it will become to get in the right frame of mind to work. Make sure you have all the equipment you need there (pens, notebooks, note cards, computer, clock) so you don't have to search for them every time you sit down. **Write down where you will study and how you can prepare your space.**

_____

Discuss the items from the preceding list with a partner. Talk about how each of you can be a successful student this semester. See how your ideas are similar to a classmate's or if one of you has thought of a different idea that may be motivating to the other.

connect

PART 1
Reading to Succeed

Pictorial Press Ltd/Alamy

 Click to Connect! Visit **www.cengagebrain.com** to access study resources for this chapter through CourseMate, which includes audio, video, quizzes, and a searchable, interactive eBook version of the text.

1 Connecting to the Reading Process

> *People with goals succeed because they know where they're going. It's that simple.*
>
> —EARL NIGHTINGALE

Connect with Ideas

Do you agree with Nightingale? Is having a plan critical to success? Explain.

Activate Your Knowledge

Share one goal you worked hard to accomplish. Explain how having a plan helped you succeed. Share any other elements that helped you succeed.

Engage with the Chapter

Take a moment to skim through pages 4–26, reading only the headings. What are the topics this chapter will discuss?

Getting Motivated to Read

Reading is the most important skill you can develop to help you succeed in college. You will do a tremendous amount of reading in your college classes. No matter what courses you take, you will read textbooks and other materials as a primary way to acquire new knowledge and to gain new perspectives on knowledge you already have. In fact, all students earning a degree must take basic classes in fields like art, psychology, history, government, math, science, and English. Here are just a few examples of required reading in some of the fields students choose as their major.

- ▶ To earn a degree in computer science, a student reads material in the field of computer science, but also in algebra, physics, and engineering.
- ▶ To earn a business management degree, a student reads in the fields of accounting, finance, business law, human resources, management, and marketing.
- ▶ To become an elementary school teacher, a student reads in the areas of child growth and development, classroom management, the history of education, and methods of teaching particular subjects.
- ▶ To get into the medical field, ranging from becoming a licensed practical nurse (LPN) in 9–15 months, a registered nurse (RN) in 2–3 years, or a medical doctor (MD) in 10–12 years, a student could read textbooks in anatomy, physiology, pharmacology, microbiology, chemistry, nutrition, and psychology.

Taking a class in any of these subjects requires that you read the course textbook and related books, articles, and online sources. To complete your degree requirements, you'll need to learn an effective reading and thinking process to understand these materials. This book will help you. But keep in mind this book is not teaching you how to read. You already know how to do that. Rather, it will equip you with a process for reading that you can apply in each class you take. In addition, you will learn how to think critically about new ideas and concepts—in other words, how to analyze and evaluate what you read.

Interaction 1–1 ▶ **What Do You Want to Do When You Get Out of School?**

With a classmate or as a class, discuss the following questions.

1. What career are you thinking of pursuing? _____

_____

2. Why do you want to earn this degree, or what interests you about this career? (If you are not sure exactly what degree you want to get, that's okay! Just discuss what you think you might want to do.)

_____

_____

3. What is the minimum degree requirement to be competitive in this field?

_____

4. Name some specific classes or types of classes that are needed to pursue this career/degree.

_____

_____

Motivation to Complete Your Degree: Earning More Money

Learning to read better is going to help you complete your certificate or degree program. And completing your program of choice is going to help you earn more money, which will help you build the life you envision for yourself. Look at the comparison of earnings for full-time workers below.

Figure 1.1   Average Earnings Based Upon Level of Education

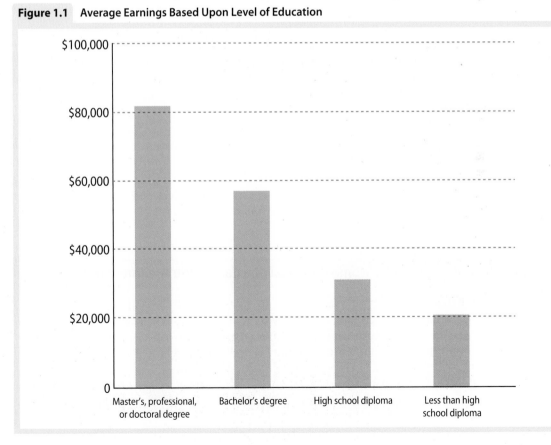

Figure 1.2   **Education Pays**

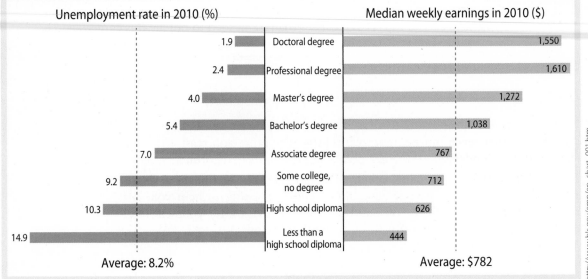

Unemployment rate in 2010 (%)   Median weekly earnings in 2010 ($)

	Unemployment rate		Median weekly earnings
Doctoral degree	1.9		1,550
Professional degree	2.4		1,610
Master's degree	4.0		1,272
Bachelor's degree	5.4		1,038
Associate degree	7.0		767
Some college, no degree	9.2		712
High school diploma	10.3		626
Less than a high school diploma	14.9		444

Average: 8.2%   Average: $782

As you can see from **Figure 1.1,** on average, those with a master's degree earned four times more than those who completed only high school. How much more did those with a bachelor's degree earn than those with only a high school diploma? Even though this data is from 2007, the trend remains the same: the more schooling you complete, the more money you're likely to make.

Figure 1.2 shows another influence education has on employment.

Did you notice the red bars? They indicate the unemployment rates for those with different levels of education. See the trend? Not only do degrees give you the potential to earn more money, but also they offer a greater chance of keeping your job! These two factors together should provide a powerful motivation for making your education a high priority.

Interaction 1–2 ▶ **Find Out the Income Potential of a Career You Are Interested In**

Do an Internet search for a career you might want to pursue. Type "Occupational Outlook Handbook" in your search bar and then look for your career at the Bureau of Labor Statistics site: www.bls.gov/oco. If you have not chosen a specific career, then search for any career you think you might be interested in. Find the following information and bring it to the next class.

1. What is the starting salary for the career you are interested in? _____

2. What is the median income for a person after five to ten years of experience in this
   career? _____

3. What is the top earning potential of someone in this field? How many years does it take to reach this level? _____

4. Do you think this income range is worth the effort of sacrifice that attending school will require from you? _____

But money isn't everything. Reading is an important part of a college education for another (even more important) reason. The more you read, the better you become at understanding other points of view. In turn, this understanding will help enrich your connections to other people and enhance your life by showing you all the possibilities that are available to you in the worlds of work, community, family, and personal interests.

Seeing clearly what you want to achieve will help you stay motivated. The next section shows you how.

Fast Forward to Your Future

Scientists who study the brain have made some surprising discoveries. One fascinating piece of information they have gained is that when a person fully imagines an activity, the brain responds as though that activity were actually occurring. Olympic athletes have taken advantage of this knowledge by adding visualization practices to their workouts. Now, in addition to actually swimming, skiing, or skating for five or six hours a day, many athletes also spend several periods of time each day visualizing themselves performing these activities exactly how they want to do them—in great detail and in living color. You can use this Olympian strategy to fine-tune your present and future so that you can get what you want out of life.

Interaction 1–3 ▸ Fine-tune Your Present and Future

1. **Imagine Yourself in the Future.** Imagine that five years have passed and you are now living out your future exactly as you want it to be at that time. Everything is going beautifully. You feel wonderful. Now feel that good feeling fully. Take your time with this—let the good feeling build. And for each of the next questions, take your time to fine-tune the details of your answer. Imagine the details as large as life, and in living color.

   ▶ How is your health?
   ▶ Where are you living?
   ▶ What is your dating, partnership, or family situation?

▶ What is your work life like? How's your financial situation?

▶ What is a typical day like?

Imagine your life as fully as you can, in as much detail as possible. Paint a rosy picture!

Now sit down and write a comment to the self you are today. What do you want to tell yourself? Make a post on your current self's wall about what you want from that person *now*.

Now step back into your current self. Read your comment. Be sure to act on any advice or encouragement you have received. Your future self has only your best interests at heart!

📝 **Update Status**　🖼 **Add Photo / Video**

> What's on your mind?

Your future self_____

_____

_____

_____

Like · Comment · See Friendship · February 7 at 12:23pm

Your present self _____

_____

_____

February 7 at 7:30pm · Like

> Write a comment...

---

2. **Make That Future Happen.** Now that you've developed a sense for where you want to be in five years, answer this question: What can you do to make that future happen? Only list things that you personally can do—don't include any actions that other people would have to take.

I can make this future happen by . . .

▶ EXAMPLE: taking classes to get my nurse practitioner degree._____

▶ _____

▶ _____

▶ _____

▶ _____

---

3. **Make a Social Commitment.** Now that you have imagined your future and written some specific tasks you have taken responsibility for, why don't you make an actual post of what you wrote for question 2 on your Facebook page, declaring your intentions to your social world. (If you do not use Facebook, then tell at least three of your close friends or family members of your intentions.)

4. **Consider the Value of Reading.** Now use your imagination to consider the value of reading more effectively. How does reading at the college level fit into the picture you have just painted of your future? For each of the following life contexts, name at least one benefit of knowing how to read more effectively. If you can't think of one offhand, think again. After you have responded as well as you can on your own, work with a small group and discuss your answers together. Add any new ideas you gain to your list.

Life context	Reading benefits this context by ...
Home and family (or attractiveness as a date or potential partner)	
Career and earning ability	
Self-confidence and self-esteem	
Health and well-being	
Other contexts that matter to you (name them here)	

As you work through this book, you may have other ideas about how reading more effectively will help you enjoy your life and understand more about the world around you and other people. If you do, we recommend that you add those new ideas to this chart. Then, if you ever get discouraged about the course, turn back and reread all your responses to Interaction 1–3. Reviewing your goals periodically will help you stay on course to the future you want to achieve.

Reading Selections and Talking with Classmates

Every chapter in this book starts with a "Read and Talk" activity that will help to prepare your mind for the ideas to come in the reading selections at the end of the chapter. A second purpose is to give you something to talk about. When you have reading assignments in your college classes, reading the material is just the beginning. After reading, you, your instructor, and your classmates will often talk about the ideas the assignment has raised.

Read and Talk

Article

Social media is part of most of our daily lives. We post on "FB" or tweet or text. Read about how social media, specifically YouTube, has changed how people communicate with the world around them.

Visit www.cengagebrain.com to access the CourseMate for this chapter to hear vocabulary words from this reading and an audio recording of it.

The Power of Three Little Words

1   Words are powerful. A single word like "stop," "no," or "yes" can send a powerful message. If you have ever heard the classic song "RESPECT" by Aretha Franklin, you know that one word certainly sends a **compelling** message. A shouted "help" can benefit someone in need or even save a life.

compelling strong

2   In the early days of YouTube and video sharing, a street magician named "MadV" offered his audience a chance to share their word in an uploaded video. This simple **solicitation** generated one of the most responded to videos on YouTube of all time. MadV turned some of the multitude of responses he received into a video compilation called "The Message." Most people wrote a word or phrase on their hand in marker or pen. One responder wrote "hope," another wrote "love," and yet another wrote "equality."

solicitation request

3   If one word holds such power, what about three? Some of our most common and **impactful** statements are made up of three words. A simple "I love you" can change someone's life or just make his or her day. An "I am sorry" can excuse an accidental bump or start to heal a broken heart. "How are you?" can be simple **etiquette**, or it can show deep concern.

> impactful meaningful
>
> etiquette rules of polite behavior

4   This seems to be the idea behind a segment *Good Morning America* did called "Your 3 Words." The segment also generated an incredible response. The words on the videos ranged in tone from fun ("love my ride" was written in the sand as a group galloped down the shoreline on their horses) to serious (two cancer victims saying "fighting cancer together") to excited ("Finally got married!") to **introspective** ("no more tears"). According to the executive producer of the show, Andrew Morse, "It's rare that you can get such insight into your viewers' lives in such a simplistic, powerful, emotional way."

> introspective inward looking

5   If you took a moment to share your thoughts with the world in just "three little words," what would your message be?

Talking about Reading

Respond in writing to the questions below and then discuss your answers with your classmates.

1. If you were to respond to MadV's video request to share your hopes or dreams with the world, what would your message be? (Remember, it has to fit on the palm of your hand.)

_____

2. If you were asked to describe this past week in three words, which words would you use?

_____

3. If you put your words with an image, what would the image be? Why? Explain your thinking.

_____

_____

_____

4. How many different scenes can you imagine where "I am sorry" or "I love you" or "How are you?" can be used? Write a brief description of each scene. _____

_____

5. 🎬 **Scan to Connect!** Use your smart phone to scan this code to watch a video. (See the inside front cover for more information on how to use this.) Think about each of the three words used in the video compilation. Share which one meant the most to you.

Reading Is an Interaction

What do you do to stay focused when you read? The simple answer is that you need to connect to what you are reading. Reading is an active process. You cannot be passive when you read and expect to be successful. There are several basic ways you can interact with what you read.

Use Your Imagination. Using your imagination while you read is one way to actively participate in reading. Interactivity is the ability of two (or more) things or people to act on one another and affect one another. When you read, you have a better chance of understanding the text if you interact with it. Let what you are reading affect you. Place yourself within the text. Form a mental picture of what the author is saying. Involve your senses: see, smell, feel, touch, and hear what you are reading. Your imagination is powerful. In fact, Albert Einstein said imagination is more important than knowledge because it takes you beyond the limits of knowledge.

Use Your Body. Another way to interact with your reading is to use your body. This doesn't mean hitting your head against the book in frustration! Rather, when you read, keep a pencil (or pen or highlighter) in your hand. This automatically puts you in a different frame of mind than if you are just sitting there like stone, moving only your eyes. And use your pencil! Mark the important parts while you read. When you get to a point in the text that you don't understand, underline it and scribble your question in the margin. When you disagree with the author, write "No way!" and then add your own explanation. When you read something completely new, try to figure out how it fits with your prior knowledge.

Use a Familiar Process. Let's apply the principle of interactivity to something you probably do every day, or at least a couple of times a week—watch TV. Applying an interactive approach to watching TV will help you transfer this principle over to reading. (If you don't watch TV, you can take the same steps in relation to movies.) In both watching TV and reading, you can have interactions before you view or read, while you view or read, and after you view or read.

Interaction 1–4 ▶ What Do You Do When You View?

Talk with a classmate about the interactions you have in the following situations.

1. What do you do *before* you watch a TV show or movie?

   ▶ _____

   ▶ _____

▶ _____

▶ _____

2. What do you do *while* you watch a movie or TV show?

▶ _____

▶ _____

▶ _____

▶ _____

3. What do you do *after* you watch a movie or TV show?

▶ _____

▶ _____

▶ _____

▶ _____

Before You View or Read

Before you view or read, you can use several strategies that will dramatically improve your comprehension (that is, understanding):

▶ Survey it to get an overview of what will be coming.
▶ Guess at the purpose of the movie, TV program, or reading selection.
▶ Predict what's going to happen.
▶ Think about your prior knowledge of the subject matter.

We will discuss each strategy separately.

Surveying a Reading Is Like Watching a Preview

When you go to a movie, often you have already seen the preview for it several times. The preview shows you some of the highlights of the movie. You often know who the main characters are (and which actors play them), you've viewed some of the scenery and settings, and you have a sense of the film's genre— whether the movie is going to be a fast-paced action adventure, a romantic comedy, or a horror flick.

Similarly, if you take a few moments to survey or preview a reading selection, you will tremendously improve your chances of comprehending it. When you preview, you do not read the whole selection; you only examine selected parts. Following are the parts to look at, shown on an article from *The Ultimate PC Guide* magazine.

Read These Parts Quickly When You Survey

Title: What do these words reveal about the subject?

Subtitle or sentence in large type: What do these words reveal about the subject?

Headings: This reading has several blue headings. These help organize key ideas. Read each heading and think about it for a moment.

Images and captions: What information can you gather from this image?

First sentences of paragraphs: Read the first sentence of each paragraph quickly.

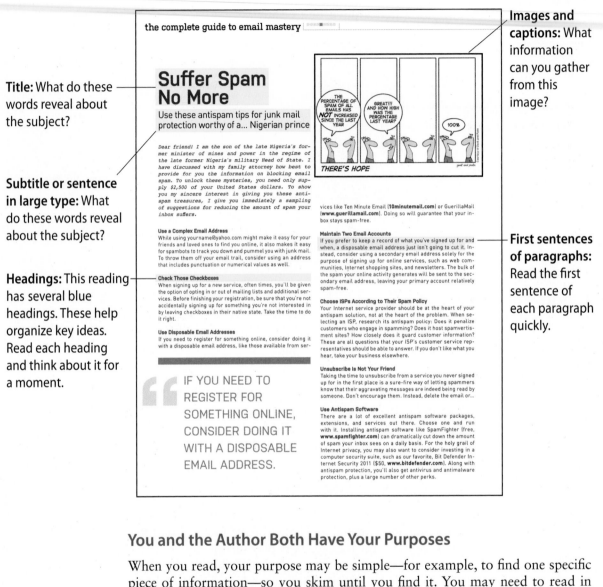

the complete guide to email mastery

Suffer Spam No More

Use these antispam tips for junk mail protection worthy of a... Nigerian prince

Dear friend! I am the son of the late Nigeria's former minister of mines and power in the regime of the late former Nigeria's military Head of State. I have discussed with my family attorney how best to provide for you the information on blocking email spam. To unlock these mysteries, you need only supply $2,500 of your United States dollars. To show you my sincere interest in giving you these antispam treasures, I give you immediately a sampling of suggestions for reducing the amount of spam your inbox suffers.

Use a Complex Email Address
While using yourname@yahoo.com might make it easy for your friends and loved ones to find you online, it also makes it easy for spambots to track you down and pummel you with junk mail. To throw off your email trail, consider using an address that includes punctuation or numerical values as well.

Check Those Checkboxes
When signing up for a new service, often times, you'll be given the option of opting in or out of mailing lists and additional services. Before finishing your registration, be sure that you're not accidentally opting in for something you're not interested in by leaving checkboxes in their native state. Take the time to do it right.

Use Disposable Email Addresses
If you need to register for something online, consider doing it with a disposable email address, like those available from ser-

vices like Ten Minute Email (**10minutemail.com**) or GuerillaMail (**www.guerillamail.com**). Doing so will guarantee that your inbox stays spam-free.

Maintain Two Email Accounts
If you prefer to keep a record of what you've signed up for and when, a disposable email address isn't going to cut it. Instead, consider using a secondary email address solely for the purpose of signing up for online services, such as web communities, Internet shopping sites, and newsletters. The bulk of the spam your online activity generates will be sent to the secondary email address, leaving your primary account relatively spam-free.

Choose ISPs According to Their Spam Policy
Your Internet service provider should be at the heart of your antispam solution, not at the heart of the problem. When selecting an ISP, research its antispam policy: Does it penalize customers who engage in spamming? Does it host spamvertisment sites? How closely does it guard customer information? These are all questions that your ISP's customer service representatives should be able to answer. If you don't like what you hear, take your business elsewhere.

Unsubscribe Is Not Your Friend
Taking the time to unsubscribe from a service you never signed up for in the first place is a sure-fire way of letting spammers know that their aggravating messages are indeed being read by someone. Don't encourage them. Instead, delete the email or...

Use Antispam Software
There are a lot of excellent antispam software packages, extensions, and services out there. Choose one and run with it. Installing antispam software like SpamFighter (free, **www.spamfighter.com**) can dramatically cut down the amount of spam your inbox sees on a daily basis. For the holy grail of Internet privacy, you may also want to consider investing in a computer security suite, such as our favorite, Bit Defender Internet Security 2011 ($50, **www.bitdefender.com**). Along with antispam protection, you'll also get antivirus and antimalware protection, plus a large number of other perks.

> " IF YOU NEED TO REGISTER FOR SOMETHING ONLINE, CONSIDER DOING IT WITH A DISPOSABLE EMAIL ADDRESS.

THERE'S HOP

You and the Author Both Have Your Purposes

When you read, your purpose may be simple—for example, to find one specific piece of information—so you skim until you find it. You may need to read in order to carry on a class discussion. Or you may need to read for deep understanding in order to ace a test. Regardless, in school, all academic reading is given to you with a built-in purpose. You must understand that purpose so you can accomplish your reading tasks successfully.

In addition, whatever you are reading has a purpose. The author had a specific purpose in mind when he or she was writing. Let's connect reading purpose with viewing purpose. Like readings, TV programs have different purposes as well. Readings, movies, and TV shows generally have one or more of these purposes: to persuade, to inform, and to express. You can remember these by using the acronym PIE.

Three Purposes for Writing (Think PIE!)

Persuasive Attempt to change the reader's or viewer's thoughts, attitudes, or behaviors.

Informative Attempt to inform the reader or viewer about key information, usually factual.

Expressive Attempt to engage the reader's or viewer's emotions, whether happy or sad, angry or delighted, comic or tragic.

Interaction 1–5 ▸ Your Purposes for Viewing

1. Name five TV programs that you watch or have watched at least three or four times. Next to each program's name, note what kind of program it is—for example, a talk show, a reality show, a sporting event, a cartoon, and so on.

Name of program you watch	Type of program
EXAMPLE: 30 Rock	comedy
1.	
2.	
3.	
4.	
5.	

2. What is your main purpose for watching each program? _____

_____

3. In question 2 you were thinking about your purpose for watching certain TV programs. What about the purpose of that particular *type* of program? Can types of programs also be divided into those meant to be persuasive, informative, or expressive? To answer this question, try to

put different types of programs you've watched (not just those you listed on the previous page) into the three categories given below.

Types of programs meant to persuade viewers	Types of programs meant to inform or teach viewers	Types of programs meant to express emotion or evoke emotions from viewers
EXAMPLE: Political commentary and debate programs (e.g., *Real Time with Bill Maher*)	EXAMPLE: News programs	EXAMPLE: Cartoons

4. Discuss your findings with the class or in a small group. What have you learned?

You can see that different types of programs, called **genres**, have distinctive purposes. The same is true for different kinds of reading material. For example, news stories have the main purpose of informing readers about current events. College textbooks have the main purpose of teaching students; their purpose, too, is to inform. What about *People* magazine? The articles in *People* do inform readers about celebrities, but why? To entertain readers, and thus their main purpose is to be expressive.

At times you can tell the purpose of a reading selection just from the title. For example, an article called "The President Should Be Ashamed" is a persuasive reading; the word *should* clearly shows that the writer wants readers to believe the president did something wrong. The article is not simply reporting information. (An informative title would state "The President Is Ashamed.")

Other times, you can make an educated guess based on where the reading selection appears—for example, if it's part of a newspaper, it may be in the news section, on the opinion page, or part of the want ads. When an article is printed in the Letters to the Editor section, the writer's main purpose is to persuade readers. The publishing context can reveal a lot about the author's purpose.

In addition, understanding the author's purpose can help you make inferences about his or her point of view, assumptions, biases (one-sided views), and beliefs.

Interaction 1–6 ▸ Predict Purposes with Images and Text

Examine the three words and images in the photographs that follow. Answer the questions that follow each photo.

1.

Andreas Gradin/Shutterstock.com

A. Predict the author's purpose:

Persuasive	Informative	Expressive

B. Explain the meaning of the words based on the purpose and the context.

_____

_____

C. What can you infer about the author's point of view, assumptions, or beliefs?

_____

_____

2.

Chad Ehlers/Alamy

A. Predict the author's purpose:

Persuasive	Informative	Expressive

B. Explain the meaning of the words based on the purpose and the context.

_____

_____

C. What can you infer about the author's point of view, assumptions, or beliefs?

_____

_____

3.

Clearviewstock/Shutterstock.com

A. Predict the author's purpose:

| Persuasive | Informative | Expressive |

B. Explain the meaning of the words based on the purpose and the context.

_____

_____

_____

_____

C. What can you infer about the author's point of view, assumptions, or beliefs?

_____

_____

As you can see, words and images can be used independently or together to make inferences about what the author means and even what he or she feels, believes, or assumes. You will learn more about these concepts in Part Three. In the meantime, let's practice predicting the author's purpose based on the first thing you usually read in any article or book: the title.

Interaction 1–7   Purposes in Reading

For each of the following types of reading material, decide whether the main purpose is likely to be persuasive, informative, or expressive. Consider both the title and the publishing context. Circle the best answer, and be prepared to discuss the reasons for your answer.

1. A news article called "House Fire Kills Five in Connecticut" from *New York Times* online

    P   I   E

2. A chapter in a health textbook called "Personal Nutrition"

    P   I   E

3. An editorial in the *Washington Post* called "Mormon Church Needs Reform"

    P   I   E

4. A graphic novel called *Diablo III: The Book of Cain* by Deckard Cain

    P   I   E

5. An article called "Schistosomiasis Affects 230 Million Each Year" on the World Health Organization's website

    P   I   E

6. "Big California, Little Fixes," an editorial in the *Los Angeles Times* online

    P   I   E

7. *Through My Eyes,* a book by Tim Tebow and Nathan Whitaker

    P   I   E

8. A movie preview or trailer for *The Dark Knight Rises*

    P   I   E

9. An article in *National Geographic* magazine called "Last of the Cave People," by Mark Jenkins

    P   I   E

10. A feature article in *Outside* magazine called "50 Years on Everest: The Unsung Heroes of the World's Highest Mountain," by Jenny Dubin

    P   I   E

As you can see, when you are preparing to read, it helps to spend a moment thinking about the likely purpose of the reading selection, based on the context in which the reading selection is presented and its title.

More than One Purpose. Authors often have more than one purpose for a piece of writing. As an example, writing intended to persuade readers frequently contains informative facts or an emotional story. An article, book, advertisement, TV show, or movie can have elements of each purpose, but there is usually a main purpose. To give an illustration, let's look at item 10 in Interaction 1–7: a magazine article called "50 Years on Everest: The Unsung Heroes of the World's Highest Mountain" by Jenny Dubin. The article's main purpose is to inform readers about the heroes who have climbed Mount Everest. It gives factual information about these climbers, their experiences, and why they are heroes. But readers are also fascinated by stories of what real people have struggled through, survived, and overcome to climb Mount Everest—and so the article also has a second purpose: to be expressive.

You Already Know Something about This

When you sit down to watch an episode of your favorite show, you have the combined prior knowledge of all the other episodes you have watched.

When you've just surveyed a reading, you've learned something already from the title, the images, the captions, and the headings. Aside from these obvious pieces of information, though, it's quite likely you know much more. Before you read the article on p. 14, for example, you probably had one or more strategies for dealing with the spam you receive in your email inbox. As you surveyed (and read) the article, you connected what you already knew with what you read. All of this knowledge that you bring to your viewing or reading is called your **prior knowledge**. (*Prior* means "before.") You want to activate, or set in motion, your prior knowledge as much as you can before you start reading. Doing this takes advantage of a natural pattern of learning for people: fitting what they are learning about into what they already know.

A mental strategy you can use to trigger your prior knowledge is to ask questions. Here are several questions that can activate your mind to make connections.

- ► Do I know anything about this? What is it?
- ► Have I read anything about this? What was it?
- ► Have I watched anything about this? What was it?
- ► Have I experienced anything like this? When?
- ► Do I know anyone else who has experienced something like this? Who?

Practicing intentional engagement before you read by using your imagination and focus can really enrich your reading experiences.

| Interaction 1–8 | Connect to Your Prior Knowledge |

Circulate around your class, talking to several of your classmates. Share with each other the prior knowledge you have about the following.

- ► Star-crossed lovers
- ► *Carpe diem*
- ► Langston Hughes
- ► World Heritage Sites
- ► *The Hunger Games*
- ► Add your own.

- ► Metaphor
- ► *The Great Gatsby*
- ► Impressionism
- ► "The Boy Who Cried Wolf"
- ► West Bank
- ► Add your own.

Once you have had a chance to talk to several people, share what you knew or learned with the class.

While You Are Viewing or Reading

Have you ever gone to a movie like *The Hunger Games* with a hard-core fan? This person has read not only the first book three times already, but the whole series as well, and knows all the characters, all the actors who portray the characters, where the film was made, and all the gossip surrounding the stars, the film, and the author. Or have you ever gone to a professional sporting event or watched a game with a hard-core fan? This person knows all the players, the history of each of them and the team, the coach, and the strengths or weaknesses of everyone involved! Or maybe you have gone to a concert with a die-hard fan of Lady Gaga, Bruno Mars, Jay-Z, George Strait, or Aerosmith. They know all the words to all the songs on every album the singer or group has made. (Maybe *you* are one of these dedicated people!) If so, you'll understand that there are differences between what a casual viewer sees and what a dedicated viewer knows and sees.

One of the differences is that the casual viewer might get caught up emotionally in the moment-by-moment movie scenes, but the dedicated viewer retains a broader, more critical perspective on what is happening. Or a casual spectator might get wrapped up in what looks like a bad plan by the coach, but the die-hard fan knows it is all part of the bigger strategy. Due partly to their greater experience and partly to their intense curiosity, dedicated fans know more about the movie director's or coach's options, and thus, they are in a better position to know why a particular choice was made and whether the choice was a good one.

The same kinds of differences are true for casual and dedicated readers. While the casual reader may be reading one sentence at a time and thinking about its meaning, the dedicated reader is not only doing that but also staying interactive by asking the types of questions shown in **Table 1.1** on page 22.

Refer back to Table 1.1 the next few times you read, and practice the following strategies.

- ▶ Actively try to understand what the author is saying.
- ▶ Monitor your own comprehension.
- ▶ Search for the relevance and significance of the information you are reading.
- ▶ Remain open to learning something new.

The rest of the chapters in this book will suggest strategies you can use to improve your comprehension, but the most important factor of all is your active participation.

Table 1.1 Learning Tasks to Accomplish While Reading	To accomplish these learning tasks while reading . . .	the interactive reader thinks these thoughts:
	The reader tries to imagine what he or she are reading	1. Can I see or hear this in my head?
	The reader tries to understand what the author is saying.	1. What does it mean when the author says this? 2. Can I explain this using my own words?
	The reader monitors (tracks) whether he or she comprehends the material and applies strategies to aid comprehension. You may be losing comprehension 1. if you have to slow your reading considerably, 2. if you go back to reread a section several times, or 3. if you can't tell what is important and what is not.	1. I don't understand. I'll keep reading to see if this becomes clearer. 2. I don't know this word. I wonder if I can figure it out from the surrounding words. If not, I'll use the dictionary. 3. I have read this same paragraph three times already and I don't get it. What is the main idea here?
	The reader searches for the relevance of the reading to his or her own life and to other ideas and situations.	1. How does this connect to what I already know? 2. What examples of this have I experienced or do I know about?
	The reader is open to learning something new that doesn't necessarily fit easily into known information.	1. How is this different from what I thought was true?
	The reader searches for the significance of the ideas.	1. Why is this important? 2. What effects do these ideas have? What are the consequences?

After You View or Read

What you do after you watch a TV program, movie, or YouTube video depends partly on why you were watching it to begin with. If you were watching Ellen DeGeneres, you may just laugh a final laugh and change the channel. But if you were watching local politicians debate whether to build a superhighway through your neighborhood next year, you would probably spend some time afterward thinking about what each person had said and whether you wanted to vote for them. Similarly, if you read a selection that is meant to be persuasive, you would probably ask yourself if the writer had convinced you of his or her point, and why. If you were reading a textbook or other informative reading material, it would make sense after you read to ask yourself what you had just learned—and why it mattered.

In college, you will be expected to carry on conversations about the information you read. And even if you don't speak up in class, you will still probably be required to take at least one test on the material you have read. So you need effective strategies that will help you learn, study, and remember the information. You should develop the following after-reading strategies.

▶ Think carefully about the ideas you have read.
▶ Talk about the ideas in class or with your classmates or study partners.
▶ Turn your annotations into notes.

Chapter 7 in this book will help you develop a strong connection between your during and after reading strategies.

Interaction 1–9   Practice the Reading Process

Find an article in a magazine or journal. Here are the rules for your search.

▶ The subject must interest you.
▶ The article must have an informative purpose.
▶ The article must have at least ten paragraphs.

To find it, look in your campus library's periodicals section (in the physical library or on its website); visit your local bookstore, newsstand, pharmacy, coffee shop, or grocery store; or go online. (Hint: Numerous special-interest magazines exist. You may want to think about subjects you care about and then see if you can find a magazine for people who share one of these interests.) You are going to use the article to answer questions on the next couple of pages.

Before You Read

A. Survey Your Article

1. What is your purpose for choosing this article? In other words, why are you interested in this topic? What do you hope to learn?_____

_____

2. What is the title of the article?_____

3. Check which of the following appear in your article:

_____ Title

_____ Headings and/or subheadings

_____ Words in bold or italics

_____ Visuals

B. Support the Informative Purpose

1. Explain how you know the purpose is informative._____

_____

C. **Predict What You Expect the Article to Cover**

Based on your survey of the article, what information do you expect to find?

▶ _____

▶ _____

▶ _____

▶ _____

▶ _____

D. **Activate Your Prior Knowledge**

For each item you predicted, think of at least one piece of prior knowledge that you hold about that subject—even if the information is somewhat vague. List these pieces of prior knowledge here.

▶ _____

▶ _____

▶ _____

▶ _____

▶ _____

While You Read

Monitor Your Comprehension

Read the informative article you chose. As you read, mark your article using the following guidelines.

1. Put a ✔ next to each paragraph that you read and understood while staying focused.

2. Put an ✗ next to a paragraph that you had to reread due to lack of understanding or focus.

3. Circle words you don't know.

After You Read

A. **Think about What You Learned, Its Relevance, and Its Significance**

Review what you said about your purpose for selecting your article and what you expected to find on p. 23, and then answer the following questions.

1. What did you learn from the article? List at least three major details or pieces of information.

   ▶ _____

   ▶ _____

   ▶ _____

2. Was the article as relevant as you expected it to be? Why or why not? _____

_____

_____

3. What did you find significant about the article? What was important about it to you? _____

_____

_____

4. Who else might find this article relevant? What audience was this article probably written for?

_____

_____

B. **Reflect on Your Reading Process**

1. After you read, compare the paragraphs that have ✔'s and those that have ✗'s. What makes some paragraphs easy to understand or stay focused on while other paragraphs are not? List your ideas, and then share them with a classmate to get more ideas.

   ▶ _____

   ▶ _____

   ▶ _____

2. In a dictionary, look up the meanings of three words you circled, and write the words and definitions here.

   ▶ _____

   ▶ _____

   ▶ _____

3. Reread the parts of the article where the circled words appeared. Did looking up the definitions help you understand those parts? Why or why not? _____

_____

_____

Beyond Skills: Knowledge

Much of this book will discuss skills to use while you are reading and after you have finished reading—skills that will improve your comprehension, help you understand text structure, and, in general, make reading college textbooks a more deliberate and interactive experience. There is another factor besides reading skills, however, that affects how well you read college-level material. That factor is *prior knowledge,* which we've already defined as knowledge you already have about a particular subject. Each person's prior knowledge is somewhat different from that of every other person. Thus, readings that seem easy to you may be more difficult for your classmate, or vice versa.

When an author and readers share prior knowledge, reading becomes easier and comprehension improves. For example, often authors assume that members of a particular culture will share certain pieces of information. Former professor E. D. Hirsch has written several books in which he notes that literate Americans typically know what the phrase *Independence Day* refers to (July 4, the day America declared independence from the British back in 1776). They know what the term *civil rights movement* means. They know certain stories from the Bible, not necessarily because they are Jews or Christians who study the Bible, but because the Bible is a source of many stories that form part of the background of our culture. Hirsch calls this shared background knowledge *cultural literacy.*

We have no way of knowing which pieces of information you already have that might be considered cultural literacy. But a very important predictor of reading comprehension is prior knowledge. So whenever one of the readings in the book refers to a story, idea, or fact about our culture that seems especially important to know, a Common Knowledge box appears. Why would we consider certain ideas more important to know than others? If we find that many writers assume their readers will know a certain fact or understand a particular idea, then we think you should take the time to learn about it. That way, when you find a reference to it in another reading sometime in the future, you will hold that information as prior knowledge.

The more prior knowledge you bring to a reading, the more easily you will understand it. The more you read, the more knowledge you will hold in common with others.

Interaction 1–10 > **Common Knowledge**

In each of the other classes you are taking, ask your professors for a list of terms they feel are "common knowledge" for their class or within their field. Share these lists with this class. Make sure you have prior knowledge of the words on your list so you can briefly explain their meaning to your classmates, if needed.

- ▶ Did you know some of these terms already? If so, which ones?
- ▶ Do your classmates know these terms?
- ▶ Share any prior knowledge you have.
- ▶ Discuss whether these different terms seem important to know.

Connect Your Skills

Connecting to the Reading Process

A. Before You Read. Survey the following movie review and answer the pre-reading questions.

1–5. Surveying the Reading

Survey the textbook selection that follows. Then check the elements that are included in this reading.

_____ Title   _____ Words in bold or italic type

_____ Headings   _____ Images and captions

_____ First sentences of paragraphs

6. Guessing the Purpose

Based on the source and the title of the excerpt below, do you think the author's purpose is mostly to persuade, inform, or express?

_____

_____

7–8. Predicting the Content

Based on your survey, what are two things you expect the reading selection to discuss?

▶ _____

▶ _____

9–10. Activating Your Knowledge

Have you seen *Moneyball*? If so, what did you think of the film? If not, did you hear anything about the film? What do you know about the meaning of the name of the movie? What do you know about baseball? Consult your memory to find any prior knowledge you may have.

▶ _____

▶ _____

▶ Reading with Pen in Hand

Students who annotate as they read are more successful than those who do not. That's why you will annotate each selection in *Connect* as you read. In the reading that follows, use the following symbols:

★ or Point   to indicate a main idea

① ② ③   to indicate major details

Movie Review: *Moneyball*
Brad Pitt stars as Oakland Athletics General Manager Billy Beane in this surprise success with a story that goes beyond baseball.

Kenneth Turan

1   Winning isn't everything, voracious Vince Lombardi used to say, it's the only thing. But what if Lombardi was wrong? What if other things mean more, last longer, have more significance than victories, not only in life but also in the particular lives of the people who play the games?

2   This is the heretical premise of the thoughtful and entertaining *Moneyball*, based on the equally iconoclastic bestseller by Michael Lewis. Starring Brad Pitt in top movie star form, it's a film that's impressive and surprising.

3   It's a surprise because *Moneyball* is that rare sports movie that doesn't end with a rousing last-second victory or a come-from-behind celebration. Fittingly for a book its author calls "a biography of an idea," it deals not only with wins and losses but also with the quixotic quest of a man who wanted to revolutionize a sport, someone who was willing, in Lewis' words, "to rethink baseball: how it is managed, how it is played, who is best suited to play it, and why."

4   That man was Billy Beane, charmingly played by Pitt, the provocative general manager of the Oakland Athletics whose unconventional ideas about what a team with limited resources could do to compete with profligate powerhouses like the New York Yankees continue to infuriate the sport's traditionalists. It's not for nothing that *Moneyball* starts with a quote from Yankees star Mickey Mantle: "It's unbelievable how much you don't know about the game you've been playing all your life."

Melinda Sue Gordon/Columbia Pictures/Everett Collection

5   *Moneyball* is also a surprise success because this has been a famously troubled production, one on which Sony pulled the plug just before shooting was to begin despite having Steven Soderbergh set to direct from a script by Steven Zaillian. The project should have died right there, but Pitt, who must have had a sense of how good a role this was for him, refused to let it go. With Aaron Sorkin aboard as co-writer and Bennett Miller shrewdly installed as director, the film unexpectedly flourished.

6   Miller, whose only previous features are the subtle, nuanced *Capote* and a documentary, has a restrained but dead-on storytelling style that is an ideal counterpoint for a tale set in the emotional, volatile world of professional sports. He's a filmmaker who knows how to make stories involving without overstating them, and, like Billy Beane, he sees value in situations others might miss.

7   *Capote* won a lead actor Oscar for Philip Seymour Hoffman (who returns here, letter-perfect as Oakland Manager Art Howe), and Miller's focused style once again creates an atmosphere where actors can flourish. Chief among these is Pitt, who does wonders with a role of a good guy in a tough space, a man who combines the confidence and charisma of the former professional athlete Beane is with an unexpected questioning nature. This is low-key star power at its best.

8   Pitt, of course, does not do it alone. Aside from Hoffman, he has an ideal foil in an unexpectedly dramatic Jonah Hill, who makes the perfect odd couple complement to Pitt's Beane as the awkward, pudgy Peter Brand, a computer geek who studied economics at Yale but eats baseball statistics for breakfast and ends up as Oakland's assistant general manager.

9   The actors and director Miller have the benefit of a strong script that feels seamless despite having had both Zaillian and Sorkin work on it. (Stan Chervin gets story credit.) Though it departs at times from the way things happened—Brand is a fictional character because Oakland's real assistant general manager, Paul DePodesta, later with the Dodgers, refused to allow his name to be used—the screenplay has great pungent dialogue and a strong sense of drama that couldn't have been easy to distill from Lewis' discursive book.

10   *Moneyball* begins on Oct. 15, 2001, with Beane's Oakland team in serious trouble: It's losing the American League division series to the much wealthier Yankees. The A's general manager gets more bad news when he meets with the team owner. Not only are the A's relinquishing one of their top players to the Yankees via free agency, but there is also no money to replace him.

11   As Beane runs a meeting with his scouts and player development people (several of whom are played by real-life weathered baseball veterans), the general manager is a picture of frustration. Because the A's are one of the sport's poorer teams, they can't buy their way out of trouble. "We got to think differently," Beane insists, but just what would differently mean?

12   Beane gets a hint when he meets young Brand, then working for the Cleveland Indians, who introduces the general manager to the world of sabermetrics, a statistical analysis of baseball pioneered by Bill James. The notion is that traditional ways of looking at player value have led to individuals being misjudged, to some players being overvalued and, most important for the A's, to others being undervalued and thus available for poor but enlightened teams to purchase.

13   *Moneyball* sets off this inside baseball stuff with segments about Beane's private life, about his failed marriage (Robin Wright plays the ex-wife) and his tenuous relationship with his young daughter (a very fine Kerris Dorsey). Most critically, the film takes us back to Beane's own odyssey

as a professional player, showing how the past was prologue to actions he takes in the here and now.

14   Once Beane, a nervy guy who believes in wheeling, dealing and rolling the dice, gets James' system in his blood, the great fun of *Moneyball* begins as we watch Beane and Brand assemble, in classic "Seven Samurai" fashion, a team of unwanted players. People like Scott Hatteberg (Chris Pratt), a catcher whose overall baseball abilities Beane valued so much that he changed him into a first baseman because Hatteberg could no longer throw well enough to be behind the plate.

—From Kenneth Turan, Movie Review in the *Los Angeles Times*, September 23, 2011.
Copyright © 2012 by the *Los Angeles Times*. Reprinted with permission.

B. Use the material you annotated to answer the following questions about the movie review.

11. What kind of movie is *Moneyball*? _____

12. What other movies of this kind have you seen? _____

   _____

13. Who is the story about? _____

   _____

14–16. Who are the three actors in the movie, and what roles do they play?

   ▶ _____

   ▶ _____

   ▶ _____

17–18. Have you seen any of these actors in other movies? Name the actor and the movie, and describe your thoughts about them.

   ▶ _____

   ▶ _____

19. Who is the director? _____

20. What action drives *Moneyball*? _____

   _____

   _____

 Click to Connect! To check your comprehension of chapter concepts, visit **www.cengagebrain.com** to access the CourseMate for this chapter.

Chapter Summary Activity

Chapter 1 has discussed reading as an active process, showing you strategies you can use before, during, and after you read to increase your comprehension. Fill in the Reading Guide to Connecting to the Reading Process below by completing each idea on the left with information from Chapter 1 on the right. You can return to this guide throughout the course as a reminder of how to use the reading process to your advantage.

Reading Guide to Connecting to the Reading Process

Complete this idea with …	information from Chapter 1.
Two common motivators for reading well	1. _____ 2. _____
Four things to do before reading	3. _____ 4. _____ 5. _____ 6. _____
Parts of a reading to pay attention to while surveying	7. _____ 8. _____ 9. _____ 10. _____ 11. _____
Three general purposes an author may have	12. _____ 13. _____ 14. _____
Prior knowledge—definition	15. _____
Six learning tasks to accomplish while reading	16. _____ 17. _____ 18. _____

	19. _____
	20. _____
	21. _____
Three questions for monitoring comprehension	22. _____
	_____
	_____
Three ways to review and rehearse what you've read	23. _____
	24. _____
	25. _____

Compared to interactive reading strategies you used before you read this chapter, what is one thing you will do differently because you find it more effective? Write down your thoughts.

_____

_____

_____

Reading 1–1 | Newspaper Article

▶ Pre-Reading the Selection

In August 2007, the article "Amid War, Passion for TV Chefs, Soaps and Idols," about the increasing popularity of television in Afghanistan, appeared in the *New York Times*.

Surveying the Reading

Survey the following article. Then check the elements that are included in this reading.

_____	Title	_____	Words in bold or italic type
_____	Headings	_____	Images and captions
_____	First sentences of paragraphs		

Guessing the Purpose

Based on the title of the article that begins on page 34 and the fact that it was published in a newspaper, what two main purposes do you suppose the author has: to persuade, inform, and/or express? _____

Predicting the Content

Based on your survey, what are three things you expect the reading selection to discuss?

► _____

► _____

► _____

Activating Your Knowledge

Search your memory for knowledge you have on any of the following topics: Afghanistan, the Taliban, television in developing countries, or how democracy and television are related. Write down at least two of these pieces of prior knowledge.

► _____

► _____

Scan to Connect! Use your smart phone to scan this code to watch a video. (See the inside front cover for more information on how to use this.) The program *Afghan Star* is the Afghan equivalent of our *American Idol*. Compare and contrast what you see and hear in this music video with what you see and hear on the American show. Discuss at least three particular similarities or differences.

Common Knowledge

Read these terms and their definitions to help you understand the reading selection.

Taliban (*paragraph 1*) A group of religious fundamentalists who ruled Afghanistan from 1994 to 2001, introducing very strict Sharia law (Islamic law), including many laws that negatively affected women's rights.

the call to prayer (*paragraph 9*) Muslims (people who follow Islam) pray five times each day; a man known as the *muezzin* calls the faithful to prayer each time.

taboos (*paragraph 21*) Actions, words, objects, and the like that are banned in a particular society. For example, cannibalism (eating human flesh) is a taboo in many cultures.

democracy (*paragraph 30*) A government led by the people, usually through voting periodically for political leaders.

▶ Reading with Pen in Hand

Students who annotate as they read are more successful than those who do not. That's why you will annotate each selection in *Connect* as you read. In the reading that follows, use the following symbols:

★ or (Point)   to indicate a main idea

① ② ③   to indicate major details

 Visit www.cengagebrain.com to access the CourseMate for this chapter to hear pronunciations of vocabulary words from this reading.

Amid War, Passion for TV Chefs, Soaps and Idols

Barry Bearak

▶ Paragraphs 1–3 focus on one person. Who? Why is he important?

1   KABUL, Afghanistan, July 25—Twelve years ago, during a very different time in a very different Afghanistan, a medical student named Daoud Sediqi was bicycling from campus when he was stopped by the Taliban's whip-wielding religious police.

2   The young man immediately felt an avalanche of regret, for he was in violation of at least two laws. One obvious offense was the length of his hair. While the ruling Taliban insisted that men sprout untrimmed beards, they were otherwise opposed to scruffiness and the student had allowed his locks to grow shaggy. His other **transgression** was more serious. If his captors searched his possessions, they would find a CD with an X-rated movie.

transgression What synonym (word with similar meaning) is in the second sentence of this paragraph?

3   "Fortunately, they didn't look; my only punishment was to have my head shaved because of my long hair," recalled Mr. Sediqi, now at age 31 one of this nation's best-known men, someone sprung from a new wellspring of fame—not

a warlord or a mullah, but a television celebrity, the host of "Afghan Star," this nation's "American Idol."

4   Since the fall of the Taliban in late 2001, Afghanistan has been developing **in fits and starts**. Among the unchanging circumstances that still leave people fitful: continuing war, inept leaders, corrupt police officers and woeful living conditions. According to the government's latest surveys, only 43 percent of all households have nonleaking windows and roofs, 31 percent have safe drinking water and 7 percent have sanitary toilets.

in fits and starts This phrase could be misunderstood as it is used in this sentence. So look it up online (try www.Bartleby.com), in a good dictionary (under *fit*), or in an idiom dictionary. What does it mean?

5   But television is off to a phenomenal start, with Afghans now engrossed, for better or worse, in much of the same escapist fare that seduces the rest of the world: soap operas that pit the unbearably conniving against the implausibly virtuous, chefs preparing meals that most people would never eat in kitchens they could never afford, talk show hosts wheedling secrets from those too shameless to keep their troubles to themselves.

6   The latest national survey, which dates from 2005, shows that 19 percent of Afghan households own a television, a remarkable total considering not only that owning a TV was a crime under the Taliban but that a mere 14 percent of the population has access to public electricity. In a study this year of Afghanistan's five most urban provinces, two-thirds of all people said they watched TV every day or almost every day.

▶ Paragraphs 4–8 suggest three reasons people in Afghanistan are watching TV. What are they?

7   "Maybe Afghanistan is not so different from other places," said Muhammad Qaseem Akhgar, a prominent social analyst and newspaper editor. "People watch television because there is nothing else to do."

8   Reading is certainly less an option; only 28 percent of the population is literate. "Where else can one find amusement?" Mr. Akhgar asked.

9   Each night, people in Kabul obey the beckoning of prime time much as they might otherwise answer the call to prayer. "As you can see, there is truth on the television, because all over the world the mother-in-law is always provoking a fight," said Muhammad Farid, a man sitting in a run-down restaurant beside the Pul-i-Khishti Mosque, his attention fixed on an Indian soap opera that had been dubbed into Dari.

▶ Paragraphs 9–11 quote two Afghans. What point do the Afghans make?

10   Women, whose public outings are constrained by custom, most often watch their favorite shows at home. Men, on the other hand, are free to make TV a **communal** ritual. In one restaurant after another, with deft fingers dipping into mounds of steaming rice, patrons sit cross-legged on carpeted platforms, their eyes fixed on a television set perched near the ceiling. Profound metaphysical questions hover in the dim light: Will Prerna find happiness with Mr. Bajaj, who is after all not the father of her child?

communal Based on the contrast between women's and men's actions set up in the previous sentence and this one, what do you think *communal* might mean?

11   "These are problems that teach you about life," said Sayed Agha, who sells fresh vegetables from a pushcart by day and views warmed-over melodramas by night.

12   What to watch is rarely contested. At 7:30, the dial is turned to Tolo TV for "Prerna," a soap opera colloquially known by the name of its female protagonist.

Afghan boys and men watching TV

Joao Silva/The New York Times/Redux

intrafamily Notice the two parts of this word: *intra-* + *family. Intra-* means "within." What does the whole word mean?

extramarital This word, too, has two parts: *extra-* + *marital. Extra-* means "outside of." *Marital* means "related to marriage." What does the whole word mean?

gestate A human baby takes forty to forty-one weeks to *gestate* inside the mother's uterus. Look at the context here. What is a general definition of *gestate*?

hackneyed What does this word mean? Use a dictionary.

At 8, the channel is switched for "The Thief of Baghdad." At 8:30, it is back to Tolo for the **intrafamily** and **extramarital** warfare waged on "Tulsi," the nickname for a show whose title literally means "Because the Mother-in-Law Was Once the Daughter-in-Law."

13   Kabul has eight local television stations, including one feebly operated by the government. "The key time slots are from 6 to 9 p.m. because that's when people switch on their generators for electrical power," said Saad Mohseni, who runs Tolo, the channel that dominates the market in most of the country. "People love the soap operas."

14   "We've just bought the rights to '24,' the American show," he said. "We had some concerns. Most of the bad guys are Muslims, but we did focus groups and it turns out most people didn't care about that so long as the villains weren't Afghans."

15   Mr. Mohseni, a former investment banker, and his three siblings started Tolo TV (Tolo means "dawn" in Dari) in 2004, assisted by a grant from the United States Agency for International Development. After living most of their adult lives in exile in Australia, the Mohsenis returned to post-Taliban Kabul looking for investment opportunities and discovered a nearly prehistoric television wilderness ready for settlement. A used color TV cost only $75.

16   But what did they want to watch? Afghan tastes had not been allowed to **gestate** over decades, passing from Milton Berle to Johnny Carson to Bart Simpson. Everything would be brand-new. "We let ourselves be guided by what we liked," Mr. Mohseni said.

17   For the most part, that means that Tolo has harvested the **hackneyed** from television's vast international landscape. True-crime shows introduce Afghans to the sensationalism of their own pederasts and serial killers. Reality shows

pluck everyday people off the streets and transform them with spiffed-up wardrobes. Quiz shows reward the knowledgeable: How many pounds of mushrooms did Afghanistan export last year? A contestant who answers correctly earns a free gallon of cooking oil.

18   Some foreign shows, like those featuring disasters and police chases, are so nonverbal that Tolo is able to rebroadcast them without translation. Other formats require only slight retooling.

▸ Paragraphs 12–19 discuss different genres of TV shows that Afghans watch. What are they?

19   Mr. Sediqi is about to begin his third season with "Afghan Star." He has never seen "American Idol" and said he had never heard of his American counterpart, Ryan Seacrest. Nevertheless, he ably manages to introduce the competing vocalists and coax the audience to vote for their favorites via cellphone.

20   "I must tell you that I am having very good fun," Mr. Sediqi said, employing his limited English. He is one of several young stars at Tolo whose hipness is exotic enough to seem almost extraterrestrial to an average Afghan. Older men who prefer soap operas to singing competitions are likely to want to give Mr. Sediqi a good thrashing. "People in the countryside and the mosques say that the show is ruining society," Mr. Sediqi admitted.

▸ What seems to be the main point of paragraph 20?

21   Tolo has drawn a huge audience while testing the bounds of certain taboos. Zaid Mohseni, Saad's younger brother, said: "When we first put a man and woman on the air together, we had complaints: this isn't legal, this isn't Islamic, blah, blah, blah. Then the criticism softened. It was O.K. as long as they don't talk to each other. Finally, it softened more: O.K., they can talk as long as they don't laugh."

▸ What is the main point of paragraphs 21–25?

22   The bounds are pushed but not broken. A live talk show called "Woman" is co-moderated by a psychiatrist, Dr. Muhammad Yasin Babrak. While female callers are frank in their laments, the therapist limits himself to being Dear Abby to the lovelorn rather than Dr. Ruth to the sexually frustrated. "I won't talk about incest or homosexuality," he said.

23   Music videos, primarily imports from India, are broadcast regularly. With a nod to Afghan tradition, the bare arms and midriffs of female dancers are obscured with a milky strip of electronic camouflage. And yet, sporting events are somehow deemed less erotic. Maria Sharapova was shown at Wimbledon with the full flesh of her limbs unconcealed.

24   Whatever the constraints, some observers consider TV a portal to promiscuity. "Forty million people are living with H.I.V.-AIDS, and television is finally helping Afghanistan contribute to those figures," the Ayatollah Asif Mohseni said with sarcasm.

25   He is an elderly white-bearded man, and while he is not related to the family who runs Tolo TV, he, too, has entered the television business, starting a station more inclined to showcase Islamic chanting. "We have an economy that is in ruins," Ayatollah Mohseni said. "Do you think rubbish Indian serials with half-naked people are the answer?"

26   But the strongest complaints against Tolo have come from politicians, including members of the government. Tolo's news coverage, while increasingly

▸ What is the main point of paragraphs 26–30?

professional, is very often unflattering and even irreverent. Members of Parliament have been shown asleep at their desks or in overheated debate throwing water bottles. One lawmaker was photographed picking his nose and then guiltily cleaning his finger.

27   In April, when Attorney General Abdul Jabar Sabet thought he had been quoted out of context, he sent policemen to Tolo's headquarters to arrest the news staff. The ensuing contretemps had to be mediated by the United Nations mission in Kabul.

28   "It has been quite odd," said Saad Mohseni, Tolo's chief. "This is Afghanistan, a young democracy, and we don't have problems with the drug dealers or the Taliban or even the local populace. Our problems are all with the government, either because of red tape or attempted censorship or someone with a vested interest trying to extract money."

29   He paused for effect.

30   "With democracy comes television. It's hard for some people to get used to."

—"Amid War, Passion for TV Chefs, Soaps and Idols" by Barry Bearak, *New York Times*, August 1, 2007. Copyright © 2007 by *New York Times*. All rights reserved. Reprinted by permission.

▶ Check Your Skills While Continuing to Learn

The questions that follow will check your understanding (comprehension) of the reading selection. They address all the skills you will learn throughout the book. Here in Chapter 1, each skill is first described briefly. Then a sample question, answer, and reason for the answer are given.

A Suggested Learning Process

- ▶ Read and think about the skill.
- ▶ Study all three parts of the example: the question, the answer, and the explanation.
- ▶ Look back at the reading selection so you can understand the example.
- ▶ Answer the second question as a check for yourself of how well you can already apply this skill.
- ▶ Note that you can keep track of your progress in applying the different skills by filling in the chart in the inside back cover of the book.

▶ Comprehension Questions

Write the letter of the answer on the line. Then explain your thinking.

Main Idea

Skill

Think of the main idea as the "point" of the paragraph or passage. The main idea dominates the paragraph. To find the main idea, notice which sentence explains the author's most important point about the subject. The other sentences in the paragraph should offer explanations, examples, and details about the main idea. Sometimes a main idea may cover the supporting details from several paragraphs.

Example

<u>a</u>   1. What is the best statement of the main idea of paragraph 12?

    a. What to watch is rarely contested.

    b. At 7:30, the dial is turned to Tolo TV for "Prerna."

    c. At 8, the channel is switched for "The Thief of Baghdad."

    d. At 8:30, it is back to Tolo for the intrafamily and extramarital warfare waged on "Tulsi."

Why? What information in the selection leads you to give that answer? The first sentence is the point of the paragraph: Everyone in Kabul watches the same programs. The other sentences list the programs that everyone watches at different times.

Practice

____   2. What is the best statement of the main idea of the group of paragraphs 21–23?

    a. Tolo has drawn a huge audience while testing the bounds of certain taboos.

    b. They can talk as long as they don't laugh.

    c. The therapist limits himself to being Dear Abby for the lovelorn rather than Dr. Ruth to the sexually frustrated.

    d. Maria Sharapova was shown at Wimbledon with the full flesh of her limbs unconcealed.

Why? What information in the selection leads you to give that answer? _____

_____

_____

Supporting Details

Skill

Think of the supporting details as the "proof" for the main idea. To locate the supporting details, find the main idea and then look for the information the author uses to explain it in more detail. Sometimes, if a main idea covers more than one paragraph, you will find the supporting details in several paragraphs.

Example

<u>b</u>   3. In paragraph 2, what are the two major supporting details?

    a. Men's untrimmed beards; his captors searched Sediqi's possessions.

    b. Sediqi's long, shaggy hair; his possession of an X-rated movie

    c. The ruling Taliban; his possession of a CD

    d. He felt an avalanche of regret; he was scruffy.

Why? What information in the selection leads you to give that answer? The main idea of paragraph 2 is "The young man immediately felt an avalanche of regret, for he was in violation of at least two laws." Answer B gives the two major supporting details; it lists the two laws Sediqi broke. His hair was long and shaggy, and he had an X-rated movie with him.

Practice

_____ 4. Paragraph 5 has a single sentence. Nevertheless, it has a main idea and three supporting details. What are the supporting details?

    a. Television is off to a phenomenal start; Afghans are engrossed in television programs; soap operas pit evil against good.

    b. Afghans are engrossed in television programs; soap operas that pit evil against good; chefs who prepare too-expensive meals on TV.

    c. The same escapist shows seduce the rest of the world; soap operas that pit evil against good; chefs who prepare too-expensive meals on TV

    d. Soap operas that pit evil against good; chefs who prepare too-expensive meals on TV; talk shows hosts who expose people's secrets

Why? What information in the selection leads you to give that answer? _____

_____

_____

Author's Purpose

Skill

The author's general purpose may be to persuade (change the reader's mind or behavior), inform (share information with the reader), or express (evoke emotion, often through stories); or it may be a combination of these purposes. At specific points in a text, an author may use a variety of methods to achieve the general purpose. You should always assume that the author has a particular reason for what he or she wrote.

Example

_d_ 5. In the first sentence of paragraph 6, why does the author give the statistics (that is, facts stated as percentages)?

    a. to entertain readers by sharing how few Afghans have televisions

    b. to inform readers that televisions are run using private rather than public electricity

    c. to persuade readers that it was good for the Afghan people that the Taliban left power

    d. to inform readers of how quickly watching television has become a major occupation, despite other shortages

Why? What information in the selection leads you to give that answer? The author says that 19 percent ownership of TVs is "remarkable" for two reasons: previously, owning a TV was a crime, and only 14 percent
of the people have access to public electricity. In paragraph 4, the author says the Taliban government fell in late
2001, and here in paragraph 6, he notes that the latest national survey was taken in 2005, only four years later.

Practice

_____ 6. In paragraph 22, what is the author's purpose in saying that Dr. Babrak limits himself to
being Dear Abby rather than Dr. Ruth?

   a. to inform readers how popular the live talk show "Woman" is

   b. to persuade readers that Afghan women do not want to discuss their sexual needs on
   television

   c. to inform readers to what extent Dr. Babrak pushes the bounds of Afghan custom but
   does not break them

   d. to persuade readers that Dr. Babrak is one of the most conservative Muslims in Afghanistan

Why? What information in the selection leads you to give that answer? _____

_____

_____

Relationships

Skill

The ideas in a reading selection are related to one another in different ways. For instance, one sentence might discuss the causes of an event mentioned in a different sentence. Some relationships have
to do with time, space, comparisons and contrasts, causes and effects, and so on. You may see the
relationships between the ideas in different parts of one sentence, in different sentences, or even in
different paragraphs. Many times, these relationships are indicated with signal words or transitions
such as *but, and, however, for example,* and so on.

Example

b   7. In paragraph 10, what signal word or words indicate a difference (a contrast) between
how and where women and men watch television?

   a. most often

   b. on the other hand

   c. after

   d. not

Why? What information in the selection leads you to give that answer? *On the other hand* is used to say that
while women usually have to watch TV at home alone, men can watch TV together in public. Sometimes, although
not here, the first part of this expression is also used: *on the one hand.*

Practice

_____ 8. In the second sentence of paragraph 13, what is the relationship between the first part of the sentence—"The key time slots are from 6 to 9 p.m." and the second part—"because that's when people switch on their generators for electrical power"?

   a. The first part is an example of the second part.

   b. The second part is a contrast with the first part.

   c. The second part is the cause of the first part.

   d. The first part happened earlier in time than the second part.

Why? What information in the selection leads you to give that answer? _____

_____

Fact, Opinion, and Inference

Skill

A fact is a true statement that can be verified by using another source of information: *It is 85 degrees outside*. An opinion is an individual's personal reaction: *It's too hot to play baseball*. An inference is an idea the reader gets from the other ideas the author has stated: *That person must be from up north*. To be valid, an inference must be a logical extension of what the author has written.

Example

_a_ 9. Which statement below is an opinion?

   a. All over the world, the mother-in-law is always provoking a fight.

   b. Seven years ago, Daoud Sediqi had his head shaved.

   c. Only 28 percent of the Afghan population is literate.

   d. Attorney General Abdul Jabar Sabet sent policemen to arrest the news staff at Tolo TV.

Why? What leads you to give that answer? There are two overly broad ideas in answer A: *all* over the world and *always*. Often, such broad statements cannot be verified and thus cannot be considered facts. Also, very few things are always true all around the world. True statements tend to be more specific. Answers B, C, and D are facts that can be verified either by this newspaper article or by the author's sources of information.

Practice

_____ 10. Which of the following inferences is valid—that is, supported by the information in the article?

   a. Afghan society will remain as it is, despite the influence of television.

   b. Afghan society is changing due to the influence of television.

   c. People around the world use television mostly as a way to forget their troubles.

   d. Television contributes to the spread of HIV-AIDS.

Why? What information in the selection leads you to give that answer? _____

_____

_____

_____

_____

▸Vocabulary in New Contexts

Review the vocabulary words in the margins of the reading selection and then complete the following activities.

Relationships Between Words

Circle *yes* or *no* to answer the question. Then explain your answer.

1. Can an **extramarital** affair be deduced from the **gestation** period of a baby?

   Yes   No

   Why or why not? _____

2. Would the phrase *in fits and starts* be considered **hackneyed**?

   Yes   No

   Why or why not? _____

3. Would leaving a **communal** bathroom a mess be considered a **transgression** of etiquette?

   Yes   No

   Why or why not? _____

4. Could **intrafamily** drama manifest itself **in fits and starts**?

   Yes   No

   Why or why not? _____

Language in Your Life

Write short answers to each question. Look at the vocabulary words closely before you answer.

1. Name an activity or idea that required some **gestation** for you to appreciate it better.

_____

2. Name one idea or saying that you find to be **hackneyed**. _____

_____

3. Name an activity that you have attempted **in fits and starts**. _____

_____

4. Name what you think is the most serious **transgression** someone can commit. _____

_____

5. Name a **communal** activity that you enjoy. _____

_____

Language in Use

Select the best word to complete the meaning of each sentence.

communal	extramarital	gestated	hackneyed
in fits and starts	intrafamily	transgression	

1. The hippies in the 1960s and 1970s made _____ living famous in America.

2. They tried to overcome the idea that people should live in nuclear families and have sexual relationships only with their husband or wife. Instead of considering _____ sex a _____, they celebrated it as an expression of free love.

3. Although living in community was a fresh idea then, by now some of the hippies' notions of communes seem _____, even ridiculous. But the idea has _____, and now other kinds of communities have formed in the United States, such as cohousing, an idea that started in Denmark.

4. Forming an intentional community can be a process that happens _____. So many difficult tasks are involved, such as finding land that the group can afford, that the effort can easily stop short of success.

5. In successful communities, however, the group can come to feel like a family. And as in all families, _____ tensions can skyrocket over matters like agreeing on how to make decisions.

Reading 1–2 | Sociology Textbook

▸ Pre-Reading the Selection

The reading that follows, "Mass Media and Body Image," is part of a sociology textbook chapter on sexuality and gender.

Surveying the Reading

Survey the selection. Then check the elements that are included in this reading.

_____ Title	_____ Words in bold or italic type
_____ Headings	_____ Images and captions
_____ First sentences of paragraphs	

Guessing the Purpose

Judging from the genre of the book from which this reading is taken, what do you suppose is the purpose of the selection? _____

Predicting the Content

Predict three things this selection will discuss.

▸ _____

▸ _____

▸ _____

Activating Your Knowledge

Think of two friends or relatives who have been influenced by the media to view their bodies in a certain way. Briefly note the kinds of influence the media has had on them.

▸ _____

▸ _____

🔵 **Scan to Connect!** Use your smart phone to scan this code to watch a video. (See the inside front cover for more information on how to use this.) As you watch this video, apply your prior knowledge of the effect of media on your body image (or of people you know). Is it similar to or different from the video? Explain.

Common Knowledge

Read these terms and their definitions to aid your understanding of the reading selection.

revenue (*paragraph 4*) Income produced from a particular source

industry (*paragraph 4*) A specific type of manufacture

▶ Reading with Pen in Hand

Students who annotate as they read are more successful than those who do not. That's why you will annotate each selection in *Connect* as you read. In the reading that follows, use the following symbols:

★ or Point   to indicate a main idea

① ② ③   to indicate major details

 Visit www.cengagebrain.com to access the CourseMate for this chapter to hear pronunciations of vocabulary words from this reading.

The Mass Media and Body Image

Robert J. Brym and John Lie

gender Notice that the authors didn't use the word *sex*. Also notice they say the *social construction of gender*. Take a guess at the meaning of *gender*, or use a dictionary to find the meaning.

▶ On TV, what roles do women and men fill?

1   The social construction of **gender** does not stop at the school steps. Outside school, children, adolescents, and adults continue to negotiate gender roles as they interact with the mass media. If you systematically observe the roles played by women and men in TV programs and ads one evening, you will probably discover a pattern noted by sociologists since the 1970s. Women will more frequently be seen cleaning house, taking care of children, modeling clothes, and acting as objects of male desire. Men will more frequently be seen in aggressive, action-oriented, and authoritative roles. They reinforce the normality of traditional gender roles. As you will now see, many people even try to shape their bodies after the body images portrayed in the mass media.

▶ What difference in the two girls' diaries is Joan Jacobs Brumberg interested in?

2   The human body has always served as a sort of personal billboard that advertises gender. However, historian Joan Jacobs Brumberg (1997) makes a good case for the view that the importance of body image to our self-definition has grown over the past century. Just listen to the difference in emphasis on the body in the diary resolutions of two typical white, middle-class American girls, separated by a mere 90 years. From 1892: "Resolved, not to talk about myself or feelings. To think before speaking. To work seriously. To be self restrained in conversation and actions. Not to let my thoughts wander. To be dignified. Interest myself more in others." From 1982: "I will try to make myself better in any way I possibly can with the help of my budget and baby-sitting money. I will lose weight, get new lenses, already got new haircut, good makeup, new clothes and accessories" (quoted in Brumberg, 1997: xxi).

3   As body image became more important for one's self-definition in the course of the twentieth century, the ideal body image became thinner, especially for women. Thus, the first American "glamour girl" was Mrs. Charles Dana Gibson, who was famous in advertising and society cartoons in the 1890s and 1900s as the "Gibson Girl." According to the Metropolitan Museum of Art's Costume Institute, "[e]very man in America wanted to win her" and "every woman in America wanted to be her. Women stood straight as poplars and tightened their corset strings to show off tiny waists" (Metropolitan Museum of Art, 2000). As featured in the *Ladies Home Journal* in 1905, the Gibson Girl measured 38-27-45—certainly not slim by today's standards. During the twentieth century, however, the ideal female body type thinned out. The "White Rock Girl," featured on the logo of the White Rock beverage company, was 5'4" and weighed 140 pounds in 1894. In 1947 she had slimmed down to 125 pounds. By 1970 she was 5'8" and 118 pounds (Peacock, 2000).

▶ What do the examples of the Gibson Girl and the White Rock Girl show about the changing definition of the ideal female body?

4   Why did body image become more important to people's self-definition during the twentieth century? Why was slimness stressed? Part of the answer to both questions is that more Americans grew overweight as their lifestyles became more **sedentary**. As they became better educated, they also grew increasingly aware of the health problems associated with being overweight.

▶ What are two reasons that a slimmer body image became the ideal in the twentieth century?

sedentary Look at the context. What is the meaning?

Lou Chardonnay/Surf/Corbis

The low-calorie and diet food industry promotes an idea of slimness that is often impossible to attain and that generates widespread body dissatisfaction.

unattainable *Attain* means "reach." What does *unattainable* mean?

The desire to slim down was, then, partly a reaction to bulking up. But that is not the whole story. The rake-thin models that populate modern ads are not promoting good health. They are promoting an extreme body shape that is virtually **unattainable** for most people. They do so because it is good business. In 1990 the United States diet and low-calorie frozen entrée industry alone enjoyed revenues of nearly $700 million. Some 65 million Americans spent upward of $30 billion in the diet and self-help industry in the pursuit of losing weight. The fitness industry generated $43 billion in revenue, and the cosmetic surgery industry another $5 billion (Hesse-Biber, 1996: 35, 39, 51, 53). Bankrolled by these industries, advertising in the mass media blankets us with images of slim bodies and makes these body types appealing. Once people become convinced that they need to develop bodies like the ones they see in ads, many of them are really in trouble because these body images are very difficult for most people to attain.

▶ Did Gardner's 1997 study indicate that a majority of women and a majority of men were dissatisfied with their appearance?

5   Survey data show just how widespread dissatisfaction with our bodies is and how important a role the mass media play in generating our discomfort. For example, a 1997 survey of North American college graduates showed that 56 percent of women and 43 percent of men were dissatisfied with their overall appearance (Garner, 1997). Only 3 percent of the dissatisfied women, but 22 percent of the dissatisfied men, wanted to gain weight. This reflects the greater desire of men for muscular, stereotypically male **physiques**. Most of the dissatisfied men, and even more of the dissatisfied women (89 percent), wanted to lose weight. This reflects the general societal push toward slimness and its greater effect on women.

physiques Use the context to determine the meaning of *physiques*.

▶ How does Figure 1.3 reveal gender differences in body ideals?

6   **Figure 1.3** reveals gender differences in body ideals in a different way. It compares women's and men's attitudes toward the appearance of their stomachs. It also compares women's attitudes toward their breasts with men's attitudes toward their chests. It shows, first, that women are more concerned about their stomachs than men are. Second, it shows that by 1997 men were more concerned about their chests than women were about their breasts. Clearly, then,

▶ What is the main idea of this figure?

Figure 1.3   Body Dissatisfaction, United States, 1972–1997 (in percentage, N=4000)

Note: The N of 4000 refers only to the 1997 survey. The number of respondents in the earlier surveys was not given.

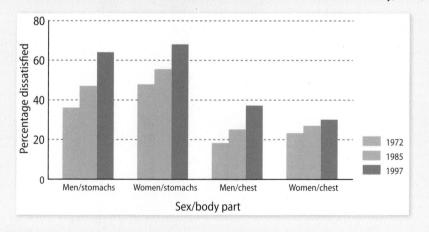

Table 1.2 The Influence of Fashion Models on Feelings about Appearance, North America (in percent, N=4000)

	Men	Women	Extremely Dissatisfied Women
I always or often:			
Compare myself to models in magazines	12	27	43
Carefully study the shape of models	19	28	47
Very thin or muscular models make me:			
Feel insecure about my weight	15	29	67
Want to lose weight	18	30	67

people's body ideals are influenced by their gender. Note also that Figure 1.3 shows trends over time. North Americans' anxiety about their bodies increased substantially between 1972 and 1997.

7   **Table 1.2** suggests that advertising is highly influential in creating anxiety and insecurity about appearance, particularly about body weight. Here we see that in 1997 nearly 30 percent of North American women compared themselves with the fashion models they saw in advertisements, felt insecure about their own appearance, and wanted to lose weight as a result. Among women who were dissatisfied with their appearance, the percentages were much larger, with about 45 percent making comparisons with fashion models and two-thirds feeling insecure and wanting to lose weight. It seems safe to conclude that fashion models stimulate body dissatisfaction among many North American women.

8   Body dissatisfaction, in turn, motivates many women to diet. Because of anxiety about their weight, 84 percent of North American women said they had dieted in the 1997 survey. The comparable figure for men was 54 percent. Just how important is it for people to achieve their weight goals? According to the survey, it's a life or weight issue: 24 percent of women and 17 percent of men said they would trade more than three years of their lives to achieve their weight goals.

9   Body dissatisfaction prompts some people to take dangerous and even life-threatening measures to reduce. In the 1997 survey, 50 percent of female smokers and 30 percent of male smokers said they smoked to control their weight. Other surveys suggest that between 1 percent and 5 percent of American women suffer from anorexia, or refusal to eat enough to remain healthy. About the same percentage of American female college students suffer from bulimia, or regular self-induced vomiting. For college men, the prevalence

▶ How do fashion models stimulate body dissatisfaction among North American women?

▶ What percentage of North American women and men have dieted, according to the 1997 study?

▶ What is the percentage difference between men's and women's insecure feelings when they compare themselves to models?

▶ What are two dangerous methods people use to lose weight?

voluntary This adjective relates to the noun *volunteer.* What does it mean?

of bulimia is between 0.2 percent and 1.5 percent (Averett and Korenman, 1996: 305–6). In the United Kingdom, eating disorders are just as common, and the British Medical Association warned that celebrities such as *Ally McBeal* star Calista Flockhart were contributing to a rise in anorexia and bulimia. However, U.K. magazine editors are taking some responsibility for the problem. They recognize that waif-thin models are likely influencing young women to feel anxious about their weight and shape. As a result, the editors recently drew up a **voluntary** code of conduct that urges them to monitor the body images they portray, impose a minimum size for models, and use models of varying shapes and sizes ("British Magazines": 2000). Whether similar measures are adopted in the United States remains to be seen.

—From Brym/Lie, *Sociology in Today's World*, 2e (p. 362). Copyright © 2012 Cengage Learning, Inc. Reproduced by permission. www.cengage.com/permissions

▶ Comprehension Questions

Write the letter of the answer on the line. Then explain your thinking.

Main Idea
Skill

Think of the main idea as the "point" of the paragraph or passage. The main idea dominates the paragraph. To find the main idea, notice which sentence explains the author's most important point about the subject. The other sentences in the paragraph should offer explanations, examples, and details about the main idea. Sometimes a main idea may cover the supporting details from several paragraphs.

Example

___c___   1. What is the main idea of this selection?

a. TV actors reinforce gender roles.

b. Self-improvement is a North American trait.

c. Many people try to shape their bodies to look like bodies portrayed in the media.

d. Slimness has been stressed as an ideal body image in the twentieth century.

Why? ▶ What information in the selection leads you to give that answer? Choices A and D are given as supporting details; neither is broad enough to cover the entire selection. Choice B was never mentioned. Choice C covers all the details in the piece.

Practice

_____ 2. What is the main idea of paragraphs 2–4, taken together?

   a. Body image has become more important to our self-definition during the twentieth century.

   b. The Gibson Girl and the White Rock Girl demonstrate how body image has changed.

   c. As people became more sedentary, they gained weight.

   d. The diet food and fitness industries make billions of dollars from women dissatisfied with their bodies.

Why? What information in the selection leads you to give that answer? _____

_____

_____

Supporting Details

Skill

Think of the supporting details as the "proof" for the main idea. To locate the supporting details, find the main idea and then look for the information the author uses to explain it in more detail. Sometimes, if a main idea covers more than one paragraph, you will find the supporting details in several paragraphs.

Example

__d__ 3. From 1972 to 1997, what was the increase in the percentage of men who were dissatisfied with their stomachs?

   a. about 10 percent

   b. about 15 percent

   c. about 20 percent

   d. about 25 percent

Why? What information in the selection leads you to give that answer? Figure 1.3 shows that about 63 percent of men were dissatisfied with their stomachs in 1997 and about 37 percent in 1972. The difference is about 26 percent.

Practice

_____ 4. What proportion of men compare themselves to models in magazines always or often?

   a. 12 percent

   b. 19 percent

   c. 15 percent

   d. 18 percent

Why? What information in the selection leads you to give that answer? _____

_____

Author's Purpose

Skill

The author's general purpose may be to persuade (change the reader's mind or behavior), inform (share information with the reader), or express (evoke emotion, often through stories); or it may be a combination of these purposes. At specific points in a text, an author may use a variety of methods to achieve the general purpose. You should always assume that the author has a particular reason for what he or she wrote.

Example

b   **5.** What is the author's purpose for discussing the Gibson Girl and the White Rock Girl in paragraph 3?

    a. They show how advertising images promote glamour in harmful ways.

    b. They are media images that illustrate the change in the ideal body type of women over time.

    c. They promote extreme body shapes that are virtually unattainable for most people.

    d. They demonstrate the impact of media on women's self-esteem.

Why? What information in the selection leads you to give that answer? The first sentence of paragraph 3 states the main idea. Only choice B covers all the information given in paragraph 3 about the Girls. The other choices are not supported by this selection.

Practice

    6. Which general statement is the author supporting by listing the amounts of money that the diet, low-calorie frozen entrée, self-help, fitness, and cosmetic surgery industries make?

    a. Slimness is stressed in the 20th century because it is good business.

    b. These industries are supporting an extreme body shape that few people can attain.

    c. Overweight people will do anything to lose weight.

    d. People in general are not satisfied with their bodies.

Why? What information in the selection leads you to give that answer? _____

_____

_____

Relationships

Skill

The ideas in a reading selection are related to one another in different ways. For instance, one sentence might discuss the causes of an event mentioned in a different sentence. Some relationships have to do with time, space, comparisons and contrasts, causes and effects, and so on. You may see the relationships between the ideas in different parts of one sentence, in different sentences, or even in different paragraphs. Many times, these relationships are indicated with signal words or transitions such as *but, and, however, for example,* and so on.

Example

_d_   7. What is the relationship between the first two sentences of paragraph 2?
- a. similarity
- b. cause
- c. example
- d. difference

Why? What information in the selection leads you to give that answer? The word *however* at the beginning of the second sentence signals contrast or difference.

Practice

_____   8. What is the relationship of Table 1.2 to paragraph 7?
- a. Table 1.2 is the main idea and paragraph 7 gives the details.
- b. Paragraph 7 states the main ideas and Table 1.2 gives the details.
- c. Paragraph 7 gives the causes and Table 1.2 gives the effects.
- d. Table 1.2 gives the causes and paragraph 7 gives the effects.

Why? What information in the selection leads you to give that answer? _____

_____

_____

Fact, Opinion, and Inference

Skill

A fact is a true statement that can be verified by using another source of information: *It is 85 degrees outside.* An opinion is an individual's personal reaction: *It's too hot to play baseball.* An inference is an idea the reader gets from the other ideas the author has stated: *That person must be from up north.* To be valid, an inference must be a logical extension of what the author has written.

Example

_c_   9. Which of the following statements expresses an opinion?
- a. Advertising in the mass media blankets us with images of slim bodies.
- b. About the White Rock Girl: By 1970 she was 5'8" and 118 pounds (Peacock, 2000).
- c. About the Gibson Girl: "Every man in America wanted to win her."
- d. Body dissatisfaction motivates many women to diet.

Why? What leads you to give that answer? The word *every* in choice C is a clue that this is an opinion, since statements with absolute words like *every*, *all*, and *none* are rarely factual.

Practice

_____ 10. According to the information in this reading selection, which of the following statements is true?

   a. Seventeen percent of women would exchange at least three years of their lives to become their ideal weight.

   b. Only women compare themselves to fashion models in magazines.

   c. About 75 percent of women would not give up three years of their lives to achieve their weight goals.

   d. Nearly one-tenth of college women are in danger of becoming bulimic.

Why? What information in the selection leads you to give that answer? _____

_____

▶ Vocabulary in New Contexts

Review the vocabulary words in the margins of the reading selection and then complete the following activities.

Relationships Between Words

Circle *yes* or *no* to answer the question. Then explain your answer.

1. Do large non-profit organizations like United Way or the Red Cross find **voluntary** contributions **unattainable**?

   Yes   No

   Why or why not? _____

2. Does **gender** determine whether a person is **sedentary**?

   Yes   No

   Why or why not? _____

3. Is **gender voluntary**?

   Yes   No

   Why or why not? _____

   _____

4. Can a strong **physique** be built through **sedentary** activities?

   Yes   No

   Why or why not? _____

Language in Your Life

Write short answers to each question. Look at the vocabulary words closely before you answer.

1. Name an accomplishment that you believe is **unattainable** for you. _____

_____

2. Name your favorite **sedentary** activity. _____

3. Name an actor or actress whose **physique** you find attractive. _____

_____

4. Name some **voluntary** activities you enjoy participating in. _____

_____

5. Name the **gender** of pet you prefer. _____

_____

Language in Use

Select the best word to complete the meaning of each sentence.

genders	physique	sedentary	unattainable	voluntary

1. "Boxing," George Foreman says, "is the sport all others aspire to." While practitioners of other sports may disagree, it is clear that boxing demands a well-conditioned _____.

2. Boxing probably became an organized sport when it was included as part of the ancient Greek Olympics. And even though it was referred to as the "manly art of self defense" in the 19th century, both _____ have been putting on the gloves since at least the 1700s.

3. Despite evidence of female boxing beginning in London in 1720, many countries had made the sport _____ to 20th century women, at least until the 1970s.

4. In 1977, the ban on female boxing in America was lifted. However, discrimination against female boxers continued—limited fight opportunities and low pay being two examples. In 1987, a former female boxing champion, Marian "Lady Tyger" Trimiar underwent a _____ month-long hunger strike to advocate for equality in the boxing world.

5. Today, from the efforts of "Lady Tyger" and others like her, the sport of female boxing is alive and well and growing. And like their male counterparts, these women are not _____; most train harder, longer, and more intensely than men because they have something to prove: in a male dominated sport, women can pack a punch.

 Click to Connect! For more practice applying the skills you learned in this chapter, visit **www.cengagebrain.com** to access the CourseMate for this chapter.

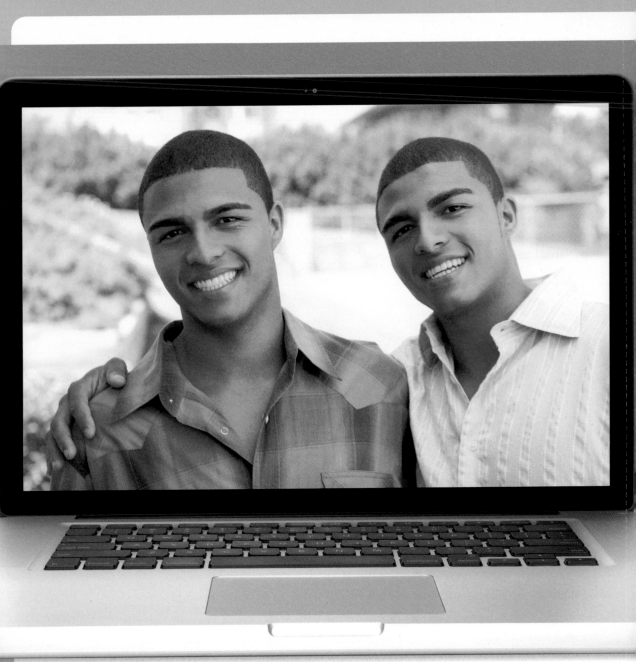

Click to Connect! Visit **www.cengagebrain.com** to access study resources for this chapter through CourseMate, which includes audio, video, quizzes, and a searchable, interactive eBook version of the text.

2
Asking Questions

> *When I was in college, I was working for a savings-and-loan association as a security guard at night. One evening, my identical twin brother stopped by, and one of my not-so-bright coworkers was amazed:*
>
> **Coworker** *Wow, are you guys twins?*
> **Me** *Yeah.*
> **Coworker** *How do you tell each other apart?*

Connect with Ideas

Did the coworker ask good questions? Why or why not?

Activate Your Knowledge

Have you used questions effectively to help yourself learn something? What kinds of questions did you ask?

Engage with the Chapter

Survey pages 60–68. What kinds of questions would you ask to find key information from these pages?

Read and Talk

Online Magazine

The following magazine article is about an athlete, Oscar Pistorius, who is without legs from the knee down. It poses the question "What does it mean to be disabled?" Read to find out how he competes and what some think about his athleticism.

Visit www.cengagebrain.com to access the CourseMate for this chapter to hear vocabulary words from this reading and an audio recording of it.

Oscar Pistorius Has a Huge Carbon Footprint

Christopher Keyes

1   In August [2011], Oscar Pistorius, a 24-year-old South African whose nonfunctioning lower legs were severed below the knee by doctors when he was 11 months old, raced in the 400 at the Track and Field World Championships in Daegu, South Korea. He not only competed, but he beat 22 of the fastest runners on the planet and reached the semifinals. Pistorius also ran the first **leg** of the 4×400 relay, helping South Africa advance to the finals. Assuming he runs another qualifying time of 45.25 seconds, he'll be competing at the 2012 Summer Olympic Games in London.

Chris McGrath/Getty Images

leg part of a trip

2   "When I was small," Pistorius has said, "I'd ask my mother why I didn't have any legs. And she'd say, 'You do. In the morning, your brother puts on his shoes and you put on your legs. There's no difference.'"

3   No difference! It was a perfectly understandable lie told by a parent facing unthinkable circumstances. But here's the most amazing part: she was right. And maybe if we could all block out the distractions swirling around Pistorius, we could be reminded again of sport's **infinite** ability to blow our minds.

infinite without end

4   Of course, that's more difficult than it sounds. It was easy to enjoy the success of Jim Abbott, the major league pitcher who thrived with just one

good arm. We had to wring our hands a bit during the saga of Casey Martin, the disabled golfer who was denied permission by the PGA to use a cart, but he disappeared quietly after failing to qualify for the tour. Pistorius is different. He and his **prosthetic** Cheetahs force us to deal with uncomfortable questions we've never had to ponder before. If a man without legs can challenge the best athletes in the world, what does it mean to be disabled? And what will it mean in the coming decades, when technological advances **annihilate** handicaps and create amputee athletes who can run faster than their able-bodied competition? Is it fair? How will the advantages of one athlete's carbon-fiber shinbones be weighed against another's surgically corrected vision?

> prosthetic artificial body part

> annihilate completely destroy

5   These are all questions that the man in question has grown weary of. When I scheduled a call with Pistorius, his manager, Peet van Zyl, asked me to e-mail my interview topics in advance. I declined. "Well, I can tell you right now that if you want to talk about advantages or the science of his Cheetahs, he's done," he said **tersely**. "He's so done talking about that."

> tersely abruptly

6   I reached Pistorius on August 16, just a few days before he would fly to Daegu. He was sick with the flu. Even though rigorous testing has cleared Pistorius of having an advantage, a well-known blogger and sports scientist in South Africa had just made headlines by calling the amputee's inclusion at the championships "a farce." As I dialed Pistorius's South African cell-phone number, I pictured him in a defensive crouch. Instead, he came across the way he's always described: humble, easygoing, and incredibly open. When I asked him about the controversy, he didn't **flinch**.

> flinch a quick, nervous reaction of fear

7   "It has been tiring in the past," he admitted. "I've tried to educate people about the tests, and there are some people who don't want to accept anything you say. I don't really think it's my job to do that. The scientists have done that already. I'm putting my focus on the running."

—From "Oscar Pistorius Has a Huge Carbon Footprint," *Outside* Magazine, Oct–Nov 2011. Copyright © 2011 *Outside* Magazine. Reprinted with permission.

Talking about Reading

Respond in writing to the questions that follow and then discuss your answers with your classmates.

1. Is it fair for an athlete with artificial legs to compete against athletes who have their own? Why or why not? If not, who is it unfair to? _____

_____

_____

_____

2. Reread in paragraph 2 what Oscar's mother used to tell him about putting on his Cheetahs. If she had not said this, do you think Oscar would have become a world-class runner?

_____

_____

3. In paragraph 3, the writer says that the statement by Oscar's mother is an "understandable lie." Was it a lie nor not? _____

_____

_____

4. How important is it to Pistorius's success that he says, "I'm putting my focus on the running" (paragraph 7)? _____

_____

5.  **Scan to Connect!** Use your smart phone to scan this code to watch a video. (See the inside front cover for more information on how to use this.) What advantage besides those discussed in the article does Pistorius discuss in this video?

Asking Questions to Establish Your Purpose for Reading

When you genuinely want to know something, you ask a lot of questions about it. Asking questions leads to learning more. So when you need to learn from a reading selection, ask questions about it. Searching for the answers to your questions gives you a well-defined purpose for reading. Stating your purpose for reading will motivate you to read actively and clarify what information you are looking for.

Turn Headings or Titles into Questions

Start with the title or heading; turn it into a question and then look for the answer as you read. **Table 2.1** gives some titles of nonfiction trade books (non-textbooks) and some headings from college textbooks, along with questions that you might form from them. Notice that to form the questions, you use the main words of the title or heading. These are the words that carry much of the meaning. For example, in the last row of headings, the subtitle is "A Time of Transition." The two main words, *Time* and *Transition,* are connected somehow to the main words of the title, *Fourteenth Century.* But how? That is the information to look for while you read.

Book title or textbook heading	Question
The Innocent Man: Murder and Injustice in a Small Town (book title)	Who is the innocent man, what was the injustice, and in what small town did this happen?
The Week That Changed the World (book title)	What week changed the world? How did it change the world?
"Material and Nonmaterial Culture" (sociology textbook heading)	How are material and nonmaterial culture different?
"Solving Equations Containing Fractions" (mathematics textbook heading)	How do you solve equations containing fractions?
"Why Hills Look Steeper Than They Are" (psychology textbook heading)	Why do hills look steeper than they are?
"The Fourteenth Century: A Time of Transition" (humanities textbook heading)	Why (or how) was the fourteenth century a time of transition?

Table 2.1 Questions Formed from Titles and Headings

Notice how the questions try to figure out what kind of information might be coming. For example, in the third heading, since the two kinds of culture, *material* and *nonmaterial*, seem to be opposites, the word *different* is used in forming the question about them. Sometimes asking more than one question seems necessary, especially when there is a title and a subtitle.

Interaction 2–1 ▶ Form Questions and Activate Your Prior Knowledge

For each textbook heading, form a question that you think would be answered in the section that follows it. Take a moment to think about some possible answers to the question before moving on to the next item. In other words, activate your prior knowledge on the topic.

1. "The Causes of Obesity" (psychology). Question: <u>EXAMPLE: What are the causes of obesity?</u>

   Predict some possible causes: <u>EXAMPLE: eating too much, exercising too little, genetic influence.</u>

2. "The Process of Management" (business management). Question: _____

   Predict some possible processes: _____

3. "Comparing American and Metric Units of Measurements" (math). Question: _____

Predict some possible comparisons: _____

_____

4. "Muscles, Exercise, and Aging" (biology). Question: _____

_____

Predict some possible relationships: _____

_____

5. "The Great Balancing Act: The Rights of the Accused versus the Rights of Society" (American government). Question: _____

_____

Predict some possible contrasts: _____

_____

_____

Just asking a question is not precise enough. You want to ask a good question that will help you find the main or key ideas of what you are reading. Keep in mind that many of your questions will be related to the title or topic. However, only one leads you to the main idea. Once you are in the practice of asking good questions, you will be able to clearly define your reading purpose, which is to find the answer to your question.

Interaction 2–2 ▸ Turn a Title or Heading into the Best Question

Following is a list of titles or headings from a variety of articles. Circle the question that would best lead you to the key idea(s) of the article.

1. Three Ways to Cook Root Vegetables
   a. What are root vegetables?
   b. Why cook root vegetables?
   c. How do you cook root vegetables?
   d. What are the three ways to cook root vegetables?

2. Cake for Breakfast? Study Says Go for It.
   a. Why can you have cake for breakfast?
   b. What kind of cake can you eat for breakfast?
   c. Why would you want cake for breakfast?
   d. Who did the cake study?

3. Top Pet Names of 2012
   a. What are the best pet names?
   b. What is the most popular pet name?
   c. What are the top pet names of 2012?
   d. Which pet names are not popular?

4. The Good and the Bad of Working from Home
   a. What is the good about working from home?
   b. What is the bad about working from home?
   c. What is good and bad about working from home?
   d. Why should you work from home?

5. How to De-Spam Everything in Your Life
   a. What is spam?
   b. How do you de-spam your life?
   c. How do you de-spam your e-mail?
   d. Why would you want to de-spam every part of your life?

Interaction 2–3   Form Questions and State a Purpose for Reading

The heading and four subheadings that follow are from one section of a chapter in a college biology textbook. Turn each one into a question and write the question next to the heading. You may need to form two questions if a heading has two ideas. Then make a statement about what will be your purpose for reading. Finally, take a moment to recall any prior knowledge you may have about the answer to each question.

1. Section heading: Overview of Life's Unity

   Question: EXAMPLE: What is included in an overview of life's unity? _____

   My purpose for reading: EXAMPLE: I want to get an overview of the unity of life. _____

2. First subheading: DNA, The Basis of Inheritance

   Question: _____

   My purpose for reading: _____

3. Second subheading: Energy, The Basis of Metabolism

   Question: _____

   My purpose for reading: _____

4. Third subheading: Energy and Life's Organization

   Question: _____

   My purpose for reading: _____

5. Fourth subheading: Life's Responsiveness to Change

Question: _____

My purpose for reading: _____

Read to Answer the Question, and Then Mark the Answer

After you have formed a question from the heading, stated a purpose for reading, and thought about any prior knowledge you might have, you are ready to read to find the answer. The parts of the answer to the question are the main ideas of the section. When you reach an idea or fact that helps to answer the question you formed from the heading, mark it in some way: highlight it, underline it, or otherwise mark it as a main idea. Be careful to mark only the ideas that directly answer the question.

Interaction 2–4   Mark the Answer to the Question

Here is the first part of section 1.2 of *Biology: Today and Tomorrow,* which you just asked questions about in Interaction 2–3. The two questions we asked about the main heading and the first subheading are written in the margin. The different parts of the answers to these questions are highlighted in the reading.

What is included in an overview of life's unity?	## 1.2 Overview of Life's Unity
	1 "Life" is not easy to define. It is too big, and it has been changing for 3.9 billion years! Even so, you can frame a definition in terms of its unity and diversity. Here is the unity part: All living things grow and reproduce with the help of DNA, energy, and raw materials. They sense and respond to their environment. But details of their traits differ among many millions of kinds of organisms. That is the diversity part—variation in traits.
What is DNA, and how is it the basis of inheritance?	**DNA, the Basis of Inheritance**
	2 You will never, ever find a rock made of nucleic acids, proteins, and complex carbohydrates and lipids. In the natural world, only living cells make these molecules. The signature molecule of life is the nucleic acid called DNA. No chunk of granite or quartz has it.
	3 DNA holds information for building proteins from smaller molecules: the amino acids. By analogy, if you follow suitable instructions and invest enough energy in the task, you might organize a pile of a few kinds of ceramic tiles (representing amino acids) into diverse patterns (representing proteins), as in **Figure 2.1.**

Figure 2.1   Examples of objects built from the same materials according to different assembly instructions.

⁴   Why are the proteins so important? Many kinds are structural materials, and others are enzymes. Enzymes are the main worker molecules in cells. They build, split, and rearrange the molecules of life in ways that keep a cell alive. Without enzymes, the information held in DNA could not be used. There would be no new organisms.

⁵   In nature, each organism inherits its DNA—and its traits—from parents. Inheritance means an acquisition of traits after parents transmit their DNA to offspring. Think about it. Why do baby storks look like storks and not like pelicans? Because storks inherit stork DNA, not pelican DNA.

⁶   *Reproduction* refers to actual mechanisms by which parents transmit DNA to offspring. For slugs, humans, trees, and other multicelled organisms, information in DNA guides *development*—the transformation of the first cell of a new individual into a multicelled adult, typically with many different tissues and organs.

Using the knowledge you gained from reading, answer these questions formed from the headings. The second question has been split into its two components (parts).

1. What is included in an overview of life's unity? _____

_____

2. What is DNA? _____

_____

3. How is DNA the basis of inheritance? _____

_____

Mark Only the Most Important Ideas

Notice that answering the questions posed about the headings did *not* require rewriting the whole reading selection. That's because most of the words a writer uses are details and examples that help readers understand the main ideas. It's the main ideas that you are searching for now. The only marking or highlighting you'll want to do to answer your questions is on the main ideas. The main ideas are the answers to the questions.

When you think about one of the purposes for highlighting, you will see why you should mark only the main ideas. Long after you have read a selection, you may need to review it as you study for a test on the material. If you highlight too much material, you will have to reread a great deal of it, which is an inefficient way to study. Mark no more than 10–15 percent of a reading selection to make your highlighting the most effective.

Interaction 2–5 ▸ **Read to Answer Your Question**

The next subsection of "Overview of Life's Unity" is printed here. Review the heading and the question you formed from it (see Interaction 2–3), and mark the parts of the answer to the question. Then answer the questions that follow.

Question:

Energy, the Basis of Metabolism

1   DNA is only part of the picture. Becoming alive and maintaining life requires energy—the capacity to do work. Each normal living cell has ways to obtain and convert energy from its surroundings. By the process called metabolism, a cell acquires and uses energy to maintain itself, grow, and make more cells.

2   Where does the energy come from? Nearly all of it flows from the sun into the world of life, starting with **producers**. Producers are plants and other organisms that make their own food from simple raw materials. All other organisms are **consumers**. They cannot make their own food; they must eat other organisms.

3   When, say, zebras browse on plants, some energy stored in plant tissues is transferred to them. Later on, energy is transferred to a lion as it devours the zebra. It gets transferred again as decomposers go to work, acquiring energy from the remains of zebras, lions, and other organisms.

4   Decomposers are consumers, mostly bacteria and fungi that break down sugars and other molecules to simpler materials. Some of the breakdown products are cycled back to producers as raw materials. Over time, energy that plants originally captured from the sun returns to the environment.

—From Starr, *Biology: Today and Tomorrow with Physiology*, 2e (p. 4).
Copyright © 2007 CENGAGE Learning, Inc. Reproduced by permission. www.cengage.com/permissions

1. What is energy? _____

2. How is energy the basis of metabolism? _____

   _____

3. What are paragraphs 2 to 4 mainly about? _____

4. What are two main kinds of organisms, grouped in terms of how they get energy? _____

   _____

5. What example does the author give of each kind of organism? _____

   _____

6. Since these paragraphs have been mostly about energy, what is the next topic you expect the author to cover? _____

Asking Questions to Improve Your Thinking

The questions you have been forming from headings are a natural way to start an interaction with the author of the selection. They help you comprehend the main ideas, which you need to be able to do before you can work with them further. Once you have understood the author's ideas, using an organized method for asking questions and thinking about them will allow you to compare and contrast these ideas with other ideas, follow the thoughts to their logical conclusions, and apply the ideas to other areas of your life. Critical thinking is the vehicle.

Critical Thinking Is a Learning Process

Critical thinking is a systematic process of thinking and learning that includes the following kinds of activities:

- ▶ Gathering information about a subject and remembering it accurately.
- ▶ Gaining clarity about what the subject means or how it acts.
- ▶ Thinking about how ideas can be applied in different situations.
- ▶ Analyzing the parts of the subject to find out how they are related.
- ▶ Evaluating the usefulness or worth of the subject based on relevant criteria.
- ▶ Forming new ideas or creating something new based on this thinking process.

When you read textbooks, articles, and other materials in college and in your career, and when you listen to lectures in your courses or during work-related training, you will dramatically increase the amount you learn if you make it a habit to systematically apply these six thinking activities to the subject matter.

Reading is not an activity you can do on autopilot. You need to:

▶ Actively question the author's words.
▶ Think about the ideas behind the words.
▶ Add your own thoughts into the mix.
▶ Make decisions or solve problems based on the understanding you have formed.

To help you form the habit of using a critical thinking process, you will next explore a series of six critical thinking levels. The levels are arranged according to a format of increasing complexity that Benjamin Bloom, a professor at the University of Chicago, devised. His critical thinking levels are often referred to as Bloom's Taxonomy. (Lorin W. Anderson and David R. Krathwohl revised the system. Their labels for each level are used here.) **Figure 2.2** shows the six levels.

You can use this thinking process to help you make decisions, solve problems, investigate majors or job offers, and read books, articles, and websites. You can also use this thinking process in your own life. In fact, you probably already do.

Figure 2.2   Bloom's Taxonomy with Questions. Each thinking action depends on mastering the steps below it. In order to draw conclusions from your reading, for example, you need to recall it, understand it, use it, grasp how its parts work together, and evaluate its worth.

Level 6 Create	You use the information to create something new or you draw conclusions. "What other explanations or solutions are there?"
Level 5 Evaluate	You decide what value the information has or make choices based on it. "What factors should I consider to decide whether these ideas are worthwhile?"
Level 4 Analyze	You understand the parts and how they relate to one another. "How do the parts or sections fit together to make up the whole?"
Level 3 Apply	You can use the information in a new situation or solve problems with it. "How can I apply this knowledge or procedure to produce a certain result?"
Level 2 Understand	You understand the information and can explain it to someone else. "How can I retell this using my own words?"
Level 1 Remember	You can recall and repeat basic information. "Who? What? When? Where? How? Why?"

Interaction 2–6 ▸ Reasons Why You Decided to Attend School

Pair up with another student. Write your own answers to the Level 1 question and then discuss your answers with your partner. Then move to Level 2, and discuss each level's question until you reach Level 6. When you are finished, be prepared to discuss with the class how your answers became more involved as you moved from Level 1 to Level 6.

Level 1—Remember: You can recall and repeat basic information.

What are your reasons for attending school?

_____

_____

_____

Level 2—Understand: You understand the information and can explain it to someone else.

How would you explain your reasons for attending school to someone who doesn't think school is important?

_____

_____

_____

Level 3—Apply: You can use the information in a new situation or solve problems with it.

How can your reasons for attending school apply in this class?

_____

_____

_____

Level 4—Analyze: You understand the parts and how they relate to one another.

What are the steps you have to take in order to reach your educational goal?

_____

_____

_____

Level 5—Evaluate: You decide what value information has or make choices based on it.

What factors should you consider when deciding whether school is worthwhile?

_____

_____

_____

Level 6—Create: You use information to create something new or draw conclusions.

What are some solutions to obstacles you will face while attending school (such as getting sick, not having enough time, getting distracted, or lacking motivation)?

_____

_____

_____

Interaction 2–7   **Ask Reading and Thinking Questions**

Use the reading process you summarized in the Chapter Summary Activity in Chapter 1 on page 31 to read the following selection from a sociology textbook. (The selection continues in Interaction 2–8.) Turn the headings into questions, and write them in the margin. Read for the answers, and then mark them. Finally, answer the critical thinking questions that follow.

Question:

Applying the Four Theories: The Problem of Fashion

MGM/Everett Collection

> Oh. Two weeks ago I saw Cameron Diaz at Fred Siegel and I talked her out of buying this truly heinous angora sweater. Whoever said orange is the new pink is seriously disturbed.
>
> —Elle Woods (Actor Reese Witherspoon) in *Legally Blond* (2001)

1   In December 2002 the *Wall Street Journal* announced that Grunge might be back (Tkacik, 2002). Since 1998, one of the main fashion trends among white, middle-class, and preteen and young teenage girls was the Britney Spears look: bare midriffs, highlighted hair, wide belts, glitter purses, big wedge shoes, and Skechers "Energy" sneakers. But in 2002 a new pop star, Avril Lavigne, was rising on the pop charts. Nominated for a 2003 Grammy Award in the "Best New Artist" category, the 17-year-old skater-punk from the small Canadian town of Napanee (2001 population: 15,132), affects a shaggy, unkempt look (Statistics Canada, 2002). She sports worn-out T-shirts, 1970s-style plaid Western shirts with snaps, low-rise blue jeans, baggy pants, undershirts, ties, backpacks, chain wallets, and, for shoes, Converse Chuck Taylors. The style is similar to the Grunge look of the early 1990s, when Nirvana and Pearl Jam were the big stars on MTV and Kurt Cobain was king of the music world.

2   Why in late 2002 were the glamorous trends of the pop era giving way in one market segment to "neo-Grunge"? Why, in general, do fashion

shifts take place? Sociological theory has interesting things to say on this subject (Davis, 1992).

The Functionalist Approach to Fashion Trends

Question:

3   Until the 1960s, the standard sociological approach to explaining the ebb and flow of fashion trends was functionalist. In the functionalist view, fashion trends worked like this: Every season, exclusive fashion houses in Paris and, to a lesser extent, Milan, New York, and London would show new styles. Some of the new styles would catch on among the exclusive clientele of Chanel, Dior, Givenchy, and other big-name designers. The main appeal of wearing expensive, new fashions was that wealthy clients could distinguish themselves from people who were less well off. Thus, fashion performed an important social function. By allowing people of different rank to distinguish themselves from one another, fashion helped preserve the ordered layering of society into classes ("It is an interesting question," wrote 19th-century American writer Henry David Thoreau in *Walden*, "how far [people] would retain their relative rank if they were divested of their clothes.") By the 20th century, thanks to technological advances in clothes manufacturing, it didn't take long for inexpensive knockoffs to reach the market and trickle down to lower classes. New styles then had to be introduced frequently so that fashion could continue to perform its function of helping to maintain an orderly class system. Hence the ebb and flow of fashion.

4   The functionalist theory was a fairly accurate account of the way fashion trends worked until the 1960s. Then, fashion became more democratic. Paris, Milan, New York, and London are still hugely important fashion centers today. However, new fashion trends are increasingly initiated by lower classes, minority racial and ethnic groups, and people who spurn "high" fashion altogether. Napanee is, after all, pretty far from Paris, and today big-name designers are more likely to be influenced by the inner-city styles of hip-hop than vice versa. New fashions no longer just trickle down from upper classes and a few high-fashion centers. Upper classes are nearly as likely to adopt lower-class fashion trends that emanate from just about anywhere. As a result, the functionalist theory no longer provides a satisfying explanation of fashion cycles.

Critical Thinking Level 1 ▸ Remember

Recall the ideas presented in the reading about the following topics. If you don't remember much about an item, skim the reading, quickly looking for the key phrase listed here. When you find it, reread that section to refresh your memory. Then return to recollecting (remembering). Jot down a few notes on a separate sheet of paper if doing so will help you remember the points the authors are making.

▶ The functionalist view
▶ The main appeal of wearing expensive, new fashions
▶ The important social function that fashion performs
▶ The effect of technological advances in clothes manufacturing
▶ The change in the fashion industry that began in the 1960s

Critical Thinking Level 2 › Understand

Using the list of topics from Critical Thinking Level 1 to spark your memory and help you organize the ideas, *explain* the ideas in the selection to a classmate. Then turn to another classmate and listen to his or her explanation.

Critical Thinking Level 3 › Apply

Apply functionalism to Avril Lavigne's look as described in paragraph 1. Can functionalism explain the success of her look? _____

_____

Critical Thinking Level 4 › Analyze

Analyze the quotation from Henry David Thoreau that is given in paragraph 3. Does it support a functionalist approach to fashion? Why or why not? _____

_____

Critical Thinking Level 5 › Evaluate

Judge how much the opening quotation from the *Legally Blond* character Elle Woods contributes to the main idea of this reading selection. _____

_____

Critical Thinking Level 6   Create

Construct an alternative explanation for the change in the fashion cycle that has taken place since the 1960s (since functionalism can't explain it very well). _____

_____

_____

Critical thinking level	Tasks you can do to help you think about any reading or lecture
Level 1: Remember	Recall (remember) the ideas.
Level 2: Understand	Explain the ideas using your own words.
Level 3: Apply	Use the ideas in a new situation or think of problems you could solve with them.
Level 4: Analyze	Figure out how the parts relate to one another.
Level 5: Evaluate	Decide how valuable you find the ideas. Think about what choices you can make based on the ideas.
Level 6: Create	Draw conclusions from the ideas. Create something new from them.

Table 2.2   General Critical Thinking Tasks

Tasks are organized here in the order you should do them. For instance, be sure you know and understand the information before you apply it.

A Shift from the Author's Ideas to Your Ideas

You may have noticed that when you were answering questions on levels 1 and 2, you were merely recalling and restating material that came directly from the reading selection. At level 3, you had to take the knowledge you had gained and apply it to a new situation, a task that involved more of *you*. When you got to level 4, the balance really started to shift toward you, the reader, and away from the information in the reading. Now you had to think on your own, not just repeat or apply what the reading said. Your ability to think was stretched further in level 5, when the question became broader and more open-ended. By the time you reached level 6, you were on your own! You had to think up an entirely different explanation for the recent fashion cycle, perhaps by considering broader ideas about how things have changed since the 1960s.

You can use these ways of thinking as you study any reading selection (or any lecture) using the critical thinking tasks in **Table 2.2**. Adapt these tasks as needed to fit the situation.

Interaction 2–8 ▸ Ask More Reading and Thinking Questions

The rest of the sociology selection on fashion is printed here. Before you read it, turn the headings into questions and search for the answers as you read. When you find parts of the answer, mark them. Then answer the questions that follow.

Conflict Theory's View of the Fashion World

Question:

5   Some sociologists have turned to conflict theory as an alternative view of the fashion world. Conflict theorists typically view fashion cycles as a means by which industry owners make big profits. Owners introduce new styles and render old styles unfashionable because they make more money

when many people are encouraged to buy new clothes often. At the same time, conflict theorists think fashion keeps people distracted from the many social, economic, and political problems that might otherwise incite them to express dissatisfaction with the existing social order and even rebel against it. Conflict theorists, like functionalists, thus believe that fashion helps maintain social stability. Unlike functionalists, however, they argue that social stability bestows advantages on industrial owners at the expense of nonowners.

6   Conflict theorists have a point. Fashion is a big and profitable business. Owners do introduce new styles to make more money. They have, for example, created The Color Marketing Group (known to insiders as the "Color Mafia"), a committee that meets regularly to help change the national palette of color preferences for consumer products. According to one committee member, the Color Mafia makes sure that "the mass media, fashion magazines and catalogs, home shopping shows, and big clothing chains all present the same options" (Mundell, 1993).

7   Yet the Color Mafia and other influential elements of the fashion industry are not all-powerful. Remember what Elle Woods said after she convinced Cameron Diaz not to buy that heinous angora sweater: "Whoever said orange is the new pink is seriously disturbed." Like many consumers, Elle Woods rejected the advice of the fashion industry. And in fact some of the fashion trends initiated by industry owners flop, one of the biggest being the introduction of the midi-dress with a hemline midway between knee and ankle) in the mid-1970s. Despite a huge ad campaign, most women simply would not buy it.

8   This points to one of the main problems with the conflict interpretation: It incorrectly makes it seem like fashion decisions are dictated from above. Reality is more complicated. Fashion decisions are made partly by consumers. This idea can best be understood by thinking of clothing as a form of symbolic interaction, a sort of wordless "language" that allows us to tell others who we are and learn who they are.

Question:

Clothing as a Form of Symbolic Interaction

9   If clothes speak, sociologist Fred Davis has perhaps done the most in recent years to help us see how we can decipher what they say (Davis, 1992). According to Davis, a person's identity is always a work in progress. True, we develop a sense of self as we mature. We come to think of ourselves as members of one or more families, occupations, communities, classes, ethnic and racial groups, and countries. We develop patterns of behavior and belief associated with each of these social categories. Nonetheless, social categories change over time, and so do we as we move through them and as we age. As a result, our identities are always

in flux. We often become anxious or insecure about who we are. Clothes help us express our shifting identities. For example, clothes can convey whether you are "straight," sexually available, athletic, conservative, and much else, thus telling others how you want them to see you and indicating the kinds of people with whom you want to associate. At some point you may become less conservative, sexually available, and so forth. Your clothing style is likely to change accordingly. (Of course, the messages you try to send are subject to interpretation and may be misunderstood.) For its part, the fashion industry feeds on the ambiguities within us, investing much effort in trying to discern which new styles might capture current needs for self-expression.

10   For example, capitalizing on the need for self-expression among many young girls in the late 1990s, Britney Spears hit a chord. Feminist interpretations of the meaning and significance of Britney Spears are especially interesting in this respect because they focus on the gender aspects of fashion.

Feminist Interpretations of Britney Spears

Question:

11   Traditionally, feminists have thought of fashion as a form of patriarchy, a means by which male dominance is maintained. They have argued that fashion is mainly a female preoccupation. It takes a lot of time and money to choose, buy, and clean clothes. Fashionable clothing is often impractical and uncomfortable, and some of it is even unhealthy. Modern fashion's focus on youth, slenderness, and eroticism diminishes women by turning them into sexual objects, say some feminists. Britney Spears is of interest to traditional feminists because she supposedly helps lower the age at which girls fall under male domination.

12   In recent years, this traditional feminist view has given way to a feminist interpretation that is more compatible with symbolic interactionism ("Why Britney Spears Matters," 2001). Some feminists now applaud the "girl power" movement that crystallized in 1996 with the release of the Spice Girls' hit single, "Wannabe." They regard Britney Spears as part of that movement. In their judgment, Spears's music, dance routines, and dress style express a self-assuredness and assertiveness that resonate with the less submissive and more independent role that girls are now carving out for themselves. With her kicks, her shadow boxing, and songs like the 2000 single "Stronger," Spears speaks for the empowerment of young women. Quite apart from her musical and dancing talent, then, some feminists think that many young girls are wild about Britney Spears because she helps them express their own social and sexual power. Of course, not all young girls agree. Some, like Avril Lavigne, find Spears "phony" and too much of a "showgirl." They seek "more authentic" ways of asserting their identity through fashion (Pascual, 2002). Still, the symbolic interactionist

and feminist interpretations of fashion help us see more clearly the ambiguities of identity that underlie the rise of new fashion trends.

Question:

The Usefulness of the Four Theoretical Perspectives

13   Our analysis of fashion shows that each of the four theoretical perspectives—functionalism, conflict theory, symbolic interactionism, and feminism—can clarify different aspects of a sociological problem. This does not mean that each perspective always has equal validity. Often, the interpretations that derive from different theoretical perspectives are incompatible. They offer competing interpretations of the same social reality. It is then necessary to do research to determine which perspective works best for the case at hand. Nonetheless, all four theoretical perspectives usefully illuminate some aspects of the social world.

—From Brym/Lie, *Sociology: Your Compass for a New World*

Critical Thinking Level 1 **Remember**

Including the material in Interaction 2–7 as well as this one, what four theories are applied to the fashion industry in this reading selection?

▶ _____

▶ _____

▶ _____

▶ _____

Critical Thinking Level 2 **Understand**

What aspects of fashion do each of the four theories explain particularly well, according to the authors?

▶ _____

_____

▶ _____

_____

▶ _____

_____

▶ _____

_____

Critical Thinking Level 3 ▸ Apply

Choose a movie character whose clothing seems like a statement of who they are. Using some of the categories of identity from the section "Clothing as a Form of Symbolic Interaction," write a paragraph in which you describe the person's clothing and how it seems to identify them. What do you think their clothes say about their family, occupation, community, class, ethnic group, sexual orientation or availability, athleticism, political viewpoint, or anything else? Be sure to use plenty of details to describe their clothing and to support your points.

_____

_____

_____

Critical Thinking Level 4 ▸ Analyze

What example is used to support the point that conflict theorists make about fashion? What counter-example (opposing example) is then given to show the limits of the first example?

▸ Example: _____

▸ Counterexample: _____

Critical Thinking Level 5 ▸ Evaluate

Certain working situations seem to call for particular ways of dressing. For example, a day care provider might dress in roomy, comfortable clothes that won't be damaged by food or dirt. Consider three occupations you might want to have. Suggest appropriate dress for each one. How does dressing in that particular way help fulfill the needs of the job?

▸ _____

▸ _____

▸ _____

Critical Thinking Level 6 ▸ Create

Before you read this selection, what did you think about the fashion industry—its quickly changing trends, its origins in the upper or lower classes, its emphasis on profits, its usefulness in identifying yourself, or any other aspect? Write for ten minutes to explore your thoughts.

Now that you have read the selection, would you say that your earlier viewpoint was similar to any of the theories presented here? Different from one of them? Write for five more minutes to establish where among these theories your ideas fit.

What Level of Critical Thinking Are You Being Asked to Use?

Tests in your college classes, such as literature, history, and even math, will probably include one or more of the following types of questions: multiple choice, true/false, short answer, and essay. Multiple choice requires choosing an answer from a list of possible answers (usually a, b, c, d), true/false gives you one of the two choices, short answer requires you to write out the answer yourself in a few short sentences (think short summary), and essay questions require multiple paragraphs.

A good strategy for approaching how to answer your test questions is to pay attention the key **critical thinking verb** in the question and then make sure that your answer demonstrates the appropriate level of thinking. Earlier in the chapter, you learned about the six levels of critical thinking and verbs that are linked to each one (see Table 2.2 on p. 73). Following are some other verbs that may be used in questions to describe these thinking and writing tasks.

Level 1: *remember, identify, list, reproduce, define*

Level 2: *understand, paraphrase, conclude, match, exemplify*

Level 3: *apply, diagram, demonstrate, solve, illustrate*

Level 4: *analyze, compare, examine, explain, investigate*

Level 5: *evaluate, assess, rank, critique, justify*

Level 6: *create, develop, design, adapt, imagine*

When you read a question, identify the critical thinking level by looking at key verbs to decide what level of thinking is called for.

Interaction 2–9 ▸ Identify the Bloom's Taxonomy Level

Underline the key critical thinking verbs and circle the correct critical thinking level based on the task of each question. Note that the verbs may not be identical to those listed above, but they will be synonyms (have a similar meaning), so pay attention to the task of each question.

1. Which of the following justifies the term *enculturation*?
   a. Level 1: Remember
   b. Level 2: Understand
   c. Level 3: Apply
   d. Level 4: Analyze
   e. Level 5: Evaluate
   f. Level 6: Create

2. According to the passage, which step occurs first?
   a. Level 1: Remember
   b. Level 2: Understand
   c. Level 3: Apply
   d. Level 4: Analyze
   e. Level 5: Evaluate
   f. Level 6: Create

3. Write a paper on the following topic: Your First Crush.
   a. Level 1: Remember
   b. Level 2: Understand
   c. Level 3: Apply
   d. Level 4: Analyze
   e. Level 5: Evaluate
   f. Level 6: Create

4. Summarize paragraph 6.
   a. Level 1: Remember
   b. Level 2: Understand
   c. Level 3: Apply
   d. Level 4: Analyze
   e. Level 5: Evaluate
   f. Level 6: Create

5. Find a solution to the following problem: Simplify $(5x^2)(-2x^3)$.
   a. Level 1: Remember
   b. Level 2: Understand
   c. Level 3: Apply
   d. Level 4: Analyze
   e. Level 5: Evaluate
   f. Level 6: Create

6. Contrast Renoir's paintings with Monet's.
   a. Level 1: Remember
   b. Level 2: Understand
   c. Level 3: Apply
   d. Level 4: Analyze
   e. Level 5: Evaluate
   f. Level 6: Create

Connect Your Skills

Asking Questions

A. Circle the level of critical thinking required for each of the following questions.

1. What is the topic of the following reading?
   a. Level 1: Remember
   b. Level 2: Understand
   c. Level 3: Apply
   d. Level 4: Analyze
   e. Level 5: Evaluate
   f. Level 6: Create

2. Explain the term *social distance scale*.
   a. Level 1: Remember
   b. Level 2: Understand
   c. Level 3: Apply
   d. Level 4: Analyze
   e. Level 5: Evaluate
   f. Level 6: Create

3. Design an experiment to rank the buoyancy of various liquids.
   a. Level 1: Remember
   b. Level 2: Understand
   c. Level 3: Apply
   d. Level 4: Analyze
   e. Level 5: Evaluate
   f. Level 6: Create

4. Distinguish between inductive and deductive reasoning.
   a. Level 1: Remember
   b. Level 2: Understand
   c. Level 3: Apply
   d. Level 4: Analyze
   e. Level 5: Evaluate
   f. Level 6: Create

5. Prioritize the following list from most important to least.
   a. Level 1: Remember
   b. Level 2: Understand
   c. Level 3: Apply
   d. Level 4: Analyze
   e. Level 5: Evaluate
   f. Level 6: Create

6. Put the important ideas of the following reading into a visual map.
   a. Level 1: Remember
   b. Level 2: Understand
   c. Level 3: Apply
   d. Level 4: Analyze
   e. Level 5: Evaluate
   f. Level 6: Create

7. Which of the following animals is a consumer?
   a. Level 1: Remember
   b. Level 2: Understand
   c. Level 3: Apply
   d. Level 4: Analyze
   e. Level 5: Evaluate
   f. Level 6: Create

8. Make a PowerPoint of the key concepts in Chapter 2 for the class.
   a. Level 1: Remember
   b. Level 2: Understand
   c. Level 3: Apply
   d. Level 4: Analyze
   e. Level 5: Evaluate
   f. Level 6: Create

9. Judge the validity of the following argument.
   a. Level 1: Remember
   b. Level 2: Understand
   c. Level 3: Apply
   d. Level 4: Analyze
   e. Level 5: Evaluate
   f. Level 6: Create

B. Read the following passage, turn the headings into questions, and answer the critical thinking questions that follow.

Pseudopsychologies—Palms, Planets, and Personality

10. Question: _____

[1] A **pseudopsychology** (SUE-doe-psychology) is any unfounded system that resembles psychology. Many pseudopsychologies give the appearance of being scientific but are actually false. (*Pseudo* means "false.") Pseudopsychologies are types of **superstitions**, unfounded beliefs held without evidence or in the face of falsifying evidence.

2   Unlike "real" psychology, pseudopsychologies change little over time because followers seek evidence that appears to confirm their beliefs and avoid evidence that falsifies them. Critical thinkers, scientists, and psychologists, in contrast, are skeptical of their own theories (Schick & Vaughn, 2011). They actively look for contradictions as a way to advance knowledge.

3   *Can you give some examples of false psychologies?* One pseudopsychology, known as *phrenology*, was popularized in the nineteenth century by Franz Gall, a German anatomy teacher. Phrenology claimed that personality traits are revealed by the shape of the skull. Psychological research has long since shown that bumps on the head have nothing to do with talents or abilities. In fact, the phrenologists were so far off that they listed the part of the brain that controls hearing as a center for "combativeness"! *Palmistry* is a similarly falsified system that claims lines on the hand reveal personality traits and predict the future. Despite the overwhelming evidence against phrenology and palmistry, these pseudopsychologies are still practiced today. Palmists, in particular, can still be found separating the gullible from their money in many cities.

4   At first glance, a pseudopsychology called *graphology* might seem more reasonable. Some graphologists claim that personality traits are revealed by handwriting. Based on such claims, some companies even use graphologists to select job candidates. This is troubling because graphologists score close to zero on tests of accuracy in rating personality (Dazzi & Pedrabissi, 2009; Furnham, Chamorro-Premuzic, & Callahan, 2003). In fact, graphologists do no better than untrained college students in rating personality and job performance (Neter & Ben-Shakhar, 1989). Even a graphological society recommends that handwriting analysis should not be used to select people for jobs (Simner & Goffin, 2003). (By the way, graphology's failure at revealing personality should be separated from its value for detecting forgeries.)

5   Graphology might seem harmless enough until you imagine being denied a job because a graphologist didn't like your handwriting. This false system has been used to determine who is hired, given bank credit, or selected for juries. In these and similar situations, pseudopsychologies do, in fact, harm people.

6   *If pseudopsychologies have no scientific basis, how do they survive and why are they popular?* There are several reasons, all of which can be illustrated by a critique of astrology.

Problems in the Stars

11. Question: _____

7   Arguably the most popular pseudopsychology, astrology holds that the positions of the stars and planets at the time of one's birth determine personality traits and affect behavior. Like other pseudopsychologies, astrology has repeatedly been shown to have no scientific validity, either theoretically or empirically (Kelly, 1999; Rogers & Soule, 2009):

8   **1. The theory of astrology is unconvincing.** Astrology is based on a zodiac map invented several thousand years ago in an ancient civilization called Babylon. Unlike scientific theories, which are regularly falsified and rejected or revised accordingly, the basic underpinnings of astrology have remained relatively unchanged. To date, no astrologer has offered a convincing explanation of *how* the positions of the planets at a person's birth could affect his or her future. Astrologers have also failed to explain *why* the moment of birth should be more important than, say, the moment of conception. (Perhaps it is because it is relatively easy to figure out the moment of birth and much

trickier to determine the moment of conception.) Besides, the zodiac has shifted in the sky by one full constellation since astrology was first set up. (In other words, if astrology calls you a Scorpio you are really a Libra, and so forth.) However, most astrologers simply ignore this shift (Martens & Trachet, 1998).

9   **2. The evidence against astrology *is* convincing.** One study of more than 3,000 predictions by famous astrologers found that only a small percentage were fulfilled. These "successful" predictions tended to be vague ("There will be a tragedy somewhere in the east in the spring") or easily guessed from current events (Culver & Ianna, 1988). Similarly, if astrologers are asked to match people with their horoscopes, they do no better than would be expected by chance. In one famous test, astrologers could not even use horoscopes to distinguish murderers from law-abiding people (Gauquelin, 1970). In fact, there is no connection between people's astrological signs and their intelligence or personality traits (Hartmann, Reuter, & Nyborg, 2006). There is also no connection between the "compatibility" of couples' astrological signs and their marriage and divorce rates or between astrological signs and leadership, physical characteristics, or career choices (Martens & Trachet, 1998).

10   In short, astrology doesn't work.

11   Then why does astrology often seem to work? Even the daily horoscopes printed in newspapers can seem uncannily accurate. For many people this apparent accuracy can only mean that astrology is valid. Unfortunately, such uncritical acceptance overlooks a much simpler psychological explanation (see, for example, Rogers & Soule, 2009). The following discussion explains why.

Uncritical Acceptance

12. Question: _____

12   Perceptions of the accuracy of horoscopes are typically based on **uncritical acceptance**—the tendency to believe claims because they seem true or because it would be nice if they were true. Horoscopes are generally made up of mostly flattering traits. Naturally, when your personality is described in *desirable* terms, it is hard to deny that the description has the "ring of truth." How much acceptance would astrology receive if a birth sign read like this:

> **Virgo:** You are the logical type and hate disorder. Your nitpicking is unbearable to your friends. You are cold, unemotional, and usually fall asleep while making love. Virgos make good doorstops.

Confirmation Bias

13. Question: _____

13   Even when an astrological description contains a mixture of good and bad traits, it may seem accurate. To find out why, read the following personality description.

> **Your Personality Profile**
> You have many personality strengths, with some weaknesses to which you can usually adjust. You tend to be accepting of yourself. You are comfortable with some structure in your life but do enjoy

diverse experiences from time to time. Although on the inside you might be a bit unsure of yourself, you appear under control to others. You are sexually well-adjusted, although you do have some questions. Your life goals are more or less realistic. Occasionally you question your decisions and actions because you're unsure that they are correct. You want to be liked and admired by other people. You are not using your potential to its full extent. You like to think for yourself and don't always take other people's word without thinking it through. You are not generally willing to disclose to others because it might lead to problems. You are a natural introvert, cautious, and careful around others, although there are times when you can be an extrovert who is the "life of the party."

14   Does this describe your personality? A psychologist read a similar summary individually to college students who had taken a personality test. Only 5 students out of 79 felt that the description was inaccurate. Another classic study found that people rated the "personality profile" as more accurate than their actual horoscopes (French et al., 1991).

15   Reread the description and you will see that it contains both sides of several personality dimensions ("You are a natural introvert . . . although there are times when you can be an extrovert..."). Its apparent accuracy is an illusion based on **confirmation bias**, in which we remember or notice things that confirm our expectations and forget the rest (Lilienfeld, Ammirati, & Landfield, 2009). The pseudopsychologies thrive on this effect. For example, you can always find "Aquarius characteristics" in an Aquarius. If you looked, however, you could also find "Gemini characteristics," "Scorpio characteristics," or whatever. Perhaps this explains why, in an ironic twist, 94 percent of those sent the full 10-page horoscope of a famous mass murderer accepted it as their own (Gauquelin, 1970).

16   Confirmation bias is also relied on by various "psychic mediums" who claim that they can communicate with the deceased friends and relatives of audience members. An analysis shows that the number of "hits" (correct statements) made by these people tends to be very low. Nevertheless, many viewers are impressed because of our natural tendency to remember apparent hits and ignore misses. Of course, particularly embarrassing misses are often edited out before such shows appear on television (Nickell, 2001).

The Barnum Effect

14. Question: _____

17   Pseudopsychologies also take advantage of the **Barnum effect**, which is a tendency to consider personal descriptions accurate if they are stated in general terms (Kida, 2006). P. T. Barnum, the famed circus showman, had a formula for success: "Always have a little something for everybody." Like the all-purpose personality profile, palm readings, fortunes, horoscopes, and other products of pseudopsychology are stated in such general terms that they can hardly miss. There is always "a little something for everybody." To observe the Barnum effect, read *all 12* of the daily horoscopes found in newspapers for several days. You will find that predictions for other signs fit events as well as those for your own sign do. Try giving a friend the wrong horoscope sometime. Your friend may still be quite impressed with the "accuracy" of the horoscope.

18   Astrology's popularity shows that many people have difficulty separating valid psychology from systems that seem valid but are not. The goal of this discussion, then, has been to make you a more critical

observer of human behavior and to clarify what is, and what is not, psychology. Here is what the "stars" say about your future:

> Emphasis now on education and personal improvement. A learning experience of lasting value awaits you. Take care of scholastic responsibilities before engaging in recreation. The word *psychology* figures prominently in your future.

19   Pseudopsychologies may seem like no more than a nuisance, but they can do harm. For instance, people seeking treatment for psychological disorders may become the victims of self-appointed "experts" who offer ineffective, pseudoscientific "therapies" (Kida, 2006; Lilienfeld, Ruscio, & Lynn, 2008). Valid psychological principles are based on scientific theory and evidence, not fads, opinions, or wishful thinking.

—From Coon/Mitterer, *Introduction to Psychology: Gateways to Mind and Behavior with Concept Maps and Reviews*, 13e (pp. 18–20).
Copyright © 2013 Cengage Learning, Inc. Reproduced by permission. www.cengage.com/permissions

15. Level 1: Remember

Define the following terms:

▶ Pseudopsychology _____

▶ Phrenology _____

▶ Palmistry _____

▶ Graphology _____

▶ Astrology _____

_____

16. Level 2: Understand

Each New Year's day, "psychics" make predictions about what will happen over the coming year. Most of these predictions are wrong, yet this practice continues. Can you explain why? _____

_____

_____

17. Level 3: Apply

An "uncritical acceptance" applies to the phrase, "you cannot teach an old dog new tricks." Can you explain how? Can you think of another saying that many people accept uncritically? _____

_____

_____

_____

18. Level 4: Analyze

Explain why this cartoon depicts "the most accurate fortune ever told." Use information from the passage to support your thoughts. _____

_____

19. Level 5: Evaluate

Every day you encounter people who make claims that could be described as pseudopsychology. How carefully do you evaluate what others say? How carefully do you think about your own beliefs? Explain your thoughts.

_____

_____

_____

20. Level 6: Create

Pick your favorite legend and do some research to see if there is any science behind it. Some examples might include UFOs, the Loch Ness Monster, Bigfoot, or the Legend of Bloody Mary.

Click to Connect! To check your comprehension of chapter concepts, visit **www.cengagebrain.com** to access the CourseMate for this chapter.

Chapter Summary Activity

This chapter has discussed how asking questions can help you read and think more effectively. Fill in the Reading Guide to Asking Questions below by completing each main idea on the left with specific supporting details from the chapter on the right. You can use this guide later as you work on other reading assignments.

Reading Guide to Asking Questions

Complete this idea with...	information from Chapter 2.
How titles can be used to aid comprehension	1. _____ _____
Two benefits of asking questions	2. _____ _____ 3. _____ _____
What you do after you ask questions	4. _____ _____
Two things to do while reading after asking questions	5. _____ _____ 6. _____ _____
How to avoid overmarking	7. _____ _____
Six levels of critical thinking, organized from easiest to most difficult	8. _____ 9. _____ 10. _____ 11. _____ 12. _____ 13. _____

Two verbs for level 1	14. _____
	15. _____
Two verbs for level 2	16. _____
	17. _____
Two verbs for level 3	18. _____
	19. _____
Two verbs for level 4	20. _____
	21. _____
Two verbs for level 5	22. _____
	23. _____
Two verbs for level 6	24. _____
	25. _____

Think about what your reading comprehension strategies were before you read this chapter. What have you learned that will be helpful? Write down your thoughts.

_____

_____

_____

Reading 2–1 | Nonfiction Book

▶ Pre-Reading the Selection

The reading that begins on page 89 is from a nonfiction book called *Willpower: Rediscovering the Greatest Human Strength*, written by psychologist Roy Baumeister and journalist John Tierney.

Surveying the Reading

Survey the selection that follows. Then check the elements that are included in this reading.

_____	Title	_____	Words in bold or italic type
_____	Headings	_____	Images and captions
_____	First sentences of paragraphs		

Guessing the Purpose

Based on the title of the book and the reading selection, do you think the author's purpose is mostly to persuade, inform, or express? _____

Predicting the Content

Based on your survey, what are three things you expect the reading selection to discuss?

▶ _____

▶ _____

▶ _____

Activating Your Knowledge

Think about how people set and achieve goals, how athletes train for marathons or similar events, and what you have heard or read about David Blaine. Take notes about some of this prior knowledge.

▶ _____

▶ _____

▶ _____

🎞 **Scan to Connect!** Use your smart phone to scan this code to watch a video. (See the inside front cover for more information on how to use this.) Watch at least the first four minutes of this TED Talk by David Blaine. What do you learn about Blaine that may help to explain his feats of endurance?

▶ Reading with Pen in Hand

Students who annotate as they read are more successful than those who do not. That's why you will annotate each selection in *Connect* as you read. In the reading that follows, use the following symbols:

★ or ⟨Point⟩   to indicate a main idea

① ② ③   to indicate major details

 Visit www.cengagebrain.com to access the CourseMate for this chapter to hear pronunciations of vocabulary words from this reading.

David Blaine's Feats of Will

Roy F. Baumeister and John Tierney

"The more the body suffers, the more the spirit flowers."

—David Blaine's philosophy, borrowed from St. Simeon Stylites, a fifth-century ascetic who lived for decades atop a pillar in the Syrian desert

1   We wish to consider a scientific explanation for David Blaine. We don't mean an explanation for *why* Blaine does what he does. That's impossible, at least for psychologists, and probably for psychiatrists, too. When he is not doing his famous magic tricks, Blaine works as a self-described endurance artist, performing **feats** involving willpower instead of illusion. He stood for thirty-five hours more than eighty feet above New York's Bryant Park, without a safety harness, atop a round pillar just twenty-two inches wide. He spent sixty-three sleepless hours in Times Square encased in a giant block of ice. He was entombed in a coffin with six inches of headroom for a week, during which he consumed nothing except water. He later went on to conduct another water-only fast, whose results were published in the *New England Journal of Medicine*:

▶ Why do the authors call Blaine's actions "feats involving will-power"?

feats Read the examples in the next sentences. What kinds of acts are *feats*?

DENNIS VAN TINE/Landov

In 2006, David Blaine was shackled to a spinning gyroscope suspended five stories above the ground in New York City without netting or safety harnesses. It took him 52 hours of spinning (with no food or water) to escape and jump 30 feet to a wooden platform below him.

a loss of fifty-four pounds in forty-four days. He spent those forty-four days without food suspended above the Thames River in a sealed transparent box, inside which the temperatures ranged from subfreezing to 114 degrees Fahrenheit.

2   "Breaking the comfort zone seems to be the place where I always grow," says Blaine, echoing St. Simeon's notion that suffering makes the spirit flower. We won't attempt to analyze that rationale. The *why* is beyond our ken.

3   We're interested in the *how* of Blaine's feats. How he endures is a mystery that matters to people who aren't endurance artists. Whatever one thinks of his **ordeals** (or his psyche), it would be useful to figure out what keeps him going. If we could isolate his secret for fasting forty-four days, maybe the rest of us could use it to last until dinner. If we knew how he endured a week of being buried alive, we might learn how to sit through a two-hour budget meeting. Exactly what does he do to build and **sustain** his willpower? How, for instance, did Blaine not immediately give up when everything went wrong during his attempt to break the world record for breath holding? He'd spent more than a year preparing for this feat by learning to fill his lungs with pure oxygen and then remain immobile under water, conserving oxygen by **expending** as little energy as possible. Blaine could relax so completely, both mentally and physically, that his heart rate would drop to below fifty beats per minute, sometimes below twenty. During a practice session at a swimming pool at Grand Cayman Island, his pulse dropped by 50 percent as soon as he began the breath-hold, and he kept his head under water for sixteen minutes with little apparent stress. He emerged just shy of the world record of 16:32, looking **serene** and reporting that he hadn't felt any pain, and had barely been aware of his body or surroundings.

4   But several weeks later, when he went on *Oprah* to try to break the world record in front of judges from Guinness, there were a couple of complications in addition to the pressure of performing for a television audience. Instead of floating facedown in a pool, he had to face the studio audience from the inside of a giant glass sphere. To remain vertical and not float to the surface, he had to keep his feet wedged into straps at the bottom of the sphere. As he filled his lungs with oxygen, he worried that the muscular effort to keep his feet in place would eat up too much oxygen. His pulse was higher than usual, and when he started holding his breath, it stayed above 100 instead of **plummeting**. To make matters worse, he could hear his racing pulse on a heart-rate monitor that had inadvertently been placed too close to the sphere, continually distracting and distressing him with its rapid *beep-beep-beep*. By the second minute, his pulse was 130 and he realized he wasn't going to be able to control it. It remained above 100 as the minutes ticked by and his body used up its oxygen. Instead of being lost in a state of meditative bliss, he was acutely aware of his racing pulse and the excruciating buildup of carbon dioxide inside his body.

5   By the eighth minute, he was barely halfway to the record and convinced he wouldn't make it. By the tenth minute, his fingers were tingling as his body

---

▶ Look for the question the authors ask and then look for the answer.

ordeals Based on the examples given, what kinds of experiences are *ordeals*?

sustain Look for a synonym in the next sentence. What does *sustain* mean?

expending This sentence contains several clues to the meaning of *expend*. What does *expending* mean?

serene If Blaine looked like he hadn't been in pain, would he be calm or agitated?

▶ What complications did Blaine face?

plummeting Use the contrast clue here, and a clue at the end of paragraph 3, to decide the meaning of *plummeting*.

▶ Imagine what this would be like.

shunted blood from the extremities to preserve vital organs. By the twelfth minute, his legs were throbbing and his ears were ringing. By the thirteenth minute, he feared that the numbness in his arm and the pain in his chest were **precursors** to a heart attack. A minute later he felt contractions in his chest and was nearly overwhelmed with the impulse to breathe. By the fifteenth minute his heart was skipping beats and his pulse was **erratic**, jumping to 150, down to 40, back over 100. Now convinced that a heart attack was coming, he released his feet from the straps so that the emergency team could pull him out of the sphere when he blacked out. He floated upward, forcing himself to remain just below the surface, still expecting to black out any second, when he heard the audience cheer and realized that he'd broken the old record of 16:32. He looked at the clock and held on until the next minute, emerging from the water with a new Guinness record of 17:04.

6   "This was a whole other level of pain," he said shortly afterward. "I still feel as if somebody hit me in the stomach with the hardest punch they could."

7   So how did he will his way through it?

8   "That's where the training comes in," he said. "It gives you the confidence to pull through a situation that isn't so easy."

9   By training, he didn't mean simply his recent exercises in breath holding, although there had been plenty of them during the previous year. Each morning he'd do a series of ordinary breath-holds (starting with regular air instead of pure oxygen) separated by short intervals, gradually increasing the duration and the pain. Over the course of an hour, he'd end up holding his breath for forty-eight minutes, and then he'd have a pounding headache for the rest of the day. Those daily breathing drills got his body used to the pain of carbon dioxide buildup. But just as important were the other kinds of exercises he'd been conducting for more than three decades, since the age of five. He had long been a believer in the notion that willpower is a muscle that can be strengthened. He picked up this idea partly through reading about the Victorian training of his childhood hero, Houdini, and partly by trial and error.

10   Growing up in Brooklyn, Blaine forced himself to practice card tricks hour after hour, day after day. He learned to win swimming races by not coming up for air the entire length of the pool—and then, with practice, eventually won five hundred dollars in bets by swimming five lengths under water. In the winter, he **eschewed** a coat, wearing only a T-shirt even when walking for miles on bitterly cold days. He regularly took cold baths and conducted the occasional barefoot run in the snow. He slept on the wooden floor of his bedroom, and once spent two straight days in a closet (his tolerant mother brought him food). He got in the habit of continually setting goals that had to be met, like running so far every day, or jumping to grab a leaf from the branch of a certain tree every time he walked under it. At age eleven, after reading about fasting in the novel *Siddhartha* by Hermann Hesse, he tried it himself and soon got up to four days on just water. By age eighteen he managed a ten-day fast with just

precursors Which came first, the numbness and pain or the thought that he was having a heart attack? What is a *precursor*?

erratic The specific example here explains *erratic*. What does it mean?

▶ Is this new or repeated information?

▶ What can you learn from this description about reaching your own goals?

▶ Think of a time when you kept testing something about yourself.

eschewed Use your logic. What does *eschewed* mean?

water and wine. Once he became a professional endurance artist, he reverted to the same techniques before a stunt, including little rituals that had nothing directly to do with the stunt.

▶ What compulsions do you have?

11   "Some sort of OCD [obsessive-compulsive disorder] kicks in whenever I'm about to do a long-term challenge," he told us. "I make tons of weird goals for myself. Like, when I'm jogging in the park in the bike lane, whenever I go over a drawing of a biker, I have to step on it. And not just step on it—I have to hit the head of the biker perfectly with my foot, so that it fits right under my sneaker. Little things like that annoy anyone running with me, but I believe if I don't do them, I won't succeed."

12   But why believe that? Why would stepping on the drawing of a biker help you hold your breath longer?

13   "Getting your brain wired into little goals and achieving them, that helps you achieve the bigger things you shouldn't be able to do," he said. "It's not just practicing the specific thing. It's always making things more difficult than they should be, and never falling short, so that you have that extra reserve, that tank, so you know you can always go further than your goal. For me that's what disci-

▶ How does Blaine define discipline?

pline is. It's repetition and practice."

—From *Willpower: Rediscovering the Greatest Human Strength* (pp. 124–128) by Roy F. Baumeister and John Tierney, copyright © 2011 by Roy F. Baumeister and John Tierney. Used by permission of The Penguin Press, a division of Penguin Group (USA) Inc.

▶ **Comprehension Questions**

Write the letter of the answer on the line. Then explain your thinking.

Main Idea

____ 1. Which of these sentences from paragraph 1 is the statement of its main idea?

a. We wish to consider a scientific explanation for David Blaine.

b. We don't mean an explanation for *why* Blaine does what he does.

c. That's impossible, at least for psychologists, and probably for psychiatrists, too.

d. When he is not doing his famous magic tricks, Blaine works as a self-described endurance artist, performing feats involving willpower instead of illusion.

Why? What information in the selection leads you to give that answer? _____

_____

_____

____ 2. What is the main idea of paragraphs 4 and 5?

a. But several weeks later, when he went on *Oprah* to try to break the world record in front of judges from Guinness, there were a couple of complications in addition to the pressure of performing for a television audience.

b. Instead of floating facedown in a pool, he had to face the studio audience from the inside of a giant glass sphere.

c. To make matters worse, he could hear his racing pulse on a heart-rate monitor that had inadvertently been placed too close to the sphere, continually distracting and distressing him with its rapid *beep-beep-beep*.

d. Instead of being lost in a state of meditative bliss, he was acutely aware of his racing pulse and the excruciating buildup of carbon dioxide inside his body.

Why? What information in the selection leads you to give that answer? _____

_____

_____

Supporting Details

_____ 3. In paragraph 9 the authors state that Blaine believes willpower is a muscle that can be strengthened. Where are the supporting details for this statement located?

a. Paragraph 2

b. Paragraphs 6 and 7

c. Paragraph 9

d. Paragraphs 9 and 10

Why? What information in the selection leads you to give that answer? _____

_____

_____ 4. Which of the following statements is true about paragraph 5?

a. There are no supporting details.

b. There are only supporting details.

c. Every sentence except the first one is a supporting detail.

d. Every sentence except the last one is a supporting detail.

Why? What information in the selection leads you to give that answer? _____

_____

_____

Authors' Purpose

_____ 5. What is the authors' overall purpose in this passage from their chapter "Can Willpower Be Strengthened"?

a. to persuade readers of the reasons David Blaine performs endurance feats

b. to entertain readers with amazing stories of a master illusionist

    c. to inform readers how one person strengthens his willpower in case knowing how he does it will help them strengthen theirs

    d. to persuade readers that everyone can be a David Blaine if they'll only practice a little

Why? What information in the selection leads you to give that answer? _____

_____

_____

_____

_____ **6.** What is the authors' purpose in listing Blaine's endurance feats in paragraph 1?

    a. to persuade readers to keep reading in order to find out how Blaine was able to do them

    b. to teach readers that Blaine's feats are so remarkable that only he could ever do them

    c. to entertain readers with Blaine's odd, extreme choice of actions

    d. to inform readers of actions they can take when they are in the mood to do crazy stunts

Why? What information in the selection leads you to give that answer? _____

_____

_____

Relationships

_____ **7.** What is the relationship between the last sentence of paragraph 3 and the first sentence of paragraph 4?

    a. The last sentence of paragraph 3 begins a story and the first sentence of paragraph 4 finishes it.

    b. The last sentence of paragraph 3 gives a positive example and the first sentence of paragraph 4 introduces a contrast.

    c. The first sentence of paragraph 4 gives the effect of the cause introduced in the last sentence of paragraph 3.

    d. The two sentences demonstrate a similarity between two events.

Why? What information in the selection leads you to give that answer? _____

_____

_____

_____ **8.** What pattern of organization is used in paragraph 10?

    a. space order

    b. time order

    c. comparison

    d. definition

Why? What information in the selection leads you to give that answer? _____

_____

_____

Fact, Opinion, and Inference

____ 9. Choose the statement that is an opinion.

  a. We're interested in the *how* of Blaine's feats.

  b. How he endures is a mystery that matters to people who aren't endurance artists.

  c. He had long been a believer in the notion that willpower is a muscle that can be strengthened.

  d. Those daily breathing drills got his body used to the pain of carbon dioxide buildup.

Why? What information in the selection leads you to give that answer? _____

_____

_____

____ 10. David Blaine's philosophy is shared in the epigraph "The more the body suffers, the more the spirit flowers." Which of the following statements would Blaine most likely support?

  a. Not all pain is gain.

  b. "Choose rather to be strong of soul than to be strong of body." —Pythagoras

  c. "The body is shaped, disciplined, honored, and in time, trusted." —Martha Graham, "I Am a Dancer"

  d. "It is a great ability to be able to conceal one's ability."—Francois de La Rochefoucauld

Why? What information in the selection leads you to give that answer? _____

_____

_____

▶ Critical Thinking Questions

Critical Thinking Level 1 ▷ **Remember**

Besides taking as his philosophy the epigraph that begins this article, *specify* what else David Blaine has in common with St. Simeon Stylites, whom this quotation is from. _____

_____

_____

Critical Thinking Level 2 ▸ Understand

Describe a time when you were successful at using or strengthening your willpower.

_____

_____

_____

Critical Thinking Level 3 ▸ Apply

Use what you have learned from Blaine's methods to think of three things you can do to help yourself achieve a long-term goal. (You may want to review your long-term goals on pages xxix–xxx.)

_____

_____

Critical Thinking Level 4 ▸ Analyze

In paragraph 11, Blaine is reported to say, "Some sort of OCD kicks in whenever I'm about to do a long-term challenge." Below is printed the definition of OCD from the Mayo Clinic website. Based on this definition, *analyze* whether Blaine has OCD. Explain your answer.

> Obsessive-compulsive disorder (OCD) is an anxiety disorder characterized by unreasonable thoughts and fears (obsessions) that lead you to do repetitive behaviors (compulsions). With obsessive-compulsive disorder, you may realize that your obsessions aren't reasonable, and you may try to ignore them or stop them. But that only increases your distress and anxiety. Ultimately, you feel driven to perform compulsive acts in an effort to ease your stressful feelings.
>
> —Mayo Clinic

_____

_____

Critical Thinking Level 5 ▸ Evaluate

With a classmate or group, *explain* what is missing from the thoughts of the man sitting on the bench in the cartoon on the next page. Then, on your own, evaluate whether this has ever been a problem for you.

_____

_____

_____

Robert Mankoff/Cartoonbank.com

Critical Thinking Level 6   Create

Create a new goal. Make sure it is something you care about. Ask three classmates to suggest practices or habits you could develop in order to help achieve it. Give them ideas for achieving their goals.

_____

_____

_____

▶ Vocabulary in New Contexts

Review the vocabulary words in the margins of the reading selection and then complete the following activities.

Relationships Between Words

Circle *yes* or *no* to answer the question. Then explain your answer.

1. Is it a **feat** to **sustain** your love when your partner cheats on you?

   Yes   No

   Why or why not? _____

2. Does a **serene** person act **erratically**?

   Yes   No

   Why or why not? _____

3. Is **eschewing** violence a **precursor** to a peaceful life?

   Yes   No

   Why or why not? _____

4. Does a person usually have to **expend** energy to learn from an **ordeal**?

   Yes   No

   Why or why not? _____

Language in Your Life

Write short answers to each question. Look at the vocabulary words closely before you answer.

1. Name one **serene** person you know. _____

   _____

2. Name one **ordeal** that you have successfully passed through. _____

   _____

3. Name one time when you saw someone or something **plummet**. _____

   _____

4. Name one action you expect to take as a **precursor** to success. _____

   _____

5. Name one thought you have that **sustains** you through hard times. _____

   _____

Language in Use

Select the best word to complete the meaning of each sentence.

erratic	eschew	expend	feat	ordeal
plummet	precursor	serene	sustain	

1. Louis Zamperini's plane *The Green Hornet* _____ into the Pacific in May 1943.

2. He and a fellow soldier lived through the _____ of floating on a raft for 47 days, at one point killing a shark with a pair of pliers, but this turned out to be only a _____ to a much more difficult time after they were captured by the Japanese.

3. As a prisoner of war, Zamperini had to _____ himself through times when he was made to clean a pigsty by hand, be punched repeatedly in the face, and tolerate the abuse of a sadistic guard who enjoyed tormenting Zamperini in particular.

4. It was a real _____ to survive such treatment.

5. Prisoners of war have reported that they just had to do their best to remain _____ despite _____ treatment from their captors.

6. If they _____ too much energy on thinking of revenge, they can't focus on their main goal of getting out alive. They must _____ negativity as much as humanly possible. In Zamperini's case, he shared Italian recipes with his fellow prisoners to help them keep their minds off their situation.

Reading 2–2   Psychology Textbook

▶ Pre-Reading the Selection

The reading on page 100 about motivation is from a textbook called *What Is Psychology?*

Surveying the Reading

Survey the article that follows. Then check the elements that are included in this reading.

_____	Title	_____	Words in bold or italic type
_____	Headings	_____	Images and captions
_____	First sentences of paragraphs		

Guessing the Purpose

Based on the type of book this reading is from, do you suppose the author's purpose is mostly to inform, persuade, or express? _____

Predicting the Content

Survey the first sentence of each paragraph and predict three things that the selection will discuss.

▶ _____

▶ _____

▶ _____

Activating Your Knowledge

What do you know about different kinds of motivation? Do you have any personal stories from your past about when you have felt most motivated? List two or three things you know about motivation.

▶ _____

▶ _____

▶ _____

Scan to Connect! Use your smart phone to scan this code to watch a video to activate your knowledge about motivation. (See the inside front cover for more information on how to use this.) As you watch the video, consider who you relate to better, Rocky or his son.

▶Reading with Pen in Hand

Students who annotate as they read are more successful than those who do not. That's why you will annotate each selection in *Connect* as you read. In the reading that follows, use the following symbols:

★ or (Point)   to indicate a main idea

① ② ③   to indicate major details

 Visit www.cengagebrain.com to access the CourseMate for this chapter to hear pronunciations of vocabulary words from this reading.

What Is Motivation?

Ellen Pastorino

▶What four viewpoints are introduced?

1   Over the years, psychologists have viewed motivation in several different ways—as *instincts* that direct our behavior, as uncomfortable biological states called *drives* that motivate us to find ways to feel better, as the desire to maintain an optimal level of *arousal* in our body, or as *incentives* that guide us to seek reward from the world. However, none of these theories seems to fully explain all aspects of motivation. Today psychologists do not expect any single theory to explain all our motivations. Instead, we recognize that each of these theories has its strengths and weaknesses. Let's take a closer look at these different theories of motivation.

drives A definition precedes the word. What is it?

Motivation as Instinct

▶What did James believe motivation was based on?

2   One of the earliest views on motivation was one that was heavily influenced by the work of Charles Darwin and the theory of natural selection. Back in the 1800s, American psychologist William James proposed that motives are, in fact, **genetically** determined **instincts** that have evolved in humans because they support survival and procreation. According to William James, instincts are impulses from within a person that direct or *motivate* that person's behavior.

genetically James said these behaviors evolved. What does that suggest *genetically* means?

▶What two problems did his theory have?

3   Over time, the idea that motives are inborn instincts gradually fell out of favor with psychologists. One problem with James's view was that the list of proposed instincts kept getting longer and longer. Taken to its logical extreme, instinct theory could be used to argue that all behavior is due to instinct. Furthermore, it is impossible to determine whether many of the proposed instincts are truly inborn. Many of our so-called instincts may result from learning.

Motivation as a Drive

▶Think of another example of drive reduction you have experienced.

4   Instinct theory was followed by **drive reduction theories** of motivation. According to the drive reduction approach, motivation stems from the desire to reduce an uncomfortable internal state, called a **drive**, that results when our needs are not fulfilled. For instance, when we do not have enough food in our system, we feel the uncomfortable state of *hunger*, which *drives* us to eat until we have taken in the food that our bodies require. Then, when we have taken in enough food, the hunger drive **dissipates**, and we stop eating. In this fashion, our drives can help us survive by creating what psychologists call a *drive state*, which ensures that we will be motivated to meet our biological needs.

dissipates What does your logic tell you this means?

5   **Primary drives**, such as the need for food, water, and warmth, motivate us to maintain certain bodily processes at an internal state of equilibrium, or **homeostasis**. Obviously, it would be desirable for us to take in just the right amount of food and water, to sleep just enough, and to maintain our body temperature at 98.6 degrees. Without the motivation from drives, we would not keep our bodies at homeostasis because we would not know when to eat, sleep, drink, and so on. **But what causes a drive state in the first place?**

▶ What is the purpose of primary drives?

6   Primary drives begin in the body when the brain recognizes that we are lacking in some biological need. The brain recognizes need based on the *feedback* that it receives from the body's systems and organs. One type of feedback system is called a **negative feedback loop (Figure 2.3)**. Negative feedback loops are information systems in the body that monitor the level of a bodily process and adjust it up and down accordingly. A good analogy for a negative feedback loop is the action of a thermostat. In your home, you set the thermostat at a desired level, and the thermostat monitors the air temperature and compares it to that set level. If the room gets too cold, the heater turns on. If the room gets too warm, the heater turns off. Many primary drives in the body work in the same fashion.

▶ How do primary drives work?

7   The idea that motivation in the form of primary drives serves to maintain homeostasis makes a great deal of sense. Without primary drives, our biological needs would likely not be met, and we might not survive. **But how well does the idea of drive explain some of our other motivations?** For example, does

▶ How would you answer the question printed in blue?

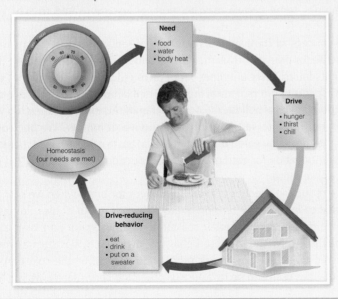

Figure 2.3   How do negative feedback loops maintain homeostasis?

Figure 2.4   Which drives do you feel strongly? Weakly, or not at all?

Achievement (the need to achieve success in life)	**Affiliation** (the need to be close to others)
Counteraction (the need to overcome one's fears and failures)	**Rejection** (the need to reject those you do not like)
Abasement (the need to admit inferiority)	**Defendance** (the need to defend oneself against others)
Narcissism (the need to be self-absorbed)	**Nurturance** (the need to be nurturing and care for others)
Autonomy (the need to be independent)	**Succorance** (the need to have others care for you)
Understanding (the need to understand one's world)	**Sex** (the need to engage in sexual relations)
Play (the need to have fun)	**Blamavoidance** (the need to avoid being blamed or rejected by others)
Sentience (the need to seek out experiences that are pleasing to the senses)	**Aggression** (the need to be aggressive and to fight)
Order (the need to be neat and organized)	**Dominance** (the need to control your environment and the people in it)
Harmavoidance (the need to avoid pain and harm to oneself)	**Exhibition** (the need to have others notice you)
Infavoidance (the need to avoid humiliation and embarrassment)	**Deference** (the need to defer to others)

presumed What other word could you plug in here that would make sense? What is *presumed*?

▶ What are secondary drives?

▶ How does overeating call drive reduction theory into question?

sole What do logic and prior knowledge of similar words tell you this means?

▶ How does riding a roller coaster call drive reduction theory into question?

drive reduction theory explain academic achievement motivation, or motivation to be loved? To help explain what motivates those behaviors not directly related to survival, drive reduction theorists developed the notion of **secondary drives**, or drives that motivate us to perform behaviors that are not directly related to biological needs.

8   Secondary drives are **presumed** to develop as we begin to associate things like achievement with satisfaction of primary drives—for example, receiving a candy bar for doing well in school satisfies hunger. As a result, we may also become more motivated to achieve academically. **Figure 2.4** shows a list of secondary needs that were identified by psychologist Henry Murray back in the 1930s. According to some psychologists, the need to fulfill certain secondary drives differs from person to person, like any other personality characteristic. For example, some people may be more or less motivated to achieve than others.

9   The concept of motivation as a means of reducing drives seems to make more sense for primary drives than for secondary drives, but even here it is not without its faults. There are times when drive reduction theory cannot explain certain aspects of our biological motives. For example, what about overeating? Think about a typical holiday meal in your family. At holiday dinners, do you eat only enough food to satisfy your primary drive of hunger? We bet not. How many times have you eaten until you felt ill because it was a special occasion? If our **sole** motivation for eating were drive reduction, we would not "pig out" in instances like these.

10   Drive reduction theories also fail to account for times when we seem to be motivated to *increase* the tension or arousal levels in our bodies. For instance, when you decide to ride a roller coaster at an amusement park or to skydive, what possible drive could these behaviors lower? Activities such as these do not appear to reduce any of our primary drives. Rather, the sole purpose of these activities seems to be to *arouse* us physiologically. Clearly, we will have to

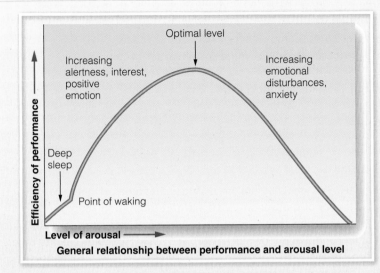

Figure 2.5 How could you tell if you had an arousal level that was too high?

General relationship between performance and arousal level

conceptualize motivation in some other way to account for these types of behavior.

Arousal Theory of Motivation

11   The **arousal theory** of motivation states that each of us has a level of physiological arousal at which we operate best, an *optimal* level of arousal. In general, we perform best on tasks when we are moderately aroused **(Figure 2.5)**; too much or too little arousal generally weakens performance. Therefore, each of us is motivated to seek out arousal when we find ourselves underaroused and to reduce our arousal level when we are overaroused.

12   Although most of us perform best at moderate levels of arousal, some people seem to **crave** arousal, seeking out higher levels of arousal than the rest of us. In fact, sometimes they seek out levels of arousal that the rest of us would find *aversive*. For example, think of adventurers who handle dangerous animals, climb skyscrapers without protective gear, or bungee-jump off bridges. Many of us wouldn't try these activities even if we were *paid to*! So what motivates some people to **habitually** seek out such arousing activities? Some people are what psychologists call **sensation seekers**; they habitually tend to seek out high levels of physiological arousal by engaging in intensely stimulating experiences. Some sensation seekers pursue daring activities such as mountain climbing, skydiving, and fast driving, whereas others may be stimulated by engaging in problem behaviors such as drug use, aggression, and delinquency.

13   One theory that seeks to explain the causes of sensation seeking looks at biological differences in the brains of sensation seekers. Psychologist Marvin Zuckerman found that sensation seekers tend to have low levels of a substance called *monoamine oxidase* (MAO). MAO is an enzyme that breaks down neurotransmitters such as serotonin, dopamine, and norepinephrine. One of these

conceptualize A *concept* is an idea; *conceptual* means related to an idea; when you add *–ize*, what meaning do you arrive at?

optimal Based on the words before this one, what does *optimal* mean?

▶ How would you rate your own ideal arousal level: high, medium, low?

crave What would cause someone to seek out higher levels of arousal? What does *crave* mean?

aversive Use the contrast in this sentence to decide what *aversive* means.

habitually The root of this word is *habit*. What does *habitually* mean?

▶ How does a low level of MAO affect sensation-seeking activity?

neurotransmitters, dopamine, seems to be responsible for motivating us to obtain rewards. The low level of MAO in the brains of sensation seekers may mean that they experience more dopamine activity than other people. Without MAO to break it down, the dopamine would remain in the synapse longer, continuing to stimulate the neuron. This increased dopamine action may be related to the sensation seeker's motivation to experience reward from intense arousal.

Self-Determination Theory of Motivation

▶ What three feelings does self-determination theory say we need?

14   Perhaps jumping out of airplanes and skiing off mountainsides is not your cup of tea. The idea that humans have different types of motivation is part of a broad theory of motivation called **self-determination theory**. According to self-determination theory, humans need to feel *competent* (skilled), *autonomous* (in control of our own behavior), and *related* (or connected) to others. As we live our lives, actively trying to meet these needs, we will at times experience *autonomous motivation* and *controlled motivation*. When we are autonomously motivated, we are self-motivated to engage in a behavior. For example, you might study for an exam because you want to do well on the exam. When we experience controlled motivation, our behavior is externally regulated. For example, you may study for an exam because you want to please your professor.

incentives Reread the example just given. What are *incentives*?

▶ What are two kinds of incentives?

15   These examples show the power that **incentives** have to motivate us into action. You can think of incentives as goals or desires that you wish to satisfy or fulfill. For example, someone who desires money will be motivated to engage in behaviors that will likely lead to obtaining money, such as taking a job or buying lottery tickets. Incentives can be either *intrinsic* (coming from within us) or *extrinsic* (coming from outside us). Intrinsic incentives, such as wanting to make a good grade to please yourself, provide **intrinsic motivation** for behavior whereas extrinsic incentives, such as wanting to please others or desiring monetary rewards, provide **extrinsic motivation** for behavior.

▶ Are you oriented to intrinsic or extrinsic motivation?

16   People differ in their orientation toward either an intrinsic or an extrinsic motivation. Some of us tend to be more motivated by intrinsic rewards in life, such as a sense of accomplishment and pride. Others of us tend to be more motivated by extrinsic rewards, such as grades and money. Which motivates you more? Although all of us are motivated at times by both intrinsic and extrinsic motives, some studies suggest an advantage to having a more intrinsic orientation. For example, research has indicated that intrinsically motivated college students are less likely to use drugs and alcohol. And, intrinsic motivation has been shown to predict success in sticking to an exercise program and doing well in school. It appears that intrinsic rewards, such as a sense of accomplishment, are more likely to keep us working hard for success.

—From Pastorino, *What Is Psychology*, 3e. Copyright © 2012 Cengage Learning, Inc. Reproduced by permission. www.cengage.com/permissions

▶ Comprehension Questions

Write the letter of the answer on the line. Then explain your thinking.

Main Idea

_____ 1. What is the best statement of the main idea of the entire selection?

    a. Over the years, psychologists have viewed motivation in several different ways—as instincts, as drives, as the desire to maintain arousal, or as incentives.

    b. However, none of these theories seems to fully explain all aspects of motivation.

    c. Today psychologists do not expect any single theory to explain all our motivations.

    d. Motivation as Instinct

Why? What information in the selection leads you to give that answer? _____

_____

_____

_____

_____ 2. What is the best statement of the main idea of the section "Motivation as a Drive"?

    a. Instinct theory was followed by **drive reduction theories** of motivation.

    b. According to the drive reduction approach, motivation stems from the desire to reduce an uncomfortable internal state, called a **drive**, that results when our needs are not fulfilled.

    c. Primary drives, such as the need for food, water, and warmth, motivate us to maintain certain bodily processes at an internal state of equilibrium, or **homeostasis**.

    d. Secondary drives are presumed to develop as we begin to associate things like achievement with satisfaction of primary drives.

Why? What information in the selection leads you to give that answer? _____

_____

_____

Supporting Details

_____ 3. Which of the following is <u>not</u> an example of a primary drive?

    a. food

    b. warmth

    c. water

    d. achievement

Why? What information in the selection leads you to give that answer? _____

_____

_____

____   4. According to this passage, which detail is an example of problematic sensation seeking?

    a. mountain climbing

    b. skydiving

    c. taking drugs

    d. bungee jumping

Why? What information in the selection leads you to give that answer? _____

_____

_____

Author's Purpose

____   5. What is the author's purpose in putting certain questions in bold blue type?

    a. to direct readers' attention to only the most important ideas

    b. to help students read actively for the answers and thus keep them engaged

    c. to call out the most important terms and definitions

    d. to show how the three figures are linked to the text

Why? What information in the selection leads you to give that answer? _____

_____

_____

_____

____   6. What is the overall purpose of this selection?

    a. to inform readers how to distinguish primary and secondary drives

    b. to inform readers about practical steps they can take to reduce negative feedback loops

    c. to inform readers about the biological differences in the brains of sensation seekers

    d. to inform readers of different theories of motivation, including their strengths and their weaknesses

Why? What information in the selection leads you to give that answer? _____

_____

_____

_____

Relationships

____   7. What pattern of organization is used in the first two sentences of paragraph 2?

    a. time order

    b. comparison

c. definition

d. classification

Why? What information in the selection leads you to give that answer? _____

_____

8. Overall, Figure 2.3 describes which of the following?

a. a contrast

b. an example

c. a process

d. a comparison

Why? What information in the selection leads you to give that answer? _____

_____

_____

Fact, Opinion, and Inference

9. Choose the statement that is a fact.

a. Secondary drives are presumed to develop as we begin to associate things like achievement with satisfaction of primary needs.

b. William James proposed a theory of motivation based on instinct.

c. But what causes a drive state in the first state?

d. Arousal Theory of Motivation

Why? What information in the selection leads you to give that answer? _____

_____

_____

_____

10. What can you infer about theories from this selection?

a. Theories are all based on undeniable facts.

b. Once a theory is proposed, that line of inquiry halts.

c. Each theory is built on the one that came before it.

d. A theory is an explanation of why and how a behavior occurs, but it may not explain every single instance of that behavior.

Why? What information in the selection leads you to give that answer? _____

_____

_____

_____

▸Critical Thinking Questions

Critical Thinking Level 1 ▸ Remember

Identify the appropriate term for each definition given below.

1. _____ : an internal state of equilibrium
2. _____ : the need for food, water, and warmth
3. _____ : the need to be close to others
4. _____ : an enzyme that breaks down neurotransmitters
5. _____ : theory that proposes that people need to feel competent, autonomous, and related

Critical Thinking Level 2 ▸ Understand

Using your own words, *explain* two different kinds of incentives and give an example of each one.

_____

_____

_____

Critical Thinking Level 3 ▸ Apply

On a separate piece of paper, write a paragraph in which you *apply* the self-determination theory of motivation to the following situation. Your goal is to explain Ernestine Shepherd's motivations using any of the following terms that apply: *autonomous motivation, controlled motivation, incentives, intrinsic motivation, extrinsic motivation.*

Ernestine Shepherd: World's Oldest Female Bodybuilder

At age 56, Ernestine Shepherd found herself in a changing room trying on bathing suits with her sister Velvet. When they saw what they looked like, they had to laugh. Velvet said "Tina, we're going to have to do something about this." So they started working out together. Unfortunately, about a year into their training, Velvet died suddenly of an aneurysm. For a long time, Ernestine could not bring herself to work out. Her blood pressure increased, she started having panic attacks, and she didn't want to attend church. However, Raymond Day, who had trained her and her sister, came to visit her at home. He told her she needed to get her life back together. Her other sister Bern recommended that she start walking. Ernestine says about this time: "Strength training and walking each day, I slowly noticed a change in my mood.... I noticed how clear-headed I became after exercising.... One night my sister came to me in a dream. She said she was happy I was carrying on our dream."

Today, Ernestine Shepherd runs ten miles a day, has a daily weight training program, and is the oldest female bodybuilder in the world.

Critical Thinking Level 4 › Analyze

Think of a goal that you would like to motivate yourself to achieve. Write it down:

_____

Use Figure 2.4 to *analyze* at least two secondary needs this goal would fulfill. Explain.

_____

_____

_____

_____

Critical Thinking Level 5 › Evaluate

Evaluate which theory of motivation discussed in this selection has the most specific and detailed evidence associated with it. On a separate piece of paper, contrast this theory with at least one other theory that is described to prove your point. _____

Critical Thinking Level 6 › Create

List at least ten behaviors you were motivated to do in the past week. Decide which ones were the hardest to get motivated to do. For each difficult one, *create* a short plan of action that you can use the next time you need to do this action.

▶ Vocabulary in New Contexts

Review the vocabulary words in the margins of the reading selection and then complete the following activities.

Relationships Between Words

Circle *yes* or *no* to answer the question. Then explain your answer.

1. In its present form, the cockroach has been around for 144 million years. Would you call it **genetically optimal**?

   Yes   No

   Why or why not? _____

2. If your manager gives you the proper **incentives**, will you **habitually** do a good job?

   Yes   No

   Why or why not? _____

3. Can you **conceptualize** a chocolate **craving** as being **aversive**?

   Yes   No

   Why or why not? _____

   _____

4. Does the **sole** owner of a business have a way to **dissipate** decision-making responsibility?

   Yes   No

   Why or why not? _____

   _____

5. When people feel **driven** to succeed, can we **presume** they want to be powerful?

   Yes   No

   Why or why not? _____

   _____

Language in Your Life

Write short answers to each question. Look at the vocabulary words closely before you answer.

1. Name an **incentive** that would get you to study for two hours every day. _____

   _____

2. Name one experience or thing that you **crave**. _____

   _____

3. Name one person whom you **habitually** encounter. _____

   _____

4. Name one trait that you consider part of your **genetic** inheritance. _____

   _____

5. Name an emotion that you consider **optimal**. _____

   _____

Language in Use

Select the best word to complete the meaning of each sentence.

aversive	conceptualize	crave	dissipates	drives	genetically
habitually	incentives	optimal	presumed	solely	

1. Cardiology professor Barbara Natterson-Horowitz and writer Kathryn Bowers have written a book called *Zoobiquity: What Animals Can Teach Us About Health and the Science of Healing.* In it, they note that many different species of animals, just like humans, _____ eat plants and parts of plants that make them intoxicated.

2. In fact, the bighorn sheep found in the Canadian Rockies so _____ the hallucinogenic lichen they scrape off rocks that they will grind their teeth nearly off to get it.

3. People and animals also get the same kinds of diseases, and the authors suggest that there are _____ for physicians and veterinarians to consult on cases for _____ understanding.

4. However, physicians find that idea _____; all their training points them to _____ that human medical needs are different from those of animals, not similar to them.

5. Physicians are _____ to somehow be superior to veterinarians, or at least they think so. As Natternson-Horowitz notes, though, a joke that several veterinarians told her reveals their stance: "What do you call a physician? A veterinarian who treats only one species."

6. This emphasis _____ on human disease might mean doctors aren't aware, for example, that teen "cutting" behavior is very similar to overlicking and overbiting behaviors found in dogs, cats, and horses. Both species do this to _____ stress and anxiety that they don't have other ways to get rid of.

7. Do humans and animals share the same primary _____? Absolutely. Food, water, warmth, and procreation are _____ necessary for life on Planet Earth.

 Click to Connect! For more practice applying the skills you learned in this chapter, visit **www.cengagebrain.com** to access the CourseMate for this chapter.

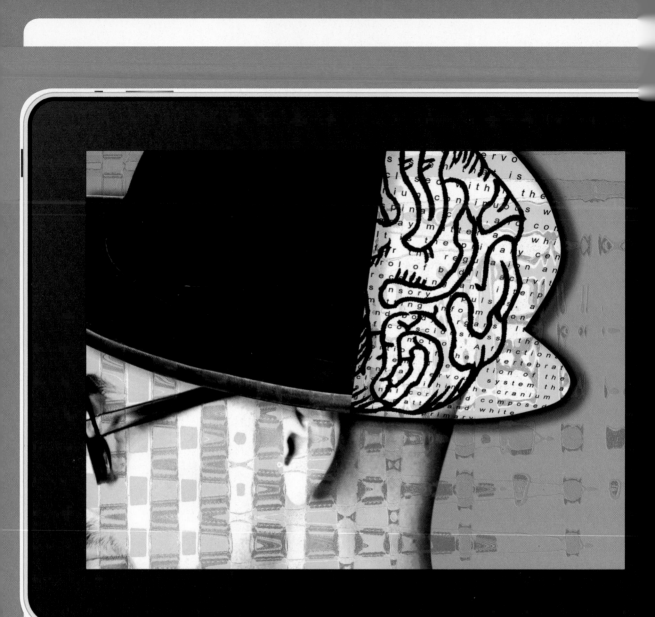

Click to Connect! Visit **www.cengagebrain.com** to access study resources for this chapter through CourseMate, which includes audio, video, quizzes, and a searchable, interactive eBook version of the text.

▶ What are the differences in sound and meaning between the two words that are spelled the same?

▶ What clues help you decide what each word means?

▶ Can you identify the part of speech of each word?

1. We must *polish* the *Polish* furniture. _____

_____

_____

2. The farm was used to *produce produce.* _____

_____

_____

3. The soldier decided to *desert* in the *desert.* _____

_____

_____

4. When shot at, the *dove dove* into the bushes. _____

_____

_____

5. **Scan to Connect!** Use your smart phone to scan this code to watch a video. (See the inside front cover for more information on how to use this.) Suppose you moved to a land where everyone communicated using American Sign Language. Watch this video several times to decide what steps you could take to begin to learn the language. What would you do, and why?

Vocabulary Strategies

As you work through this chapter, you will learn strategies to help you determine the meanings of words you do not know based on the context in which they are used. But before we introduce these strategies, we want to talk about what to do with the new words you are exposed to. How can you learn them? How can you remember them? This is important to know now so that as you work through this chapter (and this book), you can practice the strategies you need to make new words your own.

Learning words in their naturally occurring context is more effective than memorizing them from, say, a list of vocabulary words. We learn words better when we see them in an article or a book or hear them in a conversation because in those contexts, we understand their connections with other ideas. Learning words in context also helps us connect them to our own prior knowledge. So how is it that you will most effectively learn new words? You have to read!

The next step is to incorporate new words into your daily life. You could *read* twenty new words a day and never *learn* one of them. The only way to truly learn a new word is to actively make it a part of your writing and speech. As you write in your college courses, use the vocabulary you are learning. You can also use new words in a vocabulary notebook, a journal, letters, your Facebook wall, blogs, and text messages—anywhere you write. And you can transfer new words into your speaking vocabulary by learning how they are pronounced. The audio files that accompany this book online through the CourseMate can help. Listen to the words, practice them on your own, and then introduce them into your conversation. You can access these audio files by going to www.cengagebrain.com and searching for this textbook and its available study resources.

Organize Your Vocabulary Study with EASY Note Cards

You need an easy way to keep your study of vocabulary organized, and it's a smart idea to keep reminding yourself of the meanings of new words so you can commit them to memory. Creating and then studying EASY note cards is a simple way to learn and remember enough about a new word so you can start to use it comfortably.

Here is the format of an EASY note card.

The word

(the part of speech—
noun, verb, adjective, adverb)

FRONT

Example—Write a sentence using the word that shows you know its meaning.

Antonym—the word's opposite (if there is one)

Synonym—a word with a similar meaning (If there is one)

Your Logic—Use your logic to make up a definition in your own words

BACK

As you learn about each word, you may find that other words are related to it. You can add this information to the front of the card as you learn it. You may also choose to draw a picture on the front of the card that reminds you of the meaning, or you can write how to pronounce the word.

Here is a sample note card for the word *refuse* from "Why English Is So Hard to Learn."

Refuse

(noun)
Pronunciation: **REF**use

Examples: The dumpster was overflowing with refuse.
Hoarders can't let go of their refuse.

Antonyms: property, assets, stuff you still want

Synonyms: garbage, junk, rubbish, trash

Your logic: If you would refuse to bring it in your house, it may be refuse!

FRONT

BACK

Throughout the next section you'll practice making EASY note cards.

Context Clues

What do you do when you are reading and come across a word whose meaning you don't know? One option is to stop reading and find your dictionary, which is probably in the other room. By the time you make it back to the room where you were reading, chances are you have forgotten the word you went to look up. So now you have to find the word in your reading again. You look it up, read the definition, and close the dictionary. Now you have to reread the paragraph because you have forgotten what it was about. You finally get back to the word, and you have already forgotten what it meant!

There is an easier option. You can use **context clues**. Let's unpack the meaning of *context clue*, starting with the easy word. What is a synonym for **clue**? How about *sign*, *hint*, or *evidence*? What does **context** mean? It means *environment* or *setting*. In other words, a context clue is a hint (clue) about the meaning of a word that is located in the surrounding words or sentences (context).

When you are trying to figure out what a word means, look in the sentences surrounding the word. Clues to your word's meaning can be found anywhere within a paragraph, but they are often found in one or more of the following three places:

- ▶ The actual sentence in which the unknown word appears.
- ▶ The sentence before the one in which the word appears.
- ▶ The sentence after the one in which the word appears.

Students often pressure themselves by thinking they have to come up with a specific definition for a word they do not know. But when you use context clues, you are not looking for the exact meaning of a word; you are simply looking for an approximate meaning that will give you enough of an understanding to keep reading. That way you won't have to stop and get distracted every time you come across a word you do not know.

There are several types of context clues. The most common ones are examples, antonyms, synonyms, and your own logic interacting with the words on the page. Context clues are *easy*. Literally—as **EASY as 1, 2, 3**. Check out the following **mnemonic**. (Can you guess the meaning of **mnemonic** based on the *example* context clue?)

Example

Antonym

Synonym

Your Logic

As

1. Look for signal words, or transitions.

2. Focus on what you know.

3. Pay attention to punctuation.

You may not always look for clues in EASY order, but all four kinds of clues are important to remember.

Examples

Examples are probably the most straightforward kind of context clue. First, the author uses a word and then gives an example that describes or explains it, often using signal words.

> ### Words that signal examples:
>
> *for example, for instance, such as, like, to illustrate*
> Felix is convinced Jessica is clairvoyant. **For example**, she has saved him from getting a ticket three times by telling him she had a feeling there was a police officer ahead.

As you can see, the word *clairvoyant* has something to do with being able to see things that haven't happened yet. You can tell because of the example given: *she had a feeling there was a police officer ahead.*

Interaction 3–1 ▸ Use Example Context Clues with Signal Words

Each sentence includes a **boldfaced** vocabulary word. Underline the example that provides a clue to its meaning. Circle the signal word. Then guess the meaning of the vocabulary word and write it on the line.

1. Roy's friends tell him he will never get a date because he is too **reticent**. For example, he almost never talks to anyone other than his closest friends. _____

2. Many pregnant women are convinced that they will not **exhibit** basic maternal behaviors, such as holding their baby correctly, nursing them, or even keeping them safe. _____

3. One classic example of **integrity** is Abraham Lincoln, who is said to have walked several miles to return a few cents he had overcharged a customer. _____

4. Depending on one's preference, the **grandeur** of nature can be illustrated by sunrises and sunsets, mountain vistas, or beach scenery. _____

5. Actions like stabbing a friend in the back or cheating on a partner often cause the victim to become **incensed**. _____

Now create EASY note cards (on pp. 116–117) for the words you did not know. Bring your note card(s) to class to share your ideas.

Signal Words May Not Be Present. One important thing to know about context clues is that signal words are optional. Suppose you read a sentence that does not include any signal words. You can figure out if there are examples by adding example signal words to different places to see if they make sense. If they do, that's an example context clue. See how it works here:

> Felix is convinced Jessica is clairvoyant. [**for example**] She has saved him from getting a ticket three times by telling him she had a feeling there was a police officer ahead.

This won't always work, but it works often enough that you can use it to search for example context clues. However, use your common sense. Sometimes the way a sentence is put together doesn't allow you to insert *for example* or *such*, but it can still include examples.

Interaction 3–2 ▸ Use Example Context Clues without Signal Words

Each item includes a **boldfaced** vocabulary word. First, add example signal words where they fit best in the sentence. Then underline the example that provides a clue to its meaning. Finally, guess the meaning of the vocabulary word and write it on the line.

1. **Ageism** predisposes us to discriminate against old people by avoiding them or in some way victimizing them primarily because of their age. We might think all elderly are senile, or they cannot contribute to society, or they are not open to change.

—From Corey, *I Never Knew I Had A Choice: Explorations in Personal Growth*, 8e (p. 119). Copyright © 2006 Cengage Learning, Inc. Reproduced by permission. www.cengage.com/permissions

_____

2. A **neutral mutation** has no effect on survival or reproduction. It neither helps nor hurts the individual. If you carry a mutation that keeps your earlobes attached to your head instead of swinging freely, attached earlobes should not in itself stop you from surviving and reproducing as well as anybody else.

—From Starr, *Biology*

_____

Now create EASY note cards for the words you did not know. Bring your note card(s) to class to share your ideas.

Antonyms

Antonyms are words that have opposite meanings, such as *light* and *dark*. Sometimes you can figure out the meaning of a word by finding its antonym in a context that shows the author means to contrast (show the difference between) the two words.

> ### Words that signal contrast:
> *on the other hand, in contrast, however, but, yet, instead, even though, although, unlike*
> **Although** the lawyer's question seemed innocuous enough, its true intent was to harm the character of the witness.

The word *although* signals a contrast between the two parts of the sentence that are divided by the comma. To figure out the meaning of *innocuous*, you can use that signal word as a clue. You might also notice that the sentence shows contrast in its wording: <u>seemed</u> innocuous..., its <u>true</u> intent was to harm.... The word with an opposing meaning is *harm*. So *innocuous* means "not harmful." Once you determine the opposite word, you can put *not* or *doesn't* in front of it; this will often help you form a working definition. Sometimes, a working definition is all you need in order to understand what you are reading.

Interaction 3–3 ▶ Use Antonym Context Clues

Each sentence includes a **boldfaced** vocabulary word. Underline the antonym that provides a clue to its meaning. If there are signal words that indicate contrast, circle them. Then guess the meaning of the vocabulary word and write it on the line.

1. Looking for a new car can be quite frustrating. There are so many choices. The sporty model I like loses its value quickly. However, the model that looks like every other car on the road **retains** its value.

   A. What is your "working definition" for **retains**? _____

   B. What does **retains** mean? _____

2. To become an efficient reader, you must practice active reading strategies. On the other hand, **passive** reading requires nothing more than running your eyes over a page.

   A. What is your "working definition" for **passive**? _____

   B. What does **passive** mean? _____

3. John bought a rental property, thinking that collecting a monthly rent would make it a nice investment, but it has turned into an enormous **liability** because there have been no tenants and tons of repairs.

   A. What is your "working definition" for **liability**? _____

   B. What does liability mean? _____

4. In a breakup, would it be more painful if the person you cared for **deceived** you, rather than admitting the truth?

   —From Hales, *An Invitation to Health*, 15e (p. 135). Copyright © 2013 Cengage Learning, Inc. Reproduced by permission. www.cengage.com/permissions

   A. What is your "working definition" for **deceived**? _____
   B. What does **deceived** mean? _____

5. Despite the impressive collection of research findings for personality **stability** using the five-factor model, there is growing evidence for personality change.

   —From Kail, *Human Development: A Life-Span View*, 4e (p. 512). Copyright © 2007 Cengage Learning, Inc. Reproduced by permission. www.cengage.com/permissions

   A. What is your "working definition" for **stability**? _____

   B. What does **stability** mean? _____

   Now create EASY note cards for the words you did not know. Bring your note card(s) to class to share your ideas.

Synonyms

Synonyms are words that have a similar meaning or the same meaning, such as *small* and *little*. Sometimes you can figure out the meaning of a word by finding its synonym in a context that shows the author means to compare (show the similarities between) the two words. Other times the author actually defines the word, so be on the lookout for phrases that mean the same thing as the word.

Words that signal similarity:

like, as, also, as well, or, in other words, that is, in the same way

Hominids were bipedal—**that is**, two-legged, a trait that enabled them to move over long distances and make use of their arms and legs for different purposes.

—From Duiker, *World History*, 5e. Copyright © 2007 Cengage Learning, Inc.
Reproduced by permission. www.cengage.com/permissions

The words *that is* signal that the author is going to repeat the same idea using different words. The word *bipedal* means the same thing as "two-legged." These words are synonyms.

| Interaction 3–4 | **Use Synonym Context Clues** |

Each sentence includes a **boldfaced** vocabulary word. Underline the synonym (or definition) that provides a clue to its meaning. If there is a transition to signal the synonym, circle it. Then guess the meaning of the vocabulary word and write it on the line.

1. Many young children think their parents know everything. In the same way, people who have faith in God believe that God is **omniscient**. _____

2. The amount of light that enters a camera is determined by the size of the **aperture**, or opening, in the shutter.

   —From Fichner-Rathus, *Understanding Art*, 8e. Copyright © 2007 Cengage Learning, Inc.
   Reproduced by permission. www.cengage.com/permissions

   _____

3. Banks today try to convince consumers that their ATMs are **ubiquitous**, that is, that they can find one on every corner. _____

4. Glass is usually made from molten sand, or **silica**, mixed with minerals such as lead, copper, cobalt, cadmium, lime, soda, or potash. Certain combinations of minerals afford the glass a rich quality as found in stained-glass windows of the great cathedrals and in the more recent stained-glassworks of Henri Matisse and Marc Chagall.

—From Fichner-Rathus, *Understanding Art*, 8e

_____

5. President Theodore Roosevelt once made the following statement: "People used to say to me that I was an astonishingly good politician and **divined** what the people are going to think…. I did not [predict] how the people were going to think; I simply made my mind up what they ought to think and then did my best to get them to think it."

—From Schmidt, *American Government and Politics Today, 2007–2008*, 13e. Copyright © 2007 Cengage Learning, Inc. Reproduced by permission. www.cengage.com/permissions

_____

Now create EASY note cards for the words you did not know. Bring your note card(s) to class to share your ideas.

Your Logic

We said earlier that context clues for the meaning of a word are found in the surrounding words or sentences—that is, in the context of the reading selection. However, the reader's context plays a role, too, especially the context of how you think—your logic. Your ability to understand logical connections as you interact with the words on the page will help you make meaning as you read. Starting with what you already understand, actively try to figure out what you don't yet know. This process of making inferences is one you should always be using as you read.

> Despite his **valiant** effort, the young boxer was no match for the defending champion.

Here, you can assume that the young boxer tried his best to beat the champion. The sentence also says the young boxer was "no match" for the champion. Trying hard even when losing marks a person as brave, which is the meaning of *valiant*.

Interaction 3–5 ▸ Use Your Logic

Each sentence includes a **boldfaced** vocabulary word. Underline the part of the sentence that provides a clue to the word's meaning. Then use your logic and any prior knowledge you may have to guess the meaning of the word and write it on the line.

1. Janice and Renee are both Pilates instructors who work at the YMCA. They have decided that if they **collaborate**, they might be able to open their own studio.

A. What does **collaborate** mean? _____

B. How did your logic help? _____

_____

2. The artist had created an interesting display of black-and-white photos of homeless men and women **juxtaposed** with color images of celebrities.

A. What does **juxtaposed** mean? _____

B. How did your logic help? _____

_____

3. Remember that you will almost never memorize a speech or read it from a manuscript. Most often, you will choose the exact words of your speech as you are speaking it. Therefore, you need a **speaking outline** to help remember specific information that you plan to include in your speech.

—From Griffin, *Invitation to Public Speaking*, 2e. Copyright © 2006 Cengage Learning, Inc.
Reproduced by permission. www.cengage.com/permissions

A. What is a **speaking outline**? _____

B. How did your logic help? _____

_____

4. Hurricane Katrina created **havoc** in the north central Gulf coast region when it struck in the summer of 2005.

A. What does **havoc** mean? _____

B. How did your logic help? _____

_____

5. A **lackadaisical** defense in the first half of the game left the defending Super Bowl champs in a weakened position.

A. What does **lackadaisical** mean? _____

B. How did your logic help? _____

_____

Now create EASY note cards for the words you did not know. Bring your note card(s) to class to share your ideas.

EASY as 1, 2, 3

Regardless of whether you are using an example, antonym, synonym, or your logic to figure out what an unknown word means, you should follow these three steps:

1. Look for signal words (which lead to *example*, *antonym*, and *synonym* context clues).

2. Focus on what you know (which leads to *your logic*).

3. Pay attention to punctuation (which turns grade school rules into college assets).

1. Look for signal words

Signal words or transitions that help you find context clues are a good place to start determining the meanings of words. Remember that signal words often lead to example, synonym, and antonym context clues.

Interaction 3–6   Look for Signal Words

Each sentence includes a **boldfaced** vocabulary word. Underline the word or words that provide a clue to its meaning. Circle any signal words. Then guess the meaning of the word and write it on the line.

1. In daily life, we quickly **habituate**, or respond less, to predictable and unchanging stimuli.

   —From Coon/Mitterer, *Introduction to Psychology*

   A. What does **habituate** mean? _____

   B. What kind of context clue was used? _____

2. Despite the serious **allegations** against him, Mr. Smith's only crime was being in the wrong place at the wrong time.

   A. What does **allegations** mean? _____

   B. What kinds of context clue were used? _____

3. Meenu's big sister often **patronized** her; Meenu looked down on their little brother as well.

   A. What does **patronized** mean? _____

   B. What kind of context clue was used? _____

4. In his book *The Prophet*, Kahlil Gibran points out that love is two-sided: as it can give you great **ecstasy**, so it can cause you great pain.

   A. What does **ecstasy** mean? _____

   B. What was the context clue? _____

5. **Secularization** is one of the dominant trends influencing religion throughout the world. We can detect **secularization** in survey data that track religious attitudes and practices over time. For example, between 1972 and 2000, the percentage of Americans expressing no religious preference increased from 5 to 14 percent, while the percentage of people attending religious services once a month or more fell from 57 to 45 percent.

—National Opinion Research Center, 2002

A. What does **secularization** mean? _____

B. What kind of context clue was used? _____

Now create EASY note cards for the words you did not know. Bring your note card(s) to class to share your ideas.

2. Focus on what you know

Readers often pay attention to what they *do not* know rather than to what they *do* know. Your knowledge connects to many fields of study and types of information. Start training yourself to look for the connections between your prior knowledge and the new information you read. By focusing on what you know, you will be able to understand more of what you read than if you focus on what you do not know.

Interaction 3–7   Focus on What You Know

Each sentence includes a **boldfaced** vocabulary word. Underline the word or words that provide a clue to its meaning. Then guess the meaning of the word and write it on the line.

1. While one late credit card payment is not usually a problem, a habitual pattern can lead not only to your card being **revoked** but also to long-term damage to your credit report. _____

_____

2. Traditional Western doctors are now more frequently **advocating** the use of acupuncture, a Chinese medical practice of puncturing the body with needles at particular pressure points to relieve pain or treat disease.

—From Hales, *An Invitation to Health*, 12e. Copyright © 2007 Cengage Learning, Inc. Reproduced by permission. www.cengage.com/permissions

_____

3. During my first years in college, Martin Luther King's message of love as the path to ending racism and healing the wounds of racial domination had been replaced by a black power movement stressing militant resistance. While King had called for nonviolence and compassion, this new movement called on us to harden our hearts, to wage war against our enemies.

Loving our enemies, militant leaders told us, made us weak and easy to **subjugate**, and many turned their backs on King's message.
—From Hooks and Nhat, "Building a Community of Love"

_____

4. Having two or more wives in a **polygynous** society is usually seen as a mark of prestige or high status. In highly stratified kingdoms, **polygyny** is one of the privileges of royalty and aristocrats, as was the case with the late King Sobhuza of Swaziland, who, it was estimated, had well over a hundred wives.
—From Ferraro, *Cultural Anthropology: An Applied Perspective*, 6e. Copyright © 2006 Cengage Learning, Inc.
Reproduced by permission. www.cengage.com/permissions

A. What is a **polygynous society**? _____

B. What does **polygyny** mean? _____

5. At least 260,000 species of flowering plants live in **diverse** habitats. They bloom in **spacious** meadows and **aromatic** forests, in **parched** deserts and on **craggy** mountaintops.
—From Starr, *Biology: Concepts and Applications*, 6e

A. What does **diverse** mean? _____

B. What does **spacious** mean? _____

C. What does **aromatic** mean? _____

D. What does **parched** mean? _____

E. What does **craggy** mean? _____

F. What prior knowledge helped you determine the meaning of **diverse, spacious, aromatic, parched,** and **craggy**? _____

Now create EASY note cards for the words you did not know. Bring your note card(s) to class to share your ideas.

3. Pay attention to punctuation

Punctuation may not be the most exciting topic you'll ever read about, but it is important. Here's a humorous example that shows how punctuation alone can change the meaning of the same words:

An English professor wrote the words, "Woman without her man is nothing" on the blackboard and directed his students to punctuate it correctly. The men wrote: "Woman, without her man, is nothing." The women wrote: "Woman! Without her, man is nothing."
—Author unknown

Both sentences are correctly punctuated, but because of their punctuation, they have very different meanings. However, when it comes to context clues, punctuation does not have to be this tricky. Look at the following examples.

1. **dashes**—Material within dashes may provide a definition of the word that came before. Or a dash may introduce or follow an example.

> Triathlons—races that include biking, swimming, and running—have become popular in recent years.

> Iron, bronze, wood, ivory, terra-cotta—sculptors from the kingdom of Benin used all these materials with great skill.
>
> —From Fichner-Rathus, *Understanding Art*, 8e

2. **(parentheses)** Parentheses may enclose definitions.

> Trans fat (hydrogenated or partially-hydrogenated oil) is called "trans" because it is a process that "transfers" fat from a non-saturated to a saturated state.

3. **, commas,** The words enclosed by commas may restate the meaning of the previous word.

> Mariel is a chatty, even garrulous, person.

4. **colons (:)** Words after a colon often are examples or illustrations of the words before it.

> The most important skill for college graduates entering the work force is effective oral communication: listening, following instructions, conversing, and giving feedback.
>
> —From Williams, *Management*, 4e. Copyright © 2007 Cengage Learning, Inc. Reproduced by permission. www.cengage.com/permissions

---

Interaction 3–8 ▶ Pay Attention to Punctuation

Each sentence includes a **boldfaced** vocabulary word. Underline the word or words that provide a clue to its meaning. Circle any punctuation marks that act as clues. Then guess the meaning of the word and write it on the line.

1. To have a championship team requires the perfection of certain **tactics:** speed, skill, effective execution of plays, and, most of all, teamwork.

   What are **tactics**? _____

   _____

2. To be an **advocate**, or supporter, for the rights of an unpopular group of people requires courage, determination, and grace.

   What does **advocate** mean (other than supporter)? _____

   _____

3. Devin's little brother Cameron creates such a **disruption**—whenever Devin tries to study, Cameron sneaks up behind him and shouts in his ear.

   What does **disruption** mean? _____

   _____

4. The growing use of technology has created a **bifurcated workforce**, two tiers of workers whose different skills with technology have resulted in two distinct levels of income, even at the entry level.

   —From Segal, *An Introduction to the Profession of Social Work: Becoming a Change Agent*, 2e.
   Copyright © 2007 Cengage Learning, Inc. Reproduced by permission. www.cengage.com/permissions

   What is a **bifurcated workforce**? _____

   _____

5. One of the earliest, and perhaps the most primitive, methods of enhancing sound is **onomato-poeia**, which occurs when the sound of a word echoes its meaning, as it does in common words (*bang*, *crash*, and *hiss*).

   —From Kirszner/Mandell, *Literature*, 6e

   What does **onomatopoeia** mean? _____

   _____

Now create EASY note cards for the words you did not know. Bring your note card(s) to class to share your ideas.

Word Parts

There are three basic word parts: roots, prefixes, and suffixes. All words are made up of one or more of these pieces.

▶ Root. The root carries the main meaning of the word. A word has at least one root. It can have more than one. The root can be found at the beginning, middle, or end of a word.

▶ Prefix. Placed before a root, a prefix changes the word's meaning. Not all words have prefixes. Some words have one prefix; others have more than one.

▶ **Suffix.** Placed after a root, the suffix often changes the part of speech (such as noun, verb, or adjective) and thus changes the way the word acts in the sentence. Not all words have suffixes. Some words have only one suffix; others have more than one.

Sometimes students have trouble keeping the meanings of *root, prefix,* and *suffix* straight. Keep in mind that in the alphabet, P comes before R, and S comes after R (p, q, r, s…). So prefixes come at the beginning of a word (first in the alphabet order), suffixes come at the end of a word (last in the alphabet order), and roots are what prefixes and suffixes attach to (in the middle of R and S in the alphabet order).

Example: *undeniable*

Prefix	Root	Suffix
un-	deny	-able
(not)	(declare untrue)	(able to be)

In the word *undeniable*, the root *deny* carries the main meaning. To deny something is to declare that it isn't true. The prefix *un-* changes the meaning to its opposite. The suffix *-able* changes the word *deny*, which is a verb, into an adjective and also changes its meaning. Often, you need to change the order of the meaning of the word parts to create a definition that makes sense. *Undeniable* means "not able to be declared untrue." In other words, it means "definitely true."

The benefit of learning word parts is that by knowing a single part, you have a clue to the meaning of multiple words. Take the prefix *un-*, used in the example above. Did you know that *un-* is used in more than 2,000 words? Just by knowing one 2-letter prefix, you have partial knowledge of thousands of words. List as many words as you can think of that use the prefix *un-*.

_____	_____	_____	_____
_____	_____	_____	_____
_____	_____	_____	_____
_____	_____	_____	_____

You can use note cards as you learn word parts, just as you did in the EASY note card vocabulary strategy, but the layout on the cards will be a bit different since you are learning one part rather than a whole word. Also, you'll keep adding words that use the word part as you find them in your reading. See the following example.

Example for the Root *duc*

duc / duce / duct (lead, bring, take)

deduce   de- (from) + duce (take)—take from
           understand; conclude

produce   pro- (forward) + duce (bring)—bring forward
           make; manufacture; show

induce   in- (in, into) + duce (lead)—lead into
           urge; cause

FRONT

Notice that this root can be spelled three different ways and that it has three related meanings. These sample words consist of a prefix plus a root, but of course, words may also have suffixes.

When you make a word part card, your focus is mainly on the one word part at the top. However, in order to understand how a whole word uses that part, you'll also need to find out what the other word parts mean. So for each word part card, you may also be learning several other word parts. This is an efficient way to learn lots of word parts.

On the back of the card, use any technique that will connect the sample words to other things you know. The more connections you make, the easier it will be to understand the meanings of new words you encounter.

▶ Connect words to people, places, or things, or to other words (like antonyms) you already know.

▶ Connect words to visuals: Use a picture or an example that creates a mental visual for you.

▶ Connect words to other new words you are learning: Use two new words in one sentence that shows you know their meaning.

BACK

Roots

English is sort of a "mutt" language—many of its words come from several other languages, including Latin and Greek. **Table 3.1** displays ten common Latin roots.

From the sample words in the Latin roots table, it is easy to see how roots combine with prefixes to form new words. For example, the root *tract*, meaning

Table 3.1 Common Latin Roots

Latin root	Basic meaning	Example words
dict	to say	contradict, dictate, diction, edict, predict
duc	to lead, bring, take	conduct, deduce, produce, reduce
gress	to walk	digress, progress, transgress
ject	to throw	eject, inject, interject, project, reject, subject
pel	to drive	compel, dispel, impel, repel
pend	to hang	append, depend, impend, pendant, pendulum
port	to carry	comport, deport, export, import, report, support
scrib, script	to write	describe, description, prescribe, prescription, subscribe, subscription, transcribe, transcription
tract	to pull, drag, draw	attract, contract, detract, extract, protract, retract, traction
vert	to turn	convert, divert, invert, revert

"to pull," can be combined with a number of prefixes, including *de-* and *re-*. *Detract* means "to pull away" (*de-* means "away, off") and *retract* means "to pull back" (*re-* means "again, back").

Interaction 3–9 ▶ **Use Common Latin Roots to Develop Your Vocabulary**

Make a word part note card for each of the following roots. The sample words on the note card will be the three word choices for each numbered item below. (You may use a dictionary if you need to.) Then circle the correct word in each of the following sentences.

dict	gress	pel	port	tract

1. An addict's need for a drug (edicts/contradicts/dictates) his or her daily activities.

2. Michael's speech topic was the environmental impact of oil on birds, but for some reason he (transgressed/digressed/progressed) in the middle of his speech and began to discuss fish.

3. When the sun broke through the clouds, it (dispelled/repelled/impelled) the gloom.

4. The United States and other countries (deport/export/import) residents if they don't have a "green card" or other official documentation of their right to remain.

5. After giving birth, a mother's uterus (extracts/contracts/protracts) back to its smaller, pre-pregnancy size.

Greek root	Basic meaning	Example words
anthrop	human	misanthrope, philanthropy, anthropomorphic
bio	life	biology, biological, biography, autobiography
chron	time	anachronism, chronic, chronicle, synchronize, chronometer
dem	people	democracy, demography, demagogue, endemic, pandemic
log, logue	word, thought, or speech	dialogue, monologue, epilogue, logic
morph	form	amorphous, metamorphic, morphology
path	feeling, suffering	empathy, sympathy, sympathetic, apathy, apathetic, psychopathic
pedo, ped	child, children	pediatrician, pedagogue
philo, phil	having a strong affinity or love for	philanthropy, philharmonic, philosophy
phon	sound	polyphonic, cacophony, phonetics

Table 3.2   Common Greek Roots

From the sample words in the Greek roots table (**Table 3.2**), you can see how roots combine with suffixes to form words that are a different part of speech (such as a noun, verb, adjective, or adverb). For example, the root *path*, meaning "feeling," can be combined with a number of suffixes that change its part of speech. For example, *sympathy* is a noun; *sympathetic* is an adjective; and *sympathetically* is an adverb. The basic meaning does not change, but the suffix changes how the word is used.

Interaction 3–10   Use Common Greek Roots to Develop Your Vocabulary

Make a word part note card for each of the following roots. The sample words on the note card will be the three word choices for each numbered item below. (You may use a dictionary if you need to.) Then circle the correct word in each of the following sentences.

anthrop	chron	log	morph	philo

1. There is not much (anthropology/anthropological/misanthropic) evidence to suggest that a Paleolithic diet is healthier for modern people than other diets.

2. The newspaper (chronicles/synchronizes/chronometers) the day-by-day events of the campaigns of all the Presidential hopefuls.

3. The (logic/dialogues/epilogue) to the final movie of the Harry Potter series reveals that Hermione and Ron wind up getting married and having children.

4. Prefixes, roots, and suffixes are all building blocks of language, and when linguists study languages they look at these and other (amorphous/morphology/morphological) elements.

5. Although it hurts that her boyfriend broke up with her, Ananda is able to look at the situation (philosophically/philharmonic/philanthropical).

Prefixes

One key way to improve your vocabulary is to learn common prefixes. In fact, by knowing just the five most common prefixes in English (*un-*, *re-*, *in-*, *dis-*, and *en-*), you will have a partial understanding of more than 60 percent of all English words that have prefixes (see **Table 3.3**). Notice that the spelling of some prefixes changes depending on the root they are attached to. For example, the *il-* in *illogical* and the *im-* in *impossible* mean the same thing: "not."

Table 3.3   Prefixes

Prefix	Meaning
un-	not
re-	again, back
in-, im-, ir-, il-	not
dis-	not, apart
en-, em-	cause to
non-	not
in-, im-	in, into
fore-	before
inter-	between, among
mis-	wrongly
over-	too much
pre-	before

Prefix	Meaning
sub-	under
de-	reverse, remove, reduce
trans-/tres-:	across
anti-	against
mid-	middle
semi-	half
super-	above
under-	too little

Interaction 3–11 ▸ Use Prefixes to Develop Your Vocabulary

Make a word part note card for each of the following prefixes from **Table 3.3**. The sample words on the note card will be the three word choices for each numbered item below. (You may use a dictionary if you need to.) Then circle the correct word in each of the following sentences.

| un- | re- | in-, im-, ir-, il- | dis- | en-, em- |

1. Attending college but never studying outside of class is (unforgettable/unproductive/ unremarkable).

2. The karate instructor's angry outburst (reduced/recognized/reverted) his student to tears.

3. To make sure her brother would understand what she meant, Tia (impelled/incurred/injected) her innocent-sounding words with a heavy dose of sarcasm.

4. We (distracted/disloyal/disjointed) the birthday boy's attention while the guests sneaked in.

5. "Walking a mile in someone else's shoes" is a saying that encourages (embarrassment/ enchantment/empathy).

Suffixes

Table 3.4 is a list of frequently used suffixes. The most commonly used suffixes, -s and -es, are used to form the plurals of most nouns. The suffixes -ed and -ing are added to verbs to change their tense.

The list of common suffixes includes some suffixes that change the part of speech of a word. For example, if you add -ful to a noun, the noun becomes an adjective: *helpful, wishful, graceful.* There are many other suffixes that indicate the part of speech of a word.

Table 3.4 Suffixes

Nouns	
Suffix	**Meaning**
-ance, -ence	state, condition, action of
-er, -or	person who
-ion, -tion, -ation, -ition	condition, process of
-ism	state, quality, or condition of
-ity	state of
-ment	action or process of
-ness	state of, condition of
-s, -es	plural (more than one)
Verbs	
Suffix	**Meaning**
-ate	act upon
-ed	past participle of verb
-ing	present participle of verb
-ize, -ise, -yze	make
-s	third-person singular verb
Adjectives	
Suffix	**Meaning**
-able, -ible	able to
-al, -ial	characteristic of
-ic	characteristic of
-ish	kind of
-ly	characteristic of
-ous, -eous, -ious	possessing the qualities of
Adverbs	
Suffix	**Meaning**
-fully	In full degree
-ly	characteristic of
-wise	In a specified direction, manner, or position

Interaction 3–12 ▶ Use Suffixes to Develop Your Vocabulary

Make a word part note card for each of the following suffixes. The sample words on the note card will be the three word choices for each numbered item below. (You may use a dictionary if you need to.) Then circle the correct word in each of the following sentences.

-ance	-ity	-eous	-ly	-yze

1. (Governance/Ignorance/Assistance) of the law is no excuse for breaking it.

2. A Roman sculpture, thought to be an ancient (clarity/charity/rarity), was purchased in 2008 for $25.5 million, but doubts about its authenticity soon arose.

3. The house was located on a piece of land between the ocean and the bay, and the (erroneous/aqueous/beauteous) environment perfectly suited the owner, who loved to fish.

4. Some languages can be sounded out (loudly/sympathetically/phonetically) from the written words; in other languages there are too many differences between the spoken and written words.

5. To (analyze/paralyze/revitalize) the experiment, the scientists checked the results at each step and took careful notes.

Denotation and Connotation

Denotation is the literal meaning of a word. It is straightforward. When you see denotation, think "d"—denotation is the dictionary definition. When you look up a word in the dictionary, the definition is the denotation of that word.

> ret·i·cent [ret-*uh-suhnt*] –*adjective* 1. disposed to be silent or not to speak freely; reserved. 2. reluctant or restrained.

Connotation, on the other hand, is the emotional meaning of a word. When you see connotation, think "conn": connotation is the emotional **conn**ection of a word. Connotation is the feeling associated with a word. Some words have positive connotations, and others have negative connotations.

Take the words *slender*, *thin*, and *skinny*. They have similar denotative meanings, and they are considered synonyms. But their connotations are quite different. *Slender* implies a generally attractive thinness. *Thin* can suggest a reduced state, for example, from being sick. *Skinny* connotes "too thin" or even "emaciated." Of the three words, then, *slender* is the most complimentary, and *skinny* the least.

Connotations are also dependent on the context in which they appear. Here are three words with the same denotation, or dictionary definition. They are considered synonyms even though they have different connotations.

eat	consume food
gobble	eat greedily and quickly
nibble	take small or hesitant bites

Now read the sentences below. What does each sentence connote about the guests?

A. The guests, who arrived close to midnight, ate some snacks.

B. The guests, who arrived close to midnight, gobbled some snacks.

C. The guests, who arrived close to midnight, nibbled some snacks.

No particular connotation is suggested by the verb *ate* in sentence A. *Gobbled* in sentence B suggests that the guests were extremely hungry, or rude, or so tired that they just wanted to get eating out of the way so they could get to bed. *Nibbled* in sentence C suggests they were not hungry, or very polite, or possibly even eating only to please their hosts who had made the snacks for them. In addition, people don't often say that men nibble, so the sentence may also connote that the guests were female or at least effeminate.

Interaction 3–13 ▶ Understand Connotation

Each passage includes two words in bold that have the same denotative meaning but different connotative meanings. Write the definition they share, discuss the difference in connotation, and answer the comprehension question.

A.   One fighter **jabbed** the other with his left hand, but then his opponent **pummeled** him.

1. Shared denotation: _____

2–3. Connotations: _____

_____

4. Who probably won?

the first fighter   his opponent

B. From *The Hunger Games*

> I give Cato time to **hoist** himself into the tree before I begin to climb again. Gale always says I remind him of a squirrel the way I can **scurry** up even the slenderest branches. Part of it's my weight, but part of it's practice. You have to know where to place your hands and feet. I'm another thirty feet in the air when I hear the crack and look down to see Cato flailing as he and a branch go down. He hits the ground hard and I'm hoping he possibly broke his neck when he gets back to his feet, swearing like a fiend.
>
> —Suzanne Collins, p. 182

5. Shared denotation: _____

6–7. Connotations: _____

_____

8. Who made it up the tree more easily?

Cato   Katniss (here, "I")

C. "I **forecast** that the economic situation in Europe will improve within six months," the advisor said. "I **hope** you are right," the banker responded.

9. Shared denotation: _____

_____

10–11. Connotations: _____

_____

12. Who knew more about the economic situation?

the advisor   the banker

D. They walked into the **bar** but walked right back out when they realized it was a strip **joint**.

13. Shared denotation: _____

_____

14–15. Connotations: _____

_____

16. Where are drinks more likely to be watered down?

a bar   a joint

E. The dolphin **startled** the swimmer, but the octopus's arrival **terrified** her.

17. Shared denotation: _____

18–19. Connotations: _____

_____

20. Which sea creature does the swimmer believe is friendlier?

the dolphin   the octopus

Interaction 3–14 ▶ **Understand Denotation and Connotation in a Quotation**

Read the words of comic strip creator Jules Feiffer, and answer the questions that follow.

> I used to think I was poor. Then they told me I wasn't poor—I was needy. Then they told me it was self-defeating to think of myself as needy. I was deprived. (Oh not deprived but rather underprivileged.) Then they told me that *underprivileged* was overused. I was disadvantaged. I still don't have a dime. But I have a great vocabulary.

1. Are there any differences in the denotations of *poor, needy, deprived, underprivileged,* and *disadvantaged*? Use a dictionary to answer this question. _____

_____

2. Are there any differences in the connotations of *poor, needy, deprived, underprivileged,* and *disadvantaged*? _____

3. Form a group with two or three other students. Each of you should have your dictionary handy. Using your dictionaries and discussing any prior knowledge each of you may have about the words listed in question 2, arrange the words from most negative connotation to most positive connotation. _____

_____

Interaction 3–15 ▶ **Determine Denotation and Connotation While You Read**

Read the following paragraphs from a sociology textbook and answer the questions that follow.

Paragraph A

> Language reflects the assumptions of a culture. This can be seen and exemplified in several ways:
> **Language affects people's perceptions of reality.** Example: Researchers have found that men tend to think that women are not included when terms such as "man" are used to refer to all people. Studies

find that when college students look at job descriptions written in masculine pronouns, they assume that women are not qualified for the job.

A quote by Alma Graham illustrates this gender bias created by language: If a woman is swept off a ship into the water, the cry is 'Man overboard!' If she is killed by a hit-and-run driver, the charge is 'manslaughter.' If she is injured on the job, the coverage is 'workmen's compensation.' But if she arrives at a threshold marked 'Men Only,' she knows the admonition is not intended to bar animals or plants or inanimate objects. It is meant for her.

—From Andersen/Taylor, *Sociology: Understanding a Diverse Society*, 4e. Copyright © 2006 Cengage Learning, Inc. Reproduced by permission. www.cengage.com/permissions

Can you think of any other examples of words we use that connote a gender bias? _____

_____

Paragraph B

Language reflects the social and political status of different groups in society. Example: a term such as "woman doctor" suggests that the gender of the doctor is something exceptional and noteworthy. The term "working woman" (used to refer to women who are employed outside the home) also suggests that women who do not work for wages are not working.   —From Andersen/Taylor, *Sociology*, 4e

Ask yourself what the term *working man* connotes and how this differs from *working woman*. Discuss with your class. _____

_____

Paragraph C

Groups may advocate changing language referring to them as a way of asserting a positive group identity. Example: Some advocates for the "disabled" challenge the term "handicapped," arguing that it stigmatizes people who may have many abilities, even if they are physically distinctive. Also, though someone may have one disabling condition, they may be perfectly able in other regards.

—From Andersen/Taylor, *Sociology*, 4e

Which word has a more positive connotation, *disabled* or *handicapped*? Support your opinion. Can you think of any terms that would have a more positive connotation than either of these two words? _____

_____

Paragraph D

The implications of language emerge from specific historical and cultural contexts. Example: The naming of so-called races comes from the social and historical processes that define different groups as inferior or superior. Racial labels do not just come from physical, natural, or cultural differences.

The term "Caucasian," for example, was coined in the seventeenth century when racist thinkers developed alleged scientific classification systems to rank different societal groups. Alfred Blumenthal used the label Caucasian to refer to people from the Caucuses of Russia, who he thought were more beautiful and intelligent than any group in the world. —From Andersen/Taylor, *Sociology*, 4e

Is the term Caucasian used accurately today? _____

_____

Paragraph E

Language shapes people's perception of groups and events in society. Example: Native American victories during the nineteenth century are typically described as "massacres"; comparable victories by White settlers are described in heroic terms. The statement that Columbus "discovered" America implies that Native American societies did not exist before Columbus "found" the Americas. —From Andersen/Taylor, *Sociology*, 4e

Discuss the connotation of *massacre*. _____

_____

What are some words that connote the actions or people associated with the word *heroism*?

_____

Discuss how describing Columbus as *discovering* America creates a negative connotation of the Native American societies. _____

_____

Connect Your Skills

Developing Your Vocabulary

A. As you read the following selection from an introduction to psychology textbook, use context clues to determine the meanings of the colored words. Make an EASY note card for each word. Then answer the questions that follow.

Overcoming the Gambler's Fallacy

Seventeen-year-old Jonathan just lost his shirt again. This time, he did it playing online Blackjack. Jonathan started out making $5 bets and then doubled his bet over and over. Surely, he thought, his luck would eventually change. However, he ran out of money after just eight straight hands, having lost more than $1000. Last week, he lost a lot of money playing Texas Hold 'Em. Now Jonathan is in tears—he has lost most of his summer earnings, and he is worried about having to drop out of school and tell his parents about his losses. Jonathan has had to admit that he is part of the growing ranks of underage gambling addicts.

Like many problem gamblers, Jonathan suffers from several cognitive distortions related to gambling. Here are some of his mistaken beliefs:

► *Magnified gambling skill*: Your self-confidence is exaggerated, despite the fact that you lose persistently.
► *Attribution errors*: You ascribe your wins to skill but blame losses on bad luck.
► *Gambler's fallacy*: You believe that a string of losses soon must be followed by wins.
► *Selective memory*: You remember your wins but forget your losses.
► *Overinterpretation of cues*: You put too much faith in irrelevant cues such as bodily sensations or a feeling that your next bet will be a winner.
► *Luck as a trait*: You believe that you are a "lucky" person in general.
► *Probability biases*: You have incorrect beliefs about randomness and chance events.

Do you have any of these mistaken beliefs? Taken together, Jonathan's cognitive distortions created an illusion of control. That is, he believed that if he worked hard enough, he could figure out how to win. Fortunately, a cognitive therapist helped Jonathan cognitively restructure his beliefs. He now no longer believes he can control chance events. Jonathan still gambles a bit, but he does so only recreationally, keeping his losses within his budget and enjoying himself in the process.

—From Coon/Mitterer, *Introduction to Psychology*, 13e

1. What synonym is used for the phrase **cognitive distortions**? _____

2. What synonym is used for **magnified**? _____

3. Does **attribution** relate to the causes or effects of actions? _____

4. What is the general definition of **fallacy**? _____

5. A belief in **irrelevant** cues, in general, is called _____

6. Is a **trait** temporary or permanent? _____

7. When you throw a coin into the air, what is the **probability** that it will land heads up? _____

8. Why was Jonathan's sense of control an **illusion**? _____

_____

9. The use of the word **restructure** assumes that beliefs have _____

10. Does the use of the word **recreationally** in the last sentence suggest that previously Jonathan was, or was not, enjoying himself? _____

B. Use word parts, context clues, and your prior knowledge to understand the meanings of each colored word. Make word parts note cards. Then answer the questions that follow.

> Like the English countryside the **colonists** left behind them, Chesapeake Bay had been **refashioned** by its **inhabitants** into a working landscape. And just as the tidy English checkerboard of fields and woodlots was essential to English culture—indeed, to England's **survival**—the jumbled patchwork of **ecological** zones in coastal Virginia was essential to Powhatan culture and survival. But to the newcomers the Virginia coastline was not a **humanized** place. They saw it as a random snarl of marches, beaver ponds, **unkempt** fields, and hostile forest. If the English wanted to live and prosper in this new place in their **accustomed** manner, they would have to **transform** the land into something more **suitable** for themselves.
> —Charles C. Mann, *1493*, p. 49

11. Do **colonists** typically get to live in their accustomed manner?

    Yes   No

    Why or why not? _____

    _____

12. Is an **unkempt** appearance **suitable** for a job interview?

    Yes   No

    Why or why not? _____

    _____

13. Do different creatures **inhabit** distinct **ecological** zones?

    Yes   No

    Why or why not? _____

    _____

14. Does **humanization** involve a **transformation**?

    Yes   No

    Why or why not? _____

    _____

15. When the **inhabitants** of one land form a new **colony** in another, is their **survival** guaranteed?

Yes   No

Why or why not? _____

_____

C. Circle the word in each pair that is more connotative than the other. Use a dictionary if you need to.

16. frown   grimace

17. jog   run

18. forgetful   oblivious

19. top   pinnacle

20. gorgeous   good-looking

 Click to Connect! To check your comprehension of chapter concepts, visit **www.cengagebrain.com** to access the CourseMate for this chapter.

Chapter Summary Activity

This chapter has discussed how using context clues and word parts can help you develop your vocabulary, and it has introduced how reading for connotations can improve your comprehension. Fill in the Reading Guide to Developing Your Vocabulary below by completing each main idea on the left with specific supporting details from the chapter on the right. You can use this guide later as you work on other reading assignments.

Reading Guide to Developing Your Vocabulary

Complete this idea with ...	information from Chapter 3.
Definition of context clues	1. _____ _____
Four types of context clues and their definitions	2. _____ _____ 3. _____ _____

4. _____

   _____

5. _____

   _____

Signal words or phrases for three
types of context clues

6. _____

   _____

7. _____

   _____

8. _____

   _____

Three steps to take when using
context clues

9. _____

   _____

10. _____

    _____

11. _____

    _____

Definitions of three kinds of
word parts

12. _____

    _____

13. _____

    _____

14. _____

    _____

Difference between denotation
and connotation

15. _____

    _____

Think about what your vocabulary development strategies were before you read this
chapter. What have you learned that will be helpful? Write your thoughts.

_____

_____

_____

Reading 3–1 | Online Magazine Article

▶ Pre-Reading the Selection

The size of your vocabulary affects your professional success. Read the article on page 148 by Ken Olan, who is an executive with Every Advantage Business Solutions in Houston, Texas.

Surveying the Reading

Survey the following article. Then check the elements that are included in this reading.

_____	Title	_____	Words in bold or italic type
_____	Headings	_____	Images and captions
_____	First sentences of paragraphs		

Guessing the Purpose

Judging from the title of this article, what do you suppose are Ken Olan's purposes for writing?__
_____

Predicting the Content

Predict three things this selection will discuss.

▶ _____

▶ _____

▶ _____

Activating Your Knowledge

Think about several people you know who have a large vocabulary. What kinds of jobs do they have?

▶ _____

▶ _____

▶ _____

Scan to Connect! Use your smart phone to scan this code to watch a video. (See the inside front cover for more information on how to use this.) Discuss why the changed language made such a difference.

Common Knowledge

Reader's Digest (*paragraph 2*) A general-interest family magazine published monthly by the Reader's Digest Association

Americans with Disabilities Act (*paragraph 8*) Often referred to with the acronym ADA, this 1990 federal law prohibits discrimination against persons with a disability.

▶ Reading with Pen in Hand

Students who annotate as they read are more successful than those who do not. That's why you will annotate every selection in *Connect* as you read. In the reading that follows, use the following symbols:

★ or (Point)   to indicate a main idea

① ② ③   to indicate major details

 Visit **www.cengagebrain.com** to access the CourseMate for this chapter to hear pronunciations of vocabulary words from this reading.

Vocabulary—A Treasure Chest for Success

Ken Olan

▶ What point does the author want to make?

perspective Consider the meaning of the sentence *perspective* is in to decide what the word means.

1   In my years of studying success I've learned some fascinating facts about the relationship between the size of one's vocabulary and how successful a person is in life. I think these insights may provide you with some new **perspective** on just how important it is to develop your personal vocabulary. At least I hope they will.

▶ What does Blake Clark's article say?

persons from all walks of life What does *all walks of life* suggest?

2   *Reader's Digest* published an article by Blake Clark some years ago entitled, "Words Can Do Wonders for You." In the article he wrote, "Tests of more than 350,000 **persons from all walks of life** show that, more often than any other measurable characteristic, knowledge of the exact meanings of a large number of words accompanies outstanding success."

▶ What impact did prisoners' vocabulary have?

3   The same dynamic can also be seen at the other end of the socioeconomic spectrum. Several years ago there was a study done on penitentiary prisoners to see what impact their vocabulary had on their actions. The study found that the more limited the person's vocabulary, the more limited their behavior was likely to be. In

distinctions The sentence before this one mentions that a person who knows fewer words has *fewer choices* and *fewer ideas*. A person who knows more words would be able to notice more distinctions. What are *distinctions*?

other words, they had fewer choices they could understand and therefore fewer ideas about what their potential actions could be. Vocabulary is a way of seeing things, of making **distinctions**, of understanding the world we live in. We use vocabulary to interpret

Cengage Learning

and express ourselves. The prisoners, who had a limited vocabulary, were unable to make the distinctions needed to acquire personal success. They just didn't understand. In fact, some of these prisoners may have even resorted to violence because it was their only effective way of expressing their feelings.

4   Legendary success expert Earl Nightingale wrote of a 20-year study of college graduates. The study concluded, "Without a single exception, those who had scored highest on the vocabulary test given in college were in the top income group, while those who had scored the lowest were in the bottom income group."

What is the point of the 20-year study that Earl Nightingale reported on?

5   Work done by scientist Johnson O'Connor involved tests that were given to executive and supervisory personnel in 39 large manufacturing companies. Every person who was tested scored high in basic aptitudes that go along with leadership. The differences in their vocabulary ratings, however, were dramatic and distinct. Here's how it turned out:

What did the work by scientist Johnson O'Connor show?

- ▶ Presidents and vice presidents averaged 236 out of a possible 272 points.
- ▶ Managers averaged 168 points.
- ▶ Superintendents, 140 points.
- ▶ Foremen, 86 points.

In virtually every case, the size of each person's vocabulary **correlated** with the career level they had achieved. Could it be a coincidence? Absolutely not.

correlated Based on what the previous list showed, what does correlated mean?

6   When I was in high school I remember taking weekly vocabulary tests. Although I enjoyed learning new words I didn't think I'd ever use a lot of the words very often. You know what? I was right. I don't speak a lot of those words on a daily basis. But when I hear someone else using them I know what they mean. I don't have to sit there and wonder what in the world the other person is talking about. So developing a great vocabulary isn't really all about how important or how intelligent you sound when you speak. The biggest benefit of having an understanding of what different words mean is how intelligently you can listen to and understand what others are saying. A large vocabulary is a common characteristic among all successful individuals, regardless of their occupation. That's because it **enhances** your ability to think and understand things more clearly. With the ability to make greater distinctions comes the capacity for greater understanding and knowledge.

What is the biggest benefit of having an understanding of what different words mean?

enhances Look in the previous sentence and the sentence enhances is in. Note that enhances is a verb—an action word. What does it mean?

7   Many people don't appreciate the phenomenal importance of understanding the meaning of a lot of different words until they start running into other people using words they don't comprehend. Here's an extreme example I often use to drive this point across. Imagine you had to move to a different country with a different language you didn't know. Would you be at a disadvantage to the people who did speak the language? Of course you would. Would you be able to understand everything that was going on around you?

What example does the author give about the importance of knowing a lot of words?

▶ What is the effect of a small vocabulary?

8

Definitely not. But what if you knew just some of the language? Would you be better off? Absolutely, and the more of that language you learned the better off you'd be. So then, I hope we can agree that if you went somewhere and didn't understand the language, you'd quickly realize the importance of knowing the meaning of different words … as many words as you could learn. For the exact same reason we can agree that it is just as important to understand as many words as possible in your native language. Without that advantage you can become almost as ignorant as if you didn't understand it at all.

Certainly those who have a better grasp on the language will have an advantage over you. By having a smaller vocabulary, you become handicapped, meaning that you can't do, or won't understand, things that others with a larger vocabulary can. You are at a competitive disadvantage, and the Americans with Disabilities Act does nothing to help people who are handicapped with a poor vocabulary. So grab yourself a dictionary or thesaurus and commit to learning just one new word a week, or more, and watch how your ability to operate in this place we call the "real world" gets easier and more rewarding for you.

—From "Vocabulary—A Treasure Chest for Success" by Ken Olin, from *American Chronicle*, Sept. 20, 2006. Reprinted by permission of the author.

▶ Comprehension Questions

Write the letter of the answer on the line. Then explain your thinking.

Main Idea

_____ 1. Which of the following best states the main idea of this passage?

    a. Those who have a better grasp of a language have an advantage.

    b. There is a relationship between a person's vocabulary knowledge and his or her ability to function and succeed in the "real world."

    c. Many people don't appreciate the phenomenal importance of understanding the meaning of a lot of different words.

    d. Vocabulary is a way of seeing things, of making distinctions, of understanding the world we live in.

Why? What information in the selection leads you to give that answer? _____

_____

_____

_____ 2. Which of the following statements best summarizes this passage?

    a. Work done by scientist Johnson O'Connor tells us that vocabulary knowledge is an important key to getting a good job. In fact, his research indicated that a good vocabulary was the number one factor for being successful.

b. Vocabulary is important.

c. There is a direct relationship between the size of one's vocabulary and success in life.

d. The biggest benefit of having an understanding of what different words mean is how intelligently you can listen to and understand what others are saying.

Why? What information in the selection leads you to give that answer? _____

_____

Supporting Details

____ 3. According to the passage, what is the biggest benefit of having an understanding of what different words mean?

a. success in life

b. the ability to communicate in a foreign language

c. improved listening and comprehension skills

d. a greater ability to understand what others are saying

Why? What information in the selection leads you to give that answer? _____

_____

____ 4. Based on the reading selection, which of the following does not support the idea that there is a direct relationship between the size of one's vocabulary and success in life?

a. Johnson O'Connor's research

b. Blake Clark's article

c. taking weekly vocabulary tests in high school

d. Earl Nightingale's study

Why? What information in the selection leads you to give that answer? _____

_____

_____

Author's Purpose

____ 5. What is the purpose or purposes of the passage?

a. to entertain the reader with personal stories of the author's life

b. to persuade the reader that vocabulary is integral to success by informing the reader of three studies

c. to persuade the reader to learn more vocabulary

d. to inform the reader of studies about vocabulary that link to success

Why? What information in the selection leads you to give that answer? _____

_____

_____

____ 6. Why does the author refer to Johnson O'Connor's study?

    a. to persuade the reader to obtain a position of leadership

    b. to entertain the reader

    c. to illustrate the relationship between success at work and having a large vocabulary

    d. to persuade the reader to avoid violence as a means of self-expression

Why? What information in the selection leads you to give that answer? _____

_____

_____

Relationships

____ 7. What is the overall pattern of organization of the reading selection?

    a. comparison and contrast

    b. cause-and-effect

    c. time order

    d. process

Why? What information in the selection leads you to give that answer? _____

_____

____ 8. What organizational pattern do you find in the first sentence of paragraph 6?

    a. cause-and-effect

    b. classification

    c. process

    d. time order

Why? What information in the selection leads you to give that answer? _____

_____

Fact, Opinion, and Inference

____ 9. Which of the following statements is a fact?

    a. The Americans with Disabilities Act does nothing to help people who are handicapped with a poor vocabulary.

    b. Some of these prisoners may have even resorted to violence because it was their only effective way of expressing their feelings.

    c. I think these insights may provide you with some new perspective on just how important it is to develop your personal vocabulary.

    d. I hope we can agree that if you went somewhere and didn't understand the language, you'd quickly realize the importance of knowing the meaning of different words.

Why? What leads you to give that answer? _____

_____

____   **10.** Which of the following inferences would the author be likely to agree with?

    a. Prisoners are in jail because they have a bad vocabulary.

    b. It's better to learn the language of a culture before you visit it so you can avoid being taken advantage of.

    c. The author did not enjoy high school.

    d. Vocabulary can be a contributing factor to failure.

Why? What information in the selection leads you to give that answer? _____

_____

_____

▸Critical Thinking Questions

Critical Thinking Level 1 ▸ **Remember**

Identify three studies the author mentions to illustrate the idea that there is a direct relationship between the size of one's vocabulary and success in life.

1. _____

2. _____

3. _____

Critical Thinking Level 2 ▸ **Understand**

Describe how these studies support the idea of a relationship between a person's vocabulary knowledge and his or her ability to function and succeed in the "real world."

1. _____

_____

_____

2. _____

_____

_____

3. _____

_____

_____

Critical Thinking Level 3	Apply

Ken Olan gives an example of traveling to a country where you don't know the language. Have you ever traveled to a country whose language you did not know? *Discuss* your experience. If you have not had an experience like this, *imagine* what it would be like. What kind of problems did (or might) you experience?

_____

_____

_____

Critical Thinking Level 4	Analyze

"Those who prefer their English sloppy have only themselves to thank if the advertisement writer uses his mastery of the vocabulary and syntax to mislead their weak minds."

—Dorothy L. Sayers (British writer, 1893–1957)

First, restate this quotation in your own words.

_____

_____

_____

Second, *analyze* this quotation according to the information given in Ken Olan's article. Would Olan agree with Dorothy Sayers? Explain your answer.

_____

_____

_____

Critical Thinking Level 5	Evaluate

Having a large vocabulary allows you to vary your use of language according to the situation. In each of the following pairs of sentences, evaluate whether the language is informal or formal. Write *informal* next to the sentence that would be appropriate in an informal conversation between friends. Write *formal* next to the sentence that could be used in a context such as an article in a magazine or newspaper or in a college essay.

▶ **Pair A**

1. Knowing lots of words makes you rich. _____

2. Having a large vocabulary leads to wealth. _____

▶ **Pair B**

3. The overweight Siamese lay on the lawn. _____

4. The fat cat sat on the grass. _____

▶ Pair C

5. The man is talkative. _____

6. The dude talks a lot. _____

Critical Thinking Level 6 Create

Make a word map to show other words that share each word part in the word *disruption*. Then fill in an example, antonym, and synonym. On separate paper, make a word map for a different word.

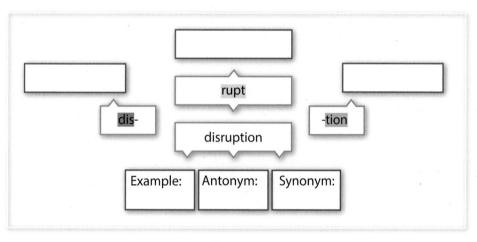

▶ Vocabulary in New Contexts

Review the vocabulary words in the margins of the reading selection and then complete the following activities.

EASY Note Cards

Make a note card for each of the vocabulary words that you did not know in the reading. On one side, write the word. On the other side, divide the card into quarters and label them E, A, S, and Y. Add a word or phrase in each area so that you wind up with an example sentence, an antonym, a synonym, and, finally, a definition that shows you have figured out the meaning of the word with your logic. Remember that an antonym or synonym may have appeared in the reading.

Relationships Between Words

Circle *yes* or *no* to answer the question. Then explain your answer.

1. Do **people from all walks of life** have the same **perspective** on marriage?

   Yes   No

   Why or why not? _____

_____

2. Would being able to notice more **distinctions enhance** your enjoyment of a painting?

Yes   No

Why or why not? _____

3. Is there a strong **correlation** between your **perspective** and your sense of accomplishment?

Yes   No

Why or why not? _____

_____

Language in Your Life

Write short answers to each question. Look at the vocabulary words closely before you answer.

1. Name one action you could take to **enhance** your appreciation of nature. _____

_____

2. Note one **distinction** you wish you were not aware of. _____

_____

3. Name one time you experienced an empowering **perspective**. _____

_____

4. Name one thing that you believe **correlates** with success or happiness. _____

_____

5. Name one place you have gone where there were **people from all walks of life.** _____

_____

Language in Use

Select the best word to complete the meaning of each sentence.

correlated	distinctions	enhance	perspective	people from all walks of life

1. Historically, the _____ that divide people have to do with ethnicity, class, and gender.

2. A more inclusive _____ allows us to find the human qualities we all share.

3. Even though steroids are illegal, many athletes take them because the drugs _____ their performances.

4. However, men's overuse of steroids is _____ with developing a sometimes frightening aggressiveness.

5. Drug abuse of any kind can negatively affect _____, of course, not just athletes taking steroids but also businesspeople drinking too much alcohol and young people smoking cigarettes.

Reading 3–2 Nonfiction Book

▶ Pre-Reading the Selection

The reading on page 158 is from a nonfiction book called *Alex & Me*. In it, scientist Irene Pepperberg describes some of the experiments she did with Alex, an African Grey parrot whose last words to Irene before he died were "You be good. I love you."

Surveying the Reading

Survey the selection. Then check the elements that are included in this reading.

_____ Title	_____	Words in bold or italic type
_____ Headings	_____	Images and captions
_____ First sentences of paragraphs		

Guessing the Purpose

Based on the title of the book this reading is from, do you suppose the author's purpose overall is to inform, persuade, or express? _____

Predicting the Content

Survey the first sentence of each paragraph and predict three things the selection will discuss. _____

_____

▶ _____

▶ _____

▶ _____

Activating Your Knowledge

Think about any related knowledge you may have: Have you seen TV shows about the language abilities of animals such as chimpanzees, dogs, and birds? What about knowledge related to how humans view animals in general? For example, what particular abilities do humans like to think they have that separate them from the other animals? List two or three things you know.

▶ _____

▶ _____

▶ _____

🔘 **Scan to Connect!** Use your smart phone to scan this code to watch a video. (See the inside front cover for more information on how to use this.) How would you compare Alex's language ability to that of a person?

▶ Reading with Pen in Hand

Students who annotate as they read are more successful than those who do not. That's why you will annotate every selection in *Connect* as you read. In the reading that follows, use the following symbols:

★ or ⟨Point⟩   to indicate a main idea

① ② ③   to indicate major details

 Visit **www.cengagebrain.com** to access the CourseMate for this chapter to hear pronunciations of vocabulary words from this reading.

Alex the Parrot: Not a Bird Brain

Irene M. Pepperberg

▶ Imagine how you might teach Alex these things.

1   The original proposal for The Alex Project that I wrote back in the spring of 1977 had been, I must concede, quite ambitious. It argued that my Grey would learn object labels (words), categories, concepts, and numbers in three years; that he would be able to communicate back and forth with a human; and that he would have some comprehension of what he was doing. I had complete confidence that my Grey would be able to do all this. But I have to admit that each time Alex met a challenge I set him, each time he did what no bird brain is supposed to be able to do, I was as thrilled as any parent can be when her child crosses a developmental **hurdle**, such as crawling, walking, or talking.

hurdle A synonym, examples, and your logic will tell you what a *hurdle* is.

garnered What word could you substitute for *garnered*?

2   As the list of scientific publications grew—and as our work **garnered** more and more public attention—I found a slowly growing acceptance that I wasn't just "that woman who talks to a parrot." I was beginning to be taken seriously in scientific circles. But the chorus of "Oh, he's just mimicking" or "He's just following her cues" still sounded loudly in my ears. At least that is how I perceived it. I found myself having to prove over and over that Alex had more going on in his bird brain than some mechanical trickery or other. One such challenge was, "Oh, he can produce labels all right, and he sounds convincing, but does he really understand what he's saying? Does he comprehend the noises coming from his beak?"

▶ Make a mental movie of what Pepperberg's experience was like.

▶ Why wouldn't people just accept that Alex knew what he was saying?

3   It seemed quite clear to me from my hundreds and hundreds of hours watching and listening to Alex that he did indeed know what he was saying. A simple example: if Alex said "Want grape" and you gave him banana, he'd spit it right back at you and repeat insistently, "Want grape." He wouldn't stop until you gave him a grape. If you were dealing with a child, you would accept without question that he or she really wanted a grape, and that banana simply wouldn't do. But that's not science. Science needs numbers. Science needs tests to be done over and over again—actually, sometimes sixty times or more—before the answer has statistical **legitimacy**, and before scientists will take you seriously. Poor Alex.

legitimacy This noun is based on the adjective *legitimate*. What does it mean?

Irene Pepperberg with Alex

Rick Friedman/Corbis

4   A few years into our Northwestern period—my initial temporary job ultimately stretched out to six and a half years—we embarked on a **rigorous** series of tests of Alex's comprehension ability. Scientifically I can report that he passed each test, and move on to the next part of our story. But how he did it gives us insights into his mind that are striking, if not always quite so easily classified as scientific.

5   The tests involved putting various of his "toys" on a tray and asking questions such as "What object is green?" "What matter is blue and three-corner?" "What shape is purple?" "How many four-corner wood?" At first, Alex answered correctly most of the time: "key" or "wood" or "wool" or "three," et cetera. But before too long, he started to act up. He would say "green" and then pull at the green felt lining of the tray, hard enough that all the objects would fall off. Or he would say "tray" and bite the tray. Sometimes he'd say nothing and suddenly start preening. Or he'd turn around and lift his butt in my direction, a gesture too obvious to need translation. Once he grabbed the tray out of my hand and flung it on the floor, saying, "Wanna go back," which meant, *I'm done with this. Take me back to my cage.*

6   Who can blame him? None of the objects were new to him. He'd answered these kinds of questions dozens of times, and yet we still kept asking them, because we needed our statistical sample. You could imagine him thinking, *I've already told you that, stupid,* or simply, *This is getting* very *boring.* He was like the bright little kid at school who finds none of the work challenging and so passes the time by making trouble.

7   Sometimes, however, Alex chose to show his opinion of the boring task at hand by playing with our heads. For instance, we would ask him, "What color key?" and he would give every color in his repertoire, skipping only the correct color. Eventually, he became quite **ingenious** with this game, having more fun getting us agitated rather than giving us the answers we wanted and he surely knew. We were pretty certain he wasn't making mistakes, because it was statistically near to impossible that he could list all but the

rigorous You may have heard of rigor mortis (the stiffness of death). What does *rigorous* mean?

▶ What do you suppose Pepperberg is about to discuss?

▶ What emotions do you feel about Alex's reactions to the tests?

▶ Have you known any people who acted this way?

ingenious Read the description of Alex's responses again. What word describes his responses?

correct answer. These observations are not science, but they tell you a lot about what was going on in his head; they tell you a lot about how sophisticated his cognitive processes really were. Whether you would describe what he did as something to amuse himself or as making a joke at our expense, I cannot say. But he was definitely doing something other than routinely answering questions.

▶ Does this information surprise you? Why or why not?

8   We became ever more ingenious in presenting our questions, to keep a step ahead of his boredom. Sometimes we succeeded, sometimes we didn't. In the end we did arrive at a statistically valid answer to the question "Does Alex know what he's saying?" Yes, he did. His level of comprehension was equal to that of chimpanzees and dolphins, no small achievement for so small a brain.

▶ How do you tell whether two things are the same or different?

9   Alex faced the same boredom with the next major challenge we gave him: namely, would he understand the concept of "same" and "different"? It might seem like common sense that in order to survive in the wild, birds would, for example, have to identify the songs of individuals and distinguish among species. Surely this involves some grasp of "same" and "different." Yet when I embarked on the "same/different" project with Alex, the scientists who test such things thought that apes were at par or slightly below humans in this conceptual ability, monkeys were below apes, and birds … well, they hardly counted at all.

▶ Does this seem like a complex task?

10   The concept of "same/different" is fairly sophisticated cognitively. We trained Alex to use color and shape as categories with which to determine same or different. When presented with a pair of objects, such as green four-corner wood and blue four-corner wood, Alex's correct response to "What's same?" and "What's different?" would be "shape" and "color," respectively, not the specific color or shape. To answer the question correctly, Alex would have to take note of the various **attributes** of the two objects, understand exactly what I was asking him to compare, make that judgment, and then vocally tell me the answer. No small order for a bird brain.

attributes Use your logic to decide what another word for *attributes* is.

▶ Does novelty hold your attention more than the familiar?

11   It took many months to train him, but eventually he was ready to be tested. Because many of the objects were familiar, boredom again became an issue. We tried to keep his interest by **interspersing** "same/different" tests with teaching him new numbers, new labels, and other novel tasks. He was a trouper. Overall, he got the right answer—"shape" or "color"—about three-quarters of the time. (We also included a third category, "matter" or material.) When we gave him pairs of objects that were novel to him, colors he could not label, for instance, he was right 85 percent of the time, which is actually a better measure of his ability. The **novelty** obviously held his attention better.

interspersing Judging from the context and the prefix *inter-*, what does this word mean?

novelty An antonym appears earlier. What is *novelty*?

▶ Why is Pepperberg attending this conference?

12   Now, when David Premack had tested chimps on this kind of test, all the animal had to do was indicate whether two objects were the same or different. Alex went a step further in our tests. He was able to tell me exactly *what* was the same or different: color, shape, or material. When I reported our results at the International Primatological Congress in Göttingen, Germany in 1986, a senior primatology professor—we called them "silverbacks," referring to the markings of older

gorillas—lumbered to his feet and said, "You mean to tell me that your parrot can do what Premark's chimps can do, only in a more sophisticated manner?"

13   I said, "Yes, that's right," wondering what onslaught might follow. Nothing. He simply said "Oh," and sat down. I might have burst into song, with "Anything chimps can do, Alex can do better," but I **restrained** myself. Besides, my voice isn't up to it. Nevertheless, this was a moment of triumph for Alex. Pity he wasn't there to witness it.

14   From the "same/different" concept, it was natural to go on to **relative** concepts, such as size difference. Alex got that, too. I could show him two different-sized keys, each a different color, for instance, and ask him, "Alex, what color bigger?" and he could tell me. These various achievements attracted a lot of public attention. Bob Bazell, of NBC television, came to film Alex, as did crews from ABC and CBS. Alex was even on the front page of the *Wall Street Journal. Very* smart bird!

restrained Note the contrast in the sentence. What does *restrained* mean?

▶ Why was this a moment of triumph?

relative What do the examples indicate *relative* means?

▶ Why did these achievements attract so much attention?

—From Irene M. Pepperberg, *Alex & Me* (pp. 106–112). Copyright © 2008 HarperCollins. Reprinted by permission.

▶ Comprehension Questions

Write the letter of the answer on the line. Then explain your thinking.

Main Idea

_____   1. What is the best statement of the main idea of paragraph 1?

   a. The original proposal for The Alex Project that I wrote back in the spring of 1977 had been, I must concede, quite ambitious.

   b. It argued that my Grey would learn object labels (words), categories, concepts, and numbers in three years.

   c. It argued that he would be able to communicate back and forth with a human.

   d. It argued that he would have some comprehension of what he was doing.

Why?▶ What information in the selection leads you to give that answer? _____

_____

_____

_____   2. What is the best statement of the main idea of paragraph 7?

   a. For instance, we would ask him, "What color key?" and he would give every color in his repertoire, skipping only the correct color.

   b. Eventually, he became quite ingenious with this game, having more fun getting us agitated rather than giving us the answers we wanted and he surely knew.

   c. We were pretty certain he wasn't making mistakes, because it was statistically near to impossible that he could list all but the correct answer.

   d. Sometimes, however, Alex chose to show his opinion of the boring task at hand by playing with our heads.

Why? What information in the selection leads you to give that answer? _____

_____

_____

Supporting Details

_____ 3. Which detail supports the idea that Alex became bored with all the testing?

   a. I found myself having to prove over and over that Alex had more going on in his bird brain than some mechanical trickery or other.

   b. Scientifically I can report that he passed each test, and move on to the next part of our story.

   c. Or he'd turn around and lift his butt in my direction, a gesture too obvious to need translation.

   d. Overall, he got the right answer—"shape" or "color"—about three-quarters of the time.

Why? What information in the selection leads you to give that answer? _____

_____

_____

_____ 4. What aspects of objects was Alex tested on?

   a. number of corners

   b. sizes, shapes, colors, numbers, and materials

   c. how long he would continue to examine them

   d. how novel each one was

Why? What information in the selection leads you to give that answer? _____

_____

_____

Author's Purpose

_____ 5. What is Professor Pepperberg's purpose in discussing Alex's boredom?

   a. to express more about Alex than the scientific data can show using statistics

   b. to persuade readers that Alex's comprehension was as sophisticated as a person's

   c. to inform readers that even though Alex was smarter than other test animals, she was never believed

   d. to celebrate Alex's life after he died

Why? What information in the selection leads you to give that answer? _____

_____

_____

_____

____ 6. In paragraph 12, why does the author "wonder...what onslaught might follow"?

    a. She was concerned that an older gorilla (a silverback) would take offense at what she was reporting.

    b. It was well known in Germany that Alex liked to agitate his testers, and this was frowned upon.

    c. She was concerned because she was contradicting what scientists at that time believed about the cognitive ability of apes and birds.

    d. No special reason

Why? What information in the selection leads you to give that answer? _____

_____

_____

Relationships

____ 7. What is the predominant pattern of organization in this selection?

    a. contrast

    b. narration

    c. effect

    d. definition

Why? What information in the selection leads you to give that answer? _____

_____

_____

____ 8. What organizational patterns does this sentence use? *It took many months to train him, but eventually he was ready to be tested.*

    a. cause and example

    b. example and narration

    c. narration and contrast

    d. contrast and classification

Why? What information in the selection leads you to give that answer? _____

_____

_____

Fact, Opinion, and Inference

____ 9. Choose the opinion.

a. Bob Bazell, of NBC television, came to film Alex.

b. When David Premack had tested chimps on this kind of test, all the animal had to do was indicate whether two objects were the same or different.

c. He got the right answer about three-quarters of the time.

d. The original proposal was quite ambitious.

Why? What information in the selection leads you to give that answer? _____

_____

_____

____ 10. Choose the idea that is best supported by the information in this selection.

a. Alex's thinking skills were based solely on memorization.

b. Alex knew what he wanted.

c. Irene Pepperberg was too close to Alex to be objective.

d. Alex is the only African Grey parrot who was smart enough to be trained.

Why? What information in the selection leads you to give that answer? _____

_____

_____

▶Critical Thinking Questions

Critical Thinking Level 1 ▶ **Remember**

Recall at least five actions Alex took when he was bored.

_____

_____

_____

Critical Thinking Level 2 ▶ **Understand**

Explain what was more impressive about the way Alex demonstrated his understanding of "same/different" than the way Premack's chimps demonstrated theirs. Use your own words rather than words from the selection.

_____

_____

_____

Critical Thinking Level 3 ▶ Apply

Use what you have learned about Alex's intelligence to make a poster that supports the mission of the nonprofit organization Thinking Animals (thinkinganimals.com). According to the Thinking Animals Web site, "the more people understand the cognitive and behavioral complexity of animals—their intelligence, as well as the depth and nature of our evolutionary debt to them—the more they will consider the humane treatment and conservation of animals to be a priority."

Critical Thinking Level 4 ▶ Analyze

Analyze the words that Pepperberg used with Alex to discover at least one way that she simplified her language to make it easier for Alex to understand.

_____

_____

_____

Critical Thinking Level 5 ▶ Evaluate

Evaluate whether humans have the right to perform tests on animals such as those Pepperberg performed on Alex. Make a list of the kinds of tests you find acceptable or even good, and another list of the kinds of tests you consider unacceptable or bad. What is the difference between the acceptable and unacceptable tests?

_____

_____

_____

Critical Thinking Level 6 ▶ Create

Imagine you are training Alex. What would you want him to learn next, after he learned "same/different"? Explain why.

_____

_____

_____

▶ Vocabulary in New Contexts

Review the vocabulary words in the margins of the reading selection and then complete the following activities.

EASY Note Cards

Make a note card for each of the vocabulary words that you did not know in the reading. On one side, write the word. On the other side, divide the card into quarters and label them E, A, S, and Y.

Add a word or phrase in each area so that you wind up with an example sentence, an antonym, a synonym, and, finally, a definition that shows you have figured out the meaning of the word with your logic. Remember that an antonym or synonym may have appeared in the reading.

Relationships Between Words

Circle *yes* or *no* to answer the question. Then explain your answer.

1. When a person encounters a **novel** problem, does he or she need to be **ingenious**?
   Yes   No
   Why or why not? _____

2. Can the **legitimacy** of an idea be increased by **rigorous** application of the scientific process?
   Yes   No
   Why or why not? _____
   _____

3. Do people typically **restrain** themselves to different degrees based on the **relative** formality of the situation?
   Yes   No
   Why or why not? _____

4. Is it generally true that as a student overcomes **hurdles** to academic success, he or she **garners** more respect from friends and family?
   Yes   No
   Why or why not? _____

5. Might a man become confused if a woman who was asking him out on a date **interspersed** compliments about him with negative comments about his less desirable **attributes**?
   Yes   No
   Why or why not? _____
   _____

Language in Your Life

Write short answers to each question. Look at the vocabulary words closely before you answer.

1. Name a time when you had to **restrain** yourself. _____
   _____

2. Note one idea you have learned about that you consider a **novelty**. _____
   _____

3. Name one action you have taken that has **garnered** praise from others. _____

_____

4. Name one invention you think is **ingenious**. _____

_____

5. Name one **hurdle** you had to overcome to attend college. _____

_____

Language in Use
Select the best word to complete the meaning of each sentence.

attribute	garner	hurdle	ingenious	intersperse
legitimacy	novel	relative	restrained	

1. U.S. military medical teams have substantially reduced the number of deaths of soldiers who are wounded in battle, despite having no _____ medical tools or technologies to help them.

2. In recent wars in Iraq and Afghanistan, the mortality rate of 10 percent of those wounded is very low _____ to previous wars—the Vietnam War and the Persian Gulf War, for instance—in which that rate was around 25%.

3. This low rate has been achieved despite the _____ of having very few surgeons and orthopedists available near the battlefields to help wounded soldiers.

4. Researchers examined various medical records from previous wars to _____ information that has lowered the rate.

5. One _____ of soldiers' habits that has helped keep soldiers from dying is that they started actually wearing their Kevlar vests; their commanding officers have become responsible for making sure they do.

6. At least as important, though, is the _____ use of different stages of surgical care.

7. Forward Surgical Teams, small medical teams that are _____ with soldiers on the front lines, are immediately available to provide the first stage of care before sending the injured for stage-two care at Combat Support Hospitals.

8. The third stage of care is provided at hospitals in Kuwait, Spain, Germany, and the United States. The _____ of this new system is proven in the lowered death rate.

 Click to Connect! For more practice applying the skills you learned in this chapter, visit **www.cengagebrain.com** to access the CourseMate for this chapter.

PART 2
Reading to Understand

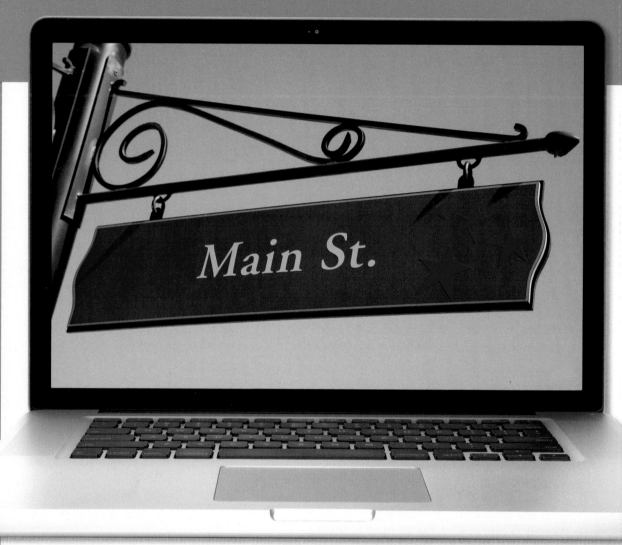

James R. Martin/Shutterstock

Click to Connect! Visit **www.cengagebrain.com** to access study resources for this chapter through CourseMate, which includes audio, video, quizzes, and a searchable, interactive eBook version of the text.

Finding the
Main Idea

> " *The main thing is
> to keep the main thing
> the main thing.* "
> —STEPHEN COVEY

Connect with Ideas

So … what is the main thing? Discuss ideas with a classmate about what "the main thing" in a movie, song, or story could be.

Activate Your Prior Knowledge

What do you think "the main thing" could refer to when it comes to reading? When it comes to your priorities in life? To different goals you have?

Engage with the Chapter

Take two minutes to skim this chapter to find some of the ideas that will be discussed. What is one idea that is new to you?

Read and Talk

Nonfiction Book

The following reading comes from the beginning of chapter five of *First Things First* by Stephen Covey. This excerpt is one suggestion Mr. Covey gives for keeping "the main thing the main thing" in life. As you read through the passage, keep the title in mind, and ask yourself what is the main thing Mr. Covey is trying to say to you, the reader.

Visit www.cengagebrain.com to access the CourseMate for this chapter to hear vocabulary words from this reading and an audio recording of it.

The Passion of Vision

Stephen Covey

capacity Think about the meaning of the sentence. What is a synonym for *capacity*?

1   Viktor Frankl, an Austrian psychologist who survived the death camps of Nazi Germany, made a significant discovery. As he found within himself the **capacity** to rise above his humiliating circumstances, he became an observer as well as a participant in the experience. He watched others who shared in the ordeal. He was intrigued with the question of what made it possible for some people to survive when most died.

2   He looked at several factors—health, vitality, family structure, intelligence, survival skills. Finally, he concluded that none of these factors was primarily responsible. The single most significant factor, he realized, was a sense of future vision—the **impelling** conviction of those who were to survive that they had a mission to perform, some important work left to do.

impelling Use your logic. If you believe you are on a mission, does your belief urge you forward or caution you to hold back? What does *impelling* mean?

3   Survivors of POW camps in Vietnam and elsewhere have reported similar experiences: a compelling, future-oriented vision is the primary force that kept many of them alive. The power of vision is incredible! Research indicates that children with "future-focused role images" perform far better scholastically and are significantly more competent in handling the challenges of life. Teams and organizations with a strong sense of mission significantly outperform those without the strength of vision. According to Dutch sociologist Fred Polak, a primary factor influencing the success of civilizations is the "collective vision" people have of their future.

manifestation This noun is related to the verb *manifest*. Another way to state the first part of this sentence is "Creative imagination manifests itself best in vision." Also examine the next sentence to figure out this word's meaning.

4   Vision is the best **manifestation** of creative imagination and the primary motivation of human action. It's the ability to see beyond our present reality, to create, to invent what does not yet exist, to become what we not yet are. It gives us capacity to live out of our imagination instead of our memory. We all have some vision of ourselves and our future. And that vision creates consequences. More than any other factor, vision affects the choices we make and the way we spend our time.

5   If our vision is limited—if it doesn't extend beyond the Friday night ball game or the next TV show—we tend to make choices based on what's right in front of us. We react to whatever's urgent, the impulse of the moment, our

Nick Koudis/Photodisc/Jupiter Images

feelings or moods, our limited awareness of our options, other people's priorities. We **vacillate** and fluctuate. How we feel about our decisions—even the way we make them—changes from day to day.

6   If our vision is based on illusion, we make choices that aren't based on "true north" principles. In time, these choices fail to create the quality-of-life results we expect. Our vision becomes no more than platitudes. We become disillusioned, perhaps cynical. Our creative imagination withers, and we don't trust our dreams anymore.

7   If our vision is partial—if we focus only on our economic and social needs and ignore our mental and spiritual needs, for example—we make choices that lead to imbalance. If our vision is based on the social mirror, we make choices based on expectations of others. It's been said that "when man discovered the mirror, he began to lose his soul." If our self-vision is no more than a reflection of the social mirror, we have no connection with our inner selves, with our own uniqueness and capacity to contribute. We're living out of scripts handed to us by others—family, associates, friends, enemies, the media.

8   And what are those scripts? Some may seem **constructive**: "You're so talented!" "You're a natural ball player!" "I always said you should be a doctor!" Some may be destructive: "You're so slow!" "You can't do anything right!" "Why can't you be more like your sister?" Good or bad, these scripts can keep us from connecting with who we are and what we're about.

9   And consider the images the media project—cynicism, skepticism, violence, indulgence, fatalism, materialism, "that important news" is bad news. If these images are the source of our personal vision, is it any wonder that many of us feel disconnected and at odds with ourselves?

—"The Passion of Vision" from *First Things First to Live, To Love, To Learn*, by Stephen Covey, A. Roger Merrill, and Rebecca R. Merrill, pp. 103–104. Reprinted by permission of Franklin Covey Co.

vacillate Look for a synonym and a definition in this sentence and the next. What does *vacillate* mean?

constructive Look at the examples that follow *constructive* and find an antonym in a later sentence to uncover this word's meaning.

Talking about Reading

Respond in writing to the questions that follow and then discuss your answers with your classmates.

1. Can you define *vision* using your own words? _____

_____

_____

2. Why is vision so powerful? List some of the results of having vision that Covey mentioned and then add any of your own. _____

_____

_____

3. Based on what you read, what factors weaken the power of vision? _____

_____

_____

4. What vision do you hold for your education? What will your education open up for you to do, have, or be? What is the "main thing" you are seeking from your college experience? Do you have a plan for manifesting your vision? _____

_____

_____

5.  **Scan to Connect!** Use your smart phone to scan this code to watch a video. (See the inside front cover for more information on how to use this.) Think about the messages in the video. Are they good examples of the future vision that Covey discusses in paragraphs 2 and 3 of "The Passion of Vision"? Why or why not?

Asking Questions to Understand What You Read

Just as vision is powerful in determining the success of your life, your ability to focus on the main idea while reading is powerful in determining your success in college. When you first read something, each word on the page may seem equally as important as the one before—but that is not the case. Every text you read has an underlying structure of ideas. Some ideas are more general; others are more specific. Some ideas are more important, and others are less important. To best understand what points the author is trying to make, keep your eye on the main idea.

Here is an example from a criminal justice textbook.

> Arrest strategies can be broken into two categories. The first category, **reactive arrests**, are arrests made by police officers, usually on general patrol, who observe a criminal act or respond to a call for service. The second category, **proactive arrests**, occur when the police take the initiative to target a particular type of criminal or behavior.
>
> —From Gaines, *Criminal Justice in Action*, 6e (p. 139). Copyright © 2011 Cengage Learning, Inc. Reproduced by permission. www.cengage.com/permissions

This paragraph includes three levels of ideas that we will discuss in this chapter.

1. The topic. The topic is who or what the reading is about. You can find the topic by asking, "What is the reading about?" The topic of the example

Figure 4.1   Three Comprehension Questions

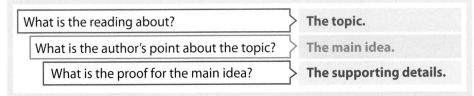

paragraph is "arrests." You can tell this is the topic because of the number of times this idea is stated: *arrest strategies, reactive arrests, arrests,* and *proactive arrests*. Every sentence in this paragraph refers to arrests.

2. The main idea. The main idea is the point the author wants to make about the topic. You can find the main idea by asking, "What is the author's point about the topic?" The main point of the example paragraph is that there are two categories of arrest. You can tell this is the main idea because two things are true:

   ▶ It is more specific than the topic: Not just "arrests," but "two categories of arrests."
   ▶ It is more general than the other ideas. Each of the other ideas is about one very specific kind of arrest. "Two categories" is more general than "the first category" and "the second category."

3. The supporting details. The major supporting details give evidence or proof for the author's point. To find the supporting details in a paragraph, ask, "What is the proof for the main idea?" The supporting details in the example paragraph are about reactive arrests and proactive arrests. These are the two categories that the author mentions more generally in the first sentence. The supporting details give the specific information about each category.

Figure 4.1 lists the three levels of ideas and the questions you can ask to find each one.

What Is the Reading About? The Topic

Asking the simple question "What is the reading about?" will lead you to the **topic.** The topic is *who* or *what* a reading is about. In longer passages, you will often find the topic stated in the title, but even in single paragraphs, words related to the topic are usually repeated throughout the paragraph in different ways. Topics are normally stated in a single word or a phrase. If your reading has a title, start by reading it to figure out what the topic is. However, if there is no title, you can still look for people, places, things, or concepts repeated throughout the reading. Look at the following example from a history book.

In 1930, <u>Mohandas Gandhi</u>, the sixty-one-year-old leader of the nonviolent movement for Indian independence from British rule, <u>began a march to the sea with seventy-eight followers</u>. Their destination was Dandi, a little coastal town some 240 miles away. <u>The group covered about 12 miles a day.</u> As they went, <u>Gandhi</u> preached his doctrine of nonviolent resistance to British rule in every village <u>he</u> passed through: "Civil disobedience is the inherent right of a citizen. He dare not give it up without ceasing to be a man." <u>By the time he reached Dandi, twenty-four days later, his small group had become a nonviolent army of thousands.</u> When they arrived at Dandi, <u>Gandhi</u> picked up a pinch of <u>salt</u> from the sand. All along the coast, thousands did likewise, openly breaking British laws that prohibited Indians from making their own <u>salt</u>. The British had long profited from their monopoly and sale of <u>salt</u>, an item much in demand in a tropical country. By their simple acts of disobedience, <u>Gandhi</u> and the Indian people had taken a bold step on <u>their long march</u> to independence. <u>The salt march</u> was but one of many nonviolent activities that <u>Mohandas Gandhi</u> undertook between World War I and World War II to win India's goal of national independence from British rule.

—From Duiker, *World History*, 5e

Gandhi's name is mentioned several times in this paragraph, and thus, it should be evident that the paragraph has something to do with him. You can also see that the passage is about a "salt march." Almost every sentence describes something about this march. Combining the *who* with the *what*, you might guess that the topic is "Gandhi's salt march." If you are marking the text as you read, you might write that phrase in the margin to spark your memory when you come back to review for a test. The marginal note acts as a title—it focuses your attention on the topic. Or you could use a highlighter to mark the words in the paragraph itself.

Determining the topic is a good starting point for comprehending a reading selection. Follow these steps to keep it simple:

1. If there is a title, consider it first.
2. Look for **bold** or *italicized* terms to see what they have in common.
3. Look for repeated words, phrases, or concepts.

Once you figure out what the reading is about, you can begin to predict what kinds of information and ideas you might find in it.

Interaction 4–1 ▶ Identify the Topic of a Paragraph

Read each paragraph and decide what the topic is. Start with the question "What is this about?" Remember to look for repeated words, and mark them as you read. When you are finished reading, create a title for the paragraph based on your findings.

Paragraph 1

There are societies where fathers play an active role in child care. For example, according to Ziarat Hossain and colleagues, Navajo fathers invest about 60 percent as much time as mothers do in direct caregiving tasks. The father role has shifted primarily from an economic provider to a more balanced partner, including playing, emotional bonding, and child-rearing. Fathers' investment in child care varies tremendously across families depending on cultural values.

—From Ferraro, *Cultural Anthropology: An Applied Perspective*, 9e (p. 267). Copyright © 2012 Cengage Learning, Inc. Reproduced by permission. www.cengage.com/permissions

What is a good title? _____

Paragraph 2

The term *wiki* derives from the Hawaiian word *wiki*, which means fast. This technology allows many users to collaborate to create and update an Internet page. A wiki Web site allows registered users to add and edit content on a specific topic. The best known wiki is Wikipedia.com, an online encyclopedia where registered contributors may post additions to any entry. Wiki technology records the original material, plus the material that contributors add over time. Wikis have great potential to gather in one place contributions worldwide from all the specialists on one subject, for example, but there are not necessarily any safeguards that the material placed on the site is accurate or reliable.

—From Biagi, *Media/Impact: An Introduction to Mass Media*, 8e. Copyright © 2007 Cengage Learning, Inc. Reproduced by permission. www.cengage.com/permissions

What is a good title? _____

Paragraph 3

Taxes are dues we pay for membership in our society; they're the cost of living in this country. Federal, state, and local tax receipts fund government activities and a wide variety of public services, from national defense to local libraries. Administering and enforcing federal tax laws is the responsibility of the IRS, a part of the U.S. Department of Treasury.

—From Gitman, *Personal Financial Planning*, 12e (p. 75). Copyright © 2011 Cengage Learning, Inc. Reproduced by permission. www.cengage.com/permissions

What is a good title? _____

Paragraph 4

Your **speech topic** is the subject of your speech. Selecting a topic for a speech can be a very creative and energizing part of putting a speech together. With a little systematic thought and inventive organization, speakers often come up with a wide range of interesting speech topics.

—From Griffin, *Invitation to Public Speaking*, 4e (p. 44). Copyright © 2012 Cengage Learning, Inc. Reproduced by permission. www.cengage.com/permissions

What is a good title? _____

Paragraph 5

What is the name of the first song on your favorite playlist? Who won the World Series last year? Who wrote *Hamlet*? If you can answer these questions, you are using **recall**, a direct retrieval of facts or information. Tests of recall often require *verbatim* (word-for-word) memory. If you study a poem until you can recite it without looking at it, you are using recall. When you answer an essay question by providing facts and ideas, you are also using recall, even though you didn't learn your essay verbatim.

—From Coon/Mitterer, *Introduction to Psychology*, 13e

What is a good title? _____

Interaction 4–2 ▶ Identify More Topics of a Paragraph

Read each paragraph and decide what the topic is. Start with the question "What is this about?" Remember to look for repeated words, and mark them as you read. When you are finished reading, create a title for the paragraph based on your findings.

Paragraph 1   History Textbook

Samuel Adams, whose family owned a Boston brewery, was the undisputed leader of the popular pro-test movement in Massachusetts during the 1760s and 1770s. Adams was one of the organizers of the Sons of Liberty, a group responsible for many of the demonstrations against British policies as well as some of the violence against British officials. After the Revolution, he served as governor of Massachusetts.

—From Berkin, *Making America: A History of the United States*, 6e (p. 116).
Copyright © 2012 Cengage Learning, Inc. Reproduced by permission. www.cengage.com/permissions

What is a good title? _____

Paragraph 2   Psychology Textbook

As a personality trait, shyness refers to a tendency to avoid others, as well as feelings of anxiety, preoccupa-tion, and social inhibition (uneasiness and strain when socializing). Shy persons fail to make eye contact, retreat when spoken to, speak too quietly, and display little interest or animation in conversations. Mild shyness may be no more than a nuisance. However, extreme shyness (which may be diagnosed as *social anxiety disorder*) is often associated with depression, loneliness, fearfulness, social anxiety, inhibition, and low self-esteem.

—From Coon/Mitterer, *Introduction to Psychology*, 13e

What is a good title? _____

Paragraph 3   Environmental Science Textbook

All animals have a home range—that is, an area in which they live that provides their daily needs. The size of this area varies greatly for different animals. Some animals require many square miles of habitat—for example, wolves and mountain lions. Others may spend their entire lives within a 1- to 2-acre area—cottontail rabbits, for example. As a general rule, small animals have small territories and larger animals have larger home ranges.

—From Burton, *Environmental Science: Fundamentals and Applications*, 1e (pp. 224–225).
Copyright © 2009 Cengage Learning, Inc. Reproduced by permission. www.cengage.com/permissions

What is a good title? _____

Paragraph 4   Criminal Justice Textbook

On a limited basis, police can certainly prevent some crimes. If a rapist is dissuaded from attacking a solitary woman because a patrol car is cruising the area, then the police officer behind the wheel has prevented a crime. Furthermore, exemplary police work can have an effect. The nation's two largest cities—New York and Los Angeles—have both experienced sharp declines in crime in recent years, a trend many attribute in large part to aggressive and innovative law enforcement.

—From Gaines/Miller, *Criminal Justice in Action*, 6e

What is a good title? _____

Paragraph 5 | Anthropology Textbook |

> As with other forms of artistic expression, the functions of dance are culturally variable. Dance is likely to function in a number of different ways both between and within societies. Dance often performs several functions simultaneously within a society, but some functions are more prominent than others. To illustrate, dance can function psychologically by helping people cope more effectively with tensions and aggressive feelings; politically by expressing political values and attitudes, showing allegiance to political leaders, and controlling behavior; religiously by various methods of communicating with supernatural forces; socially by articulating and reinforcing relationships between members of the society; and educationally by passing on the cultural traditions, values, and beliefs from one generation to the next.
>
> —From Ferraro, *Cultural Anthropology*, 6e

What is a good title? _____

What Is the Author's Point About the Topic? The Main Idea

Asking what the author's point about the topic is will lead you to the **main idea**. The main idea is, of course, the main point that the author is trying to get across to you. The main idea *limits* the topic to what the author wants to discuss. For example, suppose the topic is love. Love is a very broad topic. An author could explore any number of main ideas in regard to love. Here are a few examples.

<u>There are several health benefits associated with</u> [being in love.]

[Love] <u>is viewed differently in different cultures.</u>

[Love] <u>is more complicated than many people realize.</u>

In these sentences, the topic is in brackets and the main idea is underlined. When the topic and the main idea appear in a single sentence, that sentence is called the *topic sentence*. Use this formula as a memory aid:

$$T + MI = TS$$
topic plus main idea equals topic sentence

Notice that in these examples, the topic is always *love*. The main idea, however, is different in each topic sentence. Each main idea is about a different aspect of love. As a result, each topic sentence would lead to a paragraph with different supporting details.

A Sample Analysis

In the following paragraph, the topic sentence is in bold type. Put brackets around the topic and underline the main idea. Then, refer back to the list of three points on pages 172–173. Explain how you can be sure that you have correctly identified the topic and the main idea.

> **Disney has expanded well beyond animation to become a global entertainment giant.** The company's studio division makes films for moviegoers of all ages, produces big-budget Broadway musicals, and distributes recorded music. Its parks and resort division operates theme parks in the United States, Japan, France, and Hong Kong, as well as family resorts and cruise ships. Disney's consumer products division puts the company's well-known brand and characters on everything from toys and T-shirts to books and beverages. The company's media holdings include the ABC television network, the ESPN sports network, and the Disney Interactive Media Group, which offers online, mobile, and video games.
>
> —From Pride, *Foundations of Business*, 3e (p. 3). Copyright © 2012 Cengage Learning, Inc. Reproduced by permission. www.cengage.com/permissions

Here is the formula for the topic sentence of this paragraph:

T	+	MI	= TS
Disney	+	has expanded well beyond animation to become a global entertainment giant.	

The topic is Disney. Notice how many sentences begin with references to Disney—*the company, its,* and *Disney's.* The main idea is *has expanded well beyond animation to become a global entertainment giant.* The main idea is more specific than the topic, and it is more general than the supporting details. The supporting details give information about different divisions of Disney: the studio division, the park and resorts division, the consumer products division, and the company's media holdings. Together, they add up to Disney being "a global entertainment giant." The details support the main idea.

Interaction 4–3 ▶ Find the Main Idea

What is the main idea of each paragraph?

1. Look for repeated ideas to find the topic.

2. To figure out the main idea, think about how the author is limiting the topic to just the point he or she wants to discuss.

3. Look for a sentence in which T + MI = TS.

4. In the topic sentence, put brackets around the topic and underline the main idea.

Paragraph 1

Public Speaking Textbook

Invitational speeches are usually given in two contexts. In the first context, we give invitational speeches when there are two sides to an issue and we want to be sure we explore and understand them as fully as possible. In the second context, we give invitational speeches when an audience is polarized about an issue and we know we can't persuade them to change.

—From Griffin, *Invitation to Public Speaking*, 2e

A. What is the paragraph about? Topic: _____

B. What is the author's point about the topic? Main idea: _____

C. What is the topic sentence? T + MI = TS: _____

_____

Paragraph 2

Health Textbook

Risky remedies have been tried by millions of people in their search for a quick fix to weight problems. In the 1920s, some women swallowed patented weight loss capsules that turned out to be tapeworm eggs. In the 1960s and 1970s, addictive amphetamines were common diet aids. In the 1990s, appetite suppressants known as fen-phen became popular. They were taken off the market after being linked to heart valve problems.

—From Hales, *An Invitation to Health*, 12e

A. What is the paragraph about? Topic: _____

B. What is the author's point about the topic? Main idea: _____

C. What is the topic sentence? T + MI = TS: _____

_____

Paragraph 3

Environmental Science Textbook

Petroleum products are damaging to the environment when they leak or spill on land. Leaking underground fuel tanks have polluted groundwater, contaminating drinking water and destroying plant and animal life. Poisonous fumes from petroleum spills are hazardous to the health of humans as well as other animals and also create potential fire hazards.

—From Burton, *Environmental Science*

A. What is the paragraph about? Topic: _____

B. What is the author's point about the topic? Main idea: _____

_____

C. What is the topic sentence? T + MI = TS: _____

_____

Paragraph 4

Criminal Investigation Textbook

When a suspect has become cooperative, you can increase the amount of conversation. Once rapport is established, listen for words indicating that the suspect is in some way connected with the crime, such as "I didn't do it, but I know who did." If the suspect is not implicated in the crime but has relevant information, attempt to obtain a statement. If the suspect is implicated, try to obtain an admission or confession.

—From Hess, *Criminal Investigation*, 9e (p. 193). Copyright © 2010 Cengage Learning, Inc.
Reproduced by permission. www.cengage.com/permissions

A. What is the paragraph about? Topic: _____

B. What is the author's point about the topic? Main idea: _____

C. What is the topic sentence? T + MI = TS: _____

_____

Paragraph 5

Nonfiction Book

In the mid-1970s the world of skateboarding was turned upside down by a small group of kids who called themselves the Z-boys. A band of lanky, sun-bleached teenagers from a surf shop near Venice, California, the Z-boys skated in a way no one had ever seen. They did aerial maneuvers. They scraped their boards along curbs and handrails. They carried themselves with a punk-outsider sensibility that we now recognize as the sport's lingua franca. Most usefully, they had a gift for dramatic timing, making their debut at the Bahne-Cadillac Skateboard Championship in Del Mar, California, in the summer of 1975. —From Daniel Coyle, *The Talent Code*, pp. 58–59

A. What is the paragraph about? Topic: _____

B. What is the author's point about the topic? Main idea: _____

C. What is the topic sentence? T + MI = TS: _____

_____

Interaction 4–4 Find More Main Ideas of a Paragraph

What is the main idea of each paragraph?

1. Look for repeated ideas to find the topic.

2. To figure out the main idea, think about how the author is limiting the topic to just the point he or she wants to discuss.

3. Look for a sentence in which T + MI = TS.

4. In the topic sentence, put brackets around the topic and underline the main idea.

Paragraph 1

Public Speaking Textbook

Even though we usually think of our audience as the listeners in a speech, speakers are also listeners. When you give a speech, listen to your audience for signs of disinterest, hostility, or opposition. Also listen to make sure your style and mannerisms aren't confusing or distracting. Finally, listen for signs that your audience is confused by the information in your speech. Each of these signals helps you adapt your message so your speech is a listenable one. —From Griffin, *Invitation to Public Speaking*, 2e

A. What is the paragraph about? Topic: _____

B. What is the author's point about the topic? Main idea: _____

C. What is the topic sentence? T + MI = TS: _____

_____

Paragraph 2   Health Textbook

The major threat to the lives of college students isn't illness but injury. Almost 75 percent of deaths among Americans 15 to 24 years old are caused by "unintentional injuries" (a term public health officials prefer), suicides, and homicides. The odds of dying from an injury in any given year are about 1 in 765; over a lifetime they rise to 1 in 23. In all, injuries—intentional and unintentional—claim almost 150,000 lives a year. Accidents, especially motor vehicle crashes, kill more college-age men and women than all other causes combined; the greatest number of lives lost to accidents is among those 25 years of age.   —From Hales, *An Invitation to Health*, 12e

A. What is the paragraph about? Topic: _____

B. What is the author's point about the topic? Main idea: _____

C. What is the topic sentence? T + MI = TS: _____

_____

Paragraph 3   Sociology Textbook

Teen pregnancy is integrally linked to gender expectations of men and women in society. Some teen men consciously avoid birth control, thinking it takes away from their manhood. Teen women often romanticize motherhood, thinking that becoming a mother will give them social value they do not otherwise have. For teens in disadvantaged groups, motherhood confers a legitimate social identity on those otherwise devalued by society.   —From Andersen/Taylor, *Sociology*, 4e

A. What is the passage about? Topic: _____

B. What is the point of this paragraph? Main idea: _____

_____

C. What is the topic sentence? T + MI = TS: _____

_____

Paragraph 4   Psychology Textbook

The right hemisphere of the brain can produce only the simplest language and numbers. Working with the right side is like talking to a child who can say only a dozen words or so. To answer questions, the right hemisphere must use nonverbal responses, such as pointing at objects.

—From Coon/Mitterer, *Introduction to Psychology*, 13e

A. What is the paragraph about? Topic: _____

B. What is the author's point about the topic? Main idea: _____

C. What is the topic sentence? T + MI = TS: _____

_____

Paragraph 5 | **Government Textbook**

It is difficult to estimate how many people are homeless because the number depends on how the home-less are defined. There are *street people*—those who sleep in bus stations, parks, and other areas. Many of these people are youthful runaways. There are the so-called *sheltered homeless*—those who sleep in government-supported or privately-funded shelters. Many of these individuals used to live with their families or friends. Whereas street people are almost always single, the term *sheltered homeless* includes many families with children. Homeless families are the fastest-growing subgroup of the homeless population. There are also the *hard-core homeless*—which are those who have been on the streets a year or more.

—From Schmidt, *American Government and Politics Today 2007–2008*, 13e

A. What is the paragraph about? Topic: _____

B. What is the author's point about the topic? Main idea: _____

_____

C. What is the topic sentence? T + MI = TS: _____

_____

Location of the Topic Sentence: Anywhere

A topic sentence can appear in different places within a paragraph. In one paragraph the topic sentence may be the first sentence. In another paragraph it may come last. And you can find a topic sentence anywhere in between. The rule about topic sentences is that they can be found anywhere in a paragraph. It is not the location of the topic sentence that is important; it is the relationships between the ideas in the paragraph that matter.

Think about this analogy. Some of you may live in cities, states, or even countries far away from the rest of your family. Let's say, just for example, that you live in Dallas, Texas, and your parents live in Villahermosa, Mexico. Are you still their child? Are they still your parents? Of course! It is the relationship between you and your parents that matters, not your respective locations.

In a paragraph, it is the same for the topic, main idea, and supporting details. It does not matter where they are located; their relationship is always the same.

▶ The topic is a broad, general idea.
▶ The main idea narrows the topic to the specific point the author wants to discuss.
▶ The major and minor details support the main idea with even narrower, more specific ideas.

Let's look at an example. The topic sentence has been underlined for you. Notice that it is in the middle of the paragraph.

> ### Women and the Monastic Life
>
> We tend to think of monasticism as a masculine enterprise, but it should be remembered that the vowed religious life was open to both men and women. The entire early history of Christianity records a flourishing monastic life for women. <u>In the late Roman period, groups of religious women flourished all over the Roman Empire.</u> Saint Benedict's sister, Scholastica, was head of a monastery. Her contemporary, Brigid of Ireland, was such a powerful figure in the Irish church that legends grew up around her. In England, Hilda, abbess of Whitbey, not only ruled over a prominent monastery that was a learning center, but she also held a famous Episcopal gathering to determine church policy.
>
> —From Cunningham, *Culture and Values, Volume I: A Survey of the Humanities*, 6e.
> Copyright © 2006 Cengage Learning, Inc. Reproduced by permission. www.cengage.com/permissions

Let's put this paragraph into the following diagram to visualize these relationships (see **Figure 4.2**).

Figure 4.2   Three Levels of Information

broad `About >` **Topic:** _____

narrower `Point >` **Main Idea:** _____

narrowest `1. Proof >` **Supporting Detail:** Saint Benedict's sister, Scholastica, was head of a monastery.

`2. Proof >` **Supporting Detail:** Her contemporary, Brigid of Ireland, was such a powerful figure in the Irish church that legends grew up around her.

`3. Proof >` **Supporting Detail:** In England, Hilda, abbess of Whitbey, not only ruled over a prominent monastery that was a learning center, but she also held a famous Episcopal gathering to determine church policy.

What about the first two sentences in the paragraph? They are not in our diagram. When the topic sentence falls in the middle of a paragraph, sometimes the sentences that come before it introduce the idea even more broadly than the topic sentence does. They act as a funnel, giving readers a very broad context that quickly narrows down to the main idea. Sentences like these frequently introduce the main idea for a whole group of paragraphs. (And when a topic sentence introduces a group of paragraphs, it's often called a *thesis statement* rather than a topic sentence.)

Note that if you were to reorder the paragraph, putting the supporting details first and then ending with the topic sentence, the relationships between the ideas would be exactly the same as shown in the original paragraph and in Figure 4.2.

Saint Benedict's sister, Scholastica, was head of a monastery. Her contemporary, Brigid of Ireland, was such a powerful figure in the Irish church that legends grew up around her. In England, Hilda, abbess of Whitbey, not only ruled over a prominent monastery that was a learning center, but she also held a famous Episcopal gathering to determine church policy. <u>In the late Roman period, groups of religious women flourished all over the Roman Empire.</u>

—From Cunningham/Reich, *Culture and Values, Volume 1*, 6e

So when you are searching for the topic sentence of a paragraph, look for the relationships among the ideas—which ideas are the broadest, narrower, and narrowest—rather than expecting to find the topic sentence in a particular location. It is the relationship that matters, not the location.

Interaction 4–5 ▶ Find the Topic Sentence

Remember that T + MI = TS. Locate the topic sentence of each paragraph. Then mark the parts of the topic sentence: put brackets around the topic, and underline the main idea.

Paragraph 1   **Business Textbook**

Both businesses and nonprofits rely on four fundamental resources to achieve their objectives. Some combination of these factors is crucial for an economic system to work and create wealth. *Natural resources* include all inputs that offer value in their natural state, such as land, fresh water, wind, and mineral deposits. *Capital* includes machines, tools, buildings, information, and technology—the synthetic resources that a business needs to produce goods or services. *Human resources* encompass the physical, intellectual, and creative contributions of everyone who works within an economy. *Entrepreneurs* are people who take the risk of launching and operating their own businesses, largely in response to the profit incentive. All of these factors must be in place for an economy to thrive.

—From Kelly, *BUSN*, 3e (p. 6). Copyright © 2011 Cengage Learning, Inc. Reproduced by permission. www.cengage.com/permissions

A. What is the topic? _____

B. What is the main idea? _____

C. What is the topic sentence? _____

_____

Paragraph 2   **Health Textbook**

Women see doctors more often than men, take more prescription drugs, are hospitalized more, and control the spending of three of every four health-care dollars. In a national telephone poll, 76 percent of American women—but only 60 percent of men—said they had had a health exam in the last 12 months. The genders differ significantly in the way they use health-care services in the United States.

—From Hales, *An Invitation to Health*, 15e

A. What is the topic? _____

B. What is the main idea? _____

C. What is the topic sentence? _____

Paragraph 3   Biology Textbook

Ecstasy is a drug that makes you feel socially accepted, relieves anxiety, and sharpens the senses while giving you a mild high. It can also leave you dying in a hospital bed, foaming at the mouth and bleeding from every orifice as your temperature skyrockets. It can send your family and friends spiraling into horror and disbelief as they watch you stop breathing. Lorna Spinks ended life that way. She was nineteen years old. Her family wants you to know what Lorna did not: Ecstasy can kill.

—From Starr/Evers/Starr, *Biology Today and Tomorrow*, 2e

A. What is the topic? _____

B. What is the main idea? _____

C. What is the topic sentence? _____

Paragraph 4   Humanities Textbook

The Islamic statement of faith begins: "There is but one God, Allah...." To grasp this belief in monotheism is to understand a whole variety of issues connected to Islam. The word Islam means "submission" to God. Because God is almighty, his divinity is hidden from humanity; as a consequence Allah may not be depicted in artistic form. Because the revelation of Allah is final and definitive, Islam sees the reality of God beyond the revelation of the God of the Jewish Scriptures and is explicitly resistant to the Trinitarian faith of Christianity. The fundamental monotheism of Islam also helps explain why Islam has a tradition of missionary expansion. The omnipotent will of God is for all humanity to submit to God.

—From Cunningham/Reich, *Culture and Values, Volume 1*, 6e

A. What is the topic? _____

B. What is the main idea? _____

C. What is the topic sentence? _____

_____

Paragraph 5   Psychology Textbook

When confronted with stress, people sometimes simply give up and withdraw from the battle. Some people routinely respond to stress with fatalism and resignation, passively accepting setbacks that might be dealt with effectively. This syndrome is referred to as *learned helplessness*. Learned helplessness is passive behavior produced by exposure to unavoidable aversive events.

—From Weiten, *Psychology: Themes and Variations*, 7e. Copyright © 2007 Cengage Learning, Inc. Reproduced by permission. www.cengage.com/permissions

A. What is the topic? _____

B. What is the main idea? _____

C. What is the topic sentence? _____

_____

What Is the Proof for the Author's Main Idea?
The Supporting Details

Asking "What is the proof for the author's main idea?" leads you to the author's *supporting details*. The details are called "supporting" because they give support—evidence or proof for the author's main idea. The support might consist of examples, statistics, facts, anecdotes, or expert opinion. To find the supporting details in a paragraph, turn the topic sentence into a question and look for the answers. Each one should be a supporting detail. Let's look at an example from a finance textbook. The topic sentence is underlined.

Small Savings Mean Big Bucks!

It should be obvious: spend less than you earn, so you'll have money to invest. Yet so many people don't recognize this simple fact. They run up large credit card bills and take out loans instead of building a nest egg for the future.

Where to start? How about with the little stuff? <u>You'd be amazed at how reducing even your smallest expenses can lead to big savings!</u> Here are some examples of how reducing your discretionary spending now will yield big payoffs later, thanks to the large impact of compound interest:

▶ Instead of buying 40 $5 lottery tickets a year, invest the $200 at the end of each year at 8 percent. If you start at age 18, you'll have $106,068 by the time you reach age 67!

▶ Buy a used car instead of a new one, and invest the amount you saved at 8 percent for 40 years. If you saved $9,000 buying a used car, you'd have more than $195,000 available for your retirement fund!

▶ Stop the money drain into vending machines, espresso stands, and restaurant or fast food lunches. Buy a regular cup of coffee rather than a latte or espresso, avoid the vending machines, and take a brown-bag lunch to work several days a week. If you save $22 a week for 50 weeks a year at 8 percent for 40 years, your savings will grow by more than $284,000!

▶ Use less of things like shampoo, detergent, and toothpaste. Try cutting the amount you use in half. Then look for other areas where you can do this.

▶ Pay attention to how you spend your loose change. Limit the amount of cash and coins you carry, and you'll plug one of the biggest financial leaks in most Americans' pockets.

—From Gitman, *Personal Financial Planning*, 11e. Copyright © 2008 Cengage Learning, Inc. Reproduced by permission. www.cengage.com/permissions

To find the supporting details, form a question from the topic sentence:

How can reducing even your smallest expenses lead to big savings?

Look for each answer the author gives.

Supporting Details:

1. Don't buy lottery tickets; invest instead.
2. Buy a used car instead of a new one, and invest the difference.
3. Pack lunch and avoid expensive drinks and snacks.
4. Reduce consumption of household products.
5. Carry smaller amounts of cash and save change.

Thinking about the supporting details will help you decide whether you understand or agree with an author's main idea.

Interaction 4–6 ▶ **Find the Supporting Details**

Reread each of the following paragraphs. Mark the topic and the main idea in the paragraph itself if you haven't already done so. Then form a question from the topic sentence and answer it with the supporting details.

1. Paragraph 5 of Interaction 4–2 on page 177

   Question formed from the topic sentence: _____

   _____

   Supporting Details:

   1. _____

   2. _____

   3. _____

   4. _____

   5. _____

2. Paragraph 5 of Interaction 4–3 on page 180

   Question formed from the topic sentence: _____

   _____

   Supporting Details:

   1. _____

   _____

   2. _____

   _____

3. _____

   _____

4. _____

   _____

3. Paragraph 1 from Interaction 4–4 on page 180

Question formed from the topic sentence: _____

_____

Supporting 1. _____
Details:
   _____

   2. _____

   _____

   3. _____

   _____

Major Versus Minor Details

There are two types of supporting details: major and minor. Let's look at the difference between major and minor details by examining the details from the passage on page 186 about spending less to make more money. The major details are in **bold**; the minor details are in regular type.

> ▶ **Instead of buying 40 $5 lottery tickets a year, invest the $200 at the end of each year at 8 percent.** If you start at age 18, you'll have $106,068 by the time you reach age 67!
>
> ▶ **Buy a used car instead of a new one and invest the amount you saved at 8 percent for 40 years.** If you saved $9,000 buying a used car, you'd have more than $195,000 available for your retirement fund!
>
> ▶ **Stop the money drain into vending machines, espresso stands, and restaurant or fast food lunches. Buy a regular cup of coffee rather than a latte or espresso, avoid the vending machines, and take a brown-bag lunch to work several days a week.** If you save $22 a week for 50 weeks a year at 8 percent for 40 years, your savings will grow by more than $284,000!
>
> ▶ **Use less of things like shampoo, detergent, and toothpaste.** Try cutting the amount you use in half. Then look for other areas where you can do this.
>
> ▶ Pay attention to how you spend your loose change. **Limit the amount of cash and coins you carry,** and you'll plug one of the biggest financial leaks in most Americans' pockets.

—From Gitman/Joehnk, *Personal Financial Planning*, 11e

Notice how the major details capture the direct support for the main idea. They are all ways you can reduce your discretionary spending. The minor details give extra information about the major details. In this passage, they describe how much money each type of savings could yield.

The major details directly prove or support the main idea and give organizational structure to the paragraph. The minor details give extra information about the major details.

Interaction 4–7   **Identify the Minor Details**

Read the following selection from a health textbook. The first sentence is a thesis statement—the same as a topic sentence except that it controls a group of paragraphs, not just one paragraph. Form a question from the thesis statement to find the major supporting details. Mark these with numbers. Then answer the questions about the minor supporting details that follow.

Health-Related Fitness

There are five health-related components of physical fitness.

Question: _____

Cardiorespiratory fitness refers to the ability of the heart to pump blood through the body efficiently. It is achieved through aerobic exercise—any activity, such as brisk walking or swimming, in which sufficient or excess oxygen is continually supplied to the body. In other words, aerobic exercise involves working out strenuously without pushing to the point of breathlessness.

Muscular strength refers to the force within muscles; it is measured by the absolute maximum weight that you can lift, push, or press in one effort. Strong muscles help keep the skeleton in proper alignment, improve posture, prevent back and leg aches, help in everyday lifting, and enhance athletic performance. Muscle mass increases along with strength, which makes for a healthier body composition and a higher metabolic rate.

Muscular endurance is the ability to perform repeated muscular effort; it is measured by counting how many times you can lift, push, or press a given weight. Important for posture, muscular endurance helps in everyday work as well as in athletics and sports.

Flexibility is the range of motion around specific joints—for example, the stretching you do to touch your toes or twist your torso. Flexibility depends on many factors: your age, gender, and posture; how muscular you are; and how much body fat you have. As children develop, their flexibility increases until adolescence. Then a gradual loss of joint mobility begins and continues throughout adult life. Both muscles and connective tissue, such as tendons and ligaments, shorten and become tighter if not consistently used through their full range of motion.

Body composition refers to the relative amounts of fat and lean tissue (bone, muscles, organs, water) in the body. As discussed later in this chapter, a high proportion of body fat has serious health implications, including increased incidence of heart disease, high blood pressure, diabetes, stroke, gallbladder problems, back and joint problems, and some forms of cancer.

—From Hales, *An Invitation to Health,* 15e

_____ 1. What do the minor details of the first major supporting detail discuss?

    a. the benefits of cardiorespiratory fitness

    b. the problems of not having cardiorespiratory fitness

    c. the methods for gaining cardiorespiratory fitness

_____ 2. What do the minor details of the second major supporting detail discuss?

    a. the benefits of muscular strength

    b. the problems of not having muscular strength

    c. the methods for gaining muscular strength

_____ 3. What do the minor details of the third major supporting detail discuss?

    a. the benefits of muscular endurance

    b. the problems of not having muscular endurance

    c. the methods for gaining muscular endurance

_____ 4. What do the minor details of the fourth major supporting detail discuss?

    a. the benefits of flexibility

    b. the causes of flexibility and the effects of aging on flexibility

    c. the increase of enjoyment from flexibility

_____ 5. What do the minor details of the fifth major supporting detail discuss?

    a. the benefits of a high proportion of lean tissue in the body

    b. the problems of a high proportion of fat in the body

    c. the causes of a high proportion of fat in the body

Interaction 4–8   **Identify the Supporting Details of Paragraphs**

In each paragraph, bracket the topic, underline the main idea, and use numbers or parentheses to indicate the major supporting details. Then answer the question about minor supporting details.

Paragraph 1 | **Finance Textbook** |

    You'll soon find many other ways to "save small," such as taking public transportation, comparing prices before you buy, reading books and magazines from the library instead of buying them, and using coupons to buy groceries. Then, make saving a given, not something you do when you have money left over. Pay yourself first. Have your employer deposit the maximum amount in your 401(k) plan each pay period. It will grow even faster if your employer matches your contributions. You can also authorize withdrawals from your checking account to an investment account or to a mutual fund.

—From Gitman/Joehnk, *Personal Financial Planning*, 11e

1. Which major supporting detail does the author provide extra information about? _____

Paragraph 2

True wine lovers go through an elaborate series of steps when they are served a good bottle of wine. Typically, they begin by drinking a little water to cleanse their palate. Then they sniff the cork from the wine bottle, swirl a small amount of the wine around in a glass, and sniff the odor emerging from the glass. Finally, they take a sip of the wine, rolling it around in their mouth for a short time before swallowing it. At last they are ready to confer their approval or disapproval.

—From Weiten, *Psychology*, 7e

2. How many minor supporting details are there in this paragraph? _____

Paragraph 3

Communication apprehension, or nervousness, can take two forms. People who are apprehensive about communicating with others in any situation are said to have *trait anxiety*. People who are apprehensive about communicating with others in a particular situation are said to have *state*, or *situational*, anxiety. Take a moment to consider whether you are trait anxious or state anxious in communication situations. Do you fear all kinds of interactions or only certain kinds? Most of us experience some level of state anxiety about some communication events, such as asking a boss for a raise, verbally evaluating another's performance, or introducing ourselves to a group of strangers.

—From Griffin, *Invitation to Public Speaking*, 2e

3. Which of the major details does the author provide more detail about? _____

Paragraph 4

In many working-class and middle-class neighborhoods, many homes sprouted signs announcing a variety of services—household beauty parlors, kitchen bakeries, rooms for boarders. A Milwaukee woman recalled, "I did baking at home to supplement our income. I got 9 cents for a loaf of bread and 25 cents for an apple cake…I cleared about $65 a month." A sewing machine salesman commented that he was selling more and more machines to people who would not previously have done their own sewing. For farm families, feed sacks had long provided fabric for sewing, and companies now competed by printing attractive designs on their sacks. One woman remembered her mother making a pretty new school dress out of a sack that had "a sky-blue background with gorgeous mallard ducks on it." "Use it up, wear it out, make it do, or do without" became the motto of most American families.

—From Berkin, Miller, Cherny, and Gormly, *Making America*, 6e

4. Which of the two major supporting details does the author provide more details about? _____

_____

Paragraph 5

The notion that love will endure forever without any change is unrealistic. Although love can last over a period of time, love takes on different forms as the relationship matures. Love is complex and involves both joyful experiences and difficulties. The intensity of your love changes as you change.

You may experience several stages of love with one person, deepening your love and finding new levels of richness. Conversely, you and your partner may become stagnant and the love you once shared fades.

—From Corey/Corey, *I Never Knew I Had a Choice*, 8e

5. Which of the major supporting details does the author provide extra information about _____

_____

The Thesis Statement of a Group of Paragraphs

A thesis statement is the same as a topic sentence except that it controls a group of paragraphs, not just one paragraph. When a group of paragraphs has a thesis statement, then often the topic sentences of the individual paragraphs act as the major supporting details for the thesis. The remainder of each paragraph provides the minor supporting details.

A Sample Analysis

► Mark the thesis statement of the following selection from an anthropology textbook. Bracket the topic and underline the main idea.
► Form a question from the thesis statement and write it here. _____

_____

► Find the two topic sentences that act as major supporting details and number them. Then bracket each topic and underline each main idea.
► Identify each minor detail that supports the main idea of the topic sentence. Label each one with a letter such as (a). Double-check to make sure all the minor details support the main ideas.

Human Adaptation

Human adaptations to a particular environment are cultural and biological.
Cultural responses to cold climates include "technological" and behavioral solutions. Examples are building fires, using animal skins as clothing and blankets, and seeking refuge from the elements in caves or constructed dwellings. And let's not forget using wood fires, coal-burning stoves, and gas and electric heating systems for keeping warm. Humans who live in cold climates also engage in certain behaviors that are adaptive. They tend to eat more food, particularly fats and carbohydrates, especially during the colder months; they engage in greater amounts of activity sourcing food and getting fuel for heat, which increases their internal body temperature; and they curl up when sleeping to reduce the surface area of exposure and resulting heat loss. Some would say many cultures have gone soft with today's

modern housing and stocked refrigerators and pantries. Members of such cultures now have a hard time going without such conveniences, which is especially noted when there are long power outages.

   Adaptations to cold climates have also resulted in differences in body stature. To illustrate, Arctic people, such as the Inuit, are generally short and stocky with short extremities. People living in hot equatorial zones, by way of contrast, tend to be taller and less stocky with longer arms and legs. Although there are always exceptions to these general trends, human body weight (relative to height) tends to be higher in cold climates and lower in warmer climates.

—From Ferraro & Andreatta, *Cultural Anthropology*, 9e

The thesis statement is the first sentence because it includes both cultural and biological adaptations to environment, and each of the two supporting paragraphs discusses one of these adaptations. The first paragraph discusses cultural adaptations, and the second paragraph discusses biological adaptations having to do with body stature. In the first paragraph, sentences 2 and 3 are about technological solutions, and sentence 4 is about behavioral solutions. There are also more minor details that support that minor detail. In the second paragraph, there are three minor details.

Interaction 4–9 ▶ Find the Thesis Statement of a Group of Paragraphs

▶ Mark the thesis statement of the following selection from a psychology textbook. Bracket the topic and underline the main idea.

▶ Form a question from the thesis statement and write it here: _____

_____

▶ Find the topic sentences that act as major supporting details and number them. Then bracket each topic and underline each main idea.

▶ Identify each minor detail that supports the main idea of the topic sentence. Label each one with a letter such as (a). Double-check to make sure all the minor details support the main ideas.

Social Comparison

   If you want to know how heavy you are, you simply get on a scale. But how do you know if you are a good athlete, worker, parent, or friend? How do you know if your views on politics, religion, or hip-hop are unusual or widely shared? When there are no objective standards, the only available yardstick is provided by comparing yourself with others.

   Typically, we don't make social comparisons randomly or on some absolute scale. Meaningful evaluations are based on comparing yourself with people of similar backgrounds, abilities, and circumstances. To illustrate, let's ask a student named Wendy if she is a good tennis player. If Wendy compares herself with a professional, the answer will be no. But this tells us little about her relative ability. Within her tennis group, Wendy is regarded as an excellent player. On a fair scale of comparison,

Wendy knows she is good and she takes pride in her tennis skills. In the same way, thinking of yourself as successful, talented, responsible, or fairly paid depends entirely on whom you choose for comparison. Thus, a desire for social comparison provides a motive for associating with others and influences which groups we join.

In addition to providing information, social comparisons may, at times, be made in ways that reflect desires for self-protection or self-enhancement. If you feel threatened, you may make a downward comparison by contrasting yourself with a person who ranks lower on some dimension. For example, if you have a part-time job and your employer cuts your hours, you may comfort yourself by thinking about a friend who just lost a job.

As Wendy's tennis playing suggests, comparing yourself with people of much higher ability will probably just make you feel bad. For example, when women compare their bodies with those of beautiful women in the media, their dissatisfaction with their own bodies increases. However, upward comparisons, in which we compare ourselves to a person who ranks higher on some dimensions, are sometimes used for self-improvement. One way that Wendy can learn to improve her tennis skills is to compare herself with players who are only a little better than she is.

—From Coon/Mitterer, *Introduction to Psychology*, 13e

Outlines and Visual Maps

In this chapter you have been marking a text to show the relationships among the ideas in a paragraph or group of paragraphs. These relationships can also be shown with outlines and visual maps. Outlines use a system of indentation to show how broad or narrow an idea is. Concept maps use a different method of organization that puts each idea into a bubble and links the bubbles with arrows to show the connections between them. Both of these are strategies intended to help you note the relationships among ideas in a reading selection (or in your own thinking). They are equally valid. The one you use will depend on your preference and the organization of the material. (We will talk more about this in Chapter 6.)

Outlines

An outline is a hierarchical organization from the broadest idea (topic) to the narrowest (minor detail). You are probably familiar with the formal outline:

I. Topic + Main Idea
  A. Major Detail
    1. minor detail
    2. minor detail
  B. Major Detail
    1. minor detail
    2. minor detail

Notice the hierarchical nature of the outline. Broader ideas are supported by the narrower details. Working from bottom to top, the minor details support the major details, and the major details support the main idea.

Interaction 4–10 ▶ Use an Outline

Mark the following reading selection from a math textbook: Bracket the topic, underline the main idea, and use numbers to indicate the major supporting details. Then fill in the formal outline to show the relationships among the ideas.

Sometimes students who have had difficulty learning math in the past think that their problem is not being born with the ability to "do math." This isn't true! Learning math is a skill and, much like learning to play a musical instrument, takes daily, organized practice. Below are some strategies that will get you off to a good start.

Attend Class. Attending class every meeting is one of the most important things you can do to succeed. Your instructor explains material, gives examples to support the text and information about topics that are not in your book, or may make announcements regarding homework assignments and test dates. Getting to know at least a few of your classmates is also important to your success. Find a classmate or two on whom you can depend for information, who can help with homework, or with whom you can form a study group.

Make a Calendar. Because daily practice is so important in learning math, it is a good idea to set up a calendar that lists all of your time commitments and time for studying and doing your homework. A general rule for how much study time to budget is to allot two hours outside of class for every lecture hour. If your class meets for three hours per week, plan on six hours per week for homework and study.

Gather Needed Materials. All math classes require textbooks, notebooks, pencils (with big erasers!), and usually as much scrap paper as you can gather. If you are not sure that you have everything you need, check with your instructor. Ideally, you should have your materials by your second class meeting and bring them to every class meeting after that. Additional materials that may be of use outside of class are the online tutorial program iLrn (www.iLrn.com) and the Video Skillbuilder CD-ROM that is packaged with your textbook.

Understand What Your Instructor Expects From You. Your instructor's syllabus is documentation of his or her expectations. Many times your instructor will detail in the syllabus how your grade is determined, when office hours are held, and where you can get help outside of class. Read the syllabus thoroughly and make sure you understand all that is required.

I. Learning math is a skill that takes daily, organized practice.

   A. _____

      1. _____

      2. _____

   B. _____

      1. _____

      2. _____

   C. _____

      1. _____

      2. _____

   D. _____

      1. _____

      2. _____

Concept Maps

You may know several terms to describe this strategy: mind map, visual, bubble, or cluster. We like to use the term *concept map* because it describes very precisely what you are doing—mapping out the important concepts (that is, ideas) from a reading or lecture and showing their relationships to one another.

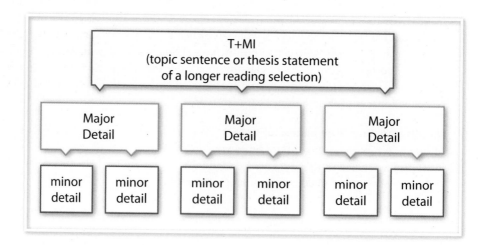

"Suns and Rays" Concept Map

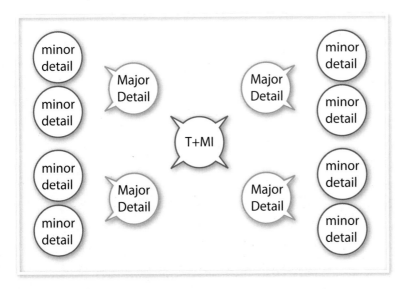

Mark the following reading selection: Bracket the topic, underline the main idea, and use numbers to indicate the major supporting details. Then fill in the concept map to show the relationships among the ideas.

Pilates for Strength and Flexibility

Used by dancers for deep-body conditioning and injury rehabilitation, Pilates (pronounced puh-LAH-teez), was developed more than seven decades ago by German immigrant Joseph Pilates. Increasingly used to complement aerobics and weight training, Pilates exercises improve flexibility and joint mobility and strengthen the core by developing pelvic stability and abdominal control.

Pilates-trained instructors offer "mat" or "floor" classes—classes that stress the stabilization and strengthening of the back and abdominal muscles. Fitness centers also may offer training on Pilates equipment, primarily a device called the Reformer, a wooden contraption with various cables, pulleys, springs, and sliding boards attached that is used for a series of progressive, range-of-motion exercises. Instructors typically work one-on-one or with small groups of two or three participants and tailor exercise sessions to individual flexibility and strength limitations. Unlike exercise techniques that emphasize numerous repetitions in a single direction, Pilates exercises involve very few, but extremely precise, repetitions in several planes of motion.

According to research from the American College of Sports Medicine, Pilates enhances flexibility and muscular endurance, particularly for intermediate and advanced practitioners, but its potential to increase cardiorespiratory fitness and reduce body weight is limited. The intensity of a Pilates workout increases from basic to intermediate to advanced levels, as does the number of calories burned. For intermediate practitioners, a 30-minute session burns 180 calories, with each additional quarter-hour burning another 90 calories. A single weekly session enhances flexibility but has little impact on body composition.

—From Hales, *An Invitation to Health*, 12e

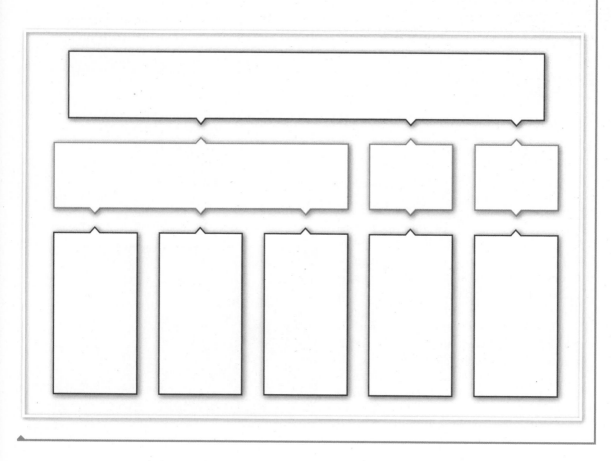

Connect Your Skills

Finding the Main Idea

A. Find the topic sentence. Bracket the topic and underline the main idea. Number each major supporting detail. Then answer the questions that follow.

Human Hearts Beat Together

Meghan Rosen

It's not always easy to follow your heart. But for human babies and their mothers, following *each other's* hearts may be as simple as sharing a smile. A new study shows that 3-month-old infants and their mothers can synchronize their heartbeats to mere milliseconds. Researchers sat 40 pairs of mothers and infants face-to-face, equipped with sticky skin electrodes on either side of their hearts. Beat for beat, mother-and-child hearts thumped together almost instantly as they shared loving looks or contented coos. This cardiac coupling worked only for moms with their own babies, and only when the duos synchronized smiles and other cheerful social behaviors, researchers report in this month's issue of *Infant Behavior and Development*. When humans mirror each other's facial expressions, they may switch on specific areas in the brain that tell the heart when to thump, the researchers suspect. Melding with mom lasts longer

Losevsky Pavel/Shutterstock.com

than just a few beats, however. Babies who don't tune in with their mothers are less empathetic as teenagers, according to previous work from the same lab. Premature infants or those whose mothers have postpartum depression may be most at risk for losing this social skill because they miss out on early opportunities to interact with mom.

—From "Human Hearts Beat Together" by Meghan Rosen. Copyright © 2011 by the American Association for the Advancement of Science. Reprinted by permission. http://news.sciencemag.org/sciencenow/2011/12/scienceshot-human-hearts-beat-to.html

1–3. What are three ways you can figure out the topic of this paragraph?

▶ _____

▶ _____

▶ _____

4. What words are clues to the topic? _____

_____

5. When exactly does sharing a smile produce two hearts beating together? _____

_____

_____

6. How many different research studies are discussed in this paragraph? _____

_____

7–8. What are two possible reasons for teens not being socially skilled?

▶ _____

▶ _____

B. Find each topic sentence. Bracket the topics, and underline the main ideas. Then complete the concept maps that follow.

Facebook's "Social Inbox" Fiasco: *Slate* Readers Respond

Sonia Tsuruoka

1   On Friday, *Slate* ran an article by Elizabeth Weingarten examining Facebook's "Social Inbox" feature, which sorts messages from friends and friends of friends into a user's main inbox, and files the rest in an "Other" folder—unbeknownst, it appears, to most Facebook users.

2   *Slate* staffers weren't the only ones missing messages. We received an outpouring of responses from readers who reported lost messages from friends, employers, and good Samaritans looking to return lost possessions. "I lost my wallet a month ago, and as soon as I read this, went to my 'Other' folder and lo and behold, there was a message from over a month ago saying that someone had found my wallet,"

wrote Michael Stafford Gelberg. "UN FREAKING BELIEVABLE. I just hope he had the heart to hold on to it for this long." At least two other readers discovered similar messages, one after losing an iPod Touch, and the other after losing a work-issued laptop last April. Melissa Zentgraf, a professional recruiter, wrote that she missed around ten messages from friends of friends who were interested in positions she was recruiting for. "So not only do I lose business, I look like a beyotch to the friends who referred them to me," she said. "Actually explains why one person has been giving me the cold shoulder lately."

3   Other missed messages were more personal. "An old acquaintance passed away and I sent flowers to the funeral," wrote a reader with the handle tnmke. "Shortly after that, his ex-girlfriend contacted me on Facebook at the request of his parents. They wondered who I was, and I guess they wanted to piece together as much of their son's life as they could. Facebook put this important message in the 'Other' folder and I didn't see it for months. I did reply and apologized for the delay, but I haven't heard back. Perhaps my message ended up in her 'Other' folder." Another reader reported that the feature intercepted messages from a potential love interest. "After reading this article on *Slate* about how Facebook hides certain messages from you, I checked to see if I had any hidden ones," wrote Julie Hill. "Lo and behold, an email from a nice guy asking me out. NINE MONTHS AGO. Thanks a lot, Zuckerberg!"

4   Some stories sounded perhaps too dramatic to believe. "Three years ago I spent a semester abroad in Argentina, where I met this woman who was studying for medical school in Seville," wrote Jason Ross. "I just checked my 'other' [folder] and found that she is back living in Spain, and the mother of my 2-year-old twins! Imagine how your life changes with one e-mail. Thank you, Facebook!!"

5   A handful of comments came from people who had noticed the Other tab before seeing the article. And plenty of the readers who had not checked the Other folder before found nothing in there but spam. Some readers suggested that, because Facebook does not charge people to use the site, it is silly to get angry at the company. But because many of the missed messages were personal in nature, emotion was hard to avoid. "Since April 2010," one reader wrote, "I have lost my 20-year-old daughter, both my parents and a sister. There were over 60 messages from old friends and relatives that I never saw. Stop treating us like children, Facebook. Epic Fail."

6   For now, it remains impossible to get e-mail notifications for your Other messages, so, as Weingarten writes, if you want to ensure you don't miss any potentially important messages, you have to make checking the folder a part of your daily Facebook routine.

—Adapted from "Facebook's "Social Inbox" Fiasco: Slate Readers Respond" by Sonia Tsuruoka. Copyright © 2011 The Slate Group, LLC. http://www.slate.com/blogs/browbeat/2011/12/12/facebook_s_social_inbox_fiasco_slate_readers_respond.html

9–12. Complete the concept map of paragraph 2.

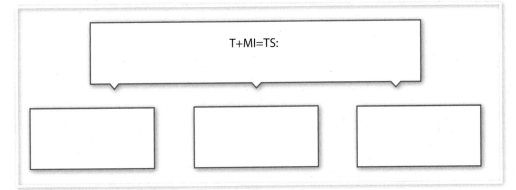

T+MI=TS:

13–15. Fill in the concept map for paragraph 3.

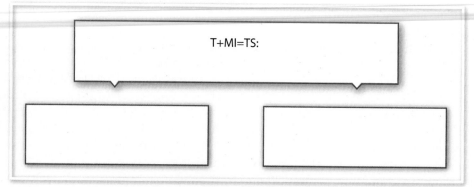

T+MI=TS:

C. Find the thesis statement. Bracket the topic and underline the main idea. Number each major supporting detail (that is, the topic sentences of the individual paragraphs). Then complete the outline that follows.

Sole Proprietors

1   Sole proprietors need certain characteristics to be successful. Sole proprietors must be willing to accept full responsibility for the firm's performance. The pressure of this responsibility can be much greater than any employee's responsibility. Sole proprietors must also be willing to work flexible hours. They are on call at all times and may even have to substitute for a sick employee. Their responsibility for the success of the business encourages them to continually monitor business operations. They must exhibit strong leadership skills, be well organized, and communicate well with employees.

2   Many successful sole proprietors have had previous work experience in the market in which they are competing, perhaps as an employee in a competitor's firm. For example, restaurant managers commonly establish their own restaurants. Experience is critical to understanding the competition and the behavior of customers in a particular market.

—From Madura, *Introduction to Business*, 4e (pp. 16–18). Copyright © 2007 Cengage Learning, Inc. Reproduced by permission. www.cengage.com/permissions

16–18.

I. _____

    A. _____

        1. They are willing to work flexible hours.

        2. They always monitor business operations.

        3. They have strong leadership skills, are well organized, and communicate well with employees.

    B. _____

        1. Restaurant managers commonly establish their own restaurants.

        2. Experience is critical to understanding the competition and the behavior of customers in a particular market.

19. What is a sole proprietor? _____

20. What word contrasts with *sole proprietor*? _____

Click to Connect! To check your comprehension of chapter concepts, visit **www.cengagebrain.com** to access the CourseMate for this chapter.

Chapter Summary Activity

This chapter has discussed how marking the answers to three comprehension questions can help you understand the relationships between ideas in a paragraph. Fill in the Reading Guide to Finding the Main Idea below by completing each main idea on the left with the specific supporting details from the chapter on the right. You can use this guide later as you work on other reading assignments.

Reading Guide to Finding Main Idea

Complete this idea with ...	information from Chapter 4.
Reading comprehension questions	1. _____
	2. _____
	3. _____
Three information levels in a reading and their definitions	4. _____
	5. _____
	6. _____
A simple process for finding the topic	7. _____
	8. _____
	9. _____
The meaning of T + MI = TS	10. _____
Relationships among topic, main idea, and supporting details in a paragraph	11. _____
	_____
	_____
Definition of thesis statement	12. _____
	_____
Three ways to show the relationships among ideas for later study	13. _____
	14. _____
	15. _____

Think about what your reading comprehension strategies were before you read this chapter. How did they differ from the suggestions here? What is one new strategy you can start using? Write down your thoughts.

_____

_____

_____

Reading 4–1 │ Website

▶ Pre-Reading the Selection

The reading on page 205 about Heifer International is from their website. Heifer International was declared one of the top fifteen NGOs (nongovernmental organizations) in the world in 2012 for its "inexpensive and uncomplicated formula" for helping people make gains in nutrition, health, income, gender equity, and family life.

Surveying the Reading

Survey the article that follows. Then check the elements that are included in this reading.

_____	Title	_____	Words in bold or italic type
_____	Headings	_____	Images and captions
_____	First sentences of paragraphs		

Guessing the Purpose

Based on the kind of organization Heifer International is and the title of the reading selection from its website, do you suppose the purpose is mostly to inform, persuade, or express? _____

Predicting the Content

Survey the first sentence of each paragraph and predict three things that the selection will discuss.

▶ _____

▶ _____

▶ _____

Activating Your Knowledge

What do you know about Heifer International, programs to end poverty and hunger, or reasons people live in poverty? List two or three things you know.

▶ _____

▶ _____

▶ _____

 **Scan to Connect!** Use your smart phone to scan this code to watch a video to activate your knowledge about vocabulary. (See the inside front cover for more information on how to use this.) This video of women in Nepal who have been helped by Heifer International discusses some of the cornerstones, or principles, that the organization adheres to. What are they?

Common Knowledge

disaster relief organizations (*paragraph 9*) Nonprofit, nongovernmental organizations devoted to providing humanitarian aid during times of crisis, such as famines and wars. Examples are the Red Cross and Doctors Without Borders.

Euro (*paragraph 29*) The official currency (money) of the eurozone, which includes 17 out of the 27 countries of Europe. The Euro is also used in five other countries, although it is not the official currency.

▶ Reading with Pen in Hand

Students who annotate as they read are more successful than those who do not. That's why you will annotate every selection in *Connect* as you read. In the reading that follows, use the following symbols:

★ or ⟨Point⟩   to indicate a main idea

① ② ③   to indicate major details

 Visit www.cengagebrain.com to access the CourseMate for this chapter to hear pronunciations of vocabulary words from this reading.

Bringing an End to World Hunger Through Unimaginable Blessings

1   Today, millions of people who were once hungry will be nourished by milk, eggs and fresh vegetables.

2   Families who for generations knew only poverty will be building new homes and starting businesses.

3   Children who once headed out to the fields to do backbreaking work will be heading into schoolrooms to learn to read.

4   And people who never thought they'd be in a position to help someone else will be experiencing the joy of **charitable** giving.

5   How is this possible?

6   With Heifer's proven approach—more than 65 years in the making—to helping people obtain a **sustainable** source of food and income.

Cornerstones guide our efforts to end world hunger and care for the earth.

Long-Term Solutions emphasizing community involvement **distinguish** our work from that of global relief organizations.

"Passing on the Gift" means **recipients** agree to share the offspring of gift animals with others in need, making them equal partners with Heifer in the fight to end world hunger.

How We Measure Success shows how people's lives have permanently changed since Heifer came along.

▶ Make mental movies of paragraphs 1 to 4.

charitable Use your logic to decide what *charitable* means.

sustainable Use word parts and your prior knowledge for this meaning.

▶ Why are the headings here underlined in blue?

distinguish Use your logic, and refer to the Common Knowledge box, to define this word.

recipients This word is based on the word *receive*. What does it mean?

The Foundation of the Heifer Model Is Our Cornerstones

▶ What do you expect to read as some of the cornerstones?

7   If you ask Heifer project partners, "What are the most fundamental principles upon which you build your life?" many would answer "Heifer's Cornerstones." Used for more than 65 years, these 12 Cornerstones guide communities to self-reliance.

8   Cornerstones stimulate group wisdom and personal insights, and they keep people's hearts, minds and actions balanced, focused and productive. Together, they form the acronym **PASSING ON THE GIFTS** and echo the practice that makes Heifer unique and its projects sustainable.

▶ Form a mental image of each cornerstone as you read.

Passing on the Gift allows families who received Heifer gifts to become donors as they pass on these gifts to other families in need.

mutually Look back at "Passing on the Gift" in paragraph 6 for an explanation.

Accountability means that we are **mutually** accountable to the communities we serve for how we achieve common goals.

Sharing & Caring embodies the belief that global problems can be solved if everyone commits to sharing resources and caring for others.

Sustainability & Self-reliance is the goal for families we work with so that they will continue to thrive after our support ends.

Improved Animal Management means that project participants learn how to keep their animals safe, healthy and productive.

consumption Look at the word parts to figure out this word's meaning.

Nutrition & Income are the rewards Heifer expects recipients to reap from their gift animal through the **consumption** and/or sale of products such as milk, eggs, cheese, honey and wool.

Genuine Need & Justice ensures that those most in need are given priority in receiving animals and training.

biogas Word parts will help you understand this word.

Improving the Environment through sustainable farming techniques, reforestation, and tree-saving **biogas** is at the core of our projects.

Full Participation is expected by all participants. Leaders at the grassroots level should involve all members in decision making.

Training & Education are key to ensuring that animals are well cared for and that self-reliance is achieved by project participants.

Spirituality is expressed in common beliefs about the value and meaning of all life, a sense of connectedness to the earth and a shared vision of the future.

Gender & Family Focus encourages women and men to share in decision making as well as in the benefits the animals and training bring.

Long-Term Solutions

9   Heifer applauds and supports the vital work of disaster relief organizations. However, in times of crisis, it's important to explain the distinction between their work and ours.

10   Ever since our founder, Dan West, came up with the phrase "not a cup, but a cow," Heifer's approach to providing global assistance to struggling countries has been characterized by long-term development, rather than short-term relief.

11   After immediate needs for food, shelter, fresh water, clothing and other necessities have been met, Heifer works within communities to empower disaster survivors with the economic means—such as livestock, training and other resources—to rebuild their families, their neighborhoods and their hope for sustainable futures.

12   **Here's how Heifer International works:**
A typical Heifer project consists of three essential components:
► Livestock and other material goods
► Training and extension work
► Organizational development, which includes planning, management, record keeping, passing on the gift, reporting and evaluation.

13   **And it all starts in a community.**
First, Heifer helps a community group analyze their situation. They ask: What do we need? What are our resources? What would we like to see happen in five years? Then, they plan specific activities to achieve their goals.

14   At this point, the Heifer "living loan" becomes reality. Farmers prepare for their animals by participating in training sessions, building sheds, and sometimes planting trees and grasses.

15   Then the livestock arrives—bringing with it the benefits of milk, wool, draft power, eggs and offspring to pass on to another farmer.

► What is the main difference discussed in paragraphs 9–11?

► What are the three components?

► What are the four steps discussed in paragraphs 13–16?

Heifer International

16   Finally, the group evaluates its progress, and the cycle repeats as the group moves to more and more ambitious goals, each time visioning, deciding, **implementing** and reflecting.

implementing Reread the previous three paragraphs and decide which word in this list describes each step. What does *implementing* mean?

▶ What is the basic method Heifer uses?

17   Every family and community that receives assistance promises to repay their living loan by donating one or more of their animal's offspring to another family in need. This practice of **"Passing on the Gift"** ensures project sustainability, develops community and enhances self-esteem by allowing project partners to become donors.

18   This is Heifer's **sustainable approach** to ending hunger and poverty—one family, one animal at a time. It's not temporary relief. It's not a handout. It's securing a future with generations of people who have hope, health and dignity.

Passing on the Gift

"Passing on the gift is fundamental to Heifer's whole approach."

▶ Describe what the author is doing in paragraphs 19–20, and then in paragraphs 21–24.

19   As people share the offspring of their animals—along with their knowledge, resources, and skills—an expanding network of hope, dignity and self-reliance is created that reaches around the globe. The women in the video mentioned on page 204 are participating in a **Passing on the Gift** ceremony in Nepal, a ceremony that demonstrates the community growth through Heifer's work.

20   "Passing on the Gift" creates a living cycle of sustainability that develops community and enhances self-esteem by allowing project partners to become donors.

21   In Rwanda, Christine Makahumure showed the true meaning of **passing on the gift.**

22   In 1994 genocidal war that raked Rwanda destroyed everything Christine had. She saw her son and husband shot to death when they were caught in a crossfire. When the fighting ended, Christine was barely able to feed her daughter and parents.

meager Based on the context, what does meager mean?

23   But then she received a Heifer cow. The milk supplemented the family's **meager** diet, and she was able to buy a small home with income from selling milk.

24   Christine gave her first calf to a neighbor—but she didn't stop there. She provided money so her neighbors could build and apply for their own Heifer cow. And she adopted four war orphans and became a living example of passing on the gift.

How We Measure Success: A Better Life in Kosovo

▶ Read paragraphs 25–30 to find out what Mevlude's life was like before and after Heifer provided her with a cow.

25   The road to Mevlude Bërbatovci's house, just outside of the village of Nakaradë-Fushë in Kosovo, was once a difficult and muddy path, but now it is stable with rocks and sand that Mevlude spread herself. This road describes Mevlude—a hard working woman full of ambition and energy, ready to overcome any obstacle.

26   The obstacles have been many as Mevlude has struggled to survive in war torn Kosovo. She lost four children shortly after childbirth and her adopted son, Besnik, is now the joy of her life.

27   Until she became involved with Heifer International, Mevlude was unable to afford her own animals. Now she has her own Holstein dairy cow that has already given birth to two calves, the first of which Mevlude passed on to another family last summer.

28   When Mevlude was asked how much her life had changed since she had received her cow from Heifer International, she said, "a hundred percent!" Her family now has more income and better nutrition than ever before. With this one animal they now have cheese, milk, cottage cheese, and yogurt on their table, adding much needed protein to their diet.

29   In addition to her Heifer, Mevlude also received a greenhouse through Heifer. Last year Mevlude cultivated peppers, tomatoes, and cucumbers and sold hundreds of Euros worth of produce. She plans to grow even more this summer and also hopes to add two more cows to her budding dairy herd.

30   Mevlude's story is that of a woman working hard to improve the life of her family. With the help of one animal and a greenhouse, her hard work is paying off toward a better future. Help other families like Mevlude's by buying a share of a Heifer today.

—Courtesy of Heifer International

▶ Comprehension Questions

Write the letter of the answer on the line. Then explain your thinking.

Main Idea

_____ 1. Which statement best expresses the main idea of the twelve cornerstones?

a. Heifer's cornerstones are the principles on which the organization operates in order to guide communities to self-reliance.

b. The cornerstones mean that the neediest families get help first.

c. The cornerstones allow recipients to become donors.

d. The cornerstones require recipients to make sacrifices.

Why? What information in the selection leads you to give that answer? _____

_____

_____

_____ 2. What is the best statement of the main idea of paragraph 12?

a. Here's how Heifer International works.

b. A typical Heifer project consists of three essential components.

c. Livestock and other material goods

d. Training and extension work

Why? What information in the selection leads you to give that answer? _____

_____

_____

Supporting Details

_____ 3. Which details support the main idea that Heifer helps communities find long-term solutions?

    a. milk, wool, draft power, eggs, offspring

    b. sharing and caring

    c. providing immediate relief in the form of food, shelter, and fresh water; planting trees and grasses for the community

    d. providing economic means to rebuild after disasters; supporting gifts with training; involving communities in all the planning for their future

Why? What information in the selection leads you to give that answer? _____

_____

_____

_____ 4. Which detail most directly supports this main idea? *In Rwanda, Christine Makahumure showed the true meaning of* **passing on the gift.**

    a. In 1994 genocidal war that raked Rwanda destroyed everything Christine had.

    b. When the fighting ended, Christine was barely able to feed her daughter and parents.

    c. The milk supplemented the family's meager diet, and she was able to buy a small house with income from selling milk.

    d. She provided money so her neighbors could build and apply for their own Heifer cow.

Why? What information in the selection leads you to give that answer? _____

_____

_____

Author's Purpose

_____ 5. What is the overall purpose of this website?

    a. to inform readers of the horrible effects of war

    b. to persuade readers that poor people around the work deserve our help

    c. to persuade readers to send money to Heifer to support their work

    d. to provide information about Heifer so that more people will want to work for them

Why? What information in the selection leads you to give that answer? _____

_____

_____

_____ 6. What purpose(s) do paragraphs 1–6 serve?

   a. to depress readers by explaining the difficulty of the task Heifer is engaged in

   b. to inspire readers and to establish the success of the Heifer program

   c. to show that sometimes, people just need a little help to get back on their feet again

   d. they are a general introduction to the topic

Why? What information in the selection leads you to give that answer? _____

_____

_____

Relationships

_____ 7. What is the general organizational pattern of paragraphs 13–16?

   a. space order

   b. definition

   c. process

   d. effect

Why? What information in the selection leads you to give that answer? _____

_____

_____

_____ 8. What is the main pattern of organization in paragraph 12?

   a. definition

   b. classification

   c. cause

   d. process

Why? What information in the selection leads you to give that answer? _____

_____

_____

Fact, Opinion, and Inference

_____ 9. Choose the statement that is an opinion.

   a. Cornerstones stimulate group wisdom and personal insights, and they keep people's hearts, minds and actions balanced, focused and productive.

   b. Passing on the Gift allows families who received Heifer gifts to become donors as they pass on these gifts to other families in need.

c. Accountability means that we are mutually accountable to the communities we serve for how we achieve common goals.

d. Sustainability and Self-reliance is the goal for families we work with so that they will continue to thrive after our support ends.

Why? What information in the selection leads you to give that answer? _____

_____

_____

_____ 10. Which idea would this organization most likely agree with?

a. We need to lay down the law.

b. Give a man a fish and you feed him for a day. Teach him how to fish and you feed him for a lifetime.

c. You are what you eat.

d. Neither a borrower nor a lender be.

Why? What information in the selection leads you to give that answer? _____

_____

_____

▶ Critical Thinking Questions

Critical Thinking Level 1 ▶ **Remember**

Identify two people whom Heifer International has helped, and name the country each one is from.

_____

_____

Critical Thinking Level 2 ▶ **Understand**

Match each heading from the website with the information that goes with it by putting the letter of the information next to the heading.

Website Heading	Information
_____ 1. The Foundation of the Heifer Model Is Our Cornerstones	A. an example of a woman helping war orphans, and an example of community growth in Nepal
_____ 2. Long-Term Solutions	B. an example of a woman who keeps expanding her family's farm through hard work
_____ 3. Passing on the Gift	C. fundamental principles of this organization
_____ 4. How We Measure Success	D. process and categories of help that Heifer gives

Critical Thinking Level 3 ▸ Apply

Heifer makes the point that they create long-term, not short-term, solutions. Think of a problem that someone you know is having. If he or she were to put the solution in terms of a longer period of time, what new methods could be *applied* to solve the problem?

_____

_____

_____

Critical Thinking Level 4 ▸ Analyze

With books, we tend to read from beginning to end. But when visiting a website, we can read the web pages in any order. There are other differences in these reading situations, too. Reflect on your experiences. Then *analyze* which features in "Bringing an End to World Hunger Through Unimaginable Blessings" would be handled differently if they were in a book instead of online.

_____

_____

_____

_____

_____

_____

Critical Thinking Level 5 ▸ Evaluate

Evaluate this idea: People should be responsible for their own success. Rate the following aspects of the idea and then write a sentence or two about your ratings. For example, how difficult or easy is it for people to be responsible for their own success?

Difficult	1	2	3	4	5	Easy
Unrealistic	1	2	3	4	5	Realistic
Not important	1	2	3	4	5	Important
I don't achieve this.	1	2	3	4	5	I do achieve this.

_____

_____

_____

Critical Thinking Level 6 ⟩ **Create**

Imagine a world where no one is ever hungry, cold, or homeless. Think about your daily life. What would you see, hear, and feel?

_____

_____

_____

▶ Vocabulary in New Contexts

Review the vocabulary words in the margins of the reading selection and then complete the following activities.

EASY Note Cards

Make a note card for each of the vocabulary words that you did not know in the reading. On one side, write the word. On the other side, divide the card into quarters and label them E, A, S, and Y. Add a word or phrase in each area so that you wind up with an example sentence, an antonym, a synonym, and, finally, a definition that shows you have figured out the meaning of the word with your logic. Remember that an antonym or synonym may have appeared in the reading.

Relationships Between Words

Circle *yes* or *no* to answer the question. Then explain your answer.

1. If you were to **implement** more **charitable** activities and decrease your **consumption**, would you be considered a kinder person?

   Yes   No

   Why or why not? _____

2. Do football coaches tend to **distinguish** between athletes who are **recipients** of Olympic gold medals and athletes who have more **meager** talents?

   Yes   No

   Why or why not? _____

3. Is a love affair better when both people in it are **mutual recipients** of the other's affections?

   Yes   No

   Why or why not? _____

4. Is a **sustainable** future for our planet dependent only on **biogas**?

   Yes   No

   Why or why not? _____

Language in Your Life

Write short answers to each question. Look at the vocabulary words closely before you answer.

1. Name one area of your life in which you want to increase (or decrease) **consumption**.

_____

2. Name one organization in your area that is **charitable**. _____

_____

3. Name one person with whom you have a **mutually** beneficial relationship. _____

_____

4. Name one person who has been a **recipient** of your love. _____

_____

5. Name one way you can **distinguish** friend from foe. _____

_____

Language in Use

Select the best word to complete the meaning of each sentence.

biogas	charitable	consumption	distinguished	implement
meager	mutually	recipient	sustainable	

1. Aside from a few superrich people like Bill Gates, richer Americans are less _____ than poor Americans.

2. A study conducted in 2001 _____ the donations of two groups. Americans whose incomes were more than $75,000 a year gave away, on average, 2.7% of their incomes. Americans with incomes less than $25,000 gave away 4.2% of theirs.

3. And when researchers in 2007 looked at how wealthier people _____ their charitable plans, they found they tended to give not to poor people, but to organizations they have connections with, such as the colleges they attended or the ballet or theater they go to.

4. A 2010 study found that lower-income people were more generous to and trusting of the _____ of charity, while upper-income people had _____ empathy for them.

5. Upper-income people may not be as generous because they can't imagine needing to be _____ supportive (since they have what they need already).

6. In the 2010 study, higher-income people's lack of interest in giving was not _____ once they were instructed to imagine being poor themselves.

Reading 4–2 | American Government Textbook

▶ Pre-Reading the Selection

Despite the American dream of liberty and justice for all, it took concerted efforts by many people to extend voting and other rights to African Americans. In the reading that begins on page 217, you will learn about how many people's actions, including Martin Luther King, Jr.'s, impacted the fight for equal rights in America.

Surveying the Reading

Survey the article that follows. Then check the elements that are included in this reading.

_____	Title		_____	Words in bold or italic type
_____	Headings		_____	Images and captions
_____	First sentences of paragraphs			

Guessing the Purpose

Judging from the title of the reading as well as the title of the book from which this selection is taken, _American Government and Politics Today_, what do you suppose the purpose for writing is? _____

_____

Predicting the Content

Predict three things this selection will discuss.

▶ _____

▶ _____

▶ _____

Activating Your Knowledge

What do you already know about the civil rights movement, Martin Luther King, Jr., sit-ins, and other related topics? Note two or three things you know.

▶ _____

▶ _____

▶ _____

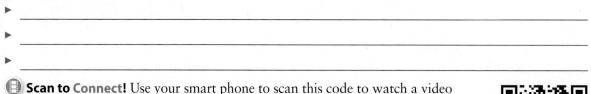

 Scan to Connect! Use your smart phone to scan this code to watch a video to activate your knowledge about the civil rights movement. (See the inside front cover for more information on how to use this.) In the video, you will learn some of the details of this period of recent history by seeing Charles Moore's photographs and by listening to his words as an eyewitness. Write a topic sentence and make a short visual outline of the key details you see.

Common Knowledge

Freedom Rides (*paragraph 3*) African American and white volunteers, many of them college students, rode public buses into segregated Southern states to test a 1960 United States Supreme Court decision outlawing racial segregation in interstate transportation facilities like bus and train stations.

Jim Crow laws (*paragraph 5*) Laws that mandated "separate but equal" status for African Americans in Southern states between 1876 and 1965. The laws allowed for inferior treatment of African Americans by segregating them from whites in many public places like restaurants, stores, schools, and public restrooms.

The Civil Rights Act of 1964 (*paragraph 5*) A bill prohibiting discrimination based on race and color in public places, schools, and government, among other things.

▶ Reading with Pen in Hand

Students who annotate as they read are more successful than those who do not. That's why you will annotate every selection in *Connect* as you read. In the reading that follows, use the following symbols:

    ★ or Ⓟⓞⓘⓝⓣ   to indicate a main idea

    ① ② ③   to indicate major details

 Visit www.cengagebrain.com to access the CourseMate for this chapter to hear pronunciations of vocabulary words from this reading.

The Civil Rights Movement

Steffen W. Schmidt, Mack C. Shelley II, and Barbara A. Bardes

1   In December 1955, a forty-three-year-old African American woman, Rosa Parks, boarded a public bus in Montgomery, Alabama. When the bus became crowded and several white people stepped aboard, Parks was asked to move to the rear of the bus (the "colored" section). She refused, was arrested, and was fined $10, but that "was not the end of the matter." For an entire year, African Americans **boycotted** the Montgomery bus line. The protest was headed by a twenty-seven-year-old Baptist minister, Dr. Martin Luther King, Jr. During the protest period, he went to jail, and his house was bombed. In the face of overwhelming odds, King won. In 1956, a federal district court issued an injunction prohibiting the segregation of buses in Montgomery. The era of civil rights protests had begun.

▶ What started the civil rights movement?

boycotted Think about how African Americans might have protested the treatment of Rosa Parks. Then guess at the meaning of this word, or use your dictionary.

King's Philosophy of Nonviolence

2   The following year, in 1957, King formed the Southern Christian Leadership Conference (SCLC). King **advocated** nonviolent civil disobedience as a means

advocated Reread the heading above this paragraph. What does it suggest is the meaning of *advocated*?

to achieve racial justice. King's philosophy of civil disobedience was influenced, in part, by the life and teachings of Mahatma Gandhi (1869–1948). Gandhi had led resistance to the British colonial system in India from 1919 to 1947. He used **tactics** such as demonstrations and marches, as well as nonviolent, public disobedience to unjust laws. King's followers successfully used these methods to gain wider public acceptance of their cause.

tactics Three examples of tactics are given in this sentence, and the next sentence includes a synonym. What are tactics?

Nonviolent Demonstrations

▶ What are some examples of King's use of nonviolence?

3   For the next decade, African Americans and sympathetic whites engaged in sit-ins, freedom rides, and freedom marches. In the beginning, such demonstrations were often met with violence, and the contrasting image of nonviolent African Americans and violent, hostile whites created strong public support for the civil rights movement. When African Americans in Greensboro, North Carolina, were refused service at a Woolworth's lunch counter, they organized a sit-in that was aided day after day by sympathetic whites and other African Americans. **Enraged** customers threw ketchup on the protesters. Some spat in their faces. The sit-in movement continued to grow, however. Within six months of the first sit-in at the Greensboro Woolworth's, hundreds of lunch counters throughout the South were serving African Americans.

▶ What did the Woolworth's sit-in achieve?

enraged Use your logic. How do people probably feel if they throw ketchup at and spit on others?

▶ What else did the sit-ins achieve?

4   The sit-in technique also was successfully used to integrate interstate buses and their terminals, as well as railroads engaged in interstate transportation.

Dr. Martin Luther King, Jr. acknowledges the crowd of nearly a quarter-million African Americans and whites at the August 1963 March on Washington for Jobs and Freedom, for which King is best remembered for his "I Have a Dream" speech.

Bettmann/CORBIS

Although buses and railroads engaged in interstate transportation were pro-hibited by law from segregating African Americans from whites, they stopped doing so only after the sit-in protests.

Marches and Demonstrations

5   One of the most famous of the violence-plagued protests occurred in Birmingham, Alabama, in 1963, when Police Commissioner Eugene "Bull" Connor unleashed police dogs and used electric cattle prods against the protesters. People throughout the country viewed the event on television with **indignation** and horror. King himself was thrown in jail. The media coverage of the Birmingham protest and the violent response by the city government played a key role in the process of ending Jim Crow in the United States. The ultimate result was the most important civil rights act in the nation's history, the Civil Rights Act of 1964.

6   In August 1963, African American leaders A. Philip Randolph and Bayard Rustin organized a massive March on Washington for Jobs and Freedom. Before nearly a quarter-million white and African American spectators and millions watching on television, King told the world his dream: "I have a dream that my four little children will one day live in a nation where they will not be judged by the color of their skin but by the content of their character."

—From Schmidt, *American Government and Politics Today, 2007–2008*, 13e

▶ What effect on Americans did the media coverage of the violence used on the protesters have?

indignation Use your logic to consider how people felt when they saw others being poked with electric cattle prods. What does *indignation* mean?

▶ What was Martin Luther King, Jr.'s dream?

▶ Comprehension Questions

Write the letter of the answer on the line. Then explain your thinking.

Main Idea

_____ 1. Which of these sentences from paragraph 3 is the statement of its main idea?

   a. For the next decade, African Americans and sympathetic whites engaged in sit-ins, freedom rides, and freedom marches.

   b. In the beginning, such demonstrations were often met with violence, and the con-trasting image of nonviolent African Americans and violent, hostile whites created strong public support for the civil rights movement.

   c. When African Americans in Greensboro, North Carolina, were refused service at a Woolworth's lunch counter, they organized a sit-in that was aided day after day by sympathetic whites and other African Americans.

   d. Enraged customers threw ketchup on the protesters.

Why? What information in the selection leads you to give that answer? _____

_____

_____

____   2. What is the main idea of paragraph 2?

    a. King advocated nonviolent civil disobedience as a means to achieve racial justice.

    b. King's philosophy of civil disobedience was influenced, in part, by the life and teachings of Mahatma Gandhi (1869–1948).

    c. Gandhi used tactics such as demonstrations and marches, as well as nonviolent, public disobedience to unjust laws.

    d. King's followers successfully used these methods to gain wider public acceptance of their cause.

Why? What information in the selection leads you to give that answer? _____

_____

Supporting Details

____   3. According to the passage, what was the most important achievement of the civil rights movement?

    a. Rosa Parks' boycott of the Montgomery bus line

    b. the formation of the Southern Christian Leadership Conference (SCLC)

    c. the March on Washington for Jobs and Freedom

    d. the Civil Rights Act of 1964

Why? What information in the selection leads you to give that answer? _____

_____

____   4. Based on the reading, which of the following was *not* a response to the Woolworth's sit-in participants in Greensboro?

    a. The customers were enraged.

    b. The customers threw ketchup on the protesters.

    c. The protesters were fined $10.

    d. Some customers spat in the protesters' faces.

Why? What information in the selection leads you to give that answer? _____

_____

Author's Purpose

____   5. What is the overall purpose of this passage?

    a. to inform the reader of a timeline of the civil rights movement

    b. to entertain readers with stories of Martin Luther King, Jr., sit-ins, and Jim Crow

    c. to persuade readers that not enough has been done for equality

    d. to evaluate the validity of the causes of the civil rights movement

Why? What information in the selection leads you to give that answer? _____

_____

____ 6. Why did the author mention Gandhi in paragraph 2?

   a. to inform readers that Gandhi led resistance to the British colonial system in India from 1919 to 1947

   b. to explain how King's philosophy of civil disobedience was influenced, in part, by the life and teachings of Mahatma Gandhi

   c. to persuade readers that the use of nonviolence is the most convenient and successful way to lead a social revolution

   d. to entertain readers with amusing anecdotes from the civil rights movement era

Why? What information in the selection leads you to give that answer? _____

_____

_____

Relationships

____ 7. What is the overall pattern of organization of this passage?

   a. narration in time order

   b. definition

   c. comparison and contrast

   d. cause-and-effect

Why? What information in the selection leads you to give that answer? _____

_____

_____

____ 8. What is the relationship between the two main parts of the following sentence? *When African Americans in Greensboro, North Carolina, were refused service at a Woolworth's lunch counter, they organized a sit-in that was aided day after day by sympathetic whites and other African Americans.*

   a. classification

   b. comparison and contrast

   c. cause-and-effect

   d. definition

Why? What leads you to give that answer? _____

_____

Fact, Opinion, and Inference

_____ 9. Which of the following statements is an opinion?

   a. Within six months of the first sit-in at the Greensboro Woolworth's, hundreds of lunch counters throughout the South were serving African Americans.

   b. "I have a dream that my four little children will one day live in a nation where they will not be judged by the color of their skin but by the content of their character."

   c. King's followers successfully used these methods to gain wider public acceptance of their cause.

   d. For an entire year, African Americans boycotted the Montgomery bus line.

Why? What information in the selection leads you to give that answer? _____

_____

_____ 10. What does the following sentence imply (suggest) about Gandhi? _King's philosophy of civil disobedience was influenced, in part, by the life and teachings of Mahatma Gandhi (1869–1948)._

   a. Gandhi had not been successful in his civil disobedience efforts.

   b. Gandhi had been successful in his civil disobedience efforts.

   c. Gandhi was an African American pioneer who inspired King.

   d. Gandhi and King were friends, who though they had never met, corresponded with each other frequently.

Why? What information in the selection leads you to give that answer? _____

_____

_____

_____

▶ Critical Thinking Questions

Critical Thinking Level 1 ▶ **Remember**

Review the annotations you made on the "The Civil Rights Movement," and jot down a few things you learned that you found interesting.

_____

_____

_____

Critical Thinking Level 2 ▷ Understand

Fill in the topic sentence in the "top to bottom" concept map for paragraph 5.

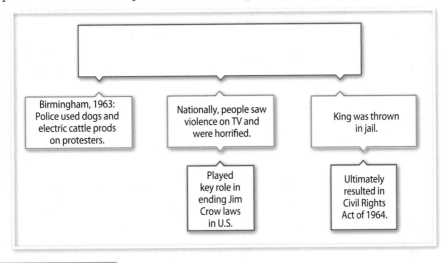

Critical Thinking Level 3 ▷ Apply

Suppose that the food choices at your school are awful. You have complained, but no one seems to be listening. Following Martin Luther King, Jr.'s lead, what are some steps you could take to change the quality of the food at your school? *Develop a plan of action* with a partner or small group in your class.

_____

_____

_____

Critical Thinking Level 4 ▷ Analyze

What *connections* can you make between Gandhi (from the reading excerpt on page 174) and King (from Reading 4–2)? How are they similar?

Gandhi   **King**

_____   _____

_____   _____

_____   _____

What differences can you list about the two men and their situations? Stay away from the obvious distinctions like, "One was in India and one was in the United States."

Gandhi   **King**

_____   _____

_____   _____

_____   _____

Critical Thinking Level 5 ▶ Evaluate

Not all African Americans agreed with Martin Luther King, Jr.'s philosophy of nonviolence. For example, in the early 1960s, Malcolm X urged African Americans to "fight back" against white supremacy. Some people have argued that such a militant approach is always counterproductive. Others believe that a militant alternative may have made King's peaceful approach more attractive. *Evaluate* these statements. Does one make more sense to you than the other? Why or why not?

_____
_____
_____

Critical Thinking Level 6 ▶ Create

One of the best-known songs from the civil rights movement is "We Shall Overcome." What can you tell about the topic of the song based on its title? Use your prior knowledge to expand your prediction. What do you think this song is about? Give some specific predictions.

_____
_____
_____

▶Vocabulary in New Contexts

Review the vocabulary words in the margins of the reading selection and then complete the following activities.

EASY Note Cards

Make a note card for each of the vocabulary words that you did not know in the reading. On one side, write the word. On the other side, divide the card into quarters and label them E, A, S, and Y. Add a word or phrase in each area so that you wind up with an example sentence, an antonym, a synonym, and, finally, a definition that shows you have figured out the meaning of the word with your logic. Remember that an antonym or synonym may have appeared in the reading.

Relationships Between Words

Circle *yes* or *no* to answer the question. Then explain your answer.

1. Is **boycotting** a company's products a good way to express your **indignation** over their unfair treatment of workers?

Yes　No

Why or why not? _____

2. When someone is **enraged**, do they sometimes use **tactics** they later regret?

   Yes   No

   Why or why not? _____

3. If you **advocated** violence, is it likely your **tactics** would backfire on you?

   Yes   No

   Why or why not? _____

Language in Your Life

Write short answers to each question. Look at the vocabulary words closely before you answer.

1. Name one kind of behavior that you like to **advocate**. _____

   _____

2. Name a **tactic** that someone has used to get you to do what he or she wants. _____

   _____

3. Name one time you felt **indignant**. _____

   _____

4. Name a piece of news that **enraged** you. _____

   _____

5. Name one product you would like to **boycott**. _____

   _____

Language in Use

Select the best word to complete the meaning of each sentence.

advocate	boycott	enraged	indignation	tactics

1. In the debate over abortion, some people _____ for the rights of an unborn child over the rights of the mother; others believe it is a woman's right to choose what to do with her body.

2. People on both sides of this debate become easily _____, probably because their deepest beliefs are at stake.

3. In a sense, each side's _____ is a sign of their sincerity.

4. Those opposed to abortion naturally _____ abortion clinics.

5. But the scare _____ used by extremists do not make it any easier for the two groups to understand each others' positions.

 Click to Connect! For more practice applying the skills you learned in this chapter, visit **www.cengagebrain.com** to access the CourseMate for this chapter.

Click to Connect! Visit **www.cengagebrain.com** to access study resources for this chapter through CourseMate, which includes audio, video, quizzes, and a searchable, interactive eBook version of the text.

5

Identifying
Implied Main Ideas

Connect with Ideas

Explain in your own words what idea or principle this saying implies (suggests without saying). Do you think this advice is good? Why or why not?

Activate Your Knowledge

Share one of your favorite memories—something you would have written on a piece of marble—with the class or a classmate. Also, if you want to, share a memory that you have written in sand—that is, if you can remember it!

Engage with the Chapter

Scan through the pages until you find the heading "What Is an Implied Main Idea?" Read to see what the difference between a main idea and an implied main idea is. If you already know, read to confirm your prior knowledge.

Read and Talk

Culinary
Textbook

What you eat depends on your culture: where you live and the beliefs you grew up with. What habits of mind do you have when it comes to food?

Visit www.cengagebrain.com to access the CourseMate for this chapter to hear vocabulary words from this reading and an audio recording of it.

What Is a Food? What's in a Meal?

constitutes Context here and in paragraph 2 will help you decide what this means.

1   The definition of what is a "food," what **constitutes** a "meal," and how meals can and should be sequenced are all part of the basic assumptions about foods that are culturally influenced and, in turn, influence diet. Dog is food in one culture and decidedly not food in another. In much of Asia, the **mucilaginous** excretion of a cow's udder is not considered appropriate food for humans. As anthropologist Marvin Harris points out, "The Chinese and other Eastern and Southeastern Asian peoples do not merely have an aversion to the use of milk, they **loathe** it intensely, reacting to the prospect of gulping down a nice, cold glass of the stuff much as Westerners might react to the prospect of a nice, cold glass of cow saliva." Aversion to milk may be, in part, the result of low lactase levels in adults in food systems that have not included dairying as a key component. Similarly, North Americans tend to **eschew** insects as food. In Mexico and Thailand, among other places, they are delicacies. No cultural group defines as "food" every edible item in their environment. And some foods seen as appropriate for adults may not be considered appropriate for children.

mucilaginous Look for word parts and guess at this meaning.

loathe A synonym is given earlier, and an example follows.

eschew Use your prior knowledge here.

2   We also have rules about what collection of edible items is considered a "meal." A hamburger, fries, and a drink may constitute a meal to North Americans. However, Japanese eating in McDonald's restaurants do not consider this a meal. Without rice, the eating event that includes the burger is a snack, not a proper meal. In Korea, however, this is not a problem. Koreans consider an eating event at McDonald's to be a meal and will even take guests to McDonald's restaurants as special treats. Think about what constitutes a meal for you. What elements must an eating event have to be defined as a meal? What constitutes a snack? What things go together? Does corned beef *need* cabbage?

3   Finally, the number and content of meals in a daily, weekly, or yearly cycle is also something that tends to follow cultural rules. When we carry out a statistical analysis of American food consumption, we find that the consumption of bacon **correlates** highly with the consumption of eggs. Bacon and eggs go together and are generally eaten early in the day. Some North Americans may like cold pizza for breakfast, but they find the Japanese custom of soup for the first meal of the day to be rather strange. The pattern of three meals per day with the largest family meal in the evening is a product of the industrial revolution and the extended school day. Farm families used to consume the largest meal at midday to help the workers sustain themselves through a long

correlates Use your prior knowledge to figure this out.

working day. "Supper" was a light meal at the end of the working day. Many cultures define two meals per day as ideal; others may have four or more.

4   Many plastic and paper plates come with three distinct compart-ments, a more-than-symbolic representation of the "ideal" American meal of meat, starch, and vegetable. It is so central to our assumptions about what constitutes a meal that we construct plates to accommodate it. Meal cycles are also part of our basic assumption about food. For many North Americans, Sunday dinner is the central meal of the week. Special foods are served at this meal. In the Italian-American community, studies by Goode et al. found that Sunday dinner included more of the ideal ele-ments of a meal than any other meal during the week. It was generally based around a "gravy" dish that combined a tomato-based sauce with pasta. Meals during the rest of the week were much less elaborate.

—From Bryant/DeWalt/Courtney/Schultz, *The Cultural Feast: An Introduction to Food and Society*, 2e (pp. 222–223). Copyright © 2004 Cengage Learning, Inc. Reproduced by permission. www.cengage.com/permissions

Talking about Reading

Respond in writing to the questions below and then discuss your answers with your classmates.

1. Is drinking milk part of your cultural heritage? What attitudes have you heard your family and friends express about drinking milk? _____

_____

_____

2. What are some edible things in your environment that you and others from your culture do not eat? Why do you choose not to eat these things?_____

_____

_____

3. Is there a meal in the week that is most important to your family? What is it? What foods are usually served? _____

_____

_____

4. Look at what the authors say in paragraph 3 about the reasons Americans started eating their largest meal at the end of the day. What characteristic(s) of Americans might help explain that Sunday dinner is their central meal of the week (paragraph 4)? _____

_____

_____

5.  **Scan to Connect!** Use your smart phone to scan this code to watch a video. (See the inside front cover for more information on how to use this.) As you watch the video, think about the connections between the foods and their cultural significance.

What Is an Implied Main Idea?

Many paragraphs and longer passages have a stated main idea; the author tells readers directly what the point is. This is especially true in certain genres, or kinds, of writing. For example, in college textbooks, the main idea is usually stated. However, even in textbooks authors don't always state the point, but rather leave it for the reader to infer.

An implied main idea is not stated directly; rather, it is suggested. To suggest the main idea, the author carefully selects which details to share. Readers then infer the main idea from the details. In a sense, it becomes your job to create a topic sentence. Another way to say this is that you summarize the details of the passage in one sentence in order to draw a conclusion about the author's meaning.

Cartoons are a good beginning point for figuring out implied main ideas since cartoonists rarely state their ideas directly. Instead, they expect viewers to look at the details and supply the main idea themselves. The following cartoon is from the Cornell University Food and Brand Lab.

▶ First, ask "Who or what is this about?" Since you have a title, turn it into a question.
▶ Next, what details do you notice? Look at each detail individually.
▶ Then, ask, "What do these details have in common?" See what generalization you can draw using each detail.
▶ What is the implied main idea of the cartoon?

Illustration by Brian Wansink, Ph.D., author of "Mindless Eating: Why We Eat More than We Think (Bantam, 2006). Used by permission of Dr. Brian Wansink.

Sample Analysis

The title at the bottom, "Beware of Big Buckets," seems prominent. A great place to start is by turning the title into a question: "Why beware of big buckets?" One important detail of the cartoon is the words the two men are exchanging. The first man asks, "Aren't you through yet?" Notice that the second man does not respond by saying, "I'm still hungry." He says instead that the popcorn isn't gone yet. What does that imply about why he is eating?

The relative size of the men's buckets seems to be another important detail. The implied main idea of the cartoon would be something like "When popcorn comes in a bigger bucket, people will eat more of it." Or "Larger servings make people eat more."

Interaction 5–1 ▶ Identify the Implied Main Idea of Cartoons

Notice the important details of the following cartoons. What is the implied main idea?

1. Cartoon by Roz Chast (*The New Yorker*)

Roz Chast/New Yorker Cartoon/Cartoonbank

Is there a title? If so, turn it into a question. _____

Important details: _____

_____

_____

Implied main idea: _____

_____

2. Cartoon by Daryl Cagle (caglepost.com)

Daryl Cagle/Cagle Cartoons

There is no title. So just focus on the details.

Important details: _____

_____

Implied main idea: _____

_____

Making Generalizations

When you start with details and then make an umbrella statement about them, you are making a generalization. Working with the cartoon "Beware of Big Buckets," we stated that the implied main idea was about "people" eating more food. This was a generalization because there is only one person in the cartoon who is eating more.

When it comes to the reading you're doing in college, you'll need to be careful about the size of the generalization you infer from the details. In fact, two typical problems that may arise when you try to formulate an implied main idea are that you will make a statement that is too broad for the details shared by the author or one that is too narrow. The generalization you make needs to be the right size. It should fit the details as closely as possible.

Interaction 5–2 ▶ Generalize from Details

On the line, write a generalization about each set of details by naming the smallest category into which all the details fit.

1. keyboard, mouse, CPU, monitor _____

2. *Keeping up with the Kardashians*, *The Voice*, *Jersey Shore* _____

3. Netflix, Apple, Redbox _____

4. Huron, Ontario, Michigan, Erie, Superior _____

5. Ghana, Nigeria, Cameroon, Guinea _____

6. Gisele Bundchen, Heidi Klum, Tyra Banks _____

7. tongue, eyes, nose, chin, cheeks _____

8. Stephen King, John Grisham, Suzanne Collins, Stephanie Meyer _____

9. Porsche Spyder, BMW M5, Mercedes-Benz McLaren, Audi R8 _____

10. *The Sorcerer's Stone*, *The Chamber of Secrets*, *The Prisoner of Azkaban* _____

You can double-check if your generalization is right by turning it into a question. For example, here is the question for number 4, "What are the Great Lakes?" The details answer the question, so we know we are right. Let's move on to a group of sentences to see if you can find the perfect generalized statement or topic sentence.

> **Interaction 5–3** ▶ Decide Whether a Topic Sentence Covers the Right Amount of Information

For each set of details, choose the topic sentence that covers the right amount of information by circling **C** for "correct". For each other possible topic sentence, circle **B** for statements that are too broad, and circle **N** for statements that are too narrow. For sentences that are too broad or too narrow, underline the part of the sentence that makes them unworkable.

1. ▶ Roman Catholic Christians go to Rome and Lourdes.
   ▶ Jewish pilgrims go to Jerusalem.
   ▶ Muslims travel to Mecca.
   ▶ Such places have religious significance.
   ▶ They might be the birthplace of a prophet, the final resting place of a saint, or the site of a miracle.

   A. People from various religions make pilgrimages to different holy places.

       C   B   N

   B. Religious fanatics make pilgrimages to different holy places.

       C   B   N

   C. The world seems to be traveling to the places members of its religions consider holy.

       C   B   N

2. ▶ Some people use the Internet to find a particular fact for a specific reason.
   ▶ Others perform transactions, such as buying, selling, or trading.
   ▶ Some users spend their time online talking with others at social networking sites.
   ▶ And at times, people go online in order to learn something new.

   A. People use the Internet to gather information.

       C   B   N

   B. There is nothing a person can do in real life that he or she can't also do online.

       C   B   N

   C. Some of the things people used to get done by talking with others in person can now be accomplished online.

       C   B   N

3. ▶ Plant-based foods contain more than 100,000 nutrients that can help prevent disease.
   ▶ The consumption of red meat increases the risk of heart disease and cancer.
   ▶ Plants are low in disease-promoting ingredients like saturated fat, cholesterol, and sugar.
   ▶ Our bodies gain more benefits from the vitamins and minerals when we directly eat plant-based foods rather than simply taking a supplement.
   ▶ Plant-based foods are a more efficient source of protein for our bodies than red meat and animal products such as milk or eggs.

   A. Meat increases the risk of heart disease.

       C   B   N

B. A diet eliminating red meats and consisting of plant-based foods has several benefits.

    C   B   N

C. The consumption of plants can prevent all disease.

    C   B   N

4. ▸ When pain messages are sent from damaged tissue through the nervous system, they pass through several "gates," starting in the spinal cord, before they get to the brain.
   ▸ But these messages travel only if the brain gives them "permission," after determining they are important enough to be let through.
   ▸ If permission is granted, a gate will open and increase the feeling of pain by allowing certain neurons to turn on and transmit their signals.
   ▸ The brain can also close a gate and block the pain signal by releasing endorphins, the narcotics made by the brain to quell pain.   —Doigne, *The Brain That Changes Itself*

A. The nervous system controls the passage of pain and pleasure to the brain through a series of "gates."

    C   B   N

B. When a person experiences tissue damage to their hands or feet, they only feel pain if the brain decides the damage is extensive enough.

    C   B   N

C. The "gate control theory of pain" proposed a series of controls, or "gates," between the site of injury and the brain.

    C   B   N

5. ▸ If a person drinks quickly, the alcohol will have a more significant effect on him or her than if the same amount was taken in over a longer period of time.
   ▸ How much a person drinks matters as well.
   ▸ Food in the stomach slows the rate at which alcohol is absorbed, and so decreases the effects of the alcohol.
   ▸ The more the drinker weighs, the less the same amount of alcohol will affect him or her.

A. The amount of alcohol, the timing of drinks, as well as the condition of the drinker, help determine how alcohol will affect the drinker.

    C   B   N

B. The way a person drinks determines how drunk he or she will get.

    C   B   N

C. A wide array of factors determines how alcohol will affect a drinker.

    C   B   N

When you are trying to decide what main idea the author is implying, be sure to consider whether your idea is too broad or too narrow by checking it against each detail. If you find that you have made either mistake, decide which part of the sentence is the problem and make that part more general or more specific, as needed. Adjust it until it fits the details.

Identifying the Implied Main Idea

Recall from Chapter 4 that there are three levels of ideas and questions you can ask to help you organize and understand what you are reading (see **Figure 5.1**).

Figure 5.1   Three Comprehension Questions

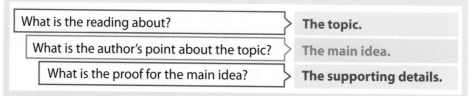

Following is a group of sentences that includes only the supporting details of a paragraph from a business management textbook. In other words, there is no topic sentence. Read the details and see if you can figure out the following information.

▶ The topic: What is the paragraph about? To figure out what the topic is, look for repeated ideas.
▶ The main idea: What is the author's point about the topic? To determine the author's main idea, a helpful question to ask yourself is: **What do all these details have in common?** Answering this question should help you make a generalized main idea.

To create a topic sentence, remember that T + MI = TS. That is, put the topic and the main idea together in one sentence to create a topic sentence.

Topic: _____

    Main Idea: _____

       Supporting Details:

       1. Background questions: Interviewers ask applicants about their work experience and education.

       2. Job-knowledge questions: Interviewers ask applicants to demonstrate job knowledge.

3. Situational questions: Interviewers ask applicants how they would respond in a hypothetical situation.

4. Behavioral questions: Interviewers ask applicants what they did in previous jobs that were similar to the job for which they are applying.

—From Williams, *Management*, 4e

Combine the topic and the main idea. (Remember that T + MI = TS.) What would a good topic sentence be?

_____

_____

Now turn your topic sentence into a question to double-check if the details support it.

Interaction 5–4 ▸ **Identify Implied Main Ideas from Lists of Details**

Read each set of supporting details. Then put the topic and main idea into the outline. Finally, write a topic sentence for the details.

1. Topic: _____

Main Idea: _____

Supporting Details:

1. In the United States, we show our agreement by nodding.

2. In Ethiopia, the same message is sent by throwing the head back.

3. The Semang of Malaya sharply thrust the head forward.

4. The Dyaks of Borneo raise the eyebrows.

—From Ferraro, *Cultural Anthropology*, 6e

Topic sentence: _____

Double-check by turning your TS into a question.

2. Topic: _____

Main Idea: _____

Supporting Details:

1. Spending for health care is estimated to account for about 15 percent of the total U.S. economy.

2. In 1965, about 6 percent of our income was spent on health care.

3. That percentage has been increasing ever since.

4. Measured by the percentage of the gross domestic product devoted to health care, America spends almost twice as much as Australia or Canada.

—From Schmidt/Shelley/Bardes, *American Government and Politics Today 2007–2008*, 13e

Topic sentence: _____

Double-check by turning your TS into a question.

3. Topic: _____

   Main Idea: _____

     Supporting Details:

1. Children in the primary grades learn about their country mostly in patriotic ways: They learn about the Pilgrims, the flag, and some of the presidents.

2. Later, in the middle grades, children learn more historical facts and come to understand the structure of the government.

3. By high school, students have a more complex understanding of the political system, may identify with a political party, and may take positions on issues.

—From Schmidt/Shelley/Bardes, *American Government and Politics Today 2007–2008*, 13e

Topic sentence: _____

Double-check by turning your TS into a question.

4. Topic: _____

   Main Idea: _____

     Supporting Details:

1. First, because of the widespread use of Spanish on signs in cities like Los Angeles and Miami, many people assume that Latinos do not speak English or have no desire to learn it.

2. But the rate of learning English for Latinos is about the same as for other immigrant groups.

3. Second, Latinos are sometimes viewed (wrongly) as not fully participating in the economy.

4. However, Mexicans and Central Americans have a labor force participation rate of 62 percent, which exceeds the Anglo rate.

5. Third, many mainstream Americans view recent immigrants as "short-timers" who are interested only in making enough money to return home.

6. But when asked in a national survey if they planned to stay permanently in the United States, more than 90 percent of the legal immigrants said yes.

—From Ferraro, *Cultural Anthropology*, 6e

Topic sentence: _____

Double-check by turning your TS into a question.

Applying the Strategy to Paragraphs

You can add a step to this same process to identify the implied main ideas of paragraphs. You will need to find the details after you find the topic.

1. Find the topic by looking for repeated ideas.

2. Search the paragraph for the details. Often, these will be specific facts, reasons, and examples. You may find it helpful to put parentheses ( ) around the major supporting details or to number them.

3. Figure out the main idea by asking what all the details have in common.

4. Create a topic sentence and then turn it into a question to double-check it.

Interaction 5–5 ⟩ **Identifying the Implied Main Ideas of Paragraphs**

Put parentheses around (or number) each major supporting detail. For each paragraph, write a topic sentence that fits the details. Remember these paragraphs do not have a topic sentence; you have to create one!

Paragraph 1   **Literature Textbook**

   In ancient China and Japan, poetry was prized above all else. One story tells of a samurai warrior who, when defeated, asked for a pen and paper. Thinking that he wanted to write a will before being executed, his captor granted his wish. Instead of writing a will, however, the warrior wrote a farewell poem that so moved his captor that he immediately released him. To the ancient Greeks and Romans, poetry was the medium of spiritual and philosophical expression. Today, throughout the world, poetry continues to delight and inspire.

—From Kirszner/Mandell, *Literature*, 6e. Copyright © 2007 Cengage Learning, Inc. Reproduced by permission. www.cengage.com/permissions

Topic: _____

Main Idea: _____

Topic Sentence: _____

Double-check by turning your TS into a question.

Paragraph 2   **Nonfiction Book**

   The largest redwoods, which are called redwood giants or redwood titans, are usually not the very tallest ones, but they are the thickest. The main trunk of a redwood titan can be as much as thirty feet in diameter near its base. The tallest redwoods are often slender, and so they aren't the thickest ones, but they can reach more than three hundred feet tall. The redwoods are rather like people. A football player is often bigger than a basketball player—more massive, that is. The basketball player is taller and more slender. So it is with redwoods.

—Adapted from Preston, *Wild Trees*

Topic: _____

Main Idea: _____

Topic Sentence: _____

Double-check by turning your TS into a question.

Paragraph 3   **Biology Textbook**

The functional activities of cells that result in growth, repair, energy release, use of food, and secretions are combined under the heading of metabolism. One process of metabolism is called Anabolism. It is the building up of complex materials from simpler ones such as food and oxygen. Another process of metabolism is called Catabolism. This is the breaking down and changing of complex substances into simpler ones, with a release of energy and carbon dioxide. The sum of all the chemical reactions within a cell is therefore called metabolism.

—From Scott/Fong, *Body Structures and Functions*, 11e (p. 7). Copyright © 2009 Cengage Learning, Inc. Reproduced by permission. www.cengage.com/permissions

Topic: _____

Main Idea: _____

Topic Sentence: _____

Double-check by turning your TS into a question.

Paragraph 4   **Speech Textbook**

Why do we ignore some messages but tune into others, opening ourselves up to new ideas and ways of thinking? Why do we willingly confirm some people but refuse to consider confirming others? Similarly, why are we sometimes surprisingly good at understanding some speakers but unable to follow others? Listening researcher Michael Nichols explains that we sometimes fail to listen because "the simple art of listening isn't always so simple." Rather, it is often work. The "sustained attention of careful listening—that may take heroic and unselfish restraint. To listen well we must forget ourselves" and give our focused attention to another. Researchers say that hindrance to listening could be coming from the listener himself or herself, the speaker, or the environment.

—From Griffin, *Invitation to Public Speaking*, 4e

Topic: _____

Main Idea: _____

Topic Sentence: _____

Double-check by turning your TS into a question.

Paragraph 5   **Sociology Textbook**

Domination represents one extreme type of interaction. In social interaction based on domination, nearly all power is concentrated in the hands of people of similar status, whereas people of a different status enjoy almost no power. In extreme cases of domination, subordinates live in a state of near-constant fear. The opposite is interaction based on cooperation. Here, power is more or less equally distributed between people of different statuses. Cooperative interaction is based on feelings of trust. Between the two extremes of interaction based on domination and interaction based on cooperation is interaction based on competition. In this mode of interaction, power is unequally distributed, but the degree of inequality is less than in systems of domination. Most of the social interactions analyzed by exchange and rational choice theorists are of this type. Envy is an important emotion in most competitive interactions.

—From Brym/Lie, *Sociology: Your Compass for a New World Brief Edition*, 2e

Topic: _____

Main Idea: _____

Topic Sentence: _____

Double-check by turning your TS into a question.

Applying the Strategy to Longer Passages

To identify the implied main idea of a longer passage, use the same strategy. Just keep in mind that when you are making a generalization that will be broad enough to cover several paragraphs or more, the major supporting details you are looking for will be the topic sentences of the individual paragraphs. And the generalization that covers several paragraphs is not called a topic sentence; instead, it's called a *thesis statement*.

Interaction 5–6   Identify the Implied Main Idea of a Longer Passage

Identify the topic of the following passages, along with the main idea. Then write a thesis statement for each.

Passage 1   Psychology Textbook

1. First, relate the question to what you know about the topic. Then, read the alternatives. Does one match the answer you expected to find? If none match, reexamine the choices and look for a partial match.

2. Read all the choices for each question before you make a decision. Here's why: If you immediately think that "a" is correct and stop reading, you might miss seeing a better answer like "both a and d."

3. Read rapidly and skip items you are unsure about. You may find "free information" in later questions that will help you answer difficult items.

4. Eliminate certain alternatives. With a four-choice multiple-choice test, you have one chance in four of guessing right. If you can eliminate two alternatives, your guessing odds improve to 50-50.

5. Unless there is a penalty for guessing, be sure to answer any skipped items. Even if you are not sure of the answer, you may be right. If you leave a question blank, it is automatically wrong. When you are forced to guess, don't choose the longest answer or the letter you've used the least. Both strategies lower scores more than random guessing does.

6. There is a bit of folk wisdom that says "Don't change your answers on a multiple-choice test. Your first choice is usually right." This is false. If you change answers, you are more likely to gain points than to lose them. This is especially true if you are uncertain of your first choice or it was a hunch, and if your second choice is more reflective (Higham & Gerrard, 2005).

7. Remember, you are searching for the one best answer to each question. Some answers may be partly true, yet flawed in some way. If you are uncertain, try rating each multiple-choice alternative on a 1–10 scale. The answer with the highest rating is the one you are looking for.

8. Few circumstances are always or never present. Answers that include superlatives such as most, least, best, worst, largest, or smallest are often false.

—From Coon/Mitterer, *Introduction to Psychology: Gateways to Mind and Behavior*, 13e

Topic: _____

Main Idea: _____

Thesis Statement: _____

Double-check by turning your TS into a question.

Passage 2 | Accounting Textbook |

Rather than pay cash for large purchases such as houses and cars, most people borrow part of the purchase price and then repay the loan on some scheduled basis. Spreading payments over time makes big-ticket items more affordable, and consumers get the use of an expensive asset right away. Most people consider the cost of such borrowing a small price to pay for the immediate satisfaction they get from owning the house, car, or whatever it happens to be. In their minds, at least, the benefits of current consumption outweigh the interest costs on the loan. Unfortunately, while the initial euphoria of the purchase may wear off over time, the loan payments remain—perhaps for many more years to come.

Some borrow to meet a financial emergency. For example, people may need to borrow to cover living expenses during a period of unemployment, or to purchase plane tickets to visit a sick relative.

Others borrow for convenience. Merchants as well as banks offer a variety of charge accounts and credit cards that allow consumers to charge just about anything—from gas and oil or clothes and stereos to doctor and dental bills and even college tuition. Further, in many places—restaurants, for instance—using a credit card is far easier than writing a check. Although such transactions usually incur no interest (at least initially), these credit card purchases are still a form of borrowing, because payment is not made at the time of the transaction.

Finally, others borrow for investment purposes. It's relatively easy for an investor to partially finance the purchase of many different kinds of investment vehicles with borrowed funds. In fact, margin loans, as they're called, amounted to nearly $220 billion in late 2005—a tidy sum, but down substantially from the $280 billion reached when the stock market peaked in March 2000.

—From Gitman/Joehnk, *Personal Financial Planning*, 11e

Topic: _____

Main Idea: _____

Thesis Statement: _____

_____

Double-check by turning your TS into a question.

Passage 3　　　　　　　　　　　　　　　　　　　| Management Textbook |

Leaders begin with the question, "What should we be doing?" while managers start with "How can we do what we're already doing better?" Leaders focus on vision, mission, goals, and objectives, while managers focus on productivity and efficiency. Managers see themselves as preservers of the status quo, while leaders see themselves as promoters of change and challengers of the status quo in that they encourage creativity and risk taking. One of the reasons for Dell, Inc.'s long-term success and profitability is that founder and chairman Michael Dell never accepts the status quo. He fervently believes that everything the company does can be changed and improved. Says Dell, "Celebrate for a nanosecond. Then move on."

Another difference is that managers have a relatively short-term perspective, while leaders take a long-term view. When Dell opened its first factory in Asia, Michael Dell congratulated the plant manager by sending him one of his old running shoes to stress that opening that plant was just the first step in the company's strategy of opening manufacturing plants in that part of the world. Managers are also more concerned with means, how to get things done, while leaders are more concerned with ends, what gets done. Managers are concerned with control and limiting the choices of others, while leaders are more concerned with expanding people's choices and options. Finally, managers solve problems so that others can do their work, while leaders inspire and motivate others to find their own solutions.

—From Williams, *Management*, 4e

Topic: _____

Main Idea: _____

Thesis Statement: _____

_____

Double-check by turning your TS into a question.

Passage 4

Subsistence agriculture, in which each family produces enough food to feed itself, accounts for more than half of tropical rainforest loss. Subsistence farmers often practice slash-and-burn agriculture in which they first cut down the forest and allow it to dry, then burn the area and immediately plant crops. The yield from the first crop is often quite high, because the minerals that were in the trees are available in the soil after the trees are burned. However, soil productivity declines rapidly so the subsequent crops are poor. In a very short time, the people farming the land must move to new forest and repeat the process.

More than 20 percent of tropical deforestation is the result of commercial logging. Vast tracts of tropical trees are being removed for export abroad, including to the United States. Most tropical countries are allowing commercial logging to proceed at a much higher rate than is sustainable.

More than 10 percent of destruction of rain forests occurs to provide open rangeland for cattle. Much of the beef raised on ranches cleared from forests is exported to fast-food chains. After the forests are cleared, cattle can be grazed on the land for 6 to 10 years, after which time shrubby plants, known as scrub savanna, take over the range.

—From Berg, *Introductory Botany: Plants, People, and the Environment, Media Edition*, 2e. Copyright © 2008 Cengage Learning, Inc. Reproduced by permissions. www.cengage.com/permissions

Topic: _____

Main Idea: _____

Thesis Statement: _____

_____

Double-check by turning your TS into a question.

Passage 5

The vast majority of financial transactions take place at depository financial institutions—commercial banks (both brick-and-mortar and Internet), savings and loan associations (S&Ls), savings banks, and credit unions. Although they're regulated by different agencies, depository financial institutions are commonly referred to as "banks" because of their similar products and services. What sets these institutions apart from others is their ability to accept deposits; most people use them for checking and savings account needs.

Other types of financial institutions that offer banking services, but don't accept deposits like traditional banks, are considered nondepository institutions. Today you can hold a credit card issued by a stock brokerage firm or have an account with a mutual fund that allows you to write a limited number of checks.

- ▶ Stock brokerage firms offer several cash management options, including money market mutual funds that invest in short-term securities and earn a higher rate of interest than bank accounts, special "wrap" accounts, and credit cards.
- ▶ Mutual funds provide yet another alternative to bank savings accounts. Like stockbrokers, mutual fund companies offer money market mutual funds.

Other nondepository financial institutions include life insurance and finance companies.

—From Gitman/Joehnk/Billingsley, *Personal Financial Planning*, 12e

Topic: _____

Main Idea: _____

Thesis Statement: _____

    Double-check by turning your TS into a question.

Connect Your Skills

A. Identifying the Implied Main Idea

Look at the visual here and answer the questions beside it.

1. Who or what is this about? _____

2. What details do you notice? _____
   _____
   _____

3. What do these details have in common? ____
   _____

4. What is the implied main idea of the cartoon? _____

Roz Chast/The New Yorker

B. Identifying the General Idea

Identify the general category from the details listed.

5. hinges, lenses, bridge, nose pads, rims   _____

6. skull, ribs, humerus, spine, pelvis, femur   _____

7. euro, rupee, yen, won, yuan   _____

8. frogs, lizards, salamanders, newts   _____

C. Deciding Whether a Topic Sentence Covers the Right Amount of Information

Choose the topic sentence that covers the right amount of information. Circle **C** for "correct," **B** for "broad," and **N** for "narrow." For the sentence that is too broad or too narrow, underline the part of the sentence that makes it unworkable.

> ▶ Around grades 9 and 10 adolescents' ideas about whether, as adults, they will focus mainly on the home, paid work outside the home, or a combination of the two become apparent.
> ▶ Boys are strongly inclined to consider only their careers in making course choices.
> ▶ Most girls are inclined to consider both home responsibilities and careers, although a minority considers only home responsibilities and another minority considers only careers.
> ▶ Consequently, boys tend to choose career-oriented courses, particularly in math and science, more often than girls do. In college, the pattern is accentuated.
> ▶ Young women tend to choose easier courses that lead to lower-paying jobs because they expect to devote a large part of their lives to childrearing and housework (Hochschild with Machung, 1989: 15–18).
>
> —From Brym/Lie, *Sociology: Your Compass for a New World, Brief Edition*

9. Adolescents often make course and career choices with gender ideologies in mind.

    C   B   N

10. Boys are more inclined to make class choices based solely on their career.

    C   B   N

11. The career choices that men and women go into always reflect their gender expectation.

    C   B   N

D. Creating a Topic Sentence

Read the following paragraphs. Identify the topic and the major details. Then formulate the main idea and create a topic sentence for each one.

> Individual racism refers to "the beliefs, attitudes and actions of individuals that support or perpetuate racism" (Wijeyesinghe, Griffin, & Love, 1997, p. 89). Institutional racism involves the manipulation of societal institutions to give preferences and advantages to Whites and restrict the choices, rights, mobility, and access of People of Color. While individual racism resides within the person, the institutional variety is wired into the very fabric of social institutions: into their rules, practices, and procedures. Some forms of institutional racism are subtle and hidden; others are overt and obvious. However, all serve to deny and limit access to those who are culturally different. Cultural racism is the belief that the cultural ways of one group are superior to those of another. In the United States, it takes the form of practices that "attribute value and normality to White People and Whiteness, and devalue, stereotype, and label People of Color as

'other,' different, less than, or render them invisible" (Wijeyesinghe, Griffin, & Love, 1997, p. 93). Cultural racism can be found in both individuals and institutions. In the former, it is often referred to as ethnocentrism. Each level of racism supports and reinforces the others, and together, they contribute to its general resistance to change.

—From Moule, *Cultural Competence: A Primer for Educators*, 2e (p. 29). Copyright © 2012 Cengage Learning, Inc.
Reproduced by permission. www.cengage.com/permissions

12. **Topic:** _____

13. **Main Idea:** _____

14. **Topic Sentence:** _____

Double-check by turning your TS into a question.

Tax software programs take much of the tedium out of tax preparation, reducing the time you spend from days to hours. If you file the long Form 1040 and some supporting forms, invest in the stock market, own real estate, or have foreign income or a home-based business, you'll probably benefit from using tax preparation programs. It's even easier and faster if you use a personal finance program to keep tabs on your income and expenses, because the tax software can extract the appropriate data. The programs automate much of the process; for example, they know that X % of the amount you entered on Line K has to be transferred to Line Q, saving you the task of remembering to do it yourself. The programs are updated annually to include the hundreds of changes in tax laws. Another advantage is that the programs feed your data to state tax returns, so you only have to enter it once.

—From Gitman/Joehnk/Billingsley, *Personal Financial Planning*, 12e

15. **Topic:** _____

16. **Main Idea:** _____

17. **Topic Sentence:** _____

Double-check by turning your TS into a question.

E. Creating a Thesis Statement for a Longer Passage

Identify the topic and major details of the following passage. Then create a main idea and formulate a thesis statement.

Is the information reliable? Check the domain in the URL. Is it .com (a commercial enterprise that might be trying to sell something), .org (a nonprofit organization, more interested in services and issues than in commerce), .edu (an educational institution), or .gov (a government agency)? What bias might those operating the site have about your topic? Do they make any disclaimers about the information they post on the site? What makes this information reliable or not?

Is the information authoritative? URLs that include a tilde (~) often indicate that a single individual is responsible for the information on a website. Can you find the person's credentials posted on the site? Can you contact the person and ask for credentials? Can you find the person's credentials in any print sources, such as a *Who's Who* reference? Regardless of whether the material was authored by a single person, an organization, an institution, or a company, is the author an expert on the subject of the site?

How current is the information? Many web pages include a date that tells you when it was posted or last updated. If you don't see such a date, you may be able to find it in your browser's View or Document menu. If you determine that the website is current, is the time frame relevant to your subject or arguments? You may find great information, but if it doesn't relate to the time frame of your speech, it's not relevant or ethical to use.

How complete is the information? Much of the text posted on the Internet consists of excerpts from printed material, and what is left out may be of more use than what is included. For example, a site may contain one paragraph from a newspaper article, but that paragraph may not reflect the overall message of the article. If you want to use an excerpted portion of a printed work, you must locate the complete work to ensure you are using that material accurately.

Is the information relevant? Many interesting facts and stories appear on the web, but be sure those you use as supporting material do more than just tell a great story. Your information must help you develop your thesis (Chapters 7 and 16). Ask yourself whether the information fits your needs. Does it help develop your main ideas, or does it take you in a different direction?

Is the information consistent and unbiased? Is the information you find consistent with information you find on other sites, from printed sources, or from interviews? Can you find other sources to support the statements, claims, and facts provided by a website? If the information is inconsistent with other sources, it may reflect new findings about a topic, but it also may reflect an unfounded or unsubstantiated claim. Many sites present only one side of an issue. To guarantee a less biased presentation and more comprehensive picture of your topic, search at a number of different sites and be sure to cross-check what you find against the information you obtain from more established sources such as books and other print documents. Be wary of outrageous or controversial claims that can't be checked for accuracy or aren't grounded in reasonable arguments or sources.   —From Griffin, *Invitation to Public Speaking*, 4e

18. Topic: _____

19. Main Idea: _____

20. Thesis Statement: _____

Double-check by turning your TS into a question.

Click to Connect! To check your comprehension of chapter concepts, visit **www.cengagebrain.com** to access the CourseMate for this chapter.

Chapter Summary Activity

This chapter has discussed how to find the implied main idea of paragraphs and longer passages. Construct a Reading Guide to Identifying Implied Main Ideas here by completing each idea on the left with information from the chapter on the right. You can use this guide later if you need to figure out a text's implied main idea.

Reading Guide to Identifying Implied Main Ideas

Complete this idea with ...	information from Chapter 5.
Difference between a stated main idea and an implied main idea	1. _____ _____
Clues for figuring out the implied main idea of a cartoon	2. _____ _____
	3. _____ _____
Generalization—definition	4. _____ _____
Two problems with making general statements	5. _____ _____
	6. _____ _____
Explain how to double-check your generalization.	7. _____ _____
Three levels of ideas and questions you can ask to help you organize and understand what you are reading	8. _____ _____
	9. _____ _____
	10. _____ _____

How to find the topic	**11.** _____ _____
The question to find the implied main idea	**12.** _____ _____
Formula to create a topic sentence	**13.** _____ _____
How to double-check your topic sentence	**14.** _____ _____
The sentence that controls multiple paragraphs	**15.** _____ _____

Think about what your reading comprehension strategies were before you read this chapter. What have you learned that will be helpful? Write your thoughts.

_____

_____

_____

Reading 5–1 | Online Article

▶ Pre-Reading the Selection

This reading comes from MSN.com's Health and Fitness section. Think about the portions you eat on a daily basis as you read through this passage.

Surveying the Reading

Survey the following selection. Then check the elements that are included in this reading.

_____ Title   _____ Words in bold or italic type

_____ Headings   _____ Images and captions

_____ First sentences of paragraphs

Guessing the Purpose

Judging from the title of the reading, what do you suppose is the author's purpose? _____
_____

Predicting the Content

Predict three things this selection will discuss.

▶ _____

▶ _____

▶ _____

Activating Your Knowledge

Share what you know about correct portion sizes. For example, how much meat, vegetables, or bread should a person eat at dinner? If you are not sure of the correct amount, then just share what you typically eat for dinner.

▶ _____

▶ _____

▶ _____

 Scan to **Connect**! Use your smart phone to scan this code to watch a video to activate your knowledge about portion size. (See the inside front cover for more information on how to use this.) What two strategies are mentioned in this video for controlling portions?

Common Knowledge

"Clean Plate Club" (*paragraph 3*) National campaigns started during wartimes to encourage schoolchildren to eat all the food on their plates in order to conserve limited resources. Parents even now still sometimes demand that children eat all they are served.

▶Reading with Pen in Hand

Students who annotate as they read are more successful than those who do not. That's why you will annotate each selection in *Connect* as you read. In the reading that follows, use the following symbols:

★ or ⟮Point⟯   to indicate a main idea

①②③   to indicate major details

  Visit **www.cengagebrain.com** to access the CourseMate for this chapter to hear pronunciations of vocabulary words from this reading.

Portion Control: Change Your Thinking or Your Plate?

Karen Collins

accustomed Look at the cause-and-effect relationship between the first and last part of the sentence to guess the meaning of this word.

▶ Which sentence states the conclusion that Brian Wansink reached?

▶ What did the research from Cornell University and Penn State show?

1   According to experts, we have become so **accustomed** to oversized portions of food and extra-large serving dishes that we can no longer tell how much we are overeating. We may have more success at reducing our excessive portions by reducing the size of our food packages and serving pieces than by trying to figure out a healthy portion size. That's essentially the conclusion Cornell University professor Brian Wansink reaches in a recent analysis published in the *Journal of the American Dietetic Association* on the problem of Americans' extra-large portions.

2   Research from Cornell University and Penn State has repeatedly shown that the larger the amount of food we are faced with—whether on our plates or in serving bowls—the more we will eat. We might not eat everything, but we still eat more than if we started with less. This has been demonstrated in single meals, such as comparing the amount eaten of different size sub sandwiches, and in totals over a period of several days.

David Young-Wolff/PhotoEdit

phenomenon Use your prior knowledge to think about what this word might mean.

3   For many people, eating more when presented with large amounts of food may be tied to the "Clean Plate Club" **phenomenon**. We have been taught to view not eating all we are given as wasteful. However, researchers suggest that we may

often be unable to even recognize extra-large portions. Studies show that when an equal amount of food is presented on a relatively large and small plate, we see the large plate as having less food than the smaller plate, which seems more full.

▶ What does the author say about our ability to recognize portion sizes?

4   Studies also show that we tend to eat in "units." If we buy a package of six cookies or crackers, we usually eat them all rather than leaving part of a package. If a "unit" or package of candy, French fries or soft drinks gets larger, we are more likely to eat the whole container anyway. And food units in the United States—packages in stores and portions in restaurants—have grown **dramatically** in the last 20 years. For example, a bottle of soda 20 years ago was 6.5 ounces and had 85 calories; today's soda comes in 20 ounce bottles that can contain about 250 calories. Along with calorie consumption, extra large portions can significantly increase the amount of fat and sodium we get.

▶ What are "units" and what is deceiving about them?

dramatically Use the example clue in the following sentence to decide what *dramatically* means.

Portion Size Management

5   One way to improve your portion size management is to learn to better judge the amount of food in front of you. Studies have shown that if people practice measuring out different portion sizes, their accuracy can improve. The American Institute for Cancer Research and the United States Department of Agriculture have both developed educational materials to help people learn to recognize serving sizes by comparing food amounts to common objects. For example, three ounces of meat, poultry or fish look like a deck of cards or a checkbook. A half-cup of pasta or rice looks like a tennis ball or a cupped handful.

▶ What suggestion is given for recognizing correct portion sizes?

6   Because of how our **perception** of portion size changes depending on the size and shape of the container, Wansink argues that we should pay more attention to our packages, plates, and serving bowls. Market research shows that single-serving packages are booming in popularity, which may be one step in this direction. Look around your kitchen at the different size plates, bowls and glasses you have available. Instead of serving ice cream in two- or three-cup cereal bowls, make half- or one-cup custard cups the official ice cream bowl. With 200 calories per cup in even many healthful cereal choices, our tendency to simply fill a bowl and then eat it all could turn that bowl of cereal into a higher-calorie breakfast than you realize if you use large bowls. You don't have to get rid of those big bowls; large portion sizes are one way to increase the amount of nutrients we get. If you want people to eat more salad, they will do so automatically with bigger salad bowls.

perception Look at the cause-and-effect relationship in this sentence to guess what *perception* means.

▶ What suggestion is given for using the dishes you have?

7   Finally, Wansink's research shows that the more food we have on hand, the more we will eat. So ignore the "common sense" of grocery store marketing **urging** you to buy two packages of cookies or chips for the price of one; you may just eat twice as much. If you find it's easier or less expensive to buy large quantities of snack foods (such as nuts or trail mix), you can separate the food into several healthful portions, or take some out and tuck the big package out of sight.

▶ What should you do when you buy larger-portion items at the grocery store?

urging The word *urging* is a verb. Based on the context, what does it mean?

—From *Portion Control: Change Your Thinking or Your Plate?* by Karen Collins, R.D., American Institute for Cancer Research. Reprinted with permission from the American Institute for Cancer Research, www.aicr.org.

▶ Comprehension Questions

Write the letter of the answer on the line. Then explain your thinking.

Main Idea

____ 1. What is the topic sentence of paragraph 3?

    a. For many people, eating more when presented with large amounts of food may be tied to the "Clean Plate Club" phenomenon.

    b. We have been taught to view not eating all we are given as wasteful.

    c. However, researchers suggest that we may often be unable to even recognize extra-large portions.

    d. Studies show that when an equal amount of food is presented on a relatively large and small plate, we see the large plate as having less food than the smaller plate, which seems more full.

Why? What information in the selection leads you to give that answer? _____

_____

_____

____ 2. What is the implied main idea of this reading passage?

    a. The more food the average person is given, the more calories he or she will consume.

    b. Training ourselves to perceive more accurately how much food we are eating will help us stop overeating.

    c. Following the example of the American Institute for Cancer Research and the United States Department of Agriculture, people should learn to recognize serving sizes by comparing food amounts to common objects.

    d. Most of us overeat due to eating strategies instilled in us while we were children, such as the "Clean Plate Club."

Why? What information in the selection leads you to give that answer? _____

_____

_____

_____

Supporting Details

____ 3. According to the reading passage, why do many people eat portions that are too large?

    a. People have become desensitized to proper portion size.

    b. Many people know when they should stop eating, but they have trouble because food is so delicious.

c. Food today has more calories in it than it did 20 years ago.

d. The dishes that we serve our food on are too small and need to be larger.

Why? What information in the selection leads you to give that answer? _____

_____

4. Which of the following is *not* a suggestion given for controlling portion size?

a. Use smaller dishes.

b. Compare correct portions to common items as an easy guideline.

c. Only buy food that is in an appropriately sized package.

d. Do not buy two-for-one deals.

Why? What information in the selection leads you to give that answer? _____

_____

Author's Purpose

5. What is the main purpose of this reading passage?

a. to inform the reader about how to avoid buying large quantities of junk food

b. to entertain readers with situations of trickery and manipulation

c. to persuade readers that they must eat meals on 9-inch plates and clean their plates

d. to persuade readers to change the size of their portions by informing them how to monitor and control their portions

Why? What information in the selection leads you to give that answer? _____

_____

_____

6. What is the purpose of the section entitled "Portion Size Management"?

a. to persuade readers to manage their portion size by informing them of some basic strategies

b. to entertain readers with anecdotal information of successful portion size management

c. to inform readers of the best strategies for managing portion size

d. to inform readers of the latest portion size management research by The American Institute for Cancer Research and the United States Department of Agriculture

Why? What information in the selection leads you to give that answer? _____

_____

_____

Relationships

_____ 7. What is the pattern of organization of this sentence?

> Ignore the "common sense" of grocery store marketing urging you to buy two packages of cookies or chips for the price of one; you may just eat twice as much.

   a. time order
   b. cause-and-effect
   c. comparison
   d. classification

Why? What leads you to give that answer? _____

_____

_____ 8. What is the main pattern of organization in the section entitled "Portion Size Management"?
   a. classification
   b. comparison and contrast
   c. cause-and-effect
   d. examples

Why? What information in the selection leads you to give that answer? _____

_____

Fact, Opinion, and Inference

_____ 9. Which of the following statements is an opinion?
   a. Wansink's research shows that the more food we have on hand, the more we will eat.
   b. It's easier and less expensive to buy large quantities of snack foods, such as nuts or trail mix.
   c. Market research shows that single serving packages are booming in popularity.
   d. According to research, if we buy a package of six cookies or crackers, we usually eat them all rather than leaving part of a package.

Why? What leads you to give that answer? _____

_____

_____ 10. With which of the following statements would Wansink probably agree?

    a. Consumers should leave packaging decisions to product developers, grocery stores, and marketing companies.

    b. With slick marketing and the large portions served at restaurants, correct portion size is impossible to decipher.

    c. By using common sense, most consumers are successfully eating properly sized portions.

    d. We will eat more if we have large portions of food piled on a small plate than if we have the correct portion size on a larger plate.

Why? What information in the selection leads you to give that answer? _____

_____

▶ Critical Thinking Questions

Critical Thinking Level 1 ▸ Remember

List three suggestions given in the passage to improve your portion size management.

1. _____

2. _____

3. _____

Critical Thinking Level 2 ▸ Understand

Summarize the reading in several sentences. Include the major details.

_____

_____

_____

_____

Critical Thinking Level 3 ▸ Apply

Think of restaurants at which you have eaten. *Apply* your knowledge of their menus to the problem of oversized portions. Do you think their portion sizes are appropriate? How big are they? On a sheet of paper, list the name of each restaurant and a few menu items served there, along with a description of the portion size. Discuss your list with a classmate. What size would be appropriate for the menu items? If you mentioned the same restaurants, see if you measured their portions in the same way.

_____

_____

Critical Thinking Level 4 ▸ Analyze

Analyze how much you eat for dinner tonight. Write down each item that you eat, and *compare* it to the size of a common object, such as a baseball, a deck of cards, or a fist. Then compare each item on your list to the following portion size guidelines provided by the Missouri Diabetes Prevention and Control Program.

Portion Size Guidelines

Below are ways you can picture a serving or portion size using everyday objects.
(Note: hands and finger sizes vary from person to person! These are GUIDES only.)

Food Portion	Looks Like
Grains, Beans, and Starchy Vegetables Group	
½ cup cooked rice or pasta	half of a baseball
½ cup cooked dry beans, lentils, or peas	cupcake wrapper full
½ cup potatoes, corn, green peas	level ice cream scoop
corn on the cob	4-inch corn cob
Vegetable	
1 cup green salad	baseball or a fist
¾ cup tomato juice	small styrofoam cup
½ cup cooked broccoli	half baseball or light bulb
½ cup serving	6 asparagus spears, 7 or 8 baby carrots
Fruit	
½ cup of fresh fruit	custard cup
1 medium size fruit	fist or baseball
¼ cup raisins	large egg
Meat and Protein Foods	
3 ounces cooked meat, fish, poultry	deck of cards
3 ounces cooked chicken	leg plus thigh or ½ whole breast
1 ounce of cheese	4 stacked dice
2 tablespoons peanut butter	ping-pong ball
1 teaspoon peanut butter	fingertip
1 tablespoon peanut butter	thumb tip
Fats, Oils and Nuts	
1 teaspoon butter, margarine	fingertip
2 tablespoons salad dressing	ping-pong ball

For each item, decide whether your portion was smaller than the guideline (such as 50 percent), 100 percent (that is, the same as the guideline), 200 percent (twice as much as the guideline), and so on. When you have compared each item, write a few sentences about what you learned.

_____

_____

_____

Critical Thinking Level 5   Evaluate

Go to the food tracker on ChooseMyPlate.gov at https://www.choosemyplate.gov/SuperTracker/food-tracker.aspx#. Track what you eat for a day (or longer). Fill in the information on the Food Tracker page. It will give you a graph based on daily food target. Bring your results to class and *evaluate* them with a classmate to determine if you should change your diet or ways you could improve your eating habits.

Critical Thinking Level 6   Create

Create a strategy list with a partner or group of classmates that helps you plan how you will control your portions based on information from the readings in this chapter. Brainstorm together two lists of portion control strategies: one list for eating at home, and the other list for eating out. Share the lists you create with your class.

_____

_____

_____

▶Vocabulary in New Contexts

Review the vocabulary words in the margins of the reading selection and then complete the following activities.

EASY Note Cards

Make a note card for each of the vocabulary words that you did not know from the reading. On one side, write the word. On the other side, divide the card into quarters and label them E, A, S, and Y. Add a word or phrase in each area so that you wind up with an example sentence, an antonym, a synonym, and, finally, a definition that shows you have figured out the meaning of the word with your logic. Remember that an antonym or synonym may have appeared in the reading.

Relationships Between Words

Circle *yes* or *no* to answer the question. Then explain your answer.

1. Would witnessing the **phenomenon** of their child's birth be something a parent becomes **accustomed** to?

   Yes   No

   Why or why not? _____

2. Would a doctor try **urging** individuals with anorexia to change how they **perceive** themselves?

Yes   No

Why or why not? _____

3. Has modern life has **dramatically** affected natural **phenomena**?

Yes   No

Why or why not? _____

Language in Your Life

Write short answers to each question. Look at the vocabulary words closely before you answer.

1. Name one item that you think would **dramatically** improve your life. _____

_____

2. Name one word that describes how people often **perceive** you. _____

_____

3. Name one food you often have an **urge** for. _____

_____

4. Name one amazing natural **phenomenon** you have either seen or want to see. _____

_____

5. Name something you have become **accustomed** to. _____

_____

Language in Use

Select the best word to complete the meaning of each sentence.

accustomed	dramatically	perceived	phenomenon	urging

1. Old Ralph Higgins has lived in Circle, Alaska (located about 75 miles south of the Arctic circle with only around a hundred residents), for more than forty years. He's been photographing the aurora borealis for at least half that time, but has still not grown _____ to its beauty.

2. The aurora borealis, commonly called northern lights, is a natural _____ caused when charged particles from the sun's solar wind enter the earth's atmosphere and collide with gaseous atoms.

3. The color most commonly _____ is a pale green, but depending on how high in the atmosphere the particles interact, colors of yellow, pink, red, blue, or purple may be also be seen.

4. It doesn't take much _____ for Ralph to gather his camera gear, bundle up, get in his old pick-up truck and head off into the night in search of the perfect northern lights photo.

5. And even though life can be rough in the great frozen north, Ralph can forget all the hardships when he sees the aurora borealis _____ dancing across the night sky, lifts his camera lens, and quietly says, "I wouldn't want to be anywhere else!"

Reading 5–2 | Health Textbook

▶ Pre-Reading the Selection

This reading comes from a textbook entitled *An Invitation to Health*. Think about your health as you read through this passage and do the exercises associated with it.

Surveying the Reading

Survey the following selection. Then check the elements that are included in this reading.

_____ Title   _____ Words in bold or italic type

_____ Headings   _____ Images and captions

_____ First sentences of paragraphs

Guessing the Purpose

Judging from the title of the reading and the book from which it was taken, what do you suppose is the purpose for writing? _____

Predicting the Content

Predict three things this selection will discuss.

▶ _____

▶ _____

▶ _____

Activating Your Knowledge

Share what you know about the epidemic of obesity in America and the world. Do you know its causes and effects? On a separate sheet of paper, create a list with a partner.

 Scan to Connect! Use your smart phone to scan this code to watch a video to activate your knowledge about an alternative eating plan to the typical American diet. (See the inside front cover for more information on how to use this.) What is your reaction to this eating plan? How do you think you would fare following this lifestyle change?

Common Knowledge

The World Health Organization (*paragraph 2*) An agency of the United Nations responsible for coordinating health efforts around the world.

▶Reading with Pen in Hand

Students who annotate as they read are more successful than those who do not. That's why you will annotate each selection in *Connect* as you read. In the reading that follows, use the following symbols:

★ or (Point)   to indicate a main idea

① ② ③   to indicate major details

 Visit www.cengagebrain.com to access the CourseMate for this chapter to hear pronunciations of vocabulary words from this reading.

The Global Epidemic

Dianne Hales

▶ How many people around the world are overweight or obese?

1   For the first time in history, more than half of the people on the planet are overweight. Obesity, as headlines blare and health experts warn, is emerging as the number-one public health problem of the twenty-first century. An estimated 1.1 billion people around the world—seven in ten of the Dutch and Spanish, two in three Americans and Canadians, and one in two Britons, Germans, and Italians—are overweight or obese. In Europe, excess weight ranks as the most common childhood disorder. Since 1980, obesity rates have tripled in parts of Eastern Europe, the Middle East, China, and the Pacific Islands. In many poor countries, obesity is common among city dwellers, while people in rural areas remain underweight and **malnourished**.

malnourished The prefix *mal-* means "bad or badly." What does *malnourished* mean?

▶ What does the World Health Organization recommend governments do to fight obesity?

2   The World Health Organization, in its first global diet, exercise, and health program to combat obesity, recommends that governments promote public knowledge about diet, exercise, and health; offer information that makes healthy choices easier for consumers to make; and require accurate, comprehensible food labels. Although ultimately each individual decides what and how much to eat, policy makers agree that governments also must act to reverse the obesity epidemic.

susceptibility The clue for this word hinges on the cause-and-effect relationship between *susceptibility* and *Western lifestyle*.

▶ What factor significantly impacts obesity?

3   Exposure to a Western lifestyle seems to bring out **susceptibility** to excess weight. Obesity is much more common among the Pima Indians of Arizona compared to Pimas living in Mexico, who have maintained a more traditional lifestyle, with more physical activity and a diet lower in fat and richer in complex carbohydrates. Native Hawaiians who follow a more traditional diet and lifestyle also have lower rates of obesity and cardiovascular disease. Simply moving to America increases the risk of obesity. In a study of immigrants, the rate of obesity more than doubled within 15 years—from 8 percent among recent immigrants to 19 percent.

Supersized Nation

▶ How many American adults are overweight?

4   Two-thirds of American adults, up from fewer than half 20 years ago, are overweight. About one in every three Americans is obese. Since the 1970s, the obesity rate has doubled for teens and tripled for children between the ages of

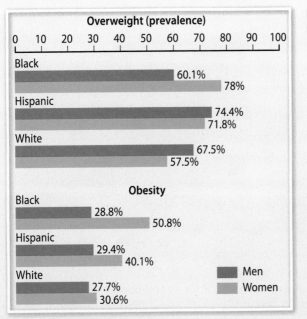

Figure 5.2   Weight Problems by Race/Ethnic Group and Gender

6 and 11. Although more men than women are overweight, more adult women (38 percent) are obese than men (28 percent). Non-Hispanic black women have the highest obesity rate (50 percent), compared with 40 percent of Hispanic women and 30 percent of white women (**Figure 5.2**). In some Native American communities, up to 70 percent of all adults are dangerously overweight. Differences in metabolic rates may be one factor.

5   Weight problems are starting earlier than ever. One in ten preschoolers and one in five grade schoolers are seriously overweight. According to federal estimates, some 6 million American youngsters are so heavy that their health is in jeopardy. Another 5 million are on the threshold of this danger zone. Not only are more children overweight today, but they're 30 to 50 percent heavier than "fat" kids were a decade ago. The percentage of obese teenagers has tripled in the last 20 years.

▶ How many children face potential health problems because they are overweight?

6   Not all Americans are equally likely to be overweight or obese. As **Figure 5.3** shows, the southern states have the highest concentration of obese residents. Mississippi is home to the county with the highest percentage of people with a body mass index (BMI) between 30 and 40. (BMI is defined as the ratio between weight and height that correlates with percentage of body fat.)

▶ Which region of the United States has the most obese residents?

7   States also vary in their efforts to control obesity. According to an ongoing evaluation program at the University of Baltimore, no states deserve an A overall. Only one state—California—earned an A in the report card. For the high grade, the researchers credited the state's legislative package targeted at the nutrition and diets of schoolchildren at risk of becoming obese.

▶ Why did California receive an A from the University of Baltimore's evaluation program?

Figure 5.3   Obesity in the United States

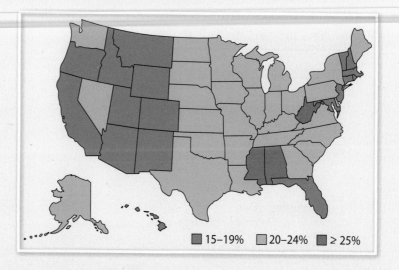

15–19%   20–24%   ≥ 25%

Overall, California earned a B for its anti-obesity work for all populations. Five states—Idaho, Nevada, South Dakota, Utah, and Wyoming—received an F on the report card for failing to take any action in combating obesity.

How Did We Get So Fat?

▶ What three general factors influence obesity?

8   A variety of factors, ranging from heredity to environment to behavior, played a role in the increase in overweight and obesity. They include:

bombarded If Americans are eating more calories than they used to and the commercials are nonstop, what do you think *bombarded* means?

A. More calories. Bombarded by nonstop commercials for tasty treats, tempted by foods in every form to munch and crunch, Americans are eating more—some 200 to 400 calories more a day than they did several decades ago. Many of these extra calories come from refined carbohydrates, which can raise levels of heart-damaging blood fats called triglycerides and increase the risk of diabetes as well as obesity.

B. Bigger portions. The size of many popular restaurant and packaged foods has increased two to five times during the past 20 years. Some foods, like chocolate bars, have grown more than ten times since they were first introduced. Popular 64-ounce sodas can pack a whopping 800 calories. According to studies of appetite and **satiety**, people presented with larger portions eat up to 30 percent more than they otherwise would.

satiety *Satiety* is presented here with its antonym, *appetite*. What does it mean?

C. Fast food. Young adults who eat frequently at fast-food restaurants gain more weight and develop metabolic abnormalities that increase their risk of diabetes in early middle age. In a recent study, those who ate fast food at least twice a week gained an extra 10 pounds and had a two-fold greater increase in insulin resistance, a risk factor for diabetes. The men in the study visited fast-food restaurants more often than the women; blacks did so more frequently than whites.

Food/Beverage	Original Size (year introduced)	Today (largest available)
Budweiser (bottle)	7 oz. (1976)	40 oz.
Nestle's Crunch	1.6 oz. (1938)	5 oz.
Soda (Coca Cola)	6.5 oz. (1916)	34 oz.
French fries (Burger King)	2.6 oz. (1954)	6.9 oz.
Hamburger (McDonald's) (beef only)	1.6 oz. (1955)	8 oz.

Matthew Farruggio (both)

Figure 5.4   Supersized Portions

D. Physical inactivity. As Americans eat more, they exercise less. Experts estimate that most adults expend 200 to 300 fewer calories than people did 25 years ago. The most dramatic drop in physical activity often occurs during the college years.

E. Passive entertainment. Television is a **culprit** in an estimated 30 percent of new cases of obesity. TV viewing may increase weight in several ways: It takes up time that otherwise might be spent in physical activities. It increases food intake since people tend to eat more while watching TV. And compared with sewing, reading, driving, or other relatively sedentary pursuits, television watching lowers metabolic rate so viewers burn fewer calories. The combination of watching television (at least two and one-half hours a day) and eating fast food more than twice a week triples the risk of obesity, according to a 15-year study of more than 3,700 white and black young adults.

culprit This noun is part of a cause-and-effect relationship. Determine what effect television viewing has on obesity to predict the meaning of *culprit*.

F. Modernization. The growth of industry and technology has led to an abundance of food, less need for physical activity, urbanization, labor-saving devices, and a more sedentary lifestyle. Suburban sprawl directly contributes to obesity, according to a recent study. People who live in neighborhoods where they must drive to get anywhere are significantly more likely to be obese than those who can easily walk to their destinations. Each hour spent in a car was associated with a 6 percent increase in the likelihood of obesity and each half-mile walked per day reduced those odds by nearly 5 percent.

G. Socioeconomics. The less money you make, the more likely you are to be overweight. One in four adults below the poverty level is obese, compared with one in six in households earning $67,000 or more. Minorities are at even greater risk. One in three poor African Americans is obese.

H. Prenatal factors. A woman's weight before conception and weight gain during pregnancy influence her child's weight. A substantial number of children are prone to gaining weight because their mothers developed gestational diabetes during their pregnancies. Children born to obese women are more than twice as likely to be overweight by age four.

I. Childhood development. Today's children don't necessarily eat more food than in the past, but they eat more high-fat, high-calorie foods and they exercise much, much less. On days when they eat fast food, youngsters consume an average of 187 more calories per day. Fewer than half of grade schoolers participate in daily physical education classes. Many spend five hours or more a day in front of a computer or television screen.

J. Genetics. Although scientists have identified genes involved in appetite and metabolism, they have not found a genetic cause for obesity. It may be that various genes contribute a small increase in risk or that rare abnormalities in many genes create a predisposition to weight gain and obesity.

K. Emotional influences. Obese people are neither more nor less psychologically troubled than others. Psychological problems, such as irritability, depression, and anxiety, are more likely to be the result of obesity than the cause. Emotions do play a role in weight problems. Just as some people reach for a drink or a drug when they're upset, others cope by overeating, bingeing, or purging.

—From Hales, *An Invitation to Health*, 12e

▶ Comprehension Questions

Write the letter of the answer on the line. Then explain your thinking.

Main Idea

_____ 1. What is the topic sentence of paragraph 6?

a. Not all Americans are equally likely to be overweight or obese.

b. As Figure 5.3 shows, the southern states have the highest concentration of obese residents.

c. Mississippi is home to the county with the highest percentage of people with a body mass index (BMI) between 30 and 40.

d. (BMI is defined as the ratio between weight and height that correlates with percentage of body fat.)

Why? What information in the selection leads you to give that answer?_____

_____

____   2. Which of the following sentences states the main idea of this reading passage?

    a. For the first time in history, more than half of the people on the planet are overweight.

    b. The World Health Organization, in its first global diet, exercise, and health program to combat obesity, recommends that governments promote public knowledge about diet, exercise, and health.

    c. A variety of factors, ranging from heredity to environment to behavior, played a role in the increase in overweight and obesity.

    d. Although scientists have identified genes involved in appetite and metabolism, they have not found a genetic cause for obesity.

Why? What information in the selection leads you to give that answer? _____

_____

_____

Supporting Details

____   3. According to the reading passage, which of the following is *not* a confirmed cause of obesity?

    a. sedentary pursuits

    b. suburban sprawl

    c. high-fat, high-calorie foods

    d. genetics

Why? What information in the selection leads you to give that answer? _____

_____

_____

____   4. Based on Figure 5.2 on page 263, which of the following details is accurate?

    a. White males have a higher rate of obesity than black males.

    b. Hispanic women have the highest obesity rate among female minorities.

    c. White and Hispanic males have a higher prevalence of being overweight and obese than their female counterparts.

    d. Black, white, and Hispanic women all have a higher obesity rate than their male counterparts.

Why? What information in the selection leads you to give that answer? _____

_____

_____

_____

Author's Purpose

____ 5. What is the main purpose of this reading passage?

    a. to inform readers about the causes of global obesity

    b. to entertain readers with the evolution of portion sizes

    c. to persuade readers that they are in danger of becoming fat and should change their diets

    d. to inform readers that obesity is not caused by psychological issues

Why? What information in the selection leads you to give that answer? _____

_____

____ 6. What is the purpose of Figure 5.4 on page 265?

    a. to persuade readers to eat original portion sizes

    b. to inform readers about why they are getting fat

    c. to inform readers of how the available sizes of popular food products have increased since they were first introduced

    d. to entertain students with fun facts about the benefits of eating larger portion sizes

Why? What information in the selection leads you to give that answer? _____

_____

Relationships

____ 7. What is the overall pattern of organization of this reading passage?

    a. time order

    b. listing

    c. comparison and contrast

    d. cause-and-effect

Why? What information in the selection leads you to give that answer? _____

_____

____ 8. What relationship is found in the following sentence?

> Obese people are neither more nor less psychologically troubled than others.

    a. classification

    b. comparison and contrast

    c. cause-and-effect

    d. narration

Why? What leads you to give that answer? _____

_____

Fact, Opinion, and Inference

____ 9. Which of the following information is stated as a fact in the reading passage?

    a. Less than 50 percent of the earth's human population is obese.

    b. The percentage of obese women has tripled in the last 20 years.

    c. Native Americans may have different metabolic rates than other Americans, causing their communities to have very high percentages of overweight adults.

    d. Wyoming has the lowest obesity rate among adults in the United States.

Why? What leads you to give that answer? _____

_____

_____

____ 10. Which of the following can be inferred from this reading passage?

    a. The government is ultimately responsible for the obesity rates in the United States because it allows people the choice of what they eat.

    b. Obesity may be caused partly by cheap food.

    c. This author is overweight, if not obese. That is why she knows so much about obesity.

    d. The World Health Organization is winning the war against obesity.

Why? What information in the selection leads you to give that answer? _____

_____

_____

_____

▶ Critical Thinking Questions

Critical Thinking Level 1   ▶ Remember

Recall two examples of how exposure to a Western lifestyle influenced groups to become overweight.

1. _____

_____

2. _____

_____

Critical Thinking Level 2   ▶ Understand

Summarize the reading. You will need to think about the three comprehension questions (What is the reading about? What is the author's point about the topic? What is the proof for the author's main idea?). In your summary, note examples of each important point in the main idea.

What is the reading about? _____

What is the author's point about the topic? <u>A variety of factors, ranging from heredity to environment to behavior, played a role in the increase in overweight and obesity.</u>

What is the proof for the author's main idea?

1. _____

_____

2. _____

_____

3. _____

_____

4. _____

_____

Summary: _____

_____

_____

_____

_____

Critical Thinking Level 3 ‣ Apply

Apply what you have been reading about to yourself and your family. What kinds of choices that affect your weight do you and your family make? Explain your thoughts.

_____

_____

_____

Critical Thinking Level 4 ‣ Analyze

Compare and contrast this idea from the passage with the idea about guns that follows:

> Although ultimately each individual decides what and how much to eat, policy makers agree that governments also must act to reverse the obesity epidemic.

People who shoot and kill others would never be able to do that if they couldn't purchase a gun. And they couldn't buy guns if gun manufacturers didn't make them. So gun manufacturers should be held legally responsible for the deaths of shooting victims.

List all the similarities and differences you can find between these two ideas.

_____

_____

_____

Critical Thinking Level 5 ‣ Evaluate

With classmates, *evaluate* who is responsible for obesity. Is it the government, the individual, fast food restaurants, or someone or something else? If you can't agree on an answer, try to rank the various answers in terms of who is most responsible, next most responsible, and so on.

_____

_____

_____

Critical Thinking Level 6 ‣ Create

Imagine you are on the World Health Organization task force to create a global diet, exercise, and health program to combat obesity. Work with a group of classmates to create a list of suggestions you would include in this plan.

_____

_____

_____

▶Vocabulary in New Contexts

Review the vocabulary words in the margins of the reading selection and then complete the following activities.

EASY Note Cards

Make a note card for each of the vocabulary words that you did not know from the reading. On one side, write the word. On the other side, divide the card into quarters and label them E, A, S, and Y. Add a word or phrase in each area so that you wind up with an example sentence, an antonym, a synonym, and, finally, a definition that shows you have figured out the meaning of the word with your logic. Remember that an antonym or synonym may have appeared in the reading.

Relationships Between Words

Circle *yes* or *no* to answer the question. Then explain your answer.

1. Would a person who is **malnourished** be **satiated**?

   Yes   No

   Why or why not? _____

2. Would a typical **culprit** be **bombarded** by guilt?

   Yes   No

   Why or why not? _____

3. Could not exercising be a **culprit** in increasing one's **susceptibility** to disease?

   Yes   No

   Why or why not? _____

Language in Your Life

Write short answers to each question. Look at the vocabulary words closely before you answer.

1. Name something you are **bombarded** with on a daily basis. _____

   _____

2. Name something that increases your **susceptibility** to feeling compassionate. _____

   _____

3. Name one time when you were the **culprit**. _____

   _____

4. Name some images that come to mind when you think of the word **malnourished**. _____

   _____

5. What is the perfect meal to leave you feeling **satiated**? _____

   _____

Language in Use

Select the best word to complete the meaning of each sentence.

| bombarded | culprits | malnourished | satiated | susceptibility |

1. While no one knows for sure, the United Nations Food and Agriculture Organization estimates there are 925 million _____ people in the world.

2. With about 7 billion people in the world, that means 1 in 7 people do not know what it means to be _____ on a daily basis.

3. The group with the highest chance of _____ to malnutrition is children.

4. Being undernourished causes these children to be _____ by disease, which leads to approximately 5 millions deaths per year.

5. The cause of hunger varies, but the usual _____ include poverty, harmful economic systems, conflict, and climate change.

 Click to Connect! For more practice applying the skills you learned in this chapter, visit **www.cengagebrain.com** to access the CourseMate for this chapter.

Shutterstock.com

6

Recognizing Patterns of Organization

> " *Design is not just what it looks like and feels like. Design is how it works.* "
>
> —STEVE JOBS

Connect with Ideas

Think about Jobs's idea about design in relation to a couple of objects that you use every day. How does design matter in "how it works"?

Activate Your Knowledge

Consider a piece of writing that you've read; it could be from a magazine, book, newspaper, or online. What can you say about its design?

Engage with the Chapter

Survey the box on page 280. Are these paragraph patterns only designs for writing, or also for thinking? Discuss your ideas.

Read and Talk

Online Article

Fashion designers show their new creations and within moments, it seems, others are making quick, less expensive copies of the clothing and accessories. How is this done and what is being done to prevent it? Read to find out.

Visit www.cengagebrain.com to access the CourseMate for this chapter to hear vocabulary words from this reading and an audio recording of it.

To Copy or NOT to Copy…

1   To copy or NOT to copy…that is the question, although the question is not new. As early as the 1700s, French silk weavers insisted on protection for their designs. And high-end fashion designers in the United States have been trying since 1914 to gain design protection. Designers have **reiterated** their need for protection some 93 times; the current legislation is the Innovative Design Protection and Piracy Prevention Act ("IDPPPA"), introduced to Congress in 2010. This bill attempts to make illegal copied garments that are "substantially similar" to the original. Supporters argue that this standard of similarity should apply to fashion just as it has been used for other kinds of creative works, like books, movies, and music.

reiterated Use the context for the meaning of this word.

2   The debate on the need for fashion piracy protection has gone back and forth. Some think that the law would bring restrictions and more litigation into every aspect of design, thereby **stifling** creativity. Others think it would open up creativity since designers could be sure their work would be valued at a fair price. Some say that the sale of knockoffs steals $12 billion per year from designers, and should be stopped. Others say that the U. S. fashion market is worth a **robust** $196 billion per year, so what's a few billion here or there? Still others say that "knocking off" a designer is the highest form of flattery. However, many top couturiers say it is not a compliment they enjoy getting. They simply consider it theft.

stifling An antonym is used in the next sentence.

robust Think about the size of the US fashion market to determine the meaning.

3   One example is the fashion label Foley + Corinna. They are the most commonly copied label despite the fact that many people have never heard of them. It is because of the frequency of knockoffs of their designs that this duo has become central in the debate of fashion piracy. The co-founder Anna Corinna gives one example of how knockoffs affect their business. She tells of a regular customer who had purchased four dresses for her bridesmaids to wear. She paid $300 for each dress. Later the customer saw the "same dress" in a discount designer's store window. She returned the dresses. Corinna says, "When one of our designs gets knocked off, the dress is cheapened—customers won't touch it." Even though this does illustrate an effect knockoffs has, it is hard to feel too badly about Foley + Corinna; their annual sales total more than $20 million.

High-couture fashion designs like this dress from designer Zac Posen, which might sell for several thousand dollars, are often pirated and sold for a fraction of the price.

4   Still, it is not really fair to justify theft simply because it is from a successful company. In particular, many smaller designers cannot absorb the losses they **sustain** due to knockoffs. If it is illegal to copy (steal) music, movies, ideas, logos, art, and this paragraph, it should also be illegal to steal fashion designs. As it stands now, copyright law might protect the printed fabric, but it does not apply to the underlying design of the clothing, which is considered a "useful article" rather than a creation.

sustain Use the context to understand this word's meaning.

5   However, designers aren't asking for the shape of the garment to be protected. It is the style, creative design, and process that should be thought of as intellectual property worth protecting. Many factors about the design and manufacturing of a garment, such as the type and quality of the material, whether the piece is handmade or machine made, and whether the print is exclusive, affect the cost of a fashion item. When confronted with the question of fashion piracy, judges have tended to rule it's piracy if the knockoff can fool someone within the fashion industry. But maybe a fairer standard is the "squint test" proposed by two law professors, Hemphill and Suk. If a reasonable person squints and cannot tell the difference between the real item and the knockoff, then the knockoff should be illegal.

Talking about Reading

Respond in writing to the questions below and then discuss your answers with your classmates.

1. What conflict does the article describe, and who is involved in it? _____

   _____

2. What are some of the distinctions between designer pieces and the knockoffs? _____

   _____

3. Do you or anyone you know shop at stores like Forever 21? Can you think of any other stores that sell knockoffs? _____

   _____

4. Do you think knockoffs should be illegal? If so, how should courts determine what is a knockoff? Is the "squint test" a good option, or is there a better strategy? _____

   _____

5. 🎞 **Scan to Connect!** Use your smart phone to scan this code to watch a video. (See the inside front cover for more information on how to use this.) As you watch the video, think about the pros and cons mentioned about knockoffs.

Predicting Paragraph Patterns

In Chapter 2 we talked about turning titles and headings into questions in order to predict what a reading selection is going to be about. For example, you might read the heading "Characteristics of a Good Nursing Home" in a psychology book and form the question, "What are the characteristics of a good nursing home?" This allows you to reflect on what you already know about a subject before reading and prepares you to search for the parts of the answer to the question, which are the main ideas.

In addition to predicting content, you may also be able to predict the structure of the information that you will be reading. Predicting the structure is helpful because it gives you a chance to form a *schema*, that is, a framework that you can use to format the material mentally.

For example, suppose you read the sentence "The first signs of civilization in Mesoamerica appeared with the emergence of what is called Olmec culture." First, you can apply to this sentence the same questioning strategy you've been using for titles and headings: What signs of civilization appeared in Mesoamerica with the emergence of Olmec culture? Second, you can mentally prepare a structure for the answers to this question, which you are about to learn. Your mental schema might look like this:

Sign: ?

Sign: ?

Sign: ?

Sign: ?

In other words, you don't know yet what the signs of civilization are, and you don't know how many signs there are, but you have prepared yourself to pick them out from all the other details in the passage. As you are reading, you will mentally be filling in the schema with the first sign, the second sign, and so on.

Interaction 6–1 Fill in the Schema with Information

Read the following paragraph to find out what the first signs of civilization in Mesoamerica were. After you read, fill in the schema with the signs.

Early Civilizations in Central America

The first signs of civilization in Mesoamerica appeared in the first millenium B.C.E., with the emergence of what is called Olmec culture in the hot and swampy lowlands along the coast of the Gulf of Mexico south of Veracruz. Olmec civilization was characterized by intensive agriculture along the muddy riverbanks in the area and by the carving of stone ornaments, tools, and monuments at sites such as San Lorenzo and La Venta. The Olmec peoples organized a widespread trading network, carried out religious rituals, and devised a system of hieroglyphics that is similar in some respects to later Mayan writing and may be the ancestor of the first true writing systems in the New World.

—From Duiker, *World History*, 5e

First signs of civilization in Mesoamerica

Sign: _____

Sign: _____

Sign: _____

Sign: _____

Sign: _____

As you can see from Interaction 6–1, if you mentally form a blank schema before you read, then as you read you can be actively searching for the information to fill it in. Taking the time to form a schema as you read is an important part of improving your reading comprehension. Noticing the paragraph pattern will help you grasp which details are more important than others to the author's main idea.

Examining Paragraph Patterns

The paragraph structure you studied in Chapter 4 gives you a way to visualize the relationships between the general and specific ideas in paragraphs. Once you see in outline form what the paragraph is About (topic) and what the author's Point about the subject is (main idea), you can examine what Proof (supporting details) the author offers to support the point. In this chapter we will discuss eight different patterns in which supporting details may be organized.

Patterns of Support

▶ **Description** shows readers what something looks, sounds, feels, tastes, or smells like. Descriptions are often arranged in space order.

▶ **Narration** tells readers how something happened. Narratives use time order. Stories and timelines are examples of narration.

▶ **Process** reveals to readers what steps need to occur for something to happen, and in what order. Events that happen in steps and stages may be written using the process pattern.

▶ **Cause-and-effect** lets readers know what made something happen (causes), or what an event leads to (effects). Another way to put this is that cause-and-effect addresses the reasons why or the results of.

▶ **Examples** are used to illustrate general ideas and make them come alive for readers. They may be preceded by the words "for example."

▶ **Comparison and contrast** describes for readers how things are the same (comparison) and/or different (contrast).

▶ **Definition** tells readers what something means. In textbooks, words that will be defined may be called "terms" or "key words."

▶ **Classification** notes for readers what kinds or types of an event or thing exist.

Description: What Does This Look, Sound, Feel, Taste, and Smell Like?

People learn about the world through their senses of sight, hearing, feeling, tasting, and smelling. No matter where you are right now, you can use your senses to orient yourself. If you look up from this book, you can move your eyes around the room or landscape and say things like, "You left your keys beside your iPod on the desk" or "The tires of the trucks are squealing, and I can smell the exhaust of all the traffic." What you are sensing may remind you of something else that seems similar: "The clock's ticking sounds like a child's heartbeat." This use of the word *like* to link two very different thoughts is called a *simile*. When a writer emphasizes sensory details, the writing pattern is called *description*.

Description answers questions such as "What does this look like?" "What does it sound like?" and "What does it feel like?" Description sometimes relies on spatial (space) order to organize details.

Reading Strategy for | Description

As you read, mentally use your senses of sight, hearing, feeling, smelling, and tasting and your sense of movement to re-create the scene the author is describing.

Description Paragraphs   Nonfiction Book

Using the reading strategy for description, read the passage. Then go back and read the highlighted words and the annotations that explain their function in the description pattern. More explanation follows the paragraph.

From the Wild

He came out of the night, appearing suddenly in my headlights, a big, golden dog, panting, his front paws tapping the ground in an anxious little dance. Behind him, tall cottonwoods in their April bloom. Behind the grove, the San Juan River, moving quickly, dark and swollen with spring melt.

▶ Spatial arrangement

▶ Signal words (transitions) for space order, for example, *behind* and *next to*

It was nearly midnight, and we were looking for a place to throw down our sleeping bags before starting our river trip in the morning. Next to me in the cab of the pickup sat Benj Sinclair, at his feet a midden of road-food wrappers, smeared with the scent of corn dogs, onion rings, and burritos. Round-cheeked, Buddha-bellied, thirty-nine years old, Benj had spent his early years in the Peace Corps, in West Africa, and had developed a stomach that could digest anything. Behind him in the jump seat was Kim Reynolds, an Outward Bound instructor from Colorado known for her grace in a kayak and her long braid of brunette hair, which held the odor of a healthy, thirty-two-year-old woman who had sweated in the desert and hadn't used deodorant. Like Benj and me, she had eaten a dinner of pizza in Moab, Utah, a hundred miles up the road where we'd met her. Like us, she gave off the scents of garlic, onions, tomato sauce, basil, oregano, and anchovies.

▶ Sensory details

—Kerasote, *Merle's Door: Lessons from a Freethinking Dog*

Spatial arrangement. Placement in space often is an important method for organizing sensory details. When you are reading, look for words that signal how the elements of the scene are arranged.

Signal Words (Transitions) for Space Order

- ▶ in the foreground, in the background
- ▶ on the left, in the middle, on the right
- ▶ in front of, behind, in back of
- ▶ north, south, east, west
- ▶ above, below, underneath, behind, forward, in front of
- ▶ off in the distance, beyond, up close
- ▶ farther away, near, nearby, closer, through
- ▶ at, in, on (as in *at the store, in the wilderness, on the table*)
- ▶ here, there
- ▶ inward, outward

Sensory details. Words that describe sights, sounds, smells, feelings, tastes, and movements help descriptive writing come alive: *a big, golden dog; dark and swollen with spring melt; gave off the scents of garlic, onions, tomato sauce.* Combinations of sensory details create word-pictures with emotional overtones. For example, *his front paws tapping the ground in an anxious little dance* includes sights, sounds, and the writer's interpretation of the dog's emotional state (*anxious*).

Interaction 6–2 ▶ Recognize Words That Signal Space Order

In the following sentences, underline words that signal space order. (Consult the list above as needed.)

1. In the Verkhoyansk Mountains of northeast Siberia, Eveny nomads are on the move.

2. Teams of reindeer pull caravans of sledges down the steep slide of a frozen mountain river.

3. Bells tinkle on the lead reindeer while dogs on short leashes dive closely alongside through the snow like dolphins beside a boat.

4. One man sits on the lead sledge of each caravan, his right foot stretched out in front of him and his left foot resting on the runner ready to fend off hidden rocks and snagging roots. Passengers or cargo sit on the sledges behind.

5. The passage of each caravan is visible from afar by a cloud of frozen reindeer breath.

—Vitebsky, *The Reindeer People*

Narration: How Did That Happen?

For all of human history, people have been telling stories. When stories are made up, we call them *fiction*, and the pattern of events in the story or novel is called the *plot*. But any time people recount events, whether the events actually occurred or not, we call the pattern *narration*.

Narration answers the questions: "How did that happen?" or "How is that happening now?" or even "How will that happen in the future?" Narration relies on time order. Time order indicates which events happened first, second, third, and so on. Writers who use time order use various kinds of words and phrases to indicate what happened when.

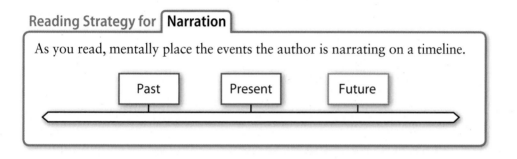

Reading Strategy for **Narration**

As you read, mentally place the events the author is narrating on a timeline.

Past   Present   Future

A Narration Paragraph   Magazine Article

Using the reading strategy for narration, read the paragraph. Then go back and read the highlighted words and the annotations that explain their function in the narration pattern. More explanation follows the paragraph.

A few years ago, a major Asian shopping mall chain realized that since pregnant mothers spent a great deal of time shopping, the potential for "priming" these women was significant. Pregnancy, after all, is among the most primal, emotional periods in women's lives. Between the hormonal changes and the nervous anticipation of bringing another life into the world, it's also one of the times when women are most vulnerable to suggestion. So the shopping mall chain began experimenting with the unconscious power of smells and sounds. First, it began spraying Johnson & Johnson's baby powder in every area of the mall where clothing was sold. Then it infused the fragrance of cherry across areas of the mall where one could buy food and beverages. Then it started playing soothing music from the era when these women were born (in order to evoke positive memories from their own childhoods, a popular tactic). The mall executives were hoping this would boost sales among pregnant mothers (which it did).

▶ Specific time words and dates

▶ Signal words (transitions) for time order, such as *first* and *then*

▶ Verbs and verb phrases

—Lindstrom, *Brandwashed*, p. 13

Specific time words and dates. Time is a crucial element in narration. When you are reading, look for phrases that will help you figure out when things have occurred.

Signal Words (Transitions) for Time Order

- ▶ Monday through Friday
- ▶ during that time
- ▶ before, during, after
- ▶ first, second, third
- ▶ first, next, then, later
- ▶ since [a date]: since 1976
- ▶ on Wednesday; on March 17, 2012
- ▶ in the period from 1865 to 1877
- ▶ ever since [something happened]: ever since she graduated
- ▶ as, meantime, meanwhile
- ▶ preceding, immediately, following, afterward
- ▶ as soon as, when, until
- ▶ still
- ▶ subsequently, eventually

Verbs and verb phrases. Verbs are a major indicator of when things happened in relation to other events. Here, the chain of malls *infused* the smell of cherry in the eating areas. The verb *infused* is in the simple past tense. That means that the event already occurred. A couple of sentences later, *were hoping* is a verb phrase that shows duration in time: executives hoped for a while, not just for a moment. In general, *-ing* verbs (such as *experimenting* and *spraying*) describe continuing actions. They are happening over a period of time.

Interaction 6–3 ▶ **Recognize Time Words and Verb Tenses**

In the following sentences, underline words that signal time order. (Consult the list above as needed.) Circle the verbs, and on the line after each sentence, write the time period indicated by the verb: past, present, or future.

Examples of verbs

Past tense: was, did, had, baked, filmed, hoped, burnt, spoken

Present tense: is, does, has, bakes, film, hope, burn, speaks

Future tense: will be, will do, will have, will bake, will hope

1. In 1999, Ken Burns made a documentary film, *Not for Ourselves Alone,* on the women's rights movement. _____

2. Part One tells the story from about 1840 through the Civil War. _____

3. The film focuses on the collaboration between Susan B. Anthony and Elizabeth Cady Stanton.

   _____

4. In 1848, after a visit with her friend and fellow activist Lucretia Mott, Stanton helped organize the first Women's Rights Convention in Seneca Falls. _____

5. Stanton demanded civil and legal equality for women, including the right to vote.

   _____

—From Murrin et al., *Liberty, Equality, Power,* 5e. Copyright © 2011 Cengage Learning, Inc.
Reproduced by permission. www.cengage.com/permissions

Process: What Steps Need to Occur, and in What Order?

In science courses and other technical contexts, you will often find a special version of narration called *process writing.* The point of process writing is to tell readers what steps to follow to achieve a certain result or to describe the stages that lead to a certain event or result. For example, a biology book may describe the process of how a cell divides. Process writing answers the question: "What steps need to occur, and in what order, to make something else happen?" To be sure that readers understand a process thoroughly, a writer makes it plain what has to happen first, second, and third. So just like narration, process writing relies on time order. Sometimes the writer also needs to outline general conditions that need to be true before the process can occur.

Reading Strategy for | Process

To keep the order of events clear as you read, mentally fill in the events on a generalized timeline.

First event	Second event	Third event	Fourth event	and so on

Process Paragraphs   Sociology Textbook

Using the reading strategy for process writing, read the paragraph. Then go back and read the highlighted words and the annotations that explain their function in the process pattern. More explanation follows the paragraph.

Ecological Theory

Nearly a century ago, Robert Park proposed an influential theory of how race and ethnic relations change over time (Park, 1914; 1950). His ecological theory focuses on the struggle for territory.

It distinguishes five stages in the process by which conflict between ethnic and racial groups emerges and is resolved:

▶ **Ordering devices.** Numbers help readers keep track of the stages, and labels summarize each stage.

1. *Invasion.* The territory may be as large as a country or as small as a neighborhood in a city.
2. *Resistance.* The established group tries to defend its territory and institutions against the intruding group. It may use legal means, violence, or both.
3. *Competition.* If the established group does not drive out the newcomers, the two groups begin to compete for scarce resources. These resources include housing, jobs, public park space, and political positions.

▶ **Narrative elements.** After some labels is a narrative explaining what usually happens.

4. *Accommodation and Cooperation.* Over time, the two groups work out an understanding of what they should segregate, divide, and share. **Segregation** involves the spatial and institutional separation of racial or ethnic groups. For example, the two groups may segregate churches, divide political positions in proportion to the size of the groups, and share public parks equally.
5. *Assimilation.* Assimilation is the process by which a minority group blends into the majority population and eventually disappears as a distinct group. Park argued that assimilation is bound to occur as accommodation and cooperation allow trust and understanding to develop. Eventually, goodwill allows ethnic groups to fuse socially and culturally. Where two or more groups formerly existed, only one remains.

▶ **Conditions.** Sometimes processes work only under certain conditions.

Park's theory stimulated important and insightful research. However, it is more relevant to some ethnic groups than others.

—From Brym/Lie, *Sociology: Your Compass for a New World*, 3e. Copyright © 2007 Cengage Learning, Inc. Reproduced by permission. www.cengage.com/permissions

---

Ordering devices. Authors Brym and Lie use two main ordering devices in this passage to clearly distinguish the five stages of the process they are describing: numbers, which help readers understand the order of the stages; and labels, which act as a summary of what each stage consists of. In process writing that is printed as a paragraph instead of as a numbered list, the stages or steps might be ordered with letters such as (a), (b), and (c), or with words such as those in the following list.

Signal Words (Transitions) for Process Writing

- ▶ first step, second step, third step
- ▶ first stage, second stage, third stage
- ▶ phases
- ▶ that (these, those) stages or steps
- ▶ first, then, eventually, last
- ▶ start, continue, end
- ▶ as [one thing happens, another thing happens], during, meanwhile, while
- ▶ any of the words from the narration list on page 284

Narrative elements. If you don't read the numbers and the labels, and instead just read the rest of each stage of the ecological theory, you will see that it is a kind of narration. In this particular piece of writing, the events are described at a level of generality that is broader than in the narratives you read in the narration section. The highlighted sentence in number 4, for instance, does not refer specifically to how particular groups decide to segregate, divide, and share. Instead it generalizes about any such interaction between two ethnic groups.

Conditions. Sometimes processes only work under certain conditions—for instance, water changes to ice only at 32°F. Here, the theory is outlined in the textbook before the conditions under which it proves true are given. We haven't reprinted the next section here, but Brym and Lie go on to say that ecological theory is an accurate description of what happened when white Europeans immigrated to America, but it has not proved to be accurate regarding other ethnic groups who have come here.

Interaction 6–4 **Recognize Words That Signal a Process**

Underline words that signal the stages of a process. (See pages 286–287 for a list.) One sentence doesn't include any.

1. The theory of *assortative mating* states that people find partners based on their similarity to each other along many dimensions, such as age and intelligence.

2. When people meet, according to Murstein's (1987) classic theory, they apply three filters, representing discrete stages.

3. The first stage is represented by the idea of *stimulus*. The question asked about a potential mate in this step is "Do the person's physical appearance, social class, and manners match your own?"

4. Second, people want to know about possible mates' *values:* "Do the person's values regarding sex, religion, politics, and so on match your own?"

5. The third stage or filter is *role:* "Do the person's ideas about the relationship, communication style, gender roles, and so on match your own?"

—From Kail/Cavanaugh, *Human Development,* 4e

Cause-and-Effect: What Made This Happen? What Does This Lead To?

Cause-and-effect paragraphs may focus on the causes of an event, in which case they answer questions such as "What made this happen?" or "What's the reason this occurred?" When they focus on the effects that came about because of something else that happened, cause-and-effect paragraphs answer questions like "What does this lead to?" or "What is the result of this action?" Another kind of variation is that a cause-and-effect paragraph may describe how a single cause leads to multiple effects, or how multiple causes create a single effect. A piece of writing may even describe how one cause leads to an effect, which then becomes the cause of a second effect, which then becomes the cause of yet another effect, and so on. This last type is called a *causal chain*.

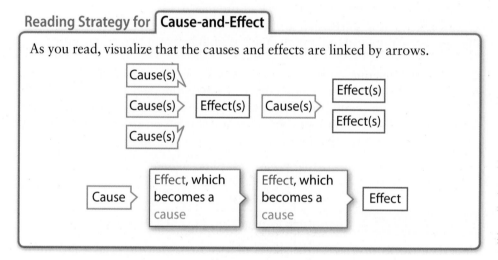

Reading Strategy for Cause-and-Effect

As you read, visualize that the causes and effects are linked by arrows.

Cause(s)
Cause(s) → Effect(s)   Cause(s) → Effect(s) / Effect(s)
Cause(s)

Cause → Effect, which becomes a cause → Effect, which becomes a cause → Effect

A Cause-and-Effect Paragraph   Anthropology Textbook

Using the reading strategy for cause-and-effect, read the paragraph. Then go back and read the highlighted words and the annotations that explain their function in the cause-and-effect pattern. More explanation follows the paragraph.

Cell Phones and Pedestrian Behavior

▶ Time order is not necessarily followed. A writer may choose to discuss an effect before a cause, as in the first sentence.

[1]In some U.S. cities there has been a dramatic rise in automobile accidents caused by inattentive pedestrians crossing the street while talking on their phones. [2]In addition to the dangers involved, the sidewalks of cities like New York are losing some of their civility. [3]In pre-cell phone days, crowded rush-hour sidewalks were reasonably easy to navigate because most people were looking where they were going....

⁴Today, however, with their minds elsewhere, phone-using pedestrians bump into other walkers, confuse others with their public conversations, and accidentally hit other pedestrians with their unrestrained hand gestures. ⁵The widespread use of cell phones, in other words, is making normal pedestrian traffic flow increasingly more difficult. ⁶Moreover, the rise of personal isolation caused by extensive cell phone use makes it less likely that pedestrians will help strangers in need or exchange pleasantries in a chance encounter—two occurrences that make urban living invigorating. ⁷These developments raise an important question: just how aware are we of the negative social consequences of our signing a one-year contract with a cell-phone company offering us 5,000 "anytime" minutes per month?

—From Ferraro, *Cultural Anthropology, 6e*

▸ Words that express degrees of uncertainty

▸ Signal words indicating that one thing causes another, such as *is making, caused by,* and *consequences*

Words indicating that one thing leads to another. In sentence 1, the words *caused by* point to a cause-and-effect relationship between people talking on cell phones crossing the street and car accidents: The first causes the second. Sentences 5, 6, and 7 use other words that indicate cause-and-effect: *is making, makes, caused by,* and *consequences* (which is another word for *effects*). Words that indicate cause-and-effect include the following. The lines tell you where you will find the cause or effect.

Signal Words (Transitions) for Causes:

_____ causes

_____ creates

_____ allows for

_____ leads to

_____ makes

because _____

are due to _____

reason is _____

is/are shaped by a number of factors: _____, _____, _____ .

brought about by _____

Signal Words (Transitions) for Effects:

causes _____

leads to _____

makes (or made) _____

consequences are _____

_____ depends on

_____ were the effects

_____ is the result

Words that express degrees of uncertainty. It's hard to be sure what causes what, and the writer here is careful to say that personal isolation makes it *less likely* that walkers with cell phones will help a stranger or strike up a conversation—not that personal isolation makes it *impossible*. Here are some words that express degrees of uncertainty:

- ▶ may [cause, affect]
- ▶ might, could [be a reason, lead to, be an effect]
- ▶ tends to
- ▶ possibly
- ▶ to a degree, to some degree

Time order is not necessarily followed. Even though logically, causes must precede (come before) effects in time, writers may choose to discuss the effect first, as Ferraro does in the first sentence. The accidents come after people talking on their cells cross the street without noticing what's going on, but the sentence puts the accidents first.

Interaction 6–5 ▶ **Recognize Cause-and-Effect Words**

Underline the transitions that signal cause-and-effect in the following sentences.

1. When Hernan Cortes and his fellow conquistadors arrived in Mesoamerica in 1519, the local inhabitants were frightened of the horses and the firearms that accompanied the Spaniards.

2. But the most lethal effects were caused by invisible disease-bearing microbes brought by these strange new arrivals. Diseases have made the lives of human beings, in the words of the English philosopher Thomas Hobbes, "nasty, brutish, and short."

3. Illnesses such as malaria and tuberculosis caused our immediate ancestors to sicken and die.

4. With the explosive growth of the human population brought about by the agricultural revolution, the problems posed by the presence of disease intensified.

5. People started living in close quarters in villages and cities, and this allowed bacteria to settle in their piles of refuse. Lice also carried bacteria around in people's clothing.

—From Duiker, *World History*, 5e

Interaction 6–6 ▶ **Apply Your Knowledge of Patterns**

Circle the signal words in each selection. If the signal words relate to the major details, use this information to determine which paragraph pattern is being used. However, for some selections, signal words won't help much. You will also need to think about the three comprehension questions (What is the reading about? What is the author's point about the topic? What is the proof for the author's main idea?).

Choose from these paragraph patterns:

description	narration	process	cause-and-effect

Selection A   **Ecology Textbook**

Pattern: _____

Scientists use logical reasoning and critical thinking to learn about the natural world. Such skills help scientists and the rest of us to distinguish between facts and opinions, evaluate evidence and arguments, and develop informed positions on issues.

Thinking critically involves three important steps:

1. Be skeptical about everything we read or hear.

2. Look at the evidence to evaluate it and any related information and opinions that may come from various sources. Validating information is especially important in the Internet age where we can be exposed to unreliable data, some of which may be just opinions from uninformed amateurs posing as experts.

3. Identify and evaluate our personal assumptions, biases, and beliefs. As the American psychologist and philosopher William James observed, "A great many people think they are thinking when they are merely rearranging their prejudices." We can also heed the words of the American writer Mark Twain: "It's what we know is true, but just ain't so, that hurts us."

—From Miller/Spoolman, *Essentials of Ecology*, 6e (p. 34). Copyright © 2012 Cengage Learning, Inc. Reproduced by permission. www.cengage.com/permissions

Selection B   **Magazine Article**

Pattern: _____

"Not many people can say a guitar saved their life—me and B. B. King, maybe," says musician and legendary long-distance hiker "Walkin'" Jim Stolz. In June 1982, Stolz was trekking the length of Utah (about 700 miles from Arizona to Idaho) when he scaled snowy Mt. Timpanogos near Provo and spent the night looking down on the twinkling city lights. Downclimbing the next morning proved dicier: Lacking an ice axe and crampons, Stolz slipped and started sliding on his belly toward a sheer cliff. He kicked and clawed at the ice, but to no avail. "In a way, I gave up," Stolz recalls. "I rolled onto my back, thinking at least I'd see what I was about to hit, and that's when I was jerked to a halt." The neck of his guitar—which he had lashed to his backpack upside down, without a case—had plowed into the ice like an axe, stopping him just short of certain death. The guitar still played, too.

—From *Backpacker* magazine, October 2006, p. 32. Reprinted by permission of the author.

Selection C   **Health Textbook**

Pattern: _____

Two-thirds of American adults, up from fewer than half 20 years ago, are overweight. About one in every three Americans is obese. Since the 1970s, the obesity rate has doubled for teens and tripled for children between the ages of 6 and 11. How did we get so fat? A variety of factors played a role. Here are some of them.

1. **More calories.** Bombarded by nonstop commercials for taste treats, tempted by foods in every form to munch and crunch, Americans are eating more—some 200 to 400 calories more a day than they did several decades ago.

2. **Bigger portions.** The size of many popular restaurant and packaged foods has increased two to five times during the past 20 years. According to studies of appetite and satiety, people presented with larger portions eat up to 30 percent more than they otherwise would.

3. **Fast food.** Young adults who eat frequently at fast-food restaurants gain more weight and develop metabolic abnormalities that increase their risk of diabetes in early middle age. In a recent study, those who ate fast food at least twice a week gained an extra 10 pounds and had a two-fold increase in insulin.

4. **Physical inactivity.** As Americans eat more, they exercise less. Experts estimate that most adults expend 200 to 300 fewer calories a day than people did 25 years ago. The most dramatic drop in physical activity often occurs during the college years.

5. **Passive entertainment.** Television is a culprit in an estimated 30 percent of new cases of obesity. TV viewing may increase weight in several ways: It takes up time that otherwise might be spent in physical activities. It increases food intake since people tend to eat more while watching TV. And compared with sewing, reading, driving, or other relatively sedentary pursuits, television watching lowers metabolic rate so viewers burn fewer calories.

—From Hales, *An Invitation to Health*, 12e

Selection D | **World History Textbook** |

Pattern: _____

    Three hundred years later, a new power, the kingdom of Chimor, with its capital at Chan Chan, at the mouth of the Moche River, emerged in the area. Built almost entirely of adobe, Chan Chan housed an estimated thirty thousand residents in an area of over 12 square miles that included a number of palace compounds surrounded by walls nearly 30 feet high. One compound contained an intricate labyrinth that wound its way progressively inward until it ended in a central chamber, probably occupied by the ruler. Like the Moche before them, the people of Chimor relied on irrigation to funnel the water from the river into their fields. An elaborate system of canals brought the water through hundreds of miles of hilly terrain to the fields near the coast.

—From Duiker, *World History*, 5e

Examples: What Are Examples of This General Idea?

Examples give the specific, down-to-earth details that help readers understand the general statements a writer is making. For example, if you tell a friend that you had a fabulous Caribbean vacation, you might use as examples the warm sun, which was always shining; the food, all freshly caught fish and local fruits and vegetables; the snorkeling, where you met a new romantic interest; and your hotel, which was right on the beach. Examples help make general statements come alive.

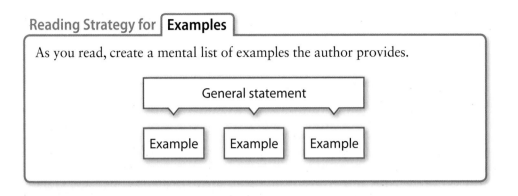

Reading Strategy for Examples

As you read, create a mental list of examples the author provides.

General statement

Example   Example   Example

An Example Paragraph   Health Textbook

Using the reading strategy for examples, read the paragraph. Then go back and read the highlighted words and the annotations that explain their function in the example pattern. More explanation follows the paragraph.

Stress on Campus

You've probably heard that these are the best years of your life, but being a student—full-time or part-time, in your teens, early twenties, or later in life—can be extremely stressful. For example, you may feel pressure to perform well to qualify for a good job or graduate school. To meet steep tuition payments, you may have to juggle part-time work and coursework. You may feel stressed about choosing a major, getting along with a difficult roommate, passing a particularly hard course, or living up to your parents' and teachers' expectations. If you're an older student, you may have children, housework, and homework to balance. Your days may seem so busy and your life so full that you worry about coming apart at the seams. One thing is for certain: you're not alone.

—From Hales, *An Invitation to Health*, 12e

▸ General idea that examples will support

▸ Signal words such as *For example* may introduce examples

▸ Examples

General idea. This first sentence offers the general statement that the rest of the passage will support; in other words, this is the topic sentence. The last part of the sentence leads into the examples: being a student can be extremely stressful.

The examples. The author lists seven different examples of how students may feel stressed. Some sentences describe a single example; one of them describes four different stressors.

Signal words for examples and lists. In example paragraphs, examples are often given in a list: here is one example, here is the second example, and here is the third example. In this paragraph, the repeated use of the word *may* is an indication that each sentence is performing a similar function. Transitions are sometimes used to let the reader know an example is coming.

Signal Words (Transitions) for Examples

- ▶ for instance
- ▶ to illustrate
- ▶ namely
- ▶ for example

Notice that example phrases are often followed by a comma.

Listing words may be used to list the examples, although they are not used in this paragraph.

Signal Words (Transitions) for Lists

- ▶ in addition, also, add to this
- ▶ first, second, third
- ▶ first, and, then

Interaction 6–7 ▶ **Recognize Words That Signal Examples**

In the following sentences, underline words and phrases that signal an example has just been given or will follow. (See the list above.)

1. Gender-specific interaction styles have serious implications for who is heard and who gets credit at work. For instance, a female office manager doesn't want to seem bossy or arrogant, so she spends a good deal of time soliciting coworkers' opinions before making an important decision. But her boss considers her approach indecisive and selects an assertive man for a senior job.

2. As another example, male managers tend to say "I" in situations where female managers tend to say "we"—as in "I'm hiring a new manager." The male phrasing emphasizes personal accomplishments.

3. The contrasting interaction styles illustrated previously often result in female managers not getting credit for competent performance.

4. As background to this issue, the gender roles that children learn in their families, at school, and through the mass media form the basis for their social interaction as adults. For instance, by playing team sports, boys tend to learn that social interaction is often about competition, conflict, self-sufficiency, and hierarchical relationships. Girls play with dolls and tend to learn that socialization is about maintaining cordial relationships, avoiding conflict, and resolving differences of opinion through negotiation.

5. Based on these patterns, misunderstandings between men and women are common. A stereotypical example: Harold is driving around lost. However, he refuses to ask for directions because doing so would amount to an admission of inadequacy. Meanwhile, it seems perfectly "natural" to Sybil to want to share information, so she urges Harold to ask for directions. Conflict results.

—From Brym/Lie, *Sociology*, 3e

Comparison and Contrast: How Are These the Same? How Do They Differ?

Comparisons show how two things are similar. Contrasts show how they are different. Sometimes the word *comparison* is used more generally to indicate both of these moves. Comparison and contrast are two of the most important patterns of thought that we have. The formation of words and the use of language, and therefore thought itself, depends on comparison and contrast. Comparison and contrast is the basis for several other patterns covered in this chapter. It is used to show what is and what is not part of a term's definition, and it is used as a basis for organizing ideas or items into categories for classification.

Reading Strategy for | Comparison and Contrast

Mentally or on paper, form two lists, one for each item being compared or contrasted. As the author gives each piece of information for an item, place it in the appropriate list.

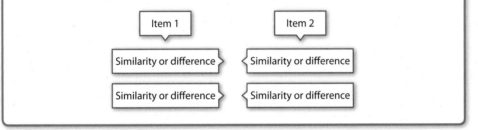

A Comparison Paragraph   Government Web Site

Using the reading strategy for comparison, read the paragraph. Then go back and read the highlighted words and the annotations that explain their function in the comparison pattern. More explanation follows the paragraph.

Heart-Healthy Diets

Heart disease is the No. 1 killer of adult Americans. To improve heart health, the U.S. Department of Health and Human Services recommends following a heart-healthy diet. Two such diets are the Heart Healthy Diet and the Therapeutic Lifestyle Changes (TLC) Diet; they are nearly identical. Both of these diets are designed to maintain healthy levels of cholesterol or reduce unhealthy levels of cholesterol. Cholesterol, a waxy substance, comes in two versions: LDL, or "bad" cholesterol, which causes arteries to narrow and become blocked; and HDL, or "good" cholesterol, which does the opposite. The diets both call for choosing foods that are low in saturated fat, which raises LDL more than any other food. The Heart Healthy Diet calls for getting only 8 to 10 percent of total daily

▶ Words that indicate sameness

▶ Similar phrasing may be used to indicate similarity, such as *Both of these diets* and *The diets both*

▶ Minor differences may be noted.

calories from saturated fat, and the TLC, less than 7 percent. The two diets also recommend the same daily amounts of fat, dietary cholesterol, and sodium (salt): roughly 30 percent or less of total calories from fat, less than 300 milligrams (mg) of dietary cholesterol, and no more than 2400 mg of sodium. Not surprisingly, given the fact that people who are overweight have higher blood cholesterol than people who are not overweight, another similarity of the diets is that they call for eating just enough calories to achieve or maintain a healthy weight.

—Adapted from "Heart Healthy Eating," WomensHealth.gov

Words that indicate sameness. Comparison shows how things are alike, and thus writing organized in this pattern often includes words such as those in the following list.

Signal Words (Transitions) for Comparisons
- ▶ the same, identical, equivalent
- ▶ similar, similarly, a similarity
- ▶ alike, like, likewise
- ▶ both
- ▶ share
- ▶ agree
- ▶ not only … but also

Similar phrasing. At times, similar ideas are stated in sentences that have similar patterns. Here, look for the sentences that begin *Both of these diets, These diets both, The two diets, similarity of the diets.* The sentence patterns are not exactly the same, but they are similar enough to point out that the ideas in the sentences may be similar as well.

Minor differences may be noted. Two things are never exactly the same—think about it. If they were, would they be two things, or one? So even in a paragraph that's mainly about similarities, you will often find information about differences, too.

Interaction 6–8 ▶ Recognize Words That Indicate Sameness

In the following sentences, underline words and phrases that indicate sameness. (Consult the list above as needed.)

1. The epic of Gilgamesh has as its hero Gilgamesh, who is similar to King Arthur in British legends in that nobody knows whether he actually existed, but lots of stories were told about him.

2. Like the Greek hero Odysseus (Ulysses) and the Arabian hero Sinbad the Sailor, Gilgamesh went on epic travels, and he met many strange things and people on his journeys.

3. One of them was a centuries-old man called Utnapashtim, who told Gilgamesh a story that shares many similarities with the story of Noah's Ark.

4. In both stories, gods were angry with humans and sent a great flood to destroy everybody.

5. And like Noah was warned by God to build an ark, in the older tale, the water god Ea told Utnapashtim to build a boat to withstand the flood.

—Adapted from Dawkins, *The Magic of Reality* (pp. 140–141)

Contrast Paragraphs   Nonfiction Book

Using the reading strategy for contrast, read the passage. Then go back and read the highlighted words and the annotations that explain their function in the contrast pattern. More explanation follows the paragraph.

Video Games versus Traditional Games

Most video games differ from traditional games like chess or Monopoly in the way they withhold information about the underlying rules of the system. When you play chess at anything beyond a beginner's level, the rules of the game contain no ambiguity; you know exactly the moves allowed for each piece, the procedures that allow one piece to capture another. The question that confronts you sitting down at the chessboard is not: What are the rules here? The question is: What kind of strategy can I concoct that will best exploit those rules to my advantage?

In the video game world, on the other hand, the rules are rarely established in their entirety before you sit down to play. You're given a few basic instructions about how to manipulate objects or characters on the screen, and a sense of some kind of immediate objective. But many of the rules—the identity of your ultimate goal and the techniques available for reaching that goal—become apparent only through exploring the world. You literally learn by playing.

—Johnson, *Everything Bad Is Good for You*

▶ Words that indicate differences

▶ Sentence patterns that point out differences, such as the ones highlighted here and in the next paragraph

Words that indicate differences. Contrast is a pattern that emphasizes differences, so you will often see words like the following in writing that contrasts.

Signal Words (Transitions) for Contrast

▶ differs from, differs by, a difference
▶ contrasts with, in contrast, to the contrary
▶ on the one hand…on the other hand
▶ however, although, but, while
▶ instead, rather

Sentence patterns that point out differences. These patterns may take obvious forms such as "On the one hand,…" and "On the other hand,…" but they may also be more subtle. Notice here that the first paragraph is about traditional games and the second paragraph is about video games. If you compare some of the sentences from each paragraph, you can see that Johnson used similar phrasing in order to make the differences stand out.

From first paragraph	From second paragraph
The rules of the game contain no ambiguity.	The rules are rarely established in their entirety.
You know exactly the moves allowed for each piece.	You're given a few basic instructions about how to manipulate objects.

Notice also the two sentences at the end of the first paragraph that suggest a contrast through the use of the pairing *is not … is*.

Interaction 6–9 ▶ **Recognize Words That Indicate Difference**

In the following sentences, underline words that indicate difference. If necessary, refer to the list on page 297. Some sentences may not have any such words.

1. Harvard University professor Jeffrey Frankel points out that budget deficits rose during the administrations of Republicans Ronald Reagan (1981–1989) and George W. Bush, but fell under Bill Clinton.
2. Other observers have noted a contrast in Democratic and Republican budgets.
3. Reagan faced a Congress controlled by the Democrats; Clinton in turn faced a Republican Congress for most of his administration.
4. Reagan regularly submitted budgets larger than the ones that the Democratic Congress eventually passed, however, while Clinton's budgets were typically smaller than those approved by the Republican Congress.
5. The perception is that the Democrats still tend to favor the less well-off, while the Republicans tend to favor the prosperous.

—From Schmidt/Shelley/Bardes, *American Government and Politics Today 2007–2008*, 13e

Definition: What Does This Mean?

Definition answers the question: "What does this mean?" Definitions include the term being taught and a description of its meaning. Examples are often given to illustrate the meaning of the term. Sometimes, illustrations of what the term does *not* include are also provided.

Reading Strategy for | **Definition**

As you read a definition, mentally slot the various parts of the definition into these categories:

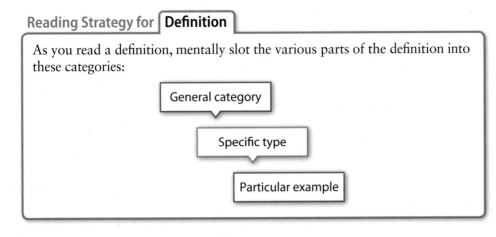

A Definition Paragraph   Mathematics Textbook

Using the reading strategy for definition, read the paragraph. Then go back and read the highlighted words and the annotations that explain their function in the definition pattern. More explanation follows the paragraph.

The Fair-Division Problem

Often you must share something you want with other people. As a child, you probably shared toys, space in a room, and parents' attention. Adults might share living space, inherited property, vacation homes, and valuables from a divorce settlement. In this chapter we study the fair-division problem, that is, the problem of finding ways in which two or more people can fairly divide something among themselves without the aid of an outside arbitrator. By tradition, the people who are trying to share the desirable object or objects are called players.

▶ Examples that readers can relate to

▶ A definition that includes a general term and then the specifics

▶ Words that signal a definition or a term is coming, such as *that is* and *are called*

—From Parks, *A Mathematical View of Our World*, 1e. Copyright © 2007 Cengage Learning, Inc. Reproduced by permission. www.cengage.com/permissions

Examples that readers can relate to. Writers usually try to help readers understand new ideas by showing how they relate to familiar ideas. Here, the writer gives seven different examples of when the fair-division problem might come up in everyday life, both for children and for adults. And although this paragraph doesn't include them, sometimes the following phrases are used to indicate that the writer is providing examples in support of a definition:

- ▶ for example, for instance
- ▶ to illustrate, to exemplify
- ▶ as an illustration, as an example

Words that signal a definition or a term is coming. Sometimes a term is simply followed by the word *is* and the definition: *A fair-division problem is a problem of finding....* Here, the authors have given readers a clue that a definition is coming by using the phrase *that is* after the term being defined. In the next sentence, the words *are called* indicate that a definition has just been given and that the term being defined will follow.

Signal Words (Transitions) for Definitions

  ▶ is
  ▶ that is
  ▶ are called
  ▶ means, has come to mean
  ▶ can be understood as

A definition that includes a general term and then the specifics. The fair-division problem is called, first, a problem, which is a general term, and then is described very specifically as a certain type of problem: *a problem of finding ways in which two or more people can fairly divide something among themselves without the aid of an outside arbitrator.* If any part of the definition were not matched by the real-life scenario, for example, if an outside arbitrator were to be called in to help solve the problem, it would no longer be considered *a fair-division problem.*

| Interaction 6–10 | Recognize the Words That Signal Terms, Definitions, and Examples |

In the following sentences, underline words and phrases that signal a term, definition, or example. (Consult the lists on pages 299–300 as needed.)

1. A *business entity* is an individual, association, or organization that engages in economic activities and controls specific economic resources. For instance, General Motors is a business entity.

2. Three basic accounting elements exist for every business entity: assets, liabilities, and owner's equity. These elements are defined below.

3. *Assets* are items that are owned by a business and will provide future benefits. Examples include cash, merchandise, buildings, and land.

4. *Liabilities* represent something owed to another business entity. One kind of liability are formal written promises to pay suppliers or lenders specified sums of money at definite future times, known as *notes payable.*

5. *Owner's equity* is the amount by which the business assets exceed the business liabilities. An owner's personal assets, such as a house and clothing, are not considered in the business entity's accounting records.

—From Heintz/Parry, *College Accounting*, 19e. Copyright © 2008 Cengage Learning, Inc. Reproduced by permission. www.cengage.com/permissions

Classification: What Kinds Are There?

Classification answers the question "What kinds are there?" Suppose someone asked you, "What kinds of movies do you like?" You might answer, "I like romantic comedies, psychological thrillers, and espionage movies." These are categories, or kinds, of movies. In other words, a general topic, movies, has been divided up into different types.

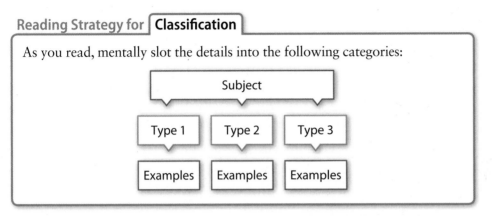

Reading Strategy for **Classification**

As you read, mentally slot the details into the following categories:

Subject

Type 1   Type 2   Type 3

Examples   Examples   Examples

A Classification Paragraph   **Mass Media Textbook**

Before you read this paragraph, survey the title and first sentence, and note the words and parts of words that are in *italics*. Then read the paragraph, using the reading strategy for classification. Finally, go back and read the highlighted words and the annotations that explain their function in the classification pattern.

> ### Ways People Communicate
>
> Three ways to describe how people communicate are intrapersonal, interpersonal, and mass communications. Each form of communication involves different numbers of people in specific ways. If you are in a market and you silently debate with yourself whether to buy a package of double-chunk chocolate chip cookies, you are using what scholars call *intra*personal communication—communication within one person. To communicate with each other, people rely on their five senses—sight, hearing, touch, smell and taste. Scholars call this direct sharing of experience between two people *inter*personal communication. **Mass communication** is communication from one person or group of persons through a transmitting device (a medium) to large audiences or markets. In *Media/Impact* you will study *mass* communication.
>
> —From Biagi, *Media/Impact*, 8e

▶ Words that indicate divisions into kinds, such as *Three ways*

▶ Information on the principle behind the classification

▶ Definitions of the types according to the principle of classification

Words that indicate division into kinds. The first words of this paragraph, *Three ways*, immediately tell us that it will offer classification. Many classification paragraphs have this combination of a number and a word indicating kinds, such as the examples in the following list.

Signal Words (Transitions) for Classification

- ▶ several kinds
- ▶ certain forms
- ▶ three patterns
- ▶ four types
- ▶ different groups

Other kinds of words that indicate classification are verbs that show the action of dividing up:

- ▶ divided into
- ▶ classified by
- ▶ split up

Information on the principle behind the classification. The second sentence tells us that this classification is going to be based on the number of people involved.

Definitions of the types according to the principle of classification. Often, definitions of each type are provided. Notice that these definitions are based on the principle of classification. If the intended readers already know what the types are, the writer might just give some examples instead of definitions. But in textbooks, you'll usually find definitions of each type.

Interaction 6–11 ▶ Recognize Words That Signal Division into Kinds

Underline words in the following sentences that indicate division into kinds. Consult the lists above as needed.

1. Cultural anthropologists have identified three major types of marriage based on the number of spouses permitted.
2. *Monogamy,* the practice of having only one spouse at a time, is the kind of marriage one finds in the United States and Canada.
3. A second form of marriage is *polygamy*: the practice of one man having more than a single wife. Approximately 70 percent of the world's cultures prefer polygamy; however, within those cultures, only about a third of men will actually have more than one wife.
4. The third kind of marriage, which is much rarer than polygamy, is *polyandry*. Polyandry involves the marriage of a woman to two or more men at a time.

—From Ferraro, *Cultural Anthropology,* 6e

Interaction 6–12 ▶ Apply Your Knowledge of Patterns

Circle the signal words in each selection. If the signal words relate to the major details, use this information to determine which paragraph pattern is being used. However, for two selections, signal words won't help much. You will also need to think about the three comprehension questions (What is the reading about? What is the author's point about the topic? What is the proof for the author's main idea?).

Choose from these paragraph patterns:

examples	comparison	contrast	definition	classification

Selection A   **Psychology Textbook**

Pattern: _____

Prosocial behavior is any behavior that benefits another person. Cooperation—that is, working together toward a common goal—is one form of prosocial behavior. Of course, cooperation often "works" because individuals gain more than they would by not cooperating. In contrast, altruism is behavior that is driven by feelings of responsibility toward other people, such as helping and sharing, in which individuals do not benefit directly from their actions. If two youngsters pool their funds to buy a candy bar to share, this is cooperative behavior. If one youngster gives half of her lunch to a peer who forgot his own, this is altruism.

—From Kail/Cavanaugh, *Human Development*, 4e

Selection B   **Public Speaking Textbook**

Pattern: _____

The power to influence others through opposition and even anger seems quite common and almost normal. But there are other ways to influence people when you give speeches. As you've watched and listened to combative exchanges, you may have heard critics of this approach call for more civility in public exchanges. The word *civility* comes from a root word meaning "to be a member of a household." In ancient Greece, *civility* referred to displays of temperance, justice, wisdom, and courage. Over time, the definition has changed only slightly, and in public speaking, **civility** has come to mean care and concern for others, the thoughtful use of words and language, and the flexibility to see the many sides of an issue. To be civil is to listen to the ideas and reasons of others and to give "the world a chance to explain itself."

—From Griffin, *Invitation to Public Speaking*, 4e

Selection C   **Health Textbook**

Pattern: _____

Two depressants of the central nervous system that are commonly abused are Xanax and Halcion. Prescribed for people who are experiencing anxiety, tension, panic attacks, acute stress reactions, and sleep disorders, Xanax and Halcion both have the effect of slowing brain activity, which produces a sense of calm. In the short term, using these depressants causes people to feel sleepy and uncoordinated; after a few days, the body becomes used to the effects and these feelings diminish. In the long term, these drugs may cause physical dependence and addiction.

—From Hales, *An Invitation to Health*, 12e

Selection D   **Biology Textbook**

Pattern: _____

Most plants and animals have cells, tissues, organs, and organ systems that split up the task of survival.... In other words, the plant or animal body shows a division of labor. A **tissue** is a community of cells and intercellular substances that are interacting in one or more tasks. For example, wood and bone are tissues that function in structural support. An **organ** has at least two tissues that are organized in certain proportions and patterns and that perform one or more common tasks. A leaf adapted for photosynthesis and an eye that responds to light in the surroundings are examples. An **organ system** has two or more organs interacting physically, chemically, or both in the performance of one or more common tasks. A plant's shoot system, with organs of photosynthesis and reproduction, is like this. So is an animal's digestive system, which takes in food, breaks it up into bits of nutrients, absorbs the bits, and expels the unabsorbed leftovers.

—From Starr/Evers/Starr, *Biology*, 2e

Selection E   Mass Media Textbook

Pattern: _____

   Today's media markets are increasingly global. U.S. media companies are looking for markets overseas at the same time that overseas media companies are purchasing pieces of media industries in the United States and other countries. MTV, for example, is available 24 hours a day in St. Petersburg, Russia. In the U.S., Yahoo Inc. paid $1 billion to buy a 40 percent interest in China's biggest online commerce firm, alibaba.com. The U.S. TV network ABC and the British Broadcasting Corporation have formed a news-gathering partnership to share television and radio news coverage worldwide. This service will compete with CNN to deliver news by satellite. Jim Murai, who has been called "the father of Japan's Internet," created a non-profit network to connect all of Japan's universities to the Internet, without government approval. Ultimately, he says, he "wants to connect all the computers in this world."

—From Biagi, *Media/Impact*, 8e

Transition Words and the Patterns They Signal

The following chart lists signal words that point to different patterns of organization. You may want to consult the chart when you are trying to figure out how a reading is organized.

Signal Words	Organizational Patterns
above	space order
after, afterward	time order
agree	comparison
alike	comparison
allows for	cause and effect
although	contrast

Signal Words	Organizational Patterns
are called	definition
as	time order
as soon as	time order
at	space order
because	cause and effect
before	time order
behind	space order
below	space order
beyond	space order
both	comparison
brought about by	cause and effect
but	contrast
can be understood as	definition
categories	classification
cause, causes	cause and effect
closer	space order
consequences are	effect
consists of	definition
continue	time order
contrasts with	contrast
creates	cause and effect
defined as	definition
depends on	cause and effect
difference	contrast
different groups	classification
differs by, differs from	contrasts
due to	cause and effect
during, during that time	time order

Signal Words	Organizational Patterns
effect	effect
end	time order
eventually	time order
ever since	time order
factors	causes
farther away	space order
first (or second, third, fourth, etc.)	time order, example
first stage, first step	time order (process)
first type	classification
following	time order
for example	example
for instance	example
forms (used as a noun)	classification
forward	space order
here	space order
however	contrast
identical	comparison
if … then …	cause and effect
immediately	time order
in	space order, time order
in addition	example
in back of, in the background	space order
in contrast	contrast
in front of, in the foreground	space order
in the middle	space order
inside	space order
instead	contrast
is	definition
kinds	classification

Signal Words	Organizational Patterns
last	time order
later	time order
leads to	cause and effect
like, likewise	comparison
makes, made	cause and effect
means, has come to mean	definition
meantime, meanwhile	time order
namely	definition
near, nearby	space order
next	time order
not only … but also	comparison
off in the distance	space order
on	space order, time order
on the one hand … on the other hand	contrast
outside, outward	space order
phases	process, classification
preceding	time order
rather	contrast
reason is	cause
result is	effect
second, second stage or step	time order, example
second type	classification
share	comparison
similar, similarity, similarly	comparison
since	time order
start	time order
still	time order
subsequently	time order
that is	definition

Signal Words	Organizational Patterns
the same	comparison
then	time order
there	space order
third, third stage or step	time order, example
third type	classification
through	space order, time order
to illustrate	example
to the contrary	contrast
types	classification
under, underneath	space order
until	time order
up close	space order
when	time order, cause
while	time order, contrast

Connect Your Skills

Recognizing Patterns of Organization

On each line next to a paragraph or a part of a paragraph, note the pattern of organization the author has used.

Illness and Evolution: Work in Progress?

1. _____

1   Predators aren't the only things that are out to get us. Parasites are a more sneaky threat, but they are just as dangerous. Parasites include tapeworms and flukes, bacteria and viruses, which make a living by feeding off our bodies. Predators such as lions also feed off bodies, but the distinction between a predator and a parasite is usually clear. Parasites feed off still-living victims (though they may eventually kill them) and they are usually smaller than their victims. Predators are either larger than their victims (as a cat is larger than a mouse) or, if smaller (as a lion is smaller than a zebra), not very much smaller. Predators kill their prey outright and then eat them. Parasites eat their victims more slowly, and the victim may stay alive a long time with the parasite gnawing away inside.

2   Parasites often attack in large numbers, as when our body suffers a massive infection with a flu or cold virus. Parasites that are too small to see with the naked eye are often called "germs," but that's rather an imprecise word. They include viruses, which are very very small indeed; bacteria, which are larger than viruses but still very small (there are viruses that act as parasites on bacteria); and other single-celled organisms like the malarial parasite, which are much larger than bacteria but still too small to be seen without a microscope. Ordinary language has no general name for these larger single-celled parasites. Some of them can be called "protozoa," but that's now rather an outdated term. Other important parasites include fungi, for example ringworm and athlete's foot (big things like mushrooms and toadstools give a false impression of what most fungi are like).

3   Examples of bacterial diseases are tuberculosis, some kinds of pneumonia, whooping cough, cholera, diphtheria, leprosy, scarlet fever, boils and typhus. Viral diseases include measles, chickenpox, mumps, smallpox, herpes, rabies, polio, rubella, various varieties of influenza and the cluster of diseases that we call the "common cold." Malaria, amoebic dysentery and sleeping sickness are among those diseases caused by "protozoa." Other important parasites, larger still—large enough to be seen with the naked eye—are the various kinds of worms, including flatworms, roundworms and flukes. When I was a boy living on a farm, I would quite often find a dead animal like a weasel or a mole. I was learning biology at school, and I was interested enough to dissect these little corpses when I found them. The main thing that impressed me was how full of wriggling, live worms they were (roundworms, technically called nematodes). The same was never true of the domesticated rats and rabbits we were given to dissect at school.

4   The body has a very ingenious and usually effective system of natural defense against parasites, called the immune system. The immune system is so complicated that it would take a whole book to explain it. Briefly, when it senses a dangerous parasite the body is mobilized to produce special cells, which are carried by the blood into battle like a kind of army, tailor-made to attack the particular parasites concerned. Usually the immune system wins, and the person recovers. After that, the immune system "remembers" the molecular equipment that it developed for that particular battle, and any subsequent infection by the same kind of parasite is beaten off so quickly that we don't notice it. That is why, once you have had a disease like measles or mumps or chickenpox, you're unlikely to get it again. People used to think it was a good idea if children caught mumps, say, because the immune system's "memory" would protect them against getting it as an adult—and mumps is even more unpleasant for adults (especially men, because it attacks the testicles) than it is for children. Vaccination is the ingenious technique of doing something similar on purpose. Instead of giving you the disease itself, the doctor gives you a weaker version of it, or possibly an injection of dead germs, to stimulate the immune system without actually giving you the disease.

2. _____

3. _____

4. _____

5. _____

6. _____

7. _____

8. _____

9. _____

10. _____

11. _____

12. _____

13. _____

The weaker version is much less nasty than the real thing: indeed, you often don't notice any effect at all. But the immune system "remembers" the dead germs, or the infection with the mild version of the disease, and so is forearmed to fight the real thing if it should ever come along.

5   The immune system has a difficult task "deciding" what is "foreign" and therefore to be fought (a "suspected" parasite), and what it should accept as part of the body itself. This can be particularly tricky, for example, when a woman is pregnant. The baby inside her is "foreign" (babies are not genetically identical to their mothers because half their genes come from the father). But it is important for the immune system not to fight against the baby. This was one of the difficult problems that had to be solved when

14. _____

pregnancy evolved in the ancestors of mammals. It was solved—after all, plenty of babies do manage to survive in the womb long enough to be born. But there are also plenty of miscarriages, which perhaps suggests that evolution had a hard time solving it and that the solution isn't quite complete. Even today, many babies survive only because doctors are on hand—for example, to change their blood completely as soon as they are born, in some extreme cases of auto-immune overreaction.

6   Another way in which the immune system can get it wrong is to fight too hard against a supposed "attacker." That is what allergies are: the immune

15. _____

16. _____

system needlessly, wastefully and even damagingly fighting harmless things. For example, pollen in the air is normally harmless, but the immune system of some people overreacts to it—and that's when you get the allergic reaction called "hay fever": you sneeze and your eyes water, and it is very unpleasant. Some people are allergic to cats, or to dogs: their immune systems are overreacting to harmless molecules in or on the hair of these animals. Allergies can sometimes be very dangerous. A few people are so allergic to peanuts that eating a single one can kill them.

7   Sometimes an overreacting immune system goes so far that a person is

17. _____

18. _____

allergic to himself! This causes so-called auto-immune diseases (*autos* is Greek for "self"). Examples of auto-immune diseases are alopecia (your hair falls out in patches because the body attacks its own hair follicles) and psoriasis (an overactive immune system causes pink scaly patches on the skin).

8   It is not surprising that the immune system sometimes overreacts, because there's a fine line to be trodden between failing to attack when you should and attacking when you shouldn't. It's the same problem we met over the

19. _____

antelope trying to decide whether to run away from the rustle in the long grass. Is it a leopard? Or is it a harmless puff of wind stirring the grass? Is this a dangerous bacterium, or is it a harmless pollen grain? I can't help wondering whether people with a hyperactive immune system, who pay the penalty of allergies or even auto-immune diseases, might be less likely to suffer from certain kinds of viruses and other parasites.

9   Such "balance" problems are all too common. It is possible to be too "risk averse"—too jumpy, treating every rustle in the grass as danger, or unleashing a massive immune response to a harmless peanut or to the body's own tissues. And it is possible to be too gung-ho, failing to respond to danger when it is very real, or failing to mount an immune response when there really is a dangerous parasite. Treading the line is difficult, and there are penalties for straying off in either direction.

20. _____

10   Cancers are a special case of a bad thing that happens: a strange one, but a very important one. A cancer is a group of our own cells that have broken away from doing what they are supposed to do in the body and have become parasitic. Cancer cells are usually grouped together in a "tumor," which grows out of control, feeding on some part of the body. The worst cancers then spread to other parts of the body (that's called metastasis) and eventually often kill it. Tumors that do this are called malignant.

21. _____

22. _____
23. _____

11   The reason cancers are so dangerous is that their cells are directly derived from the body's own cells. They are our own cells, slightly modified. This means the immune system has a hard time recognizing them as foreign. It also means it is very difficult to find a treatment that kills the cancer, because any treatment you can think of—like a poison, say—is likely to kill our own healthy cells as well. It is much easier to kill bacteria, because bacterial cells are different from ours. Poisons that kill bacterial cells but not our own cells are called antibiotics. Chemotherapy poisons cancer cells, but it also poisons the rest of us because our cells are so similar. If you overdo the dose of the poison, you may kill the cancer, but not before killing the poor patient.

24. _____

12   We're back to the same problem of striking a balance between attacking genuine enemies (cancer cells) and not attacking friends (our own normal cells): back to the problem of the leopard in the long grass again.

13   Let me end this chapter with a speculation. Is it possible that auto-immune diseases are a kind of byproduct of an evolutionary war, over many ancestral generations, against cancer? The immune system wins many battles against pre-cancerous cells, suppressing them before they have a chance to become fully malignant. My suggestion is that, in its constant vigilance against pre-cancerous cells, the immune system sometimes goes too far and attacks harmless tissues, attacks the body's own cells—and we call this an auto-immune disease. Could it be that the explanation of auto-immune diseases is that they are evidence of evolution's work-in-progress on an effective weapon against cancer?

25. _____

14   What do you think?

—From Richard Dawkins, *The Magic of Reality* (pp. 242–245). Copyright © 2011 The Free Press, a division of Simon & Schuster. Reprinted by permission.

Click to Connect! To check your comprehension of chapter concepts, visit **www.cengagebrain.com** to access the CourseMate for this chapter.

Chapter Summary Activity

This chapter has discussed how preparing your mind to receive information in certain patterns and then recognizing those patterns in writing leads to better comprehension. Construct a Reading Guide to Recognizing Patterns of Organization here by completing each main idea on the left with specific supporting details from the chapter on the right. You can use this guide later as you complete other reading assignments.

Reading Guide to Recognizing Patterns of Organization

Complete this idea with...	information from Chapter 6.
Predicting paragraph patterns:	
Why?	1. _____ _____
	2. _____ _____
How?	
Eight patterns of support:	**Definition and signal words for each pattern**
Description	3. **Definition:** _____ _____
	4. **Signal words:** _____ _____
Narration	5. **Definition:** _____ _____
	6. **Signal words:** _____ _____
Process	7. **Definition:** _____ _____
	8. **Signal words:** _____ _____
Cause and effect	9. **Definition:** _____ _____

Examples

Comparison

Contrast

Definition

Classification

10. **Signal words:** _____

_____

11. **Definition:** _____

_____

12. **Signal words:** _____

_____

13. **Definition:** _____

_____

14. **Signal words:** _____

_____

15. **Definition:** _____

_____

16. **Signal words:** _____

_____

17. **Definition:** _____

_____

18. **Signal words:** _____

_____

19. **Definition:** _____

_____

20. **Signal words:** _____

_____

Think about what your reading comprehension strategies were before you read this chapter. How did they differ from the suggestions here? What is one new strategy you can start using? Write down your thoughts.

_____

_____

_____

Reading 6–1 | Nonfiction Book

▸ Pre-Reading the Selection

The following selection is taken from a book called *The Wal-Mart Effect*, by Charles Fishman. Fishman is a senior editor for the business magazine *Fast Company*, and he wrote many articles about Wal-Mart for the magazine that he later turned into *The Wal-Mart Effect*.

Surveying the Reading

Survey the selection that follows. Then check the elements that are included in this reading.

_____	Title	_____	Words in bold or italic type
_____	Headings	_____	Images and captions
_____	First sentences of paragraphs		

Guessing the Purpose

Based on the title of the book and the information about the author, do you suppose the book's purpose is to express, inform, persuade, or a combination of these purposes? _____

_____

Predicting the Content

Predict three things this selection will discuss.

▸ _____

▸ _____

▸ _____

Activating Your Knowledge

What experiences with Wal-Mart have you had? What have you seen on TV or read about Wal-Mart? What do you know about factory conditions around the world? List two or three things you know.

▸ _____

▸ _____

▸ _____

🎬 **Scan to Connect!** Use your smart phone to scan this code to watch a video to activate your knowledge about Wal-Mart and sweatshops. (See the inside front cover for more information on how to use this.) What were Kalpona Akter's working conditions at the Bangladeshi sweatshop in which she used to work?

Common Knowledge

global economy (*paragraph 1*) Businesses manufacturing (making) and selling their goods and services around the world, that is, not being limited to any one country.

sweatshop (*paragraph 3*) A place of work where employees work long hours for little money under poor working conditions (for example, in a place without windows, or in a smoky room).

developing country (*paragraph 4*) A country with a relatively low standard of living and not much industrial development.

▶ Reading with Pen in Hand

Students who annotate as they read are more successful than those who do not. That's why you will annotate each selection in *Connect* as you read. In the reading that follows, use the following symbols:

★ or (Point)   to indicate a main idea

① ② ③   to indicate major details

  Visit www.cengagebrain.com to access the CourseMate for this chapter to hear pronunciations of vocabulary words from this reading.

Dark Bargains of the Global Economy

Charles Fishman

1   One of the dark bargains of the global economy is that while the familiar stuff, like clothes, toys, and food, continues to arrive at the local Wal-Mart without interruption, and often with prices steadily dropping, the way that stuff is made is less and less familiar, more and more remote, and perhaps less and less acceptable, all the time. The factories themselves would be illegal in the United States because of the way those factories treat their workers and their communities; but the products of those factories are perfectly legal; indeed, the very unappealing manner in which they are produced makes them cheaper all the time, and so more appealing all the time.

▶ Where do you assume these factories are? Why?

2   "Because of the pressure of cost," says S. Prakash Sethi, an expert on global factory conditions, "factories do everything possible to save on the third decimal of a penny. Wal-Mart is one of the primary, if not the most important, engines that pushes those costs down."

▶ What is Sethi saying about Wal-Mart?

3   In **a world long gone**, we could step onto the fishing wharf, we could step into the dress shop, we could stop at the roadside vegetable stand and have some sense, however modest, of the conditions under which the food and

a world long gone What two words could you substitute for this phrase? Hint: Contrast this with the opening of the next sentence.

▶ What can't we do any more that
we could do before?

▶ What is meant by "the view
inside is unsettling"?

allegations Based on the example
that follows, what does this word
mean?

▶ Why did the two women come
to the United States in fall 2004?

products we bought were created. Today we rely on the laws, and on the companies themselves, sometimes to our disappointment and disgust. Nike, the Gap, Reebok, Disney, and Wal-Mart have all had to face, explain, and recover from sweatshop problems in the last twenty years.

4   And every time the door of a factory in a developing country that makes stuff for Americans is cracked open, the view inside is unsettling. The prices suddenly make sense, and not in a reassuring way. Both Kathie Lee Gifford and Wal-Mart denied the **allegations** that a Honduran factory using children was making clothing for the Kathie Lee Gifford line. The denials were both true and a lie. By the time of the congressional hearing, the clothes were no longer being made by children. But they had been.

5   In the fall of 2004, two women from Bangladesh spent a month touring college campuses, talking about their experiences working in clothing factories in Dhaka, the capital of Bangladesh. They were brought to the United States by a labor rights group, the National Labor Committee (NLC), which works to uncover and publicize inhumane factory conditions around the world. It was the NLC's executive director, Charles Kernaghan, who told Congress about the child labor that had been making Kathie Lee Gifford clothing. The two factory workers from Bangladesh spoke no English; their translator for the tour was an NLC staffer who came over with the women from the NLC's Dhaka office. The details of the women's lives as Bangladeshi garment workers—lives they described over and over again, at Yale, at Harvard, at the University of Iowa, at the University of Wisconsin—are like something not just from around the world, but from a different century.

6   As a sixteen-year-old junior sewing operator at the Western Dresses factory in Dhaka, Robina Akther's job was to sew pocket flaps on the back pockets of pants that Western Dresses was making for Wal-Mart. She says she earned 13 cents an hour—fourteen hours of work a day, $26.98 a month. If she didn't

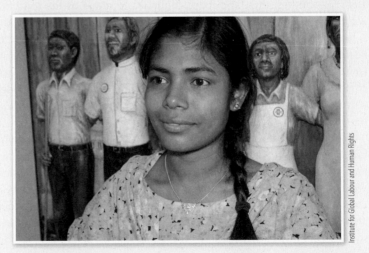

Institute for Global Labour and Human Rights

sew to the **mandated** pace, 120 pairs of pants an hour, here is what Akther said would happen: A supervisor would slap her across the face with the pants she was sewing. "If you made any mistakes or fell behind on your goal, they beat you," says Akther's translated account, which is posted on the NLC's Web site. "They slapped you and lashed you hard on the face with the pants. This happens very often. They hit you hard. It is no joke."

7   If what Akther says is true—Wal-Mart did not challenge the account as it was published in college newspapers, nor have they challenged the account that is posted on the NLC's Web site—then it is possible that Wal-Mart's customers were buying pants off the display racks that might literally have been used to beat the people who made them. Who is wearing those pants now?

8   As Akther describes it, life in the Western Dress factory was an **unending** series of days making clothes, starting before 8:00 A.M., lasting until 10:00 P.M. or 11:00 P.M., seven days a week. Ten days off in a year—not even one a month. No talking at the sewing tables, no drinking water at the sewing tables. No going to the bathroom except at the moment when permission is given, and then, "the bathrooms are filthy with no toilet paper or soap."

9   Despite the **relentless** work, Akther told college audiences, "I clean my teeth with my finger, using ash. I can't afford a toothbrush or toothpaste." Do Americans need clothing to be so inexpensive that the people making it cannot afford a toothbrush?

10   At the wages she described—typical for garment workers in Bangladesh—if Robina Akther were to have worked for fifty years as she did for those twenty months at the Western Dresses factory, if she could have survived fifty years, her total wages for the half century would have been $16,200. Wal-Mart's profit in 2004—profit, not sales—is $19,597 per minute.

11   Robina Akther's account now appears in a new forum: In September 2005, she sued Wal-Mart in court in the United States, **alleging** that in a factory making clothing for Wal-Mart, she was not even provided with the basic wages, overtime pay, and protection from physical abuse that Bangladeshi law provides. Actually, in the lawsuit, Akther is identified only as Jane Doe II—she is anonymous, along with fourteen other workers from five countries who are plaintiffs against Wal-Mart. The fifteen factory workers—from China, Indonesia, Swaziland, and Nicaragua, as well as Bangladesh—all make or made merchandise for Wal-Mart, and all have nearly identical claims of sweatshop mistreatment. In the suit, Jane Doe II—Robina Akther—is arguing that Wal-Mart didn't just have a contract to buy clothes from the Western Dresses factory; Wal-Mart had a contract with her and her fellow factory workers, and that their **systematic** mistreatment is Wal-Mart's responsibility. Not Wal-Mart's ethical responsibility, Wal-Mart's legal responsibility. It is possible that Robina Akther is going to reach out from Dhaka and turn the Wal-Mart effect on its head.

—From *The Wal-Mart Effect* by Charles Fishman. Copyright © 2006 by Charles Fishman. Used by permission of The Penguin Press, a division of Penguin Group (USA) Inc.

mandated Based on the detail that follows, what does this word mean?

▶ Are the rewards and demands of Akther's job well balanced? Why or why not?

▶ Does the writer imply (suggest) here that Akther is telling the truth? If so, how?

unending Based on its use here, what does the prefix *un-* mean?

▶ What one word would you use to describe the work conditions related here?

relentless Based on the details in paragraph 8, what does this word mean?

▶ How would you answer the last question here? Why?

▶ What conclusion does the writer want us to come to by providing these sets of numbers?

alleging What word earlier in the reading passage relates to this word? What part of speech is each word?

▶ What is the new forum mentioned in the first sentence of paragraph 11?

▶ What are the workers who are suing Wal-Mart trying to achieve?

systematic The suffix *-ic* makes nouns into adjectives. What noun is part of this word?

▶ Comprehension Questions

Write the letter of the answer on the line. Then explain your thinking.

Main Idea

_____ 1. Which of the following statements best describes the main idea of this passage?

    a. Foreign factories should operate the way U.S. factories do.

    b. The low prices of goods in stores such as Wal-Mart are only possible because of the low wages and poor working conditions of factory workers around the world.

    c. Robina Akther worked for 13 cents an hour, fourteen hours a day, and in a month's time, all she made was $26.98.

    d. Fifteen factory workers are suing Wal-Mart in U.S. courts for the mistreatment of workers in factories in China, Indonesia, Swaziland, and Nicaragua.

Why? What information in the selection leads you to give that answer? _____

_____

_____

_____ 2. What is the main idea of paragraph 4?

    a. Clothing for the Kathie Lee Gifford line was made by children in Honduras.

    b. Kathie Lee Gifford and Wal-Mart lied about the use of child labor.

    c. Child labor stopped once investigations by Congress began.

    d. Prices in the United States depend on what happens inside factories in developing countries.

Why? What information in the selection leads you to give that answer? _____

_____

_____

Supporting Details

_____ 3. The main idea of paragraph 6 is stated in the last sentence of paragraph 5. What are the major supporting details in paragraph 6?

    a. Akther earned 13 cents an hour; she worked fourteen hours a day; she had to sew 120 pairs of pants an hour; if she didn't reach that goal, she got beaten.

    b. The two women spent a month touring college campuses; Akther earned 13 cents an hour; Akther's job was to sew pocket flaps on pants.

    c. Akther's remarks had to be translated by an NLC staff member; Charles Kernaghan told Congress about children making Kathie Lee Gifford clothing; the women seemed to be working in a different century.

    d. Akther worked at the Western Dresses factory in Dhaka; her job was to sew pocket flaps on the back pocket of pants being made for Wal-Mart; she made $26.98 a month.

Why? What information in the selection leads you to give that answer? _____

_____

_____

____ 4. Which comprehension question does the information about Kathie Lee Gifford in paragraph 4 answer?

    a. What is the reading about?

    b. What is the author's point about the topic?

    c. What is the proof for the main idea?

    d. All of the above.

Why? What information in the selection leads you to give that answer? _____

_____

_____

_____

Author's Purpose

____ 5. What is one possible reason Fishman includes paragraph 7?

    a. to give an example of his main point that Wal-Mart didn't challenge Akther's account

    b. to make readers feel emotionally involved

    c. to cast doubt on Akther's story

    d. to laugh at the person who is wearing the pants now

Why? What information in the selection leads you to give that answer? _____

_____

____ 6. What is one way the author makes sure that we feel, not just think about, the role of sweatshops in the global economy?

    a. He describes the National Labor Committee's work.

    b. He contrasts the way things used to be with the way they are now.

    c. He recounts Robina Akther's experiences in a sweatshop.

    d. He gives the facts about the factory workers suing Wal-Mart.

Why? What information in the selection leads you to give that answer? _____

_____

_____

Relationships

_____ 7. In paragraph 3, what is the relationship between the first two sentences?

   a. The two sentences offer a contrast.

   b. The second sentence is an example of the first sentence.

   c. The two sentences are in a cause-and-effect relationship.

   d. The first sentence is a major detail and the second sentence is a minor detail.

Why? What information in the selection leads you to give that answer? _____

_____

_____ 8. What pattern of organization provides structure for the supporting details in paragraph 5?

   a. narration

   b. comparison

   c. classification

   d. cause-and-effect

Why? What information in the selection leads you to give that answer? _____

_____

Fact, Opinion, and Inference

_____ 9. In paragraph 6, Akther's wages are said to be 13 cents an hour. Given that she works for fourteen hours a day and in a typical month has only one day off, how much money should she be making in a month?

   a. $26.98

   b. $73.25

   c. $12.33

   d. $54.60

Why? What leads you to give that answer? _____

_____

_____ 10. In paragraph 11 the author notes that workers from several developing countries are suing Wal-Mart in a U.S. court for the "systematic mistreatment" they have suffered. What does their action imply (suggest without stating outright)?

   a. Wal-Mart cannot be held responsible for the actions of another company.

   b. They hope to leave their jobs once they collect the financial settlements they want the court to award them.

   c. They believe a U.S. court has the right to rule on what happens in other countries.

   d. Wal-Mart should win because their contracts are with the companies who own those factories, not with the workers at the factories.

Why? What information in the selection leads you to give that answer? _____

_____

_____

▶ Critical Thinking Questions

Critical Thinking Level 1 ▸ Remember

Recount (tell) the details of the conditions of the factory in which Robina Akther worked.

_____   _____

_____   _____

_____   _____

_____   _____

_____   _____

Critical Thinking Level 2 ▸ Understand

Four kinds of organizations in the United States are mentioned in this reading selection as having an interest in the dark bargain of the global economy. Name them, and *identify* their interests in the chart that follows.

U.S. Organizations and Their Interests

Group 1: _____   Their interests: _____

_____   _____

Group 2: _____   Their interests: _____

_____   _____

Group 3: _____   Their interests: _____

_____   _____

Group 4: _____   Their interests: _____

_____   _____

Critical Thinking Level 3 ▸ Apply

Fishman mentions in paragraph 4 that Honduran children were making Kathie Lee Gifford clothing to be sold at Wal-Mart. An article that the *New York Times* published about that case noted that in the Honduran factory, Global Fashions, "15-year-old girls earn 31 cents an hour and work 75-hour weeks." Do those pieces of information indicate that Global Fashions is a sweatshop? *Examine* each fact in the quotation and discuss how it relates to sweatshop conditions, as you understand them.

What Constitutes Sweatshop Conditions?

Fact	A sweatshop condition? Why or why not?
15-year-old girls	_____ _____
earn 31 cents an hour	_____ _____
work 75-hour weeks	_____

Critical Thinking Level 4 ▷ Analyze

Consider a product that you use every day. Name the product: _____

1. Look on the label. Where was it made? _____

_____

2. Is this a developing country? If you don't know, use an Internet search engine and type in the question "Is X a developing country?" into the search box. You'll find the answer on the results page. _____

_____

3. If you found out that the people making this product were paid less than the U.S. minimum wage, would you still use the product? Why or why not? _____

_____

4. If the workers were paid so little that *they* couldn't afford to buy the same product, would you still use it? Why or why not? _____

_____

5. If they were paid so little that they couldn't feed their children well, would you still use it? Why or why not? _____

_____

Critical Thinking Level 5 ▷ Evaluate

Fishman uses Robina Akther's story to show readers the working conditions in sweatshops. He gives other bits of evidence that sweatshops exist, which are listed in the left column below. Some kinds of evidence can be considered stronger than other kinds. Which piece of evidence most strongly supports the idea that sweatshops exist? Give the strongest piece of evidence an A, the second strongest a B, and the third strongest a C. Then *explain* your ratings. Why is one piece of evidence more convincing than another?

Evidence That Sweatshops Exist

Evidence that sweatshops exist (with paragraph number)	Rating (A, B, and C) and explanation of rating
Nike, the Gap, Reebok, Disney, Wal-Mart have all faced sweatshop problems in the last 20 years (para. 3)	_____ _____ _____
Kathie Lee Gifford example (para. 4)	_____ _____
Factory workers from China, Indonesia, Swaziland, and Nicaragua involved in the suit against Wal-Mart (para. 11)	_____ _____

Critical Thinking Level 6 > Create

Suppose you were on a committee set up to monitor sweatshop conditions in factories around the world. With a group of classmates, *develop* a method that could be used by inspectors sent in to monitor the factories. Think about how an inspector going into a factory could find out about the workers' pay, hours, and working conditions, without putting workers in danger, and perhaps without the cooperation of the factory owners or managers.

▶Vocabulary in New Contexts

Review the vocabulary words in the margins of the reading selection and then complete the following activities.

EASY Note Cards

Make a note card for each of the vocabulary words that you did not know from the reading. On one side, write the word. On the other side, divide the card into quarters and label them E, A, S, and Y. Add a word or phrase in each area so that you wind up with an example sentence, an antonym, a synonym, and, finally, a definition that shows you have figured out the meaning of the word with your logic. Remember that an antonym or synonym may have appeared in the reading.

Relationships Between Words

Circle *yes* or *no* to answer the question. Then explain your answer.

1. Would allegations of misconduct always indicate systematic problems?

   Yes   No

   Why or why not? _____

2. Does **relentless** pressure seem **unending** to the person being pressured?

Yes   No

Why or why not? _____

3. Was the **mandate** of religion stronger in **a world long gone**? Answers will vary.

Yes   No

Why or why not? _____

_____

Language in Your Life

Write short answers to each question. Look at the vocabulary words closely before you answer.

1. Name one action you would like to **mandate** for everyone in your family. _____

_____

2. Name one problem someone you know has that seems **unending**. _____

_____

3. Name one area of your life in which you are **relentless**. _____

_____

4. Name one thing you wish were still true even though it is from **a world long gone**. _____

_____

5. Name one way you are **systematic**. _____

_____

Language in Use

Select the best word to complete the meaning of each sentence.

a world long gone	allegations	mandated	systematically	unending

1. Amid _____ that the chief of police was involved in a burglary ring, he was caught trying to remove a kilo of cocaine from the evidence room.

2. The court _____ that he stay in the country while his bank records were searched.

3. Then a seemingly _____ series of discoveries came to light.

4. The chief and five other senior officers had been _____ shaking down local drug dealers in exchange for letting them operate in the city.

5. It reminded a newspaper reporter of another police scandal two decades earlier, which by now seems from _____ .

Reading 6–2 | Online Newsletter Article

▶ Pre-Reading the Selection

When it comes to items we purchase, we care about what others think. Read the following article written by Martin Lindstrom, a branding and marketing specialist who wrote the bestselling book *Brandwashed*, to find out how what strangers want becomes the same thing we want, too. More information on Martin Lindstrom can be found at martinlindstrom.com.

Surveying the Reading

Survey the article that follows. Then check the elements that are included in this reading.

_____	Title	_____	Words in bold or italic type
_____	Headings	_____	Images and captions
_____	First sentences of paragraphs		

Guessing the Purpose

Judging from the title of the reading, what do you suppose is the author's purpose? _____

_____

Predicting the Content

Predict three things this selection will discuss.

▶ _____

▶ _____

▶ _____

Activating Your Knowledge

Think about what factors affect your purchasing. List them below. (Do you think other people are a factor that affects what you buy?)

▶ _____

▶ _____

▶ _____

🔘 **Scan to Connect!** Use your smart phone to scan this code to watch a video to activate your knowledge about portion size. (See the inside front cover for more information on how to use this.) What manipulation strategies used by retailers to encourage purchasing are mentioned in this video? Have you fallen prey to any of these?

▶ Reading with Pen in Hand

Students who annotate as they read are more successful than those who do not. That's why you will annotate each selection in *Connect* as you read. In the reading that follows, use the following symbols:

★ or (Point)   to indicate a main idea

① ② ③   to indicate major details

Visit www.cengagebrain.com to access the CourseMate for this chapter to hear pronunciations of vocabulary words from this reading.

Thou Shalt Covet What Thy Neighbor Covets

Martin Lindstrom

▶ Predict how these strangers "help dictate our purchasing choices."

1   When it comes to the things we buy, what other people think matters. A lot. Here's how the desires of strangers—inflamed by branders and marketers—mysteriously become our desires, too.

2   Many of us spend our days—or at least part of them—quietly cursing our fellow human beings. The guy in the Hummer who cuts us off at the intersection. The old woman in the supermarket line counting out pennies one by one. The tourist consulting a map *right in front of the subway entrance*. They may be annoying, but when all is said and done we actually rely on these people, and others like them, to help **dictate** our purchasing choices—with more than a little help from companies and marketers, of course.

dictate The rest of the sentence should give you a clue to the meaning of *dictate*.

▶ Do you check consumer reviews on products before you purchase them?

3   When it comes to the things we buy, what other people think matters. A lot. Even when those people are complete strangers. One survey, by Opinion Research, shows that "61% of respondents said they had checked online reviews, blogs and other online customer feedback before buying a new product or service," and a similar 2008 study commissioned by PowerReviews showed that "nearly half of U.S. consumers who shopped online four or more times per year and spent at least $500 said they needed four to seven customer reviews before making a purchase decision." So persuasive are the opinions of others that while many of us are well aware that roughly 25% of these reviews are fakes written by friends, company staffers, marketers, and so forth, we purposely overlook this. We'd rather not think about that. And, frankly, we don't seem to care. As the *Times of London* points out, we are born to believe, in part, because a collective belief helps us to bond with others. In short, we want to trust in these messages, even when we may also be deeply **skeptical**.

skeptical Use your logic and the previous two sentences to decide what *skeptical* means.

sway Use the example of bestseller lists to understand the meaning of *sway*.

4   To see just how powerfully complete strangers' preferences and purchases can **sway** our decisions, consider the phenomenon of best-seller lists. Best-seller lists work so well in persuading us that they can be found everywhere

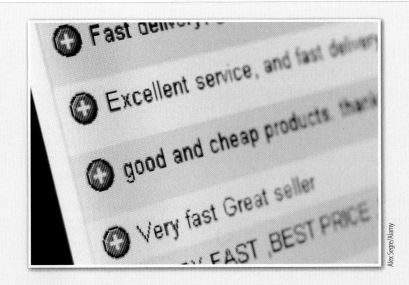

Alex Segre/Alamy

from, famously, *The New York Times'* lists of best-selling books to Sephora's list of best-selling cosmetics to *Entertainment Weekly*'s Ten Most Popular TV shows to *Variety*'s list of the ten highest-grossing movies of the week to the Apple iTunes music store's list of best-selling or recommended singles, albums, movies, and music videos. And on and on—well past the break of dawn.

5   Let's talk for a moment about iTunes. Not unlike a Barnes & Noble super-store, the iTunes start page is a chaotic place **teeming with** choices. Luckily for the overwhelmed shopper, however, these endless offerings are organized into tidy recommended categories like "What We're Watching," "What's Hot," "What We're Listening To," "New and Noteworthy," and, of course, "Top Songs" and "Top Albums."

6   An **intriguing** study published in the journal *Science* shows just how well this can work. The researchers invited 27 teenagers to visit a website where they could sample and download songs for free. Some of the teens were told what songs previous visitors had downloaded, while other teens were not told. Those told what songs their peers had chosen tended to download those very songs. And part two of the study was even more telling. This time, the teens were divided into eight groups and told only what had been down-loaded by people from their own group. The researchers found that not only did the teens tend to choose the songs that had been previously downloaded by members of their groups, but the songs that became "hits" varied across all the groups. The **implications** were clear: Whether or not a song became a "hit" was determined solely by whether it was perceived as already being popular.

7   But this still doesn't explain precisely why our buying decisions are so unduly influenced by a brand's supposed popularity. So the authors of the

▶ Do you pay attention to best-seller lists or "top tens"?

▶ Think about the songs you down-load. How do you choose them?

teeming with Do the iTunes cat-egories that follow suggest a page that is full of choices or one that has few choices?

intriguing How could the findings of this study be described?

▶ What conclusion can be drawn from this study?

implications Use your prior knowledge. Once researchers make observations, what do they form?

succumbed Use the context clue of *impressionable* to figure out the meaning.

▶ Have you ever changed your mind because your choice wasn't popular?

consensus Use a synonym in this sentence to decide on this meaning.

hordes Who is buying the tickets?

▶ Had you ever heard of "The Hollywood Stock Exchange"? Go to http://www.hsx.com/ to find out more.

consciously Use the example of the experiment to determine the meaning of *consciously*.

▶ How much do you think the "cool factor" affects your purchasing decisions?

study decided to use an fMRI to see what was really going on in these impressionable teenagers' brains when they **succumbed** to peer pressure. They had 12–17-year-olds rate 15-second clips of songs downloaded from MySpace. Then they revealed to some the songs' overall popularity. The results showed that when the participants' own ratings of the music matched up with what they had been told about the song (e.g., if they liked a popular song), there tended to be activity in the caudate nucleus, an area of the brain connected to rewards. When there was a mismatch, however (e.g., the teen liked the song but discovered it was unpopular), areas associated with anxiety lit up. The researchers concluded that "this mismatch anxiety motivates people to switch their choices in the direction of the **consensus**, suggesting that this is a major force behind conformity observed in music tastes in teenagers."

8   Early popularity is so closely tied to a brand or product's ultimate success that even Hollywood is leveraging the predictive power of the ticket-buying **hordes**. According to *New Scientist*, one of the most widespread new techniques for predicting the box-office performance of a film is by using something called "artificial markets." On The Hollywood Stock Exchange, for example, movie fans can buy and sell virtual shares in celebrities and in forthcoming or recently released films. This virtual market, which operates with a virtual currency called Hollywood Dollars, uses these predictions to create a stock rating reflecting the aggregate view of each film's popularity or likely popularity (obviously, people only buy virtual shares in things they expect to be hits) becoming the gold standard in the industry for predicting likely box office receipts, political campaigns, and share prices.

9   Of course, we generally aren't **consciously** aware that perceived popularity is driving our preferences. So for my new book, *Brandwashed*, I decided to team up with Murray Hill Center, one of the top focus group companies in the country, in order to find out what *we think* attracts us to products. "Why do you love Louis Vuitton so much?" we asked 30 women. In answering, each of them began talking about the quality of the zipper, the leather, and finally, the brand's timelessness. But had we heard the whole truth? To be sure, we decided to scan the brains of 16 of them using fMRI to uncover another layer of their answers. In each case, when the women were shown pictures of Louis Vuitton products, the Brodmann area 10, the region of the brain that's activated when respondents are observing something they perceive as "cool," lit up. The women had rationalized their purchases by telling themselves that they liked the brand for its good quality, but their brains knew that they really chose it for its "coolness," perhaps explaining why we're all so addicted to those top 10 lists—because deep deep inside we want to be on the top of the cool list.

—From "Thou Shalt Covet What Thy Neighbor Covets." Reprinted by permission of Martin Lindstrom. More information on Martin Lindstrom can be found at www.martinlindstrom.com.

▸ Comprehension Questions

Write the letter of the answer on the line. Then explain your thinking.

Main Idea

_____ 1. What is the topic sentence of paragraph 3?

    a. When it comes to the things we buy, what other people think matters.

    b. One survey, by Opinion Research, shows that "61% of respondents said they had checked online reviews, blogs and other online customer feedback before buying a new product or service."

    c. As the *Times of London* points out, we are born to believe, in part, because a collective belief helps us to bond with others.

    d. In short, we want to trust in these messages, even when we may also be deeply skeptical.

Why? What information in the selection leads you to give that answer? _____

_____

_____

_____ 2. What is the topic sentence of paragraph 7?

    a. But this still doesn't explain precisely why our buying decisions are so unduly influenced by a brand's supposed popularity.

    b. So the authors of the study decided to use an fMRI to see what was really going on in these impressionable teenagers' brains when they succumbed to peer pressure.

    c. When there was a mismatch, however (e.g., the teen liked the song but discovered it was unpopular), areas associated with anxiety lit up.

    d. The researchers concluded that "this mismatch anxiety motivates people to switch their choices in the direction of the consensus, suggesting that this is a major force behind conformity observed in music tastes in teenagers."

Why? What information in the selection leads you to give that answer? _____

_____

_____

Supporting Details

_____ 3. According to the reading passage, which of the following is not a factor that drives our purchasing?

    a. We want to be seen as cool.

    b. A product's perceived popularity

    c. Other people's preferences

    d. The purchasing domain

Why? What information in the selection leads you to give that answer? _____

_____

_____

_____ 4. What comprehension questions does the information about The Hollywood Stock
Exchange answer?

   a. What is the reading about?

   b. What is the author's point about the topic?

   c. What proof supports the author's main idea?

   d. None of the above.

Why? What information in the selection leads you to give that answer? _____

_____

Author's Purpose

_____ 5. What is the main purpose of this reading passage?

   a. to inform readers of what affects their purchasing behavior

   b. to entertain readers with intriguing studies of our retail behavior

   c. to persuade readers to purchase products that are perceived as cool

   d. to persuade readers that they should not let the opinions of others affect their
   purchasing behavior

Why? What information in the selection leads you to give that answer? _____

_____

_____ 6. What is the purpose of paragraph 5?

   a. to persuade readers to download songs from iTunes

   b. to make readers aware of the best entertainment site on the Web

   c. to give readers an example of how iTunes uses lists on their start page

   d. to inform readers of the similarities and differences between iTunes and Barnes & Noble

Why? What information in the selection leads you to give that answer? _____

_____

Relationships

_____ 7. What is the main pattern of organization found in paragraph 2?

   a. time order

   b. cause-and-effect

c. contrast

d. classification

Why? What leads you to give that answer? _____

_____

____ 8. What is the main pattern of organization for this reading selection?

a. classification

b. comparison and contrast

c. time order

d. examples

Why? What information in the selection leads you to give that answer? _____

_____

Fact, Opinion, and Inference

____ 9. Which of the following statements is an opinion?

a. When it comes to the things we buy, what other people think matters. A lot.

b. The iTunes start page is a chaotic place teeming with choices.

c. Whether or not a song became a "hit" was determined solely by whether it was perceived as already being popular.

d. The women had rationalized their purchases by telling themselves that they liked the brand for its good quality, but their brains knew that they really chose it for its "coolness."

Why? What leads you to give that answer? _____

_____

____ 10. With which of the following statements would Lindstrom agree?

a. Teenagers are more easily influenced by others' opinions than other age groups.

b. Slick marketing is the main influence dictating our purchasing choices.

c. When purchasing, consumers are affected more by unconscious factors than stated reasons.

d. The Hollywood Stock Exchange is an unethical ploy created by the film industry.

Why? What information in the selection leads you to give that answer? _____

_____

_____

_____

▶ Critical Thinking Questions

Critical Thinking Level 1 ▷ **Remember**

List three studies that show how others influence our purchasing choices.

1. _____

2. _____

3. _____

Critical Thinking Level 2 ▷ **Understand**

Summarize the reading in several sentences. Include the major details.

_____

_____

_____

_____

_____

Critical Thinking Level 3 ▷ **Apply**

Make a list of your favorite brands and products. *Choose* products and brands from your lists that match those of your classmates. Discuss why you think you like and purchase this brand or product. See if the reasons discussed in the article *apply* to your reasons for purchase.

_____

_____

_____

_____

Critical Thinking Level 4 ▷ **Analyze**

Watch a commercial. *Analyze* what the commercial is trying to sell and what strategies are being used to attempt to sell you the product. Bring this information to class to share.

_____

_____

_____

Critical Thinking Level 5 ▸ **Evaluate**

Do you have chronic halitosis? Well of course you do. We all do. It simply means bad breath. Before 1921, bad breath was just an accepted part of life and *halitosis* was a barely known term. But in 1921, The Lambert Pharmacal Company, the maker of Listerine (originally used as a surgical antiseptic and later a floor cleaner), began a marketing campaign. They claimed Listerine was the cure for "chronic halitosis." In seven years, their sales went from $115,000 to $8 million. They had invented a problem (halitosis) and provided the perfect solution (Listerine). *Evaluate* whether this is marketing or manipulation. Provide evidence for whichever side you choose.

_____

_____

_____

Critical Thinking Level 6 ▸ **Create**

Create a commercial for your favorite product. Use some of the factors that affect purchasing that were discussed in this reading. You can also use some strategies mentioned in the video that goes along with this reading, or you can do a web search. You could even check out Martin's book *Brandwashed* if you want! Share the commercial you create with your class.

_____

_____

_____

▸Vocabulary in New Contexts

Review the vocabulary words in the margins of the reading selection and then complete the following activities.

EASY Note Cards

Make a note card for each of the vocabulary words that you do not know from the reading. On one side, write the word. On the other side, divide the card into quarters and label them E, A, S, and Y. Add a word or phrase in each area so that you wind up with an example sentence, an antonym, a synonym, and, finally, a definition that shows you have figured out the meaning of the word with your logic. Remember that an antonym or synonym may have appeared in the reading.

Relationships Between Words

Circle *yes* or *no* to answer the question. Then explain your answer.

1. Is it accurate to describe a street filled with a **horde** as "**teeming**"?

Yes   No

Why or why not? _____

2. Should facts **sway** the **skeptical**?

Yes   No

Why or why not? _____

3. Do military leaders **consciously dictate** their orders?

Yes   No

Why or why not? _____

Language in Your Life

Write short answers to each question. Look at the vocabulary words closely before you answer.

1. Name something that people **succumb** to. _____

_____

2. Name one thing you find **intriguing**. _____

_____

3. Name one thing that is **dictated** to you. _____

_____

4. Name one thing you are **skeptical** of. _____

_____

5. Name something that could be described as **teeming**. _____

_____

Language in Use

Select the best word to complete the meaning of each sentence.

consciously	consensus	dictate	hordes	implication
intriguing	skeptical	succumbed	teeming	

1. In 2006, the International Astronomical Union (IAU) reached a _____ : Pluto is not a planet.

2. "But why not?" ask the _____ of students who grew up learning that there were nine planets in their solar system.

3. According to the IAU, there are three rules that _____ whether a mass in space gets labeled as a planet.

   ▸ "It needs to be in orbit around the Sun."
   ▸ "It needs to have enough gravity to pull itself into a spherical shape."
   ▸ "It needs to have 'cleared the neighborhood' of its orbit."

4. Pluto meets the first two criteria, but fails to satisfy the third one. The _____? Pluto is not a full planet but rather a "dwarf planet."

5. It appears that Pluto's gravitational orbit is _____ with other masses of a similar size.

6. Unfortunately for the _____, it seems there is enough scientific data to say that until Pluto absorbs these other masses in its "neighborhood" and becomes king of its gravitational pull, it will remain a dwarf planet.

 Click to Connect! For more practice applying the skills you learned in this chapter, visit **www.cengagebrain.com** to access the CourseMate for this chapter.

Ronfromyork, Dreamstime LLC

Click to Connect! Visit **www.cengagebrain.com** to access study resources for this chapter through CourseMate, which includes audio, video, quizzes, and a searchable, interactive eBook version of the text.

7
Reading and Taking Notes on Textbook Chapters

> " *There is an art of reading,*
> *as well as an art of thinking,*
> *and an art of writing.* "
>
> —ISAAC D'ISRAELI

Connect with Ideas

What does D'Israeli mean when he says there is an "art" of reading, thinking, and writing? Explain. How do these three activities go together?

Activate Your Knowledge

Have you ever read anything you would consider art? Share your thoughts.

Engage with the Chapter

Look ahead at pages 340–355. What can you say about how reading, thinking, and writing apply to textbooks?

Read and Talk

Psychology Textbook

How can you tell the difference between a real smile and a fake one? You can probably do it, but do you know how? Read the following article from a psychology textbook and find out.

 Visit www.cengagebrain.com to access the CourseMate for this chapter to hear vocabulary words from this reading and an audio recording of it.

Crow's-Feet and Smiles Sweet

Dennis Coon and John O. Mitterer

pageant Use your prior knowledge to infer what *pageant* means.

1   The next time you see an athletic contest or a beauty **pageant** on television, look closely at the winner's smile and the smile of the runner-up. Although both people will be smiling, it is likely that the winner's smile will be **authentic** and the loser's smile will be forced (Thibault et al., 2009).

authentic Why would a winner's smile be authentic? There is an antonym clue and a synonym clue in the next two paragraphs.

2   We smile for many reasons: to be polite or because of embarrassment, or sometimes to deceive (Frank, 2002; Frank & Ekman, 2004). These "social smiles" are often intentional or forced, and they only involve lifting the corners of the mouth. What does a genuine smile look like? A real smile involves not only the mouth, but also the small muscles around the eyes. These muscles lift the cheeks and make crow's-feet or crinkles in the outside corners of the eyes.

posed There is an antonym within the sentence. What does *posed* mean?

3   Authentic smiles are called Duchenne smiles (after Guilluame Duchenne, a French scientist who studied facial muscles). The muscles around the eyes are very difficult to tighten on command. Hence, to tell if a smile is authentic, or merely **posed**, look at the corners of a person's eyes, not the mouth

The face on the left shows a social smile; the one on the right is an authentic, or Duchenne, smile. (Gladstone & Parker, 2002.)

Juice Images/Alamy

(Williams et al., 2001). To put it another way, crow's-feet mean a smile is sweet.

4   Duchenne smiles signal genuine happiness and enjoyment (Soussignan, 2002). In one study, women who had authentic smiles in their college yearbook photos were contacted 6, 22, and 31 years later. At each **interval**, real smiles in college were associated with more positive emotions and a greater sense of competence. We can only **speculate** about why this is the case. However, it is likely that smiling signals that a person is helpful or nurturing. This leads to more supportive social relationships and, in a self-fulfilling manner, to greater happiness.

interval *Interval* refers to the years mentioned. What does *interval* mean?

speculate The word *why* gives a big clue.

—From Coon/Mitterer, *Introduction to Psychology: Gateways to Mind and Behavior*, 13e

Talking about Reading

Respond in writing to the questions below and then discuss your answers with your classmates.

1. So how do you tell the difference between a real smile and a fake one? _____

   _____

   _____

2. Discuss someone you know who smiles a lot; do they have crow's feet (or some other indicator of their "smiliness")? _____

   _____

3. The article mentions "social smiling." Explain this term in your own words and give an example.

   _____

   _____

4. What makes you fake smile? What makes you smile for real? List a couple of examples for each.

   _____

   _____

5. 🔘 **Scan to Connect!** Use your smart phone to scan this code to watch a video. (See the inside front cover for more information on how to use this.) Did the baby's laughter make you laugh for real? What makes laughter contagious?

Applying the Reading Process to Textbooks

Do you read to remember? Or do you read to forget? One is intentional. The other is the result of simply going through the motions. You're expected to do a lot of reading in college, and much of what you read will not be discussed in class. You will still be responsible for knowing the material, however, so you need to be intentional when you read. Applying the skills covered so far in this textbook will help make reading your textbooks a more efficient and productive activity.

1. In Chapter 1, you learned to use the reading process to your advantage.

2. In Chapter 2, you practiced a strategy for picking out the main ideas: they are the ideas that answer the questions you formed from the headings. Once you find these ideas, you highlight or mark them in some way. When you study for a test, you review the marked ideas.

3. In Chapter 3, you learned how to use word parts and context clues to help you make sense of the words you are reading.

4. In Chapters 4 and 5, you learned how paragraphs are structured and how to identify the topic, main idea (stated or implied), and supporting details.

5. In Chapter 6, you worked on identifying how readings are organized in patterns.

You have been practicing enough to internalize these processes. Remember that you can always refer back to the Reading Guide you created for each chapter to remind yourself of the strategies you can use before, during, and after reading. Applying each of these skills holistically to a textbook reading will help you be a great student.

In addition, textbooks are deliberately constructed to help make your reading and learning process easier. Make sure to use the learning aids in your textbooks during each stage of the reading process. Also take notes when you read, making brief annotations in the margins of your textbooks and taking longer notes in a notebook.

Two writing strategies to improve reading comprehension and help you remember what you have read are:

▶ annotating—that is, writing in the margin of the text
▶ writing Cornell notes in your notebook

In this chapter we will give you a chance to refine some of those earlier strategies and also will show you how to effectively annotate a text and use Cornell notes.

Forming Questions from Headings and Reading for the Answers

You have been using a reading strategy in which you read a heading, turn it into a question, and then read the text to find the answer to the question. Once you find parts of the answer, then you mark them in some way—highlight them or underline them. This method helps you identify main ideas. You can use it for each major section of a chapter that you read.

But what can you do if there are no headings and thus no questions to answer? In this case, read one paragraph or one section at a time and then pause to think about what the main idea was. Then go back and highlight the main idea, turn it into a question, and read to find the most important supporting details. Read first, and then return to mark the text once you are sure which ideas should be highlighted. Be selective: highlight only the most important ideas (you normally should only be highlighting 20% or less of the text).

Another helpful strategy is to create your own heading for a section. You can write it in the margin. When you return to study for a test, you can use the headings you wrote as a guide to the most important ideas.

Interaction 7–1 ▶ Refine Your Reading Strategy

Read the following textbook excerpt. While you read, turn headings into questions, read for the answers, and then highlight the answers when you find them. Two headings have been deleted so you can create them.

The Nature of Resources

Question:

1   In a very real sense, everything in our environment could be considered a natural resource. Rocks may be used as gravel for our roads, facings for our buildings, or material for our statues. Wind, falling water, still air, resting water, minerals, insects—virtually everything around us can be considered a resource. When someone takes an object and uses it to perform work or change other parts of the environment, that object has become a resource. Even before its use, the potential for use makes the object a natural resource.

2   Those things that have become or show promise of becoming important to us are the natural resources we are concerned about in this book. Those natural resources may take many forms. More important, they may be capable of going on forever. On the other hand, they may be extremely limited. They may be usable over and over, or they may be gone forever with a single use. Let us look at these a little closer.

Nonexhaustible Resources

Question:

3   Natural resources that can last forever regardless of human activities are nonexhaustible resources. They renew themselves continuously. This does not mean that such resources are not limited or that human misuse cannot damage such resources—it certainly can.

4   A good example is surface water. If a gallon of water is taken from a river, another gallon will replace it. If a stream is dammed, the water will simply go elsewhere. If a watershed is damaged so that its rainfall does not

soak into the ground, then the rainfall will simply go elsewhere. Little that we do will affect the total amount of water that comes to Earth in the form of precipitation.

5   Water supplies may be limited. We face many problems, however, as a result of the damage done to our water supply by pollution. Nevertheless, our water supply remains nonexhaustible for all practical purposes.

6   Another example is air. We use air to breathe, to grow plants, to fly airplanes, to power windmills, and to dry food and clothes. We can damage the air with pollution. We could even make it unusable, as many environmentalists would argue, but we cannot use it up. It also is non-exhaustible for all practical purposes.

Question:

Create a Heading: _____

7   Natural resources that can be replaced by human efforts are considered to be renewable resources. On the one hand, simply because a resource is renewable does not mean it will never be used up. On the other hand, it is possible to use such resources and yet have as much left afterward as before that use. Conservation practices for renewable resources should restrict their use to ensure that they are used no faster than they are regenerated. This rate of use is expected to sustain a constant resource supply for as long as they may be needed.

8   A forest is one example of a renewable resource. In this country, we use more wood today than ever before, yet we produce more wood each year than we use. The types of wood, however, have changed. We no longer harvest as many large hardwoods as we once did, but we have no foreseeable shortage of wood or wood products. This is true because of the advances made in forestry in both woodland management and genetics.

9   Another example is our fish and wildlife population. In our nation's past, there have been times of great waste. Huge droves of passenger pigeons were destroyed, and the popular food bird became extinct. Great herds of

bison, or buffalo, were killed for their hides and meat, and this great American natural resource neared extinction. With techniques of game management, however, the numbers of bison have rebounded. Fish populations, too, respond readily to fisheries management techniques.

Create a Heading: _____   *Question:*

10   Many of our natural resources exist in finite quantities. Those limited resources that cannot be replaced or reproduced are known as nonrenewable resources or exhaustible resources. In the case of exhaustible resources, we cannot manage them for renewal. They do not renew themselves; once they are gone, they are gone forever. We can conserve our exhaustible resources. We can learn how to use less. We may try to find more of them. We may even be able to recycle some of them; but once these resources are gone, we simply have to do without them.

11   Conservation of nonrenewable resources is accomplished by reducing the rate at which these resources are used so that they last longer. This can involve recycling metals or even plastics (derived from petroleum) to reduce the necessity for extracting new materials. Conservation of these resources must ensure that they are not used up before we learn to replace them with other resources.

12   Even though an exhaustible resource exists in a finite (limited) supply that does not mean it is necessarily a limited resource. Many exhaustible resources exist in such huge amounts that they are practically nonexhaustible. For instance, there is so much coal on the planet that, even though it is exhaustible, there is no practical limit. In addition, there is so much iron ore that, although iron is an exhaustible resource, it has no practical limit.

13   One especially important exhaustible resource is oil. We constantly hear of the "energy crisis." There is only so much oil in the ground, and when we have removed all we can find, it is gone, so we must develop other sources of energy. Another example is our mineral resources. We use lead, cobalt, zinc, and other minerals to make our goods. We depend on these mineral resources for our way of life. We must manage those resources to make them last as long as possible.

14   Soil also probably fits into this category. Soil is constantly being formed by nature. We can improve existing soil, make it more fertile, move water to it, and supply missing minerals. We can even make soil substitutes in small quantities, but we cannot really make soil. Only nature can do that. Why, then, is soil not a nonexhaustible resource? It is exhaustible because nature makes soil so slowly. A soil destroyed by improper use will probably be replaced—in 500,000 years—but that is not renewal that is useful to us. Thus, soil is a nonrenewable or exhaustible resource.

—From Burton, *Environmental Science: Fundamentals and Application*

Annotating (Taking Marginal Notes) As You Read

While you are reading, you can annotate the text. That is, you can write brief notes, symbols, and abbreviations in the margin to point out important ideas that you want to review the next time you look at the chapter. For instance, you might put all the definitions of important terms in (parentheses), or note the most important examples of main ideas with asterisks (*). Develop your own personal list of symbols and abbreviations. The actual abbreviations are not important, as long as you can remember them and use them consistently. Some possibilities are presented in **Table 7.1**.

Table 7.1
Use Symbols and Abbreviations to Point Out Important Ideas

Use this symbol or abbreviation	to indicate ...
main (or) *key* (or) *	A main idea or important point
① ② ③ (or) *(1) (2) (3)*	A list of details or steps in a sequence
def	The definition of a key term
imp ex	An important example
! (or) *?*	Personal reactions to the material
Exam	A possible exam question

You can also write short responses to the author's ideas, engaging in a dialogue to keep your mind working actively while you read. The following example from a sociology textbook chapter on aging includes symbols, abbreviations, and short responses combined with highlighting.

Age Prejudice and Discrimination

def.

Age prejudice refers to a negative attitude about an age group that is generalized to all people in that group. Prejudice against the elderly is prominent. As an example, people may talk "baby talk" to the elderly. Doing so defines the elderly as childlike and incompetent. Prejudice relegates people to a perceived lower status in society and stems from the stereotypes associated with different age groups.

ex.
language use important!

Remember Aunt Donna and the nurse. (prior knowledge)

—From Andersen/Taylor, *Sociology*, 4e

Interaction 7–2 ▸ Annotate Paragraphs

Annotate the paragraphs that follow. Use the abbreviations from Table 7.1 or create your own.

1.

Age discrimination is the different and unequal treatment of people based solely on their age. While age prejudice is an attitude, age discrimination involves actual behavior. Some forms of age discrimination are illegal. The Age Discrimination Employment Act, first passed in 1967 but amended several times since, protects people from age discrimination in employment. An employer can neither hire nor fire someone based solely on age, nor segregate or classify workers based on age. Age discrimination cases have become one of the most frequently filed cases through the Equal Employment Opportunity Commission (EEOC), the federal agency set up to monitor violations of civil rights in employment.

—From Andersen/Taylor, *Sociology*, 4e

2.

There are several ways to build credit. First, open checking and savings accounts. They signal stability to lenders and indicate that you handle your financial affairs in a businesslike way. Second, use credit: open one or two charge accounts and use them periodically, even if you prefer paying cash. For example, get a Visa card and make a few credit purchases each month (don't overdo it, of course). You might pay an annual fee or interest on some (or all) of your account balances, but in the process, you'll build a record of being a reliable credit customer. Third, obtain a small loan, even if you don't need one. If you don't actually need the money, put it in a liquid investment, such as a money market account or certificate of deposit. The interest you earn should offset some of the interest expense on the loan; you can view the difference as a cost of building good credit. You should repay the loan promptly, perhaps even a little ahead of schedule, to minimize the difference in interest rates. However, don't pay off the loan too quickly because lenders like to see how you perform over an extended period of time. Keep in mind that your ability to obtain a large loan in the future will depend, in part, on how you managed smaller ones in the past.

—From Gitman, Joehnk, Billingsly, *Personal Financial Planning*, 12e

3.

While you can certainly recognize a business when you see one, more formal definitions may help. A business is any activity that provides goods and services in an effort to earn a profit. Profit is the financial reward that comes from starting and running a business. More specifically, a profit is the money that a business earns in sales (or revenue), minus expenses such as the cost of goods and the cost of salaries. But clearly, not every business earns a profit all of the time. When a business brings in less money than it needs to cover expenses, it incurs a loss. If you launch a music label, for instance, you'll need to pay your artists, buy or lease a studio, and purchase equipment, among other expenses. If your label generates hits, you'll earn more than enough to cover all your expenses and make yourself rich. But a series of duds could leave you holding the bag.

Just the possibility of earning a profit provides a powerful incentive for people of all backgrounds to launch their own enterprise. Despite the economic meltdown of 2008, nearly 19% of American adults were engaged in entrepreneurial activity—either launching or managing their own businesses. The numbers among your peers are probably even higher, since more than two thirds of college students plan to launch their own business at some point in their career. People who risk their time, money, and other resources to start and manage a business are called entrepreneurs.

—From Kelly/McGowen, *BUSN*, 3e

4.

The capabilities of the patrol car, perhaps the most important piece of policing technology of the past century, continue to expand. Project 54, a voice-recognition system developed at the University of New Hampshire, allows police officers to "multitask" without having to divert their attention from the road or to take a hand off the wheel. The officer simply presses a button, and all the technological equipment in the car becomes voice activated. Four Andrea digital array microphones positioned in the cab of the automobile cancel all noise except the sound of the officer's voice. So, for example, if the officer witnesses a hit-and-run accident, he or she simply says the word "pursuit" to activate the automobile's siren and flashing lights. Then the officer can call for an ambulance and run a check on the suspect's license plate—all by voice command. Other recent innovations include Automatic License Plate Recognition, a three-camera computer-operated system that performs a "20-millisecond" background check on every license plate it sees, and the StarChase launcher, a small, laser-guided cannon that shoots a sticky radio transmitter at a fleeing vehicle. Once the offending car has been "tagged" with this device, police can track the fugitive at a safe distance without the need for a dangerous high-speed pursuit.

—From Gaines/Miller, *Criminal Justice in Action*, 6e

5.

In many homes, the television, computer, and video game sets have replaced adult supervision. Consider these facts (Nielsen Media Research, 2008):

▶ Ninety-eight percent of the homes in the United States contain at least one television.
▶ The average set is on for more than 6 hours each day.
▶ Children spend more time watching television (15,000 hours) than they do in school (11,000 hours).
▶ Children will likely witness on screen 180,000 murders, rapes, armed robberies, and assaults.

What happens to children when they are this plugged into media? Common Sense Media and the National Institutes of Health (NIH) analyzed 173 studies about the effect of media consumption on children, finding a strong correlation between greater exposure and adverse health outcomes. "Couch potato does, unfortunately, sum it up pretty well," states E. J. Emanuel, chair of bioethics at NIH. "The research is clear that exposure to media has a variety of negative health impacts on children and teens.…We found very few studies that had any positive association for children's health" (Common Sense Media, 2008).

Hazards of Too Much Media Violence

▶ Increased aggressiveness and antisocial behavior
▶ Increased fear of becoming a victim
▶ Increased desensitization to violence and victims of violence
▶ Increased appetite for more violence in entertainment and real life

—From Gordon/Browne, *Beginning Essentials in Early Childhood Education*, 2e (pp. 16–17).
Copyright © 2013 Cengage Learning, Inc. Reproduced by permission. www.cengage.com/permissions

Organizing Information with Visual Maps

In Chapter 6, we suggested a visual reading strategy for each pattern of organization. For example, the narration strategy is used to visualize a timeline of events being described. You can create these maps in your notebook as aids to comprehension and memory. They can be used to organize information from longer texts as well as from single paragraphs.

1. Mapping events on a timeline

2. Mapping the order of steps in a process

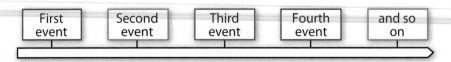

3. Mapping causes and effects

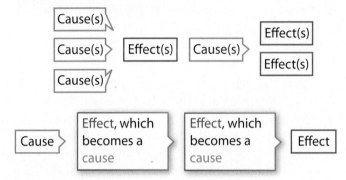

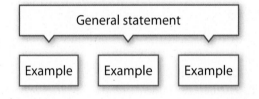

4. Mapping examples

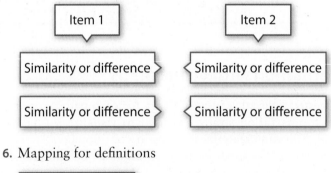

5. Mapping for comparison and/or contrast

6. Mapping for definitions

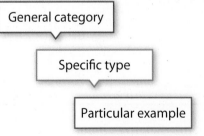

7. Mapping for classification

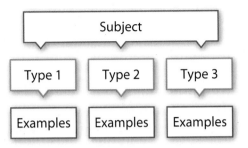

It is helpful to use a format that visually reminds you of the relationships among the different pieces of information you are mapping.

Interaction 7–3 ▷ Match Organization with a Visual Map

Pick a visual map that would work well with each paragraph from Interaction 7–2. Be prepared to discuss why you picked the visual map you chose.

1. Map for Paragraph 1: _____

   Why? _____

   _____

2. Map for Paragraph 2: _____

   Why? _____

   _____

3. Map for Paragraph 3: _____

   Why? _____

   _____

4. Map for Paragraph 4: _____

   Why? _____

   _____

5. Map for Paragraph 5: _____

   Why? _____

   _____

Interaction 7–4 ▸ **Organize with Visual Maps**

Identify the pattern of organization and then create an appropriate visual map for each of the following paragraphs using the topic, main idea, and major details.

1.

> In 1968, Israeli psychologist Sara Smilansky proposed four stages of play. The first was functional play. This play is repetitive and focuses on objects—what they are like and what can be done with them. This stage of play is common among infants and toddlers and would consist of playing with blocks or a squeaky toy. Constructive play comes next. An older toddler or child might play take the blocks and build something with them. Legos would be a good toy to represent this stage. The third stage is dramatic play, which is where a child begins pretending. For example, a child may have tea with her stuffed animals. The final stage is games with rules. This is typical of older children and might consist of games like tag or a game that children make up and agree upon rules.

What pattern best fits this paragraph? _____

Visual Map

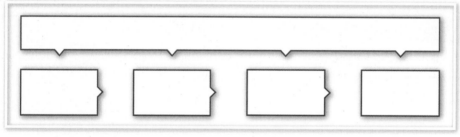

2.

> It is widely believed that humans are sensitive to at least four different types of tastes: bitter, sweet, salty, and sour (Bartoshuk & Beauchamp, 1994). It makes good sense that our tongues are designed to detect these tastes, because they are associated with certain types of foods that have implications for our survival (T. R. Scott & Plata-Salaman, 1991). Sweet flavors are associated with organic molecules that contain hydrogen, carbon, and oxygen. Sugars are organic molecules, so our ability to taste sugars may ensure that we take in enough to fuel our bodies. Salty flavors are associated with foods that release ions, or charged particles. Ions such as sodium are crucial for normal functioning of the nervous system. Our ability to taste salts ensures that we take in enough of these critical ions. Sour tastes are generally associated with acidic substances, and bitter flavors are often found in substances that contain nitrogen. Our ability to sense sour and bitter tastes may help us to regulate the level of acidity (pH) in our bodies. Bitter tastes are often associated with toxic substances. Therefore, tasting bitterness may steer us away from certain poisons.
>
> In addition to these four basic tastes, some researchers have proposed that humans may be sensitive to a **fifth** taste called *umami*, or glutamate (Rolls, 2000). Umami is a meaty, brothy flavor that is more common in Asian foods than it is in Western cuisine (MSG, or monosodium glutamate, is a common ingredient in Asian dishes). So, Westerners are not likely to be as familiar with umami's flavor as they are with the other basic tastes. Nonetheless, preliminary studies indicate that the ability to taste umami exists (Damak et al., 2003; Hodson & Linden, 2006).
>
> —From Pastorino, *What Is Psychology?*, 3e (pp. 107–108). Copyright © 2013 Cengage Learning, Inc. Reproduced by permission. www.cengage.com/permissions

What pattern best fits this paragraph? _____

Visual Map

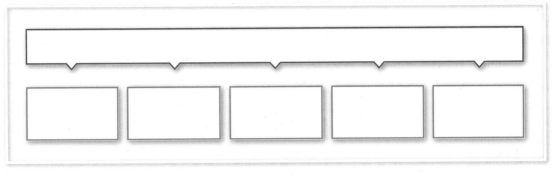

3.

> There is great diversity among cultural groups in regard to how they perceive and experience time. European Americans are dominated by an orientation toward the future. Planning, producing, and controlling what will happen are all artifacts of a future time orientation. What was and what is are always a bit vague and are subordinated to what is anticipated. At the same time, European Americans view time as compartmentalized and incremental, and being on time and being efficient with time are positive values.
>
> Asian and Latino/a cultures are described as past/present–oriented. For both, history is a living entity. Ancestors and past events are felt to be alive and impacting present reality. The past flows imperceptibly into and defines the present. In turn, both Native Americans and African Americans are characterized as present-oriented. The focus is the here and now, with less attention to what led up to this moment or what will become of it.
>
> —From Moule, *Cultural Competence: A Primer for Educators*, 2e

What pattern best fits this paragraph? _____

Visual Map

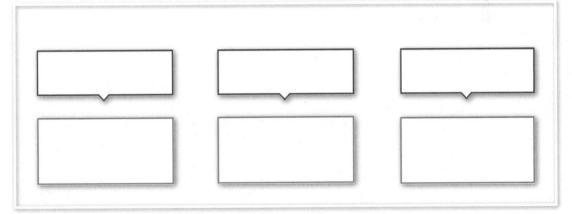

4.

> There is a good deal of truth in the adage "Necessity is the mother of invention." Often an invention is developed because there is a pressing need for it. Linton (1936) relates a classic example of an invention that occurred around the year 1900 on the island of Hiva Oa. A man from the neighboring Gilbert

Islands took up residence on Hiva Oa, married a local woman, and became a fisherman. It soon became apparent to him, however, that theft of outrigger canoes was rampant on the island. Motivated by the desire to avoid having his own boat stolen, he invented a new type of outrigger canoe with a detachable outrigger. By removing the outrigger assemblage, he could safely leave the canoe on the beach unattended. Within a short time, this new detachable outrigger almost totally replaced the previous model because there was a perceived need for this particular invention.

Sometimes inventions occur as a result of a person simply following his or her chosen profession of inventor. One of the most widely known (and successful) professional inventors is the television pitchman, Ron Popeil, president of Ronco Products. Coming from a long line of pitchmen who have sold household products by demonstrating their usefulness at department stores, chain stores, state fairs, and more recently on television, Popeil spends a lot of time in his kitchen thinking up new kitchen appliances that are time saving, convenient, efficient, and affordable and will help people prepare delicious and nutritious meals for their families. Over the years he has invented slicing and dicing devices, food dehydrators, automatic pasta and sausage makers, and meat smokers, and then he has sold them via TV infomercials in which the *product* is the star of the show, not Ron Popeil.

One of Popeil's most successful inventions is his Showtime Rotisserie. Seeing the lines of people waiting for rotisserie chickens at Costco, Popeil decided to build a personal rotisserie that could be used in the average American kitchen. Because meats cooked on a rotisserie (rotating spit) are more nutritious and flavorful than meats prepared by other techniques, Popeil wanted to enable the general population to cook a chicken at home that is as delicious as a Costco rotisserie chicken. When he set out to build the prototype kitchen rotisserie, Popeil had certain features in mind. For example, he wanted it to be large enough to hold a 15-pound turkey, but small enough to sit on the average kitchen counter underneath the cabinets; it needed a powerful electric motor to turn a horizontal spit, rather than a vertical rod that tends to dry out the meat at the top; he insisted on a heavy-duty ceramic drip pan that doesn't stick and is easy to clean; and it needed to be so well built that it would be virtually indestructible. The Showtime Rotisserie may be the best kitchen appliance ever invented, with sales in the hundreds of millions of dollars (Gladwell 2009: 3-31).

—From Ferraro/Andreatta, *Cultural Anthropology: An Applied Perspective*, 9e

What pattern best fits this passage? _____

Visual Map

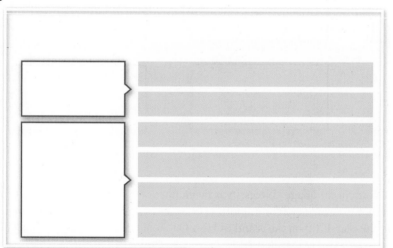

5.

The brain's ability to change as a result of experience is known as *brain plasticity*. Brain plasticity has been studied more in animals than in humans. For example, in monkeys each finger is served by a different area in the cortex. If a monkey loses a finger, the cortex reorganizes itself so the neurons in the area that once served the missing finger now respond to the adjacent fingers instead (Beatty, 2001). Also, when monkeys are trained to pick up a small object from a cup, the cortex area for that finger increases. Human brains also respond to experience—jugglers and musicians develop greater density in areas of the brain related to those skills (Paus, 2005). Similarly, in blind people the area of the brain that processes vision adapts to process other things instead (Amedi, Merabet, Bermpohl, & Pascual-Leone, 2005). Much of the cortex is *not* dedicated to a specific function and can adapt to other functions.

Is there an age when the brain no longer responds to experience? There is a subtle, gradual diminishing in the brain's plasticity. Learning is not equally easy over time (Thomas & Johnson, 2008). This is why early deprivation can have long-lasting effects in spite of later intervention. Plasticity begins to be lost at about 10 years of age. For example, if there is damage to the language areas of the brain before age 10, there is better recovery of language skills than if damage occurs after age 10. The ability to acquire language is not completely lost after age 10, but the potential is diminished. The plasticity of children's brains may help them learn subjects like algebra or second languages more efficiently than adults (Luna, 2004). However, keep in mind that the brain remains plastic across the life span to some extent, or you could not be learning about child development right now.

—From Bergin/Bergin, *Child and Adolescent Development in Your Classroom*

What pattern best fits this passage? _____

Visual Map

Using Cornell Notes to Record Ideas

Once you have asked the questions and marked the answers in a reading or have annotated it, you can either use a visual map or take notes on the main points and key details you want to remember. A classic and helpful system is the Cornell note-taking system; it is named for the university at which Walter Pauk, the creator of the system, taught. This system is highly effective for both notes on reading assignments and notes from lectures in class. To use this system, make two columns in your notebook. Here is what it looks like:

Cornell Notes	
Main points, big ideas, key terms, and questions: ⬇	**Notes: Key details, examples, explanations** 1. During reading/lecture Take notes in this space. ←——— 6 inches ———→
2. Soon after reading/ lecture Read through your notes soon after taking them and pull out the main ideas in the form of key terms, phrases, or questions to create clues to help yourself recall the details. ⬇ ←— 2.5 inches —→	To study, cover this section with your hand and attempt to recall the details of the main points, big ideas, key terms, or questions written on the left.
Summary: 3. Recall your notes on the lecture/reading when studying for a test. Summarize your notes into a few sentences. This can be done at the bottom of each page of notes, after a section, or after a chapter.	↕ 2 inches

There are several advantages of the Cornell note-taking system:

▶ It helps you get an overview of key ideas in longer readings or lectures.
▶ It allows you to organize your ideas from big to small.
▶ It gives you a chance to summarize concepts you might be tested on.
▶ It gives you a structure for effective studying.

Look at the following example of a Cornell note-taking entry. It is based on the article "The Nature of Resources" from pages 341–343.

Nature of Resources	Natural resources may be limitless or limited.
Nonexhaustible	Last forever (unless polluted) ▶ surface water, air
Renewable	Can be replaced by humans. ▶ forests and wildlife
Nonrenewable	Cannot be replaced. ▶ coal, iron ore, oil, soil, minerals
There are three kinds of natural resources. Nonexhaustible resources, like water and air, can last forever (as long as they are not polluted). Renewable resources, like forests and wildlife, can be replaced through human effort. Nonrenewable resources, like coal, iron ore, oil, soil, and minerals, are limited and gone once used.	

In the right column, you can see the detailed notes. In the left column, headings or key words summarize a main idea or identify key terms. At the bottom you find a summary of the key information. A summary consists of the topic plus main idea plus major details (T + MI + MD). Following are some other hints for creating effective Cornell notes.

▶ Use words or images that will help you remember the pattern of relationship between the ideas. Ideas are easier to remember when you understand their relationship.

▶ Use numbered lists. After you have reviewed your notes several times, you will remember how many points there are in a particular answer. You can use that knowledge as a check to see whether you are remembering all of the points.

▶ Abbreviate as you like. Develop a system of abbreviations you can use in all your classes to make note taking more efficient.

When you are reviewing for a test, cover the right column with a sheet of paper and read the key phrases on the left. See if you can say or write all the major examples from the right column. Then check your answer by reviewing the right column. You can also see if you can reproduce a summary from memory once you have studied the columns.

Interaction 7–5 ▸ Apply Cornell Note-Taking

Read the following passages. Annotate or highlight the main ideas and key details. Then turn your markings into Cornell notes in the spaces provided.

1.

> If a man walks down a busy street wearing nothing on the top half of his body, he is violating a folkway. If he walks down the street wearing nothing on the bottom half of his body, he is violating a more (the Latin word for "custom," pronounced MORE-ay). Folkways are norms that specify social preferences. Mores are norms that specify social requirements. People are usually punished when they violate norms, but the punishment is usually minor if the norm is a folkway. Some onlookers will raise their eyebrows at the shirtless man. Others will shake their head in disapproval. In contrast, the punishment for walking down the street without pants is bound to be moderately harsh. Someone is bound to call the police, probably sooner than later (Sumner (1940 [1907]). The strongest and most central norms, however, are taboos. When someone violates a taboo, it causes revulsion in the community, and punishment is severe. Incest is one of the most widespread taboos.
>
> Social scientists generally agree that folkways, mores, and most taboos change over time and vary from one society to the next. However, they traditionally single out the incest taboo as an exception. They hold that sexual relations between close relatives have been strictly forbidden throughout the history of all societies, because the prohibition is grounded in biological necessity. In this view, people have always observed that sexual relations between close relatives result in a relatively high incidence of congenital birth defects. As a result, people have always made sexual relations between close relatives taboo.
>
> —From Brym/Lie, *Sociology in Today's World*, 2e

3 Types of _____		
_____	▸ _____	
_____	▸ _____	
_____	▸ _____	

2.

Benefits of Life Insurance

Despite the importance of life insurance to sound financial planning, many people put off the decision to buy it. This happens partly because life insurance is associated with something unpleasant in many people's minds—namely, death. People don't like to talk about death or the things associated with it, so they often put off considering their life insurance needs. Life insurance is also intangible. You can't see, smell, touch, or taste its benefits—and those benefits mainly happen after you've died. However, life insurance does have some important benefits that should not be ignored in the financial planning process.

▶ Financial protection for dependents: If your family or loved ones depend on your income, what would happen to them after you die? Would they be able to maintain their current lifestyle, stay in their home, or afford a college education? Life insurance provides a financial cushion for your dependents, giving them a set amount of money after your death that they can use for many purposes. For example, your spouse may use your life insurance proceeds to pay off the mortgage on your home, so your family can continue living there comfortably, or set aside funds for your child's college education. In short, the most important benefit of life insurance is providing financial protection for your dependents after your death.

▶ Protection from creditors: A life insurance policy can be structured so that death benefits are paid directly to a named beneficiary rather than being considered as part of your estate. This means that even if you have outstanding bills and debts at the time of your death, creditors cannot claim the cash benefits from your life insurance policy, which provides further financial protection for your dependents.

▶ Tax benefits: Life insurance proceeds paid to your heirs, as a rule, aren't subject to state or federal income taxes. Furthermore, if certain requirements are met, policy proceeds can pass to named beneficiaries free of any *estate* taxes.

▶ Vehicle for savings: Some types of life insurance policies can serve as a savings vehicle, particularly for those who are looking for safety of principal.

—From Gitman, Joehnk, & Billingsley, *Personal Financial Planning*, 12e

Benefits of _____

_____   1. _____
                       2. _____
                       3. _____
                       4. _____

3.

In the mid-sixteenth century, some thirty years after the Spanish Conquest, a learned and industrious monk named Bernardino de Sahagun undertook a remarkable mission: to create an ethnographic portrait of the Aztecs as they lived before the European invasion. Sahagun held many interviews with Indians of all social classes and ages, to hear their own versions of their culture and beliefs. Included below are several thumbnail summaries of what was expected of men and women, of family members, of the upper and lower strata of Aztec society, and even of some professions.

The Father: the father is the founder of lineage. He is diligent, compassionate, sympathetic, a careful administrator of his household. He is the educator, the model giver, the teacher. He saves up for himself and for his dependents. He cares for his goods, and for the goods of others....He is thrifty and cares for the future. He regulates and establishes good order....

The bad father is not compassionate, he is neglectful and not reliable. He is a poor worker and lazy....

The Mother: the mother has children and cares for them. She nurses them at her breast. She is sincere, agile, and a willing worker, diligent in her duties and watchful over others. She teaches, and is mindful of her dependents. She caresses and serves others, she is mindful of their needs. She is careful and thrifty, ever vigilant of others, and always at work.

The bad mother is dull, stupid and lazy. She is a spend-thrift and a thief, a deceiver and a cheat. She loses things through her neglect. She is frequently angry, and not heedful of others. She encourages disobedience in her children....

The Nobleman: the man who has noble lineage is exemplary in his life. He follows the good example of others....He speaks eloquently, he is mild in speech, and virtuous...noble of heart and worthy of gratitude. He is discreet, gentle, well reared in manner. He is moderate, energetic, inquiring....He provides nourishment for others, comfort. He sustains others....He magnifies others and diminishes himself from modesty. He is a mourner for the dead, a doer of penances....

The bad nobleman is ungrateful, a debaser and disparager of others' property, he is contemptuous and arrogant. He creates disorder....

The Physician: the physician is knowledgeable of herbs and medicines from roots and plants; she is fully experienced in these things. She is a conductor of examinations, a woman of much experience, a counselor for the ill. The good physician is a restorer, a provider of health, one who makes the ill feel well. She cures people, she provides them with health again. She bleeds the sick...with an obsidian lancet she bleeds them and restores them.

—From Adler/Pouwels, *World Civilizations*, 6e (p. 192). Copyright © 2012 Cengage Learning, Inc. Reproduced by permission. www.cengage.co/permissions

Aztec Expectations of _____

_____   ▸ _____

_____   ▸ _____

_____   ▸ _____
                     _____

_____   ▸ _____

_____   ▸ _____
                     _____

_____   ▸ _____

_____   ▸ _____
                     _____

4.

The three broad views that shape modern psychology are the biological, psychological, and sociocultural perspectives.

The **biological perspective** seeks to explain our behavior in terms of biological principles such as brain processes, evolution, and genetics. By using new techniques, *biopsychologists* are producing exciting insights about how the brain relates to thinking, feelings, perception, abnormal behavior, and other topics. Biopsychologists and others who study the brain and nervous system, such as biologists and biochemists, together form the broader field of **neuroscience.**

The **psychological perspective** views behavior as the result of psychological processes within each person. This view continues to emphasize objective observation, just as the early behaviorists did. However, the psychological perspective now includes cognitive psychology, which seeks to explain how mental processes affect our thoughts, actions, and feelings (Goldstein, 2011). Cognitive psychology has gained prominence in recent years as researchers have devised ways to objectively study covert behaviors, such as thinking, memory, language, perception, problem solving, consciousness, and creativity. With a renewed interest in thinking, it can be said that psychology has finally "regained consciousness" (Robins, Gosling, & Craik, 1998).

As you can see, it is helpful to view human behavior from more than one perspective. This is also true in another sense. The **sociocultural perspective** stresses the impact that social and cultural contexts have on our behavior. We are rapidly becoming a multicultural society, made up of people from many nations. How has this affected psychology? Meet Jerry, who is Japanese American and is married to an Irish-Catholic American. Here is what Jerry, his wife, and their children did one New Year's Day:

> We woke up in the morning and went to Mass at St. Brigid's, which has a black gospel choir....Then we went to the Japanese-American Community Center for the Oshogatsu New Year's program and saw Buddhist archers shoot arrows to ward off evil spirits for the year. Next, we ate traditional rice cakes as part of the New Year's service and listened to a young Japanese-American storyteller. On the way home, we stopped in Chinatown and after that we ate Mexican food at a taco stand (Njeri, 1991).

Jerry and his family reflect a new social reality: Cultural diversity is becoming the norm. Over 100 million Americans are now African American, Hispanic, Asian American, Native American, or Pacific Islander (U.S. Census Bureau, 2007). In some large cities, such as Detroit and Baltimore, "minority" groups are already the majority.

Imagine that you are a psychologist. Your client, Linda, who is a Native American, tells you that spirits live in the trees near her home. Is Linda suffering from a delusion? Is she abnormal? Obviously, you will misjudge Linda's mental health if you fail to take her cultural beliefs into account. Cultural relativity—the idea that behavior must be judged relative to the values of the culture in which it occurs—can greatly affect the diagnosis and treatment of mental disorders (Lum, 2011). Cases like Linda's teach us to be wary of using narrow standards when judging others or comparing groups.

In addition to cultural differences, age, ethnicity, gender, religion, disability, and sexual orientation all affect the **social norms** that guide behavior. Social norms are rules that define acceptable and expected behavior for members of various groups. As we mentioned earlier, often, the unstated standard for judging what is "average," "normal," or "correct" has been the behavior of white, middle-class Western males (Henrich, Heine, & Norenzayan, 2010). To fully understand human behavior, psychologists need to know how people differ, as well as the ways in which we are all alike. To be effective, psychologists must be sensitive to people who are ethnically and culturally different from themselves (American Psychological Association, 2003b). For the same reason, an appreciation of human diversity can enrich your life, as well as your understanding of psychology (Denmark, Rabinowitz, & Sechzer, 2005).

Today, many psychologists realize that a single perspective is unlikely to fully explain complex human behavior. As a result, they are *eclectic* (ek-LEK-tik) and draw insights from a variety of perspectives.

—From Coon/Mitterer, *Introduction to Psychology: Gateways to Mind and Behavior,* 13e

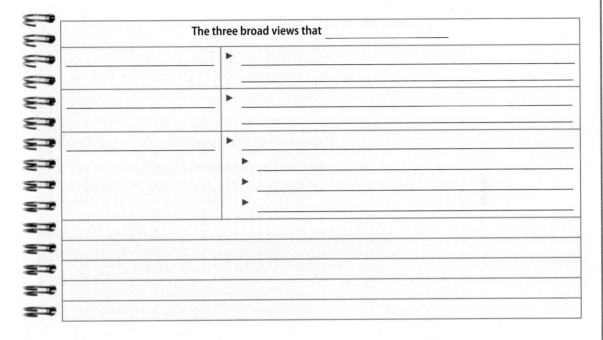

The three broad views that _____

5.

Advantages of Franchising

Both the franchisee and the franchisor must believe they'll benefit from the franchise arrangement; otherwise they wouldn't participate. The advantages of franchising for the franchisor are fairly obvious. It allows the franchisor to expand the business and bring in additional revenue (in the form of franchising fees and royalties) without investing its own capital. Also, franchisees—business owners who are motivated to earn a profit—may have a greater incentive than salaried managers to do whatever it takes to maximize the success of their outlets. From the franchisee's perspective, franchising offers several advantages:

▶ Less Risk: Franchises offer access to a proven business system and product. The systems and methods offered by franchisors have an established track record. People who are interested in buying a franchise can do research to see how stores in the franchise have performed and can talk to existing franchisees before investing.

▶ Training and Support: The franchisor normally provides the franchisee with extensive training and support. For example, Subway offers two weeks of training at its headquarters and additional training at meetings. The franchisor also sends out newsletters, provides Internet support, maintains a toll-free number for phone support, and provides on-site evaluations.

▶ Brand Recognition: Operating a franchise gives the franchisee instant brand name recognition, which can be a big help in attracting customers.

▶ Easier Access to Funding: Bankers and other lenders may be more willing to loan you money if your business is part of an established franchise than a new, unproven business.

Disadvantages of Franchising

Franchising also has some drawbacks. From the franchisor's perspective, operating a business with perhaps thousands of semi-independent owner–operators can be complex and challenging. With such a large number of owners it can be difficult to keep all of the franchisees satisfied, and disappointed franchisees sometimes go public with their complaints, damaging the reputation of the franchisor. In fact, it isn't unusual for disgruntled franchisees to sue their franchisors. Franchisees are also likely to find some disadvantages:

▶ Costs: The typical franchise agreement requires franchisees to pay an initial franchise fee when they enter into the franchise agreement and an ongoing royalty (usually a percentage of monthly sales revenues) to the franchisor. In addition, the franchisor may assess other fees to support national advertising campaigns or for other purposes. These costs vary considerably, but for high-profile franchises, they can be substantial.

▶ Lack of Control: The franchise agreement usually requires the franchisee to follow the franchisor's procedures to the letter. People who want the freedom and flexibility to be their own boss can find these restrictions frustrating.

▶ Negative Halo Effect: The irresponsible or incompetent behavior of a few franchisees can create a negative perception that adversely affects not only the franchise as a whole but also the success of other franchisees.

▶ Growth Challenges: While growth and expansion are definitely possible in franchising (many franchisees own multiple outlets), strings are attached. Franchise agreements usually limit the franchisee's territory and require franchisor approval before expanding into other areas.

▶ Restrictions on Sale: Franchise agreements normally prevent franchisees from selling their franchises to other investors without prior approval from the franchisor.

▶ Poor Execution: Not all franchisors live up to their promises. Sometimes the training and support are of poor quality, and sometimes the company does a poor job of screening franchisees, leading to the negative halo effect we mentioned previously.

These considerations suggest that before buying a franchise, potential owners should carefully research the franchise opportunity.

—From Kelly/McGowen, *BUSN*, 3e

_____ **of Franchising for the Franchisee**

_____	1. _____
	2. _____
	3. _____
	4. _____
_____	1. _____
	2. _____
	3. _____
	4. _____
	5. _____
	6. _____

Learning Aids in Textbook Chapters

Textbooks differ from other kinds of nonfiction books in that they provide many aids to help you learn the most that you can. In the introductory textbooks that you will read for your general education courses, each chapter typically has a wide variety of features to help you learn the material. These features help textbooks fulfill their almost purely informative purpose.

Chapter Outlines, Objectives, Focus Questions, or FAQs

Chapters often start with an outline or a series of questions designed for you to use as a chapter preview. These learning aids give you an overview of the chapter's scope (breadth of coverage) and sequence (order). Here is a combined chapter outline and set of focus questions from a world history textbook.

Chapter Outline and Focus Questions

tenets Guess the meaning of the word here based on its context.

Look up the word in a dictionary. What does it mean?

successors Break this word down into three parts, a root and two suffixes.

What does each suffix mean?

The word means:

The Rise of Islam
What were the main tenets of Islam, and how does the religion compare with Judaism and Christianity?

The Arab Empire and Its Successors
Why did the Arabs undergo such a rapid expansion in the seventh and eighth centuries, and why were they so successful in creating an empire?

Islamic Civilization
What were the main features of Islamic society and culture during its era of early growth?

The Byzantine Empire
What were the main features of Byzantine civilization, and why did it follow a separate path from that taken by Christian societies in the West?

Critical Thinking
In what ways did Byzantine and Islamic civilizations resemble and differ from each other? Was their relationship overall based on cooperation or conflict?

—From Duiker, *World History*, 5e

Interaction 7–6 **Integrate Your Knowledge of Patterns**

For each focus question above, name the pattern(s) of organization or level of critical thinking that is (are) suggested. Refer to Chapters 2 and 6 as needed.

1–2. The two patterns in the question under "Rise of Islam" are _____

 3. The pattern in the question under "Arab Empire" is _____

 4. The pattern in the question under "Islamic Civilization" is _____

5–6. The two patterns in the question under "Byzantine Empire" are _____

7–8. The pattern in the first critical thinking question asks for _____

9. The type of critical thinking that is asked for in the second critical thinking question is _____

10. Overall, what pattern of organization do you expect to find in the chapter? _____

_____

Interaction 7–7 ▸ **Read for Content**

1. What three religions are going to be discussed in this chapter? _____

2. When did the Arabs expand rapidly into neighboring territories? _____

3. Was the Byzantine Empire in the East or the West? _____

Using the Chapter Outline and Focus Questions to Learn

You can see that the chapter outline and focus questions give you a wealth of information about what is coming in the chapter. You can use the chapter outline or similar features in several different ways:

1. **Survey and Predict.** When you are getting ready to read the chapter, take about five minutes to read and study the chapter outline. Use the strategies you've learned for turning headings into questions, searching for patterns of organization, and figuring out what content is to come. Reflect on anything you've seen in the movies or on television (which, you realize, may or may not be accurate), and anything you've heard or read about the topics.

2. **Read One Section at a Time.** Textbook chapters can be long and complex, so it's wise to break up a chapter into its parts and read one at a time. For instance, in the world history chapter, you would read the section "The Rise of Islam" as if it were a separate reading selection, using the full reading process on it and taking notes. Only then would you proceed to the next section, "The Arab Empire and Its Successors."

3. **Put the Pieces of the Puzzle Together.** After you read a section of the chapter, refer back to the chapter outline so that you can see once again how that piece fits into the larger puzzle. Learn to move back and forth from specific details to big picture to specific details to big picture. You need to understand both.

4. **Use the Outline to Structure a Study Session for a Test.** After you have studied your notes in preparation for a test, use the chapter outline and any focus questions as a way to test yourself. One way to do this is to write the heading or question and then list all the information you can about it. If you like to study with other people, take turns asking the questions and answering them. Do take the step of writing the questions and answers down, however, if your test will be written.

Headings

Most college textbooks include several levels of headings. Major headings show the most important chapter divisions. A second level of headings divides the content within each major section. There may be a third and even a fourth level of headings in a chapter, depending on the complexity of the topic. Here are the three levels of headings from one part of a chapter from a public speaking textbook.

This is the major heading.	TYPES OF PUBLIC SPEAKING
These three headings are the main divisions of the topic, "Types of Public Speaking."	Informative Speeches
	Invitational Speeches
	Persuasive Speeches
This section is divided into three subsections.	Speaking on Special Occasions
	Introductory speeches. When you present information about…
	Commemorative speeches. When you give a **commemorative**…
	Acceptance speeches. Speeches of acceptance are delivered…

—From Griffin, *Invitation to Public Speaking*, 2e

Notice that the headings are designed to make it clear which ones represent the broadest ideas in the chapter. In this public speaking book, the major headings are signaled by the use of all capital letters in a large type size. The second-level headings include both capital and lower-case letters; they are a smaller size; they are a different color; and they are underlined. The third-level headings are not set off above the text like the first- and second-level headings; they are part of the paragraph that follows them, even though they are distinguished from the text by color and type style.

Using the Headings to Stay Oriented

1. **Remember to form questions from the headings before you read each section, and to quickly survey the section before you read it.**

2. **Stay aware of where you are in a section and in a chapter.** The headings provide you with valuable information about how experts in a field of study think about their topic and classify its subtopics. The headings act as an outline for the ideas you are learning about, and thus you can use them as an aid while you study, just as we suggested for the chapter outlines on page 365.

Interaction 7–8 ▸ Learn from Textbook Headings

The following headings come from a chapter of a sociology textbook. Study them and answer the questions that follow.

THE IMPORTANCE OF GROUPS

CHARACTERISTICS OF SOCIAL GROUPS

Group Size and Structure

PRIMARY AND SECONDARY GROUPS

GROUP SIZE AND RELATIONSHIPS

DYADS AND TRIADS

Communities Networks

IN-GROUPS AND OUT-GROUPS

REFERENCE GROUPS

SOCIAL NETWORK ANALYSIS

INTERACTION IN GROUPS

Principles of Interaction

THE PLEASURE PRINCIPLE

THE RATIONALITY PRINCIPLE

THE RECIPROCITY PRINCIPLE

THE FAIRNESS PRINCIPLE

The Economic Person Versus the Social Person

Communication and Behavior in Groups

—From Kornblum, *Sociology in a Changing World*, 7e. Copyright © 2005 Cengage Learning, Inc.
Reproduced by permission. www.cengage.com/permissions

1–3. What are the three main topics this chapter covers?

▸ _____

▸ _____

▸ _____

4–5. For the first main topic, what question would you form as a guide to reading that section? What does the question reveal about the pattern of organization you can expect to find in the section? (Refer to Chapter 6 if needed.)

Question: _____

Pattern: _____

6–8. What are three considerations about group size and structure that this chapter covers?

▶ _____

▶ _____

▶ _____

9. How many principles of group interaction are listed? _____

10. Based on this information, would you say that people always act fairly in groups? What information in the headings makes you say so? _____

_____

Boxed Material or Sidebars

Many textbooks include special-interest material in boxes or sidebars. These may be stories that illustrate the chapter concepts, summaries of research studies that relate to the chapter topic, interesting "real-world" applications of the chapter ideas, or material to help students learn to think more critically. Some may include questions; others may be cases in which you are asked to apply the chapter concepts in particular ways. Don't skip this material! The information is featured for a reason: it's important to know.

Here is an example of an illustrative anecdote from a cultural anthropology textbook.

Cross-Cultural Miscue

Tony Manza, a high-level sales executive with a Canadian office furniture company, was in Kuwait trying to land a large contract with the Kuwaiti government. Having received an introduction from a mutual friend, Manza made an appointment with Mr. Mansour, the chief purchasing agent for the government. In his preparation for the trip, Manza had been told to expect to engage in a good deal of small talk before actually getting down to business. So Manza and Mansour chatted about the weather, golf, and Tony's flight from Toronto. Then, quite surprisingly, Mansour inquired about Manza's 70-year-old father. Without giving it much thought, Manza responded by saying that his father was doing fine but that the last time he had seen him four months ago in the nursing home, he had lost some weight. From that point onward, Mansour's attitude changed abruptly from warm and gracious to cool and aloof. Manza never did get the contract he was after.

Although Manza thought he was giving Mansour a straightforward answer, his response from Mansour's perspective made Manza an undesirable business partner. Coming from a society that places very high value on family relationships, Mansour considered putting one's own father into a nursing home (to be cared for by total strangers) to be inhumane. If Manza could not be relied upon to take care of his own father, he surely could not be trusted to fulfill his obligations in a business relationship.

—From Ferraro, *Cultural Anthropology*, 6e

This feature appeared in a chapter on marriage and the family. The chapter compares family life in different countries, and this feature gives one example of how cultural differences regarding family can influence people even when they are outside the family environment.

Interaction 7–9 **Think about the Feature**

1–2. What country is Tony Manza from? _____ Mr. Mansour? _____

3. What did Manza understand about doing business in Kuwait before he arrived? _____
_____

4–5. What are two things Manza did not understand about Kuwaiti culture that led to his not getting a contract?

▶ _____

▶ _____

Using Boxed Features to Learn

When you read a boxed feature or sidebar, don't just read it and move on. First read the information carefully, and then ask and answer questions about it:

▶ How does this information relate to the chapter topic?
▶ Which chapter concepts does this information illustrate?
▶ Does the feature provide leads to other interesting information about this topic?

Review Questions or Self-Quiz

Review questions, sometimes including multiple choice answers, can often be found at the end of a textbook chapter. These questions are designed to help you decide whether or not you have learned the material. If you find that you cannot answer some questions or have answered them incorrectly, then go back to the section of the chapter where the material was covered and review it. Later, answer the review questions again to see if you now remember the material.

Another way to use such questions is to read them before you read the chapter; in other words, use them to check your prior knowledge. As you read the chapter, refer back to your answers and correct any that you answered incorrectly.

Interaction 7–10 ▸ Check Prior Knowledge with a Self-Quiz

Here are five of the ten questions from a chapter on alcohol use, misuse, and abuse from a college health textbook. As you read them, suppose you are using the questions as a check of your prior knowledge. Circle the letter of the answers you think are correct.

Making This Chapter Work for You

Review Questions

1. An individual's response to alcohol depends on all of the following *except*
   a. the rate at which the drink is absorbed into the body's tissues.
   b. the blood alcohol concentration.
   c. socioeconomic status.
   d. gender and race.

2. Responsible drinking includes which of the following behaviors?
   a. Avoiding eating while drinking because eating speeds up absorption of alcohol
   b. Limiting alcohol intake to no more than four drinks in an hour
   c. Taking aspirin while drinking to lower your risk of a heart attack
   d. Socializing with individuals who limit their alcohol intake

3. Which of the following statements about drinking on college campuses is true?
   a. The percentage of students who abstain from alcohol has increased.
   b. The number of women who binge drink has decreased.

   c. Because of peer pressure, students in fraternities and sororities tend to drink less than students in dormitories.
   d. Students who live in substance-free dormitories tend to binge-drink when alcohol is available.

4. Which of the following statements about the effects of alcohol on the body systems is true?
   a. In most individuals, alcohol sharpens the responses of the brain and nervous system, enhancing sensation and perception.
   b. Moderate drinking may have a positive effect on the cardiovascular system.
   c. French researchers have found that drinking red wine with meals may have a positive effect on the digestive system.
   d. The leading alcohol-related cause of death is liver damage.

5. Health risks of alcoholism include all of the following *except*
   a. hypertension.
   b. lung cancer.
   c. peptic ulcers.
   d. hepatitis.

—From Hales, *An Invitation to Health*, 12e

The answers to the questions from the health textbook are as follows: (1) c, (2) d, (3) a, (4) b, and (5) b. Once you discovered which questions you answered correctly and incorrectly, you would focus carefully on the sections that explained the information you didn't know.

Chapter Summary

Sometimes when reading a lot of information, a person can get bogged down in details. Often a chapter summary is included to help you remember the big picture of the chapter topics. The chapter summary may be a bulleted list of key points, or one or more paragraphs that pull together the main ideas of the chapter. Sometimes the summary is a list of questions and answers. The chapter summaries in one introductory biology textbook summarize each chapter section by section. Here is the summary of the first of one chapter's seven sections.

Summary

Section 1.1 Life shows many levels of organization. All things, living and non-living, are made of atoms. Atoms join to form molecules, and molecules of life assemble into cells. Cells are the smallest living units. An organism may be a single cell or multicellular. In most multicelled species, cells are organized as tissues and organs.

A population consists of individuals of the same species in a specified area. A community consists of all populations occupying the same area. An ecosystem is a community and its environment. The biosphere includes all regions of Earth's atmosphere, waters, and land where we find living organisms.

—From Starr/Evers/Starr, *Biology*, 2e

These two short paragraphs summarize two whole pages of the chapter. Notice that each statement in the summary is quite general.

Using the Chapter Summary to Review and to Survey

Review. If you are reading the summary after you have read the chapter, read each sentence and then pause. Can you fill in the details that explain the general statement? If not, review that section of the chapter again and search for the explanation. After you have explained each general statement with the proof that supports it, check your understanding by skimming through the chapter again. Have you missed anything major? Once you can explain the general statements in the chapter summary using details, you can feel assured that you understand much of the chapter content.

Survey. You can read the chapter summary before you read the chapter itself as part of your survey of the material. This will help you form a structure, or schema, in which to place information as you come to it in the reading. It will also help you immediately see the similarities and differences between your prior knowledge and the ideas you will be reading about.

Interaction 7–11 ▶ Survey Using a Chapter Summary

Read the Review of Key Points on pages 385–386.

What ideas are similar to what you already know or believe? _____

_____

_____

What ideas are different from or contradict what you know and believe? _____

_____

_____

Key Terms

Key terms, or key concepts, may be listed at the beginning or end of a chapter. In some books, the term and its definition are provided in that section. In other books, a list of key terms is given with the numbers of the pages on which you will find their definitions. Any terms that are called *key* or *important* are terms that you should be able to define and provide examples for.

Using Key Terms to Review

Use the list of key terms to be sure you understand the important concepts in a chapter. Four instances in particular can cue you that the term is important to know:

▶ The term is in **boldface**.
▶ It is called an *Important Term* or a *Key Term*.
▶ The term is included in a major heading.
▶ The author spends a paragraph or more explaining a term.

When the chapter emphasizes a certain concept, then in addition to knowing the definition of the term, be sure you can discuss specific examples of it.

Connect Your Skills

Reading and Taking Notes on Textbook Chapters

A. Perform the following tasks on the chapter outline excerpt from a history textbook.

- ▶ Create a focus question for the first section.
- ▶ Name the pattern of organization for each focus question, including the one you created.
- ▶ Identify the level of thinking for the critical thinking question.

Chapter Outline and Focus Questions

The Road to World War I

The Great War
Why did the course of World War I turn out to be so different from what the belligerents had expected? How did World War I affect the belligerents' governmental and political institutions, economic affairs, and social life?

War and Revolution
What were the causes of the Russian Revolution of 1917, and why did the Bolsheviks prevail in the civil war and gain control of Russia?

Critical Thinking
What was the relationship between World War I and the Russian Revolution?

1. _____

2. What pattern is used in the question you asked? _____

3. What pattern is used in both questions under "The Great War"? _____

4. What pattern is used in both questions under "War and Revolution"? _____

5. What critical thinking level is asked for in the critical thinking question? _____

B. Read the following excerpt from a college history text. We have kept the section title but removed the other headings. However, note that paragraphs 2 to 4 are related to one another, and paragraphs 5 and 6 are related to each other. Consider each of these as separate groups of text.

- ▶ Before you read, turn the title into a question and write it in the margin.
- ▶ As you read, look for the answers to the question. Read all the paragraphs in a group before marking any of their main ideas.
- ▶ When you mark the main ideas, highlight just a few key words—enough so that if you were reading only the highlights later, they would remind you of the main ideas.
- ▶ Write your own heading for each group of paragraphs on the lines given.
- ▶ Double-check your heading by turning it into a question to see if the details answer it.

The Road to World War I

6. Question: _____

_____

1   On June 28, 1914, the heir to the Austrian throne, the Archduke Francis Ferdinand, was assassinated in the Bosnian city of Sarajevo. Although this event precipitated the confrontation between Austria and Serbia that led to World War I, underlying forces had been propelling Europeans toward armed conflict for a long time.

Topical Press Agency/Getty Images

7. Heading for paragraphs 2–4: _____

_____

8. Question: _____

2   The system of nation-states that had emerged in Europe in the second half of the nineteenth century had led to severe competition. Rivalries over colonies and trade intensified during a frenzied imperialist expansion, while the division of Europe's great powers into two loose alliances (Germany, Austria, and Italy; France, Great Britain, and Russia) only added to the tensions. The series of crises that tested those alliances in the 1900s and early 1910s had left European states embittered, eager for revenge, and willing to revert to war as an acceptable way to preserve the power of their national states.

3   The growth of nationalism in the nineteenth century had yet another serious consequence. Not all ethnic groups had achieved the goal of nationhood. Slavic minorities in the Balkans and the polyglot Habsburg Empire, for example, still dreamed of creating their own national states. So did the Irish in the British Empire and the Poles in the Russian Empire.

4   National aspirations, however, were not the only source of internal strife at the beginning of the twentieth century. Socialist labor movements had grown more powerful and were increasingly inclined to use strikes, even violent ones, to achieve their goals. Some conservative leaders, alarmed at the increase in labor strife and class division, even feared that European nations were on the verge of revolution. Did these statesmen opt for war in 1914 because they believed that "prosecuting an active foreign policy" as some Austrian leaders expressed it, would smother "internal troubles"?

Some historians have argued that the desire to suppress internal disorder may have encouraged some leaders to take the plunge into war in 1914.

9. Heading for paragraphs 5–6: _____

10. Question: _____

5   The growth of large mass armies after 1900 not only heightened the existing tensions in Europe but also made it inevitable that if war did come, it would be extremely destructive. **Conscription**—obligatory military service—had been established as a regular practice in most Western countries before 1914 (the United States and Britain were major exceptions). European military machines had doubled in size between 1890 and 1914. With its 1.3 million men, the Russian army had grown to be the largest, but the French and Germans were not far behind, with 900,000 each. The British, Italian, and Austrian armies numbered between 250,000 and 500,000 soldiers.

6   **Militarism**, however, involved more than just large armies. As armies grew, so did the influence of military leaders, who drew up vast and complex plans for quickly mobilizing millions of men and enormous quantities of supplies in the event of war. Fearful that changing these plans would cause chaos in the armed forces, military leaders insisted that the plans could not be altered. In the crises during the summer of 1914, the generals' lack of flexibility forced European political leaders to make decisions for military instead of political reasons.

—From Duiker, *World History*, 5e

C. Create Cornell notes for the "Road to World War I" reading based on your highlighting or annotating.

11–20.

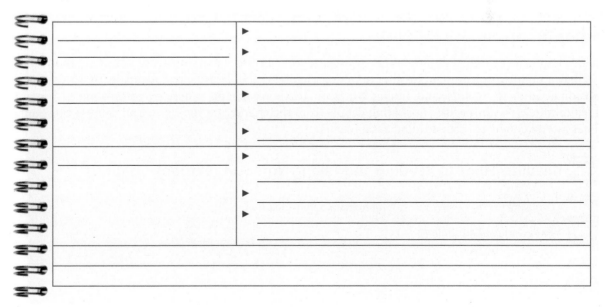

D. Identify the pattern of organization and create a visual map to reflect that pattern.

21. What main pattern of organization is reflected? _____

22–25.

Chapter Summary Activity

This chapter has discussed note-taking strategies you can use when you read college textbooks, as well as a number of learning aids that textbook chapters include to help students learn. Construct a Reading Guide to Reading and Taking Notes on Textbook Chapters here by completing each main idea on the left with specific supporting details from the chapter on the right. You can use this guide later as you complete other reading assignments.

Reading Guide to Reading and Taking Notes on Textbook Chapters

Complete this idea with...	information from Chapter 7.
Three-part reading strategy	1. _____ _____

	2. _____
	_____
	3. _____
	_____
Strategy for readings without headings	4. _____
	_____
	5. _____
	_____
	6. _____
	_____
	7. _____
	_____
Annotating	8. _____
	_____
Common items to annotate	9. _____
	_____
Four benefits of Cornell notes	10. _____
	_____
	11. _____
	_____
	12. _____
	_____
	13. _____
	_____
Three parts of a summary	14. _____
	_____
	15. _____
	_____

16. _____

Three hints for effective Cornell notes

17. _____
    _____

18. _____
    _____

19. _____
    _____

Nine learning aids in textbooks

20. _____

21. _____

22. _____

23. _____

24. _____

25. _____

26. _____

27. _____

28. _____

Two uses for the chapter outline

29. _____
    _____

30. _____
    _____

Think about what your reading comprehension strategies were before you read this chapter. How did they differ from the suggestions here? What are some new strategies you can start using? Write down your thoughts.

_____

_____

_____

Reading 7–1 | Psychology Textbook

▶ Pre-Reading the Selection

People tend to be very interested in the question, "What will make me happy?" The following reading from a psychology textbook, *Psychology: Themes and Variations*, addresses some of the research into this question.

Surveying the Reading

Survey the following article. Then check the elements that are included in this reading.

_____	Title	_____	Words in bold or italic type
_____	Headings	_____	Images and captions
_____	First sentences of paragraphs		

Guessing the Purpose

Judging from the title of the selection and the publication context, what do you suppose is the purpose of this selection? _____

Predicting the Content

Predict two things that this selection will discuss.

▶ _____

▶ _____

Activating Your Knowledge

Think about a person you know who seems happy. Of the predictors of happiness covered in this reading, which do you think most apply to them?

▶ _____

▶ _____

▶ _____

Scan to Connect! Use your smart phone to scan this code to watch a video to activate your knowledge about the ingredients of happiness. (See the inside front cover for more information on how to use this.) Quickly read the section on money in "Exploring the Ingredients of Happiness." Does the information in the video support, partially support, or contradict the information in the reading? Explain your answer.

Entries from the Glossary of *Psychology*

Refer to these entries as you read.

correlation the extent to which two variables are related to each other

empiricism the premise that knowledge should be acquired through observation

hypothesis a tentative statement about the relationship between two or more variables

▸ Reading with Pen in Hand

Students who annotate as they read are more successful than those who do not. That's why you will annotate each selection in *Connect* as you read. In the reading that follows, use the following symbols:

★ or ⟨Point⟩   to indicate a main idea

① ② ③   to indicate major details

 Visit **www.cengagebrain.com** to access the CourseMate for this chapter to hear pronunciations of vocabulary words from this reading.

Exploring the Ingredients of Happiness

Wayne Weiten

1   Answer the following "true" or "false."

_____ 1. The empirical evidence indicates that most people are relatively unhappy.

_____ 2. Although wealth doesn't guarantee happiness, wealthy people are much more likely to be happy than the rest of the population.

_____ 3. People who have children are happier than people without children.

_____ 4. Good health is an essential requirement for happiness.

_____ 5. Good-looking people are happier than those who are unattractive.

▸ What seems to be the main idea of the reading selection?

2   The answer to all these questions is "false." These assertions are all reasonable and widely believed hypotheses about the correlates of happiness, but they have not been supported by empirical research. Recent years have brought a surge of interest in the correlates of **subjective well-being**—individuals' personal perceptions of their overall happiness and life satisfaction. The findings of these studies are quite interesting. As you have already seen from our true-false questions, many commonsense notions about happiness appear to be inaccurate.

subjective well-being This expression is defined in the same sentence. What does it mean?

How Happy Are People?

▸ How would you answer the question that the heading poses?

3   One of these inaccuracies is the apparently widespread assumption that most people are relatively unhappy. Writers, social scientists, and the general public seem to believe that people around the world are predominantly dissatisfied and unhappy, yet empirical surveys consistently find that the vast majority

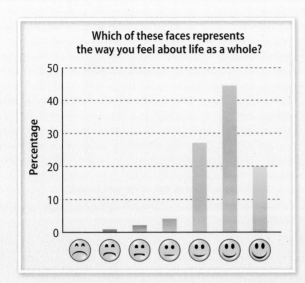

Figure 7.1   Measuring Happiness with a Nonverbal Scale
Researchers have used a variety of methods to estimate the distribution of happiness. For example, in one study in the United States, respondents were asked to examine the seven facial expressions shown and select the one that "comes closest to expressing how you feel about your life as a whole." As you can see, the vast majority of participants chose happy faces. (Data adapted from Myers, 1992.)

of respondents—even those who are poor or disabled—characterize themselves as fairly happy (Diener & Diener, 1996; Myers & Diener, 1995). When people are asked to rate their happiness, only a small minority place themselves below the neutral point on the various scales used (see **Figure 7.1**). When the average subjective well-being of entire nations is computed, based on almost 1000 surveys, the means cluster toward the positive end of the scale, as shown in **Figure 7.2** (Veenhoven, 1993). That's not to say that everyone is equally happy. Researchers find substantial and thought-provoking disparities among people in subjective well-being, which we will analyze momentarily, but the overall **picture seems rosier** than anticipated.

> **picture seems rosier** A person who looks out of "rose-colored glasses" is an optimist. What does this phrase mean in this sentence?

Factors That Do Not Predict Happiness

4   Let us begin our discussion of individual differences in happiness by highlighting those things that turn out to be relatively unimportant determinants of subjective well-being. Quite a number of factors that you might expect to be influential appear to bear little or no relationship to general happiness.

> ▶ What pattern of organization is implied throughout this reading selection?

5   **Money.** There is a positive correlation between income and subjective feelings of happiness, but the association is surprisingly weak (Diener & Seligman, 2004). For example, one study found a correlation of just .13 between income and happiness in the United States (Diener et al., 1993). Admittedly, being very poor can make people unhappy, but once people **ascend** above the poverty level, little relation is seen between income and happiness. On the average, wealthy people are only marginally happier than those in the middle classes. The problem with money is that in this era of voracious consumption, pervasive advertising and rising income fuel escalating material desires (Frey & Stutzer, 2002; Kasser et al., 2004). When these growing material desires outstrip what people can afford, dissatisfaction is likely (Solberg et al., 2002).

> ▶ Give examples of what makes people happier and less happy.

> **ascend** Given the immediate context, what does *ascend* mean?

> What is the antonym of *ascend*?

Figure 7.2   The Subjective Well-Being of Nations

Veenhoven (1993) combined the results of almost 1000 surveys to calculate the average subjective well-being reported by representative samples from 43 nations. The mean happiness scores clearly pile up at the positive end of the distribution, with only two scores falling below the neutral point of 5. (Data adapted from Diener and Diener, 1996.)

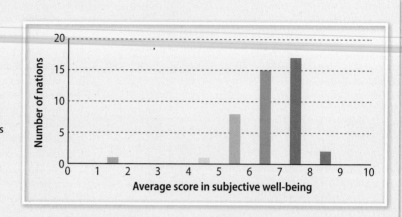

materialistic Break this word into a root and two suffixes—*material + ist + ic.* What does it probably mean?

▶ Does age have a big impact on happiness?

▶ Does parenthood have an impact on happiness?

▶ Do intelligence and attractiveness have an impact on happiness?

▶ Does this paragraph include a thesis statement?

▶ Are the next three predictors stronger or weaker than the ones discussed in the previous section?

6

7

8

9

10

Thus, complaints about not having enough money are routine even among people who earn hefty six-figure incomes. Interestingly, there is some evidence that people who place an especially strong emphasis on the pursuit of wealth and **materialistic** goals tend to be somewhat less happy than others (Kasser, 2002; Ryan & Deci, 2001), perhaps in large part because they are so focused on financial success that they don't derive much satisfaction from their family life (Nickerson et al., 2003).

Age. Age and happiness are consistently found to be unrelated. Age accounts for less than 1 percent of the variation in people's happiness (Inglehart, 1990; Myers & Diener, 1997). The key factors influencing subjective well-being may shift some as people grow older—work becomes less important, health more so—but people's average level of happiness tends to remain remarkably stable over the life span.

Parenthood. Children can be a tremendous source of joy and fulfillment, but they can also be a tremendous source of headaches and hassles. Compared to childless couples, parents worry more and experience more marital problems (Argyle, 1987). Apparently, the good and bad aspects of parenthood balance each other out, because the evidence indicates that people who have children are neither more nor less happy than people without children (Argyle, 2001).

Intelligence and Attractiveness. Intelligence and physical attractiveness are highly valued traits in modern society, but researchers have not found an association between either characteristic and happiness (Diener, 1984; Diener, Wolsic, & Fujita, 1995).

Moderately Good Predictors of Happiness

Research has identified three facets of life that appear to have a moderate association with subjective well-being: health, social activity, and religious belief.

Health. Good physical health would seem to be an essential requirement for happiness, but people adapt to health problems. Research reveals that individuals who develop serious, disabling health conditions aren't as unhappy as one might guess (Myers, 1992; Riis et al., 2005). Good health may not, by itself, produce happiness, because people tend to take good health for granted. Considerations such as these may help explain why researchers find only a moderate positive correlation (average = .32) between health status and subjective well-being (Argyle, 1999).

11   **Social Activity.** Humans are social animals, and **interpersonal** relations do appear to contribute to people's happiness. Those who are satisfied with their social support and friendship networks and those who are socially active report above-average levels of happiness (Diener & Seligman, 2004; Myers, 1999). Furthermore, people who are exceptionally happy tend to report greater satisfaction with their social relations than those who are average or low in subjective well-being (Diener & Seligman, 2002).

12   **Religion.** The link between religiosity and subjective well-being is modest, but a number of large-scale surveys suggest that people with heartfelt religious convictions are more likely to be happy than people who characterize themselves as nonreligious (Argyle, 1999; Ferriss, 2002). Researchers aren't sure how religious faith fosters happiness, but Myers (1992) offers some interesting **conjectures**. Among other things, he discusses how religion can give people a sense of purpose and meaning in their lives, help them accept their setbacks gracefully, connect them to a caring, supportive community, and comfort them by putting their ultimate **mortality** in perspective.

Strong Predictors of Happiness

13   The list of factors that turn out to have fairly strong associations with happiness is surprisingly short. The key ingredients of happiness appear to involve love, work, and personality.

14   **Love and Marriage.** Romantic relationships can be stressful, but people consistently rate being in love as one of the most critical ingredients of happiness (Myers, 1999). Furthermore, although people complain a lot about their marriages, the evidence indicates that marital status is a key correlate of happiness. Among both men and women, married people are happier than people who are single or divorced (Myers & Diener, 1995), and this relationship holds around the world in widely different cultures (Diener et al., 2000). However, the causal relations underlying this correlation are unclear. It may be that happiness causes marital satisfaction more than marital satisfaction promotes happiness. Perhaps people who are happy tend to have better intimate relationships and more stable marriages, while people who are unhappy have more difficulty finding and keeping mates.

15   **Work.** Given the way people often complain about their jobs, one might not expect work to be a key source of happiness, but it is. Although less critical than love and marriage, job satisfaction has a substantial association with general happiness (Warr, 1999). Studies also show that

interpersonal Break this word into a prefix, a root, and a suffix—*inter + person + al.* Based on the meaning of these words—*international, interweave, interoffice*—what does *inter-* mean?

What does *interpersonal* mean?

▶ When people are isolated, are they less happy than others?

▶ How many possible reasons does Myers give for how having heartfelt religious convictions makes people somewhat happier?

conjectures Based on the meaning of the sentence it is in, what does *conjectures* mean?

mortality Although this word consists of more than two word parts, consider it as *mortal + ity.* What does *mortal* mean?

What do you guess is the purpose for the *–ity* ending?

▶ Does this paragraph include a topic sentence?

▶ What are two important points in this paragraph?

▶ Do unemployed people typically have a strong sense of well-being?

unemployment has strong negative effects on subjective well-being (Lucas et al., 2004). It is difficult to sort out whether job satisfaction causes happiness or vice versa, but evidence suggests that causation flows both ways (Argyle, 2001).

▶ Are external or internal factors more important in whether a person is happy?

16   **Personality.** The best predictor of individuals' future happiness is their past happiness (Diener & Lucas, 1999). Some people seem destined to be happy and others unhappy, regardless of their triumphs or setbacks. The limited influence of life events was apparent in a stunning study that found only marginal differences in overall happiness between recent lottery winners and recent accident victims who became quadriplegics (Brickman, Coates, & Janoff-Bulman, 1978). Investigators were amazed that such extremely fortuitous and horrible events didn't have a dramatic impact on happiness. Several lines of evidence suggest that happiness does not depend on external circumstances—buying a nice house, getting promoted—so much as internal factors, such as one's outlook on life (Lykken & Tellegen, 1996). With this fact in mind, researchers have begun to look for links between personality and subjective well-being, and they have found some intriguing correlations. For example, extraversion is one of the better predictors of happiness. People who are outgoing, upbeat, and sociable tend to be happier than others (Fleeson, Malanos, & Achille, 2002). Additional positive correlates of happiness include self-esteem and optimism (Lucas, Diener, & Suh, 1996).

Conclusions about Subjective Well-Being

▶ Does this paragraph include a topic sentence?

17   We must be cautious in drawing inferences about the causes of happiness, because the available data are correlational (see **Figure 7.3**). Nonetheless, the empirical evidence suggests that many popular beliefs about the sources of happiness are unfounded. The data also demonstrate that happiness is shaped by a complex constellation of variables. In spite of this complexity, however, a number of worthwhile insights about the ingredients of happiness can be gleaned from the recent flurry of research.

▶ What is the main idea of this paragraph?

18   First, research on happiness demonstrates that the determinants of subjective well-being are precisely that: subjective. Objective realities are not as important as subjective feelings. In other words, your health, your wealth, and your job are not as influential as how you feel about your health, wealth, and job (Schwarz & Strack, 1999). These feelings are likely to be influenced by what your expectations were. Research suggests that bad outcomes feel worse when unexpected than when expected and good outcomes feel better when unexpected than when expected (Shepperd & McNulty, 2002). Thus, the same objective event, such as a pay raise of $2000 annually, may generate positive feelings in someone who wasn't expecting a raise and negative feelings in someone expecting a much larger increase in salary.

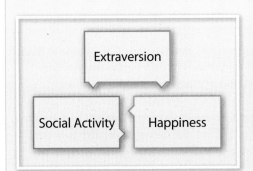

Figure 7.3   Possible Causal Relations Among the Correlates of Happiness
Although we have considerable data on the correlates of happiness, it is difficult to untangle the possible causal relationships. For example, we know that a moderate positive correlation exists between social activity and happiness, but we can't say for sure whether high social activity causes happiness or whether happiness causes people to be more socially active. Moreover, in light of the research showing that a third variable—extraversion—correlates with both variables, we have to consider the possibility that extraversion causes both greater social activity and greater happiness.

19   Second, when it comes to happiness, everything is relative (Argyle, 1999; Hagerty, 2000). In other words, you evaluate what you have relative to what the people around you have. Generally, we compare ourselves with others who are similar to us. Thus, people who are wealthy assess what they have by comparing themselves with their wealthy friends and neighbors. This is one reason for the low correlation between wealth and happiness. You might have a lovely home, but if it sits next door to a neighbor's palatial mansion, it might be a source of more dissatisfaction than happiness.

▶ How do people decide if they have enough?

20   Third, research on subjective well-being indicates that people often adapt to their circumstances. This adaptation effect is one reason that increases in income don't necessarily bring increases in happiness. Thus hedonic adaptation occurs when the mental scale that people use to judge the pleasantness/unpleasantness of their experiences shifts so that their neutral point, or baseline for comparison, changes. Unfortunately, when people's experiences improve, hedonic adaptation may sometimes put them on a hedonic treadmill—their neutral point moves upward, so that the improvements yield no real benefits (Kahneman, 1999). However, when people have to grapple with major setbacks, hedonic adaptation probably helps protect their mental and physical health. For example, people who are sent to prison and people who develop debilitating diseases are not as unhappy as one might assume, because they adapt to their changed situations and evaluate events from a new perspective (Frederick & Loewenstein, 1999). That's not to say that hedonic adaptation in the face of life's difficulties is inevitable or complete (Lucas et al., 2003). People who suffer major setbacks, such as the death of a spouse or serious illness, often are not as happy as they were before the setback, but generally they are not nearly as unhappy as they or others would have predicted.

▶ What is the main message of this paragraph?

REVIEW OF KEY POINTS

▶ Research on happiness reveals that many commonsense notions about the roots of happiness appear to be incorrect, including the notion that most people are unhappy. Factors such as income, age, parenthood, intelligence, and attractiveness are largely uncorrelated with subjective well-being.

▶ Physical health, good social relationships, and religious faith appear to have a modest impact on feelings of happiness. The only factors that are good predictors of happiness are love and marriage, work satisfaction, and personality.

▶ Research on happiness indicates that objective realities are not as important as subjective feelings and that subjective well-being is a relative concept. The evidence also indicates that people adapt to their circumstances.

—From Weiten, *Psychology: Themes and Variations*, 8e. Copyright © 2010 Cengage Learning, Inc. Reproduced by permission. www.cengage.com/permissions

▶ Comprehension Questions

Write the letter of the answer on the line. Then explain your thinking.

Main Idea

____ 1. The four statements that follow are a main idea and three supporting details. Select the letter of the main idea.

   a. Wonderful and horrible life events don't necessarily affect happiness much.

   b. Extraversion, self-esteem, and optimism are linked to happiness.

   c. People's happiness seems to depend on internal factors, not external factors.

   d. Buying a nice house and getting promoted don't necessarily lead to happiness.

Why? What information in the selection leads you to give that answer? _____

_____

____ 2. Myers (1992) speculates that having a sense of purpose and meaning, the ability to accept setbacks gracefully, and connections to community may foster happiness. Which of the factors discussed provides these three traits?

   a. parenthood

   b. social activity

   c. religion

   d. work

Why? What information in the selection leads you to give that answer? _____

_____

Supporting Details

_____ 3. What is the single most important factor in predicting someone's future happiness?

a. marriage

b. work

c. religious beliefs

d. past happiness

Why? What information in the selection leads you to give that answer? _____

_____

_____ 4. Of the following, which is the most important determinant of happiness?

a. subjective feelings

b. intelligence

c. money

d. objective realities

Why? What information in the selection leads you to give that answer? _____

_____

_____

Author's Purpose

_____ 5. What is the author's purpose in beginning this feature with the true/false quiz?

a. to make students realize they must read this section

b. to demonstrate that commonsense ideas about happiness are often incorrect

c. to show how unhappy most people around the world are

d. to help students understand they should have children if they want to be happy

Why? What information in the selection leads you to give that answer? _____

_____

_____ 6. What seems to be the general purpose of Figures 7.1 to 7.3?

a. to support the conclusions of the text with more specific details

b. to demonstrate times when the conclusions of the text do not hold true

c. to provide an overall framework for the more specific words in the text

d. to suggest the conditions under which the conclusions of the text are true

Why? What information in the selection leads you to give that answer? _____

_____

Relationships

____ 7. In the third conclusion about subjective well-being, the author notes that "when people's experiences improve, hedonic adaptation may *sometimes* put them on a *hedonic treadmill*—their neutral point moves upward, so that the improvements yield no real benefits (Kahneman, 1999)." What is the relationship of the next sentence, which begins with "However, when…" to this one?

    a. cause

    b. definition

    c. contrast

    d. exemplification

Why? What information in the selection leads you to give that answer? _____

_____

____ 8. In the next sentence, which begins "For example, people who…," what relationship is established between the two parts of the sentence with the word *because*?

    a. definitions-term

    b. effect-cause

    c. cause-effect

    d. definition-examples

Why? What information in the selection leads you to give that answer? _____

_____

Fact, Opinion, and Inference

____ 9. Which of the following statements is the author's opinion?

    a. The findings of these studies are quite interesting.

    b. Recent years have brought a surge of interest in the correlates of subjective well-being.

    c. One study found a correlation of just .13 between income and happiness in the United States (Diener et al., 1993).

    d. The key ingredients of happiness appear to involve love, work, and personality.

Why? What leads you to give that answer? _____

_____

____ 10. The author writes, "Some people seem destined to be happy and others unhappy, regardless of their triumphs or setbacks." What does the verb *destined* imply?

    a. that personality is not or cannot be shaped by the individual

    b. that happiness is temporary

c. that setbacks lead to unhappiness in general

d. that environment is more important than heredity

Why? What leads you to give that answer? _____

_____

▶ Critical Thinking Questions

Critical Thinking Level 1 ▷ **Remember**

If I am happy that I bought a new house, but later, find that I am not as happy as I expected to be, what are three possible explanations you can *recall* from the article? _____

_____

Critical Thinking Level 2 ▷ **Understand**

Fill in the outline to show you *understand* the relationship among the ideas in the reading selection.

About = Topic: _____

Point = Main Idea: _____

Proof = Supporting Details:

1. _____

_____

2. _____

_____

3. _____

_____

4. _____

_____

5. _____

_____

6. _____

_____

7. _____

_____

Critical Thinking Level 3 ▸ Apply

Apply the findings from the reading to your own life: If you knew that having more money wasn't going to make you any happier, but that job satisfaction would be an important factor, what job would you seek?

_____

Critical Thinking Level 4 ▸ Analyze

Choose two time periods in your life: one period in which you were generally happy and another in which you were generally unhappy. Use the moderately good predictors of happiness and the strong predictors of happiness to take notes on each period of your life. You might want to set up your notes in a table format as shown here. Do your individual results support the research results that love, work, and personality strongly predict happiness and that health, social activity, and religion moderately predict happiness? *Compare* your findings with the reading.

Moderate and Strong Predictors of Happiness

Predictors	Generally happy time	Generally unhappy time
Health		
Social activity		
Religion		
Love and marriage		
Work		
Personality		

Critical Thinking Level 5 ▸ Evaluate

Rate the usefulness of the information on happiness to you, personally, on a scale of 1 to 10, with 10 being "very useful." Write a paragraph on a separate sheet of paper to explain your rating.

Critical Thinking Level 6 ▸ Create

Based on the three conclusions about subjective well-being, *create* a list of at least three suggestions to give to a friend about how to be happy. Make sure that each suggestion is something that your friend can do, not something that another person would have to do, or a way the world would have to change.

1. _____
   _____
   _____

2. _____
   _____
   _____

3. _____
   _____
   _____

▶ Vocabulary in New Contexts

Review the vocabulary words in the margins of the reading selection and then complete the following activities.

EASY Note Cards

Make a note card for each of the vocabulary words that you did not know from the reading. On one side, write the word. On the other side, divide the card into quarters and label them E, A, S, and Y. Add a word or phrase in each area so that you wind up with an example sentence, an antonym, a synonym, and, finally, a definition that shows you have figured out the meaning of the word with your logic. Remember that an antonym or synonym may have appeared in the reading.

Relationships Between Words

Circle *yes* or *no* to answer the question. Then explain your answer.

1. Would having a **rosy picture** of the world affect someone's **subjective well-being**?

   Yes   No

   Why or why not? _____

   _____

2. Would the **mortality** rate **ascend** during an armed conflict?

   Yes   No

   Why or why not? _____

3. Would a **materialistic** person likely be concerned with **conjectures** about next year's hottest fashion?

   Yes   No

   Why or why not? _____

Language in Your Life

Write short answers to each question. Look at the vocabulary words closely before you answer.

1. Name something that people **ascend**. _____

   _____

2. Name a specific person or type of person who is **materialistic**. _____

   _____

3. Make a **conjecture** about your life. _____

   _____

4. Name some common causes of **mortality**. _____

   _____

5. Name some things that affect your **subjective** well-being. _____

   _____

Language in Use

Select the best word to complete the meaning of each sentence.

ascend	conjectured	materialistic	mortality
rosy picture	subjective well-being		

1. A study by the American Pet Products Association tells us that in 2011–2012 there were approximately 78.2 million owned dogs in the U.S. Though there was no hard data, it is _____ that approximately 10% of our pets die each year.

2. The _____ rate of large dogs is greater than that of small dogs. On average only 13% of large breed dogs live beyond 10 years, whereas almost 40% of small dogs live longer than 10 years.

3. Despite the fact that our animals die before we do, many people swear that owning a dog improves their _____. In fact, single people who are dog lovers often will not even date someone who does not share their view.

4. It can be easy to see why people who own dogs love them so much. Most dogs have endearing personalities and see the world as one big _____.

5. In addition to giving love, most pet owners become downright _____ when it comes to their dogs; the average dog owner will spend about $2000 on Fido or Fifi this year! Collectively, this comes to about $50 billion per year.

Reading 7–2 | Management Textbook

▶ Pre-Reading the Selection

The next reading comes from a college business management textbook, *Management*. The chapter it comes from is titled "Managing Individuals and a Diverse Work Force."

Surveying the Reading

Survey the article that follows. Then check the elements that are included in this reading.

_____	Title	_____	Words in bold or italic type
_____	Headings	_____	Images and captions
_____	First sentences of paragraphs		

Guessing the Purpose

Judging from the title of the chapter, the title of the selection, and the publication context in a textbook on business management, what do you suppose is the main purpose of this selection?

_____

Predicting the Content

Predict two things this selection will probably discuss.

▶ _____

▶ _____

Activating Your Knowledge

Read the first paragraph and answer the questions about a boss you have or used to have. If you've never had a boss, answer the questions about a teacher you've had.

_____

_____

_____

🎬 **Scan to Connect!** Use your smart phone to scan this code to watch a video to activate your knowledge about basic types of personalities. (See the inside front cover for more information on how to use this.) Long before social scientists discovered the "big five" dimensions of personality that you will read about in Reading 7–2, people were sometimes classified according to whether they were "sanguine," "choleric," "melancholic," or "phlegmatic." In the video you will see an instance of each. See if you can match up the four types in the video with any of the five dimensions from the reading.

▶Reading with Pen in Hand

Students who annotate as they read are more successful than those who do not. That's why you will annotate each selection in *Connect* as you read. In the reading that follows, use the following symbols:

★ or (Point)   to indicate a main idea

① ② ③   to indicate major details

 Visit www.cengagebrain.com to access the CourseMate for this chapter to hear pronunciations of vocabulary words from this reading.

Big Five Dimensions of Personality

Chuck Williams

▶Why does the author start with this paragraph?

1   Stop for a second and think about your boss (or the boss you had in your last job). What words would you use to describe him or her? Is your boss introverted or extraverted? Emotionally stable or unstable? Agreeable or disagreeable? Organized or disorganized? Open or closed to new experiences? When you describe your boss or others in this way, what you're really doing is describing dispositions and personality.

▶Why are the Big Five called that?

2   A **disposition** is the tendency to respond to situations and events in a predetermined manner. **Personality** is the relatively stable set of behaviors, attitudes, and emotions displayed over time that makes people different from each other. For example, which of your aunts or uncles is a little offbeat, a little out of the ordinary? What was that aunt or uncle like when you were small? What is she or he like now? Chances are she or he is pretty much the same wacky person. In other words, the person's core personality hasn't changed. For years, personality researchers studied thousands of different ways to describe people's personalities. In the last decade, however, personality research conducted in different cultures, different settings, and different languages has shown five basic dimensions of personality account for most

marekuliasz/Shutterstock.com

of the differences in people's behaviors, attitudes, and emotions (or for why your boss is the way he or she is!). The Big Five Personality Dimensions are extraversion, emotional stability, agreeableness, conscientiousness, and openness to experience.

3   **Extraversion** is the degree to which someone is active, assertive, **gregarious**, sociable, talkative, and energized by others. In contrast to extraverts, introverts are less active, prefer to be alone, and are shy, quiet, and reserved. For the best results in the workplace, introverts and extroverts should be correctly matched to their jobs. For example, the Peabody Hotel in Memphis, Tennessee, solved one of its problems by having job applicants complete an introversion/extraversion personality measure. Ken Hamko, a manager at the hotel, explained how this worked: "We had hostesses who wouldn't stay by the door or greet guests or smile. When we gave them the personality profile, we found they didn't like being in front of people. So we moved them into other positions and replaced them with extraverts."

gregarious Notice that a list of traits is given, and then their antonyms, in the same order. There are three antonyms for *gregarious*. What does *gregarious* mean?

▶ To what kinds of jobs are extraverts well suited?

4   **Emotional stability** is the degree to which someone is not angry, depressed, **anxious**, emotional, insecure, or excitable. People who are emotionally stable respond well to stress. In other words, they can maintain a calm, problem-solving attitude in even the toughest situations (e.g., conflict, hostility, dangerous conditions, or extreme time pressure). By contrast, under only moderately stressful situations, emotionally unstable people find it difficult to handle the most basic demands of their jobs and become distraught, tearful, self-doubting, and anxious. Emotional stability is particularly important for high-stress jobs, such as police work, fire fighting, emergency medical treatment, or piloting planes. John S. Blonsick, a captain with Delta Air Lines, said:

anxious Use an antonym clue to decide what *anxious* means.

▶ In what general conditions is it important to have emotional stability?

5   *From the first day of flight training, pilot aspirants are tested for their ability to separate their emotions from their operational environment. The process allows a pilot to erect psychological barriers to avoid distractions in an environment in which the decision-making process is conducted at slightly under the speed of sound.... Abnormal and emergency situations are handled in a cool and professional manner. Voice-recorder transcripts of accidents invariably read like training manuals, despite the life-threatening situations they depict. Crew members are focused and actively working to correct the situation as they have been trained to do right up to the very last moment before impact.*

▶ Does the information here suggest that emotional stability can be learned?

6   **Agreeableness** is the degree to which someone is cooperative, polite, flexible, forgiving, good-natured, tolerant, and trusting. Basically, agreeable people are easy to work with and be around, whereas disagreeable people are distrusting and difficult to work with and be around. A number of companies have made general attitude or agreeableness the most important factor in their hiring decisions. Small business owner Roger Cook says, "Hire nice people. I'm looking for personal—not professional—traits. I want a good or nice person. I can teach the skills. I call their references and ask, 'Is he or she a nice person?' I take a close look at how applicants answer questions and carry themselves. Why nice people? Because they're trustworthy; they get along with other crew members: they are good with customers and they are usually hard workers."

▶ Why would a manager want to hire an agreeable person?

persevering Use a dictionary to define this word.

▶ Define a conscientious person.

7   **Conscientiousness** is the degree to which someone is organized, hardworking, responsible, **persevering**, thorough, and achievement oriented. One management consultant wrote about his experiences with a conscientious employee:

8   *He arrived at our first meeting with a typed copy of his daily schedule, a sheet bearing his home and office phone numbers, addresses, and his email address. At his request, we established a timetable for meetings for the next four months. He showed up on time every time, day planner in hand, and carefully listed tasks and due dates. He questioned me exhaustively if he didn't understand an assignment and returned on schedule with the completed work or with a clear explanation as to why it wasn't done.*

▶ Is openness to experience an important trait for a job that requires a person to follow rules all day long?

ambiguity Use a dictionary to define this word.

9   **Openness to experience** is the degree to which someone is curious, broad-minded, and open to new ideas, things, and experiences; is spontaneous, and has a high tolerance for **ambiguity**. Most companies need people who are strong in terms of openness to experience to fill certain positions, but for other positions, this dimension is less important. People in marketing, advertising, research, or other creative jobs need to be curious, open to new ideas, and spontaneous. By contrast, openness to experience is not particularly important to accountants, who need to consistently apply **stringent** rules and formulas to make sense out of complex financial information.

stringent Use a dictionary to define this word.

▶ In terms of job performance, which of the Big Five is most important?

10   Which of the Big Five Personality Dimensions has the largest impact on behavior in organizations? The cumulative results indicate that conscientiousness is related to job performance across five different occupational groups (professional, police, managers, sales, and skilled or semiskilled jobs). In short, people "who are dependable, persistent, goal directed, and organized tend to be higher performers on virtually any job; viewed negatively, those who are careless, irresponsible, low-achievement striving, and impulsive tend to be lower performers on virtually any job." The results also indicate that extraversion is related to performance in jobs, such as sales and management, which involve significant interaction with others. In people-intensive jobs like these, it helps to be sociable, assertive, and talkative and to have energy and be able to energize others. Finally, people who are extraverted and open to experience seem to do much better in training. Being curious and open to new experiences, as well as sociable, assertive, talkative, and full of energy, helps people perform better in learning situations.

—From Williams, *Management*, 4e

▶ **Comprehension Questions**

Write the letter of the answer on the line. Then explain your thinking.

Main Idea

_____   1. Which of the following is the main idea of the entire reading selection?

 a. Stop for a second and think about your boss (or the boss you had in your last job).

 b. The Big Five Personality Dimensions are extraversion, emotional stability, agreeableness, conscientiousness, and openness to experience.

c. A disposition is the tendency to respond to situations and events in a predetermined manner.

d. In other words, the person's core personality hasn't changed.

Why? What information in the selection leads you to give that answer? _____

_____

____ 2. What is the implied main idea of the last paragraph?

    a. Conscientiousness has the largest impact on behavior in organizations, and extraversion also plays a large role in certain situations.

    b. Which of the Big Five Personality Dimensions has the largest impact on behavior in organizations?

    c. The results also indicate that extraversion is related to performance in jobs, such as sales and management, which involve significant interaction with others.

    d. Finally, people who are extraverted and open to experience seem to do much better in training.

Why? What information in the selection leads you to give that answer? _____

_____

_____

Supporting Details

____ 3. The paragraphs on extraversion, emotional stability, agreeableness, and conscientiousness all have the same kind of supporting details. What kind?

    a. statistics

    b. process writing

    c. classification

    d. examples

Why? What information in the selection leads you to give that answer? _____

_____

_____

____ 4. What are some situations in which emotional stability is especially important?

    a. police work, fire fighting, and emergency medical treatment

    b. filing, interviewing prospective employees, and warehouse work

    c. acting, dancing, and singing

    d. selling insurance, owning a small business, and managing others

Why? What information in the selection leads you to give that answer? _____

_____

Author's Purpose

_____ 5. What is the author's general purpose?

    a. to highlight the importance of hiring mostly extraverts in sales positions

    b. to ensure that future managers don't hire emotionally unstable people

    c. to emphasize that creative positions require people who are open to new experiences

    d. to share information with students that they can use in hiring decisions later, when they are managers

Why? What information in the selection leads you to give that answer? _____

_____

_____

_____ 6. Why does the author ask readers to think about their bosses in the first paragraph?

    a. to encourage employee dissatisfaction

    b. to help readers understand their bosses

    c. to help readers connect the information to their own experience

    d. to persuade readers that, if they like their bosses, they are likely to be promoted

Why? What information in the selection leads you to give that answer? _____

_____

Relationships

_____ 7. What relationship does the word _whereas_ establish in this sentence:

> Basically, agreeable people are easy to work with and be around, whereas disagreeable people are distrusting and difficult to work with and be around.

    a. effect

    b. definition

    c. comparison

    d. contrast

Why? What information in the selection leads you to give that answer? _____

_____

_____ 8. Two paragraphs in this reading are in _italic_ type. What relationship to the paragraph that precedes each one does the italic type represent?

    a. example

    b. cause

c. process writing

d. classification

Why? What information in the selection leads you to give that answer? _____

_____

Fact, Opinion, and Inference

____   9. Which of the following statements is a fact?

a. Ken Hamko said the hostesses who wouldn't greet customers were extraverts.

b. In stressful job situations, openness to experience is the most important quality.

c. Small business owner Roger Cook likes to hire nice people.

d. Accountants should be curious and spontaneous.

Why? What information in the selection leads you to give that answer? _____

_____

____   10. Which of the following statements is a good summary of the selection?

a. A person's disposition doesn't matter as much as their personality.

b. When hiring employees, try to find conscientious people. Also, match the needs of the position with the personality traits of the potential employee.

c. Bosses should be extraverted, stable, agreeable, conscientious, and open to experience.

d. When a worker is conscientious, he or she will also be extraverted and open to experience.

Why? What information in the selection leads you to give that answer? _____

_____

▶ Critical Thinking Questions

Critical Thinking Level 1 ▸ Remember

Recall a person you have enjoyed working or studying with. Which of the Big Five personality traits did he or she have?

_____

_____

_____

Critical Thinking Level 2 ▷ **Understand**

Fill in the outline to show you *understand* the relationship among the ideas in the reading selection.

About = Topic: _____

   Point = Main Idea: _____

      Proof = Supporting Detail:

        1. _____

           _____

        2. _____

           _____

        3. _____

           _____

        4. _____

           _____

        5. _____

           _____

        6. _____

           _____

Critical Thinking Level 3 ▷ **Apply**

Based on this passage, what traits should you *cultivate* to do well in college? _____

_____

Critical Thinking Level 4 ▷ **Analyze**

Determine which two of the Big Five personality traits would be very important for a door-to-door salesperson to have. Give your reasons for saying so.

▷ _____

▷ _____

Critical Thinking Level 5 ▶ Evaluate

Rate yourself from 1 to 10 on each of the following characteristics.

Where Are You on the "Big Five"?

Extravert									Introvert
10	9	8	7	6	5	4	3	2	1
Emotionally stable									Unstable
10	9	8	7	6	5	4	3	2	1
Agreeable									Disagreeable
10	9	8	7	6	5	4	3	2	1
Conscientious									Not conscientious
10	9	8	7	6	5	4	3	2	1
Open to experience									Not open to experience
10	9	8	7	6	5	4	3	2	1

Based on your responses, write down three jobs you might be (or are) good at, and explain why. If you can't think of particular jobs, then discuss the types of jobs you might be good at.

▶ _____

▶ _____

▶ _____

Critical Thinking Level 6 ▶ Create

Create a job description for a position that would be a good fit for a person who is introverted, conscientious, and open to experience. _____

_____

_____

_____

_____

▶ Vocabulary in New Contexts

Review the vocabulary words in the margins of the reading selection and then complete the following activities.

EASY Note Cards

Make a note card for each of the vocabulary words that you do not know from the reading. On one side, write the word. On the other side, divide the card into quarters and label them E, A, S, and Y. Add a word or phrase in each area so that you wind up with an example sentence, an antonym, a synonym, and, finally, a definition that shows you have figured out the meaning of the word with your logic. Remember that an antonym or synonym may have appeared in the reading.

Relationships Between Words

Circle *yes* or *no* to answer the question. Then explain your answer.

1. Might a person who is **gregarious** still feel **ambiguous** about public speaking?

   Yes   No

   Why or why not? _____

2. Does it take **perseverance** to follow a **stringent** diet?

   Yes   No

   Why or why not? _____

   _____

3. Could a **stringent** work schedule produce **anxiety**?

   Yes   No

   Why or why not? _____

Language in Your Life

Write short answers to each question. Look at the vocabulary words closely before you answer.

1. Name something that makes you **anxious**. _____

   _____

2. Name a specific person you know who is **gregarious**. _____

   _____

3. Name the most **stringent** rule you have ever heard of. _____

   _____

4. Name an achievement that requires **perseverance**. _____

   _____

5. Name a person you feel some **ambiguity** about. _____

   _____

Language in Use

Select the best word to complete the meaning of each sentence.

ambiguity	anxious	gregarious	perseverance	stringent

1. The famous motto printed on the New York James A. Farley Post Office building is all about _____ : "Neither snow nor rain not heat nor gloom of night stays these couriers from the swift completion of their appointed rounds."

2. And it certainly would take a _____ process or set of rules to ensure that this motto was indeed carried out.

3. However, post office officials are _____ to point out that this is not actually the motto of the post office; it was simply used as an inscription by the architect who built the building.

4. This quotation is actually a paraphrase from Herodotus, who lived approximately 484–425 B.C. He has been called "The Father of History" and while some find _____ in his historical writings, there is no doubt the quotation was used by him to describe a system of mounted postal carriers operated by the Persians.

5. So the next time a _____ mail carrier quotes this phrase to you, you can impress him or her with your knowledge of the history concerning this famous inscription.

 Click to Connect! For more practice applying the skills you learned in this chapter, visit **www.cengagebrain.com** to access the CourseMate for this chapter.

PART 3
Reading Critically

8

Distinguishing
Fact and Opinion

> " *The fact that an opinion
> has been widely held is
> no evidence whatever that
> it is not utterly absurd.* "
>
> —BERTRAND RUSSELL

Connect with Ideas

What does the quotation from Bertrand Russell mean? Restate it using your own words. Discuss the quotation and your opinion of it with your classmates.

Activate Your Knowledge

What are some strategies you use to tell the difference between fact and opinion?

Engage with the Chapter

Think about what you "know" about pirate life. Then survey Reading 8–1 on page 429 and Reading 8–2 on page 439. Was your knowledge correct? Did you know the facts?

Read and Talk

Online
Newspaper
Article

When you hear the words "notorious cyber-criminal," what comes to mind? The following article tells a little bit about a cyber-criminal. See if her story matches what came to your mind.

Visit www.cengagebrain.com to access the CourseMate for this chapter to hear vocabulary words from this reading and an audio recording of it.

Jammie Thomas-Rasset: The Download Martyr
RIAA fines Brainerd woman $220,000 for 24 songs.

Nick Pinto

1   At the very end of a snowbound dead-end road outside Brainerd, in a small beige single-story house out in the woods, lives one of the world's most **notorious** cyber-criminals.

notorious Use your logic to infer the meaning of this word.

2   Sitting in her den with her family and dog on a recent weekend, Jammie Thomas-Rasset doesn't seem quite so threatening. Short and sturdily built, she wears her long dark hair parted down the middle.

3   She's got an ordinary job, as a brownfields coordinator for the Mille-Lacs band of Ojibwe in Brainerd. She spends most of her time figuring out how to get petroleum **seepage** out of former gas station properties. Weekends she spends shuttling her kids back and forth to their father, who lives in Superior.

seepage Where is petroleum stored in gas stations? Use your logic and word parts as well to define *seepage*.

4   There's not a lot of time in her life to be either the hero or the villain that so many people want her to be.

5   Ever since she was sued by the Recording Industry Association of America five years ago, Thomas-Rasset has become a central figure in the revolutions **convulsing** the music business. She's been featured in documentaries about remix culture and gets recognized in the supermarket from her appearances on the evening news.

convulsing The context is a revolution. What do revolutions cause? *Convulsing* is a verb. How would you state its meaning?

6   Almost everyone who received a threatening letter from the RIAA in those days settled with the record labels instead of going to court. Not Thomas-Rasset—she was the first person to fight.

7   The result has been a seemingly endless legal battle, with three separate trials and the promise of more to come.

8   But as she's lost case after case, Thomas-Rasset has become something of a **martyr** to the digital revolution, a symbol of the lengths to which a powerful industry will go to protect an outdated business model.

martyr The rest of paragraph 8 gives you a clue to this word.

9   What Thomas-Rasset has going for her is a quality the record industry never expected: a complete refusal to surrender.

10   "In a lot of ways, this case is a vestige from another era," says Rebecca Jeschke of the Electronic Frontier Foundation, which tracks digital copyright issues. "The industry has recognized this was a bad idea, but her case is still working its way through the system."

11   In 2005, the recording industry was in a full-fledged panic. Global sales were down for the fifth year in a row and showed no sign of hitting bottom any time soon.

12   The reason seemed pretty clear: Six years after suing the file-sharing service Napster into submission, the industry's business model was still being shaken to its foundations. In Napster's place, new networks for sharing mp3s sprung up like the heads of a hydra: Bearshare, Morpheus, Grokster, KaZaA, Gnutella, and dozens of other networks with equally silly names provided the young and tech-savvy with all the free music they could download.

13   It was as if the labels' most **lucrative** demographic of customers had suddenly turned against them.

lucrative Paragraphs 11 and 12 set up the situation. Use your logic to infer the meaning of *lucrative*.

14   So the labels decided to raise the stakes. They began suing music fans. By the beginning of 2005, the labels had filed 7,437 lawsuits against fans suspected of uploading copyrighted music.

15   Thomas-Rasset remembers the day the letter came. It was August 2005. Bringing the mail in from the porch before starting dinner, one envelope stood out at her. The letterhead looked imposing. It was from the law firm of Shook, Hardy and Bacon.

—From "Jammie Thomas-Rasset: The download martyr: RIAA fines Brainerd woman $220,000 for 24 songs," by Nick Pinto. Copyright © 2012 City Pages, LLC. Reprinted by permission.

Talking about Reading

Respond in writing to the questions that follow and then discuss your answers with your classmates.

1. What would you do if you were in Jammie's shoes? Would you pay or go to court? (Keep in mind the fine was $220,000.) Explain. _____

_____

_____

2. What are your music consumption habits? Do you buy, pay a monthly fee, download for free, or use some other method? _____

_____

3. Explain your personal view of downloading music for free. _____

_____

_____

4. Explain whether you admire Jammie or feel her stand is foolish. _____

_____

_____

5.  **Scan to Connect!** Use your smart phone to scan this code to watch a video. (See the inside front cover for more information on how to use this.) What is your reaction to the $1.5 million fine imposed by the jury? What is your reaction to the $54,000 fine countered by the judge? Imagine you were Jammie; how would these fines make you feel? Discuss your reactions to this video.

Fact and Opinion

The last paragraph of the Read and Talk selection is a good example of how writers mix fact and opinion all the time. The writer explains that the letter arrived in August and that it was from the law firm of Shook, Hardy and Bacon (facts), but also says the letterhead looked "imposing" (an opinion). It is often difficult to figure out whether a statement is based on an individual's opinion or on a widely accepted fact. For this reason, you should always read with a questioning mind. And it is not only in reading that this blurring of fact and opinion occurs. When you talk with others, watch television, and even when you get second opinions at the doctor's office, stay alert for opinions pretending to be facts.

Facts

Fact = **object**, as in **object**ive. *Objective* means not influenced by personal judgments or feelings. Facts exist externally. They are physical, observable things (like any object in the physical world). They exist separately from you and are outside of you. They are independent of you. They can be verified—you can check to see if they are true. No matter what you do, believe, or feel, facts will still be facts. Facts are objective reality.

The films listed in **Table 8.1** on page 409 and the money they made are factual. Each item on the list can be proven true (or false). You can verify this information from many different sources, such as Worldwide Box Office online or the *World Almanac and Book of Facts* in the library. Or the list—or items on it—could be proven false. Say, for example, that the numbers for the movies in positions 4 and 5 were reversed. That error would not make the information an opinion; it would just make it wrong. Once corrected, the information would be factual. Also, this is a list that has been "adjusted for inflation." A list that is not adjusted for inflation would have different titles and orders listed (as of April 2012, *Avatar* is #1, *Titanic* is #2, and *Harry Potter and the Deathly Hallows Part 2* is #3). In addition, as this is being written (April 2012), *Titanic* is back in the theaters. So this information will have to be updated. But it can still be verified (proven to be accurate), or corrected. Information that is proven to be correct is fact. Information that is proven to be wrong is fiction, false, make believe, an assumption, or even a lie. A fact must be verifiable.

Rank	Title	Worldwide Gross (constant $)	Year
1	Gone with the Wind	$3,301,400,000	1939
2	Avatar	$2,782,300,000	2009
3	Star Wars	$2,710,800,000	1977
4	Titanic	$2,413,800,000	1997
5	The Sound of Music	$2,269,800,000	1965
6	E.T. the Extra-Terrestrial	$2,216,800,000	1982
7	The Ten Commandments	$2,098,600,000	1956
8	Doctor Zhivago	$1,988,600,000	1965
9	Jaws	$1,945,100,000	1975
10	Snow White and the Seven Dwarfs	$1,746,100,000	1937

Table 8.1 Highest Grossing Films Adjusted for Inflation, as of April 2012

Interaction 8–1 ▶ Identify Information That Can Be Verified

Put a check mark beside each sentence that contains information that could be verified by research, such as by consulting encyclopedias, other reference works, or Web sites.

_____ 1. According to rankings compiled by Billboard, the most popular song of 2011 was "Rolling in the Deep" by Adele.

_____ 2. Adele's song lyrics are depressing and her voice is whiny.

_____ 3. The U.S. market for brain fitness software, or neurosoftware, is worth more than $225 million.

_____ 4. The polar bear is considered an endangered species.

_____ 5. Hunting polar bears is an act of cruelty that should be banned.

Sentence Stems That Introduce Facts

The following sentence beginnings typically introduce facts that should be verifiable—that is, they can be shown to be true or false.

▶ *According* to a study by…
▶ The research *demonstrated*…
▶ The results of the test *showed*…
▶ Scientists *confirmed*…
▶ The poll *discovered*…

Even when you see these kinds of sentence stems, be sure to think critically about what you are reading. Remember that the writer could be mistaken. If you're in a situation where big decisions are resting on the facts, always verify that they are, in fact, true.

Opinions

Opinion = **subject**, as in **subjec**tive. *Subjective* means based on or influenced by personal beliefs, feelings, or tastes. Opinions are internal. They exist inside you (or me, or someone else). They depend upon the person who holds the opinion. So where does "subject" come in? Think of your self as the "subject" of your life. Just like the subject of a sentence controls the action of a sentence, you control your opinions. Think of the ways you express your beliefs, feelings, preferences, or desires: those are all opinions. Without you, they do not exist. Opinions are subjective reality. There is a difference between reality and "your reality." Reality is fact. "Your reality" is opinion.

Read this excerpt from a review of the movie *Titanic*:

Movies this grand are hard to pull off. First you have the great financial risk, and then you have incredibly complex technical aspects, a captivating love story to develop, all the while paying attention to the historical details of the story. It was a big risk, but Cameron pulls it off beautifully. The script is seamlessly written. You find yourself being mesmerized by the story. And the cast? Well, the cast is extraordinary. Leonardo DiCaprio shines in his role, and Kate Winslet makes us all fall in love with her. Billy Zane is a villain you despise, but who has a valiant surprise up his sleeve in the end, which you can't help but admire.

What words in this part of the review tell you that the author is giving an *opinion* of the movie *Titanic*? Here are the first two opinion words in sentence one: *grand, hard*. Underline the opinion words in the rest of the paragraph.

Unlike facts, opinions can't be verified by looking in dictionaries, encyclopedias, or newspapers. Because opinions are personal, they may be held by only one person, several people, or many people. A person can give reasons for holding a certain opinion, and another person might still disagree.

Interaction 8–2 ▸ **Compare Facts and Opinions**

For each pair of sentences, decide which one is the opinion. Underline the opinion word or words, and write **O** on the line.

1. You should stop using jackhammers when you're working on the road. _____

   Repeated exposure to loud noise can lead to permanent hearing loss. _____

2. California is the best state to live in. _____

   California is the most populous state in the United States. _____

D.Coral/Shutterstock.com

3. The Subaru STI looks awesome in blue, has great horsepower, but is lacking in interior quality. _____

   The Subaru STI has a turbocharged 4-cylinder boxer engine that has 305 horsepower. _____

4. There are more than 1 billion Google searches each day. _____

   A lot of Internet users have a serious addiction to online games. _____

5. You will get sunburned! _____

   Ultraviolet rays of the sun can cause sunburn. _____

Sentence Stems That Introduce Opinions

The following words introduce opinions that may be held by one person or by a group of people.

- The defendant *claims*...
- The author *argues* that...
- My *point of view* is...
- Police *suspect*...
- Many *believe*...

A good habit to get into when you read a sentence that expresses an author's opinion is to pause and ask yourself whether the author has given you enough facts so you can decide whether you agree with the opinion. If there are enough facts, do you agree? If there aren't enough facts, what else would you need to know before you could decide?

Interaction 8–3 ▸ Create Fact and Opinion Sentences

For each topic, create one factual sentence and one opinion sentence. Then exchange sentences with a classmate and circle all the opinion words you find. Do you agree on which sentences state facts and opinions?

1. Children

   a. Fact: _____

   b. Opinion: _____

2. A balanced budget

   a. Fact: _____

   b. Opinion: _____

3. Cats

   a. Fact: _____

   b. Opinion: _____

4. Voting

   a. Fact: _____

   b. Opinion: _____

5. Music

   a. Fact: _____

   b. Opinion: _____

Words That Can Express Opinions

Fact and opinion are not always easy to distinguish. In this section you'll read about the kinds of words you should pay close attention to. When you encounter them in your reading, be very careful to think about whether you would be able to verify the information in other sources of information. If you can verify the information, you are reading facts. If you cannot, you are reading opinions. Also, be smart and consider the context of how a word is used. Connotative meaning would lead to an opinion, whereas denotative meaning would be factual. Ultimately, when you are evaluating fact and opinion, you need to remember two questions.

1. Can this be verified?

2. What is the context?

Adjectives

Many of the words that reveal to you that an opinion is being expressed are adjectives. Adjectives describe nouns. (You may recall that nouns are people, places, things, and ideas.) In the following sentence, the adjective refers to the writer's opinion.

The death penalty is immoral.

The word *immoral* is an adjective. It describes the noun phrase *death penalty*. Since you could not look in a reference book to find out whether the death penalty is, indeed, immoral, this is the opinion of the writer. One person might think the death penalty is immoral because no one should ever kill another, but a second person might believe it is moral because it prevents more serious crimes from occurring. Other people might think it's moral sometimes and immoral other times. Since an absolute answer is not definitive and many people may disagree, it's an opinion.

Here are some adjectives.

abnormal	classical	implicit	prime
abstract	compatible	incompatible	professional
academic	conservative	inherent	radical
accurate	considerable	irrational	random
adequate	consistent	isolated	rational
advocate	constant	liberal	relevant
afraid	contrary	modern	reluctant
aggressive	cooperative	mature	restricted
alternative	definite	maximum	short
ambiguous	different	minimum	stable
appropriate	dramatic	marginal	subjective
arbitrary	dynamic	modified	sufficient
attached	enhanced	normal	sustainable
attractive	enormous	objective	symbolic
bad	expert	passive	unique
beautiful	explicit	persistent	visible
big	finite	precise	voluntary
capable	immature	primary	widespread

Not all adjectives point to opinions, however. Sometimes they merely describe facts. For example, read this sentence.

> As the world population gets larger, there is increased demand for oil.

There are two adjectives here, *larger* and *increased*. But they both refer to facts that can be verified by checking an encyclopedia or other reference book. You could look in an almanac and find out when the population has grown larger, and by how much. You could also look in reference books to find out whether during those times, more oil was sold around the world. So these adjectives do not point to opinions.

When you see adjectives, think carefully about whether they point to facts or opinions.

Interaction 8–4 ▸ Identify Adjectives

A. Underline the adjectives in the following sentences. Remember that adjectives describe nouns. Then circle **F** or **O** based on whether the information can be verified. Be sure to support your reasoning.

1. Economic growth in China, India, and elsewhere has led to increased demand for food.

   F   O

   Explain if this can be verified or not: _____

   _____

2. That's a good thing because it means people are able to eat more.

   F   O

   Explain if this can be verified or not: _____

   _____

3. However, soaring food prices mean the poorest people can't even afford food.

   F   O

   Explain if this can be verified or not: _____

   _____

4. It's ridiculous that some people are becoming obese while others are starving.

   F   O

   Explain if this can be verified or not: _____

5. In Egypt, people are calling for the army to step in and distribute wheat in a fair manner.

   F   O

   Explain if this can be verified or not: _____

   _____

Interaction 8–5 Use Adjectives with an Image

▶ Select one of the photos shown here. On a separate sheet of paper, write two short paragraphs about it.

▶ Write one paragraph that uses adjectives that all point to opinions.

▶ Write a second paragraph in which some adjectives point to facts.

▶ Exchange your two paragraphs with a classmate without revealing which has factual adjectives and which has only opinion adjectives.

▶ Circle the adjectives in your partner's paragraphs that you think point to facts. Do you and your partner agree?

vilainecrevette/Shutterstock

Dustie/Shutterstock.com

One more thought about adjectives. Many times, as you read, you will get both fact and opinion together. Here is an example:

> I have a smart dog that does extraordinary tricks, like playing dead, rolling over, and catching Frisbees in mid-air.

Which words indicate opinions? _____

What happens if you read the sentence again without the adjectives? _____

Remember to carefully evaluate adjectives as you read to distinguish between facts and opinions.

Qualifiers

Some statements are qualified. That is, the writer describes how often something happens or how many members of a group are being discussed. *Qualifiers* may be used to express an opinion or a fact. Often, they are used to limit the extent of whatever the writer is describing.

- She *rarely* cries at the movies. (The sentence carefully qualifies how often she cries there.)
- *Some* police officers are corrupt. (The number isn't definite, but it's fewer than all the police officers.)
- You ate *all* the ice cream! I didn't get *any*! (Facts that were verified at the time.)

Here are some qualifiers that tell how often or how many.

a few	all	always	any	every	frequently	never
none	normally	often	rarely	some	sometimes	usually

Another group of qualifiers modify, or change, the meanings of the verbs following them:

| can | could | may | might | must | have to | shall | will | should | would |

These qualifiers indicate degrees of certainty, permission, and necessity. Notice how none of the following statements could really be called a "fact."

- I might do the laundry. (It's not too certain that I will.)
- I must do the laundry. (I really should, but I can wear my cleanest dirty shirt.)
- I will do the laundry. (I'm going to do it.)

These statements are all opinions. The last one is considered an opinion because the event has not yet occurred. Future events can't be considered facts—not yet.

▶ The war *will be* over by September.
▶ You *are going to be* sorry you said that!

Some qualifiers, such as *all, always, never, none, must,* and *have to,* are absolute. In conversation, people often use absolute qualifiers when they are exaggerating.

▶ He is *always* late. (Has he never been on time, even once?)
▶ She *never* cleans her room. (Has she ever cleaned her room, even one time?)
▶ You *must* do it my way! (Is there any other way to do it?)

Statements using absolute qualifiers are often not true. So if you see a statement with an absolute qualifier on a test, the statement is usually false (unless the facts of the passage prove it is true). The more extreme the qualifier (*all* or *none*), the more likely it is to be an opinion or simply incorrect.

Interaction 8–6 ▶ Think about Qualifiers

The qualifiers in the following sentences are in bold type. If the sentence is true, write **T** on the line. If it is false, write **F**. If a statement is false, rewrite it using a different qualifier to make it true.
Example:

__F__   I am **always** tired.

Often is a less extreme word and more likely to be true.
_____

_____   1. **Every** person in the world needs water to survive.

_____

_____   2. It is **always** warm in Hawaii.

_____

_____   3. Children are **always** brats.

_____

_____   4. Parents are **often** mean.

_____

_____   5. **All** turtles are green.

_____

_____   6. Laughter is **frequently** an effective medicine.

_____

_____ 7. Black pepper **often** makes a good ingredient for a smoothie.

_____

_____ 8. In golf, the person with the highest score **never** wins.

_____

_____ 9. In the United States, wedding rings are **usually** made from gold.

_____

_____ 10. In America, dessert is **normally** served at the end of a meal.

_____

Comparatives and Superlatives

Comparatives and superlatives are words you should think about carefully as you decide what is fact and what is opinion. A *comparative* is typically used to compare two items. Comparatives usually end with *-er* or have *more* before a word, as in *more powerful*. Some examples of comparatives are *better, greater, stronger, more helpful,* or *more beautifully*. A *superlative* compares one thing to all the other things of the same kind. Superlatives usually end with *-est* or have *most* before a word, as in *most intelligent*. Some examples of superlatives are *best, greatest, strongest, most clearly,* and *most often*. (As you may have noticed, comparatives and superlatives can be adjectives or adverbs.)

Now, as always, the question is whether we can find proof for a comparison so that we can consider it a fact. If a child says, *My dad is stronger than your dad*, we can verify whether this is a true statement simply by having a weight-lifting contest. But what about the next statement? *My dad is better than your dad*. How do we prove this? Can we? No. The statement is just too broad and general. So sometimes, superlatives and comparatives are opinions, and other times they are verifiable as fact (or just plain wrong). You always have to come back to the question: Can I verify this statement?

Interaction 8–7 ▶ Think about Comparisons

Write **F** for fact in the blank if the sentence can be proven (true or false). Write **O** for opinion if it cannot be proven. If you aren't sure, discuss the sentence with classmates to see if you can agree on an answer. Explain your answer.

_____ 1. Exxon/Mobil is the **largest** publicly traded oil and gas company in the world. Your

explanation: _____

_____ 2. Michael Jordan is a **better** basketball player than Kobe Bryant. Your explanation: ___

_____

_____ 3. George W. Bush was a **more influential** president than his father, George Bush Sr. Your explanation: _____

_____

_____ 4. The **Bhut Jolokia**, or "ghost" pepper, is the **hottest** pepper in the world. Your explanation:

_____

_____

blickwinkel/Alamy

_____ 5. The Inland Taipan or Fierce Snake is the world's **deadliest** snake. Your explanation:

_____

_____

_____

_____

_____

_____

_____ 6. *Go Fish* is the **best** card game to play with children. Your explanation: _____

_____

_____ 7. Mobile, Alabama, is the **rainiest** city in the contiguous forty-eight states. Your explanation:

_____

_____

_____ 8. Grandparenthood is **tougher** today than it used to be. Your explanation: _____

_____

_____

Sources of Information

Before you start this section, let's pause and have a little fun with how fact and opinion relate to sources of information. Here are two sentences about one of your book authors, Ivan Dole. Which one is true?

1. In 1998, Ivan went scuba diving off the coast of Destin, Florida, with a 20-foot whale shark and held on to its dorsal fin while it swam around feeding on plankton.

2. In 2002, Ivan became a certified yoga instructor even though he cannot do a headstand.

Which one is true? #1 is true, although, the picture is not of me. I grew up in Florida and am a certified Dive Master with PADI. I can prove it with a card from PADI that has my name on it. FYI, whale sharks don't eat people! And in regards to #2, I practice yoga weekly and can do a headstand (could demonstrate), but I am not a certified yoga instructor (costs $3,000—yikes!).

How did you determine which sentence was true? First, since you do not know me outside of the classroom, you would probably guess, but since you do not really know, ultimately you would have to ask me. I told you, and you have a choice: you can trust me or not. Your choice would be based on what you know about me and how credible you think I am. If you are not sure about me, you might ask for proof to verify my statement. Trust, credibility, and proof are key elements when it comes to sources.

Interaction 8–8 ▸ Fun with Fact and Opinion

Create two factual sentences—one that is true and one that is false. Do not reveal which factual sentence is true—make your classmates guess. Include your instructor in this Interaction.

1. _____

   _____

2. _____

   _____

Suppose someone says, "That's not what I heard. I heard that *she* left *him*!" While the speaker might have heard that "she left him," if you want to decide whether you believe the statement is true, you first have to determine if the speaker is trustworthy. Does this person usually speak honestly, often exaggerate, or have a reason to lie? Even if you trust the speaker, ultimately you would need to go to the people involved to determine what was true.

There are many sources for information. Generally they fall into two categories: trustworthy ("A balanced diet and sensible exercise program will help you lose weight.") and not trustworthy ("Lose weight and still eat whatever you want!"). But there are shades of trust in between. Also keep in mind that mistakes and errors are always possible. Regardless, it is the author's *ethos*, or credibility, that makes him or her believable. In order to decide whether you trust someone's facts or should consider his or her opinion carefully, you should think about how credible the source is likely to be.

To simplify sources, we will break them into three categories: experts, people with informed opinions, and people on the street.

Expert Opinion

An *expert* is someone who earns our trust because he or she has acquired extensive education and/or gained experience in a particular field of study. Or the expert may hold a position of authority or respect in the field. It is important to note that people are experts only in their own fields. Just because Chuck "The Iceman" Liddell is an Ultimate Fighting Championship (UFC) light heavyweight champion, holding the record for most knockouts, does not mean we should follow his advice about skydiving or writing an English paper.

Examples of Experts

▶ Tony Horton, developer of *P90X*, is an expert on exercise and fitness.
▶ Rafia Zakaria, member of the international executive board of Amnesty International, is an expert on human rights.

▶ Natalie Goldberg, novelist, poet, and writing instructor, is an expert on teaching fiction writing.
▶ Basil Davidson, a historian who has written extensively about Africa, is an expert on African history.
▶ Dale Earnhardt Jr., NASCAR racer, is an expert on stock car racing.

Experts get their information from other experts and from direct study or experience with the facts of their field of study. Experts usually build their opinions upon facts that they have studied intently. However, experts are not infallible: at times, they can be wrong. Also, sometimes experts build opposing opinions or interpretations from the same factual information.

Informed Opinion

People who are informed have researched or experienced something we have not and are sharing what they have learned. Included in this category are news journalists, TV news anchors, and other media people who gather and relay the news to the public. We expect them to know more than we do, but we don't necessarily accept their opinions.

Examples of Informed People

▶ a student who researches a local environmental issue online and at local meetings
▶ a person who shares firsthand travel tips for a place he or she has been recently
▶ a newspaper reporter who interviews people in order to write a story
▶ a person who is concerned about an issue and who has read several books and articles on the topic
▶ a journalist or news anchor who has discussed a topic with several experts

People who are informed get their information directly from experts, from the media, and/or from personal experience. Informed opinions are often based on fact mixed with emotional experience. Informed people are often credible, but they don't have the extensive knowledge of the expert. More of their knowledge comes from other people's descriptions and interpretations of events.

People on the Street

People on the street are just ordinary people whose expertise is unknown. If you have ever seen interviews with sports fans after a big game, you know that every person has an opinion, but you may or may not care what it is. Is the opinion based on the most important and relevant facts? It's often impossible to know.

Examples of People on the Street

▶ a celebrity sharing his or her personal views on a political position or candidate
▶ regular people who are interviewed about any recent event as they walk down the street

- people who write blogs to give their opinions on a wide variety of topics
- "reporters" for newspapers that publish stories about alien babies and virgin pregnancies

People on the street are not necessarily uninformed; it's just difficult to know whether they are informed or not—sometimes. The alien babies aren't real!

Interaction 8–9 ▸ Identify the Credibility of Sources

Write **E** for expert sources, **I** for informed sources, and **S** for people on the street.

_____ 1. Bruno Mars talking about the music industry

_____ 2. Bruno Mars on what to do in Honolulu, where he grew up

_____ 3. Bruno Mars on whom to vote for in the next presidential election

_____ 4. Suzanne Collins, who is Roman Catholic, talking about Lent

_____ 5. Suzanne Collins conducting a writing workshop

_____ 6. Suzanne Collins on how to train a puppy

_____ 7. Barack Obama on life in the White House

_____ 8. A college student's research paper on Obama's political career

_____ 9. Obama on the chances of the Chicago Bulls winning the championship

_____ 10. Tiger Woods on golf

_____ 11. Tiger Woods on golf course design

_____ 12. Tiger Woods on human-animal communication

Interaction 8–10 ▸ Distinguish Fact and Opinion

Analyze the use of fact and opinion in the following paragraphs. As you read, underline any words that you think express opinions. Then, in the space provided, note whether each sentence contains fact or opinion. Some sentences include both fact and opinion.

Zapping

The image has lost all intensity. It produces no surprise or intrigue; in the end, it is not especially mysterious or especially transparent. It is there for but a moment, filling up the time it takes to wait for the next image that follows. Likewise this subsequent image fails to surprise or intrigue; it too turns out to lack mystery or even much in the way of transparency. It stays there only a fraction of a second before being replaced by a third image, one that is again unsurprising and unintriguing, as indifferent as the previous two images. This third image lasts an infinitesimal fraction of a second, then dissolves as the screen turns bluish gray. You've intervened by using the remote control.

—Beatriz Sarlo

We will get you started on the first few:

The image has lost <u>all</u> intensity. <u> opinion </u>

It produces <u>no</u> surprise or intrigue; in the end, it is <u>not especially mysterious or especially</u> <u>transparent</u>. <u> opinion </u>

You finish the rest:

1. It is there for but a moment, filling up the time it takes to wait for the next image that follows.

   _____

2. Likewise this subsequent image fails to surprise or intrigue; it too turns out to lack mystery or even much in the way of transparency. _____

3. It stays there only a fraction of a second before being replaced by a third image, one that is again unsurprising and unintriguing, as indifferent as the previous two images. _____

4. This third image lasts an infinitesimal fraction of a second, then dissolves as the screen turns bluish gray. _____

5. You've intervened by using the remote control. _____

The Power of Marriage

Anybody who has several sexual partners in a year is committing spiritual suicide. He or she is ripping the veil from all that is private and delicate in oneself, and pulverizing it in an assembly line of selfish sensations.

But marriage is the opposite. Marriage joins two people in a sacred bond. It demands that they make an exclusive commitment to each other and thereby takes two discrete individuals and turns them into kin.

Few of us work as hard at the vocation of marriage as we should.

—David Brooks

Analysis

6. Anybody who has several sexual partners in a year is committing spiritual suicide. _____

7. He or she is ripping the veil from all that is private and delicate in oneself, and pulverizing it in an assembly line of selfish sensations. _____

8. But marriage is the opposite. _____

9. Marriage joins two people in a sacred bond. _____

10. It demands that they make an exclusive commitment to each other and thereby takes two discrete individuals and turns them into kin. _____

11. Few of us work as hard at the vocation of marriage as we should. _____

About the Word "Theory"

So what exactly constitutes the truth? Or proof of it? Most scientists carefully avoid the word "truth" when discussing science, preferring instead to use "accurate" in reference to data. In science, there is only evidence that supports a hypothesis.

For example, the hypothesis that the sun comes up every day has been supported by observable evidence for all of recorded history. Scientists no longer attempt to disprove that hypothesis, for the simple reason that after thousands of years of observation, no one has yet seen otherwise. The hypothesis is consistent with all of the data that has been collected, and it is now used to make different predictions. When a hypothesis meets these criteria, it has become a scientific theory.

—From Starr/Evers/Starr, *Biology Today and Tomorrow*, 2e

Analysis

We will skip the first two sentences, which are questions and can't be fact or opinion. They make no statement at all.

12. Most scientists carefully avoid the word "truth" when discussing science, preferring instead to use "accurate" in reference to data. _____

13. In science, there is only evidence that supports a hypothesis. _____

14. For example, the hypothesis that the sun comes up every day has been supported by observable evidence for all of recorded history. _____

15. Scientists no longer attempt to disprove that hypothesis, for the simple reason that after thousands of years of observation, no one has yet seen otherwise. _____

16. The hypothesis is consistent with all of the data that has been collected, and it is now used to make different predictions. _____

17. When a hypothesis meets these criteria, it has become a scientific theory. _____

Connect Your Skills

Distinguishing Fact and Opinion

A. Below are two reviews of *Pirates of the Caribbean: At World's End*. Read each review, giving careful attention to which parts are fact and which are opinion. As you read, underline any words (adjectives, qualifiers, comparatives, and superlatives) you think suggest an opinion. Then summarize the reviewer's evaluation.

1–15. Review #1 (There are 15 words to underline.)

I cannot put into words how disappointed I am with this movie. The series has sunk. The first one was incredible, the second was ridiculous and this third installment is ludicrous. *World's End* has no plot and is boring and flat. Even the characters, who were so fresh in the first one, are stale now. A dozen Jack Sparrows could not save this film. Keira Knightley looks horrible and acts horribly! The fight scenes are recycled. The only saving grace is Keith Richards' cameo as Jack's pirate daddy. Haven't we learned by now that trilogies never live up to the fans' expectations?

16. Summarize the author's opinion in your own words.

_____

_____

17–31. Review #2 (There are 15 words or phrases to underline.)

Why do critics always tear down the *Pirates of the Caribbean* franchise? Of course they are not perfect films, few are. But what is it audiences see that critics don't? Credit Johnny Depp for creating one of the most endearing characters ever to grace the screen as Jack Sparrow. Credit some wonderful chemistry from Orlando Bloom and Keira Knightley. And credit the magnificent score by Hans Zimmer, some eye-popping direction by Gore Verbinski, and a mass of talented character actors having a blast. And don't forget what may be the best visual effects in the series, from an angry Calypso to an imaginative and fierce battle at sea. With that, you get the final (for now) installment of one of the most popular franchises ever to invade the screen, critics be damned. *At World's End*, the best of the series, is an action-packed adventure that will please most of the fans.

32. Summarize the author's opinion in your own words.

_____

_____

33. If you have seen the movie *Pirates of the Caribbean: At World's End*, with which critic do you agree and why? _____

_____

_____

B. Pick a movie you have seen recently. On separate paper, write a review. It can be positive, negative, or a combination of both. Express your opinion and support it with facts about the movie. Use adjectives, qualifiers, comparatives, and superlatives in your paragraph. Exchange your paragraph with a classmate to see if they can circle your opinion words and restate your opinion of the movie you chose.

 Click to Connect! To check your comprehension of chapter concepts, visit **www.cengagebrain.com** to access the CourseMate for this chapter.

Chapter Summary Activity

This chapter has discussed some of the factors that you should consider as you try to distinguish facts and opinions as you read. Construct a Reading Guide to Fact and Opinion here by completing each idea on the left with information from the chapter on the right. You can use this guide as a reminder for how to distinguish fact from opinion.

Reading Guide to Fact and Opinion

Complete this idea with …	information from Chapter 8.
Three qualities of facts	1.
	2.
	3.
Three qualities of opinions	4.
	5.
	6.
Four types of words that can express opinion	7.
	8.
	9.
	10.
Two questions to always ask to determine fact versus opinion	11.
	12.

Three types of sources

13. _____

14. _____

15. _____

Think about what your strategies for distinguishing fact and opinion were before you read this chapter. How did they differ from the suggestions given here? What have you learned that will be useful in the future? Write down your thoughts.

_____

_____

_____

_____

Reading 8–1 | Online Newspaper Article

▶ Pre-Reading the Selection

The reading that follows, "Grim Life Cursed Real Pirates of Caribbean," may be an eye-opener about what pirate life was really like.

Surveying the Reading

Survey the article that follows. Then check the elements that are included in this reading.

_____	Title	_____	Words in bold or italic type
_____	Headings	_____	Images and captions
_____	First sentences of paragraphs		

Guessing the Purpose

Judging from the title of the reading, what do you suppose is the purpose for writing? _____

_____

Predicting the Content

Predict three things this selection will discuss.

▶ _____

▶ _____

▶ _____

Activating Your Knowledge

Make a list of three or four things that you know (or think you know) about the life of pirates.

▶ _____

▶ _____

▶ _____

📹 **Scan to Connect!** Use your smart phone to scan this code to watch a video to activate your knowledge about the lives of female pirates. (See the inside front cover for more information on how to use this.) Take notes on the factual details discussed in this video and then compare these to the information presented in the reading "Grim Life Cursed Real Pirates of Caribbean."

Common Knowledge

Robinson Crusoe (*paragraph 8*) A famous English novel about a man, Robinson Crusoe, who is shipwrecked on an island for many years before being rescued. He endures many adventures on the island, including rescuing a native from cannibals.

▶ Reading with Pen in Hand

Students who annotate as they read are more successful than those who do not. That's why you will annotate every selection in *Connect* as you read. In the reading that follows, use the following symbols:

★ or (Point)   to indicate a main idea

① ② ③   to indicate major details

 Visit **www.cengagebrain.com** to access the CourseMate for this chapter to hear pronunciations of vocabulary words from this reading.

Grim Life Cursed Real Pirates of Caribbean

Stefan Lovgren

▶ Describe what real pirate life was like.

1   Pirates have been figures of fascination and fear for centuries. The most famous buccaneers have been shrouded in legend and folklore for so long that it's almost impossible to distinguish between myth and reality. Hollywood movies—filled with buried treasures, eye patches, and the Jolly Roger—depict pirate life as a swashbuckling adventure. In Disney's *Pirates of the Caribbean: The Curse of the Black Pearl*, the pirate hero, played by Johnny Depp, is a lovable rogue. But what was life really like for an early 18th-century pirate? The answer: pretty **grim**. It was a world of staggering violence and poverty, constant danger, and almost inevitable death. The life of a pirate was never as glorious and exciting as depicted in the movies, said David Moore, curator of nautical archaeology at the North Carolina Maritime Museum in Beaufort. "Life at sea was hard and dangerous, and interspersed with life-threatening storms or battles. There was no air conditioning, ice for cocktails, or clean sheets aboard the typical pirate ship."

grim Look at the examples in the next sentence to guess the meaning of *grim*.

▶ When was the "Golden Age of Piracy"?

2   While the period from the late 1600s to the early 1700s is usually referred to as the "Golden Age of Piracy," the practice existed long before Blackbeard and other famous pirates struck terror in the hearts of merchant seamen along the

Sarah Nicholl/Shutterstock.com

Eastern Seaboard and Caribbean. And it exists today, primarily in the South China Sea and along the African coast.

Valuable Loot

3   One of the earliest and most high profile incidents of piracy occurred when a band of pirates captured Julius Caesar, the Roman emperor-to-be, in the Greek islands. Instead of throwing him overboard, as they did with most victims, the pirates held Caesar for ransom for 38 days. When the money finally arrived, Caesar was let go. When he returned to port, Caesar immediately fitted a squadron of ships and set sail in pursuit of the pirates. The criminals were quickly caught and brought back to the mainland, where they were hanged.

> What did Julius Caesar do to the pirates who captured him?

4   It's no coincidence that piracy came to **flourish** in the Caribbean and along America's Eastern Seaboard during piracy's heyday. Traffic was busy and merchant ships were easy pickings. Although pirates would search the ship's cabins for gold and silver, the main loot consisted of cargo such as grain, molasses, and kegs of rum. Sometimes pirates stole the ships as well as the cargo.

flourish Look at the rest of the paragraph for a logical clue to figure out what *flourish* means.

> Why did piracy flourish in the Caribbean and along America's Eastern Seaboard?

5   Neither Long John Silver nor Captain Hook actually existed, but the era produced many other infamous pirates, including William Kidd, Charles Vane, Sam Bellamy, and two female pirates, Anne Bonny and Mary Read. The worst and perhaps cruelest pirate of them all was Captain Edward Teach or Thatch, better known as "Blackbeard." Born in Britain before 1690, he first served on a British privateer based in Jamaica. Privateers were privately owned, armed ships hired by the British government to attack and plunder French and Spanish ships during the war.

> Who was Captain Edward Teach or Thatch?

6   After the war, Blackbeard simply continued the job. He soon became captain of one of the ships he had stolen, *Queen Anne's Revenge*, and set up base in North Carolina, then a British colony, from where he preyed on ships traveling the American coast. Tales of his cruelty are legendary. Women who didn't relinquish their diamond rings simply had their fingers hacked off. Blackbeard even shot one of his lieutenants so that "he wouldn't forget who he was." Still, the local townspeople tolerated Blackbeard because they liked to buy the goods he stole, which were cheaper than imported English goods. The colony's ruling officials turned a blind eye to Blackbeard's violent business. It wasn't until Alexander Spotswood, governor of neighboring Virginia, sent one of his navy commanders to kill Blackbeard that his reign finally came to an end in 1718.

> In what ways was Blackbeard cruel?

True or False

7   The most famous pirates may not have been the most successful. "The reason many of them became famous was because they were captured and tried before an Admiralty court," said Moore. "Many of these court proceedings were published, and these pirates' **exploits** became legendary. But it's the ones who did not get caught who were the most successful in my book."

> Who does Moore think are the best pirates?

exploits Ask yourself, "What became legendary?"

8   *Treasure Island*, by Robert Louis Stevenson, may be the most famous pirate story. But the most important real-life account of pirate life is probably a 1724

tome Look in the previous sentence for a synonym.

▶ Who do some people think Captain Charles Johnson was?

▶ What myths about pirate life do movies spread?

ubiquitous Look at the sentence where you find the word *ubiquitous* for a general context clue.

▶ Which characteristics of piracy that we "know" from movies are actually true?

marooned Think about where a person was *marooned*, and guess at the word's meaning.

stipulates Look for examples and punctuation context clues in the sentence where you find *stipulates*.

▶ How accurate is the character Jack Sparrow?

▶ What earned respect among pirates in the pirate world?

notorious Use two context clues in this sentence to help guide you to its meaning.

book called *A General History of the Robberies and Murders of the Most Notorious Pyrates*, by Captain Charles Johnson. The **tome** depicts in gruesome detail the lives and exploits of the most famous pirates of that time. Much of it reads as a first-hand account by someone who sailed with the pirates, and many experts believe Johnson was actually Daniel Defoe, the author of *Robinson Crusoe*, which was published in 1719. What is not in doubt is the book's commercial success at the time and the influence it had on generations of writers and filmmakers who adopted elements of his stories in creating the familiar pirate image.

9   So what part of the movie pirate is true and what is merely Hollywood fiction? What about, for example, the common practice of forcing victims to "walk the plank"? "Not true," said Cori Convertito, assistant curator of education at the Mel Fisher Maritime Museum in Key West, Florida. The pirates' favorite form of punishment was to tie their victims to the boat with a length of rope, toss them overboard, and drag them under the ship, a practice known as "keel hauling." Sadly, buried treasures—and the **ubiquitous** treasure maps—are also largely a myth. "Pirates took their loot to notorious pirate hang-outs in Port Royal and Tortuga," said Convertito. "Pirates didn't bury their money. They blew it as soon they could on women and booze."

Eye Patches, Peg Legs, and Parrots

10   On the other hand, pirate flags, commonly referred to as Jolly Rogers, were indeed present during the Golden Age. And victims were often **marooned** on small islands by pirates. Eye patches and peg legs were also undoubtedly worn by pirates, and some kept parrots as pets. Some pirates even wore earrings, not as a fashion statement, but because they believed they prevented sea sickness by applying pressure on the earlobes.

11   In the movie *Pirates of the Caribbean*, prisoners facing execution can invoke a special code, which **stipulates** that the pirate cannot kill him or her without first consulting the pirate captain. Indeed pirates did follow codes. These varied from ship to ship, often laying out how plundered loot should be divided or what punishment should be meted out for bad behavior. But Jack Sparrow, Johnny Depp's hero, probably wouldn't have lasted very long among real pirates. In the movie, he will do anything possible to avoid a fight, something real-life pirates rarely did.

12   The endless sword duels, a big part of all pirate movies, probably happened on occasion. But real-life encounters were often far more bloody and brutal, with men hacking at each other with axes and cutlasses. In one legendary account, a **notorious** pirate, trying to find out where a village had hidden its gold, tied two villagers to trees, facing each other, and then cut out one person's heart and fed it to the other. As Captain Johnson wrote in his book:

> *In the commonwealth of pirates, he who goes to the greatest length of wickedness is looked upon with a kind of envy amongst them, as a person of a more extraordinary gallantry, and is thereby entitled to be distinguished by some post, and if such a one has but courage, he must certainly be a great man.*

—"Grim Life Cursed Real Pirates of Caribbean" by Stefan Lovgren. *National Geographic*, July 11, 2003. Copyright © 2003 National Geographic. Reprinted by permission.

▶ Comprehension Questions

Write the letter of the answer on the line. Then explain your thinking.

Main Idea

_____ 1. Which sentence best summarizes the main idea for the section entitled "Eye Patches, Peg Legs, and Parrots"?

   a. Pirates were a bloody lot who enjoyed fighting more than eating, which is why Jack Sparrow would not have lasted very long.

   b. Several characteristics of movie pirates are true of real pirates.

   c. Pirates wore eye patches and peg legs.

   d. Although some pirate lore is true, most is fictitious.

Why? What information in the selection leads you to give that answer? _____

_____

_____

2. Which sentence is the topic sentence of paragraph 3?

   a. One of the earliest and most high profile incidents of piracy occurred when a band of pirates captured Julius Caesar, the Roman emperor-to-be, in the Greek islands.

   b. Instead of throwing him overboard, as they did with most victims, the pirates held Caesar for ransom for thirty-eight days.

   c. When he returned to port, Caesar immediately fitted a squadron of ships and set sail in pursuit of the pirates.

   d. The criminals were quickly caught and brought back to the mainland, where they were hanged.

Why? What information in the selection leads you to give that answer? _____

_____

_____

Supporting Details

_____ 3. Which of the following statements about pirates is not true?

   a. Pirates wore earrings because they believed it prevented seasickness.

   b. Pirates probably did have peg legs and eye patches.

   c. The battles of pirates were often bloody and brutal.

   d. The "Jolly Roger" was the common nickname of the ship that pirates sailed.

Why? What information in the selection leads you to give that answer? _____

_____

_____

_____ 4. Which of the following is least relevant to the main idea of this passage?

   a. It was a world of staggering violence and poverty, constant danger, and almost inevitable death.

   b. *Treasure Island*, by Robert Louis Stevenson, is probably the most famous pirate story.

   c. There was no air conditioning, ice for cocktails, or clean sheets aboard the typical pirate ship.

   d. The life of a pirate was never as glorious and exciting as depicted in the movies.

Why? What information in the selection leads you to give that answer? _____

_____

_____

Author's Purpose

_____ 5. What is the purpose of the section titled "Valuable Loot"?

   a. to focus the reader's attention on Julius Caesar's plight

   b. to entertain the reader with true stories from history about piracy

   c. to persuade readers that piracy was a lucrative business

   d. to inform the reader that obtaining valuables was one of the main reasons for piracy

Why? What information in the selection leads you to give that answer? _____

_____

_____

_____ 6. What is the overall purpose of this passage?

   a. to entertain the reader with true stories about the life of pirates

   b. to inform readers about the reality of pirate life based on true accounts of pirate life

   c. to persuade the reader that he or she should not watch movies about pirates because they are mostly untrue

   d. to emphasize the brutality of pirate battles

Why? What information in the selection leads you to give that answer? _____

_____

_____

Relationships

_____ 7. Identify the pattern of organization found in the following two sentences:

> The endless sword duels, a big part of all pirate movies, probably happened on occasion. But real-life encounters were often far more bloody and brutal, with men hacking at each other with axes and cutlasses.

    a. time order

    b. listing

    c. contrast

    d. cause-and-effect

Why? What leads you to give that answer? _____

_____

____ 8. What is the pattern of organization of paragraph 6?

    a. definition

    b. narration

    c. cause-and-effect

    d. example

Why? What information in the selection leads you to give that answer? _____

_____

Fact, Opinion, and Inference

____ 9. Which of the following statements is an opinion?

    a. Pirates believed earrings prevented seasickness by applying pressure on the earlobes.

    b. Traffic was busy and merchant ships were easy pickings.

    c. The worst and perhaps cruelest pirate of them all was Captain Edward Teach or Thatch, better known as "Blackbeard."

    d. The pirates' favorite form of punishment was to tie their victims to the boat with a length of rope, toss them overboard, and drag them under the ship, a practice known as "keel hauling."

Why? What leads you to give that answer? _____

_____

_____

____ 10. Which of the following can be inferred from information found in this passage?

    a. Alexander Spotswood was responsible for Blackbeard's death.

    b. Pirates living in the 1600s were crueler than those who lived in the 1700s.

    c. *Pirates of the Caribbean* is a movie filled with more pirate fact than myth.

    d. Julius Caesar became a dedicated pirate hunter after his abduction in Greece, practically eradicating piracy in his day.

Why? What information in the selection leads you to give that answer? _____

_____

▶ Critical Thinking Questions

Critical Thinking Level 1 ▷ Remember

Write as many details as you *remember* about the book *A General History of the Robberies and Murders of the Most Notorious Pyrates.*

_____

_____

_____

Critical Thinking Level 2 ▷ Understand

Fill in the following contrast visual (sometimes called a "T-Chart") for this reading selection.

Truth About Pirates	Myth About Pirates
_____	_____
_____	_____
_____	_____
_____	_____
_____	_____
_____	_____
_____	_____

Critical Thinking Level 3 ▷ Apply

Using your prior knowledge and logic, see if you can come up with some other popular movie characters that are stereotyped and different from reality. For example, you might think of a Western you may have seen, or another type of movie. Are the cowboys or Indians portrayed realistically? Brainstorm with one or more classmates and use the chart here to come up with a list of myths versus facts.

Myths Versus Reality

Myth	Reality
_____	_____
_____	_____
_____	_____

Critical Thinking Level 4 ▷ Analyze

Look back at the Read and Talk article at the beginning of this chapter regarding Jammie Thomas-Rasset. *Analyze* why computer file sharing has been called "piracy." Discuss your thoughts on this issue with your class or group.

Critical Thinking Level 5 ▷ Evaluate

In the *Activating Your Knowledge* question on page 429 you were asked to share what you knew (or what you thought you knew) about the life of pirates. Using the table here, *evaluate* whether your knowledge was correct and list what you learned from the reading passage.

Evaluating Your Knowledge

What you knew	Were you right?	Something new you learned
1.		
2.		
3.		
4.		

Critical Thinking Level 6 ▷ Create

In small groups, imagine you are pirates and *create* your own "code of honor." What are the rules by which you will abide? Once you have written your rules, compare them with the other groups' rules to see how they are similar and different.

▶ Vocabulary in New Contexts

Review the vocabulary words in the margins of the reading selection and then complete the following activities.

EASY Note Cards

Make a note card for each of the vocabulary words that you did not know in the reading. On one side, write the word. On the other side, divide the card into quarters and label them E, A, S, and Y. Add a word or phrase in each area so that you wind up with an example sentence, an antonym, a synonym, and, finally, a definition that shows you have figured out the meaning of the word with your logic. Remember that an antonym or synonym may have appeared in the reading.

Relationships Between Words

Circle *yes* or *no* to answer the question. Then explain your answer.

1. Is poverty **grim** even though it is **ubiquitous**?

   Yes   No

   Why or why not? _____

2. Might a student who is **notorious** wind up feeling emotionally **marooned**?

   Yes   No

   Why or why not? _____

3. Is it fair to say that the Constitution **stipulates** the right to **flourish**?

   Yes   No

   Why or why not? _____

Language in Your Life

Write short answers to each question. Look at the vocabulary words closely before you answer.

1. Name one **notorious** criminal. _____

   _____

2. Name something that can **flourish**, and under what conditions. _____

   _____

3. Name a situation that you find **grim**. _____

   _____

4. Name a common **stipulation** that your parent or guardian gave when you were growing up. _____

   _____

5. Name an item that is **ubiquitous** in your environment. _____

   _____

Language in Use

Select the best word to complete the meaning of each sentence.

flourish	grim	notorious	stipulates	ubiquitous

1. In today's media-driven world, there is no shortage of _____ celebrities.

2. You cannot go too many places where you will not find someone talking about the latest celebrity tragedy; they are _____.

3. In fact, it would almost seem that tragedies _____ in the environment of fame, fortune, excess, and no boundaries.

4. Inevitably, some stars reap what they sow and face _____ realities, like fines, jail time, loss of work, loss of status, or even loss of life.

5. Just remember that while we as mere mortals often wish we could live without consequences like many of the celebrities we see, there is a law that _____ that what goes up eventually must come down.

Reading 8–2 | Online Newspaper Article

▶ Pre-Reading the Selection

To listen to the news, modern pirates are vile, money-hungry, and bloodthirsty. The following reading offers an alternative set of details. Please read carefully as you get another side of the story.

Surveying the Reading

Survey the article that follows. Then check the elements that are included in this reading.

_____   Title   _____   Words in bold or italic type

_____   Headings   _____   Images and captions

_____   First sentences of paragraphs

Guessing the Purpose

Judging from the title of the article, what do you suppose the purpose for writing is? _____

Predicting the Content

Predict three things this selection will discuss.

▶ _____

▶ _____

▶ _____

Activating Your Knowledge

What do you know about modern-day pirates? Note two or three things you already know.

▶ _____

▶ _____

▶ _____

🎞 **Scan to Connect!** Use your smart phone to scan this code to watch a video to activate your knowledge about modern-day pirates. (See the inside front cover for more information on how to use this.) Why is the issue of piracy in Somalia complicated? Listen for what K'Naan says are the original reasons piracy started in Somalia. What happened after that?

Common Knowledge

Somalia (*paragraph 1*) An African country on the easternmost "horn" of Africa bordering Ethiopia. It borders the Gulf of Aden and the Red Sea, which is a popular international shipping route.

Cat o' nine tails (*paragraph 3*) A whip with nine strands of knotted cord or leather used to inflict punishment.

Alexander the Great (*paragraph 13*) Ruler of one of the largest empires of the ancient world, he lived from 356–323 BCE. He is considered to be one of the greatest military commanders in history.

▶ Reading with Pen in Hand

Students who annotate as they read are more successful than those who do not. That's why you will annotate every selection in *Connect* as you read. In the reading that follows, use the following symbols:

★ or (Point) to indicate a main idea

① ② ③ to indicate major details

 Visit www.cengagebrain.com to access the CourseMate for this chapter to hear pronunciations of vocabulary words from this reading.

You Are Being Lied to about Pirates

Johann Hari

▶ Where is the war on pirates?

1   Who imagined that in 2009, the world's governments would be declaring a new War on Pirates? As you read this, the British Royal Navy—backed by the ships of more than two dozen nations, from the US to China—is sailing into Somalian waters to take on men we still picture as parrot-on-the-shoulder pantomime villains. They will soon be fighting Somalian ships and even chasing the pirates onto land, into one of the most broken countries on earth. But behind the arrr-me-hearties oddness of this tale, there is an untold **scandal**. The people our governments are labelling as "one of the great menaces of our times" have an extraordinary story to tell—and some justice on their side.

scandal The author says the story he is going to tell will lead to a *scandal*. What might this word mean?

▶ What are some stereotypes of pirates?

lingers Notice the time periods mentioned. What might *lingers means*?

2   Pirates have never been quite who we think they are. In the "golden age of piracy"—from 1650 to 1730—the idea of the pirate as the senseless, savage Bluebeard that **lingers** today was created by the British government in a great propaganda heave. Many ordinary people believed it was false: pirates were often saved from the gallows by supportive crowds. Why? What did they see that we can't? In his book *Villains Of All Nations*, the historian Marcus Rediker pores through the evidence.

3   If you became a merchant or navy sailor then—**plucked** from the docks of London's East End, young and hungry—you ended up in a floating wooden Hell. You worked all hours on a cramped, half-starved ship, and if you slacked off, the all-powerful captain would whip you with the cat o' nine tails. If you slacked often, you could be thrown overboard. And at the end of months or years of this, you were often cheated of your wages.

> plucked The powerful British Navy was allowed to force men into serving on ships. What does *plucked* mean?
>
> ▶ Can you imagine what it would be like working under these conditions?

4   Pirates were the first people to rebel against this world. They mutinied—and created a different way of working on the seas. Once they had a ship, the pirates elected their captains, and made all their decisions collectively, without torture. They shared their bounty out in what Rediker calls "one of the most **egalitarian** plans for the disposition of resources to be found anywhere in the eighteenth century."

> ▶ How does the information from paragraphs 4 and 5 match with your prior concept of pirates?
>
> egalitarian Read the description of how pirates treated each other. What does *egalitarian* mean?

5   They even took in escaped African slaves and lived with them as equals. The pirates showed "quite clearly—and subversively—that ships did not have to be run in the brutal and oppressive ways of the merchant service and the Royal Navy." This is why they were romantic heroes, despite being unproductive thieves.

6   The words of one pirate from that lost age, a young British man called William Scott, should echo into this new age of piracy. Just before he was hanged in Charleston, South Carolina, he said: "What I did was to keep me from perishing. I was forced to go a-pirateing to live." In 1991, the government of Somalia collapsed. Its nine million people have been **teetering** on starvation ever since—and the ugliest forces in the Western world have seen this as a great opportunity to steal the country's food supply and dump our nuclear waste in their seas.

> ▶ How does William Scott's reason to become a pirate match that of modern-day Somalians?
>
> teetering Use your prior knowledge of the teeter-totter, often found on playgrounds, to determine what *teetering* means.

7   Yes: nuclear waste. As soon as the government was gone, mysterious European ships started appearing off the coast of Somalia, dumping vast barrels into the ocean. The coastal population began to sicken. At first they suffered strange rashes, nausea and **malformed** babies. Then, after the 2005 tsunami, hundreds of the dumped and leaking barrels washed up on shore. People began to suffer from radiation sickness, and more than 300 died.

> ▶ What is the effect of the dumping of nuclear waste in Somalian waters?
>
> malformed Use word parts to understand what *malformed* means.

8   Ahmedou Ould-Abdallah, the UN envoy to Somalia, tells me: "Somebody is dumping nuclear material here. There is also lead, and heavy metals such as cadmium and mercury—you name it." Much of it can be traced back to European hospitals and factories, who seem to be passing it on to the Italian mafia to "dispose" of cheaply. When I asked Mr. Ould-Abdallah what European governments were doing about it, he said with a sigh: "Nothing. There has been no clean-up, no **compensation**, and no prevention."

> ▶ Where is the nuclear waste coming from?
>
> compensation Along with clean-up and prevention, what could European countries be offering to offset the waste they are dumping into the sea near Somalia?

9   At the same time, other European ships have been looting Somalia's seas of their greatest resource: seafood. We have destroyed our own fish stocks by overexploitation—and now we have moved on to theirs. More than $300m-worth of tuna, shrimp, and lobster are being stolen every year by illegal **trawlers**. The local fishermen are now starving. Mohammed Hussein, a fisherman in the town

> ▶ What are two effects from the theft of seafood in Somalian waters?
>
> trawlers A synonym is used in this paragraph, and you can use your logic, too. What are *trawlers*?

ALI MUSA/AFP/GETTY IMAGES/Newscom

▶ What percentage of Somalians support piracy?

dissuade Use the example given. Also use the prefix to help you. What does *dissuade* mean?

10   of Marka 100 km south of Mogadishu, told Reuters: "If nothing is done, there soon won't be much fish left in our coastal waters."

This is the context in which the "pirates" have emerged. Somalian fishermen took speedboats to try to **dissuade** the dumpers and trawlers, or at least levy a "tax" on them. They call themselves the Volunteer Coastguard of Somalia—and ordinary Somalis agree. The independent Somalian news site WardheerNews found 70 per cent "strongly supported the piracy as a form of national defense."

▶ What justification does the pirate leader give for his actions?

11   No, this doesn't make hostage-taking justifiable, and yes, some are clearly just gangsters—especially those who have held up World Food Programme supplies. But in a telephone interview, one of the pirate leaders, Sugule Ali, said: "We don't consider ourselves sea bandits. We consider sea bandits [to be] those who illegally fish and dump in our seas." William Scott would understand.

▶ What is your personal response to the questions posed in this paragraph?

12   Did we expect starving Somalians to stand passively on their beaches, paddling in our toxic waste, and watch us snatch their fish to eat in restaurants in London and Paris and Rome? We won't act on those crimes—the only sane solution to this problem—but when some of the fishermen responded by disrupting the transit-corridor for 20 per cent of the world's oil supply, we swiftly send in the gunboats.

▶ Whom does the 4th century pirate represent and whom does Alexander the Great represent?

13   The story of the 2009 war on piracy was best summarized by another pirate, who lived and died in the fourth century BC. He was captured and brought to Alexander the Great, who demanded to know "what he meant by keeping possession of the sea." The pirate smiled, and responded: "What you mean by seizing the whole earth; but because I do it with a petty ship, I am called a robber, while you, who do it with a great fleet, are called emperor." Once again, our great imperial fleets sail—but who is the robber?

—"You Are Being Lied to about Pirates" by Johann Hari. Copyright © 2009 by independent.co.uk. Reprinted by permission. http://www.independent.co.uk/opinion/commentators/ johann-hari/johann-hari-you-are-being-lied-to-about-pirates-1225817.html#

▶ Comprehension Questions

Write the letter of the answer on the line. Then explain your thinking.

Main Idea

_____ 1. Which of these sentences from paragraph 1 is the best thesis for this article?

    a. Who imagined that in 2009, the world's governments would be declaring a new War on Pirates?

    b. As you read this, the British Royal Navy—backed by the ships of more than two dozen nations, from the US to China—is sailing into Somalian waters to take on men we still picture as parrot-on-the-shoulder pantomime villains.

    c. They will soon be fighting Somalian ships and even chasing the pirates onto land, into one of the most broken countries on earth.

    d. The people our governments are labeling as "one of the great menaces of our times" have an extraordinary story to tell—and some justice on their side.

Why? What information in the selection leads you to give that answer? _____

_____

_____ 2. What is the main idea of paragraph 13?

    a. The story of the 2009 war on piracy was best summarized by another pirate, who lived and died in the fourth century BC.

    b. He was captured and brought to Alexander the Great, who demanded to know "what he meant by keeping possession of the sea."

    c. The pirate smiled, and responded: "What you mean by seizing the whole earth; but because I do it with a petty ship, I am called a robber, while you, who do it with a great fleet, are called emperor."

    d. Once again, our great imperial fleets sail—but who is the robber?

Why? What information in the selection leads you to give that answer? _____

_____

Supporting Details

_____ 3. According to the passage, which is not a reason why some Somalians have become pirates?

    a. Some are gangsters.

    b. Some are protecting their waters from pollution.

    c. Some are fighting for their very survival.

    d. Some are working for the Italian mafia.

Why? What information in the selection leads you to give that answer? _____

_____

_____ 4. Which of the following details is least relevant to the topic?

    a. The people our governments are labeling as "one of the great menaces of our times" have an extraordinary story to tell—and some justice on their side.

    b. Pirates were the first people to rebel against this world.

    c. Somalian fishermen took speedboats to try to dissuade the dumpers and trawlers, or at least levy a "tax" on them.

    d. The independent Somalian news site WardheerNews found 70 per cent "strongly supported the piracy as a form of national defense."

Why? What information in the selection leads you to give that answer? _____

_____

_____

Author's Purpose

_____ 5. What is the overall purpose of this passage?

    a. to persuade readers that there may be information about the Somalian pirates that the mainstream media isn't telling us

    b. to entertain readers with tales of modern-day pirates and their adventures

    c. to inform readers of what they can do to prevent the plundering of Somalian waters

    d. to inform readers of what ancient pirates really were like

Why? What information in the selection leads you to give that answer? _____

_____

_____ 6. What is the purpose of paragraphs 3–7?

    a. to inform readers of who ancient pirates really were

    b. to give credibility to the author's claim that the Somalian pirates are not quite who we think they are

    c. to persuade readers that ancient pirates deserve their reputation

    d. to entertain readers with stories from the book *Villains of All Nations*

Why? What information in the selection leads you to give that answer? _____

_____

_____

Relationships

_____ 7. What is the overall pattern of organization of this passage?

    a. narration in time order

    b. definition

c. comparison and contrast

d. cause-and-effect

Why? What information in the selection leads you to give that answer? _____

_____

____ 8. What relationship is found in the following sentence? *"Because I do it with a petty ship, I am called a robber, while you, who do it with a great fleet, are called emperor."*

a. classification

b. contrast

c. cause-and-effect

d. narration in time order

Why? What leads you to give that answer? _____

_____

Fact, Opinion, and Inference

____ 9. Which of the following statements is an opinion?

a. The story of the 2009 war on piracy was best summarized by another pirate, who lived and died in the fourth century BC.

b. More than $300m-worth of tuna, shrimp, and lobster are being stolen every year by illegal trawlers.

c. As soon as the government was gone, European ships started appearing off the coast of Somalia, dumping barrels into the ocean.

d. Pirates took in escaped African slaves and lived with them as equals.

Why? What information in the selection leads you to give that answer? _____

_____

____ 10. Which of the following statements would the author agree with?

a. Due to their support of piracy, at least 70% of Somalians are morally bankrupt.

b. Every act of piracy committed by Somalians is justifiable.

c. The priorities of some Western governments are misaligned.

d. The author wishes he could be a Somalian pirate.

Why? What information in the selection leads you to give that answer? _____

_____

_____

_____

▶ **Critical Thinking Questions**

Critical Thinking Level 1 ▷ Remember

Recall two causes that have contributed to the creation of Somali pirate fleets.

_____

_____

_____

Critical Thinking Level 2 ▷ Understand

Fill in the details to support the thesis statement from paragraphs 2–5.

Pirates have never been quite who we think they are.

Critical Thinking Level 3 ▷ Apply

Suppose you woke up one morning and found you were a Somalian fishing captain. What would you do if mysterious ships were stealing your food and polluting your water, and causing your friends and family to become sick? *Develop a plan of action* with a partner or small group to effectively combat these problems.

_____

_____

_____

_____

_____

Critical Thinking Level 4 ▷ Analyze

What *relationships* do you see? Give one sentence from the article as an example for each pattern listed below.

Time order (narration): _____

Cause and effect: _____

_____

Contrast: _____

_____

Critical Thinking Level 5 ▷ Evaluate

Evaluate the validity of this author's argument. Did he support his position well? Why or why not? Include evidence for your reasoning.

_____

_____

_____

_____

Critical Thinking Level 6 ▷ Create

Write a letter or e-mail to your congressperson outlining your opinion about this issue and what you believe he or she should do.

▶ Vocabulary in New Contexts

Review the vocabulary words in the margins of the reading selection and then complete the following activities.

EASY Note Cards

Make a note card for each of the vocabulary words that you did not know in the reading. On one side, write the word. On the other side, divide the card into quarters and label them E, A, S, and Y. Add a word or phrase in each area so that you wind up with an example sentence, an antonym, a synonym, and, finally, a definition that shows you have figured out the meaning of the word with your logic. Remember that an antonym or synonym may have appeared in the reading.

Relationships Between Words

Circle *yes* or *no* to answer the question. Then explain your answer.

1. Would it be reasonable to say that the fallout from a major **scandal** could **linger** in the lives of those involved?

   Yes   No

   Why or why not? _____

2. Would a person who is **egalitarian** try to **dissuade** a person from treating others with equality?

   Yes   No

   Why or why not? _____

3. If fish could talk, might they describe their fish friends as being **plucked** out of the ocean by **trawlers**?

   Yes   No

   Why or why not? _____

Language in Your Life

Write short answers to each question. Look at the vocabulary words closely before you answer.

1. Name one behavior that you would **dissuade** a younger sibling from engaging in. _____

   _____

2. Name a scent you enjoy that you wish would **linger** longer. _____

   _____

3. Name something that you could **pluck**. _____

   _____

4. Name a famous person whom you would describe as **egalitarian**. _____

_____

5. Name a **scandal** that you remember happening. _____

_____

Language in Use

Select the best word to complete the meaning of each sentence.

> dissuade   egalitarian   lingered   malformed   plucked   scandal   teetering   trawlers

1. For about a thousand years, the Chinese practiced foot binding. This bizarre custom led to the creation of _____ feet, which were considered beautiful and alluring and guaranteed an affluent mate.

2. Young girls (usually between the ages of 2 and 5) from well-to-do families would be _____ from their childhood play to begin the painful process of sculpting their feet.

3. These girls' toes would be bent forward, first breaking all toes and then twisting them under the foot. Next the arch would be broken. No pain relief was given. The process, which could take years to achieve, would continue until the girls were left _____ on feet reshaped into the desired length of about 3 inches.

4. The practice, while initially reserved for the upper class, soon became an _____ ritual, commonly practiced among all social levels until the turn of the 20th century.

5. Despite the attempted ban on foot binding, the practice _____ on until it was prohibited by the government in 1949. It is estimated that millions of young girls were subjected to this practice.

 Click to Connect! For more practice applying the skills you learned in this chapter, visit **www.cengagebrain.com** to access the CourseMate for this chapter.

Daniel Smith/Warner Bros/Everett Collection

Click to Connect! Visit **www.cengagebrain.com** to access study resources for this chapter through CourseMate, which includes audio, video, quizzes, and a searchable, interactive eBook version of the text.

9
Making Inferences

It seemed to me that a careful examination of the room and the lawn might possibly reveal some traces of this mysterious individual. You know my methods, Watson. There was not one of them which I did not apply to the inquiry. And it ended by my discovering traces, but very different ones from those which I had expected. **"**

—*THE MEMOIRS OF SHERLOCK HOLMES* (1893)
SHERLOCK HOLMES IN "THE CROOKED MAN" (DOUBLEDAY, P. 416)

Connect with Ideas

What is the basis of Sherlock Holmes's detective methods, according to this quotation?

Activate Your Knowledge

What do you do when you want to figure out why someone has acted in an unexpected way? What questions do you ask yourself, or what process do you follow?

Engage with the Chapter

Look at the diagram on page 455. Does it seem to represent the process you just discussed? How is it similar or different?

Read and Talk

Magazine Article

The following article reports on a new, digital version of a well-known phenomenon.

 Visit www.cengagebrain.com to access the CourseMate for this chapter to hear vocabulary words from this reading and an audio recording of it.

Dancing with the Avatars

Sarah Stanley

oxymoron This word has its origins in Greek; its word parts mean "sharp" and "dull." Notice the context as well to decide what *oxymoron* means.

1   Exercise video games are no longer an **oxymoron**: Witness the Nintendo Wii, which has sold more than 860 million units since it **debuted** in 2006, and Kinect for Xbox360, which **tallied** 10 million sales in four months—the fastest-selling consumer-tech product of all time. Players of "exergames" generally create digital representations of themselves and move along with the action on the screen. Now, researchers are noting the growing trend and examining how exergames can maximize performance.

debuted Figure out the meaning of this word from its context.

tallied Context can help you find the meaning of *tallied*.

2   In the virtual world, as in real life, a workout buddy can be **invaluable**. In a *Journal of Sport and Exercise Psychology* study, those who worked out while watching a Skype video of a partner doing the same moves exercised 25 percent longer than they did while toning alone—but only when their partner was about 40 percent fitter than them. A too-fit partner can be discouraging and an out-of-shape partner can bore the exerciser, while a moderately more athletic partner embodies a realistic goal.

invaluable Don't be fooled by word parts here; examine the meaning in context.

avatars The next sentence will help with the meaning of *avatars*.

3   The **avatars** players pick to represent themselves affect behavior, too. "Avatars that look similar to their real-life counterparts but are slightly more attractive or social improve real-life social behaviors," says Nick Yee of the Palo Alto Research Center. "In exergames, choosing a fit avatar could be similarly motivating."

Sarah Lee/eyevine/Redux

4 In one study, people faced a digital **doppelganger** in a virtual room while lifting weights and then standing still. When the avatars grew slimmer during the exercise portion and plumper during the **stationary** phase, users performed 10 times as many reps as those whose virtual twins didn't change.

5 Active avatars may effect change even if their real-life counterparts watch the action from a computer. "Seeing your avatar exercise gets you excited to try it afterward," says Celeste DeVaneaux, CEO of Club One Island, an online health club based in Second Life. In its virtual weight loss program, participants hop online at the same time to watch their digital stand-ins try outdoor sports, attend nutrition and fitness seminars, and discuss their progress.

6 Indiana University researchers investigated Club One Island's effectiveness in sparking real-world changes. In 12 weeks, those who completed the program lost as much weight as those in similar face-to-face programs; moreover, virtual gym-goers reported bigger confidence boosts in their ability to lose weight. As research on exergame avatars progresses, such programs are likely to become more and more effective—and enjoyable.

doppelganger A synonym was given in paragraph 3. What is a *doppelganger*?

stationary An antonym is given; look for parallel phrases.

Digital Doctors

7 These video games address health issues beyond exercise.

▶ **Re-Mission.** Young cancer patients control a **nanobot** who kills cancer cells and fights infections in fictional patients.

▶ **Packy and Marlon.** Diabetic kids who play this game (in which two elephants manage their symptoms and save a summer camp) have fewer urgent-care visits.

▶ **Lit 2 Quit.** This iPhone app uses color, sound, and breath control to simulate the rush or relaxation of smoking.

nanobot A prefix and a shortened version of a word combine in *nanobot*.

—From "Dancing with the Avatars," by Sarah Stanley. *Psychology Today* (Sept/Oct 2011, p. 40). Copyright © 2011 by Sussex Publishers. Reprinted by permission.

Talking about Reading

Respond in writing to the following questions. Then discuss your answers with your classmates.

1. Have you ever played an "exergame," and if so, what kind? Did you move as vigorously playing the exergame as you would have if you had played the real game? _____

_____

2. What are some possible reasons why people exercise more when they are with someone else?

_____
_____
_____

3. What does the information in this article suggest about some good ways to motivate yourself to do something? _____

_____

4. What are some other behavioral goals besides exercising more that might be aided by watching an avatar achieve them online? _____

_____

5.  **Scan to Connect!** Use your smart phone to scan this code to watch a video. (See the inside front cover for more information on how to use this.) What are the benefits to cancer patients in playing Re-Mission? How important are they to the patients' recovery?

The Process of Making Inferences

If you have seen *Monk* on television, you know that the former police detective has an amazing ability to figure out who murdered the victim. His success is due first to his observational skills. He notices tiny details that no one else does: a missing fishing line, the grains of cement adhering to the soles of a man's shoes, the lack of debris from the ceiling on a cabinet that supposedly fell over

Sam Jones/USA Network/NBCU Photo Bank via Getty Images

during an earthquake. Second, he has a prodigious memory: Monk remembers even the most insignificant details. For example, he once saw a man in a crowd catch a baseball, and much later was able to match that man's face with that of a murderer caught on a video camera. Observing and drawing on memories are two important aspects of making meaning.

Making an inference is the process of drawing conclusions, or making meaning, from observable details. First, you notice the specifics of the sights and sounds around you, or, if you are reading, what's on the page or screen. Then, in a very quick process that may be difficult to notice, you apply your knowledge of the world—you use your memory—to those details. Finally you arrive at an inference: a conclusion about what the details mean.

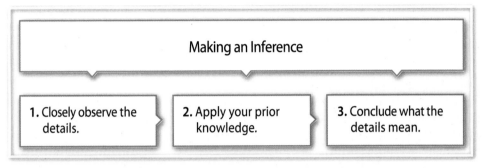

Making an Inference

1. Closely observe the details.

2. Apply your prior knowledge.

3. Conclude what the details mean.

Making inferences is a basic thinking process, and people use it all the time, not just when it's time to catch a murderer.

Making Inferences Every Day

Making inferences is the process of drawing conclusions from observable details. Every time you think, you make inferences. You use what you can see, hear, smell, taste, and touch to draw conclusions about your surroundings. For example, look at the photo below and answer the inference questions that follow.

Image Source/Alamy

What is the man doing? _____

_____

Where was this photo taken? _____

_____

When was it taken? _____

_____

What can you infer about the man? _____

_____

Asking basic questions—*who, what, when, where,* and *why*—about your observations allows you to become more conscious of the inferences you are making all the time.

| Interaction 9–1 | **Make Everyday Inferences** |

Answer the inference questions about each set of observations.

1. The maple trees have lost their leaves. The geese are flying south. The days are getting shorter.

   Where and when is this scene occurring? _____

2. My eyeballs ache. My muscles feel sore. I have a temperature of 101.9.

   What is my condition? _____

3. The woman calls out loudly "Melinda, Me-lin-da!" Her eyes are darting around. She is not smiling. Her hands are clenched.

   What is the situation? _____

4. The boy is sitting in front of a TV set. He keeps moving his thumbs and index fingers on a white object that he is holding. Occasionally he shouts "Gotcha!"

   What is the boy doing? _____

5. A man is standing by the side of the road near a shelter that has glass sides. He keeps checking his watch and then he goes to look at a sign on the shelter.

   What is the man doing? _____

Making Inferences from Images

Inferences about the photo of the man on the motorcycle in the previous section can only go so far. One reason this is true is there aren't many clues in the photo that would let viewers know exactly where the man is or exactly what he is doing. For example, he could be simply posing on a motorcycle for the photographer—it's hard to know.

   Another reason it's hard to tell is that the photographer didn't set things up in a way that suggests his or her own point of view, or interpretation, of the man on the motorcycle. For instance, the man doesn't seem particularly angry or aggressive.

His tattoos are not particularly prominent. The photo wasn't taken from straight on while the man was riding toward the camera, so the photographer doesn't seem to be implying "speed" or "danger." Thus the photographer's point of view didn't significantly affect the inferences we could make. It looks more like a snapshot taken without much thought than a photo with deliberate meaning. But what about the following image? What inferences can you draw about it?

AP Photo/Steven Senne

Here it may be handy to think in terms of layers of inferences. What can you conclude about any of these layers of implied meaning?

- ▶ Layer 1: What is happening in the photo? (the specifics: Who? What? Where? When?)
- ▶ Layer 2: What did the person who set up the flags and the podium want to suggest? (the interpretation or meaning linked to the specifics)
- ▶ Layer 3: What did the photographer want to suggest by taking the photo this way? (the creator's point of view or interpretation of the meaning of the specifics)

Think about or discuss these questions with a classmate before you read any further.

Sample Analysis

- ▶ Layer 1 asks about the most basic facts. If you have watched much news on TV or online, you can probably infer that this person is giving a speech. He is standing at a podium and gesturing, both of which imply a speech. There are American flags in front of the podium and behind the speaker, so he is probably giving a political speech. In fact, this is Presidential candidate Mitt Romney giving a speech in Chicago in March 2012.

> ▶ Layer 2 asks about the intentions of the person who arranged this scene. For example, why did he or she put the flags all around the speaker? One inference that could be made is that the person who set up the scene wants viewers to associate the speaker with the flags. National flags represent patriotism. Surrounding the speaker with flags may imply that the speaker is enfolded in his love of country. Indeed, Mitt Romney's campaign motto was "Believe in America."
>
> ▶ Layer 3 asks what the photographer wanted to suggest. Since this is a news photo, the photographer is first of all just showing viewers what happened. But he did choose a moment when the speaker has both fingers raised and is looking upward. The photo is also shot from below looking up. Of course, that may be the only angle the photographer could shoot from. But taken together, these upward fingers, eyes, and camera angle may reflect the photographer's belief that Romney was giving a good speech that would increase his chances in the election, since "up" is usually associated with good things. We don't know this for sure, however.

When you are viewing photos, cartoons, graphic novels, and artwork, think about all the possible layers of meaning and purpose. Sometimes you'll only be able to make some basic inferences, such as where something is happening or what, generally, is occurring. Other times, as in this photo, asking questions will reveal more layers of influence on the image.

Interaction 9–2 ▶ Make Inferences from Images with a Point of View

Answer the inference questions about each image.

A.

"Your magazine smells fabulous. May I kiss you?"

Robert Weber/Cartoonbank.com

1. Where can you infer this scene is occurring? _____

2. What information in the cartoon leads you to say that? _____
_____
_____

3. What can you infer the man is referring to when he says, "Your magazine smells fabulous"?
_____

4. What can you infer this reference has to do with his next question, "May I kiss you?"
_____

_____

_____

5. Why is this cartoon funny? _____

_____

B.

6. What can you infer about where this photo may have been taken? _____

7. What information in the photo leads you to say that? _____

_____

8. What does the phrase "[costs] an arm and a leg" mean? _____

9. What can you infer about the attitude of the person who changed the prices of the various grades of gasoline to "arm," "leg," and "both"? _____

10. How much does filling your vehicle up with gas cost you? _____

Heather A. Craig/Shutterstock.com

Paying Close Attention to the Details

When you make inferences about images or occurrences in your everyday life, you begin by paying close attention to the details you observe. For example, in the Mitt Romney photo, the fact that American flags surround Romney is an important detail. If he were surrounded by overflowing garbage cans, angry people, or empty chairs, the inferences that could be made about the image would be very different. Similarly, his position of standing behind a podium is a crucial detail. If he were shown sitting in the Oval Office, for instance, we would understand that he had won the election. (This is being written in April 2012, so we don't know how the election will turn out.)

In the same way, the words in a book are the details to pay close attention to when you are reading. Paying close attention to the words the author has selected and asking questions about them will reveal the author's underlying meaning. If an author uses the word "concerned," that conjures up a different mental image than if the author calls a person "frantic with worry." As you read, pay attention to each word or group of words and take the time to mentally picture what the author is implying.

Interaction 9–3   **Pay Attention to Details While Reading**

Underline the details (which may be single words or phrases) that lead you to infer, or conclude, something that is not stated. Then write down your inference.

Sentences are from various pages of the novel *One Moment, One Morning,* by Sarah Rayner.

1. Out of the corner of her eye she is watching the woman opposite her put on makeup. (p. 3)

   Inference: _____

   _____

2. She sits down heavily, head in her hands. (p. 243)

   Inference: _____

   _____

3. Should she catch up with him and confront him, or let it go? (p. 110)

   Inference: _____

   _____

4. The familiar voice takes her by surprise. (p. 294)

   Inference: _____

   _____

5. She is acutely conscious of Sofia's presence beside her. (p. 280)

   Inference: _____

   _____

Sentences are from page 31 of the nonfiction book *1776,* by David McCullough.

6. The troops were in good spirits, but had yet to accept the necessity of order or obedience.

   Inference: _____

   _____

7. Many had volunteered on the condition that they could elect their own officers, and the officers, in turn, were inclined out of laziness, or for the sake of their own popularity, to let those

in the ranks do much as they pleased. Many officers had little or no idea of what they were supposed to do.

Inference: _____

_____

8. What do you predict will happen next in this army?

_____

_____

Sentences are from page 1 of the nonfiction book *Thunderstruck*, by Eric Larson.

9. On Wednesday, July 20, 1910, as a light fog drifted along the River Scheldt, Capt. Henry George Kendall prepared his ship, the SS *Montrose*, for what should have been the most routine of voyages, from Antwerp direct to Quebec City, Canada.

Inference: _____

_____

10. At eight-thirty in the morning the passengers began streaming aboard. He called them "souls."

Inference: _____

_____

11. The ship's manifest showed 266 in all.

Inference: _____

_____

12. What are some possible inferences you can draw about what happened on the ship's journey?

_____

_____

Sentences are from pages 142–143 of the novel *Dirk Gently's Holistic Detective Agency*, by Douglas Adams (a novel).

13. The other argument was more muffled.

Inference: _____

_____

14. As Richard reached the first corridor a door slammed somewhere…. He looked into the nearest open doorway.

Inference: _____

_____

15. It led into a small ante-office. The other, inner door leading to it was firmly closed.

    Inference: _____

    _____

16. A youngish plump-faced girl in a cheap blue coat was pulling sticks of makeup and boxes of Kleenex out of her desk drawer and thrusting them into her bag.

    Inference: _____

    _____

17. "Is this the detective agency?" Richard asked her tentatively.

    Inference: _____

    _____

18. The girl nodded, biting her lip and keeping her head down.

    Inference: _____

    _____

19. "And is Mr. Gently in?"

    Inference: _____

    _____

20. "He may be," she said, throwing back her hair, which was too curly for throwing back properly, "and then again he may not be. I am not in a position to tell. It is not my business to know of his whereabouts. His whereabouts are, as of now, entirely his own business."

    Inference: _____

    _____

Understanding How Prior Knowledge Affects Inferences

Your prior knowledge and experience determine much of what you will be able to infer from an author's words. If you know a lot about something—say, the Revolutionary War—then your reading of an author's words about the Revolutionary War will lead you to make a lot more connections with existing knowledge than someone who knows little or nothing about it. (In fact, you may have realized that the second passage in Interaction 9–3 was a description of Washington's army in that war.)

Inference is the act of drawing conclusions from a variety of pieces of information, so the more information you have, the richer and more accurate are the inferences that you can draw.

Sample Analysis

List whatever prior knowledge you have that may relate to the cartoon that follows.

▶ _____
  _____

▶ _____
  _____

▶ _____
  _____

▶ _____
  _____

What inference can you draw about the cartoon based on your prior knowledge?

_____
_____

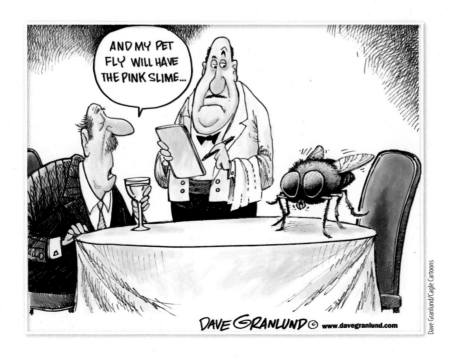

Dave Granlund/Cagle Cartoons

Interaction 9–4 ▶ Make Inferences Based on Prior Knowledge

A. Read the nonsense poem and answer the questions that follow.

Jabberwocky

'Twas brillig, and the slithy toves
Did gyre and gimble in the wabe;
All mimsy were the borogoves,
And the mome raths outgrabe.

"Beware the Jabberwock, my son!
The jaws that bite, the claws that catch!
Beware the Jubjub bird, and shun
The frumious Bandersnatch!"

He took his vorpal sword in hand:
Long time the manxome foe he sought—
So rested he by the Tumtum tree,
And stood awhile in thought.

And as in uffish thought he stood,
The Jabberwock, with eyes of flame,
Came whiffling through the tulgey wood,
And burbled as it came!

One, two! One, two! and through and through
The vorpal blade went snicker-snack!
He left it dead, and with its head
He went galumphing back.

"And hast thou slain the Jabberwock?
Come to my arms, my beamish boy!
O frabjous day! Callooh! Callay!"
He chortled in his joy.

'Twas brillig, and the slithy toves
Did gyre and gimble in the wabe;
All mimsy were the borogoves,
And the mome raths outgrabe.

—From Lewis Carroll, *Through the Looking-Glass,
and What Alice Found There* (1872)

1. In your own words, what happens in this poem? _____

   _____

   _____

2. Which four words in the first stanza name persons, places, things, or ideas (nouns)?

   ▶ _____

   ▶ _____

   ▶ _____

   ▶ _____

3. Which three words in the first stanza indicate actions (verbs)?

   ▶ _____

   ▶ _____

   ▶ _____

4. Which two words in the first stanza describe nouns (adjectives)?

    ▶ _____

    ▶ _____

5. Despite the fact that all the words you listed are not actually words in the English language, you were able, to some degree, to understand their grammatical functions in the poem. Suggest at least three kinds of prior knowledge you used to figure them out.

    ▶ _____

    _____

    ▶ _____

    _____

    ▶ _____

B. Take the following psychological quiz, and score it according to the directions that follow. Then answer the questions.

Quiz Directions: Using the scale shown below, please respond to each of the following statements according to how you would usually describe yourself. There are no right or wrong answers.

1	2	3	4	5	6	7
Strongly Disagree			Neither Agree nor Disagree			Strongly Agree

1. I would describe myself as someone who actively seeks as much information as I can in a new situation.

2. When I am participating in an activity, I tend to get so involved that I lose track of time.

3. I frequently find myself looking for new opportunities to grow as a person (e.g., information, people, resources).

4. I am *not* the type of person who probes deeply into new situations or things.

5. When I am actively interested in something, it takes a great deal to interrupt me.

6. My friends would describe me as someone who is "extremely intense" when in the middle of doing something.

7. Everywhere I go, I am out looking for new things or experiences.

Scoring: Total the scores you gave for items 1–3 and 5–7. For item 4, reverse the score. For example, if you scored yourself as 1, count it as a 7; if you scored yourself as 2, count it as a 6; if a 3, count it as a 5. If you scored 7, 6, or 5, count it as a 1, 2, or 3. A 4 remains a 4. Then add this number to your others. The highest possible score is 49; the lowest is 7.

6. What personality trait does each quiz item seems to be describing?

Item 1: _____

Item 2: _____

Item 3: _____

Item 4: _____

Item 5: _____

Item 6: _____

Item 7: _____

7. Group any qualities that seem to go together. What names would you give each group?

_____

_____

8–10. Think about the score you got and the qualities you just listed. Explain why your score makes sense by naming three specific instances in which you showed or did not show one or more of these qualities.

▶ _____

▶ _____

▶ _____

Making Tentative Inferences As You Read

Your mind is always generating tentative, or possible, inferences as you read. In fact, this is part of the excitement of reading: you make new discoveries about the author's meaning practically every other word. You read a few words, and your mind immediately starts trying to put the pieces together and figure out what the author is really saying. How does this sentence connect to what you read before and to what will come next? When you read the next few words, you realize that some of the things you originally thought might be true actually cannot be because new evidence contradicts those conclusions.

So we need to modify the basic process of making inferences that was pictured on page 455 to make it more realistic.

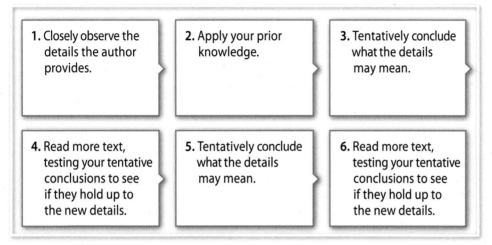

1. Closely observe the details the author provides.

2. Apply your prior knowledge.

3. Tentatively conclude what the details may mean.

4. Read more text, testing your tentative conclusions to see if they hold up to the new details.

5. Tentatively conclude what the details may mean.

6. Read more text, testing your tentative conclusions to see if they hold up to the new details.

Making Tentative Inferences As You Read

This ongoing process of inference usually happens unconsciously (beneath your awareness). As you become more aware of it, you can control the process so that your inferences become more accurate. As they do, your reading comprehension will improve.

A Sample Analysis

Here is a paragraph from *Catching Fire,* the second novel of *The Hunger Games* series. Each time you see a slash mark like this / pause and notice what conclusions you have drawn about what you just read.

> "No!" I cry, and spring forward. / It's too late to stop the arm from descending, / and I instinctively know I won't have the power to block it. / Instead I throw myself / directly between the whip and Gale. / I've flung out my arms to protect as much of his broken body as possible, / so there's nothing to deflect the lash. / I take the full force of it / across the left side of my face.
>
> —Suzanne Collins, *Catching Fire,* p. 106

Here is one reader's inference-making process about that paragraph:

> The speaker (who is Katniss) doesn't want something bad to happen, so she quickly tries to stop it. But she wasn't in time to stop—what? Someone from spanking a little kid, someone hitting somebody else? Some kind of hitting that is

too powerful for her to keep from happening. She can't block the person's arm (whose is it?), so she throws her body between the whip (ah ha) and Gale (oh, no). So she's throwing her body on top of his body, which is "broken," which means this has already been going on for some time. Her arms are spread out to cover Gale so she can't protect herself from the lash of the whip. The lash is brought down hard—on her face. Ouch!

Notice that some of the inferences this reader makes are tentative: She asks them as questions because there isn't enough information yet to be sure. She keeps her tentative conclusions in mind as she continues to read. She bases these tentative inferences on her prior knowledge (for example, about the characters), guesses about the unfolding meaning of the words and sentences, and, at times, even the emotional connection she feels with the characters or the people being written about. When this reader thinks "ouch!" she is both drawing a conclusion about the effect of the whipping on Katniss and identifying with her pain.

Notice that certain inferences weren't made because the author's words did not support them. The reader did not infer that someone was being knifed, for example, because the author wrote only "it's too late to stop the arm from descending." There was no mention of a knife. The reader might have briefly thought that might be a possibility, but it's one that has to be rejected once the reader gets to the words "the whip." All logical inferences are based in the author's words. Anything else would unfairly distort the author's intentions.

Interaction 9–5 ▶ Make Tentative Inferences as You Read

Read each paragraph, remaining conscious of the inferences you are making. Then answer the questions that follow.

A.

They were sharp, they were shrewd, they were flinty, unreasonable, calm cheaters and secret hoarders. They haunted tag sales. Bought food in bulk. Hitchhiked when gas was expensive, though they were not poor. Ate day-old rolls and bread and drank post-dated milk. Saved the rubber bands off broccoli and bananas, when they bought such luxuries. They boiled the sap from their trees and stole the corn from their neighbor's fields. They picked fiddleheads, tore fruit off stunted trees, shot and roasted raccoons. Each fall they bought and salted down or froze half a pig, devouring it from snout to hock over the course of a year. To my mind the Tatros were exactly the sort of cheap old Yankee bachelors who'd have kept a valuable collection of artifacts just because it never occurred to them to part with anything. They never would have thought of donating, or even selling; they would have simply hung on to their stuff—moldering, mothballed, packed away with cedar blocks—until Judgment Day. Or so I hoped.

—Louise Erdrich, *The Painted Drum* (New York: Harper Perennial, 2005, p. 31)

1. What do all the details about the Tatros add up to? What is their main characteristic?

   _____

   _____

2. Where do you infer that the Tatros live—in the city or the country? _____

3–6. What are four details from the selection that support your answer to question 2?

   ▶ _____

   ▶ _____

   ▶ _____

   ▶ _____

7. What does the narrator of this passage want from the Tatros? _____

   _____

8. Are the Tatros alive or dead? _____

9–10. What are two details that support your answer to question 9? *Hint*: One detail has to do with verbs.

   ▶ _____

   ▶ _____

   _____

B.

> I walk into the classroom in Elkton, Minnesota. Early April the fields around the school are wet, unplowed, not seeded yet. And the sky is deep gray. I tell the twenty-five eighth-graders that I am a Jew after I hear that *rabbis* is one of their spelling words. None of them has ever seen a Jew before. I am aware that everything I do now for the next hour represents "Jew." I walk in eating an apple: all Jews now will eat apples. I tell them I have never lived in a small town: now no Jew has ever lived in the country. One student asked if I knew anyone in a concentration camp. And we talk about the Germans: many are of German descent.
>
> —Natalie Goldberg, *Writing Down the Bones* (Boston: Shambhala, 1986, p. 27)

11. In her discussion about being Jewish, what does the author suggest about how people learn? _____

   _____

12. What does the author suggest about how people learn when she mentions the question about the concentration camp? _____

13. What tentative inference can you make about the author's use of the words "unplowed, not seeded yet" in the second sentence? _____

   _____

C.

> By the time the first English settled, other Europeans had already reached *half* of the forty-eight states that today make up the continental United States. One of the earliest arrivals was Giovanni da Verrazzano, who toured the Eastern Seaboard in 1524, almost a full century before the Pilgrims arrived. Verrazzano, an Italian in command of a French ship, smelled America before he saw it: "A sweet fragrance," he wrote, wafted out to sea from the dense cedar forests of the Carolinas.
>
> Reaching the coast, Verrazzano dispatched one of his men to swim ashore and greet some people gathered on the dunes. The natives promptly carried the Frenchman to a fire on the beach and stripped off his clothes—not to "roast him for food," as his shipmates feared, but to warm the sailor while "looking at the whiteness of his flesh and examining him from head to toe."
>
> —Tony Horowitz, *A Voyage Long and Strange* (New York: Henry Holt, 2008, p. 4)

14. Think about your own prior knowledge about the settling of the land that today is the United States. What can you infer about why the author used italics on the word "half" in the first sentence? _____

_____

15–16. What are two inferences you can make about the natives, based on their treatment of the Frenchman?

   ▶ _____

   ▶ _____

D.

The Road Not Taken

Robert Frost

Two roads diverged in a yellow wood,
And sorry I could not travel both
And be one traveler, long I stood
And looked down one as far as I could
To where it bent in the undergrowth;

Then took the other, as just as fair,
And having perhaps the better claim,
Because it was grassy and wanted wear;
Though as for that the passing there
Had worn them really about the same,

And both that morning equally lay
In leaves no step had trodden black.
Oh, I kept the first for another day!
Yet knowing how way leads on to way,
I doubted if I should ever come back.

I shall be telling this with a sigh
Somewhere ages and ages hence:
Two roads diverged in a wood, and I—
I took the one less traveled by,
And that has made all the difference.

—From *The Poetry of Robert Frost*, edited by Edward Connery Lathem.
Copyright © 1969 by Henry Holt & Co. Reprinted by permission.

17. What do you infer the two roads represent? _____

18. Is one road less traveled than the other? _____

19–20. Which two details support your answer to question 18?

   ▶ _____

   ▶ _____

21. What tentative inference can you make about why the narrator uses the word "sigh" in the first line of the last stanza? _____

22. What tentative inference can you draw from the answer you gave to question 19 and this claim: "I took the one less traveled by"? _____

   _____

   _____

E.

> Here's something about Miss Leefolt: she not just frowning all the time, she skinny. Her legs is so spindly, she look like she done growed em last week. Twenty-three years old and she lanky as a four-teen-year-old boy. Even her hair is thin, brown, see-through. She try to tease it up, but it only make it look thinner. Her face be the same shape as that red devil on the redhot candy box, pointy chin and all. Fact, her whole body be so full a sharp knobs and corners, it's no wonder she can't soothe that baby. Babies like fat. Like to bury they face up in you armpit and go to sleep. They like big fat legs too. That I know.
>
> —Kathryn Stockett, *The Help* (Penguin, 2009)

23. What tentative inferences can you make about the narrator from the kind of language she uses? Suggest at least three possibilities.

   ▶ _____

   ▶ _____

   ▶ _____

24. What are two tentative inferences you can make from the narrator's statement that "Babies like fat. . . . That I know"?

   ▶ _____

   ▶ _____

Connect Your Skills

Making Inferences

Read or view each item and answer the questions that follow.

Street Scene

Prasanta Biswas/Drik India/Majority World/The Image Works

1. What can you infer about where these people are and what has happened? _____
   _____

2. What information in the photo leads you to say that? _____

3. What can you infer from the expression on the girls' faces? _____

4. What does that imply about this situation? _____
   _____
   _____

5. What do the umbrellas imply? _____
   _____

6. What larger inference can you make about this situation, now that you have made smaller inferences about several details? _____

Knee Surgery Study

A Baylor School of Medicine study, published in 2002 in the *New England Journal of Medicine* evaluated surgery for patients with severe, debilitating knee pain. The lead author of the study, Dr. Bruce Moseley, "knew" that knee surgery helped his patients. "All good surgeons know there is no placebo effect in surgery." But Moseley was trying to figure out which part of the surgery was giving his patients relief. The patients in the study were divided into three groups. Moseley shaved the damaged cartilage in the knee of one group. For another group, he flushed out the knee joint, removing material thought to be causing the inflammatory effect. Both of these constitute standard treatment for arthritic knees. The third group got "fake" surgery. The patients were sedated, Moseley made three standard incisions and then talked and acted just as he would have during a real surgery—he even splashed salt water to simulate the sound of the knee-washing procedure. After 40 minutes, Moseley sewed up the incisions as if he had done the surgery. All three groups were prescribed the same postoperative care, which included an exercise program.

The results were shocking. Yes, the groups who received surgery, as expected, improved. But the placebo group improved just as much as the other two groups!

—From Lipton, *The Biology of Belief,* qtd. in Wayne Dwyer, *Excuses Begone!* (Carlsbad: Hays House, 2009, p. 8)

7. What can you infer about how qualified the lead author of this research study is?

He is not at all qualified.   He is reasonably qualified.   He is well qualified.

8. Name three or four details that support your inference.

   ► _____

   ► _____

   ► _____

   ► _____

9. What do you infer about the meaning of the phrase "placebo effect"? _____

   _____

10. What two details support your inference?

   ► _____

   ► _____

11. What can you infer about the placebo effect from the careful way the doctor set up the conditions around the fake surgery: the sedation, the incisions, the sound of salt water? _____

   _____

Excerpt from *Night*

Elie Wiesel

The cherished objects we had brought with us thus far were left behind in the train, and with them, at last, our illusions.

Every two yards or so an SS man held his tommy gun trained on us. Hand in hand we followed the crowd.

An SS noncommissioned officer came to meet us, a truncheon in his hand. He gave the order:

"Men to the left!" "Women to the right!"

Eight words spoken quietly, indifferently, without emotion. Eight short, simple words. Yet that was the moment when I parted from my mother. I had not had time to think, but already I felt the pressure of my father's hand: we were alone. For a part of a second I glimpsed my mother and my sisters moving away to the right. Tzipora held Mother's hand. I saw them disappear into the distance; my mother was stroking my sister's fair hair, as though to protect her, while I walked on with my father and the other men. And I did not know that in that place, at that moment, I was parting from my mother and Tzipora forever. I went on walking. My father held onto my hand....

"Here, kid, how old are you?"

It was one of the prisoners who asked me this. I could not see his face, but his voice was tense and weary.

"I'm not quite fifteen yet."

"No. Eighteen."

"But I'm not," I said. "Fifteen."

"Fool. Listen to what *I* say."

Then he questioned my father, who replied:

"Fifty."

The other grew more furious than ever.

"No, not fifty. Forty. Do you understand? Eighteen and forty."

—Excerpt from Elie Wiesel, *Night* (New York: Bantam, 1960, pp. 27–28)

12. List at least two pieces of prior knowledge you have about the events Wiesel is describing in his autobiography.

▶ _____

▶ _____

_____

13. What inference can you make about Wiesel's and his traveling companions' expectations? Use details from the first sentence to support your inference. _____

_____

_____

14. What do you infer from the presence of tommy guns "every two yards" and the truncheon? ____

_____

15. What do you infer about Wiesel's emotion when he writes (some ten years later) about leaving his mother and sister for the last time? Reread the paragraph before you respond. _____

_____

16. What do you infer from the other prisoner's insistence that Elie say that he is eighteen and that his father say that he is forty? _____

_____

Excerpt from "No Time to Read?"

David McCullough

Once upon a time in the dead of winter in the Dakota territory, Theodore Roosevelt took off in a makeshift boat down the Little Missouri River in pursuit of a couple of thieves who had stolen his prized rowboat. After several days on the river, he caught up and got the draw on them with his trusty Winchester, at which point they surrendered. Then Roosevelt set off in a borrowed wagon to haul the thieves cross-country to justice. They headed across the snow-covered wastes of the Badlands to the railhead at Dickinson, and Roosevelt walked the whole way, the entire 40 miles.

It was an astonishing feat, what might be called a defining moment in Roosevelt's eventful life. But what makes it especially memorable is that during that time, he managed to read all of *Anna Karenina*.

I often think of this when I hear people say that they haven't time to read.

—From "No Time to Read?" by David McCullough. Copyright © 2000 by David McCullough and Family Circle. First published in *Family Circle*, April 18, 2000. Reprinted by permission.

17. What inference can you make about Roosevelt's personality from these details? _____

_____

18. What do you infer that *Anna Karenina* is? _____

19. What word gives you a clue to make that inference? _____

20. What do you infer about the author's thoughts from reading the last sentence? _____

_____

 Click to Connect! To check your comprehension of chapter concepts, visit **www.cengagebrain.com** to access the CourseMate for this chapter.

Chapter Summary Activity

This chapter has discussed how to make inferences from details in the text in order to deepen your reading comprehension. Construct a Reading Guide to Making Inferences here by completing each main idea on the left with the specific supporting details from the chapter on the right. You can use this guide later as you complete other reading assignments.

Reading Guide to Making Inferences

Complete this idea with...	information from Chapter 9.
Three steps to making an inference	1. _____
	2. _____
	3. _____
Basic questions to ask about what you observe	4. _____
	5. _____
	6. _____
	7. _____
	8. _____

Details to observe when reading	9. _____
	10. _____

Think about what your inference strategies were before you read this chapter. How did they differ from the suggestions here? What strategies have you learned that you can use? Write down your thoughts.

_____

_____

_____

Reading 9–1 | News Magazine Article

▶ Pre-Reading the Selection

Poet John Donne famously wrote that "no man is an island, entire of itself," and in the article that follows, several studies are reported about exactly how true that sentiment is.

Surveying the Reading

Survey the following article. Then check the elements that are included in this reading.

_____	Title	_____	Words in bold or italic type
_____	Headings	_____	Images and captions
_____	First sentences of paragraphs		

Guessing the Purpose

Judging from the title of the reading, what do you suppose the purpose for writing is? _____

Predicting the Content

Predict three things this selection will discuss.

▶ _____

▶ _____

▶ _____

Activating Your Knowledge

What do you already know about how individuals' social life affects their health and well-being? Note two or three things you know.

▶ _____

▶ _____

▶ _____

Scan to Connect! Use your smart phone to scan this code to watch a video to activate your knowledge about social networks. (See the inside front cover for more information on how to use this.) As you watch, think about the effects of social networks in your own life. What impact do relatives, friends, and acquaintances have on your life?

▶ Reading with Pen in Hand

Students who annotate as they read are more successful than those who do not. That's why you will annotate every selection in *Connect* as you read. In the reading that follows, use the following symbols:

★ or ⟨Point⟩   to indicate a main idea

① ② ③   to indicate major details

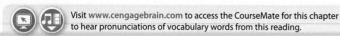

Visit www.cengagebrain.com to access the CourseMate for this chapter to hear pronunciations of vocabulary words from this reading.

How to Find Happiness on Social Networks

Philip Moeller

▶ Has there been disagreement about what social scientists have found out about social networks?

1　　Beginning nearly 40 years ago, social scientists began to look deeply and regularly at the ways people related to other people—spouses, family, friends, and others—and how different people were affected by their own social networks. What they discovered, and have consistently found in later studies, is that the diversity and numbers of our social connections are directly related to our health, happiness, and **longevity**. Social networks certainly include close friends and family members. But they extend outward from these intimate relationships to encompass extensive and often intricate networks of human ties that influence us in ways we may not even know.

longevity　Use word parts to decide the meaning.

▶ How many health issues do our social ties affect?

2　　"We would ask people, 'Are you married?' 'Do you belong to social groups?' 'Do you belong to a church?' 'Do you have friends?'" says Sheldon Cohen, a relationship researcher and psychologist at Carnegie Mellon University. "The more they have, the better off they are," he adds. Cohen rattles off a list of the ways social ties influence our well-being: "It predicts **mortality**. It predicts cardiovascular disease. It even predicts the recovery rates from cardiovascular disease. It predicts the progress of cancer. It predicts **cognitive** function [in later life]. It even predicts the common cold."

mortality　Use word parts to figure this out.

cognitive　Word parts will help you understand *cognitive*.

▶ Who usually gets sick?

3　　Cohen's own research group has exposed healthy people to a cold virus after first measuring the state of their immune systems. About a third of the people get sick. "It turns out that their social integration scale is a really good predictor of who gets sick and who doesn't," he says.

▶ Think of a personal example for each role.

4　　Claude Fischer, a sociologist at the University of California at Berkeley, divides network relationships into three roles: providing emotional support, giving practical help, and social interaction, such as going to the ball park together. "Our relationships tend to be **reciprocal** over the long run, in terms of there being a balance of giving and getting," he says.

reciprocal　A synonym (that is a phrase, not a single word) is used in the sentence.

▶ Make a mental picture of this parent.

5　　Notably, family relationships can remain significant even if they are not balanced and reciprocal. A relationship with a dominating parent, for example, can continue to be meaningful even if it's not balanced or perhaps even reciprocal. Strained or hostile relationships among family members remain significant, even though the family members may never communicate or see one another. "An **underappreciated** thing about networks," Fischer says, "is the extent to which ties can be a mixed blessing."

underappreciated　Two main word parts will be helpful here.

▶ Make a mental picture of your social network branching out all around you.

6　　However, Cohen says networks can have a positive effect on health regardless of whether the person's experiences are positive. "Every **increment** in the social network is related to an improvement in your health," he says. So, 10 ties are better than nine ties, which are better than eight, and so on. "There's just

increment　An example follows in the next sentence.

something about having these many social roles that is good for you, and the more you have, the better it is."

7   Researchers Nicholas Christakis and James Fowler, coauthors of *Connected: The Surprising Power of Our Social Networks and How They Shape Our Lives*, found that social networks affect happiness over three degrees of relationships, which they call the "three degrees of influence." First come the people you know, then the people they know, and finally, the people this second group knows. Your happiness can be affected by people in all three sets of relationships, including people you do not know and likely will never meet. Likewise, you can influence people you've never met.

▶ Think of one person in each degree.

8   If people in your direct network are happy, the odds of you being happier as well will rise by 20 percent, Christakis and Fowler say. And if people in the second layer of the network are happy, the odds that you will be happier will rise by 15 percent. The happiness effect in the third degree of removal is 10 percent. The effect is not limited to happiness but can include behavioral influences. For example, if you're gaining weight, it can influence the weights of others in your network.

▶ Make a mental movie of you changing one behavior and having the effect ripple out through your three degrees of influence.

9   Weak friendships and even encounters with people you don't know can affect your well-being, according to Karen Fingerman, professor of human development and family science at the University of Texas. She has studied interactions with what she calls "**consequential** strangers" and found that they can make or break a person's day and influence their mood. Think, for example, of the cheerful Starbucks barista you look forward to seeing on many days.

▶ Who is a consequential stranger to you?

consequential A definition follows in the sentence.

10   Casual acquaintances may also provide strong benefits. "The intimate ties give you a lot of emotional support," Fingerman says, "whereas your **peripheral** ties may help you with new information and diversions." Fingerman cites research showing that many of us find new jobs through our weaker social ties. "The people on the edge [of our social network] are the people who have access to information and to people that you do not know."

▶ Think of one benefit you've gained from a peripheral tie.

peripheral An antonym is in the first part of the quote.

11   While social networks can be extensive, our core sets of close relationships are much smaller. "We found that the average American has just four close social contacts, with most having between two and six," Christakis and Fowler say in their research. "People's social networks tend to shrink as they get older, especially as they get into middle age," Fischer says. This can increase loneliness and have an **adverse** effect on health. One **antidote** is to seek out new community groups and volunteer opportunities.

▶ Who is in your core set of close relationships?

adverse Your logic will help you here.

antidote Use your logic to understand this word.

12   Developing relationships has been made easier by the emergence of Facebook and other widely used social media sites. "What social media does is that it brings us more into contact with weaker ties," Fowler says. "The online stuff takes time away not from social ties, but from things like television and sleep," says Fischer. "There is no evidence that it undercuts face-to-face social ties."

▶ Do you agree that using Facebook puts people in touch with their weaker ties?

> ▶ Name a benefit and a disadvantage of online dating.

13   Eli Finkel, an associate professor of social psychology at Northwestern University, researches the effect of online dating services on relationships. As many as 1 in 4 romantic relationships now start online, he says, compared with less than 1 percent that were triggered 20 years ago by personal ads in newspapers. "You now have access to profiles of a large number of potential partners that you might be interested in," Finkel says, "and that's a godsend." But he feels online dating sites are misleading people when they say they've somehow "cracked the code" and can use technology to provide users with perfect matches. Neither the profiles nor the matching technology have yet replaced the value of face-to-face meetings and social interaction, Finkel says.

> ▶ Think of one example from your experience of each kind of benefit.
>
> integration Look at the example clue that follows the dash to determine this word's meaning.

14   In the end, successful networks provide people with three strong types of benefits, Cohen says. One is social **integration**—being plugged into events, trends, and experiences beyond those that directly involve you. Second, he says, is the social support provided to one another by network members. "When you care for other people, you're motivated to take better care of yourself," Cohen observes. Lastly, social networks can insulate or buffer people from negative events. "Having people who you think will provide you with help when you need it helps protect you from the effects of stress on your health," Cohen says. Even when the protection is perceived, such as believing someone would "have your back" in a crisis, the benefit is real.

—"How to Find Happiness on Social Networks," by Philip Moeller. *US News & World Report*, March 16, 2012. Copyright © 2012 Wright's Media. Reprinted by permission.

▶ Comprehension Questions

Write the letter of the answer on the line. Then explain your thinking.

Main Idea

_____ 1. Which of the following best states the main idea of this passage?

    a. Social scientists have consistently found that the diversity and numbers of our social connections are directly related to our health, happiness, and longevity.

    b. Social networks affect three degrees of influence.

    c. Weak friendships and even encounters with people you don't know can affect your well-being.

    d. Casual acquaintances may also provide strong benefits.

Why? What information in the selection leads you to give that answer? _____

_____

_____ 2. Which statement is the main idea of paragraph 14?

   a. In the end, successful networks provide people with three strong types of benefits, Cohen says.

   b. One is social integration—being plugged into events, trends, and experiences beyond those that directly involve you.

   c. Second, he says, is the social support provided to one another by network members.

   d. Lastly, social networks can insulate or buffer people from negative events.

Why? What information in the selection leads you to give that answer? _____

_____

Supporting Details

_____ 3. Which of the following details does not support this main idea?
   Diverse social ties positively influence our well-being.

   a. Having stronger social ties prevents cardiovascular disease.

   b. Having more social ties predicts cognitive function.

   c. Peripheral ties may help you with new information.

   d. One in four relationships now begin online.

Why? What information in the selection leads you to give that answer? _____

_____

_____ 4. Which researchers mentioned in this article provide information about the emotional benefits of social ties?

   a. Cohen

   b. Cohen, Fischer, and Fingerman

   c. Christakis and Fowler and Finkel

   d. Cohen, Fischer, Fingerman, Christakis and Fowler and Finkel

Why? What information in the selection leads you to give that answer? _____

_____

_____

Author's Purpose

_____ 5. What is the purpose or purposes of the passage?

   a. to express an opinion that happiness cannot be found on Facebook

   b. to inform readers how social networks can help them find happiness

   c. to persuade readers to use Facebook in order to find happiness

   d. to inform readers how the author found happiness on Facebook

____ **Why?** What information in the selection leads you to give that answer? _____

_____

_____

____ 6. Why does the author include Fowler's statement in paragraph 12 that "there is no evidence that [using social media online] undercuts fact-to-face social ties"?

    a. to persuade readers that they should not use Facebook

    b. because some people might argue that being online takes away from important social time

    c. to keep older and younger people connecting via Facebook and other social media sites

    d. to suggest that personal ads are more effective in connecting with like-minded people than using social media online

Why? What information in the selection leads you to give that answer? _____

_____

_____

_____

Relationships

____ 7. What is the overall pattern of organization of the reading selection?

    a. comparison and contrast

    b. cause-and-effect

    c. example

    d. process

Why? What information in the selection leads you to give that answer? _____

_____

_____

_____

____ 8. What organizational pattern do you find in paragraph 9?

    a. cause-and-effect

    b. classification

    c. process

    d. time order

Why? What information in the selection leads you to give that answer? _____

_____

Fact, Opinion, and Inference

_____ 9. Which of the following is the most frequently used kind of quotation in this article?

    a. fact

    b. opinion by a person on the street

    c. informed opinion

    d. expert opinion

Why? What leads you to give that answer? _____

_____

_____ 10. Which of the following can be inferred from the information in this article?

    a. It doesn't matter how you treat people you see on the street, in the bank, or in the grocery store.

    b. Each of us has the power to influence more people than we even know.

    c. Having strong social ties is the only contributing factor for a healthy body.

    d. As people age, they have met a lot of people, which expands their social circle.

Why? What information in the selection leads you to give that answer? _____

_____

_____

_____

▶ Critical Thinking Questions

Critical Thinking Level 1 ▸ Remember

Define social network. _____

_____

Critical Thinking Level 2 ▸ Understand

Describe how Cohen's and Fischer's findings overlap. _____

_____

Critical Thinking Level 3 ▸ Apply

Use the information in this article to give three pieces of advice to this person that will help her feel happier.

Lynn is a 72-year-old woman who lives alone in a small apartment complex that is designed specifically for older adults who can still live independently. Most days, Lynn stays in her apartment, watching TV or reading. She doesn't drink, but she does smoke cigarettes. Lynn eats most meals alone, although she does eat two or three meals a week with her daughter and granddaughters. _____

▶ _____

▶ _____

▶ _____

Critical Thinking Level 4 ▷ Analyze

In 1624, John Donne wrote Meditation 17 on a topic similar to the topic of the article you just read. Read the Meditation.

For Whom the Bell Tolls

No man is an island,
Entire of itself.
Each is a piece of the continent,
A part of the main.
If a clod be washed away by the sea,
Europe is the less,
As well as if a promontory were.

As well as if a manor of thine own
Or of thine friend's were.
Each man's death diminishes me,
For I am involved in mankind.
Therefore, send not to know
For whom the bell tolls,
It tolls for thee.

Analyze Meditation 17 with these questions in mind.

1. What contrast does Donne suggest when he uses the word "island" and then "continent"? ____

_____

2. What difference does Donne suggest when he uses the words "clod" and "promontory"? _____

_____

3. What is similar about the effect of the clod and the promontory being washed away by the sea?

_____

4. What does Donne mean when he says "a manor of thine own or of thine friend's"? _____

_____

5. What does Donne mean in the rest of this meditation? _____

_____

Critical Thinking Level 5   Evaluate

Evaluate who goes further in their thinking about the importance of social ties: John Donne or the researchers whose work is discussed in "How to Find Happiness on Social Networks." Support your evaluation with details. _____

_____

_____

_____

Critical Thinking Level 6   Create

Create a visual map of your social network on a separate sheet of paper. Use the ideas of Christakis and Fowler and Fingerman to set it up. Put in the names of the people you know, and short descriptors of those whose names you don't know.

▶ Vocabulary in New Contexts

Review the vocabulary words in the margins of the reading selection and then complete the following activities.

EASY Note Cards

Make a note card for each of the vocabulary words that you did not know from the reading. On one side, write the word. On the other side, divide the card into quarters and label them E, A, S, and Y. Add a word or phrase in each area so that you wind up with an example sentence, an antonym, a synonym, and, finally, a definition that shows you have figured out the meaning of the word with your logic. Remember that an antonym or synonym may have appeared in the reading.

Relationships Between Words

Circle *yes* or *no* to answer the question. Then explain your answer.

1. If you have a **reciprocal** relationship with your partner, do you wind up feeling **underappreciated**?

   Yes   No

   Why or why not? _____

   _____

2. Would an **increment** in literacy be **consequential** to the people involved?

   Yes   No

   Why or why not? _____

3. Is **cognitive** ability directly related to **longevity**?

   Yes   No

   Why or why not? _____

4. Is there an **antidote** to **mortality?**

Yes   No

Why or why not? _____

5. Can vague shapes seen in your **peripheral** vision spark an **adverse** reaction?

Yes   No

Why or why not? _____

Language in Your Life

Write short answers to each question. Look at the vocabulary words closely before you answer.

1. Name one action you could take to increase your **longevity.** _____

_____

2. Note one person whom you wish would **reciprocate** your feelings. _____

_____

3. Name an **antidote** to loneliness that has worked for you. _____

_____

4. Name a **consequential** decision you've made in the last year. _____

_____

5. Name one time when you felt your own **mortality.** _____

_____

Language in Use

Select the best word to complete the meaning of each sentence.

adversely	antidote	cognitive	consequence	increment
longevity	mortality	peripherally	reciprocal	underappreciated

1. The Centers for Disease Control (CDC) reports that 1 in every 88 children has an autism spectrum disorder that _____ affects the child's ability to interact with others.

2. Children with autism have difficulty with the _____ nature of social interactions, and sometimes they are only _____ aware, or not at all aware, of expected social behaviors.

3. Over the last twenty years, there has been a significant _____ of children receiving this diagnosis, both in the United States and in other countries.

4. The CDC believes the increase in diagnosis is not due to an increase in autism, but rather that the less severe symptoms of autism have been _____ in the past.

5. In the 1990s, the criteria for receiving the diagnosis of autism were broadened (making it easier to get such a diagnosis). In March 2012, only about a third of children with the diagnosis had a _____ disability in addition to a social disability. Ten years ago, half did.

6. One _____ of autism is a higher _____ rate than in the general population.

Reading 9–2 | Nonfiction Book

▶ Pre-Reading the Selection

Social scientist Dan Ariely discusses how what we think with our rational minds is not always the way things really are in his book, *The Upside of Irrationality: The Unexpected Benefits of Defying Logic at Work and at Home.* The selection reprinted here focuses on the irrationality of online dating.

Surveying the Reading

Survey the following selection. Then check the elements that are included in this reading.

_____	Title	_____	Words in bold or italic type
_____	Headings	_____	Images and captions
_____	First sentences of paragraphs		

Guessing the Purpose

Judging from the title of the reading as well as the title of the book from which this selection is taken, what do you suppose the purpose for writing is? _____

Predicting the Content

Predict three things this selection will discuss.

▶ _____

▶ _____

▶ _____

Activating Your Knowledge

What do you already know about online dating sites, people who have used them, and what their experiences (or yours) were like? Note two or three things you know.

▶ _____

▶ _____

▶ _____

Scan to Connect! Use your smart phone to scan this code to watch a video to activate your knowledge about online dating. (See the inside front cover for more information on how to use this.) Have you ever done any online dating? Did you "fudge" any details about yourself? Do you think it is common for people to alter their reality when they date online? Discuss possible endings to this short video with your classmates.

▶ Reading with Pen in Hand

Students who annotate as they read are more successful than those who do not. That's why you will annotate every selection in *Connect* as you read. In the reading that follows, use the following symbols:

★ or (Point)   to indicate a main idea

① ② ③   to indicate major details

Visit www.cengagebrain.com to access the CourseMate for this chapter to hear pronunciations of vocabulary words from this reading.

Online Dating: A Market Failure

Dan Ariely

▶ What difficulties are Seth and other friends having?

advent Use your logic to decide what *advent* means.

delved into What does *curious* suggest about what he did next?

1   I was troubled by the difficulties of Seth and some other friends [who couldn't find partners] until the **advent** of online dating. I was very excited to hear about sites like Match.com, eHarmony, and JDate.com. "What a wonderful fix to the problem of the singles market," I thought. Curious about how the process worked, I **delved into** the world of online dating sites.

Studio 101/Alamy

2   How exactly do these sites work? Let's take a hypothetical lonely heart named Michelle. She signs up for a service by completing a questionnaire about herself and her preferences. Each service has its own version of these questions, but they all ask for basic **demographic** information (age, location, income, and so on) as well as some measure of Michelle's personal values, attitudes, and lifestyle. The questionnaire also asks Michelle for her preferences: What kind of relationship is she looking for? What does she want in a **prospective** mate? Michelle reveals her age and weight.* She states that she is an easygoing, fun vegetarian and that she's looking for a committed relationship with a tall, educated, rich vegetarian. She also writes a short, more personal description of herself. Finally, she uploads pictures of herself for others to see.

▸ Imagine what you would say about yourself.

demographic   Read the examples that follow for this meaning.

prospective   Use word parts and context clues to determine this definition.

3   Once Michelle has completed these steps, she is ready to go window-shopping for soul mates. From among the profiles the system suggests for her, Michelle chooses a few men for more detailed investigation. She reads their profiles, checks out their photos, and, if she's interested, emails them through the service. If the interest is mutual, the two of them correspond for a bit. If all goes well, they arrange a real-life meeting. (The commonly used term "online dating" is, of course, misleading. Yes, people sort through profiles online and correspond with each other via email, but all the real dating happens in the real, offline world.)

▸ Think about what qualities would attract you.

4   Once I learned what the real process of online dating involves, my enthusiasm for this potentially valuable market turned into disappointment. As much as the singles' market needed mending, it seemed to me that the way online dating markets approached the problem did not promise a good solution to the singles problem. How could all the multiple-choice questions, checklists, and criteria accurately represent their human subjects? After all, we are more than the sum of our parts (with a few exceptions, of course). We are more than height, weight, religion, and income. Others judge us on the basis of general subjective and **aesthetic** attributes, such as our manner of speaking and our sense of humor. We are also a scent, a sparkle of the eye, a sweep of the hand, the sound of a laugh, and the knit of a brow—**ineffable** qualities that can't easily be captured in a database.

▸ Can checklists reveal who you are?

aesthetic   Based on the examples that follow, what does *aesthetic* mean?

ineffable   Use the contrast clue and the examples to decide what *ineffable* means.

5   The fundamental problem is that online dating sites treat their users as searchable goods, as though they were digital cameras that can be fully described by a few attributes such as megapixels, lens aperture, and memory size. But in reality, if prospective romantic partners could possibly be considered as "products," they would be closer to what economists call "experience goods." Like dining experiences, perfumes, and art, people can't be **anatomized** easily and effectively in the way that these dating Web sites imply. Basically, trying to understand what happens in dating without taking into account

▸ If you are an "experience good," what kind of experience are you?

anatomized   Consider the examples, as well as what scientists who study anatomy do.

*Michelle will likely shave off a few years and pounds, of course. People often tend to fudge their numbers in online dating—virtual men are taller and richer, while virtual women are thinner and younger than their real-life counterparts.

the **nuances** of attraction and romance is like trying to understand American football by analyzing the *x*'s, *o*'s, and arrows in a playbook or trying to understand how a cookie will taste by reading its nutrition label.

6   So why do online dating sites demand that people describe themselves and their ideal partners according to **quantifiable** attributes? I suspect that they pick this modus operandi because it's relatively easy to translate words like "Protestant," "liberal," "5 feet, 8 inches tall," "135 lbs.," "fit," and "professional" into a searchable database. But could it be that, in their desire to make the system compatible with what computers can do well, online dating sites force our often nebulous conception of an ideal partner to conform to a set of simple parameters—and in the process make the whole system less useful?

7   To answer these questions, Jeana Frost (a former Ph.D. student in the MIT Media Lab and currently a social entrepreneur), Zoë Chance (a Ph.D. student at Harvard), Mike Norton, and I set up our first online dating study. We placed a banner ad on an online dating site that said "Click Here to Participate in an MIT Study on Dating." We soon had lots of participants telling us about their dating experiences. They answered questions about how many hours they spent searching profiles of prospective dates (again, using searchable qualities such as height and income); how much time they spent in email conversations with those who seemed like a good fit; and how many face-to-face (offline) meetings they ending up having.

8   We found that people spent an average of 5.2 hours per week searching profiles and 6.7 hours per week emailing potential partners, for a total of nearly 12 hours a week in the screening stage alone. What was the payoff for all this activity, you ask? Our survey participants spent a mere 1.8 hours a week actually meeting any prospective partners in the real world, and most of this led to nothing more than a single, semi-frustrating meeting for coffee.

9   Talk about market failures. A ratio worse than 6:1 speaks for itself. Imagine driving six hours in order to spend one hour at the beach with a friend (or, even worse, with someone you don't really know and are not sure you will like). Given these odds, it seems hard to explain why anyone in their right mind would intentionally spend time on online dating.

10   Of course, you might argue that the online portion of dating is in itself enjoyable—perhaps like window-shopping—so we decided to ask about that, too. We asked online daters to compare their experiences online dating, offline dating, and forgetting about the first two and watching a movie at home instead. Participants rated offline dating as more exciting than online dating. And guess where they ranked the movie? You guessed it—they were so **disenchanted** with the online dating experience that they said they'd rather curl up on the couch watching, say, *You've Got Mail*.

11   So it appeared from our initial look that so-called online dating is not as fun as one might guess. In fact, online dating is a **misnomer**. If you called the activity something more accurate, such as "online searching and blurb writing," it might be a better description of the experience.

—Excerpt from pp. 217–219 from *The Upside of Irrationality* by Dan Ariely. Copyright © 2010 by Dan Ariely. Reprinted by permission of HarperCollins Publishers.

▶ Comprehension Questions

Write the letter of the answer on the line. Then explain your thinking.

Main Idea

_____ 1. Which of the following best states the main idea of this passage?

   a. Like dining experiences, perfumes, and art, people can't be anatomized easily and effectively in the way that these dating Web sites imply.

   b. So why do online dating sites demand that people describe themselves and their ideal partners according to quantifiable attributes?

   c. As much as the singles' market needed mending, it seemed to me that the way online dating markets approached the problem did not promise a good solution to the singles problem.

   d. So it appeared from our initial look that so-called online dating is not as fun as one might guess.

Why? What information in the selection leads you to give that answer? _____

_____

_____

_____

_____ 2. Which of the following is the main idea of paragraph 4?

   a. Once I learned what the real process of online dating involves, my enthusiasm for this potentially valuable market turned into disappointment.

   b. As much as the singles' market needed mending, it seemed to me that the way online dating markets approached the problem did not promise a good solution to the singles problem.

   c. After all, we are more than the sum of our parts (with a few exceptions, of course).

   d. Others judge us on the basis of general subjective and aesthetic attributes, such as our manner of speaking and our sense of humor.

Why? What information in the selection leads you to give that answer? _____

_____

_____

Supporting Details

_____ 3. Which of the following sentences from paragraph 3 is a minor supporting detail?

   a. Once Michelle has completed these steps, she is ready to go window-shopping for soul mates.

   b. From among the profiles the system suggests for her, Michelle chooses a few men for more detailed investigation.

c. If the interest is mutual, the two of them correspond for a bit.

d. (The commonly used term "online dating" is, of course, misleading. Yes, people sort through profiles online and correspond with each other via email, but all the real dating happens in the real, offline world.)

Why? What information in the selection leads you to give that answer? _____

_____

_____

___ 4. Which paragraphs include details about how the kinds of information dating sites collect are not sufficient to decide who might make a good mate?

a. 4, 5

b. 7, 8, 9

c. 10

d. 11

Why? What information in the selection leads you to give that answer? _____

_____

_____

_____

Author's Purpose

___ 5. What is the general purpose of the passage?

a. to express interesting anecdotes concerning online dating experiences

b. to persuade readers that online dating is not a good antidote to being single

c. to persuade readers that if they follow proven strategies, online dating can work for them

d. to inform readers of the benefits of online dating

Why? What information in the selection leads you to give that answer? _____

_____

_____

_____

___ 6. Why does the author give the movie *You've Got Mail* as the example at the end of paragraph 10?

a. The movie is from 1998.

b. The movie stars Meg Ryan and Tom Hanks.

c. The movie was nominated for the Golden Globe award.

d. The movie is a romantic comedy that involves email.

Why? What information in the selection leads you to give that answer? _____

_____

_____

Relationships

____ 7. What is the pattern of organization in paragraphs 2 and 3?

    a. process

    b. cause-and-effect

    c. time order

    d. definition

Why? What information in the selection leads you to give that answer? _____

_____

_____

____ 8. What is the relationship between the first two sentences of paragraph 5?

    a. cause-and-effect

    b. classification

    c. process

    d. contrast

Why? What information in the selection leads you to give that answer? _____

_____

Fact, Opinion, and Inference

____ 9. Which of the following statements is a fact?

    a. Let's take a hypothetical lonely heart named Michelle.

    b. The way the online dating markets approached the problem did not promise a good solution to the singles problem.

    c. We found that people spent an average of 5.2 hours per week searching profiles.

    d. Given these odds, it seems hard to explain why anyone in their right mind would intentionally spend time on online dating.

Why? What leads you to give that answer? _____

_____

_____

____ 10. Which of the following statements would the author be likely to agree with?

    a. Time is an investment.

    b. "There is no remedy for love but to love more."—Henry David Thoreau

c. You should judge a book by its cover.

d. Knowledge creates problems.

Why? What information in the selection leads you to give that answer? _____

_____

_____

_____

▶ Critical Thinking Questions

Critical Thinking Level 1 ▷ **Remember**

Identify four kinds of demographic data that online dating sites typically request.

1. _____

2. _____

3. _____

4. _____

Critical Thinking Level 2 ▷ **Understand**

Describe the online dating process by drawing a diagram.

Critical Thinking Level 3 ▷ **Apply**

Illustrate what the author says in paragraph 5: "dining experiences, perfumes, and art…can't be anatomized easily and effectively." Select one of the three items mentioned, and list every single element you can think of that makes up that experience. Try to capture the subtle elements as well as the obvious ones.

▶ _____ ▶ _____ ▶ _____

▶ _____ ▶ _____ ▶ _____

▸ _____   ▸ _____   ▸ _____
▸ _____   ▸ _____   ▸ _____
▸ _____   ▸ _____   ▸ _____
▸ _____   ▸ _____   ▸ _____
▸ _____   ▸ _____   ▸ _____
▸ _____   ▸ _____   ▸ _____

Critical Thinking Level 4 ▸ Analyze

Think of a person you used to date, are dating now, or have as a partner. What important attributes does this person have that first attracted you to him or her? List them on a sheet of paper. Now consider what attributes came to be most important as you got to know the person better. List these separately. *Analyze* how much overlap there is in the two lists. Explain why the two lists are not exactly the same.

Critical Thinking Level 5 ▸ Evaluate

Use percentages to *evaluate* how you assess a potential partner. Assign each important group of qualities a number of percentage points that equal 100%. Here is an example:

25%—demographic information, with special attention to location and age (has to live in the Southeast; has to be between 30 and 40).

55%—the person's identity as an individual: what he thinks of the world and himself; whether he loves his work and his place; whether he is happy; whether he is a free spirit.

20%—the person's attractiveness to me, physically; do I go weak at the knees when I'm around him?

Critical Thinking Level 6 ▸ Create

Create five questions that you think ought to be part of any online dating profile. _____

▸ _____

▸ _____

▸ _____

▸ _____

▸ _____

▶ Vocabulary in New Contexts

Review the vocabulary words in the margins of the reading selection and then complete the following activities.

EASY Note Cards

Make a note card for each of the vocabulary words that you did not know from the reading. On one side, write the word. On the other side, divide the card into quarters and label them E, A, S, and Y. Add a word or phrase in each area so that you wind up with an example sentence, an antonym, a synonym, and, finally, a definition that shows you have figured out the meaning of the word with your logic. Remember that an antonym or synonym may have appeared in the reading.

Relationships Between Words

Circle *yes* or *no* to answer the question. Then explain your answer.

1. Might **prospective** employers **delve** into job seekers' backgrounds?

   Yes   No

   Why or why not? _____

2. Did the **advent** of cell phone use create new **aesthetic** requirements for phones?

   Yes   No

   Why or why not? _____

   _____

3. Do **nuances** in your emotions sometimes seem **ineffable**?

   Yes   No

   Why or why not? _____

Language in Your Life

Write short answers to each question. Look at the vocabulary words closely before you answer.

1. Name one word that you believe is a **misnomer**. _____

   _____

2. Note one **demographic** fact about your family. _____

   _____

3. Name one time you believed in something but later became **disenchanted**. _____

   _____

4. Name one problem you have that might benefit from being **anatomized**. _____

_____

5. Name one area of life you would like to **delve** into. _____

_____

Language in Use

Select the best word to complete the meaning of each sentence.

advent	aesthetic	anatomize	delved into	demographic
disenchanted	ineffable	misnomer	nuance	prospective

1. Although the _____ of peer pressure is lost in the mists of time, writer Tina Rosenberg
   has _____ the topic as it relates to positive social change today.

2. In her 2011 book, *Join the Club: How Peer Pressure Can Transform the World*, Rosenberg
   _____ the practices of groups of people around the world who have used the positive
   desire of people to belong in order to create social progress.

3. For example, one chapter is about how teenagers, a _____ very susceptible to peer
   pressure, created in Florida the most successful anti-smoking program in the country by having a
   Students Working Against Tobacco party with teens all over the state in an anti-tobacco industry
   campaign.

4. The negative _____ considerations of smoking, such as yellowed teeth and fingers,
   had not influenced Florida teens, but when they realized how they were being manipulated by
   tobacco companies, they were more than _____. They were enraged.

5. It would be a _____ to say that the teens created an anti-smoking campaign. They
   formed an anti-smoking *industry* campaign.

6. SWAT had a "truth train" that they rode from city to city, picking up _____ peer
   networkers, training them in workshops, and holding a concert at every stop.

7. Every "truth" ad that was produced either directly reinforced the "your peers are doing it"
   message or alluded to that message in a more _____ way.

 Click to Connect! For more practice applying the skills you learned in this chapter, visit **www.cengagebrain.com** to access the CourseMate for this chapter.

Guy Erwood/Shutterstock.com

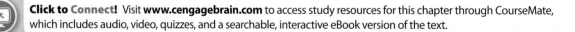

Click to Connect! Visit **www.cengagebrain.com** to access study resources for this chapter through CourseMate, which includes audio, video, quizzes, and a searchable, interactive eBook version of the text.

10 Analyzing the Author's Tone

> *One could always point to a time, a choice, an act that set the tone for a life and changed a personal destiny.*
>
> —CAROL O'CONNELL

Connect with Ideas

Do you agree with Carol O'Connell? Can a single choice set the tone for a life?

Activate Your Knowledge

Discuss a time when you misunderstood a friend's or family member's tone of voice and it caused a problem.

Engage with the Chapter

Take a minute to skim Table 10.1, "Tone Supports Purpose" on page 502 and "Words to Describe an Author's Tone" on pages 511–512. How do you think the author's purpose affects the tone?

Read and Talk

Online Newspaper Article

Read this brief article about a new child care solution for two-career couples.

Visit www.cengagebrain.com to access the CourseMate for this chapter to hear vocabulary words from this reading and an audio recording of it.

The Next Frontier of Outsourcing

The Onion Web Site

1   Increasingly, American parents are spending more time at work and less time at home. With the cost of nannies on the rise, many are turning to a new solution to their child care dilemma.

2   Susan and Mark Andelman of Portland, Oregon, started sending their son Timothy to a daycare facility in India four months ago. "It used to be quite a hassle in the morning," says Mark. "Yes, now sometimes I'm able to get him right into the box without waking him up," agrees Susan. "So it's a lot easier." Outsourcing Timothy works so well, they decided to send their three-week-old daughter Britney to infant care in Sri Lanka.

3   Though the wages earned by overseas child care workers would seem low to Americans, in countries like India they are over a billion times the average salary. As Kendra Trilson notes, "It's only twelve cents an hour in India, which is a lot cheaper than the $300 I was paying a week here in the United States."

4   "It's a big improvement," say the Andelmans, sitting on their couch and nodding their heads in unison. "Before, he was acting out, a lot of yelling and screaming," says Susan as she puts Timothy into a cardboard box and covers him with plastic peanuts. "Now, when we uncrate him, he's completely quiet." Mark nods: "Yeah, for like two or three days."

—Reprinted with permission of THE ONION. Copyright © 2012, by ONION, INC. www.theonion.com

Talking about Reading

1. What word would you use to describe the tone of this text? _____

_____

2. List four specific bits of text that let you know that the tone of the piece was not serious.

   ▶ _____

   ▶ _____

   ▶ _____

   ▶ _____

3. Were you surprised when you read these bits of text? Why? _____
   _____
   _____

4. Is surprise a necessary part of humor, do you think? Why or why not? _____
   _____
   _____

5. 🎬 **Scan to Connect!** Use your smart phone to scan this code to watch
   a video. (See the inside front cover for more information on how to use
   this.) What additional information does the video provide that the
   reading couldn't? Based on the differences between video and reading,
   which do you think is more funny? Why?

What Is Tone?

You are probably familiar with the term "tone of voice." Even if you are not, you still know how it works. You can tell if someone is mad or sad or happy or serious or playful just by how his or her voice sounds. We also "read" body language such as facial expressions to determine the tone of a speaker. We become good at this at a very young age. We all know when a parent calls our name whether or not we are in trouble!

In written language, tone has the same meaning. The difference is, of course, that you are reading words, not listening to and observing a person. So instead of the quality of the speaker's voice and the meaning of his or her body language, you have to use certain qualities of the text to figure out the tone.

Why does tone matter? If you can understand the tone, you can realize much more clearly what the author is trying to accomplish and how you will choose to respond. Let's say for a moment that you were fooled into believing that parents actually are packing their children into cardboard boxes each day to ship them off to day care in another country. You might have gotten upset, written a letter to the editor, or even started a campaign to make the practice illegal. Or you might have done nothing, but felt really bad. But if you realized that the piece was supposed to be funny, you could just make faces and laugh about it in a horrified kind of way. Your reaction would be totally different.

You have already studied some of the aspects of tone in previous chapters. First, tone is influenced by an author's purpose. Second, the author often hints at the tone by using words that have certain denotations and connotations. Two other aspects of tone that you haven't yet studied are the author's point of view and any figures of speech that an author uses. Figuring out the tone is somewhat complicated, but it's worth the effort since you can't really evaluate what an author is saying unless you can grasp whether the piece is playful or serious, arrogant or humble, optimistic or cynical.

The Author's Purpose

Throughout this book you have been identifying the author's general purpose in various reading selections. The purpose might be to entertain readers, to inform readers, or to persuade readers. The author's tone of voice supports the purpose. (See **Table 10.1**.)

Table 10.1 Tone Supports Purpose

General Purpose	General Tone
to inform (teach) readers	objective, focusing on facts and not on the author's feelings about the facts, matter-of-fact, impersonal
to entertain readers or to express the feelings or thoughts of the writer	subjective, emotional (sad, happy, funny, exciting, and every other possible emotion), personal
to persuade readers to believe or do something	subjective, often personal

Remember that looking at the language of the topic sentence (or thesis statement of longer selections) can help you figure out the author's purpose, as can examining the kinds of details used to support it. If you see the word *should* in the topic sentence, you can decide whether the author is trying to persuade readers. If you see that the details list different types of diseases, the purpose is probably informative. Always use what you know to help you figure out what you need to know.

Here are some examples of the connection between purpose and tone.

Informative purpose and objective tone

A company that makes surfboards recently started a wellness program in which employees must participate.

This sentence merely tells readers that something happened. It doesn't give the writer's thoughts or feelings about the wellness program. It just reports the facts. So it has an objective tone.

Entertainment/expressive purpose and subjective tone

CrossFit is fun, addictive, but hard. Here's how I know my CrossFit workout was a success: I didn't quit, and I didn't die!

bikeriderlondon/Shutterstock.com

The writer is expressing personal feelings about his or her own experience. The tone is subjective.

> ### Persuasive purpose and subjective tone
>
> All employees should achieve their ideal weight, stop smoking, and exercise every day.

This sentence tells readers what the writer thinks the employees should do. Others might not agree. The tone is subjective.

Interaction 10–1 ▸ **Determine an Author's Purpose and Tone**

Determine the purpose and tone of the following passages. Circle or underline any words that help you make your decision.

1.

> The word **statistics** is actually used to mean two different things. The better-known definition is that statistics are numbers measured for some purpose. A more appropriate, complete definition is the following:
>
> *Statistics is a collection of procedures and principles for gaining and analyzing information in order to help people make decisions when faced with uncertainty.*
>
> Using this definition, you have undoubtedly used statistics in your own life. For example, if you were faced with a choice of routes to get to school or work, or to get between one classroom building and the next, how would you decide which one to take? You would probably try each of them a number of times (thus gaining information) and then choose the best one according to some criterion important to you, such as speed, fewer red lights, more interesting scenery, and so on. You might even use different criteria on different days—such as when the weather is pleasant versus when it is not. In any case, by sampling the various routes and comparing them, you would have gained and analyzed useful information to help you make a decision.
>
> —From Utts, *Seeing Through Statistics*, 3e

A. What is the purpose of this paragraph? _____

B. Circle the tone words that you think best describe the tone of the passage.

objective	or	subjective
factual	or	emotional
impersonal	or	personal

2.

> Two statistics professors were flying from Topeka, Kansas, to a conference in Miami, Florida. One hour into the flight, the pilot announced that they had lost one engine, but to not worry since the plane

had two more engines. The only issue was that the flight would take 2 extra hours. A little bit later, the pilot informed the passengers that a second engine had failed, but again, to not worry because they still had one engine. The only concern was that the flight time had been increased from 6 hours to 10 hours. At this point, one statistician turned to his companion and said, "Man, I hope the last engine doesn't fail, or we will be up here forever!"

A. What is the purpose of this paragraph? _____

B. How do you know? _____

_____

3.

When you hear the word *statistics*, you probably either get an attack of math anxiety or think about lifeless numbers, such as the population of the city or town where you live, as measured by the latest census, or the per capita income in Japan. The goal of this book is to open a whole new world of understanding to the term *statistics*. By the time you finish reading this book, you will realize that the invention of statistical methods is one of the most important developments of modern times. These methods influence everything from life-saving medical advances to which television shows remain on the air.

—From Utts, *Seeing Through Statistics*, 3e

A. What is the purpose of this paragraph? _____

B. Circle the tone words that you think best describe the tone of the passage.

objective	or	subjective
factual	or	emotional
impersonal	or	personal

The Author's Point of View

Do you have any friends who are always talking about themselves—*I did this, I think that, I want, I, I, I?* Their focus on themselves may be funny or irritating, but in any case, they like to express themselves. How about friends who are always talking about you—*What did you do then? Why are you acting that way? What are you doing tonight?* You may be glad they care or wish they would go away, but you can tell that they are interested in you. What about friends who like to talk about other people (that's all of us, right?)—*Fabio and Jill are going out on Friday. Zoe is going to be a starter on the soccer team. Mr. Broderbund gave their section a five-page paper that's due on Friday.* Most of us are interested in what other people are doing and saying and what is happening in the world around us.

Point of view in an article, book, or other reading material is the same—it's how the author positions himself or herself in relation to the readers and the topic.

▶ **When an author uses the pronoun *I* or *we* as the point of view, we call it first-person point of view.**

> When I was fifteen years old, my mother died of alcoholism.

By sharing her personal experience with readers, the author makes the tone personal. First person often sounds informal. However, depending on the context, first person can also be formal.

> I asked the accused if he had ever owned a gun.

This sentence sounds formal because of the context, or circumstances, in which it is used. There is only one circumstance in which a person is called "the accused." This is when he or she has been accused of a crime but has not yet been convicted of it. This legal context has a lot of rules that must be followed, and thus it is a formal context.

▶ **When a writer directly addresses the readers as *you*, we call the point of view second person.**

> As soon as the body senses cold, it constricts the thin web of capillaries in your extremities, first your fingers and toes, then farther up your arms and legs.
>
> —From Moalem/Prince, *Survival of the Sickest*

The second-person point of view sets up a text as a conversation between the author and the reader, and so it may feel somewhat personal. This point of view is often used when giving directions about how to do something. Second person sounds informal.

▶ **When an author refers to the topic using the pronouns *he, she, it,* and *they* as the point of view, we call it third-person point of view.** Even if the words *he, she, it,* and *they* aren't present, you'll find nouns (people, places, things, ideas) that could be replaced with *he, she, it,* and *they.* For example, *the house* could be replaced by the pronoun *it, Ms. Macgiver* by the pronoun *she,* and *freedom* by the pronoun *it.*

> Scientists used to believe that "junk DNA" served no purpose, but now many of them think it may play a role in evolution.
>
> —From Moalem/Prince, *Survival of the Sickest*

The third-person point of view tends to make the tone impersonal. The writer acts as a reporter who keeps personal experience out of the writing. Also, it often sounds formal.

Now, many times all of these different pronouns—*I, he, she, it, you,* and *they*—will be in one article or book. You will need to decide which one is most important overall. One clue may be how you feel after you read the piece. Do you feel you understand the writer at a personal level? This feeling may be the result of first-person point of view. Do you feel as if the author is talking directly to you? It might be because of second-person point of view. Do you think you understand a situation better, even if neither the author nor you is involved in it? That might be because the writer used third person.

But you should check the text after you consider your feelings and thoughts and make sure you are right. Sometimes you may need to take into account other aspects of the text, such as the purpose or the particular words the author chose, to decide on the point of view.

Interaction 10–2 ▶ **Identify the Author's Point of View and Tone**

Underline all the pronouns. If there aren't any, decide which pronouns would replace the nouns (people, places, things, ideas) you do find. Decide whether each item is written in first-, second-, or third-person point of view. Then characterize each item as formal or informal, personal or impersonal. Circle your choices after each item.

1.

The psychologist Alice Isen and her colleagues have shown that being happy broadens the thought processes and facilitates creative thinking. Isen discovered that when people were asked to solve difficult problems, ones that required unusual "out of the box" thinking, they did much better when they had just been given a small gift—not much of a gift, but enough to make them feel good.

—From Norman, *Emotional Design*

first person	or	second person	or	third person
personal	or	impersonal		
informal	or	formal		

2.

Dad once told me he withheld his support so I would learn to fend for myself. He wanted me to make it on my own, to become strong. And I did.... I became, as my father hoped, strong. But I also became hard, never easy to befriend or to date; never able to accept anything from anyone—not dinner, not a movie, not a gift, not even a compliment.

—From Trussoni, *Falling Through the Earth*

first person   or   second person   or   third person
personal   or   impersonal
informal   or   formal

3.

> Food availability has increased dramatically over the past four decades. The average person in the developing world has experienced a 40 percent increase in available calories. Likewise, the proportion of malnourished has dropped from 50 percent to less than 17 percent.
>
> —From Lomborg, *Cool It*

first person   or   second person   or   third person
personal   or   impersonal
informal   or   formal

4.

> Lots of people want to ride with you in the limo, but what you want is someone who will take the bus with you when the limo breaks down.
>
> —Oprah quoted without attribution in Price, *The Best Advice Ever Given*

first person   or   second person   or   third person
personal   or   impersonal
informal   or   formal

Interaction 10–3 ▶ Distinguish Point of View from Tone

Read the two passages and answer the questions that follow. Both people are writing about the Toyota Prius. Both write subjectively, so for the questions about tone, give a more specific word that describes the writer's emotion.

PR NEWSWIRE/AP Photo

1.

> The gas mileage is not what I thought it would be. The stickers say 51 mpg on the highway and 60 in town. I assumed I would average somewhere in the middle. But in fact, I average 44 mpg. This is not bad, but not what I paid for!
>
> —http://www.epinions.com/2007_Toyota_Prius/sec_~opinion_list/display_~reviews/sort_~date/sort_dir_~des/pp_~1/pa_~1#list (accessed 7/28/07)

A. What is the author's purpose? _____

B. What is the author's point of view? _____

C. What is the tone of this passage? _____

2.

> I love the car. My commute is 40 miles each direction, a mixture of surface streets and southern California freeway, through the hills of Ventura County (including up and down the steep Conejo Grade on the 101 Freeway). Average mileage over the past year and a half when I drive like I usually do…75–80 mph (when traffic allows)…is 47 mpg. If I behave and set the cruise control on the freeway to 65 mph, my mileage averages from 52 to 54 mpg.
>
> —http://www.epinions.com/content_350201286276

A. What is the author's purpose? _____

B. What is the author's point of view? _____

C. What is the tone of this passage? _____

Positive, Neutral, and Negative Tones

If you heard someone described as *bizarre*, what kinds of actions or characteristics would you picture? What if they were called *exotic*—does that word bring the same characteristics or different ones to mind? How about just plain old *strange*? *Weird*? How about *grotesque*? (If you don't know the meanings of these words, look them up in a dictionary.)

In Chapter 3, you learned that some words have positive connotations (emotional tones), some words have negative connotations, and some words are neutral. Neutral words have no connotative tone, only the denotative, "dictionary," meaning. The following words all have connotations. They each indicate something strange. However, the attraction a person might feel toward the thing being described decreases from left to right.

(Most attractive)   exotic   bizarre   grotesque   (Least attractive)

More denotative, neutral words that describe the same basic idea as these three words are *strange* and *unusual*.

Understanding the connotations of words helps you describe the author's tone. If you read, "The *exotic* animals must have come from a place very different from here," you might consider the author fascinated by their strangeness. If, however, you read, "The *grotesque* animals must have come from a place very different from here," suddenly the author seems to be saying that there is some-thing wrong with those animals and that place. There is a tone of disgust or extreme dislike.

When an author uses words that mostly do not have connotations at all, you might say the tone is unbiased, objective, or even-handed. Since connotations suggest the author's emotional stance, the lack of such words suggests an attempt to be objective rather than subjective.

Interaction 10–4 › Identify Tone Through Connotation and Denotation

Underline words that have connotations, and on the line write a neutral word that has the same denotation. Use a dictionary as needed. Then circle the word that best describes the author's tone. Hint: One sentence might elicit more than one possible response.

1. He blathered on for hours and hours.

    Neutral word: _____   Author's tone: patient   or   impatient

2. My spirit soared as the horse galloped faster and faster.

    Neutral word: _____   Author's tone: happy   or   depressed

3. The politician's glib explanation infuriated me.

    Two neutral words: _____   Author's tone: joyful   or   angry

4. You weasel!

    Neutral word: _____   Author's tone: affectionate   or   cold

5. They flaunt their wealth.

    Neutral word: _____   Author's tone: approving   or   disapproving

---

Interaction 10–5 › Find the Tone of a Longer Passage

Determine the tone of the following passages.

1.

School Regulations, Japanese Style

▶ Boys' hair should not touch the eyebrows, the ears, or the top of the collar.
▶ No one should have a permanent wave, or dye his or her hair. Girls should not wear ribbons or accessories in their hair. Hair dryers should not be used.
▶ School uniform skirts should be ___ centimeters above the ground, no more and no less (differs by school and region).

▸ Keep your uniform clean and pressed at all times. Girls' middy blouses should have two buttons on the back collar. Boys' pant cuffs should be of the prescribed width. No more than 12 eyelets should be on shoes. The number of buttons on a shirt and tucks in a shirt are also prescribed.

▸ Wear your school badge at all times. It should be positioned exactly.

▸ Going to school in the morning, wear your book bag strap on the right shoulder; in the afternoon on the way home, wear it on the left shoulder. Your book case thickness, filled and unfilled, is also prescribed.

▸ Girls should wear only regulation white underpants of 100% cotton.

▸ When you raise your hand to be called on, your arm should extend forward and up at the angle prescribed in your handbook.

▸ Your own route to and from school is marked in your student rule handbook; carefully observe which side of each street you are to use on the way to and from school.

▸ After school you are to go directly home, unless your parent has written a note permitting you to go to another location. Permission will not be granted by the school unless this other location is a suitable one. You must not go to coffee shops. You must be home by __ o'clock.

▸ It is not permitted to drive or ride a motorcycle, or to have a license to drive one.

▸ Before and after school, no matter where you are, you represent our school, so you should behave in ways we can all be proud of.

—From Duiker, *World History*, 5e

A. What is the author's purpose? _____

B. What is the author's point of view? _____

C. Are the words used mostly denotative (and thus neutral) or connotative (emotional)?

_____

D. What is the tone of this passage? _____

2.

India's decision to allow Pepsi Foods Ltd. to open 60 restaurants in India—30 each of Pizza Hut and Kentucky Fried Chicken—marks the first entry of multinational, meat-based junk-food chains into India. If this is allowed to happen, at least a dozen other similar chains will very quickly arrive, including the infamous McDonald's.

The implications of allowing junk-food chains into India are quite stark. As the name denotes, the foods served at Kentucky Fried Chicken (KFC) are chicken-based and fried. This is the worst combination possible for the body and can create a host of health problems, including obesity, high cholesterol, heart ailments, and many kinds of cancer. Pizza Hut products are a combination of white flour, cheese, and meat—again, a combination likely to cause disease....

Then there is the issue of the environmental impact of junk-food chains. Modern meat production involves misuse of crops, water, energy, and grazing areas. In addition, animal agriculture produces surprisingly large amounts of air and water pollution.

KFC and Pizza Hut insist that their chickens be fed corn and soybeans. Consider the diversion of grain for this purpose. As the outlets of KFC and Pizza Hut increase in number, the poultry industry will buy up more and more corn to feed the chickens, which means that the corn will quickly disappear from the villages, and its increased price will place it out of reach for the common man. Turning corn into junk chicken is like turning gold into mud....

It is already shameful that, in a country plagued by famine and flood, we divert 37 percent of our arable land to growing animal fodder. Were all of that grain to be consumed directly by humans, it would nourish five times as many people as it does after being converted into meat, milk, and eggs....

Of course, it is not just the KFC and Pizza Hut chains of Pepsi Foods Ltd. that will cause all of this damage. Once we open India up by allowing these chains, dozens more will be eagerly waiting to come in. Each city in America has an average of 5,000 junk-food restaurants. Is that what we want for India?

—Gandhi, "Say No To McDonald's and KFC!"

A. What is the author's purpose? _____

B. What is the author's point of view? _____

C. Are the words used mostly denotative (and thus neutral) or connotative (emotional)? _____

_____

D. What is the tone of this passage? _____

More Specific Tone Words

It is helpful to become familiar with a range of words you can use to describe an author's tone. If you want to be able to talk in class about an author's ideas, or write about them for a college assignment, you will probably need to use words like those in the following list to describe the author's tone. Here are some possibilities.

Words to Describe an Author's Tone

alarmed	apathetic	cruel	evasive
ambitious	appalled	cynical	fearful
ambivalent	arrogant	direct	flippant
amused	bitter	disapproving	frustrated
angry	bored	elated	humorous
annoyed	celebratory	excited	hyperbolic

indignant	optimistic	righteous	thoughtful
ironic	outraged	sarcastic	urgent
irreverent	outspoken	sensational	wry
loving	pessimistic	serious	
mocking	respectful	sincere	
nostalgic	reticent	skeptical	

Interaction 10–6 ▶ Use Specific Tone Words

Circle the best tone word for each item. Use a dictionary as needed.

1.

> "I remember when my father used to get home from work," sighed Lori Price. "We would all run outside to meet him on the side porch. Today, my own children barely look up from their computers when Bruce or I walk in."

       evasive   loving   nostalgic

2.

> Sure, you'll help me. Right over the edge of a cliff, you'll help me.

       cynical   desperate   mocking

3.

> "Yes, sir, General Motors, you want to close these factories and move them to Mexico? No problem! How can we help you? You say you don't want to pay your corporate taxes? No problem! You don't have to pay *any*! So you want five of us workers to do the exact same job it used to take ten workers to do? Happy to oblige! No, we don't mind working seven days a week! Why give jobs to the unemployed when we can just work longer ourselves? We don't need to see our kids!"
>
> —Moore, *Downsize This!*

       cruel   reticent   sarcastic

4.

> "I'd much rather be a woman than a man. Women can cry, they can wear cute clothes, and they are the first to be rescued off of sinking ships."
>
> —Gilda Radner

       humorous   outspoken   sincere

5.

> "Any fine morning, a power saw can fell a tree that took a thousand years to grow."
>
> —Edwin Way Teale

skeptical   serious   respectful

Interaction 10–7 ▸ Identify Tone in a Longer Passage

Read the passage, and answer the questions that follow.

Cancer

Celine knows that she inherited her mother's brown eyes and buoyant sense of humor. She wonders whether she's also inherited "the bad gene"—the cancer-causing one that killed her grandmother and her great-grandmother. Celine's mother was 42 years old when she learned that she, too, had cancer. She died two years later, leaving behind eight sisters. Within the next decade, six had developed breast or ovarian cancer.

Unlike most college students, Celine never thinks of cancer as something that affects only people much older than she. Three of her five sisters have tested positive for what is called "the breast cancer gene." Celine is struggling to decide whether she too will undergo testing.

An estimated 10 percent of cancers are hereditary, but no one is immune from the threat of cancer or other serious diseases.

Cancer has overtaken heart disease as the number-one killer of Americans under age 85. Yet many of the almost 500,000 deaths caused by cancer each year could be prevented. A third of cancers are related to smoking; another third, to obesity, poor diet, and lack of exercise.

—From Hales, *An Invitation to Health*, 12e

A. What is the author's purpose? _____

B. What is the author's point of view? _____

C. Are the words used denotative (dictionary) or connotative (emotional connection)? _____

_____

D. What is the tone of this passage? _____

_____

Figurative Versus Literal Language

▶ "It's raining cats and dogs." This statement is a figure of speech (more specifically, it is hyperbole—an intentional exaggeration).

▶ "It's raining." This statement is literal.

Figurative language is like connotation: it reveals the author's emotions about whatever he or she is describing. Extreme uses of figurative language are sometimes called "flowery language" or "purple prose." Literal language is linked to denotation. Literal language often appears in the form of facts, and it has a matter-of-fact tone.

Sometimes a description could be figurative in one context and literal in another. For example, you could say that you "waited for hours." You could mean it literally—that is, that you *did* wait for hours (maybe you were stuck in an airport or rush hour traffic). Or you could use it figuratively to emphasize that you waited a long time, even though it wasn't actually hours. (Maybe you got impatient waiting for your date, who was twenty-five minutes late.)

Poets and novelists frequently use figurative language in their literature. We will discuss four common figures of speech—simile, metaphor, personification, and hyperbole—and share some poems that use them.

A Simile Is Like a Metaphor, but a Metaphor Is Not a Simile

Simile. An indirect comparison of two things using the words "like" or "as" (A is like B).

Metaphor. A direct comparison of two things **without** using the words "like" or "as" (A is B).

Here are some examples:

Simile:	The sun is *like* a big yellow ball bouncing from horizon to horizon.
Metaphor:	The sun *is* a big yellow ball bouncing from horizon to horizon.
Simile:	He is *like* a cat waiting to pounce on its prey.
Metaphor:	He *is* a cat waiting to pounce on its prey.

Read the following poem by Margaret Atwood. Before you begin, look at the title and predict what this poem will be about. Do you think the tone will be positive, negative, or neutral?

> **You Fit into Me**
>
> You fit into me
> like a hook into an eye
>
> a fish hook
> an open eye
>
> —"you fit into me," taken from *Power Politics* by Margaret Atwood copyright © 1971, 1996 published by House of Anansi. Reprinted by permission.

Were you surprised? The title seems to suggest that two people are perfect for each other. A "hook and eye" is a fastener for clothing, usually women's clothing. So the first hook and eye in the poem suggests "clasping together" by way of a simile. Then you get the shocker: a fish hook, an open eye! Ouch! This poem points out the power of similes to affect readers' emotions.

Personification

Personification is the act of giving an inanimate object (something that isn't alive or can't move) characteristics of an animate being (something that is alive or can move):

The *words* (inanimate) *leaped* (animate) from the page.

Think of cartoons. These are inanimate objects that are animated. Get it? Animation!

Impress your instructor and get out of trouble by using personification: "I'm sorry I couldn't finish my homework. My bed kept distracting me; it was screaming my name!" Or wiggle out of a sticky situation by explaining to your wife, husband, mom, dad, brother, sister, friend, or second cousin why you ate the last cookie: "Hey, I had no choice. The cookie pushed itself into my mouth with a force greater than my own resistance." Do you see what personification is? A bed does not literally "scream" names, but when you are tired, it sure is hard to resist lying down. Cookies do not have wills of their own. It is our own lack of willpower that gets us into trouble.

Look for examples of personification in this poem by Carl Sandburg:

Summer Grass

Summer grass aches and whispers
It wants something: it calls and sings; it pours
out wishes to the overhead stars.
The rain hears; the rain answers; the rain is slow
coming; the rain wets the face of the grass.

—"Summer Grass" from *Good Morning, America* by Carl Sandburg. Copyright © 1928 and renewed 1956 by Carl Sandburg. Reprinted by permission of Houghton Mifflin Harcourt Publishing Company.

This short poem personifies both the grass and the rain. The summer grass aches, whispers, wants, calls, sings, and pours out wishes—all actions of a living being. Sandburg uses the phrase "face of the grass," which also suggests a person or animal. And he says the rain hears, and answers, and is "slow coming."

Hyperbole

"If I've told you once, I've told you a thousand times!" If your parent or significant other ever hurled these words at you, their point was to make you realize you haven't been paying close enough attention to their wishes. Hyperbole is intentional exaggeration to make or emphasize a point. Hyperbole is meant to be taken figuratively, not literally.

Interaction 10–8 ▷ Create Hyperbole

Write two hyperboles in each category. Don't worry; they can be silly.

Family

_____

_____

Homework

_____

_____

Insects

_____

_____

Physical appearance

_____

_____

Emotions

_____

_____

Interaction 10–9 **Identify Figures of Speech**

Read the following poems. Underline any examples of metaphor, simile, personification, or hyperbole. In the margin, write which figure of speech you find. Then consider what effect they have on the author's tone.

> ### Oh, My Love Is Like a Red, Red Rose
>
> **Robert Burns**
>
> Oh, my love is like a red, red rose
> That's newly sprung in June;
> My love is like the melody
> That's sweetly played in tune.
>
> So fair art thou, my bonny lass,
> So deep in love am I;
> And I will love thee still, my dear,
> Till a' [all] the seas gang [go] dry.
>
> Till a' [all] the seas gang [go] dry, my dear
> And rocks melt wi' the sun;
> And I will love thee still, my dear,
> While the suns o' life shall run.
>
> And fare thee weel, my only love!
> And fare thee weel awhile!
> And I will come again my love
> Though it were ten thousand miles.
>
> (1796)

What words would you use to describe the poet's tone? _____

> ### My Father as a Guitar
>
> **Martin Espada**
>
> The cardiologist prescribed
> a new medication
> and lectured my father
> that he had to stop working.

And my father said: *I can't.*
The landlord won't let me.
The heart pills are dice in my father's hand,
gambler who needs cash
by the first of the month.

On the night his mother died
in far away Puerto Rico,
my father lurched upright in bed,
heart hammering
like the fist of a man at the door
with an eviction notice.
Minutes later,
the telephone sputtered
with news of the dead.

Sometimes I dream
my father is a guitar,
with a hole in his chest
where the music throbs
between my fingers.

—"My Father as a Guitar" from A MAYAN ASTRONOMER IN HELL'S KITCHEN by Martin Espada.
Copyright © 2000 by Martin Espada. Used by permission of the author and W.W. Norton & Company, Inc.

What words would you use to describe the poet's tone? _____

Harlem

Langston Hughes

What happens to a dream deferred?
Does it dry up
like a raisin in the sun?
Or fester like a sore—
And then run!
Does it stink like rotten meat?
Or crust and sugar over—
like a syrupy sweet?
Maybe it just sags
like a heavy load.
Or does it explode?

—"Harlem (2)" from *The Collected Poems of Langston Hughes* by Langston Hughes, edited by Arnold Rampersad with David Roessel,
Associate Editor. Copyright © 1994 by The Estate of Langston Hughes. Reprinted by permission of Alfred A. Knopf, a division of Random House, Inc.

What words would you use to describe the author's tone?_____

Understanding Irony

"Better slow down before the police start chasing us," your friend says as you sit in stalled traffic. "But I just love the feeling of the wind in my hair," you reply. These statements are ironic. *Irony* is the use of words or images to express the opposite of what is said. To understand irony, you need to understand what would be the expected response or action in a given situation.

For instance, if you were reading a review of a singer's new CD, for what qualities would you expect the CD to be praised?

> Pop superstar Madonna has once again wowed music critics and consumers alike with her latest offering, *Hard Candy*, an album that has garnered unanimous praise for the ease with which it can be exchanged for money.
>
> —"New Madonna Album Hailed as Available for Purchase," *The Onion*, May 20, 2008.
> Reprinted with permission of THE ONION. Copyright © 2012, by ONION, INC. www.theonion.com

You probably would not expect the CD to be praised for being for sale!

Interaction 10–10 ▶ **Identify Irony**

Identify the irony in the following passages.

1. A doctor was sued for $17 million by an angry patient after the doctor removed the wrong kidney. Asked what might have prevented the lawsuit, the patient replied, "An apology."

   What is ironic about this? _____

   _____

2. **Mislaid Plans, by Monica Ware**

   A rash of new bills came that morning. The letter from their insurance company announced the cancellation of their policies.
      She sighed and rose wearily to tell her husband. The kitchen smelled of gas. On his desk she found the note.
      "…the money from my life insurance will be enough for you and the children."

   What is ironic about this? _____

   _____

3. The story *The Gift of the Magi*, by O. Henry, is about a couple too poor to afford Christmas presents for each other. The husband wants to buy combs for his wife, who has long beautiful hair. The wife wants to buy a chain for her husband's antique pocket watch. The wife cuts and sells her hair to buy the watch chain; the husband sells his watch to buy the combs.

   What is ironic about this? _____

   _____

4. Dogs are rescued from a dog-fighting ring. However, ultimately, the dogs that were saved are put to sleep because they are deemed too dangerous.

What is ironic about this? _____

_____

As you have learned, the author's tone is not a single aspect of a book or article. Instead, it is formed from the interactions between the author's purpose, point of view, and use of denotation, connotation, and figurative language. Irony may also add a twist.

Connect Your Skills

Evaluating the Author's Tone

Read each selection and answer the questions that follow.

Population

1   Peru is essentially a bicultural society, comprised of two roughly same-sized parts: indigenous people and *criollos*. It's a division that breaks out roughly along class lines. The more affluent urban class is made up of whites and fair-skinned *mestizos* (people of mixed indigenous and Spanish descent)—all of whom generally refer to themselves as *criollos* (natives of Peru). Within this segment, a wealthy upper class has historically taken the top roles in politics and business, while the middle class has filled midlevel white-collar positions, such as clerks, teachers and entrepreneurs.

2   The other half of the population is made up primarily of indigenous *campesinos* (peasants). About 45% of Peru's population is pure *indigena* (people of indigenous descent), making one of three countries in Latin America to have such a high indigenous representation. (Note: In Spanish, *indigena* is the appropriate term; *indios* can be considering insulting, depending on how it is used.) Most *indigenas* are Quechua-speaking and live in the highlands, while a smaller percentage around the Lake Titicaca region speak Aymara. In the Amazon, which contains about 6% of the country's total population, various indigenous ethnic groups speak a plethora of other languages.

—Lonely Planet, *Peru* (p. 49)

1. What is the general purpose of this selection?

persuasive   informative   entertaining

2. More specifically, what is the author's purpose? _____

_____

3. Are there more denotative or connotative words?

   denotative   connotative

4. Is the passage subjective or objective?

   subjective   objective

5. What is the point of view of the author?

   first person   second person   third person

Rest

[1] Somewhere along a road in Indiana, I'd found a teddy bear with stuffing poking through its torn back and leg. Just as I'd done with the license plate and the horseshoe, I'd picked it up, taking a token of my run along that stretch, a mascot for the miles ahead. We'd perched him on the dashboard of the crew van along with the rest of my collection, and he's accompanied us all the way to New York. Much later, after Heather and I returned to our home in Colorado, I'd given "Indy" a bath a repaired him with black thread, making a path of careful crisscross stitches through his pale pink fuzz.

[2] Now, whenever I talk in front of a group about my run across the United States, I take Indy with me and show him to the crowd, noting that his little X's mark the spots of my own injuries. As we explore the meaning of this effort, the determination that secured the finish, the pain endured to get there, the kindess and encouragement that aided my every step, that small, soft toy serves as a reminder. This endeavor wasn't only about toughness and grit, but also about tenderness and grace. We found joy along the way, appreciated small comforts, turned to each other over and over again.

—Marshall Ulrich, *Running on Empty* (New York: Avery, 2011, pp. 233–234)

6. What is the point of view of the author?

   first person   second person   third person

7. Is the passage subjective or objective?

   subjective   objective

8. What three or four words are used to describe the qualities the author needed to succeed in running across America? _____

9. What is the general purpose of this selection?

   persuasive   informative   entertaining

10. If the teddy bear is a figure of speech, what kind is it?

    simile   metaphor   personification   hyperbole

From *Naked*

1   I was hired for the second shift, which began at 3 and ended at 11 P.M. My job was to stand in place and pull the leaves off the apples as they passed before me on the conveyor belt. There was a woman standing no more than four feet away from me, but the constant rattling din made it impossible to carry on a discussion. Forklifts droned in the background while men sawed and pounded wooden pallets. Sprayers, belts, and generators; the noise was oppressive and relentless.

—David Sedaris, *Naked*, p. 169

11. What is the point of view of the author?

| first person | second person | third person |

12. Is the passage subjective or objective?

| subjective | objective |

13. What more specific tone word describes the selection the best?

| inspirational | righteous | overwhelmed | apathetic |

We Wear the Mask

We wear the mask that grins and lies,
It hides our cheeks and shades our eyes,—
This debt we pay to human guile;
With torn and bleeding hearts we smile,
And mouth with myriad subtleties.

Why should the world be over-wise,
In counting all our tears and sighs?
Nay, let them only see us, while
    We wear the mask.

We smile, but, O great Christ, our cries
To thee from tortured souls arise.
We sing, but oh the clay is vile
Beneath our feet, and long the mile;
But let the world dream otherwise,
    We wear the mask!

—Paul Laurence Dunbar, from *Lyrics of Lowly Life* (1896)

14. What is the point of view of the author?

| first person | second person | third person |

15. Is the passage subjective or objective?

    subjective   objective

16. What more specific tone word describes the selection the best?

    sorrowful   respectful   annoyed   sincere

17. What figure of speech is "hearts" in line 4?

    simile   metaphor   personification   hyperbole

18. What does it stand for or mean? _____

19. Who do you think is the speaker of this poem? What time and place is he writing about? _____

    _____

20. Is the speaker truthful? How do you know? _____

    _____

 Click to Connect! To check your comprehension of chapter concepts, visit **www.cengagebrain.com** to access the CourseMate for this chapter.

Chapter Summary Activity

This chapter has discussed how to determine the author's tone by using purpose, point of view, denotation and connotation, and figurative language. Construct a Reading Guide to Analyzing Tone here by completing each idea on the left with information from the chapter on the right. You can use this guide anytime you need to figure out an author's tone.

Reading Guide to Analyzing Tone

Complete this idea with...	information from Chapter 10.
Four elements to examine to figure out author's tone	1. _____ _____
	2. _____ _____
	3. _____ _____

4. _____

_____

Three general purposes people have for writing

5. _____

_____

6. _____

_____

7. _____

_____

Two general kinds of tone and what the focus is

8. _____

_____

9. _____

_____

Two purposes most likely to use a subjective tone

10. _____

_____

11. _____

_____

Three points of view and the author's focus in each

12. _____

_____

13. _____

_____

14. _____

_____

Connotations of words can show these tones

15. _____

_____

16. _____

_____

Four kinds of figurative language and their definitions

17. _____

_____

18. _____
_____

19. _____
_____

20. _____
_____

Irony—definition

21. _____
_____

Compared to interactive reading strategies you used before you read this chapter, what is one thing you will do differently because you find it more effective? Write down your thoughts.

_____
_____
_____

Reading 10–1 | Essay

▶ Pre-Reading the Selection

"Why I Want a Wife" is a classic essay by Judy (Syfers) Brady. The essay first appeared in *Ms. Magazine*, a feminist magazine, in 1971.

Surveying the Reading

Survey the following article. Then check the elements that are included in this reading.

_____	Title	_____	Words in bold or italic type
_____	Headings	_____	Images and captions
_____	First sentences of paragraphs		

Guessing the Purpose

Judging from the title of the essay, what do you suppose is the purpose of the selection? _____

_____

Predicting the Content

Predict three things this selection will discuss.

▶ _____

▶ _____

▶ _____

Activating Your Knowledge

List several details you know about the role of women in modern families.

▶ _____

▶ _____

▶ _____

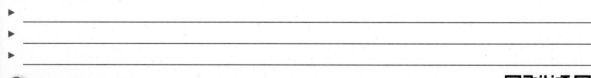

Scan to Connect! Use your smart phone to scan this code to watch a video. (See the inside front cover for more information on how to use this.) What is the overall tone of this video? What point is the author of this video trying to make? What is Evelyn Murphy's point of view about the socialization of women?

▶ Reading with Pen in Hand

Students who annotate as they read are more successful than those who do not. That's why you will annotate every selection in *Connect* as you read. In the reading that follows, use the following symbols:

★ or ⬭Point⬭   to indicate a main idea

① ② ③   to indicate major details

Visit www.cengagebrain.com to access the CourseMate for this chapter to hear pronunciations of vocabulary words from this reading.

Why I Want a Wife

Judy Brady

1   I belong to that classification of people known as wives. I am a Wife. And, not altogether incidentally, I am a mother. Not too long ago a male friend of mine appeared on the scene from the Midwest fresh from a recent divorce. He had one child, who is, of course, with his ex-wife. He is obviously looking for another wife. As I thought about him while I was ironing one evening, it suddenly occurred to me that I, too, would like to have a wife.

▸ What does the phrase "As I thought about him while I was ironing one evening" probably indicate about the author?

Why do I want a wife?

2   I would like to go back to school, so that I can become economically independent, support myself, and, if need be, support those dependent upon me. I want a wife who will work and send me to school. And while I am going to school I want a wife to take care of my children. I want a wife to keep track of the children's doctor and dentist appointments. And to keep track of mine, too. I want a wife to make sure my children eat properly and are kept clean. I want a wife who will wash the children's clothes and keep them mended. I want a wife who is a good **nurturing** attendant to my children, arranges for their schooling, makes sure that they have an adequate social life with their peers, takes them to the park, the zoo, etc. I want a wife who takes care of the children when they are sick, a wife who arranges to be around when the children need special care, because, of course, I cannot miss classes at school. My wife must arrange to lose time at work and not lose the job. It may mean a small cut in my wife's income from time to time, but I guess I can **tolerate** that. Needless to say, my wife will arrange and pay for the care of the children while my wife is working.

▸ What reasons does the author give for wanting a wife?

nurturing Based on the examples given, what is *nurturing*?

tolerate Use the context of the whole sentence to figure out the meaning.

3   I want a wife who will take care of my physical needs. I want a wife who will keep my house clean. A wife who will pick up after my children, a wife who will pick up after me. I want a wife who will keep my clothes clean, ironed, **mended**, replaced when need be, and who will see to it that my personal things are kept in their proper place so that I can find what I need the minute I need it. I want a wife who cooks the meals, a wife who is a good cook. I want a wife who will plan the menus, do the necessary grocery shopping, prepare the meals, serve them pleasantly, and then do the cleaning up while I do my studying. I want a wife who will care for me when I am sick and sympathize with my pain and loss of time from school. I want a wife to go along when our family takes a vacation so that someone can continue to care for me and my children when I need a rest and a change of scene.

▸ What reasons does the author give for wanting a wife?

mended What does *mended* mean?

4   I want a wife who will take care of the details of my social life. When my wife and I are invited out by my friends, I want a wife who will take care of the baby-sitting arrangements. When I meet people at school that I like and want to

▸ What reasons does the author give for wanting a wife?

entertain, I want a wife who will have the house clean, will prepare a special meal, serve it to me and my friends, and not interrupt when I talk about the things that interest me and my friends. I want a wife who will have arranged that the children are fed and ready for bed before my guests arrive so that the children do not bother us. I want a wife who takes care of the needs of my guests so that they feel comfortable, who makes sure that they have an ashtray, that they are passed the hors d'oeuvres, that they are offered a second helping of the food, that their wine glasses are **replenished** when necessary, that their coffee is served to them as they like it. And I want a wife who knows that sometimes I need a night out by myself.

5   I want a wife who is sensitive to my sexual needs, a wife who makes love passionately and eagerly when I feel like it, a wife who makes sure that I am satisfied. And, of course, I want a wife who will not demand sexual attention when I am not in the mood for it. I want a wife who assumes the complete responsibility for birth control, because I do not want more children. I want a wife who will remain sexually faithful to me so that I do not have to clutter up my intellectual life with jealousies. And I want a wife who understands that my sexual needs may entail more than strict **adherence** to monogamy. I must, after all, be able to relate to people as fully as possible.

6   If, by chance, I find another person more suitable as a wife than the wife I already have, I want the liberty to replace my present wife with another one. Naturally, I will expect a fresh, new life; my wife will take the children and be solely responsible for them so that I am left free. When I am through with school and have acquired a job, I want my wife to quit working and remain at home so that my wife can more fully and completely take care of a wife's duties.

7   My God, who *wouldn't* want a wife?

—"Why I Want a Wife" by Judy Brady, *Ms. Magazine*, 1971. Reprinted by permission of the author.

replenished Think about the series of tasks the wife is doing to help you guess at this word's meaning.

adherence This and the next sentence give clues to the meaning of *adherence*.

▶ What two reasons for why the author wants a wife are mentioned?

▶ Comprehension Questions

Write the letter of the answer on the line. Then explain your thinking.

Main Idea

_____   1. Which of the following sentences best states the main idea of this reading passage?

a. I want my wife to quit working and remain at home so that my wife can more fully and completely take care of a wife's duties.

b. I want a wife who will take care of the details of my social life.

c. As I thought about him while I was ironing one evening, it suddenly occurred to me that I, too, would like to have a wife.

d. I want a wife to take care of my children.

Why? What information in the selection leads you to give that answer? _____

_____

_____

____ 2. What is the main idea of paragraph 3?

   a. I want a wife who will take care of my physical needs.

   b. I want a wife who will keep my house clean.

   c. I want a wife who will keep my clothes clean, ironed, mended, replaced when need be, and who will see to it that my personal things are kept in their proper place so that I can find what I need the minute I need it.

   d. I want a wife who will care for me when I am sick and sympathize with my pain and loss of time from school.

Why? What information in the selection leads you to give that answer? _____

_____

_____

Supporting Details

____ 3. Which of the following is *not* a reason the author gives for wanting a wife?

   a. I want a wife who puts my needs above hers.

   b. I want a wife who is open to polygamy.

   c. I want a wife who understands my needs.

   d. I want a wife who will take care of all the household duties.

Why? What information in the selection leads you to give that answer? _____

_____

_____

____ 4. According to the passage, which of the following is a privilege the author reserves?

   a. entertaining guests

   b. infidelity

   c. helping clean up after meals

   d. giving the wife a night out from time to time

Why? What information in the selection leads you to give that answer? _____

_____

_____

Author's Purpose

5. What is the overall purpose of this passage?

    a. to inform the reader of the author's domestic situation

    b. to entertain the reader with a funny story

    c. to persuade readers that they should all have a wife

    d. to persuade readers through hyperbole that wives were not being treated fairly

Why? What information in the selection leads you to give that answer? _____

_____

_____

6. What is the overall tone of this passage?

    a. sincere

    b. sarcastic

    c. objective

    d. descriptive

Why? What information in the selection leads you to give that answer? _____

_____

_____

Relationships

7. What is the overall pattern of organization of this passage?

    a. time order

    b. listing

    c. comparison and contrast

    d. classification

Why? What information in the selection leads you to give that answer?_____

_____

_____

8. What is the main relationship found in the following sentence?

> I want a wife who will have arranged that the children are fed and ready for bed before my guests arrive.

    a. time order

    b. comparison and contrast

    c. cause-and-effect

    d. listing

Why? What leads you to give that answer? _____

_____

_____

Fact, Opinion, and Inference

_____ 9. How would you categorize this sentence?

It suddenly occurred to me that I, too, would like a wife.

    a. an opinion

    b. a fact

    c. both fact and opinion

    d. an expert opinion

Why? What leads you to give that answer? _____

_____

_____

_____ 10. Which of the following is a valid conclusion you could draw from reading this passage?

    a. Everyone should have a wife.

    b. The author's husband is a jerk and she should divorce him.

    c. The author uses hyperbole to make her point.

    d. The wife in this essay is meant to be a personification of a goddess.

Why? What information in the selection leads you to give that answer? _____

_____

_____

▶ Critical Thinking Questions

Critical Thinking Level 1 ▶ **Remember**

Throughout the essay, the words "I want a wife" are repeated time after time. Have you ever heard someone repeating the same phrase over and over like this? What was the effect? _____

_____

_____

Critical Thinking Level 2 Understand

Summarize the topic and main idea of this reading.

Topic: _____

 Main Idea: _____

_____

Critical Thinking Level 3 Apply

Use Brady's tone and style to write a paragraph about something you want. This desire might stem from an unequal relationship like Brady's does, but it doesn't have to. It could be about a person, a thing, an event, or anything else. Use repetition and a lot of details to explain your desire. If you want, after you write the paragraph, you can change it into a song. Consider using a refrain (repeated lines) after each stanza (group of lines) to get across the feeling of repetitiveness.

Critical Thinking Level 4 Analyze

Examine the reasons the author gives for wanting a wife. Consider what kinds of reasons she does not give that you might expect someone to want in a spouse. Discuss your ideas with your classmates. _____

_____

Critical Thinking Level 5 Evaluate

Read this pamphlet on being a good wife. (Note: Although passed around the Internet for years as a legitimate pamphlet, this is a hoax, done in the style of a mid-20th century magazine.)

The Good Wife's Guide

▸ Have dinner ready. Plan ahead, even the night before, to have a delicious meal ready on time for his return. This is a way of letting him know that you have been thinking about him and are concerned about his needs. Most men are hungry when they get home and the prospect of a good meal is part of the warm welcome needed.

▸ Prepare yourself. Take 15 minutes to rest so you'll be refreshed when he arrives. Touch up your make-up, put a ribbon in your hair and be fresh-looking. He has just been with a lot of work-weary people.

▸ Be a little gay and a little more interesting for him. His boring day may need a lift and one of your duties is to provide it.

▸ Clear away the clutter. Make one last trip through the main part of the house just before your husband arrives. Run a dust cloth over the tables.

Image courtesy of The Advertising Archives

▸ During the cooler months of the year you should prepare and light a fire for him to unwind by. Your husband will feel he has reached a haven of rest and order, and it will give you a lift too. After all, catering to his comfort will provide you with immense personal satisfaction.

▸ Minimize all noise. At the time of his arrival, eliminate all noise of the washer, dryer or vacuum. Encourage the children to be quiet.

▸ Be happy to see him.

▸ Greet him with a warm smile and show sincerity in your desire to please him.

▸ Listen to him. You may have a dozen important things to tell him, but the moment of his arrival is not the time. Let him talk first—remember, his topics of conversation are more important than yours.

▸ Don't greet him with complaints and problems.

▸ Don't complain if he's late for dinner or even if he stays out all night. Count this as minor compared to what he might have gone through at work.

▸ Make him comfortable. Have him lean back in a comfortable chair or lie him down in the bedroom. Have a cool or warm drink ready for him.

▸ Arrange his pillow and offer to take off his shoes. Speak in a low, soothing and pleasant voice.

▸ Don't ask him questions about his actions or question his judgment or integrity. Remember, he is the master of the house and as such will always exercise his will with fairness and truthfulness. You have no right to question him.

▸ A good wife always knows her place.

What do you think of this list? _____
_____

What is the author's tone? _____
_____

When would you guess this was written? _____

What is the author's purpose in writing this? _____

Critical Thinking Level 6 ▸ Create

"Why I Want a Wife" was written in the early 1970s. Single-parent households were much less common than they are today. Today, single-parent families and other nontraditional families are about equal in number to families that have a husband and a wife. Think about how the changes in culture would affect this essay if it were written today. *Write* an updated version of this essay reflecting your thoughts.

▶ Vocabulary in New Contexts

Review the vocabulary words in the margins of the reading selection and then complete the following activities.

EASY Note Cards

Make a note card for each of the vocabulary words that you did not know from the reading. On one side, write the word. On the other side, divide the card into quarters and label them E, A, S, and Y. Add a word or phrase in each area so that you wind up with an example sentence, an antonym, a synonym, and, finally, a definition that shows you have figured out the meaning of the word with your logic. Remember that an antonym or synonym may have appeared in the reading.

Relationships Between Words

Circle *yes* or *no* to answer the question. Then explain your answer.

1. Can a **nurturing** massage **replenish** a person?

   Yes   No

   Why or why not? _____

2. Does **adherence** to a political party cause a person to **tolerate** people from the other party?

   Yes   No

   Why or why not? _____

   _____

3. Does **mending** a wound usually involve causing the sides to **adhere**?

   Yes   No

   Why or why not? _____

Language in Your Life

Write short answers to each question. Look at vocabulary words closely before you answer.

1. Name one thing you do to **nurture** yourself. _____

   _____

2. Name one belief you **adhere** to. _____

   _____

3. Name one thing you have **mended**. _____

   _____

4. Name a person you merely **tolerate**. _____

_____

5. Name one way you **replenish** your energy. _____

_____

Language in Use

Select the best word to complete the meaning of each sentence.

adherence	mend	nourish	replenish	tolerate

1. Bonsai, the art of making natural tree forms in miniature, has been practiced in Japan and China for centuries. It requires proper care and _____ to specific procedures to successfully create a mature bonsai.

2. Since bonsai are totally dependent upon you for care, it is imperative that you know how to _____ them; otherwise they could die simply due to your ignorance.

3. Some examples of how finicky a bonsai can be include not being able to _____ too much heat, too much cold, too much moisture, not enough moisture, lack of fertilization, or excess fertilization…yikes!

4. Bonsais must be repotted frequently to _____ nutritious soil, avoid root rot, and allow you to trim the roots in order to keep the tree miniature.

5. You will also need to trim, train, and _____ branches to achieve the shape you want. As you can see, bonsais need patience and TLC in order to have a long and healthy life. Maybe you should buy a book on the care of a bonsais before you buy the tree!

Reading 10–2 | Essay

▶ Pre-Reading the Selection

This reading also examines the role a woman plays in the family. Kristin van Ogtrop writes about how she struggles to balance her work life with her home life.

Surveying the Reading

Survey the following article. Then check the elements that are included in this reading.

_____	Title	_____	Words in bold or italic type
_____	Headings	_____	Images and captions
_____	First sentences of paragraphs		

Guessing the Purpose

Judging from a quick scan of the reading selection and its title, what do you suppose is the purpose of this reading selection? _____

Predicting the Content

Predict three things this selection will discuss.

▶ _____

▶ _____

▶ _____

Activating Your Knowledge

Take a moment to write about what you think the life of a professional woman who has a traditional family life is like. Use someone you know as inspiration if you can. _____

_____

_____

🎬 **Scan to Connect!** Use your smart phone to scan this code to watch a video. (See the inside front cover for more information on how to use this.) Compare and contrast the points of view presented in this video and the point of view of Kristin van Ogtrop in the reading that follows.

Common Knowledge

Attila the Hun (*title*) The ruler of the Huns, who were horse-riding nomads in Central Asia, from AD 433–453. He is often referred to as a fierce, cruel, and bloodthirsty ruler.

Mr. Rogers (*paragraph 5*) The host of a popular children's television show called *Mister Rogers' Neighborhood* from 1968 to 2001. He is an icon in children's entertainment, known for being calm and gentle.

Eye of the storm (*paragraph 10*) The middle, calm part of a hurricane or tornado.

▶ Reading with Pen in Hand

Students who annotate as they read are more successful than those who do not. That's why you will annotate every selection in *Connect* as you read. In the reading that follows, use the following symbols:

★ or (Point)   to indicate a main idea

① ② ③   to indicate major details

 Visit www.cengagebrain.com to access the CourseMate for this chapter to hear pronunciations of vocabulary words from this reading.

Attila the Honey I'm Home

Kristin van Ogtrop

It's a Typical Night

1   I arrive home from work, after first stopping to pick up my two boys from my friend Gabrielle's house, where my nanny has left them on a play date. It's seven thirty. No one has had a bath. Foolishly, I have promised that we will make milkshakes. The boys have eaten dinner. I haven't. My husband is at a basketball game and won't be home until ten.

▶ Why was it "foolish" for the author to promise milkshakes?

2   Owen, who is six, tosses a bouquet of flowers—a gift from Gabrielle's garden—into the grass as we get out of the car. Three-year-old Hugo sees the moon. I mention that the sun is out, too; he runs from one end of the front walk to the other, trying to find it, getting closer to the street with each lap. Owen says he wants the milkshake *now*. I unlock the front door and step in. George the cat meows and rubs against my legs, begging to be fed.

3   I walk back outside to pick up the flowers, the wet towel (swimming lessons), and my own two bags from work (contents: three unread newspapers, two magazines, a birthday party invitation for Owen, a present for the party, and a folder of work that, ever the optimist, I'm hoping to do tonight).

▶ Why does the author describe herself as an "optimist"?

insistent Does the word itself give you any clues about its meaning? Think about who is calling. What might Hugo's tone be?

shards Use your logic and the context. What are *shards*?

▶ What figurative language is used in this paragraph?

▶ Based on the details in paragraphs 6, 7, and 8, describe the type of person the author is at work.

flustered Notice that *flustered* probably refers to an emotional state. Which emotion would fit this situation? How would you feel?

Back into the house with flowers, towel, bags. I put my keys in the bowl next to the front door (small attempt at order). I knock over a framed picture beside it. The glass in the frame shatters. Hugo calls, **insistent**, for me to come back outside.

4   Owen hovers behind me, barefoot. He wants to how why, when you combine chocolate and vanilla, does the ice cream turn brown instead of white? I maneuver Owen around the broken glass and ask him to get the Dustbuster as I begin to pick up the **shards**. He disappears into the kitchen for what seems like ten minutes. I glance out for Hugo, whose voice is fainter but *definitely* still audible. George stands on his hind legs, clawing holes in the screen. Owen reappears with the Dustbuster, revving the motor. He wants to know exactly how long until we make the milk shake, and are we sure we even have chocolate ice cream?

5   I am talking in my Mr. Rogers voice as my desperation rises. Any minute now my head is going to blast off my body, burst through the screen door, and buzz around my little town, eventually losing steam before landing with a thud somewhere near the train station, where it will be run over by one of my smiling neighbors being picked up by what I imagine are calm spouses who will drive them calmly home to houses calm and collected where the children are already bathed and ready for bed. As for me, it's time to start yelling.

The Next Day

6   I get up at 5:30 to leave the house at 6:00, to be driven to the TV studio for hair and makeup at 6:45, to go on the air, live, at 7:40. I'm the executive editor of an enormously popular women's magazine and am appearing as an "expert" on a local morning show to discuss "what your wallet says about you." I have a hairstylist I've never met and he makes the back of my head look ridiculous, like a ski jump. At 7:25 the segment producer hands me the anchor's script; it contains five questions that weren't part of yesterday's pre-interview. I make up answers that sound informed-clever-peppy enough for morning TV with two minutes to spare. Total airtime: ninety seconds.

7   By the time I get to the office at 8:30 I have six voice mail messages (boss, nanny, human resources manager, unhappy writer, underling editor wanting guidance, my mother), twenty-seven e-mails, and, on my chair, a 4,000-word article I need to edit by the end of the day. I run to the cafeteria to get something to eat, then call boss and nanny and answer most of the e-mails before my 9:30 meeting. At 10:45 two fact-checkers come into my office to describe the problems of a recent story, which kept them at work until 4:00 A.M. the night before. Are fact-checkers or editor to blame? Editor, I decide, and call her in. She is **flustered** and defensive, and starts to cry. My tissue box is empty, so I hand her a napkin. We talk (well, I talk; she nods) about the fact that she's made similar mistakes in the past, and perhaps this isn't the job for her. After she leaves I call the human resources

manager to discuss the problematic editor, a looming legal problem, and staff salaries.

8   I have lunch at my desk and a second cup of coffee while I edit the piece, until two editors visit to complain about coworkers. A third tells me she is overloaded. A fourth confesses her marital problems and starts to cry; now I'm out of napkins, too. I give her the number of a counseling service and suggest she use it. Someone calls to ask about the presentation I'm giving tomorrow; I haven't even begun to think about it, which probably should worry me but somehow doesn't. I finish the edit and drop it in my out box. Before leaving the office at 5:30 I pick up all the paper that blankets my desk and divide it into four discrete piles for the morning. I very well might forget to look through the piles and something will get overlooked, but when I return to work, the neat stacks will make me feel organized and calm. And at work, I usually am.

9   Here are a few things people have said about me at the office:

"You're unflappable."

"Are you ever in a bad mood?"

"You command respect as soon as you walk into a room."

"Your straightforward, no-nonsense style gets things done."

"You're good at **finessing** situations so people don't boil over." Here are things people—OK, the members of my family—have said about me at home:

"Mommy is always grumpy."

"Why are you so tense?"

"You just need to relax."

"You don't need to yell!"

"You're too mean to live in this house and I want you to go back to work for the rest of your life!"

10   That last one is my favorite. It's also the saddest, because it captures such a painful truth: too often I'm a better mother at work than I am at home. Of course, at work, no one shouts at me for five minutes straight in what parents universally refer to as an "outside voice." No one charges into my office, hands outstretched, to smear peanut butter all over my skirt or Vaseline all over my favorite needlepoint rug. At work, when someone is demanding something of me, I can say, "I'll call you back" or "Let's talk about that in the next meeting." When people don't listen to me, they do so after they've left my office, not right in front of me. Yet even if shouting and random acts of destruction were to become the norm at work, I probably would not respond with the angry tantrums that punctuate so many nights at home. We have our own form of chaos in the office, after all. I work with creative people—temperamental, flaky, "difficult"—but my job is to be the eye of the storm.

finessing Look at the cause and effect relationship: what does *finessing* result in? What does this mean?

▶ Why is the author "a better mother at work than I am at home"?

11   So why this angel-in-the-office, horror-at-home division? Shouldn't the skills that serve me so well at work help me at the end of the day? My friend Chrissie, heroic stay-at-home mother of four, has one explanation: My behavior simply reproduces, in the adult world, the perfect-at-school/demon-at-home phenomenon that is acted out daily among children throughout America. I am on my best behavior at work, just as Owen is on his best behavior at school, but at home we have to ask him seven times to put on his shoes and by the seventh time it's no longer a request but a shouted, boot-camp command. And I am on my worst behavior at home because that's where I can "unwind" after spending eight (or ten, or fourteen) hours at the office keeping my cool.

12   Arlie Russell Hochschild has other ideas about this apparently widespread condition. In her 1997 book *Time Bind: When Work Becomes Home and Home Becomes Work,* she writes, "In this new model of family and work life, a tired parent flees a world of unresolved quarrels and unwashed laundry for the reliable orderliness, harmony, and managed cheer of work." At the office, I do manage, in all senses of the word. I am paid to be bossy—a trait that, for better and worse, has always been a **predominant** part of my personality. But at home, that bossiness yields unpleasant dividends, both from two boys who are now officially Grade A backtalkers and from a husband who frequently lets me know he's not someone I need to supervise. Still, the impulse isn't likely to go away, as long as I remain the only one in our household who knows where the library books/soccer cleats/car keys have gone—and what to do with them. At home I am wife, mother, baby-sitting and housekeeping manager, cook, social secretary, gardener, tutor, chauffeur, interior decorator, general contractor, and laundress. That many roles is exhausting, especially at those times when my mind is still in work mode. The other night I said to Hugo, "Do you want to put on your PJs in Owen's office?" It's a messy juggling act, and when a ball drops, I'm never laughing.

13   Last Friday I picked up the cheery note that Owen's kindergarten teacher, Ms. Stenstrom, sends at the end of every week. "We had an exciting morning!" it began. "We finished our touch unit by guessing what was in all the bags—thanks for sending in SUCH mysterious objects!" I had forgotten that Owen was supposed to have taken something interesting to touch in a brown paper bag to school that day. Standing alone in the kitchen, I started to cry. I read the note again, feeling miserable for Owen, miserable for me, miserable for lovely, infinitely patient Ms. Stenstrom. Then I climbed the stairs, cornered Dean, and cried some more. Is that appropriate? To cry for an hour and then have a long, tedious, completely unproductive discussion with an equally sleep deprived husband about All The Things We're Doing Wrong? How did I turn into this?

—"Attila the Honey I'm Home" by Kristin Van Ogtrop from *The Bitch in the House: 26 Women Tell the Truth about Sex, Solitude, Work, Motherhood, and Marriage,* pp. 159–163. Reprinted by permission of the author.

- What answer does the author give for the question she asks?

predominant Use the context to determine the meaning here.

- What problems have arisen at home because of the author's "bossiness"?

- Why did the author start crying when she read Ms. Stenstrom's "cheery note"?

▶ Comprehension Questions

Write the letter of the answer on the line. Then explain your thinking.

Main Idea

_____ 1. What is the main idea of the section entitled "It's a Typical Night"?

    a. Owen is more interested in a chocolate milkshake than in helping his mom clean up the broken glass.

    b. As a harried housewife, the author struggles to keep up with two energetic boys and a cat.

    c. A working mom discusses strategies for balancing home and the office.

    d. A professional mom gives a representative description of her hectic weekday evenings.

Why? What information in the selection leads you to give that answer? _____

_____

_____

_____ 2. Which sentence best summarizes the main idea of paragraphs 9 and 10?

    a. That last one is my favorite.

    b. It's also the saddest, because it captures such a painful truth: too often I'm a better mother at work than I am at home.

    c. Of course, at work, no one shouts at me for five minutes straight in what parents universally refer to as an "outside voice."

    d. No one charges into my office, hands outstretched, to smear peanut butter all over my skirt or Vaseline all over my favorite needlepoint rug.

Why? What information in the selection leads you to give that answer? _____

_____

_____

Supporting Details

_____ 3. Which of the following helps the author feel organized at work?

    a. bossiness

    b. arranging papers into piles

    c. coming into the office early

    d. being an executive editor

Why? What information in the selection leads you to give that answer? _____

_____

_____

____ 4. Which of the following is not true about the author's children?

    a. Owen is six.

    b. Hugo is a back-talker.

    c. George is three.

    d. Owen is in kindergarten.

Why? What information in the selection leads you to give that answer? _____

_____

Author's Purpose

____ 5. What is the purpose of "such" being in all caps in this sentence in paragraph 13: "We finished our touch unit by guessing what was in all the bags—thanks for sending in SUCH mysterious objects!"?

    a. The mother had sent in some very mysterious objects.

    b. The teacher was indicating her enthusiasm.

    c. The teacher was yelling at the mother because she had her priorities wrong.

    d. The objects the mother sent in were not mysterious.

Why? What information in the selection leads you to give that answer? _____

_____

____ 6. What is the tone of the following sentence?

> I run to the cafeteria to get something to eat, then call boss and nanny and answer most of the e-mails before my 9:30 meeting.

    a. factual

    b. disorganized

    c. objective

    d. hurried

Why? What leads you to give that answer? _____

_____

Relationships

____ 7. Identify all the patterns of organization found in the following sentence:

> I am on my best behavior at work, just as Owen is on his best behavior at school, but at home we have to ask him seven times to put on his shoes and by the seventh time it's no longer a request but a shouted, boot-camp command.

    a. time order, listing, description

    b. listing, cause-and-effect

    c. comparison, contrast, and time order

    d. cause-and-effect, classification, and comparison and contrast

Why? What leads you to give that answer? _____

_____

_____

_____ 8. What is the pattern of organization of the section entitled "It's a Typical Night"?

    a. chronological

    b. comparison and contrast

    c. cause-and-effect

    d. listing

Why? What information in the selection leads you to give that answer? _____

_____

_____

Fact, Opinion, and Inference

_____ 9. Which of the following statements combines fact and opinion?

    a. I have promised that we will make milkshakes.

    b. George the cat meows and rubs against my legs, begging to be fed.

    c. I make up answers that sound informed-clever-peppy enough for morning TV with two minutes to spare.

    d. I have lunch at my desk and a second cup of coffee while I edit the piece, until two editors visit to complain about coworkers.

Why? What leads you to give that answer? _____

_____

_____

_____ 10. Which of the following can be inferred from the final paragraph?

    a. Ms. Stenstrom does not like Owen's mom.

    b. Though frustrated at times, the author is satisfied with her professional position.

    c. The author is annoyed about her husband's lack of participation in their kids' lives.

    d. The author expects that she can keep track of every single detail at home and work.

Why? What information in the selection leads you to give that answer? _____

_____

_____

▶ Critical Thinking Questions

Critical Thinking Level 1 ▸ **Remember**

State the effect "bossiness" has had on the author's work life versus her home life. _____

_____

_____

Critical Thinking Level 2 ▸ **Understand**

Summarize this reading.

_____

_____

_____

_____

_____

Critical Thinking Level 3 ▸ **Apply**

A. *Find* the following figures of speech in the selection and write them here. Note which paragraph they are in.

Hyperbole: _____

Simile: _____

Metaphor: _____

B. Is the following sentence meant figuratively or literally?

"At home we have to ask him seven times to put on his shoes…" (paragraph 11) _____

Give support for your answer. _____

Critical Thinking Level 4 ▸ **Analyze**

Analyze the tone of the reading by filling in the following information.

Point of view: _____

Objective or subjective: _____

Positive, neutral, or negative tone: _____

List a few words that have connotations that suggest why you gave that answer. _____

_____

What specific tone word from the list on pages 511–512 describes this author's tone? _____

Critical Thinking Level 5 ▸ Evaluate

Is this author's need to balance work and home life typical or atypical of contemporary U.S. life? *Support* your answer with a few pieces of evidence.

    typical   atypical

_____

_____

_____

Critical Thinking Level 6 ▸ Create

How often does your life seem out of balance? Do you have trouble balancing work, school, and home? *Create* a schedule that helps you find balance in your life. Share your thoughts with a classmate.

_____

_____

_____

▸ Vocabulary in New Contexts

Review the vocabulary words in the margins of the reading selection and then complete the following activities.

EASY Note Cards

Make a note card for each of the vocabulary words that you did not know from the reading. On one side, write the word. On the other side, divide the card into quarters and label them E, A, S, and Y. Add a word or phrase in each area so that you wind up with an example sentence, an antonym, a synonym, and, finally, a definition that shows you have figured out the meaning of the word with your logic. Remember that an antonym or synonym may have appeared in the reading.

Relationships Between Words

Circle *yes* or *no* to answer the question. Then explain your answer.

1. Does an **insistence** on the truth mean that a person cannot **finesse** an awkward situation?

   Yes   No

   Why or why not? _____

2. Would a person become **flustered** if her **predominant** beliefs were shown to be false?

   Yes   No

   Why or why not? _____

3. Can an **insistently** judgmental parent cause a child's self-respect to shatter into **shards**?

   Yes   No

   Why or why not? _____

   _____

Language in Your Life

Write short answers to each question. Look at the vocabulary words closely before you answer.

1. Name one time you were **flustered**. _____

   _____

2. Name one rule you will be (or are) **insistent** about as a parent. _____

   _____

3. Name the **predominant** color in one of the rooms in the place where you live. _____

   _____

4. Name one situation you have **finessed**. _____

   _____

5. Note the last time you saw a **shard** of glass. _____

   _____

Language in Use

Select the best word to complete the meaning of each sentence.

finessing	flustered	insistent	predominant	shards

1. The teacher was _____ that the students complete their homework perfectly.

2. When the new student did not manage to do that, he became _____, and his academic performance went downhill from there.

3. The _____ opinion in the principal's office was that the teacher's behavior had been overbearing, and the teacher was reprimanded.

4. The principal's secretary, though, was less concerned about the teacher's behavior than she was with the _____ of glass that littered the floor outside her office due to a vase being knocked off her desk.

5. Getting the children who came into the office to avoid the glass took a good deal of _____.

Click to Connect! For more practice applying the skills you learned in this chapter, visit **www.cengagebrain.com** to access the CourseMate for this chapter.

Picsfive/Shutterstock.com

 Click to Connect! Visit **www.cengagebrain.com** to access study resources for this chapter through CourseMate, which includes audio, video, quizzes, and a searchable, interactive eBook version of the text.

11

Evaluating the Author's Reasoning and Evidence

> " *I can win an argument against any opponent. People know this, and steer clear of me at parties. Often, as a sign of their great respect, they don't even invite me.* "
>
> —DAVE BARRY

Connect with Ideas

What can you infer from the quotation about Dave Barry's definition of an argument? How would you describe his tone?

Activate Your Knowledge

When you hear the word *argument*, what associations come to mind? What are some of the different meanings *argument* can have?

Engage with the Chapter

Look ahead at some of the topics in this chapter. What is needed to effectively understand and evaluate an author's reasoning and evidence?

Read and Talk

Online Article

Do you think anyone has the right to say whatever he or she wants? What about politicians, celebrities, or musicians? The following reading raises this question concerning rap artists. As you read the article, think about what constitutes free speech as covered by the First Amendment.

Visit www.cengagebrain.com to access the CourseMate for this chapter to hear vocabulary words from this reading and an audio recording of it.

Freedom of Speech in Rap Music

Brunella Irma Costagliola

controversial Look at the situation that follows this word for your clue.

1   The violent and **controversial** lyrical content of rap music has often put rappers under a bad light. While critics and politicians point their fingers to Hip-Hop artists, rappers defend themselves by recalling the First Amendment of the United States' Constitution that guarantees the freedom of speech. But, how far are rappers allowed to go with the content of their songs?

Chad Suber/Shutterstock.com

Censorship in Rap Music

misogynist There is no context clue, but you can still determine its connotation. Is it positive or negative? Look up this word or use word parts to figure it out.

2   A solution to the controversial and **misogynist** lyrical content of rap songs came after 1985 with the label "Parental Advisor" on rap albums' covers. This initiative was suggested by the Parents Music Resource Center, whose leader was Tipper Gore, Senator Al Gore's wife. Rappers rebelled against this decision, addressing their right to the freedom of speech that the First Amendment of the Unites States' Constitution grants them.

censoring This word is a verb. Look at the entire section to understand what this word means.

3   Rapper Ice-T, in a song titled Freedom of Speech, questions the legality of **censoring** rap music, asserting that if rappers are not protected by the First Amendment, then they might as well throw the Constitution away.

The Danger of Freedom of Speech in Rap Music

4   What happens when the lyrical content of rap music is believed to be true? Rapper Lawrence "Big Bad 40" White has been sent to court to defend himself against charges of being a gang member and a drug dealer. While the San Bernardino County District Attorney's office declares to have supporting evidence, such as surveillance camera recordings, to prove that the southern California rapper was actually involved in gang crimes, the rapper and his attorney declare that White has nothing to do with them.

5   Moreover, the rapper declares that the charges are in fact based on some of his songs' lyrical content, where he raps about dealing drugs and being a gang member. In a public statement, the rapper claimed that "They are using my songs against me. I thought the Constitution of the United States of America which is where I live grants me the first amendment which is freedom of speech, I mean that's what I read."

Freedom of Speech in Rap Music

6   Rap music has often been treated like the scapegoat of everything that is wrong within American society. The controversial and violent lyrical content of some rap songs has put rappers under a bad light. While rappers defend themselves citing the First Amendment and their right to free speech, the risk they put themselves into with their songs' content is exactly what happened to Big Bad 40: people might actually believe what they are talking about.

—From "Freedom of Speech in Rap Music" by Brunella Irma Cosagliola, author of *Gangster Movies in Gangsta Rap*. Reprinted with permission from http://brunella-irma-costagliola.suite101.com/ freedom-of-speech-in-rap-music-a258962.

Talking about Reading

Respond in writing to the questions that follow and then discuss your answers with your classmates.

1. What is your personal view of rap music? _____

_____

2. What does it mean to have free speech? Should there be any limits to free speech? If so, what should they be? _____

_____

_____

3. As the article states, rappers have often been attacked for the violent content of their lyrics. But don't they have the right to free speech? And if so, does this right have any limits? _____

_____

_____

_____

4. Is the content of a singer's song enough evidence to prove that he or she is a drug dealer, a gun-runner, a killer, or anything else? Why or why not? _____

_____

_____

5.  **Scan to Connect!** Use your smart phone to scan this code to watch a video. (See the inside front cover for more information on how to use this.) Do you agree with the comment that having free speech means you need to have a culture where individuals you completely disagree with are able to express their views, just as you are able to express yours? What would this mean in application?

The Author's Reasoning

Throughout this book we have been discussing how important it is to analyze and evaluate the author's words and ideas while reading. That need is especially critical when an author is trying to persuade readers to accept something different from what they already believe, or to act in a way they've never before acted—in other words, when the author is making an argument. When an author has a persuasive purpose and sets out to influence you in a particular direction, you should carefully evaluate the claim, the reasoning, and the evidence being used.

Some New Terms and Their Connection to Paragraph Structure

You should be familiar by now with the following figure (**Figure 11.1**) showing questions that lead you to the three levels, or hierarchy, of ideas found in paragraphs.

Figure 11.1   **Three Comprehension Questions**

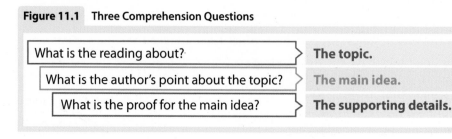

What is the reading about?	**The topic.**
What is the author's point about the topic?	**The main idea.**
What is the proof for the main idea?	**The supporting details.**

In argument, the terminology changes, but the concepts are essentially the same.

An argument is "about" an **issue**, that is, a topic that people disagree about.

The "point" in an argument is the **claim**, that is, the author's point of view concerning the topic.

The "proof" in an argument is **evidence**, that is, reasons supported by facts and other forms of support.

Usually an argument will be more than one paragraph. The sentence that contains both the issue and claim is the thesis statement, just as you learned in Chapters 4 and 5.

When you read an argument, it's a good idea to mark (highlight or annotate) the claim and evidence because it's the relationship between them you'll need to think about in order to evaluate the author's reasoning. In addition, the skill of making a **summary**, which you learned in Chapter 7 with Cornell notes, will come in handy when you are asked to respond in conversation or in writing to the argument of an author you have read. Often you will need to share the author's point of view about the argument in order to tell readers or listeners how your opinion is the same or how it is different.

Let's look at an example. Here is a short persuasive paragraph:

> Fathers, though often undervalued at the time of birth, are an important part of their child's development, especially in the first few months of life. Studies show that the bond between father and child is stronger if the father is present during the first few weeks after birth. This sets a foundation for a healthy relationship between the two. In addition, the mothers often need the extra help. The mom is tired and sore, and her chemical levels are unbalanced. If the father is present, he can be an extra set of hands, a calming presence, and emotional support. As such, men should receive paternity leave.

The topic sentence is: <u>Men should receive</u> [paternity leave].

The **issue** is: paternity leave.

   The **claim** is: men should receive.

      The **evidence** is: 1. Fathers are important to their child's development.
                       2. Studies show the bond is stronger when the father is present in the first weeks.
                       3. Early interaction sets a foundation for healthy relationships.
                       4. The father can support the mother as needed.

The formula T + MI = TS still works with persuasive or argumentative purposes. The only change is the shift in terminology: from *topic* to *issue* and *main idea* to *claim*. (Issue + Claim = Topic Sentence). You will still use the same reading and questioning process to identify these parts. Remember that you should also annotate by putting the [topic] in brackets and underlining the <u>main idea</u>. (Did you notice the claim just made?)

| Interaction 11–1 > **Identify Issues and Claims** |

In each sentence, bracket the issue (topic) and underline the author's claim (main idea). Then write an alternative claim that could be made about each issue. (You don't have to believe the claims.)

1. The drinking age should not be lowered to eighteen.

   Different claim about same issue: _____

   _____

2. The rights of an unborn child are more important than the rights of the mother.

   Different claim about same issue: _____

   _____

3. Torture, while abhorrent in most cases, should be acceptable during war.

   Different claim about same issue: _____

   _____

4. Children are negatively affected when they see violence on television or play violent video games.

   Different claim about same issue: _____

   _____

5. No scientist should be permitted to experiment on animals.

   Different claim about same issue: _____

   _____

Remember how general the topic sentence or thesis statement is compared to the specifics of the evidence? As we just saw in the earlier example, the TS is: Men should receive paternity leave. The details give specific reasons why the author thinks this should be so. In the same way that you found the supporting details for a main idea, you can turn the claim into a question to see if the evidence supports it. "Why should men receive paternity leave?" The answer to this question is the evidence the author gives.

| Interaction 11–2 > **Distinguish Between Claim and Evidence** |

Put a **C** next to the sentence that is the claim for each group and **E** for the sentences that provide evidence (support). Double-check your claim by mentally turning it into a question to see if the evidence supports it.

Dallas Events Inc/Shutterstock.com

1. _____ The cost of living in the Dallas area is among the most affordable in the United States.

_____ Dallas has a solid economy.

_____ The housing market in Dallas is the strongest in the nation.

_____ The unemployment rate is the lowest in the country.

2. _____ The behavior of the audience at last night's lecture was disrespectful.

_____ Before the talk even began, there was an atmosphere in the room of people waiting in ambush.

_____ Until a student stood up to insist that audience members be quiet, people were booing and laughing at inappropriate moments during the talk.

_____ Instead of waiting for the question-and-answer session that was to take place after the lecture, some people shouted out challenges to the lecturer's points as he spoke, causing him to lose track of his ideas.

3. _____ Alcohol causes problems with the cerebellum, which controls coordination, balance, and reflexes.

_____ Drinking too much can even limit brain signals to your body for essentials like breathing.

_____ People should not drink to excess because alcohol affects the brain.

_____ Alcohol slows down brain activity.

4. _____ The United States is the most technologically and economically advanced nation in the world.

_____ Almost every home has indoor plumbing and at least one television.

_____ Most Americans sleep in a warm bed and wake up to enough to eat.

_____ The infrastructure is well constructed and regularly maintained.

—From Segal/Gerdes/Steiner, *An Introduction to the Profession of Social Work*, 2e

5. ____   After Katrina, one insurance company found that the five hundred damaged locations that had implemented all the hurricane-loss prevention methods experienced only one-eighth the losses of those that had not done so.

____   Often, simple structural measures, like bracing and securing roof trusses and walls using straps, clips, or adhesives, can yield big benefits.

____   Hurricane Katrina did so much damage in New Orleans because of bad planning, poorly maintained levees, and environmental degradation of the city's protective wetlands.

____   Policies that are holistic in scope and include all hurricane prevention methods can help prevent the extent of such tragedies as Hurricane Katrina.   —Adapted from Lomborg, *Cool It*

Now it's time to identify an issue and claim within paragraphs.

Interaction 11–3 Annotate Issues, Claims, and Evidence

Read the following paragraphs and annotate them. Bracket [the issue], underline <u>the claim</u>, and number (insert a circled 1, 2, 3) each piece of evidence (support) given by the author. Double-check your claim by mentally turning it into a question to see if the evidence supports it.

1.

What's the difference between reading a textbook and studying it? Have you ever spent an evening "vegging out" in front of the TV? Although it was likely great fun, you may have noticed that you didn't think very much about what you were watching and that your subsequent memories were not very detailed. Psychologist Donald Norman (1993) uses the term **experiential cognition** to refer to the style of thinking that occurs during passive experience. Even though this is the appropriate way to experience entertainment, it doesn't work so well if your goal is to learn while, say, reading a textbook.

—From Coon/Mitterer, *Introduction to Psychology: Gateways to Mind and Behavior*, 13e

2.

Exercise holds a number of benefits for college students that need to be considered. Unlike middle-aged and older individuals, traditional-age college students cite improved fitness as the number one advantage that exercise offers, followed by improved appearance and muscle tone. Undergraduates who recognize the benefits of exercise are more likely to be physically active than those who focus on barriers to working out. In addition, their brains may also benefit. According to a very large recent study of more than 1.2 million men, strong cardiorespiratory fitness in young adulthood was associated with higher intelligence, better grades, and greater success in life. The reasons may be improved blood flow to the brain, diminished anxiety, enhanced mood, and less fatigue.

—From Hales, *Invitation to Health*, 15e

3.

Texting while driving is dangerous and can be fatal. In 2011, The National Safety Commission announced that it estimated that no less than 23% (1.3 million) of all crashes were caused from texting and cell phone use. These numbers mean around 6,000 deaths and at least 500,000 injuries are directly related to texting. Texting while driving reduces teenage reaction time to as slow as that of a 70-year-old person. If texting distracts for 5 seconds, this means that a person driving 50 mph would travel the length of almost 4 football fields without being aware of their surroundings. And it is not only teenagers who are at risk; 30–39-year-olds had the highest percentage of fatal crashes resulting from cell phone use in 2009. This is a danger that affects us all.

4.

"No one is immune to the folk knowledge of their culture," state Marian Friestad and Peter Wright, marketing and psychology researchers at the University of Oregon. The folk knowledge of a culture is **mythos**, the interrelated set of beliefs, attitudes, values, and feelings held by members of a particular society or culture. Friestad and Wright claim that we learn mythos not through any formal training but rather through the "whisperings of Mother culture." We listen to these whisperings as children, adolescents, young adults, and adults. They come through anecdotes and customs as well as through events and accepted norms for behavior.

America can be used to illustrate this idea. Whether you have grown up in the United States or another culture, you're likely familiar with some of the cultural myths of the United States. These cultural narratives stress the importance of freedom and democracy. They describe the United States as the land of **opportunity** and tell of journeys from rags to riches. They emphasize the value of progress and the exploration of new frontiers. They celebrate heroes and heroines who have made the United States a world leader. The mythos of any culture communicates who its people are and what values it holds most important. No one growing up within a culture can escape its mythos.

—From Griffin, *Invitation to Public Speaking*, 4e

5.

The Spartan Beast is an obstacle race from hell, truly unlike any of the other races that claim this. Our race consists of a trail that is more than 12 miles and includes more than 25 obstacles. If that doesn't sound hard enough, then factor in that most of the obstacles are unknown, so you can't train specifically for them. You literally do not know what comes next and have to be prepared for any possibility. Although you are not sure where they will be, you can expect places in the race where you will have to leap over fire or face warriors who attempt to keep you from progressing. This adversary may try to tackle you or trip you up with a padded pole. Sound like a typical day for you? Then get out of your comfort zone, visit our website, and sign up today for The Beast to see if you are Spartan tough!

Glynnis Jones/Shutterstock.com

The Relevance of the Evidence to the Claim

Relevance refers to how directly the evidence relates to the claim. Imagine that you are watching an Olympic event. An athlete who won a silver medal is contesting the gold medal decision, saying that the winner does not deserve the gold. Here are the three reasons given. Which one is the most relevant to the silver medalist's claim?

1. It's not fair.

2. I trained more hours than the gold medalist did.

3. The other athlete used performance-enhancing drugs.

As you can see, numbers 1 and 2 are emotional appeals with no relevance. However, if number 3 proved to be true, then it would be relevant. The gold medalist would be disqualified, giving the silver medalist a chance to trade up for the gold.

Interaction 11–4 ▸ Think about Relevance

1. What are some relevant skills and attitudes for being a successful student?

_____

_____

2. What are some relevant skills and attitudes for being a good parent?

_____

_____

3. Which skills have you listed that are relevant to being both a successful student and a good parent?

_____

_____

4. Which skills are relevant to being a good student that are irrelevant to being a good parent?

_____

_____

Relevance in Reading

In reading, a similar process is followed to figure out how relevant each piece of evidence is to the author's claim. The evidence can't be solely emotional, and it can't just relate to the general issue; it must directly support the claim itself. Suppose you read the following claim:

> Being a successful student takes a lot of hard work.

For evidence to be relevant, it can't simply be about "being a successful student"—that is the issue. Instead, the evidence must relate to the idea that being a successful student "takes a lot of hard work." Even within this claim, there are actually two claims—"a lot" and "hard." Some relevant evidence might be the following:

Support for the claim "Being a successful student takes a lot of work"

- ▶ Most students spend three hours outside of class for every hour in class.
- ▶ When I asked the students in my management class how long they had spent on a recent, typical assignment, more than half of them said fifteen to thirty hours.
- ▶ Most of the classes in my major require between 75 and 150 pages of reading per week.

Support for the claim "Being a successful student takes hard work"

- ▶ Professor Dubert said that students who get A's in her class usually revise their research papers three times, while students who get C's revise them only once.
- ▶ The Learning Center tutor told me that most of the Psychology 301 students he has tutored had to study a single textbook chapter alone, in a study group, and with the help of a tutor before they thought they truly understood it.
- ▶ Many students now download podcasts of instructors' lectures so they can listen to them a second time to make sure they fully grasp the important points.

The following statements would be irrelevant:

- ▶ At my school, you get free passes to the local ski resort if you are a straight-A student. (This sentence has to do with one effect of being a successful student, not the causes.)
- ▶ Successful students know how to suck up to their instructors. (This sentence suggests that being a successful student is more a matter of pandering to teachers than working hard.)

Even though these statements are about the issue, they do not directly support the claim; and thus, they are irrelevant to the claim.

Interaction 11–5 ▸ Choose Between Relevant and Irrelevant Evidence

Put a **C** next to the claim and an **R** next to the relevant evidence. Leave the blank empty if the evidence is not relevant.

1. ____ Make sure you identify the person first and then the disability.

   ____ When writing about a person with a disability, you should use language that accurately reflects the person's life circumstances and does not label the person in pejorative ways.

   ____ If a person has visual impairment, use *partial vision* or *sight* rather than *blind*, which refers to total blindness.

   ____ If you find an error in your report, please mark through it with black ink.

   —From Summers, *Fundamentals of Case Management Practice*, 2e

2. ____ One myth is "No pain, no gain."

   ____ Another is that a gym is the only good place to work out.

   ____ When working out, be careful to listen to what your body is telling you.

   ____ When working out, it is smart to avoid some common myths about exercise.

   —From Hales, *An Invitation To Health*, 12e

3. ____ Most orientations take about an hour, and they can give you the confidence you need to complete your research assignments.

   ____ If you are new to library research or are unfamiliar with the library, you should schedule a tour.

   ____ A library orientation may sound silly or boring, but it can save you hours of wandering around a facility you do not understand.

   ____ Librarians can be an excellent resource.

   —From Griffin, *Invitation to Public Speaking*, 2e

4. ____ Interviewers should use structured interviews to be sure they ask standard questions of all applicants.

   ____ Some are situational questions, which ask how an applicant might respond to a hypothetical situation.

   ____ Applicants should be prepared for the interview process both mentally and emotionally.

   ____ Others might include behavioral questions, which ask the applicant what they did in previous positions.

   —From Williams, *MGMT*, 2008 Edition

5. ____ Studies show that, generally, women commit less crime than men.

____ One important area of crime research is the relationship between class, crime, and race.

____ Arrest statistics show that the poor are more likely to be arrested for crimes.

____ Sociologists have demonstrated a strong correlation between unemployment, poverty, and crime.

—From Andersen/Taylor, *Sociology*, 4e

Interaction 11–6 ▸ Identify Irrelevant Evidence in a Paragraph

Underline the claim in the paragraph. Then evaluate each piece of evidence for relevance. Cross out any irrelevant evidence.

1.

Danica Patrick is the most popular IndyCar Series racer today. Her teammates, some of whom have won more races than Patrick, like the attention she gets. Teammate Marco Andretti says, "She's a rock star." Fans line up to buy Patrick souvenirs like sweatshirts and baseball caps with Danica's name on them. Her competitors are glad that she draws people to the sport of open-wheel racing. Patrick says, "I'm pretty girly outside the car." She wants to race for another ten years.

—Excerpted and adapted from Caldwell, "The Brickyard Is Patrick's Backyard," *New York Times*, May 25, 2008

Walter G Arce/Shutterstock.com

2.

College students should give permission for their parents to be contacted if they are experiencing difficulties. Except in certain emergencies, colleges may not contact students' parents regarding medical, psychological, or academic problems without the student's permission. Because of his violent writings, the shooter at Virginia Tech, for instance, had worried both fellow students and English faculty members, who shared their concerns with the administration. But the administration could not legally contact his parents to gain insight into Cho Seung Hui's problems. Colleges may not send report cards, even for students receiving A's and B's, to parents; they must send them to the students themselves. Students who binge drink, who are depressed, and who are having trouble socially can't get help from their families if their parents don't know they are having trouble.

3.

Amy Sutherland wrote an article called "What Shamu Taught Me about a Happy Marriage." In the article she describes how she used the techniques she learned from animal trainers to get her husband to change his habits. The technique called "approximations" was especially helpful. The trainer rewards an animal for each small step it takes toward doing the behavior the trainer wants. When her husband mimics a northern Vermont accent, Sunderland can't help but laugh. Sunderland would thank her husband for throwing a shirt in the hamper, and kiss him for putting in two. Sunderland used smaller approximations whenever she couldn't get Scott to take bigger steps. After two years, she felt she had been successful. Her marriage was smoother, and her floor was cleaner.

Credibility

Credibility means having the quality of trustworthiness. If someone is credible, then you are willing to trust or believe him or her. Credibility mostly stems from how a person is perceived. If you perceive someone as trustworthy, then it follows that you will trust him or her. However, if you do not know someone, you can still measure credibility to a certain extent. For example, in Chapter 8 you learned that an expert would usually have more credibility than a person with an informed opinion or a person on the street. Being an expert doesn't guarantee credibility; it depends on reputation as well.

In reading, credibility is often determined by the sources authors cite when they are writing. An author citing reasons based on factual evidence to support his or her claim will have more credibility than one who writes from an entirely emotional perspective.

Interaction 11–7 ▶ Evaluate Credibility

A. Create a list of five people you think have credibility. These people can be anyone—politicians, celebrities, athletes, historical figures, or personal friends and acquaintances. List the qualities you feel make them credible. Then discuss these qualities with your classmates.

_____

_____

_____

_____

B. Would you find these people persuasive on all topics or only a few? Explain.

_____

_____

_____

_____

The Types of Evidence

Authors may draw on several different kinds of evidence as support. Some forms of evidence usually seem more credible or authoritative than others, but you should ask questions about every kind as you read.

Expert Authority

As we discussed in Chapter 8 (page 421), people who are experts in their field have great authority when speaking about that field. When you are evaluating the evidence of an expert authority, ask yourself the following questions:

▶ What credentials—schooling, books they wrote, employment position— does this person have?
▶ What biases might the expert have?

Here is some insight from an experienced journalist about the problem of bias:

> There is always a tension, as a journalist, between asking open-ended questions that allow an interview subject to explain something and pressing or challenging them on accuracy or details. But if you think you already know the subject, or already have a story angle half-formed in your head, it's easy to overlook the first part.
>
> —Wallace, "The Bias of Veteran Journalists," *The Atlantic*, April 5, 2010

For example, if a journalist has been covering the technology scene, he or she may have already formed an opinion about a company or a product. This could result in an article that is not objective, but rather follows the direction of predetermined biases. That doesn't mean that you should discount his or her opinion, but you should read critically, and if you are trying to be informed, you should read more expert sources to understand the larger context. Likewise when you read, the author you are reading should ideally refer to multiple expert authorities. This gives the author a higher level of credibility.

Facts

Facts carry great weight, just as expert authorities do. That is true by definition, since a fact is a verifiable, objective piece of information. When evaluating facts, ask yourself these questions:

- First of all, is this really true? Is it a fact?
- What use is the author making of the fact?
- Does the fact apply under these conditions?
- What facts are not being stated?

To get a sense of the complicated questions that even facts can raise, consider the following paragraph from the book *How to Watch the TV News*, by Neil Postman and Steve Powers:

Every news story is a reflection of the reporter who tells the story. The reporter's previous assumptions about what is "out there" edit what he or she thinks is there. For example, many journalists believe that what is called "the intifada" is newsworthy. Let us suppose that a fourteen-year-old Palestinian boy hurls a Molotov cocktail at two eighteen-year-old Israeli soldiers. The explosion knocks one of the soldiers down and damages his left eye. The other soldier, terrified, fires a shot at the Palestinian that kills him instantly. The injured soldier eventually loses the sight of his eye. What details should be included in reporting this event? Is the age of the Palestinian relevant? Are the ages of the Israeli soldiers relevant? Was the act of the Palestinian provoked by the mere presence of Israeli soldiers? Was the act therefore justified? Is the shooting justified? Is the state of mind of the shooter relevant?

Remember that facts are selected by a person who has a particular point of view or bias.

Statistics

Statistics are numerical data. People tend to believe statistics, but they can be used to misrepresent facts just like words can. Ask yourself:

- How accurate are these numbers?
- How were they gathered, and who analyzed them?
- What use is the author making of them?

Sometimes people trying to support their Second Amendment right to bear arms use the following phrase: "Guns don't kill people, doctors do." These are the statistics behind this statement.

- There are 700,000 physicians in the United States.

  There are 120,000 accidental deaths in the United States caused by physicians every year, and the accidental death percentage per physician is 0.171.

- There are 80 million gun owners in the United States.

  There are 1,500 accidental deaths from guns every year, regardless of age group, and the accidental death percentage per gun owner is 0.0000188.

Conclusion? Doctors are 9,000 times more deadly than guns. Said another way: Doctors aren't illegal, neither should guns be!

Okay, so how does one think about these numbers? Even if they are statistically accurate, are they a credible comparison? Here are some things to think about: Almost everyone will see a doctor during his or her lifetime, but many people do not own or interact with guns. Many people who interact with doctors do so when they are ill. Was it the doctor who killed them or the illness? There is no doubt that doctors do cause accidental deaths. Just think of some stars who have overdosed on prescription medicine: Michael Jackson, Heath Ledger, and possibly Marilyn Monroe and Elvis Presley. The doubt is not about the number, but about the credibility of the comparison. It is not an "apples to apples" comparison.

Examples

Examples are used to explain ideas. Examples can be persuasive, but they do not have the same level of credibility as expert authority, facts, and statistics, especially if they alone are used to support an idea. Ask yourself:

- Are the examples true? Are they relevant?
- Are the examples representative of most of the instances of an event of this kind?
- What other forms of evidence might the author use—if there is any other evidence?

Read the following paragraph. Examine the claim and the examples used as evidence.

> Too many people these days are using the Internet as a way to meet potential partners. My friend Alex met a woman on a chat site last year, and before they even met they had decided to get married! Another friend, Josie, posted her profile on several singles sites over the weekend. She has already received twenty responses from men who would like to get to know her better. My sister Cara flirts in writing with someone she met through a blog. Why aren't people interested in meeting in person anymore?

The examples of three friends can't by themselves prove many claims. However, this particular claim would be difficult to prove at all. Who gets to define how many is "too many"? When you read a paragraph like this, realize that you are reading someone's opinion. In this case, this writer has overgeneralized from too few examples.

Personal Experiences

When an author presents personal experiences as evidence for an argument, think carefully about the same issues you would consider when reading any example. Realize that as is the case with everyone else, the author's experiences are colored by his or her own history, culture, beliefs, and so on. Ask yourself:

▶ Would another person in this situation have a similar experience? In other words, is the experience representative?
▶ How relevant to others is the author's experience?
▶ Does the author present any other kinds of evidence along with personal experience?

Consider the following examples:

▶ "If you work as hard as Michael Jordan did, you too can become a great basketball player." This sounds great and inspirational, but what if a person does not have the same athleticism as MJ? What happens then?
▶ Using Steve Jobs or Bill Gates as examples of why you should drop out of school. These two technology gurus were unique. Their experience would not work well across the board as a reason to quit school.
▶ My friend won the lottery. Wow! But the chances of winning are very small. Yes, someone will win, but one example is not valid support for playing the lottery.

Each of these examples is overgeneralized. A personal example can be great support, but it should logically relate, and an author should use other evidence as well.

Interaction 11–8 ▷ Identify the Evidence

For each group of sentences, a topic sentence is given. Bracket the issue and underline the claim in each one. Then identify the type of evidence in the other sentences, selecting from the list below. You can use an item more than once. Finally, evaluate each piece of evidence to decide which one is weakest or irrelevant to the claim, and cross it out.

opinion	expert authority	facts
examples	statistics	experience (author's personal experience)

1. Topic sentence   Buying a home is a good investment.

_____   Homes average a 3 to 6 percent increase in value yearly.

_____   You receive hefty tax benefits each year for owning a home.

_____   Owning a home makes one feel like a productive member of society.

2. **Topic sentence**   Guns should have safety locks on them.

_____   Children are naturally curious, and if a gun is in the house, then they are going to pick it up and play with it and probably end up killing themselves or a friend by accident.

_____   The U.S. Centers for Disease Control and Prevention released a report showing that 2,827 children and teens died as a result of gun violence in 2003. This number from one year is higher than the number of American fighting men and women killed in Iraq from 2003 to April 2006.

_____   National research shows that 40 percent of families with children also have a gun, and one out of four keep their guns loaded.

3. **Topic sentence**   The death penalty is expensive and all too often used on the wrong people. It should be abolished.

_____   Carrying out the death penalty costs two to five times more than keeping a person in prison for a life term.

_____   DNA testing has shown that a dozen innocent men and women have been put to death.

_____   Since the death penalty was reinstated in the United States in 1976, more than 1,000 people have been executed.

4. **Topic sentence**   You should exercise your muscles to keep them healthy.

_____   Dr. Robert H. Fitts, an exercise physiologist at Marquette University, says that both endurance and strength are important to develop.

_____   William J. Kraemer, a professor of kinesiology at the University of Connecticut, says that many people increase their endurance by walking, but few develop their strength by lifting weights, and when they do lift weights, they often do so incorrectly.

_____   Your muscles will atrophy if you don't use them.

_____   When I started lifting weights again after a five year hiatus, I felt great.

5. **Topic sentence**   Older people who want to stay in their homes should consider having remote monitors installed so that their children in other cities can track their well-being.

_____   Each morning, Lynn Pitet checks her computer when she wakes up to see if her mother is following her normal routine.

_____   Motion sensors can tell a remotely located relative whether a parent has gotten out of bed, taken medications, and is moving around the house.

_____   Only wealthier people will be able to take advantage of such a system.

_____   Because such sensors are relatively new, insurance may or may not cover the cost of installing them.

Interaction 11–9 ▶ Identify the Claim and Evaluate the Evidence

In the following passage, underline the claim (which may be in either one or two sentences). Number the pieces of supporting evidence. Discuss the relevance and strength of the evidence in supporting the claim.

Dear Friend:

Would you like to fill any kitchen with students eager to pay you $40–$50 for a 2-hour class, and show them a healthier way of eating?

If so, stop everything. Listen carefully. I've got great news.

With the right marketing strategies, you can become a popular raw foods educator. You can make a real difference. You can help people prevent or overcome disease. Best of all, teaching classes is the first step to multiple income streams.

For example, some of your students will buy your books and videos. Others will hire you to coach them.

And when you webcast your classes, people all over the world can pay you to watch them online!

Frankly, more people would improve their diets if someone showed them the ropes. Many want to eat healthier. But they don't know where to start. It seems too complicated, overwhelming, or intimidating.

That's Where You Come In!

You can introduce them to raw food meals, and show them that healthy food can be delicious. You can open their eyes to a whole new way of eating. Just imagine yourself:

▶ Surrounded by admiring students in a gourmet kitchen
▶ Inspiring people to eat better
▶ Sharing the incredible healing powers of a healthier diet
▶ Creating more harmony for humanity, animals, and the planet
▶ Empowering people to improve their health

If you've already decided to teach classes, keep reading. But if you're not sure you're ready, qualified, or have what it takes, Raw Food Riches makes it easier than you might think.

How Do You Get The Ball Rolling?

How do you plan, advertise, and deliver classes? How do you get people to find you, contact you, and prepay?

To answer these questions, we've created a groundbreaking new program called "Raw Food Riches."

For the first time ever, top chefs, educators, and coaches spill the beans on how they got started, how they became popular, and how you can follow in their footsteps.

It's all captured on four 72-minute interviews. With the trade secrets you discover, you're guaranteed to fill any kitchen with students eager to pay you $40–$50 per class.

Chef certification courses are great. They give you skills and credibility. But students don't show up at your door just because you're certified.

The main focus of those courses is culinary techniques, not marketing. So even certified chefs need easy ways to get students and fill classes.

"Raw Food Riches"

The Raw Food Riches series includes four 72-minute interviews with top chefs. Plus transcripts and the Basic Book of Trade Secrets, which organizes the information by topic and subtopic into 9 chapters.

In each recorded interview, a top chef spills the beans on how she plans, advertises, and delivers classes.

By using Raw Food Riches, you will feel confident that you can:

► Fill any kitchen with 6–8 students eager to pay you $40–50 per class.
► Earn at least $3,000 from students, customers, and clients within the next 12 months (and probably a lot more!)
► Be 100% prepared for your first class, knowing which ingredients to prep ahead of time, how long the class will take, etc.

If you don't order "Raw Food Riches," how will you learn to fill any kitchen with students eager to pay you $40–50 per class?

How will you learn to plan, advertise, and deliver your classes without a hitch?

Why struggle through months (or years) of trial and error when you can skip the hard knocks and follow a proven game plan?

So order right now!

A. Is the evidence relevant? Why or why not? _____

_____

B. Is the evidence strong? Why or why not? _____

_____

_____

How Much Is a Test Worth?

Today's high school seniors face many challenges when applying to colleges. More pressure is being put on students to go to college and get a degree due to the changes in the work force. This increases the number of students applying for college, thus creating more competition.

One of the biggest challenges students face is scoring high on standardized tests, such as the ACT and the SAT. Scores on these tests play a huge part in deciding which schools a student can or cannot attend.

Colleges put too much stock in standardized test scores. Not all students have the ability to test well, tests cannot predict how successful a student will be, and the results are not really standardized since these tests can be learned through paid practices, such as coaching.

Some students work hard for four years to keep their grade point average (GPA) high. They participate in extracurricular activities. They achieve leadership roles in important clubs. They strive to become well-rounded students.

However, they may be lacking in one important area. They may not have the ability to take and score well on a standardized test. Even the brightest student who maintains a perfect 4.0 GPA may struggle to perform well in the pressured environment that comes with taking the ACT or SAT.

Basic knowledge can easily fly out the window when a student gets nervous, knowing he only has a certain amount of time to complete each section. Many students suffer from test anxiety, a psychological condition that causes a person to become so distressed before and during a test that he performs poorly on the test.

Just knowing that their future college choices rely on how well they perform on this test may cause many students to suffer from test anxiety.

There is no test that can predict whether a student is ready for college or whether a student will be successful once he gets there. High school grades are the best indicator of how a student will do in college. Many colleges have decided to make the submission of standardized test scores optional, and these colleges have found those who did not submit their test scores performed better in college than those who did submit their test scores.

Finally, there is the issue of whether or not these tests really offer colleges standardized ways of comparing students from different high schools. There are many online study programs, study guides and tutoring programs available that promise to raise a student's standardized test score.

This removes an element of standardization, since a college is unable to determine by looking at the test score who has taken advantage of these options and who has not. There are many students who cannot afford these pricey options to ensure a higher test score, which puts them at an obvious disadvantage to those who can.

Making good grades during four years of high school with a well-rounded mixture of extracurricular activities, leadership roles, and a genuine desire to learn are much more important than a score on a four-hour test. Colleges should put less stock in standardized test scores and focus more on each individual student.

A. Is the evidence relevant? Why or why not? _____

B. Is the evidence strong? Why or why not? _____

_____

An Author's Assumptions

We all make assumptions, and authors are no exception. A dictionary typically defines an assumption as something that is believed to be true but has not been proven. This definition usually works for everyday life. You see someone behind the wheel of a car, and you assume it is his or her car. You don't ask to see the name on the title! A wedding ring or lack of one leads to certain assumptions. Styles of clothing, hair color and length, weight, age, and countless other things lead to assumptions in everyday life.

This definition needs to be added to for reading purposes. When an author assumes something, it usually means that he or she accepts certain notions as fact and so does not feel the need to support or defend them. An author's religious, cultural, ethnic, and economic background affects his or her assumptions, just as elements of your background affect yours.

Authors may assume that readers share their assumptions. For example, an article entitled "How to Turn the Tides of Global Warming" assumes that global warming can be stopped. Every aspect of an article, book, or other reading material—from its title, to its details, to things left unsaid—can provide clues to an author's assumptions.

Let's look at a puzzle to illustrate a possible assumption on your part:

> A father and son are in a terrible accident. The father dies and the son, in critical condition, is rushed to the hospital for surgery. The surgeon walks in, takes one look at the boy and says, "I can't operate on this boy. He is my son." How is this possible?
>
> _____

It is important to look at what you are reading as objectively as possible. Imagine you are having a conversation with the author and you have to understand where he or she is coming from in order to understand the text, whether it is clearly stated, implied, or assumed.

Interaction 11–10 ▸ Identify Assumptions

Identify the assumptions in each item.

1.

> How bizarre that a book on punctuation would be a bestseller in England and America!

Assumption about punctuation: _____

2.

> Never go to a doctor whose office plants have died.
>
> —Erma Bombeck

Assumption about doctors: _____

3.

> When a man comes to me for advice, I find out the kind of advice he wants, and I give it to him.
>
> —Josh Billings

Assumption: _____

4.

> More than a dozen countries have liberalized their abortion laws in recent years, including South Africa, Switzerland, Cambodia and Chad. In a handful of others, including Russia and the United States (or parts of it), the movement has been toward criminalizing more and different types of abortions. In South Dakota, the governor recently signed the most restrictive abortion bill since the Supreme Court ruled in 1973, in *Roe v. Wade*, that state laws prohibiting abortion were unconstitutional. The South Dakota law, which its backers acknowledge is designed to test *Roe v. Wade* in the courts, forbids abortion, including those cases in which the pregnancy is a result of rape or incest. Only if an abortion is necessary to save the life of the mother is the procedure permitted. A similar though less restrictive bill is now making its way through the Mississippi Legislature.
>
> —Hitt, "Pro-Life Nation," *New York Times Magazine*, April 9, 2006

Assumption of the lawmakers in countries that have liberalized their abortion laws: _____

_____

Assumption of the governor of South Dakota: _____

_____

5.

> My biological parents put me up for adoption before I was even one year old. For the rest of my childhood (until I was 18 and legal), I was passed around from family to foster family. One time, when I was 10, I had stayed with one family for almost two years before they told me I had to go. I begged with them to let me stay, but I was still sent away. I do not know why they did not love me enough to keep me (I often ask myself why my biological parents did not love me enough to keep me as well). I think it was at this point that I determined never to be hurt again. I am so fearful of being abandoned again that I do not allow myself to get close to others because then that person will leave me. I am an adult now but still feel like a scared little kid.

List this writer's assumptions about himself. _____

_____

_____

Connect Your Skills

Evaluating the Author's Reasoning and Evidence

Read the following article. Annotate the issue and claim, and pay attention to the types of evidence used as you read. Then answer the questions that follow.

How We Became a Throw-Away Society

E.A. Zimmerman

1   I once had a house guest from South America. During his visit, I happened to throw an old, broken blender in the trash. The next day it was sitting on my counter—in working order. In his world, people simply cannot afford to replace a malfunctioning item. They take the time and figure out how to fix it. In Cuba, they are still driving cars from the 1950's, mainly because they do not have a choice. New American cars have not been available since the Revolution and subsequent embargo.

Cubans put a lot of effort and ingenuity into maintaining old cars like this 1952 Ford Custom. With an average salary of $19 a month, most Cubans could not afford a new car even if they were available. Photo by Tina Gallagher.

2   In contrast, the U.S. is renowned as a "throw-away society." On average, each American generates 4.6 lbs. of garbage every day (source: U.S. EPA, 2006). I believe a combination of factors have contributed to this regrettable phenomenon, which will one day haunt us.

3   "Planned obsolescence" is not a myth. It is a manufacturing philosophy developed in the 1920's and 1930's, when mass production became popular. The goal is to make a product or part that will fail, or become less desirable over time or after a certain amount of use. This puts pressure on the consumer to buy again. Advertising trains consumers to want what is new and improved. It convinces them that the more they have, the happier they will be. Vance Packard, author of *The Waste Makers*,

a book published in 1960, called this "the systematic attempt of business to make us wasteful, debt-ridden, permanently discontented individuals."

4   Planned obsolescence does keep costs down. Instead of making an expensive product that will last a long time, businesses produce more affordable, disposable items. In addition, technological advances are happening at a breakneck pace. Some electronic items have become so inexpensive that it is cheaper to replace them. Labor and parts are pricey. Few consumers would pay $50 or more to repair a broken VCR, when they can purchase a brand new DVD player for $50.

5   Busy people often value their time and convenience more than money. It takes time, patience (and some skill) to darn socks. Complicated, computerized equipment may be difficult to repair. If a car starts to have mechanical problems, replacing it with a newer, more reliable model may be more appealing than tolerating it being in the shop for a week.

6   In a materialistic society, people may accumulate so many things that they may not value them. I will never forget watching an Ecuadorian boy absorbed in play. He had a truck made from a left-over margarine tub, pulled along his little dirt construction site on a string. I would not be surprised if it were the only toy he owned. In the U.S., most children receive so many gifts at Christmas that they do not have the time or attention span to open them all.

7   We also live in an era of fast food. In a sit down restaurant, food is served on real china and silverware that is then washed and re-used. "To go" food comes in cheap, disposable packaging. Pre-packaged frozen and canned food are increasingly popular, generating waste cardboard and tin. Milk used to come in glass bottles that were picked each up morning when fresh milk was delivered. Now, most beverages come in plastic bottles, of which less than a third are recycled (source: EPA, 2003).

8   Unlike many developing countries, we live in a world of abundance. A 2004 study by Dr. Timothy Jones of the University of Arizona also found that in the U.S., 40–50 percent of all food ready for harvest is wasted. Jones estimated that an average family of four throws out $590 worth of meat, fruit, vegetables and grain products each year. Trash is fairly cheap to dispose of. Landfills and incinerators are out of sight and out of mind. But we are already seeing negative effects of this type of lifestyle—pollution, litter, and depletion of natural resources. The question is, how long will we be able to sustain this type of living?

—E.A. Zimmerman, "How We Became a Throw Away Society." Copyright © 2012 by E.A. Zimmerman.
Reprinted by permission. http://www.ourbetternature.org/throwaway.htm

A. Identify the issue and claim.

   1. What is the issue? _____

   2. What is the claim? _____

   _____

B. What types of evidence were given? Check off each type that was given and then note the evidence and the paragraph in which it was found. Some answers may overlap.

   3. ____ expert authority

   Evidence: _____

   _____

4. ____ facts

Evidence (may overlap with expert authority): _____

_____

5. ____ statistics

Evidence: _____

_____

6. ____ examples

Evidence: _____

_____

7. ____ personal experience

Evidence: _____

_____

C. Circle **R** for relevant or **I** for irrelevant evidence as it relates to the claim.

8. R   I   Discarded trash is contributing to the pollution of our oceans.

9. R   I   The average American discards almost 7 lbs of trash daily.

10. R   I   Many repair shops have closed down due to lack of business.

D. Identify the assumptions in the following statements.

11. Give a man a fish and he will eat for a day; teach a man to fish, and he will sit in a boat all day drinking beer.

Assumption about fishing: _____

12. It's amazing that the amount of news that happens each day fits exactly into the newspaper.

Assumption about news: _____

13. Having one child makes you a parent; having two makes you a referee.

Assumption about children: _____

14. If opportunity does not knock, build a door. —Milton Berle

Assumption about opportunity: _____

15. "Don't say you don't have enough time. You have exactly the same number of hours per day that were given to Helen Keller, Pasteur, Michelangelo, Mother Teresa, Leonardo da Vinci, Thomas Jefferson, and Albert Einstein." —*Life's Little Instruction Book*, compiled by H. Jackson Brown, Jr.

Assumption about you: _____

Click to Connect! To check your comprehension of chapter concepts, visit **www.cengagebrain.com** to access the CourseMate for this chapter.

Chapter Summary Activity

This chapter has discussed how to evaluate an author's reasoning. Construct a Reading Guide to Evaluating the Author's Reasoning here by completing each idea on the left with information from the chapter on the right. You can use this guide whenever you read arguments.

Reading Guide to Evaluating the Author's Reasoning

Complete this idea with ...	information from Chapter 11.
In arguments a topic is called	1. _____ _____
In arguments a main idea is called	2. _____ _____
In arguments a detail is called	3. _____ _____
Relevant evidence–definition of	4. _____ _____
Five types of evidence	5. _____
	6. _____ _____
	7. _____ _____
	8. _____ _____

	9. _____
	_____
Two items to consider when reading an expert's opinion or judgment	**10.** _____
	_____
	11. _____
	_____
Two items to consider about facts	**12.** _____
	_____
	13. _____
	_____
Two questions to ask about statistics	**14.** _____
	_____
	15. _____
	_____
Three questions to ask about examples and personal experiences	**16.** _____
	_____
	17. _____
	_____
	18. _____
	_____
Credibility—definition of	**19.** _____
	_____
In reading material, an assumption is	**20.** _____
	_____

Think about the reading strategies you used to evaluate an author's reasoning and evidence before you read this chapter. What is one thing you will do differently because you find it more effective? Write down your thoughts.

_____
_____
_____

Reading 11–1 | American Government Textbook

▶ Pre-Reading the Selection

Have you considered what is meant by free speech in the U.S. Constitution? Does it mean you can do or say anything you want? The selection reprinted here defines free speech from a constitutional perspective. Read it to see if it says what you think it will.

Surveying the Reading

Survey the following article. Then check the elements that are included in this reading.

_____   Title   _____   Words in bold or italic type

_____   Headings   _____   Images and captions

_____   First sentences of paragraphs

Guessing the Purpose

Judging from the title of the reading as well as the title of the book from which this selection is taken, what do you suppose the purpose for writing is?

_____

Predicting the Content

Predict three things this selection will discuss.

▶ _____

▶ _____

▶ _____

Activating Your Knowledge

What do you already know about free speech as it relates to the Constitution? Note two or three things you know.

▶ _____

▶ _____

▶ _____

◉ **Scan to Connect!** Use your smart phone to scan this code to watch a video to activate your knowledge about your rights to burn the flag. As you watch, pay attention to what Penn says concerning what the Bill of Rights gives him the right to do: burn the American flag. What is your reaction to his action and what he says?

▶ Reading with Pen in Hand

Students who annotate as they read are more successful than those who do not. That's why you will annotate every selection in *Connect* as you read. In the reading that follows, use the following symbols:

★ or ⟨Point⟩   to indicate a main idea

① ② ③   to indicate major details

 Visit www.cengagebrain.com to access the CourseMate for this chapter to hear pronunciations of vocabulary words from this reading.

What Is Free Speech?

1   If most political speaking or writing is permissible, save that which actually **incites** someone to take illegal actions, what *kinds* of speaking and writing qualify for this broad protection? Though the Constitution says that the legislature may make "no law" abridging freedom of speech or the press, and although some justices have argued that this means literally *no* law, the Court has held that there are at least four forms of speaking and writing that are not automatically granted full constitutional protection: libel, obscenity, symbolic speech, and false advertising.

incites Use your logic to decide what the verb *incites* means.

▶ What four forms of speech are not automatically granted full constitutional protection?

Libel

2   A **libel** is a written statement that **defames** the character of another person. (If the statement is oral, it is called *slander*.) The libel or slander must harm the person being attacked. In some countries, such as England, it is easy to sue another person for libel and to collect. In this country, it is much harder. For one thing, you must show that the libelous statement was false. If it was true, you cannot collect no matter how badly it harmed you.

defames If you have prior knowledge of slander, use this to help you; if not, look to the word *character* for help.

▶ What is the difference between libel and slander?

3   A beauty contest winner was awarded $14 million (later reduced on appeal) when she proved that *Penthouse* magazine had libeled her. Actress Carol Burnett collected a large sum from a libel suit brought against a gossip newspaper. But when Theodore Roosevelt sued a newspaper for falsely claiming that he was a drunk, the jury awarded him damages of only six cents.

▶ How do you think Theodore Roosevelt felt?

4   If you are a public figure, it is much harder to win a libel suit. A public figure such as an elected official, a candidate for office, an army general, or a well-known celebrity must prove not only that the publication was false and damaging but also that the words were published with "actual **malice**"—that is, with reckless disregard for their truth or falsity or with knowledge that they were false. Israeli General Ariel Sharon was able to prove that the statements made about him by *Time* magazine were false and damaging but not that they were the result of "actual malice."

▶ What does "actual malice" mean?

malice What desire would a person who tells lies about someone feel?

▶ What is "libel tourism"?

5

For a while, people who felt they had been libeled would bring suit in England against an American author. One Saudi leader sued an American author who had accused him of financing terrorism even though she had not sold her book in England (but word about it had been on the Internet). This strategy, called "libel tourism," was ended in 2010 when Congress **unanimously** passed and the president signed a bill that bars enforcement in U.S. courts of libel actions against Americans if what they published would not be libelous under American law.

unanimously The prefix *un-* means "one" and the root *animus* means "mind." How did Congress vote on this issue?

Obscenity

▶ How would you define *obscenity*?

6

Obscenity is not protected by the First Amendment. The Court has always held that obscene materials, because they have no redeeming social value and are calculated chiefly to appeal to one's sexual rather than political or literary interests, can be regulated by the state. The problem, of course, arises with the meaning of *obscene*. In the period from 1957 to 1968, the Court decided 13 major cases involving the definition of obscenity, which resulted in 55 separate opinions. Some justices, such as Hugo Black, believed that the First Amendment protected all publications, even wholly obscene ones. Others believed that obscenity deserved no protection and struggled heroically to define the term. Still others shared the view of former Justice Potter Stewart, who objected to "hard-core pornography" but admitted that the best definition he could offer was "I know it when I see it."

▶ Can you paraphrase the Court's definition of what is obscene?

7

It is unnecessary to review in detail the many attempts by the Court at defining obscenity. The justices have made it clear that nudity and sex are not, by definition, obscene and that they will provide First Amendment protection to anything that has political, literary, or artistic merit, allowing the government to punish only the distribution of "hard-core pornography." Their most recent definition of this is as follows: to be obscene, the work, taken as a whole, must be judged by "the average person applying contemporary community standards" to appeal to the "prurient interest" or to depict "in a patently offensive way, sexual conduct specifically defined by applicable state law" and to lack "serious literary, artistic, political, or scientific value."

▶ What are the two contrasting approaches to obscenity within the community?

8

It is easy to make sport of the problems the Court has faced in trying to decide obscenity cases (one conjures up images of black-robed justices leafing through the pages of *Hustler* magazine, taking notes), but these problems reveal, as do other civil liberties cases, the continuing problem of balancing competing claims. One part of the community wants to read or see whatever it wishes; another part wants to protect private acts from public degradation. The first part **cherishes** liberty above all; the second values decency above liberty. The former fears that *any* restriction on literature will lead to *pervasive* restrictions; the latter believes that reasonable people can distinguish (or reasonable laws can require them to distinguish) between patently offensive and artistically serious work.

cherishes Use the example clue in the previous sentence to decide what *cherishes* means.

9   With the advent of the Internet, it has become more difficult for the government to regulate obscenity. The Internet spans the globe. It offers an amazing variety of materials—some educational, some entertaining, some sexually explicit. But it is difficult to apply the Supreme Court's standard for judging whether sexual material is obscene—the "average person" applying "contemporary community standards"—to the Internet, because there is no easy way to tell what "the community" is. Is it the place where the recipient lives or the place where the material originates? And since no one is in charge of the Internet, who can be held responsible for controlling offensive material? Since anybody can send anything to anybody else without knowing the age or location of the recipient, how can the Internet protect children? When Congress tried to ban obscene, indecent, or "patently offensive" materials from the Internet, the Supreme Court struck down the law as unconstitutional. The Court went even further with child pornography. Though it has long held that child pornography is illegal even if it is not obscene because of the government's interest in protecting children, it would not let Congress ban pornography involving computer-designed children. Under the 1996 law, it would be illegal to display computer simulations of children engaged in sex even if no real children were involved. The Court said "no." It held that Congress could not ban "virtual" child pornography without violating the First Amendment because, in its view, the law might **bar** even harmless depictions of children and sex (for example, in a book on child psychology).

> What is the problem with regulating the Internet?

bar Consider the examples that follow the verb. What does *bar* mean?

Symbolic Speech

10   You cannot ordinarily claim that an illegal act should be protected because that action is meant to **convey** a political message. For example, if you burn your draft card in protest against the foreign policy of the United States, you can be punished for the illegal act (burning the card), even if your intent was to communicate

> Define *symbolic speech*.

convey Use the synonym in the next sentence to understand *convey*.

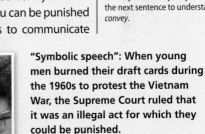

"Symbolic speech": When young men burned their draft cards during the 1960s to protest the Vietnam War, the Supreme Court ruled that it was an illegal act for which they could be punished.

Hulton Archive/Getty Images

infringement Use the context of these sentences and your logic.

▶ What is your reaction to this issue?

muster Use the context of the sentence and the two that follow, as well as your logic.

your beliefs. The Court reasoned that giving such **symbolic speech** the same protection as real speech would open the door to permitting all manner of illegal actions—murder, arson, rape—if the perpetrator meant thereby to send a message.

11   On the other hand, a statute that makes it illegal to burn the American flag is an unconstitutional **infringement** of free speech. Why is there a difference between a draft card and the flag? The Court argues that the government has a right to run a military draft and so can protect draft cards, even if this incidentally restricts speech. But the only motive that the government has in banning flag-burning is to restrict this form of speech, and that would make such a restriction improper.

12   The American people were outraged by the flag-burning decision, and in response the House and Senate passed by huge majorities (380 to 38 and 91 to 9) a law making it a federal crime to burn the flag. But the Court struck this law down as unconstitutional. Now that it was clear that only a constitutional amendment could make flag-burning illegal, Congress was asked to propose one. But it would not. Earlier members of the House and Senate had supported a law banning flag-burning with over 90 percent of their votes, but when asked to make that law a constitutional amendment they could not **muster** the necessary two-thirds majorities. The reason is that Congress is much more reluctant to amend the Constitution than to pass new laws. Several members decided that flag-burning was wrong, but not so wrong or so common as to justify an amendment.

—From Wilson/Dilulio/Bose, *American Government: Institutions and Policies*, 13e.

▶ Comprehension Questions

Write the letter of the answer on the line. Then explain your thinking.

Main Idea

_____ 1. Which of the following best states the main idea of this passage?

   a. A libel is a written statement that defames the character of another person.

   b. The Court has always held that obscene materials, because they have no redeeming social value and are calculated chiefly to appeal to one's sexual rather than political or literary interests, can be regulated by the state.

   c. The Court has held that there are at least four forms of speaking and writing that are not automatically granted full constitutional protection: libel, obscenity, symbolic speech, and false advertising.

   d. You cannot ordinarily claim that an illegal act should be protected because that action is meant to convey a political message.

Why? What information in the selection leads you to give that answer? _____

_____

_____

____ 2. Which of the following is the main idea of paragraph 9?

    a. Is it the place where the recipient lives or the place where the material originates?

    b. With the advent of the Internet, it has become more difficult for the government to regulate obscenity.

    c. But it is difficult to apply the Supreme Court's standard for judging whether sexual material is obscene—the "average person" applying "contemporary community standards"—to the Internet, because there is no easy way to tell what "the community" is.

    d. When Congress tried to ban obscene, indecent, or "patently offensive" materials from the Internet, the Supreme Court struck down the law as unconstitutional.

Why? What information in the selection leads you to give that answer? _____

_____

Supporting Details

____ 3. Which of the following sentences from paragraph 12 is a minor supporting detail?

    a. The American people were outraged by the flag-burning decision, and in response the House and Senate passed by huge majorities (380 to 38 and 91 to 9) a law making it a federal crime to burn the flag.

    b. But the Court struck this law down as unconstitutional.

    c. Earlier members of the House and Senate had supported a law banning flag-burning with over 90 percent of their votes, but when asked to make that law a constitutional amendment they could not muster the necessary two-thirds majorities.

    d. Several members decided that flag-burning was wrong, but not so wrong or so common as to justify an amendment.

Why? What information in the selection leads you to give that answer? _____

_____

_____

____ 4. Which paragraphs include the major details?

    a. 2, 6, 7, 10, 11

    b. 4, 7, 8, 9

    c. 1, 3, 5, 7, 9

    d. 1, 2, 4, 6, 7, 10, 11

Why? What information in the selection leads you to give that answer? _____

_____

Author's Purpose

____ 5. What is the general purpose of the passage?

    a. to inform the reader about the four types of speech that are not automatically guaranteed under the Constitution

b. to persuade readers that the Constitution does not cover free speech in an equitable manner

c. to entertain the reader with stories of free speech issues, like libel suits, obscenity, and symbolic speech

d. to inform the reader of the definition of libel and obscenity

Why? What information in the selection leads you to give that answer? _____

_____

_____

6. Why does the author include the Internet in the discussion of obscenity in paragraph 9?

a. to illustrate that the Internet is a haven of obscenity

b. to give examples of current obscenity cases the Court is considering

c. to illustrate the complexities that have risen in defining what is obscene since the Internet began

d. because the reader would expect it

Why? What information in the selection leads you to give that answer? _____

_____

_____

Relationships

7. What is the pattern of organization in paragraphs 10 and 11?

a. process

b. cause-and-effect

c. time order

d. contrast

Why? What information in the selection leads you to give that answer? _____

_____

_____

8. What is the relationship between the first two sentences of paragraph 5?

a. cause-and-effect

b. classification

c. example

d. contrast

Why? What information in the selection leads you to give that answer? _____

_____

Fact, Opinion, and Inference

_____ 9. Which of the following statements contains an opinion?

    a. In America it is hard to sue someone for libel and collect.

    b. If you are a public figure, it is much harder to win a libel suit.

    c. Obscenity is difficult to define, but people know it when they see it.

    d. With the advent of the Internet, it has become more difficult for the government to regulate obscenity.

Why? What leads you to give that answer? _____

_____

_____ 10. Based on the thesis statement of this reading, what topic would the author discuss next?

    a. False advertising

    b. He or she would continue discussing symbolic speech.

    c. There is no way to determine this.

    d. Constitutional amendments

Why? What information in the selection leads you to give that answer? _____

_____

_____

▶ Critical Thinking Questions

Critical Thinking Level 1 ▸ Remember

Identify four forms of speaking not automatically covered under the constitution.

1. _____

2. _____

3. _____

4. _____

Critical Thinking Level 2 ▸ Understand

Define each of the terms from this reading selection in your own words and give one example for each.

| Critical Thinking Level 3 | Apply |

Illustrate how the lack of free speech—that is, censorship—applies to at least three of the following subject areas:

- ▶ movies
- ▶ music
- ▶ books
- ▶ student speech
- ▶ religious beliefs

What are some examples of censorship in these categories? _____

_____

_____

_____

| Critical Thinking Level 4 | Analyze |

Analyze which of the following are examples of libel. Circle **Y** for yes and **N** for no and then explain your reasoning.

A reporter deliberately turns in a false story that a Senator did not pay his or her taxes, and as a result, the Senator loses a re-election.

Y   N   Explain: _____

You send an e-mail to a co-worker explaining how you know she lied about doing a report.

Y   N   Explain: _____

A magazine knowingly prints an exaggerated story about the public drunkenness and obnoxious behavior of a young actress.

Y   N   Explain: _____

A chef intentionally spreads a rumor that a competing restaurant has cockroaches in its kitchen.

Y   N   Explain: _____

A cheerleader gossips about how the captain of the football team is taking steroids (and he is).

Y   N   Explain: _____

| Critical Thinking Level 5 | Evaluate |

Evaluate the following situation: The term "wardrobe malfunction" became common in 2004 after the Super Bowl XXXVIII halftime show in which Justin Timberlake tore off part of Janet Jackson's costume, exposing her breast. The duo apologized, claiming it was an accident. However, the Federal

Communications Commission (FCC) fined CBS $550,000 for the incident. This fine was later dismissed. Many Americans were outraged by this brief (1/2 second) exposure, complaining that they found it distasteful, especially during a family show. What is your view of this situation?

_____

_____

_____

Critical Thinking Level 6 Create

Create a short story that revolves around a girl who is libeled. Create the situation and describe the result.

▶ Vocabulary in New Contexts

Review the vocabulary words in the margins of the reading selection and then complete the following activities.

EASY Note Cards

Make a note card for each of the vocabulary words that you did not know from the reading. On one side, write the word. On the other side, divide the card into quarters and label them E, A, S, and Y. Add a word or phrase in each area so that you wind up with an example sentence, an antonym, a synonym, and, finally, a definition that shows you have figured out the meaning of the word with your logic. Remember that an antonym or synonym may have appeared in the reading.

Relationships Between Words

Circle *yes* or *no* to answer the question. Then explain your answer.

1. Might **defaming** a person's character **incite** their anger?

   Yes   No

   Why or why not? _____

2. Should parents **unanimously** decide to **bar** their minor children from drinking alcohol?

   Yes   No

   Why or why not? _____

3. Could *malice* and *cherish* be considered synonyms?

   Yes   No

   Why or why not? _____

Language in Your Life

Write short answers to each question. Look at the vocabulary words closely before you answer.

1. Name one thing you **cherish**. _____

_____

2. Note one injustice that **incites** your indignation. _____

_____

3. Name one behavior that originates in **malice**. _____

_____

4. Name one activity you have trouble **mustering** the energy to undertake. _____

_____

5. Name one temptation you would like to **bar** from your life. _____

_____

Language in Use

Select the best word to complete the meaning of each sentence.

bar	cherishes	convey	defames	inciting
infringement	malice	muster	unanimously	

1. The movie *The Bourne Identity* (2002) follows an amnesiac protagonist named Jason Bourne. His struggle to _____ enough memories to know who he is drives much of the film.

2. The only clue he has to his identity is an account number to a safe deposit box in a bank in Switzerland. The trail of facts he uncovers _____ the message that he might be an assassin.

3. He learns that he failed in an attempt to assassinate an African dictator (a definite _____ of the leader's rights), and his failure incites a hunt by the CIA, who believe he has gone rogue after failing in his mission.

4. Bourne, of course, finds a woman he _____ in their opinion, but to leave his past behind and have a normal life, he must rid himself of the CIA operatives trying to kill him.

5. Moviegoers may not be _____ in their opinions, but to this reviewer at least, the chase scenes and evasive maneuvering that follow make this film a gripping, smart, fast-paced movie experience.

Reading 11–2 | Online Magazine Article

▶ Pre-Reading the Selection

Does your school allow access to social networking sites, or do you have to access them through another source, like your phone? Read the following article by Nicholas Bramble, a lecturer at Yale Law School who does research on open access in university settings, to see what reasons he gives for advocating that schools stop blocking social network sites.

Surveying the Reading

Survey the following article. Then check the elements that are included in this reading.

_____   Title   _____   Words in bold or italic type

_____   Headings   _____   Images and captions

_____   First sentences of paragraphs

Guessing the Purpose

Judging from the title of the reading and the introductory sentence, what do you suppose the purpose for writing is? _____

Predicting the Content

Predict three things this selection will discuss.

▶ _____

▶ _____

▶ _____

Activating Your Knowledge

What do you already know about how social networking sites work? Note two or three things you know (in and out of school).

▶ _____

▶ _____

▶ _____

🎬 **Scan to Connect!** Use your smart phone to scan this code to watch a video to activate your knowledge about social media in education. As you watch, think about the changes you have seen in the classroom since you started grade school.

▶ Reading with Pen in Hand

Students who annotate as they read are more successful than those who do not. That's why you will annotate each selection in *Connect* as you read. In the reading that follows, use the following symbols:

★ or (Point)   to indicate a main idea

① ② ③   to indicate major details

Visit **www.cengagebrain.com** to access the CourseMate for this chapter to hear pronunciations of vocabulary words from this reading.

Fifth Period Is Facebook
Why schools should stop blocking social network sites.

Nicholas Bramble

suburban This area is near D.C. What is a *suburban* area?

1   At a **suburban** school district near Washington, D.C., the most popular teacher happens to be a local star on YouTube. Unbeknown to him, students with cell-phone cameras have videotaped him dancing to "Soulja Boy Tell 'Em" and other songs taught to him by the students.

▶ Have you ever filmed someone unaware and posted it online? How would you feel if it were a video of you?

▶ Have you ever watched videos like those mentioned?

2   Less sweetly, when another teacher from the same school Googled the school's name, she found videos showing students getting into fights with one another. They posted the videos to their MySpace pages and debated who had the better fighting skills. The teacher also found footage from a set of girls who had filmed themselves dancing suggestively in school stairwells. These videos were disturbing, inappropriate, and often exceptionally well-produced, with multiple camera angles and **sophisticated** editing cuts.

sophisticated Use your logic to figure this out.

3   If the school administration knew of the videos, they would be deleted and the teenagers responsible for them would likely face suspension—including the ones who taught their teacher how to dance to Soulja Boy. Schools have had a nearly unanimous response to Facebook, MySpace, and YouTube: repression and silence. Administrators block access to these sites because they think it's important to keep classrooms free from the **perceived** harms associated with social networks—harassment, bullying, exploitative advertising, violence, and sexual imagery.

▶ Do you know of anyone who has been suspended for posting videos?

perceived Use your logic to figure this out.

▶ Why are educators' views about social media shortsighted?

4   But this is shortsighted. Educators should stop thinking about how to **repress** the huge amounts of intellectual and social energy kids devote to social media and start thinking about how to channel that energy away from causing trouble and toward getting more out of their classes. After all, it's not as if most kids are investing commensurate energy into, say, their math homework. Why not try to start bridging the worlds of Facebook, YouTube, and the classroom?

repress What's happening to the intellectual and social energy?

5   The main reason is fear. Megan Meier, the 13-year-old student in Missouri who committed suicide after an ex-friend's mother created a fake MySpace profile to humiliate her, stands as a warning against school involvement with the **intricacies** of kids' online social lives. In response to cyber-stalking and online solicitation of minors, the House of Representatives passed a bill in 2006—the Deleting Online Predators Act—that would require schools to block students from accessing sites like Facebook, MySpace, and LiveJournal. The Senate has put forward similar proposals. And even without a Congressional mandate, many schools have already taken the initiative to ban students—and teachers— from using these sites.

▶ Did you know of this situation or one like it?

intricacies This is a noun. It is based on the adjective *intricate*. What are *intricacies*?

6   Bad idea. Researchers have already **enumerated** the benefits that kids can get from traditional media. Watching *Sesame Street* or *Blue's Clues* improves children's problem-solving skills and school readiness. Teaching students how to use word-processing software, Web-design programs, and video-production tools is a proven way of refocusing at-risk teens on school, and, eventually, getting them jobs. Social networks can also pull in students who are otherwise disengaged, because they draw on kids' often intense interest in finding new ways to communicate with one another.

enumerated The root word is *number*. What does *enumerated* mean.

▶ What media did you interact with as a kid?

7   How can teachers bring social networking into the classroom? For starters, students could talk about what they're doing on Facebook and company, map out the ways they're making connections with one another, and share videos and software they've created. Once the conversation gets going, teachers could figure out whether some kids were being left out and find ways to increase those students' media literacy and bring them into the **fold**. Teachers can manage the project by selecting the best content and conversations, and incorporating it into other parts of the curriculum. If a student created an entry on Wikipedia for a local band or sports team, other students could work on revising the entry and building it into a larger local history project. The audience for school projects need no longer be one hurried teacher.

▶ Make a mental picture of your social network being used in the classroom.

fold Use the contrast between the previous sentence and this one to understand this rather uncommon usage of *fold*.

8   Schools could also find students like the ones who made the stairwell dance videos and get them to produce a **school-sanctioned** video with a better subject—the re-enactment of a literary or historical scene, for example. This isn't as simple as a teacher saying, "Why don't you write a poem about your frustration, rap it on video, and put it on YouTube?" Instead, a teacher could assign students the task of filming a scene from *The Scarlet Letter* in the stairwell, identifying the dynamic of shaming in the novel, and writing about how it might be playing out in their Facebook news feeds. In math class, students could develop statistical models and graphs of the patterns of information flow in their social networks. To understand how advertising works, students from different backgrounds and with different online habits could compare what's being hawked to them. And for a school journalism project, teams of students could aggregate other students' narratives from blogs, Facebook, and

school-sanctioned Your logic will help you here.

▶ Do you have the tech skills and resources to pull off an assignment like the one described here?

Twitter and compile a real-time collective analysis of the state of their educational union.

9   In the process, teachers could also gain technical skills and be in a better position to **head off** future online trouble. Consider this recent MySpace post from Washington, D.C.: "I swear man when I see Martin and Kris on the bus they going to get it, Trina u a snitch, me and Bobby going to beat the shit out of them" (names changed). A school psychologist who knew about it could talk to the kids involved in hopes of preventing a real-world fight.

10   Schools also stand to gain from harnessing students' **budding** tech expertise. Rather than relying on private companies like Blackboard for expensive software, schools can get students who are taking computer programming to develop social media tools, apps, and platforms for creating and sharing class projects. These projects could then go on a school's Web site, in an iTunes-style store. Moodle, Ck12.org, and Sakai are great examples of how schools are using this new kind of open, cost-effective learning.

11   Some teachers and administrators might object that such proposals inadvertently reward students for online misbehavior. But there are ways to discipline students other than through the typical punishment of suspension. Editing videos is slow and painstaking; a student could be made to stay after school or miss a free period to work on it.

12   Another objection is that proposals like these break down the distinction between the schoolyard and the classroom, and could allow mean and anonymous student gossip to further invade children's lives. To be sure, the classroom does serve as a sanctuary, sometimes, from **petty** concerns and conflicts. But slamming the classroom door on social media just makes the virtual world more of a wasteland. A hundred years ago, John Dewey warned that when teachers suppress children's natural interests in the classroom, they "substitute the adult for the child, and so weaken intellectual curiosity and alertness, suppress initiative, and deaden interest." By locking social networking out of school, teachers and principals are making exactly that error. Instead, they should meet kids where they live: online.

—Nicholas Bramble, "Fifth Period Is Facebook: Why schools should stop blocking social network sites."
Copyright © 2009 Slate Group, LLC. Reprinted by permission.

head off Use your logic to understand this phrase.

▶ How technologically savvy are your teachers or parents?

budding Use your logic to understand this word.

▶ Are you familiar with the sites mentioned here?

▶ What would your reaction be to this type of punishment?

▶ What is your response to this idea?

petty Use your prior knowledge to understand this word.

▶ Comprehension Questions

Write the letter of the answer on the line. Then explain your thinking.

Main Idea

_____ 1. Which of the following best states the main idea of this passage?
   a. Educators are shortsighted for several reasons.
   b. Social networks affect users negatively.

c. There are several reasons why schools should stop blocking social networking sites from the classroom.

d. School administrators block social networking sites for several reasons.

Why? What information in the selection leads you to give that answer? _____

_____

_____

2. Which statement is the main idea of paragraph 14?

a. Schools also stand to gain from harnessing students' budding tech expertise.

b. Rather than relying on private companies like Blackboard for expensive software, schools can get students who are taking computer programming to develop social media tools, apps, and platforms for creating and sharing class projects.

c. These projects could then go on a school's Web site, in an iTunes-style store.

d. Moodle, Ck12.org, and Sakai are great examples of how schools are using this new kind of open, cost-effective learning.

Why? What information in the selection leads you to give that answer? _____

_____

_____

Supporting Details

3. Which of the following details does *not* support the main idea of the passage?

a. Teaching students how to use word-processing software, Web-design programs, and video-production tools is a proven way of refocusing at-risk teens on school, and, eventually, getting them jobs.

b. If a student created an entry on Wikipedia for a local band or sports team, other students could work on revising the entry and building it into a larger local history project.

c. Editing videos is slow and painstaking; a student could be made to stay after school or miss a free period to work on it.

d. Administrators block access to these sites because they think it's important to keep classrooms free from the perceived harms associated with social networks—harassment, bullying, exploitative advertising, violence, and sexual imagery.

Why? What information in the selection leads you to give that answer? _____

_____

_____

_____   4. Which of the following contributes most to the prohibition of social sites at school?

    a. harassment

    b. bullying

    c. provocative videos

    d. fear

Why? What information in the selection leads you to give that answer? _____

_____

_____

Author's Purpose

_____   5. What is the purpose or purposes of the passage?

    a. to entertain readers with searchable topics of videos that students have posted on YouTube

    b. to inform readers of the reasons why administrators block social networking sites from students

    c. to persuade readers that schools should not prevent students from using social networking sites, but rather utilize them in the learning environment

    d. to list a series of schools whose students have violated anti-social networking rules in creative ways

Why? What information in the selection leads you to give that answer? _____

_____

_____

_____   6. Why does the author include paragraph 11?

    a. to persuade readers that social sites should not be used in the classroom because they reward bad behavior

    b. to be proactive in resolving an objection some of his readers might have

    c. to keep students and teachers from communicating through social media sites

    d. to suggest that media use in the classroom might not be such a good idea after all

Why? What information in the selection leads you to give that answer? _____

_____

_____

Relationships

_____ 7. What is the overall pattern of organization of the reading selection?

    a. comparison and contrast

    b. cause-and-effect

    c. example

    d. process

Why? What information in the selection leads you to give that answer? _____

_____

_____

_____ 8. What organizational pattern do you find in paragraph 7?

    a. cause-and-effect

    b. classification

    c. process

    d. time order

Why? What information in the selection leads you to give that answer? _____

_____

_____

Fact, Opinion, and Inference

_____ 9. How would you classify the source of this article?

    a. fact

    b. opinion by a person on the street

    c. informed opinion

    d. expert opinion

Why? What leads you to give that answer? _____

_____

_____ 10. Which of the following would the author agree with?

    a. Despite wanting to use social networking sites in the classroom, the author realizes this is an idealistic and even unrealistic idea.

    b. The specific culprit may change over time, but the issue remains the same: current students need to be met with relevant education strategies.

    c. Washington, D.C., has a bigger problem with social networking sites in their school districts than others around the country.

    d. Congress is the reason for the ban of social sites in classrooms.

Why? What information in the selection leads you to give that answer? _____

_____

_____

▶ Critical Thinking Questions

Critical Thinking Level 1 ▷ **Remember**

Explain why many schools prohibit access to social networks on campus. _____

_____

Critical Thinking Level 2 ▷ **Understand**

On your own paper, use a visual map to *enumerate* the benefits of using social networking sites.

Critical Thinking Level 3 ▷ **Apply**

Use the information in this article to think about how different teachers you have had or currently have would respond to this article. Discuss your experiences and thoughts with your classmates.

Critical Thinking Level 4 ▷ **Analyze**

Analyze the fears mentioned in paragraph 3. How could social networking sites be used to educate the students on proper behavior and eradicate the fears of school administrators?

_____

_____

_____

Critical Thinking Level 5 ▷ **Evaluate**

Evaluate each of the following statements and decide which ones the author would agree with based on the information in the article. Support your decision.

We need to replicate in the classroom the world in which students are living.

Yes   No

_____

_____

Computers are making us stupid because they do our thinking for us.

Yes   No

_____

_____

If we teach today the way we were taught yesterday, we aren't preparing students for today or tomorrow.

Yes   No

_____

_____

Kids <u>do</u> want to learn, but schools get in the way.

Yes   No

_____

_____

If we allow technology into the classroom unchecked, the effects could be detrimental to education.

Yes   No

_____

_____

Critical Thinking Level 6 ▸ Create

Recognizing, of course, that you would not necessarily want these to be assigned, *create* some class assignments that would connect your social media activities and your academic learning.

_____

_____

_____

_____

_____

▸ Vocabulary in New Contexts

Review the vocabulary words in the margins of the reading selection and then complete the following activities.

EASY Note Cards

Make a note card for each of the vocabulary words that you did not know from the reading. On one side, write the word. On the other side, divide the card into quarters and label them E, A, S, and Y. Add a word or phrase in each area so that you wind up with an example sentence, an antonym, a synonym, and, finally, a definition that shows you have figured out the meaning of the word with your logic. Remember that an antonym or synonym may have appeared in the reading.

Relationships Between Words

Circle *yes* or *no* to answer the question. Then explain your answer.

1. Would an apology be a good strategy to **head off** a full-blown fight between two couples over a **petty** conflict?

   Yes   No

   Why or why not? _____

2. Would a child in her mother's high heels and lipstick be **perceived** as **sophisticated?**

   Yes   No

   Why or why not? _____

3. Are there certain **budding** thoughts a person should work hard to **repress?**

   Yes   No

   Why or why not? _____

Language in Your Life

Write short answers to each question. Look at the vocabulary words closely before you answer.

1. Name one action you find **petty.** _____

   _____

2. Use the word *fold* in three different ways. _____

   _____

3. Explain whether you would like to live in an urban, rural, or **suburban** area and why. _____

   _____

4. **Enumerate** several benefits of education. _____

   _____

5. Name one person you feel has an appealing level of **sophistication.** _____

   _____

Language in Use
Select the best word to complete the meaning of each sentence.

budding	enumerate	fold	government-sanctioned
head off	intricacies	perceived	petty
repress	sophisticated	suburban	

1. The following is a true story: On April 10, 2012, a soldier in Afghanistan, a son of a friend of mine, stepped on an IED while on a routine, _____ patrol and lost all four limbs.

2. This soldier turned 25 four days later. What should have been a simple birthday turned into a celebration of life. With the _____ of the injuries he sustained, it was a miracle that he is still alive.

3. The good news is that he is in critical but stable condition, and his wife is now by his side ready to _____ him into her arms, and wishing with every fiber of her being that he could reciprocate.

4. It is an impossibly hard place to be: to go from one day being a _____ family, proud parents of a 6-month-old daughter, to literally holding on to dear life, lost without any answers to the unvoiced "why."

5. You can only _____ the despair and anger for so long. The mental, emotional, and physical road to recovery will be long and hard. You do not have to be religious to say a prayer for this soldier, for this family. They have paid a steep price, perhaps even costlier than death would have been, to ensure the freedom of people they do not even know.

6. So don't let _____ politics get in the way of humanity. When you see soldiers, thank them for their sacrifice; thank them for their bravery; thank them for your freedom; be kind; and recognize the hero within them.

7. _____ your blessings: being able to stand in line (you have feet), being able to run a mile (you have legs), and being able to hug those you love (you have arms). Don't take the little things for granted, and when you start to feel sorry for yourself, remember our wounded warriors.

 Click to Connect! For more practice applying the skills you learned in this chapter, visit **www.cengagebrain.com** to access the CourseMate for this chapter.

Red Circle Images/Fotosearch

Applying Your
Critical Reading
Skills to Arguments

The purpose of this casebook is to take a "hot" topic—global warming—and use it as the backdrop for you to practice the reading and thinking skills you have been developing. While thinking critically has been a part of every chapter in this book, the last few chapters have emphasized the concepts of analysis, synthesis, and evaluation. When you deal with fact and opinion, author's tone, and author's reasoning, you are using some major brain cells! And you should be proud of yourself for doing so!

Pre-Reading

Take out a sheet of paper. Jot down your thoughts on the following questions:

▶ What prior knowledge do you have about global warming?
▶ Which parts of your prior knowledge are facts, and which are opinions?

Reading

The three readings that follow each take a different approach to global warming: What causes global warming? Is this a significant problem? Is it the world's most important problem? Your job will be to read each selection critically: read to understand what the author is saying, and read to evaluate the strength of the argument.

It would be a good idea to annotate as you read. Since you are dealing with an argument, you should identify the following aspects of each reading selection:

▶ the author's claim
▶ the author's evidence (its relevance and strength)
▶ the author's assumptions

You will be asked to discuss the information in each article, so read actively.

Casebook Reading 1

Al Gore is a former vice president of the United States who served with President Bill Clinton. He has written two books on the environment, including the best-selling book *Earth in the Balance: Ecology and the Human Spirit* (1992). The following reading selection consists of excerpts from different parts of *An Inconvenient Truth*, his first book about global warming. The book was made into a documentary film of the same title; it won two Academy Awards. Gore and the Intergovernmental Panel on Climate Change (IPCC) jointly won a Nobel Peace Prize in 2007 for their work on climate change.

Excerpts from *An Inconvenient Truth*

Al Gore

▶ As you read, be sure to change the title and headings into questions and then look for the answers.

1   Many people today still assume—mistakenly—that the Earth is so big that we human beings cannot possibly have any major impact on the way our planet's ecological system operates. That assertion may have been true at one time,

but it's not the case anymore. We have grown so numerous and our technologies have become so powerful that we are now capable of having a significant influence on many parts of the Earth's environment. The most vulnerable part of the Earth's ecological system is the atmosphere. It's vulnerable because it's so thin. My friend, the late Carl Sagan, used to say, "If you had a globe covered with a coat of varnish, the thickness of that varnish would be about the same as the thickness of the Earth's atmosphere compared to the Earth itself."

▶ Summarize paragraphs 1 and 2 in a sentence to make sure you understand the argument so far.

2   The atmosphere is thin enough that we are capable of changing its composition. Indeed, the Earth's atmosphere is so thin that we have the capacity to dramatically alter the concentration of some of its basic molecular components. In particular, we have vastly increased the amount of carbon dioxide—the most important of the so-called greenhouse gases.

3   These images illustrate the basic science of global warming.

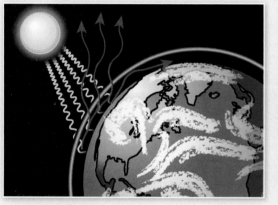 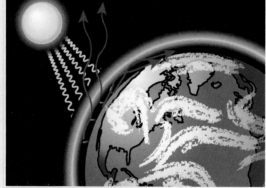

4   The Sun's energy enters the atmosphere in the form of light waves and heats up the Earth. Some of that energy warms the Earth and then is re-radiated back into space in the form of infrared waves. Under normal conditions, a portion of the outgoing infrared radiation is naturally trapped by the atmosphere—and that is a good thing, because it keeps the temperature on Earth within comfortable bounds. The greenhouse gases on Venus are so thick that its temperatures are far too hot for humans. The greenhouse gases surrounding Mars are almost nonexistent, so the temperature there is far too cold. That's why the Earth is sometimes referred to as the "Goldilocks planet"—the temperatures here have been just right.

▶ What is the purpose of the images and paragraphs 4–6? How does the tone influence credibility?

5   The problem we now face is that this thin layer of atmosphere is being thickened by huge quantities of human-caused carbon dioxide and other greenhouse gases. And as it thickens, it traps a lot of the infrared radiation that would otherwise escape the atmosphere and continue out to the universe. As a result, the temperature of the Earth's atmosphere—and oceans—is getting dangerously warmer.

6   That's what the climate crisis is all about.

What Exactly Are Greenhouse Gases?

7 When we talk about greenhouse gases and climate change, carbon dioxide usually gets the most attention. But there are also some others, although CO_2 is the most important by far.

8 What all greenhouse gases have in common is that they allow light from the sun to come into the atmosphere, but trap a portion of the outward-bound infrared radiation and warm up the air.

▶ Make sure you are noticing the pattern of organization to get the key evidence the author is presenting to support his claim. You might underline the evidence.

9 Having some amount of greenhouse gases is beneficial. Without them, the average temperature of the Earth's surface would be right around 0°F—not a very nice place to live. Greenhouse gases help keep the Earth's surface at a much more hospitable temperature—almost 59°F. But due to increasing concentrations of human-caused greenhouse gases in modern times, we are raising the planet's average temperature and creating the dangerous changes in climate we see all around us. CO_2 usually gets top billing in this because it accounts for 80% of total greenhouse gas emissions. When we burn fossil fuels (oil, natural gas, and coal) in our homes, cars, factories, and power plants, or when we cut or burn down forests, or when we produce cement, we release CO_2 into the atmosphere.

10 Like CO_2, methane and nitrous oxide both predate our presence on the Earth but have gotten huge boosts from us. Sixty percent of the methane currently in the atmosphere is produced by humans; it comes from landfills, livestock farming, fossil-fuel burning, wastewater treatment, and other industry. In large-scale livestock farming, liquid manure is stored in massive tanks that emit methane. Dry manure, left on fields, by contrast, does not. Nitrous oxide (NO_2)—another greenhouse culprit—also occurs naturally, though we have added 17% more of it to the atmosphere just in the course of our industrial age, from fertilizers, fossil fuels, and the burning of forests and crop residues.

11 Sulfur hexafluoride (SF_6), PFCs, and HFCs are all greenhouse gases that are produced exclusively by human activity. Not surprisingly, emissions of those gases are on the rise, too. HFCs are used as substitutes for CFCs—which were banned because their emissions in refrigeration systems and elsewhere were destroying the ozone layer. CFCs were also very potent greenhouse gases. PFCs and SF6 are released into the atmosphere by industrial activities like aluminum smelting and semiconductor manufacturing, as well as the electricity grid that lights up our cities.

12 And finally, water vapor is a natural greenhouse gas that increases in volume with warmer temperatures, thereby magnifying the impact of all artificial greenhouse gases.

Ice Core Samples from the Glaciers

▶ What is the importance of ice core samples to the author's argument?

13 Scientist Lonnie Thompson takes his team to the tops of glaciers all over the world. They dig core drills down into the ice, extracting long cylinders filled

with ice that was formed year by year over many centuries. Lonnie and his team of experts then examine the tiny bubbles of air trapped in the snow in the year that it fell. They can measure how much CO_2 was in the Earth's atmosphere in the past, year by year. They can also measure the exact temperature of the atmosphere each year by calculating the ratio of different isotopes of oxygen (oxygen-16 and oxygen-18), which provides an ingenious and highly accurate thermometer.

14   The team can count backward in time year by year—the same way an experienced forester can "read" tree rings—by simply observing the clear line of demarcation that separates each year from the one preceding it, as seen in this unique frozen record.

15   The thermometer to the right measures temperatures in the Northern Hemisphere over the past 1,000 years.

16   The blue is cold and the red is hot. The bottom of the graph marks 1,000 years and the current era is at the top.

17   The correlation between temperature and CO_2 concentrations over the last 1,000 years—as measured in the ice core record by Thompson's team—is striking. Nonetheless, the so-called global-warming skeptics often say that global warming is really an illusion reflecting nature's cyclical fluctuations. To support their view, they frequently refer to the Medieval Warm Period. But as Dr. Thompson's thermometer shows, the vaunted Medieval Warm Period (the third little blip from the left, next) was tiny compared to the enormous increases in temperature of the last half-century (the red peaks at the right of the chart).

18   These global-warming skeptics—a group diminishing almost as rapidly as the mountain glaciers—launched a fierce attack against another measurement of the 1,000-year correlation between CO_2 known as the "hockey stick," a graphic image representing the research of climate scientist

▶ What is the purpose of this graph?

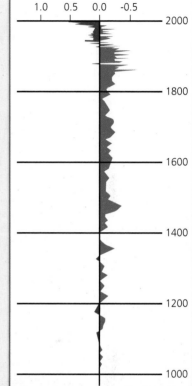

1000 Years of Northern Hemisphere Temperature (°C)

▶ What is the purpose of this graph? Hint: Notice how it differs from the previous graph.

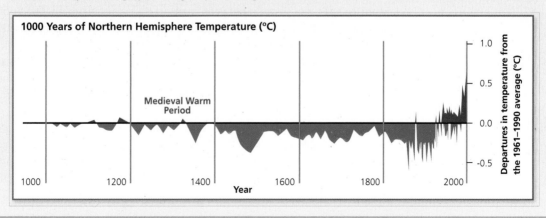

1000 Years of Northern Hemisphere Temperature (°C)

Medieval Warm Period

Departures in temperature from the 1961–1990 average (°C)

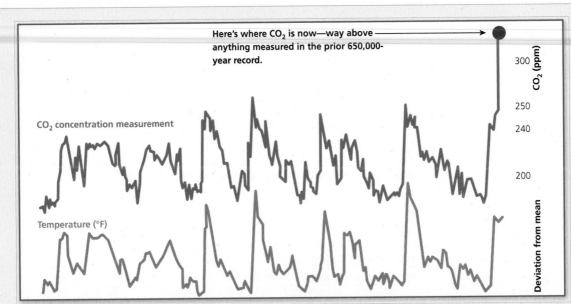

Here's where CO₂ is now—way above anything measured in the prior 650,000-year record.

CO₂ concentration measurement

Temperature (°F)

The top right point of this gray line shows current global temperatures. And the bottom right point marks the depth of the last ice age. That short distance—about an inch in the graph—represents the difference, in Chicago, between a nice day and a mile of ice over your head. Imagine what three times that much on the warm side would mean.

▶ What is the author doing in paragraphs 17–18? How does this affect the argument's credibility?

Michael Mann and his colleagues. But in fact, scientists have confirmed the same basic conclusions in multiple ways—with Thompson's ice core record as one of the most definitive.

CO₂ in Antarctica

19   In Antarctica, measurements of CO₂ concentrations and temperatures go back 650,000 years. The blue line above charts CO₂ concentrations over this period.

20   The top right side of the blue line represents the present era, and that first dip down as you move from right to left is the last ice age. Then, continuing to the left, you can see the second most recent ice age, the third and fourth most recent ice ages, and so on. In between them are periods of warming. At no point in the last 650,000 years before the preindustrial era did the CO₂ concentration go above 300 parts per million.

21   The gray line shows the world's temperature over the same 650,000 years. It's a complicated relationship, but the most important part of it is this: When there is more CO₂ in the atmosphere, the temperature increases because more heat from the Sun is trapped inside.

▶ Did you pay attention to the significance of the statement in paragraph 22?

22   There is not a single part of this graph—no fact, date, or number—that is controversial in any way or in dispute by anybody.

23   To the extent that there is a controversy at all, it is that a few people in some of the less responsible coal, oil, and utility companies say, "So what? That's not going to cause any problem."

24   But if we allow this [rise in CO_2 levels] to happen, it would be deeply and unforgivably immoral. It would condemn coming generations to a catastrophically diminished future.

25   And that is what is at stake. Our ability to live on planet Earth—to have a future as a civilization.

▶ What do paragraphs 22–25 do? What is their purpose and tone?

—Reprinted from AN INCONVENIENT TRUTH by Al Gore. Copyright © 2006 by Al Gore. Permission granted by Rodale, Inc., Emmaus, PA 18098.

Interacting with Gore's Argument

Answer the following questions based on your annotations. If you find you need to improve your annotations, please do so.

Interaction A ▶ Establishing the Author's Purpose

1. What is the author's purpose in paragraph 1? _____

_____

2. What do you think the author is trying to achieve when he calls Carl Sagan "my friend"? (If you don't know who Carl Sagan is, visit **www.carlsagan.com** and select "Carl Sagan." Read several paragraphs of his biography.) _____

_____

3. What is the purpose or purposes of the section of the text composed of paragraphs 3–6 and the section titled "What Exactly Are Greenhouse Gases?" _____

_____

4. What is the author's overall purpose? _____

_____

Interaction B ▶ Understanding the Claim and Evidence

1. What does Gore claim is the reason for global warming? Remember that a claim is controversial. You may want to consider the opposing arguments that Gore addresses in order to understand his claim completely. _____

_____

2. What evidence does Gore use to support his claim? Hint: Each of the following groups of paragraphs supports one main idea. Summarize each idea here. Doing this will show Gore's main supporting points.

   ▶ Summary of paragraphs 1–2: _____

   ▶ Summary of paragraphs 3–6: _____

▶ Summary of paragraphs 7–12: _____

_____

▶ Summary of paragraphs 13–18: _____

_____

▶ Summary of paragraphs 19–25: _____

_____

_____

3. Is the support relevant? _____

4. Reread the paragraphs in which Gore responds to people who don't agree with various parts of his argument. Tell how Gore responds to their viewpoints.

▶ Paragraph 1 _____

_____

▶ Paragraph 17 _____

_____

_____

▶ Paragraph 18 _____

_____

_____

▶ Paragraph 23 _____

_____

Interaction C ▶ Considering Fact, Opinion, and Authority

1. Carl Sagan in paragraph 1

   A. Is the Carl Sagan quotation a fact or an opinion? Explain. _____

   _____

   B. Is Carl Sagan an expert source, an informed source, or a person on the street? Explain. _____

   _____

   C. Reread Sagan's words carefully. Evaluate how well they support the point that Gore is making. _____

2. Al Gore in paragraph 9

   A. Reread paragraph 9. Is the first sentence fact or opinion? Explain. _____

   _____

B. Is Al Gore an expert source, an informed source, or a person on the street? Explain.

_____

_____

C. Which of the following statements from paragraph 9 are facts? Put a check mark beside each fact.

▶ The second sentence, which begins "Without them…" _____

▶ The fourth sentence, which begins "But due to increasing…" _____

▶ The last sentence, which begins "When we burn fossil fuels…" _____

3. Al Gore in paragraph 22

A. List all the absolute qualifiers in this paragraph. _____

B. If you had to argue that this was fact or opinion, what would you say, and why? _____

_____

_____

C. Suppose that Gore is correct when he states that all the facts, dates, and numbers in this graph are accurate and undisputed. Look back at the graph, and give at least two examples of how the graph might still be inaccurate. You will have to think about the author's purpose and the author's assumptions.

▶ _____

▶ _____

_____

Interaction D   Identifying the Author's Tone

1. What is the overall tone of this reading? Hint: You may need to use more than one adjective.

_____

2. Identify the tone in the first sentence of paragraph 18. Give two pieces of evidence from the sentence to support your argument about the tone, and explain how they contribute to the tone.

Tone: _____

Two pieces of evidence and explanations:

▶ _____

_____

▶ _____

Interaction E	Evaluating the Argument

1. Is the author credible? Support your answer. _____

_____

_____

2. Is the argument strong? Why or why not? _____

_____

_____

3. Give the argument an overall evaluation; state your opinion of how convincing it is and back up your opinion with information from Gore's argument. Are parts of it strong and others weak? If so, discuss which parts, and why. Write a paragraph in which your purpose is to inform others of your opinion, and then give your reasons. _____

_____

_____

_____

Casebook Reading 2

S. Michael Craven is the president of the Center for Christ and Culture. His weekly syndicated commentaries in Christian publications reach four and a half million readers a week. A frequent guest host of the nationally syndicated radio program *Point of View*, Craven has also appeared on Fox News, CNN, ABC, and NBC. Craven assumed a full-time ministry in 2001.

Are Man-Made Carbon Emissions Driving Climate Change?

S. Michael Craven

▶ What is the author doing to establish his credibility?

1   A recent report in Canada's *National Post* reads "The polar ice cap is shrinking, laying bare deep gullies in the landscape and the climate is the warmest it has been in decades or perhaps centuries." Sounds scary, doesn't it? Well, it is if you're a Martian! According to NASA, data collected from the Mars Odyssey mission reveals that Mars is also experiencing "global warming." NASA scientist William Feldman

said, "In some low-latitude areas, the ice has already dissipated." Following a recent analysis of the first twelve months of data collected from Mars, scientists are accumulating evidence that climatic changes similar to Earth's are also occurring on the only other planet in the solar system where climate is now being studied.

2   Now, the obvious question is "How can Mars experience global warming if global warming is caused by an increase in carbon dioxide produced by human industry?"

3   According to the proponents of "man-made" global warming, carbon dioxide emissions are the culprit in climate change. So what is the role of carbon dioxide, if any, and are there other, more plausible explanations for the half-degree centigrade temperature increase that is believed to have occurred over the last century?

▶ What purpose do the questions in paragraphs 2 and 3 serve?

4   Astrophysicist Nir Shaviv, one of Israel's top scientists, was once a proponent of the theory that man-made carbon emissions are driving climate change. In an interview with Lawrence Solomon, columnist for the *National Post*, Dr. Shaviv "described the logic that led him—and most everyone else—to conclude that SUVs, coal plants and other things man-made cause global warming." Dr. Shaviv points out that "scientists for decades have postulated that increases in carbon dioxide and other gases could lead to a greenhouse effect." Then, as if on cue, "the temperature rose over the course of the twentieth century while greenhouse gases proliferated due to human activities" and since "no other mechanism explains the warming … greenhouse gases necessarily became the cause."

▶ What is the purpose of paragraphs 4 and 5?

5   Recently however, he has recanted, saying: "Like many others, I was personally sure that CO_2 is the bad culprit in the story of global warming. But after carefully digging into the evidence, I realized that things are far more complicated than the story sold to us by many climate scientists or the stories regurgitated by the media." As Dr. Shaviv began to dig into the issue he was surprised to discover "there is no concrete evidence—only speculation—that man-made greenhouse gases cause global warming."

6   Solomon points out, "Even research from the Intergovernmental Panel on Climate Change (IPCC)—the United Nations agency that heads the worldwide effort to combat global warming—is bereft of anything here inspiring confidence. In fact, according to the IPCC's own findings, 'man's role is so uncertain that there is a strong possibility that we have been cooling, not warming, the Earth. Unfortunately, our tools are too crude to reveal what man's effect has been in the past, let alone predict how much warming or cooling we might cause in the future.'"

▶ Did you recognize the significance of the quotation from the IPCC in paragraph 6?

7   In the wake of mounting scientific evidence, Dr. Shaviv and many others now believe that solar activity offers a much more plausible explanation for global warming than man-made carbon emissions, particularly because of the evidence that has been accumulating over the past decade of the strong relationship that cosmic-ray flux has on our atmosphere.

8   Scientists have learned that the sun's magnetic field deflects some of the cosmic rays that penetrate the Earth's atmosphere, and in so doing it also limits

the immense amounts of ions and free electrons that the cosmic rays produce. But something changed in the 20th century: The sun's magnetic field more than doubled in strength, deflecting an extraordinary number of rays. A magnetically active sun boosts the number of sunspots, indicating that vast amounts of energy are being released from deep within. Typically, sunspots flare up and settle down in cycles of about 11 years. "In the last 50 years, we haven't been living in typical times: If you look back into the sun's past, you find that we live in a period of abnormally high solar activity," according to Dr. Nigel Weiss, Professor Emeritus at the Department of Applied Mathematics and Theoretical Physics at the University of Cambridge. Conversely, in the 17th century, sunspots almost completely disappeared for 70 years during what was the coldest interval of the Little Ice Age, when New York Harbor froze, allowing walkers to journey from Manhattan to Staten Island.

▶ It might be helpful to make a drawing of the cosmic ray phenomenon the author is describing.

9   It is believed that the recent diminution of cosmic rays has limited the formation of clouds, making the Earth warmer. Low-altitude clouds are particularly significant because they especially shield the Earth from the sun to keep us cool. Low cloud cover can vary by 2% in five years, affecting the Earth's surface by as much as 1.2 watts per square meter during that same period. "That figure can be compared with about 1.4 watts per square meter estimated by the IPCC for the greenhouse effect of all the increase in carbon dioxide in the air since the Industrial Revolution," according to Henrik Svensmark, director of the Centre for Sun-Climate Research at the Danish Space Research Institute.

10   Until recently the relationship between cosmic rays and cloud formation was merely a theory. That is until Dr. Svensmark and his team undertook an elaborate laboratory experiment in a reaction chamber the size of a small room. Reporting on these events Lawrence Solomon writes:

▶ How do the results of the experiment relate to the author's argument?

11   The team duplicated the chemistry of the lower atmosphere by injecting the gases found there in the same proportions, and adding ultraviolet rays to mimic the actions of the sun. What they found left them agape: A vast number of floating microscopic droplets soon filled the reaction chamber. These were ultra-small clusters of sulphuric acid and water molecules—the building blocks for cloud condensation nuclei—that had been catalyzed by the electrons released by cosmic rays. "We were amazed by the speed and efficiency with which the electrons do their work," Dr. Svensmark remarked. For the first time ever, researchers had experimentally identified a causal mechanism by which cosmic rays can facilitate the production of clouds in Earth's atmosphere. "This is a completely new result within climate science."

(*National Post*, February 2, 2007)

▶ What impact does this last question have on the author's overall purpose and tone?

12   Is it ridiculous to suggest that the largest source of heat energy in the solar system may be the cause of our present warming trend? It is certainly not the politically correct view....

—Copyright © 2007 by S. Michael Craven Responding to 'Green Politics'—Part V July 2, 2007, accessed at http://www.battlefortruth.org. Reprinted by permission of the author.

Interacting with Craven's Argument

Answer the following questions based upon your annotations. If you find you need to improve your annotations, please do so.

Interaction F   **Establishing the Author's Purpose**

1. What is the author's overall purpose? _____

   _____

2. What is the purpose of paragraphs 1–6? _____

3. What is the purpose of paragraphs 8–11? _____

4. In paragraph 12, why does the author ask a question rather than make a statement: "Is it ridiculous to suggest that the largest source of heat energy in the solar system may be the cause of our present warming trend?" _____

   _____

   _____

Interaction G   **Understanding the Claim and Evidence**

1. What does Craven claim is the reason for global warming? _____

   _____

   _____

2. What evidence does Craven use to support his claim? Hint: Each group of paragraphs below supports one main idea. Summarize each idea here. Doing so will show Craven's main supporting points.

   ▶ Summary of paragraphs 1–3: _____

   _____

   ▶ Summary of paragraphs 4–5: _____

   _____

   _____

   ▶ Summary of paragraph 6: _____

   _____

   ▶ Summary of paragraph 7: _____

▶ Summary of paragraph 8: _____

▶ Summary of paragraph 9: _____

_____

▶ Summary of paragraphs 10–11: _____

_____

▶ Summary of paragraph 12: _____

_____

3. Is the support relevant? _____

Interaction H ▸ Considering Fact, Opinion, and Authority

1. William Feldman in paragraph 1

   A. Is the William Feldman quotation a fact or an opinion? Explain. _____

_____

   B. Is William Feldman an expert source, an informed source, or a person on the street? Explain.

_____

   C. Read Feldman's words carefully. Do they directly relate to an argument about the cause of global warming on Earth? _____

2. S. Michael Craven in paragraphs 1, 2, 3, and 12

   A. Craven mostly asks questions instead of making statements in these paragraphs. What impact does this have on our ability to determine whether he seems like an author to trust? _____

_____

   B. Is Craven an expert source, an informed source, or a person on the street? Explain.

_____

_____

_____

_____

3. Nir Shaviv
Identify the following statements as fact (**F**) or opinion (**O**) or both (**F/O**). Explain your answer.

A. "Astrophysicist Nir Shaviv, one of Israel's top scientists, was once a proponent of the theory that man-made carbon emissions are driving climate change." _____

_____

B. Dr. Shaviv says "there is no concrete evidence—only speculation—that man-made greenhouse gases cause global warming." _____

_____

_____

C. "In the wake of mounting scientific evidence, Dr. Shaviv and many others now believe that solar activity offers a much more plausible explanation for global warming than man-made carbon emissions." _____

_____

_____

Interaction I ▸ Identifying the Author's Tone

1. What tone does the author create in paragraph 1 by discussing the shrinking polar ice cap and then revealing he is referring to Mars? _____

2. For each statement about the author's tone below, give one supporting quotation from the article.

A. The author's tone is subjective. _____

B. The author's tone is objective. _____

_____

C. The author uses the second person point of view. _____

Interaction J ▸ Evaluating the Argument

1. Does Craven respond to any counterarguments from people who don't agree with his argument? How does this affect his credibility? _____

2. Is this author credible? Support your answer. _____

_____

_____

3. Is the author's argument strong? Why or why not? _____

_____

4. Give the argument an overall evaluation; state your opinion of how convincing it is, and back up your opinion with information from Craven's argument. Are parts of it strong and others weak? If so, discuss which parts, and why. Write a paragraph in which your purpose is to inform others of your opinion and give your reasons. _____

_____

_____

_____

Group Interaction: Comparing the Claims and Evidence

With a group of classmates, create a visual chart or graph that compares and contrasts the claims and major evidence in the arguments presented by Gore and Craven. For an idea about how to set up the chart, see page 297. After your group has created your chart, compare it to the chart another group created. Discuss any differences you find.

Casebook Reading 3

Bjorn Lomborg is the author of two books, *The Skeptical Environmentalist,* and the book from which the following excerpt is taken, *Cool It: The Skeptical Environmentalist's Guide to Global Warming.* A former director of the Denmark Environmental Assessment Institute, in 2004 Lomborg also started the Copenhagen Consensus Center, in which economists from around the world meet to find the best solutions to the world's biggest challenges. Lomborg was named one of the 100 most influential people in the world by *Time* magazine in 2004, and in 2008 the U.K. *Guardian* called him one of the "50 people who could save the planet." Lomborg is an adjunct professor at the Copenhagen Business School.

> What does this title suggest about the author's purpose? Note: If you do not understand the reference in the title to "canaries in a coal mine," then you should try searching online for an explanation.

Polar Bears: Today's Canaries in the Coal Mine?

Bjorn Lomborg

1   Countless politicians proclaim that global warming has emerged as the preeminent issue of our era. The European Union calls it "one of the most threatening issues that we are facing today." Former prime minister Tony Blair of the United

Kingdom sees it as "the single most important issue." German chancellor Angela Merkel has vowed to make climate change the top priority within both the G8 and the European Union in 2007, and Italy's Romano Prodi sees climate change as the real threat to global peace. Presidential contenders from John McCain to Hillary Clinton express real concern over the issue. Several coalitions of states have set up regional climate-change initiatives, and in California Republican Governor Arnold Schwarzenegger has helped push through legislation saying that global warming should be a top priority for the state. And of course, Al Gore has presented this message urgently in his lectures as well as in the book and Oscar-winning movie *An Inconvenient Truth*.

2   In March 2007, while I waited to give evidence to a congressional hearing on climate change, I watched Gore put his case to the politicians. It was obvious to me that Gore is sincerely worried about the world's future. And he's not alone in worrying. A raft of book titles warn that we've reached a *Boiling Point* and will experience a *Climate Crash*. One is even telling us we will be the *Last Generation* because "nature will take her revenge for climate change." Pundits aiming to surpass one another even suggest that we face medieval-style impoverishment and societal collapse in just forty years if we don't make massive and draconian changes to the way we live.

▶ How does the first sentence of paragraph 2 impact the author's credibility?

3   Likewise, the media pound us with increasingly dramatic stories of our ever worsening climate. In 2006, *Time* did a special report on global warming, with the cover spelling out the scare story with repetitive austerity: "Be worried. Be very worried." The magazine told us that the climate is crashing, affecting us both globally by playing havoc with the biosphere and individually through such health effects as heatstrokes, asthma, and infectious diseases. The heart-breaking image on the cover was of a lone polar bear on a melting ice floe, searching in vain for the next piece of ice to jump to. *Time* told us that due to global warming bears "are starting to turn up drowned" and that at some point they will become extinct.

▶ For what purpose does the author use the first three paragraphs?

4   Padding across the ice, polar bears are beautiful animals. To Greenland— part of my own nation, Denmark—they are a symbol of pride. The loss of this animal would be a tragedy. But the real story of the polar bear is instructive. In many ways, this tale encapsulates the broader problem with the climate-change concern: once you look closely at the supporting data, the narrative falls apart.

▶ What effect does Lomborg's saying that Greenland is part of his own nation have?

5   Al Gore shows a picture similar to *Time's* and tells us "a new scientific study shows that, for the first time, polar bears have been drowning in significant numbers." The World Wildlife Fund actually warns that polar bears might stop reproducing by 2012 and thus become functionally extinct in less than a decade. In their pithy statement, "polar bears will be consigned to history, something that our grandchildren can only read about in books." *The Independent* tells us that temperature increases "mean polar bears are wiped out in their Arctic homeland. The only place they can be seen is in a zoo."

6   Over the past few years, this story has cropped up many times, based first on a World Wildlife Fund report in 2002 and later on the Arctic Climate Impact Assessment from 2004. Both relied extensively on research published in 2001 by the Polar Bear Specialist Group of the World Conservation Union.

7   But what this group really told us was that of the twenty distinct sub-populations of polar bears, one or possibly two were declining in Baffin Bay; more than half were known to be stable; and two sub-populations were actually *increasing* around the Beaufort Sea. Moreover, it is reported that the global polar-bear population has *increased* dramatically over the past decades, from about five thousand members in the 1960s to twenty-five thousand today, through stricter hunting regulation. Contrary to what you might expect—and what was not pointed out in any of the recent stories—the two populations in decline come from areas where it has actually been getting colder over the past fifty years, whereas the two increasing populations reside in areas where it is getting warmer. Likewise, Al Gore's comment on drowning bears suggests an ongoing process getting ever worse. Actually, there was a single sighting of four dead bears the day after "an abrupt windstorm" in an area housing one of the increasing bear populations.

8   The best-studied polar-bear population lives on the western coast of Hudson Bay. That its population has declined 17 percent, from 1,200 in 1987 to under 950 in 2004, has gotten much press. Not mentioned, though, is that since 1981 the population had soared from just 500, thus eradicating any claim of a decline. Moreover, nowhere in the news coverage is it mentioned that 300 to 500 bears are shot each year, with 49 shot on average on the west coast of Hudson Bay. Even if we take the story of decline at face value, it means we have lost about 15 bears to global warming each year, whereas we have lost 49 each year to hunting.

> ▶ What do paragraphs 7–9 offer to the strength and relevancy of the author's claim?

9   In 2006, a polar-bear biologist from the Canadian government summed up the discrepancy between the data and the PR: "It is just silly to predict the demise of polar bears in 25 years based on media-assisted hysteria." With Canada home to two-thirds of the world's polar bears, global warming will affect them, but "really, there is no need to panic. Of the 13 populations of polar bears in Canada, 11 are stable or increasing in number. They are not going extinct, or even appear to be affected at present."

10   The polar-bear story teaches us three things. First, we hear **vastly exaggerated and emotional claims** that are simply not supported by data. Yes, it is likely that disappearing ice will make it harder for polar bears to continue their traditional foraging patterns and that they will increasingly take up a lifestyle similar to that of brown bears, from which they evolved. They may eventually decline, though dramatic declines seem unlikely. But over the past forty years, the population has increased dramatically and the populations are now stable. The ones going down are in areas that are getting colder. Yet we are told that global warming will make polar bears extinct, possibly within ten years, and that future kids will have to read about them in storybooks.

11 Second, polar bears are **not the only story**. While we hear only about the troubled species, it is also a fact that many species will do better with climate change. In general the Arctic Climate Impact Assessment projects that the Arctic will experience increasing species richness and higher ecosystem productivity. It will have less polar desert and more forest. The assessment actually finds that higher temperatures mean more nesting birds and more butterflies. This doesn't make up for the polar bears, but we need to hear both parts of the story.

12 The third point is that **our worry makes us focus on the wrong solutions**. We are being told that the plight of the polar bear shows "the need for stricter curbs on greenhouse gas emissions linked to global warming." Even if we accept the flawed idea of using the 1987 population of polar bears around Hudson Bay as a baseline, so that we lose 15 bears each year, what can we do? If we try helping them by cutting greenhouse gases, we can at the very best avoid 15 bears dying. We will later see that realistically we can do not even close to that much good—probably we can save about 0.06 bears per year. But 49 bears from the same population are getting shot each year, and this we can easily do something about. Thus, if we really want a stable population of polar bears, dealing first with the 49 shot ones might be both a smarter and a more viable strategy. Yet it is not the one we end up hearing about. In the debate over the climate, we often don't hear the proposals that will do the most good but only the ones that involve cutting greenhouse-gas emissions. This is fine if our goal is just to cut those gases, but presumably we want to improve human conditions and environmental quality. Sometimes greenhouse-gas cuts might be the best way to get this, but often they won't be. We must ask ourselves if it makes more sense to help 49 bears swiftly and easily or 0.06 bears slowly and expensively.

▶ What is the purpose of paragraphs 10–12?

13 The argument in this book is simple.

1. **Global warming is real and man-made.** It will have a serious impact on humans and the environment toward the end of this century.
2. **Statements about the strong, ominous, and immediate consequences of global warming are often wildly exaggerated,** and this is unlikely to result in good policy.
3. **We need simpler, smarter, and more efficient solutions for global warming** rather than excessive if well-intentioned efforts. Large and very expensive CO_2 cuts made now will have only a rather small and insignificant impact far into the future.
4. **Many other issues are much more important than global warming.** We need to get our perspective back. There are many more pressing problems in the world, such as hunger, poverty, and disease. By addressing them, we can help more people, at lower cost, with a much higher chance of success than by pursuing drastic climate policies at a cost of trillions of dollars.

▶ What do paragraphs 13–16 do?

14   These four points will rile a lot of people. We have become so accustomed to the standard story: climate change is not only real but will lead to unimaginable catastrophes, while doing something about it is not only cheap but morally right. We perhaps understandably expect that anyone questioning this line of reasoning must have evil intentions. Yet I think—with the best of intentions—it is necessary that we at least allow ourselves to examine our logic before we embark on the biggest public investment in history.

15   **We need to remind ourselves that our ultimate goal is not to reduce greenhouse gases or global warming per se but to improve the quality of life and the environment.** We all want to leave the planet in decent shape for our kids. Radically reducing greenhouse gas emissions is not necessarily the best way to achieve that. As we go through the data, we will see that it actually is one of the least helpful ways of serving humanity or the environment.

16   I hope that this book can help us to better understand global warming, be smarter about solutions to it, and also regain our perspective on the most effective ways to make the world a better place, a desire we all share.

—From *Cool It: The Skeptical Environmentalist's Guide to Global Warming*, by Bjorn Lomborg, pp. 3–9.
Copyright © 2007 by Bjorn Lomborg, reprinted by permission of Alfred A. Knopf, a division of Random House.

Interacting with Lomborg's Argument

Answer the following questions based upon your annotations. If you find you need to improve your annotations, please do so.

Interaction K   **Establishing the Author's Purpose**

1. How is this author's purpose different from Gore's and Craven's? _____
_____
_____

2. What is the purpose of the first six paragraphs? _____
_____

3. What purpose does the author serve by putting paragraphs 7–9 right after 5–6? _____
_____

4. What is the author's purpose in ending this part of the book with the phrase "a desire we all share"? _____

Interaction L ▶ Understanding the Claim and Evidence

1. Paraphrase the author's claim in your own words. _____

_____

2. In which paragraph does the author start to give evidence to support his claim? _____

3. Put a check mark next to the one statement below that is a major supporting detail rather than a minor supporting detail.

   A. "Both relied extensively on research published in 2001 by the Polar Bear Specialist Group of the World Conservation Union." (para. 6) _____

   B. "Contrary to what you might expect…the two populations in decline come from areas where it has actually been getting colder over the last fifty years." (para. 7) _____

   C. "Nowhere in the news coverage is it mentioned that 300 to 500 bears are shot each year." (para. 8) _____

4. Based on the author's argument, do polar bears perform the same function as the "canaries in coal mines" mentioned in the title? _____

Interaction M ▶ Considering Fact, Opinion, and Authority

1. Identify the following statements from the reading as fact (**F**) or opinion (**O**) or both (**F/O**). Give a reason for your evaluation.

   A. "It was obvious to me that Gore is sincerely worried about the world's future." _____

   _____

   B. "Of the 13 populations of polar bears in Canada, 11 are stable or increasing in number."

   _____

   C. "…our worry makes us focus on the wrong solutions." _____

   _____

   D. "We need to remind ourselves that our ultimate goal is not to reduce greenhouse gases or global warming per se but to improve the quality of life and the environment." _____

   _____

2. What did the author do to check whether the opinions of world leaders and the media were founded on actual facts? _____

   Name the organization whose opinions about polar bears were not verified by Lomborg's research. _____

3. How did Lomborg find out that this organization was misrepresenting the facts? _____

_____

4. Is the person who made this statement an expert source, an informed source, or a person on the street? "It is just silly to predict the demise of polar bears in 25 years." (para.9) _____

_____

Interaction N ▸ **Identifying the Author's Tone**

1. What is the tone of the following sentence? What words demonstrate the tone?
The media pound us with increasingly dramatic stories of our ever worsening climate?

_____

2. What insight does this sentence give us into the author's general tone?
This doesn't make up for the polar bears, but we need to hear both parts of the story.

_____

3. What is the overall tone of this passage? _____

Interaction O ▸ **Evaluating the Argument**

1. Is the author credible? Support your answer. _____

_____

2. Is the argument strong? Why or why not? _____

_____

3. Do you find the author's support of his argument relevant? Why or why not? _____

_____

Group or Individual Interaction: Creating a Summary Slide Show

Create a summary of one of the articles on global warming using PowerPoint or Keynote slides. Give your presentation to the class, who will grade you on whether your presentation accurately summarizes the information from the article.

Group or Individual Interaction:
Write and Make a Persuasive Speech

Based on the reading selections as well as any other information you have about global warming, write your own claim to answer the question "Is human activity causing global warming?" Then take information from all the readings that you find important in supporting your claim, and prepare a brief speech presenting your claim. Try to convince your classmates that your claim is true. The class can vote on who made the best argument.

Group or Individual Interaction:
Read Some More about Global Warming

Find an article on global warming in a newspaper or magazine, and read it. As you read, note the claim, major supporting evidence, the author's purpose, tone, and point of view, and facts and opinions used. Finally, evaluate the strength and relevancy of the author's argument. Note this information on a separate sheet of paper. Then exchange articles with a partner. Take the same kind of notes on this second article. Then compare your responses with your partner's responses on both articles. Were they similar? Why or why not?

A

A Guide to
Reading Visuals

> " *It's a visual world and people respond to visuals.* "
>
> —JOE SACCO

Interpreting Visuals 625

Visuals in textbooks may provide:

- ▶ Examples of the ideas being talked about.
- ▶ Specific numerical data to support the general statements in the text.
- ▶ A comparison of large amounts of information.

In college textbooks, some visuals include information that you must understand in order to comprehend the chapter completely. Other visuals are less important for comprehension but still interesting to look at. For example, **Table A.2** from the reading, "Congresspersons and the Citizenry: A Comparison" (page 627) provides a summary of key information to help you understand the idea of the passage better. In contrast, the movie still from *Sherlock Holmes: A Game of Shadows* at the beginning of Chapter 9 (page 451) gives you a visual that relates to the quotation under the image, but you could understand the idea without the photograph.

In the rest of this resource guide, we will discuss several major types of visual material, such as tables, pie charts, line graphs, bar graphs, flowcharts, and photographs. The following points, with some adaptations, apply to reading most of these different kinds of visuals.

Interpreting Visuals

1. **Read the title of the table or graphic carefully.** The title often provides information you need in order to understand the graphic. The title may function as the topic. Captions that appear under photographs are similarly important. Often, the caption functions as the main idea or the topic sentence of the graphic. Captions can also indicate the purpose of the visual.

2. **Read the headings of rows and columns or the labels on *x*- and *y*-axes carefully.** In a table, you should read the column headings so that you will know which groups are being compared. The information in the rows often consists of the points of comparison between the groups listed in the columns.

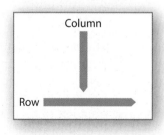

When you are reading graphs, the *y*-axis is the vertical line, and the *x*-axis is the horizontal line along the bottom of the figure. Read the labels carefully to make sure you understand how the information is set up.

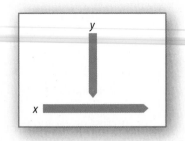

3. **If different colors are used, notice their meaning.** The parts of some graphs and charts may be printed in different colors that have specific meanings. Look for a key to tell you what the colors mean.

4. **Think critically about the implications of the headings, the numbers, and the way the information is presented.** Remember that graphics and tables summarize large amounts of data. In the process of reading so much information, sometimes it's easy to lose track of potential problems or questions that should be asked. Throughout the Interactions, we'll draw your attention to questions you might want to ask about specific graphics.

Interpret Tables

A table is an arrangement of information in rows and columns. Tables condense a lot of information into a small space, and they make pieces of information easy to compare. Tables may be composed of information reported in words or in numbers. Tables often summarize information that the author has been discussing in greater detail over the previous pages of the chapter. When you are reviewing for a test, it's a good idea to use this kind of table as a study aid.

Example: Table from a Human Development Textbook

Before you read a table, preview the title and column headings.
Notice the following kinds of information when you read a table:

▶ **What is the title of the table?** The title of **Table A.1** on page 627 is "Characteristics of Adolescents' Thinking."

▶ **What kind of information is given in each column (vertical line)?** In this table, the columns each have a heading that describes the type of information in them: "feature," "definition," and "example."

▶ **What kind of information is given in each row (horizontal line)?** If you read the first row of this table from left to right, you'll see that "adolescent egocentrism" is defined and then exemplified. Each succeeding feature is similarly defined and exemplified.

▶ **What conclusions can you draw by thinking critically?** Each of these terms explains ways that teenagers believe the world revolves around them. As a result they can be insensitive to the needs or wants of others.

Feature	Definition	Example
Adolescent egocentrism	Adolescents are overly concerned with their own thoughts and feelings.	When Levi's grandmother died unexpectedly, Levi was preoccupied with how the funeral would affect his weekend plans and ignored how upset his mother was by her own mother's death.
Imaginary audience	Adolescents believe that others are watching them constantly.	Tom had to ride his bike to football practice because his dad wouldn't let him have the car; he was sure that all his car-driving friends would see and make fun of him.
Personal fable	Adolescents believe that their experiences and feelings are unique.	When Rosa's boyfriend decided to date another girl, Rosa cried and cried. She couldn't believe how sad she was, and she was sure her mom had never felt this way.
Illusion of invulnerability	Adolescents think that misfortune only happens to others.	Kumares and his girlfriend had been having sex for about 6 months. Although she thought it would be a good idea to use birth control, he thought it was unnecessary. There was no way his girlfriend would get pregnant.

Table A.1 Characteristics of Adolescents' Thinking

—From Kall/Cavanaugh, *Human Development: A Life-Span View*, 4e

Interaction A–1 ▷ Analyze a Table from a Government Textbook

Read the following passage, which includes a table, and answer the questions that follow. Remember to follow these four steps:

1. Read the title of the table carefully.
2. Read the headings of rows and columns carefully.
3. If different colors are used, notice their meaning.
4. Think critically about the implications of the headings, the numbers, and the way the information is presented.

Congresspersons and the Citizenry: A Comparison

[1]   Members of the U.S. Senate and the U.S. House of Representatives are not typical American citizens. Members of Congress are older than most Americans, partly because of constitutional age requirements and partly because a good deal of political experience normally is an advantage in running for national office. Members of Congress are also disproportionately white, male, and trained in high-status occupations. Lawyers are by far the largest occupational group among

congresspersons, although the proportion of lawyers in the House is lower now than it was in the past. Compared with the average American citizen, members of Congress are well paid. In 2010, annual congressional salaries were $174,000. Increasingly, members of Congress are also much wealthier than the average citizen. Whereas less than 1 percent of Americans have assets exceeding $1 million, about one-third of the members of Congress are millionaires. **Table A.2** summarizes selected characteristics of the members of Congress.

Compared with the composition of Congress over the past 200 years, however, the House and Senate today are significantly more diverse in gender and ethnicity than ever before. There are 74 women in the House of Representatives (17 percent) and 17 women in the U.S. Senate (17 percent). Minority group members fill over 17 percent of the seats in the House; they include 42 African American members, 21 Hispanic members, 8 Asian or Pacific Islander Americans, and 1 Native American, Tom Cole of Oklahoma. There are 3 Hispanic members of the Senate but only 1 African American—Roland Burris of Illinois, who was appointed to fill the seat of Barack Obama after he won the presidential election. After the 2010 elections, it is unlikely that there will be any African American senators. The 111th Congress has significant numbers of members born in 1946 or later, the so-called Baby Boomers. A majority of House members and an even larger minority of the Senate belong to this postwar generation. This shift in the character of Congress may prompt consideration of the issues that will affect the Boomers, such as Social Security and Medicare.

Table A.2   Characteristics of the 111th Congress, 2009–2011

Characteristic	U.S. Population, 2008	House	Senate
Age (average)	36.8	57	63
Percent minority	25%	17.5%	7%
Religion			
Percent church members	61%	90.6%	99%
Percent Catholic	23.9%	31%	25%
Percent Protestant	51.3%	54.9%	55%
Percent Jewish	1.7%	13%	13%
Percent female	50.9%	17.8%	17%
Percent adv. degrees	5%	66.7%	76%
Lawyers	0.4%	38.6%	57%
Blue collar	30%	1.6%	3%
Percent earning more than $50,000	65%	100%	100%
Assets more than $1 million	0.7%	16%	33%

Sources: CIA World Factbook 2010; Congressional Quarterly Weekly Report; Ethnic Majority Web site, http://www .ethnicmajority.com; author's update.

—From Schmidt/Shelley/Bardes, *American Government and Politics Today*, 15e

1. What is the median age of the U.S. population? _____ Of the House of Representatives? _____ Of the Senate? _____

2. What is the percentage of church members in the U.S. population? _____ In the House? _____ In the Senate? _____

3. Compare the three populations on the basis of the percentage of people holding advanced degrees. United States: _____ House: _____ Senate: _____

4. Which of the three populations has the highest percentage of lawyers? What is the percentage? _____

5. Which of the three populations has the highest percentage of blue-collar workers? What is the percentage? _____

6. What does the paragraph explain that the table does not about the age of congresspersons?
_____

7. What does the paragraph explain that the table does not about why the family income of every single congressperson is more than $50,000? _____

8–10. A sentence in the first paragraph makes the following generalization: "Members of Congress are also disproportionately white, male, and trained in high-status occupations." In the table, what three characteristics from the first column will lead a reader to the exact percentages involved for each part of that general statement?

▶ White: _____

▶ Male: _____

▶ High-status occupation: _____

11. What pattern of organization is represented in this table? _____

12. Based on the characteristics included in this table, are the members of Congress (that is, the House and Senate combined) more similar to or more different from the general U.S. population? Does this seem important to you? Why or why not? _____
_____
_____

Interpret Pie Charts

A pie chart shows how a whole pie—100 percent of something—is divided up. Pie charts help readers compare the percentages or proportions of different components of a whole. Examine **Figure A.1** on the following page.

Example: Pie Charts from an American History Textbook

Figure A.1 Sources of Immigration

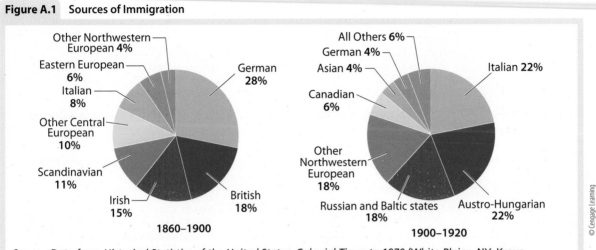

1860–1900

- Other Northwestern European 4%
- Eastern European 6%
- Italian 8%
- Other Central European 10%
- Scandinavian 11%
- Irish 15%
- British 18%
- German 28%

1900–1920

- All Others 6%
- German 4%
- Asian 4%
- Canadian 6%
- Italian 22%
- Other Northwestern European 18%
- Russian and Baltic states 18%
- Austro-Hungarian 22%

Source: Data from *Historical Statistics of the United States, Colonial Times to 1970* (White Plains, NY: Kraus International, 1989), pp. 105–109.

—From Murrin et al., *Liberty, Equality, Power,* 5e

Notice the following kinds of information when you read a pie chart:

► **What is the title?** The title of Figure A.1 is "Sources of Immigration." Based on the information that follows the title, you can tell that this information is about the United States.

► **What are the titles of the individual pie charts?** The chart on the left is called "1860–1900." The one on the right is titled "1900–1920." So from the titles alone, you can see that the purpose of the pie charts is to compare the sources of immigration during two different time periods.

► **How is the pie divided?** Let's look at the information for 1860–1900. Because the largest piece of the pie is so obvious, you can see right away that more immigrants from Germany came to the United States than any other nationality. This pie chart includes the actual percentage, 28 percent. Notice that the largest slice begins at 12:00 (if this circle were a clock face). Continuing around to the right you will find that each slice of the pie gets smaller. Thus, the second largest group of immigrants during that period was British, the next largest group was Irish, and so on.

► **What conclusions can you draw by thinking critically?** Think about all the groups represented on the pie chart for 1860–1900. What generalization can you make about where these immigrants came from? Notice that they are all from Europe, and mostly Western Europe.

Interaction A–2 ▸ Analyze a Pie Chart from a Media Textbook

Read the following passage, which includes a pie chart (**Figure A.2**), and answer the questions that follow. Remember to follow these four steps:

1. Read the title of the graphic carefully.
2. Read the names of categories carefully.
3. If different colors are used, notice their meaning.
4. Think critically about the implications of the headings, the numbers, and the way the information is presented.

Four Major Companies Dominate

1 About 5,000 companies in the United States produce music, but four companies dominate the global music business: EMI, Sony/BMG, Universal and Warner. Together these four companies, on average, have sold more than two billion recordings each year. The main recording centers in the United States are Los Angeles, New York and Nashville, but many large cities have at least one recording studio to handle local productions.

2 The recording industry, primarily concentrated in large corporations, generally chooses to produce what has succeeded before. "Increasingly, the big record companies are concentrating their resources behind fewer acts," reports *The Wall Street Journal*, "believing that it is easier to succeed with a handful of blockbuster hits than with a slew of moderate sellers. One result is that fewer records are produced."

3 Most radio formats today depend on popular music, and these recordings depend on radio to succeed. The main measurement of what is popular comes from *Billboard*, the music industry's leading trade magazine. *Billboard* began printing a list of the most popular vaudeville songs and the best-selling sheet music in 1913. In 1940, the magazine began publishing a list of the country's top-selling records.

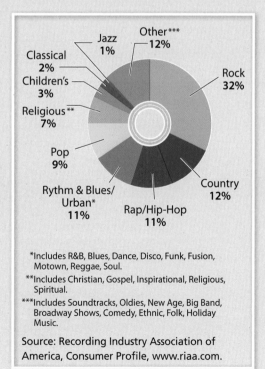

Jazz 1%
Other*** 12%
Classical 2%
Children's 3%
Religious** 7%
Pop 9%
Rythm & Blues/ Urban* 11%
Rap/Hip-Hop 11%
Country 12%
Rock 32%

*Includes R&B, Blues, Dance, Disco, Funk, Fusion, Motown, Reggae, Soul.

**Includes Christian, Gospel, Inspirational, Religious, Spiritual.

***Includes Soundtracks, Oldies, New Age, Big Band, Broadway Shows, Comedy, Ethnic, Folk, Holiday Music.

Source: Recording Industry Association of America, Consumer Profile, www.riaa.com.

Figure A.2   What Types of Music Do People Buy?
The recording industry's success rests on trends in popular music. For more than 50 years, rock music has maintained its lead as the most popular type of music.

4   Today, *Billboard* offers more than two dozen charts that measure, for example, airplay and album sales for popular artists such as Alison Krauss and Jennifer Hudson. Radio, governed by ratings and what the public demands, tends to play proven artists, so new artists are likely to get more radio attention if their recordings make one of the *Billboard* lists. This radio play, in turn, increases the artists' popularity and promotes their music.

—From Biagi, *Media Impact*, 9e

1. What is the topic of Figure A.2? _____

2. What is the main idea? _____

3. What pattern of organization is shown in the pie chart? _____

4. How much of the music that people buy is rock music? _____

5. What type of music was purchased the least? _____

6. What type of music is "other"? _____

   _____

7. What are some possible reasons that rock is the largest category? _____

   _____

8. Are there any music categories missing? _____

9. If so, where would they fit on the chart? _____

10. What is your favorite type of music? _____

Interpret Line Graphs

Line graphs are used to show how a condition or behavior changes over time. The number of people engaging in a behavior is often plotted on the y-axis (the vertical line). The units of time, such as years, are plotted on the x-axis, or horizontal line. Line graphs help make it easy to see trends in data.

Example: Line Graph from a Health Textbook

Notice the following points about the line graph on the next page (**Figure A.3**):

▶ **What is the title?** It is "Number of Cohabiting, Unmarried, Adult Couples of the Opposite Sex (United States)." Notice that the title tells us that the graph does *not* include information about couples who were not living together (cohabiting), who were married, who were not adults, who were living with same-sex partners, or who were not in the United States.

▶ **What are the headings on the x-axis and y-axis?** The y-axis is labeled "Number in Millions" and the x-axis is not labeled. The x-axis gives a

Figure A.3   Number of Cohabiting, Unmarried, Adult Couples of the Opposite Sex (United States)

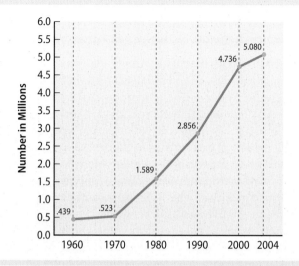

series of years starting at 1960 and ending at 2004. Notice that all the years are ten years apart except for the last two.

▶ **Think about the trend that this line graph shows.** First, notice that for each point at a particular year, the actual number is given. For instance, in 1960 less than half a million unmarried heterosexual couples were cohabitating in the United States (since the numbers are given in millions, 1 = 1 million, so the .439 means 439,000 people). Between 1960 and 1970, the number didn't change dramatically. From 1970 to 1980, however, the number tripled, approximately, and it nearly doubled in the next decade, from 1980 to 1990. In the next decade the number rose from about 2.8 million (2,800,000) to 4.7 million (4,700,000), again almost doubling. The last time period, remember, is only four years. So the small rise in numbers may be due to the fact that the time period is less than half that of the other time periods on the line graph, or it may be an indication that the numbers are increasing less rapidly than before.

Interaction A–3 ▷ Analyze a Line Graph from a Health Textbook

Read the following passage, which includes a line graph (**Figure A.4**), and answer the questions that follow. Remember to follow these four steps:

1. Read the title of the graphic carefully.
2. Read the labels on *x*- and *y*-axes carefully.
3. If different colors are used, notice their meaning.
4. Think critically about the implications of the headings, the numbers, and the way the information is presented.

Marriage

Like everything which is not the involuntary result of fleeting emotion but the creation of time and will, any marriage, happy or unhappy, is infinitely more interesting and significant than any romance, however passionate.

—W. H. Auden

1   Contemporary marriage has been described as an institution that everyone on the outside wants to enter and everyone on the inside wants to leave. The proportion of married people, especially among younger age groups, has been declining for decades. Across North America and many European countries, the age of first marriage has risen, with both men and women waiting an extra three years before saying "I do," and the rate of first marriages among men has been cut in half.

2   A generation ago nearly 70 percent of Americans were married; now only about half are (**Figure A.4**). Yet most young adults view marriage positively, and 95 percent expect to marry in the future—except for young African Americans, who have significantly lower expectations of being wed than their white counterparts, with Hispanics in between.

3   If you aren't already married, simply getting a college degree increases your odds of entering into matrimony in the future. According to a recent report, *The Decline of Marriage and Rise of New Families*, college graduates (who make up 30 percent of the adult population) are far more likely to marry (64 percent) than those without a baccalaureate degree (48 percent). Less well educated Americans are not only less likely to marry; if they do, their unions are more likely to end in divorce.

4   The median age for first marriage, which has gone up about a year every decade since the 1960s, has risen to 28.2 years for men and 26.1 years for women. Men in every age bracket through age 34 are more likely to be single than are women. Black men and women are less likely to be married than whites, with Hispanics between the two.

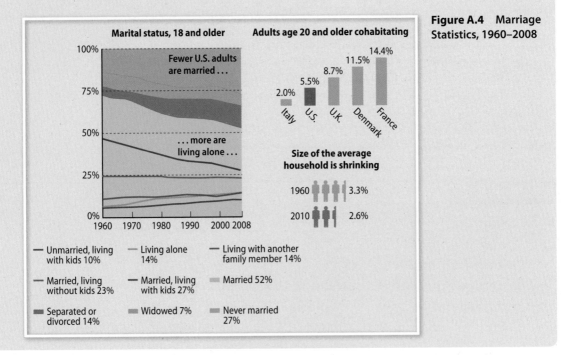

Figure A.4   Marriage Statistics, 1960–2008

1. What is the main idea of Figure A.4? _____

2. What is the purpose of the line graph? _____

3–4. What two patterns of organization are evident in this graph?

   ▶ _____

   ▶ _____

5. What is the youngest age measured in this graph? _____

6. What is the change in percentage of married Americans from 1960 to 2008? _____

7. Which category has decreased the least? _____

8. What are some possible reasons why marriage numbers have declined? _____

   _____

   _____

Interpret Bar Graphs

Bar graphs help readers compare differences between groups. A bar graph can show the relationship between two sets of numbers, such as the number of people doing two different things over a certain number of years.

Example: Bar Graph from a Business Management Textbook

Figure A.5   % of Married Women (with Children) Who Work

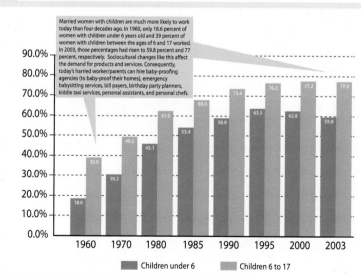

Married women with children are much more likely to work today than four decades ago. In 1960, only 18.6 percent of women with children under 6 years old and 39 percent of women with children between the ages of 6 and 17 worked. In 2003, those percentages had risen to 59.8 percent and 77 percent, respectively. Sociocultural changes like this affect the demand for products and services. Consequently, today's harried worker/parents can hire baby-proofing agencies (to baby-proof their homes), emergency babysitting services, bill payers, birthday party planners, kiddie taxi services, personal assistants, and personal chefs.

Children under 6   Children 6 to 17

—From Williams, *Management*, 4e

Let's examine the bar graph in **Figure A.5** based on the general questions.

▸ **What is the title of the bar graph?** It is "% of Married Women (with Children) Who Work." Notice that unmarried mothers are not included in this data.

▸ **What information does the *y*-axis provide?** Since there is no label, we can look at the numbers, which are percentages ranging from 0 percent at the bottom to 90 percent at the top. The title of the graph suggests that these are the percentages who work.

▸ **What information does the *x*-axis provide?** These are years, but with variable intervals between the years. The range is from 1960 to 2003.

▸ **What do the colors mean?** Notice that for each year there is a pair of bars, one blue and the other red. The key at the bottom notes that blue represents children under six, and red represents children aged six to seventeen.

▸ **What do you notice overall about the trend over time?** Has the number of married mothers who work increased or decreased over time? How about for those with young children? How about for those with older children? These have all increased over time. What does this mean? One obvious inference is that more mothers are working outside the home. A less obvious inference that might be drawn is that more families might need two incomes to survive.

Interaction A–4	Analyze a Bar Graph from a Government Textbook

Read the following passage, which includes a bar graph, and answer the questions that follow. Remember to follow these four steps:

1. Read the title of the graphic carefully.
2. Read the labels on *x*- and *y*-axes carefully.
3. If different colors are used, notice their meaning.
4. Think critically about the implications of the headings, the numbers, and the way the information is presented.

Who Participates in Politics?

1   To understand better why voter turnout declined and what, if anything, that decline may mean, we must first look at who participates in politics.

Forms of Participation

2   Voting is by far the most common form of political participation, while giving money to a candidate and being a member of a political organization are the least common. Many Americans

exaggerate how frequently they vote or how active they are in politics. In a study by Sidney Verba and Norman Nie, 72 percent of those interviewed said they voted "regularly" in presidential elections. Yet we know that since 1960, on average under 60 percent of the voting-age population has actually cast presidential ballots. Obviously, many people claim to have voted when in fact they have not. If people misreport their voting behavior, it is likely that they also misreport—that is, exaggerate—the extent to which they participate in other ways.

3   Indeed, most research shows that "politics is not at the heart of the day-to-day life of the American people." Work, family, church, and other voluntary activities come first, both in terms of how Americans spend their time and in terms of the money they donate. For example, a study by Verba and others found that a higher proportion of citizens take part in nonpolitical than political activities: "More citizens reported giving time to church-related or charitable activities than indicated contacting a government official or working informally on a community problem, two of the most frequent forms of political participation beyond the vote."

4   In an earlier study, Verba and Nie analyzed the ways in which people participate in politics and came up with six forms of participation that are characteristic of six different kinds of U.S. citizens. About one-fifth (22 percent) of the population is completely inactive: they rarely vote, they do not get involved in organizations, and they probably do not even talk about politics very much. These inactives typically have little education and low incomes and are relatively young. Many of them are African American. At the opposite extreme are the complete activists, constituting about one-ninth of the population (11 percent). These people are highly educated, have high incomes, and tend to be middle-aged rather than young or old. They tend to participate in all forms of politics.

5   Between these extremes are four categories of limited forms of participation. The *voting specialists* are people who vote but do little else; they tend not to have much schooling or income and to be substantially older than the average person. *Campaigners* not only vote but also like to get involved in campaign activities. They are better educated than the average voter, but what seems to distinguish them most is their interest in the conflicts, passions, and struggle of politics; their clear identification with a political party; and their willingness to take strong positions. *Communalists* are much like campaigners in social background but have a very different temperament: they do not like the conflict and tension of partisan campaigns. They tend to reserve their energy for community activities of a more nonpartisan nature—forming and joining organizations to deal with local problems and contacting local officials about these problems. Finally, there are some *parochial participants*, who do not vote and stay out of election campaigns and civic associations but are willing to contact local officials about specific, often personal, problems.

6   Whether participation takes the form of voting or being a complete activist, it is higher among people who have gone to college than it is among those who have not, higher among people who are employed than among the unemployed, and higher among whites and blacks than among Hispanics. The differences in voting rates for these groups are shown in **Figure A.6.**

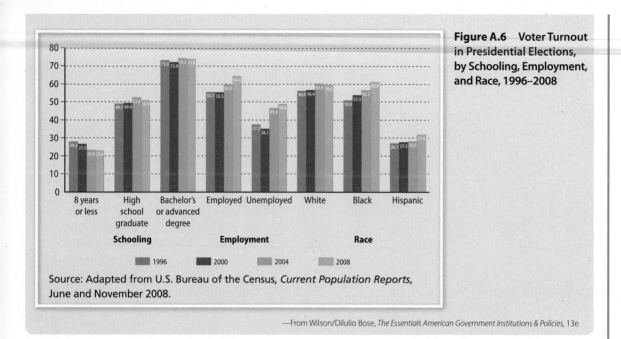

Figure A.6   Voter Turnout in Presidential Elections, by Schooling, Employment, and Race, 1996–2008

Source: Adapted from U.S. Bureau of the Census, *Current Population Reports*, June and November 2008.

—From Wilson/Dilulio Bose, *The Essentials American Government Institutions & Policies,* 13e

1. What is the pattern of organization of Figure A.6? _____

2. What is this graph measuring? _____

3. What general statement can be made about those with the least amount of education? _____

_____

4. What general statement can be made about schooling? _____

_____

5. What do the colors represent? _____

6. Why was the turnout of Black voters higher in 2008? _____

7. Why might the voter turnout of the employed be higher than that of the unemployed? _____

_____

Interpret Flowcharts

Flowcharts, also called *process charts,* show how different stages in a process are connected. You should read flowcharts from left to right and from top to bottom. Flowcharts can be simple or quite technical, with different box colors representing different aspects of the process.

Example: Flowchart from a Business Textbook

Figure A.7   How Planning Functions Are Related

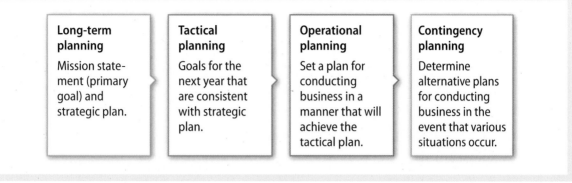

—From Madura, *Introduction to Business*, 4e

Let's examine this simple flowchart in **Figure A.7** from an introduction to a business textbook:

► **What is the title?** The title is "How Planning Functions Are Related."
► **What do the headings indicate?** There are four headings, one in each box, and they represent four different stages of planning: long-term, tactical, operational, and contingency.
► **What is the direction of flow?** The planning processes start at the left box, long-term planning, and flow through each box one by one, with contingency planning as the last box.
► **What does the flowchart mean?** In a business there are four stages of planning, each with a different goal. The one that all the others depend on is long-term planning. You can see that this consists of developing a mission statement and a strategic plan. These guide the other business plans. Tactical planning emphasizes shorter-term plans that will help make the long-term plans come into being. Then operational planning takes place to work out the "how" to make those shorter-term goals happen. Finally, after all the goal-directed planning has been done, the downside is examined in contingency planning. If things don't work out as planned, what should the company do?
► **What conclusions can you draw by thinking critically?** When you study tables and graphs, you will focus mostly on the meaning of the data for the course you are taking. But it's also smart to think how you personally might be able to make use of any and all information that you come across in your studies. Consider the flowchart in **Figure A.7** with your own goals in mind. Do you start your planning processes with your long-term goals? How will you move forward on them in the next year? Consider at least one long-term goal that you have and fill in the following chart (**Figure A.8**) with the stages of your planning as you think through how to make your goal a reality.

Figure A.8   **Planning to Achieve Your Goals**

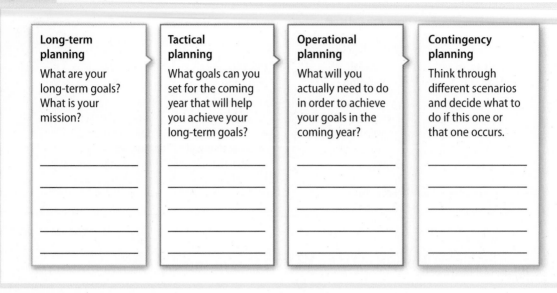

Interaction A–5   **Analyze a Flowchart from a Psychology Textbook**

Read the text that accompanies the flowchart in **Figure A.9**, and answer the questions that follow. Remember to follow these four steps:

1. Read the title of the graphic carefully.
2. Read the headings or box content carefully.
3. Notice the flow of the boxes.
4. Think critically about the implications of the headings, the flow of the boxes, and the way the information is presented.

The General Adaptation Syndrome

1   Of the many biological theories of stress, the best known may be the **general adaptation syndrome (GAS)**, developed by Hans Selye. He postulated that our bodies constantly strive to maintain a stable and consistent physiological state, called **homeostasis**. Stressors, whether in the form of physical illness or a demanding job, disturb this state and trigger a nonspecific physiological response. The body attempts to restore homeostasis by means of an **adaptive response**.

2   Selye's general adaptation syndrome, which describes the body's response to a stressor—whether threatening or exhilarating—consists of three distinct stages:

1. **Alarm.** When a stressor first occurs, the body responds with changes that temporarily lower resistance. Levels of certain hormones may rise; blood pressure may increase (Figure A.9). The body quickly makes internal adjustments to cope with the stressor and return to normal activity.

2. **Resistance.** If the stressor continues, the body mobilizes its internal resources to try to sustain homeostasis. For example, if a loved one is seriously hurt in an accident, we initially respond intensely and feel great anxiety. During the subsequent stressful period of recuperation, we struggle to carry on as normally as possible, but this requires considerable effort.

3. **Exhaustion.** If the stress continues long enough, we cannot keep up our normal functioning. Even a small amount of additional stress at this point can cause a breakdown.

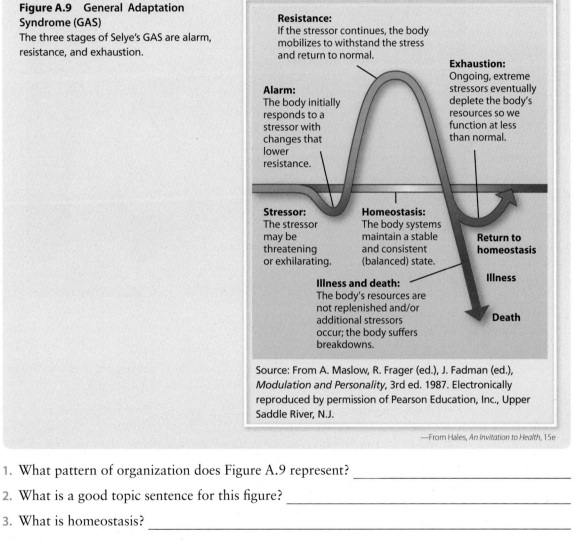

Figure A.9   General Adaptation Syndrome (GAS)
The three stages of Selye's GAS are alarm, resistance, and exhaustion.

Resistance:
If the stressor continues, the body mobilizes to withstand the stress and return to normal.

Exhaustion:
Ongoing, extreme stressors eventually deplete the body's resources so we function at less than normal.

Alarm:
The body initially responds to a stressor with changes that lower resistance.

Stressor:
The stressor may be threatening or exhilarating.

Homeostasis:
The body systems maintain a stable and consistent (balanced) state.

Return to homeostasis

Illness

Illness and death:
The body's resources are not replenished and/or additional stressors occur; the body suffers breakdowns.

Death

Source: From A. Maslow, R. Frager (ed.), J. Fadman (ed.), *Modulation and Personality*, 3rd ed. 1987. Electronically reproduced by permission of Pearson Education, Inc., Upper Saddle River, N.J.

—From Hales, *An Invitation to Health*, 15e

1. What pattern of organization does Figure A.9 represent? _____

2. What is a good topic sentence for this figure? _____

3. What is homeostasis? _____

4. What are the three stages of GAS? _____

5. How would one return to homeostasis after reaching exhaustion? _____

_____

Interpret Photographs

Photographs are used in textbooks to illustrate the ideas being discussed. Photograph captions connect the photo to the idea being illustrated and should be read just as carefully as the title of a chart, a graph, or a table.

Example: Photograph from an Anthropology Textbook

—From Ferraro, *Cultural Anthropology,* 9e

This photograph appears in a chapter on political organization and social control. It is in a section titled "Changing State Systems of Government."

- ▶ **What does the heading indicate?** There is no heading but there is a caption.
- ▶ **What does the photo caption indicate?** In order to get the most out of the photograph, you would need to know these terms from the caption: *participatory democracy* and *post-apartheid.* You could use context, word parts, a glossary, or a dictionary to determine the meanings of these terms.
- ▶ **What would the relationship of this image be to the text?** The picture would be illustrating what the text was discussing.
- ▶ **What conclusions can you draw by thinking critically?** The people in the photograph are black, so they demonstrate that apartheid is over. One is old and one is young, so perhaps they represent that the old ways have changed and the new ways are now in play. Also it is probably the first time the older woman has voted, which makes this a powerful photo!

Interaction A–6 Analyze a Photograph from an Anthropology Textbook

Read the following passage, which includes a photo, and answer the questions that follow. Remember to follow these four steps:

1. Read the heading carefully.
2. Read the photo caption carefully.
3. Notice the relationships within the image as well as between the image and the text.
4. Think critically about the implications of the headings and the way the information is presented.

Our Bodies and Culture

1   The nonmaterial aspects of our culture, such as ideas, values, and attitudes, can have an appreciable effect on the human body. Culturally defined attitudes concerning male and female attractiveness, for example, have resulted in some dramatic effects on the body. Burmese women give the appearance of elongating their necks by depressing their clavicles and scapulas with heavy brass rings, Chinese women traditionally had their feet bound, men in New Guinea put bones through their noses, and scarification and tattooing are practiced in various parts of the world for the same reasons that women and men in the United States pierce their ear lobes (that is, because their cultures tell them that it looks good). People intolerant of different cultural practices often fail to realize that had they been raised in one of those other cultures, they would be practicing those allegedly disgusting or irrational customs.

2   Even our body shape is related to a large extent to our cultural ideas. In the Western world, people go to considerable lengths to become as slender as possible. They spend millions of dollars each year on running shoes, diet plans, appetite suppressants, and health spa memberships to help them lose weight. However, our Western notion of equating slimness with physical beauty is hardly universally accepted. In large parts of Africa, for example, Western women are perceived as emaciated and considered to be singularly unattractive. This point was made painfully obvious to me (Ferraro) when I was conducting fieldwork in Kenya. After months of living in Kenya, I learned that many of my male Kikuyu friends pitied me for having such an

FRED PROUSER/Reuters /Landov

People in all cultures alter their bodies because they believe it makes them look more attractive.

unattractive wife (five feet five inches tall and 114 pounds). Kikuyu friends often came by my house with a bowl of food or a chicken and discreetly whispered, "This is for your wife." Even though I considered my wife to be beautifully proportioned, my African friends thought she needed to be fattened up in order to be beautiful.

3   Altering the body for aesthetic purposes (what is known euphemistically as "plastic surgery") has become increasingly widespread in U.S. culture over the last decade. To illustrate, 1.8 million Americans submitted to plastic surgery in 2003, a 12 percent increase from the previous year, while 6.4 million Americans opted for nonsurgical procedures such as Botox injections, an increase of 22 percent from the previous year. In fact, surgical and nonsurgical altering of our physical appearance is now so widespread and routine that it has become a wildly popular form of entertainment. Such reality TV shows as *Losing It with Jillian* and *The Biggest Loser* feature seemingly unattractive people who voluntarily submit to a host of cosmetic surgical procedures or behavioral modifications, emerging at the end of the show transformed to enjoy rave reviews from friends, family members, and the sizable viewing audience. After liposuction, nose jobs, forehead lifts, lip and breast augmentation, tooth veneers, chin implants, extreme diets, and vigorous exercise regimens, the women begin to look like Barbie dolls or Pamela Anderson, while the men take on the physical traits of action heroes (Kuczynski 2004).

—From Ferraro, *Cultural Anthropology: An Applied Perspective, 9e*

1. What is the purpose of the photo in the reading selection? _____
_____

2. What pattern of organization does the photo illustrate? _____

3. Do you find the woman in the picture to be attractive? Why or why not? _____
_____

4. How does the picture relate to the topic and main idea? _____
_____

5. Think about the accepted weights for men and women in your culture. How has this affected your view of what is attractive? _____
_____

6. What are some ways people you know have altered their bodies? _____

7. If you could, would you alter your body? If so, how? _____
_____

B

A Guide to
Reading Novels

" *Beginnings are usually scary and endings are usually sad, but it's everything in between that makes it all worth living.* "

—SANDRA BULLOCK AS BIRDEE PRUITT IN *HOPE FLOATS*

Reading novels is different from reading nonfiction, as you have been doing throughout this book. Novels are fiction. A novel represents truths about life through character, plot, setting, theme, and symbolism, among other means. Reading a novel is sometimes less straightforward than reading nonfiction, especially nonfiction that is designed to inform readers. Novels have an expressive purpose, so even if readers do wind up feeling they have learned something from a novel, the author's main purpose is to tell a story. Stories are often about how a character or characters change because of their experiences.

The reader's role, however, is similar in reading both fiction and nonfiction. As Angela Carter, a novelist and short story writer, puts it: "Reading a book is like rewriting it for yourself. You bring to a novel anything you read, all your experience of the world. You bring your history and you read it in your own terms." Your prior knowledge matters just as much in reading a novel as it does in reading nonfiction.

Your instructor may assign a particular novel for you to read and give you particular instructions for how to read it. If so, be sure to follow those directions. If not, you may want to use the following brief guide. After the guide you will find a list of novels that students around the country often read in their classes. Finally, a list of books that have been made into movies appears, along with a few suggestions for how to think about a work when it appears in two mediums.

Build Some Prior Knowledge

As Angela Carter notes, you bring your prior knowledge to reading a novel—the experiences you have had in the world and the knowledge you gained by living those experiences. Another kind of prior knowledge—knowledge of the different elements that literary authors use to develop a character and a story—is also helpful in reading fiction. In other words, knowledge of these elements will help you build a schema for reading novels.

Be Aware of Literary Elements

▶ **Characters: Fictional people.** When you read novels, notice what the characters say, what other characters say about them, how the characters look, and how the characters act. At least one of the major characters usually changes over the course of the story, usually in response to emotional or physical challenges or crises.

▶ **Point of View.** The narrator of a novel is the person who tells the story. The narrator is not the author. The author creates the narrator, and the narrator may not believe, think, or feel what the author does.

The narrator can tell the story from two different points of view: first person or third person (see pages 504–505). A first-person narrator is often a major character (but not always). First-person narrators can be reliable or unreliable (just like real people!).

A third-person narrator tells the story from a different perspective. Some are omniscient: they know everything, including what each character thinks.

Some are limited; these focus on what a single character knows. Other narrators tell the story from a greater distance. Even though they know everything that happens between characters, they can't see into characters' minds. These are called *objective narrators*.

▶ **Plot.** The plot is the pattern of events in the story. The author reveals the plot by what characters say to each other and how they interact, by how the different events that occur are arranged, and by cause and effect relationships. The plot doesn't always happen in time order. Sometimes there are flashbacks (scenes from the past).

   The plot usually includes a section called the *exposition* in which the author sets up the background for the story. It includes *complications* that arise as the characters interact, which lead to one or more small *crises*—moments of tension in which important decisions are made. These lead up to a major crisis—the *climax*. The main character(s) changes significantly because of the crisis. After the major crisis is over, the *denouement* ties up some of the plot's loose ends.

▶ **Setting.** The setting is the place and time of the story. Important elements of the setting may be the physical circumstances, the historical time period, and the country or region in which the plot takes place.

▶ **Symbolism.** A symbol is a person or thing or action that has two layers of meaning: a literal layer and a figurative layer. (You read about figures of speech in Chapter 10.) At the literal level, the symbol is exactly what is seems to be. At the figurative level, it has a more complex meaning; it stands for something more abstract or more general.

▶ **Author's Style and Tone.** The style and tone are based on some of the same aspects that you think about when reading nonfiction (see Chapter 10). How the author uses words and sentence structures creates a certain feeling. So do the figures of speech such as metaphor, simile, personification, and hyperbole. How the author uses symbols is part of the style, also. The author's tone toward the characters and the story might be optimistic, cynical, humorous, ironic (see pages 508–509), or any of the tones listed on pages 511–512.

▶ **Theme.** Theme is the central idea or point that the novel makes about life. Think about theme as an implied main idea (see Chapter 5). The author never states the theme, but it is there for readers who think about the novel and let it affect them deeply. The theme is different from the plot. The plot is what happens; the theme is what must be true for the plot to happen. The theme is also not the subject; it's a larger point. If the subject of a story is a particular person, for example, the theme is about what that person's actions reveal about people.

To Survey a Novel or Not to Survey

If your instructor gives you particular directions for surveying a novel, follow them. Otherwise, you might think about the following:

1. **Don't survey.** You can't use the same surveying techniques on a novel that you would on a piece of nonfiction. You would not get an overview of the

important points, for example, by reading only the first sentences of paragraphs. Instead, consider immersing yourself in the novel in the order in which the novelist presents it: starting on page 1.

2. **Survey the "edges" of the book.** Reading any copy on the inside and outside of the book covers (called "cover copy") may give you some insight into the main plot, reveal interesting details about the author, or reprint comments made by other authors who read the book. This is more like surveying around the book than surveying the book itself, but doing this survey gives you more of a context for starting to read.

3. **Survey the table of contents.** Sometimes novels include tables of contents. If the table of contents includes chapter titles, reading them may give you a sense of the author's tone, the settings in which the plot will unfold, or the characters' names. If you preview the table of contents, notice what predictions your mind makes out of the titles, or the movement from one chapter title to the next.

4. **Read the first paragraph of a chapter.** If you are reading a novel for class, consider reading the first paragraph of the assigned chapter as a survey. Linger over it. Squeeze out any impressions you can from the name of the character, the description of the setting, or the movement of the plot. What tone is the author setting up? Consider why the author wanted to use the beginning of the chapter—an important spot—for this particular scene. Make a prediction about the chapter. You might list all the ideas you get from the first paragraph before you read the chapter. When you finish the chapter, go back to your list and see if any of your ideas were borne out.

Entering the World of the Novel

If your instructor gives you particular directions for reading a novel, follow them. Otherwise, you might think about the following:

1. **Enter the world of the novel as a believer.** While it is the author's job to write the novel in such a way that you do believe in it, as the reader you can choose to enter this world as a believer or as a doubter. If you are going to read the novel twice, you can read it the first time as a believer, and the second time as a doubter. (Reading as a doubter is good when you need to write an analysis of the novel.) But if you are going to read it just once, then read as a believer—enter the author's world as a wholehearted participant.

2. **Read faster and then slower.** If you are reading a novel for class, you'll need to apply some strategies to make sure you understand it well enough to talk about it in terms of the elements of literature listed on pages 646–647. A strong strategy in this situation is to read the assigned section once through at your own pace with the purpose of enjoying the novel and seeing what happens to the characters. Then read the same material more slowly, pausing often to think about what the author is doing. You can assume that

the author has a reason for putting each scene and each description right where it is. Ask yourself questions that you make up from the list of literary elements. For example, you can ask yourself "Who are the major characters? Why are they doing what they are doing? Why does the author describe them in the way that he or she does?" and so on. You can make up questions from each one of the elements and think about the possible answers.

3. **Write in the margins and write on separate paper.** Using a pencil, write brief comments in the margin of the novel. Especially write comments that deal with "how" and "why" the author is doing something. On separate paper, write out your fuller responses. You might want to respond to the characters, or to the plot, or to the symbols, tone, or setting.

4. **Write a paragraph (or more) in response to any of the following questions.** These questions ask you to investigate your personal responses to the novel.

   ▶ Which character do you care about the most? Why?
   ▶ Which character do you dislike the most? Why?
   ▶ What is the most confusing part? What makes it confusing?
   ▶ What is the most interesting scene? What makes it interesting?
   ▶ What is the most important scene? What makes it important?
   ▶ What is the most important symbol? What makes it important?

Reflecting on the Novel

Once you have read the whole novel, it's a good time to take stock of what you read. Your instructor may ask you to complete certain activities to help you sum up the book. Consider these activities as well:

1. **Trace the main character's development.** Using the information from the literary elements list under "character" and "plot," write a timeline or description of the major events that the main character went through and how each one changed the character.

2. **Describe the main conflict.** What is the central conflict in the novel? Who is involved? How do you know this is the main conflict and not just one of the more minor crises?

3. **Write a statement of the novel's theme.** Review the information under "theme" on page 647. See if you can write out a statement of the theme. What is the author saying about the world, or about life, or about how people act in general under certain conditions?

4. **Talk about the novel.** In addition to or instead of writing in response to the first three activities, talk about them with a small group of classmates. Go around the circle of people, allowing each person to start off with the reactions they had as individuals. As each person listens to the others, his or her ideas will probably start changing and deepening. Keep going around the circle until no one has anything left to say about the topic.

Some Novels That People Are Reading

The following is a list of novels that students around the country are reading or have enjoyed reading. To find out more about any of these novels, go to Amazon (**http://www.amazon.com**) and type in the title. Scroll down until you see the customer reviews or editorial reviews if you want to read an overview of the plot. Be careful! You may find out what happens later in the book.

You can also just get a sense of some novels by using the "Search Inside" feature. Scroll back up to the top of the page and look above the image of the book cover. If it says "search inside," you can click on that. Then click on "front cover," "table of contents," "excerpt," "back cover," or "surprise me!" The excerpt will be the first page or two of the novel.

The Alchemist, by Paulo Coelho

Alias Grace, by Margaret Atwood

Angels and Demons, by Dan Brown

Bastard Out of Carolina, by Dorothy Allison

Beloved, by Toni Morrison

The Book Thief, by Markus Zusak

Call of the Wild, by Jack London

Catch Me If You Can, by Frank Abagnale

The Cell, by Stephen King

The Color of Water, by James McBride

The Count of Monte Cristo, by Alexandre Dumas

The Curious Incident of the Dog in the Night-Time, by Mark Haddon

Disgrace, by J. M. Coetzee

The Five People You Meet in Heaven, by Mitch Albom

Frankenstein, by Mary Shelley

Fried Green Tomatoes at the Whistle Stop Café, by Fannie Flagg

The Golden Compass, by Philip Pullman

The Great Gatsby, by F. Scott Fitzgerald

Harry Potter (series), by J. K. Rowling

Hole in My Life, by Jack Gantos

Holes, by Louis Sachar

The House on Mango Street, by Sandra Cisneros

The Hunt for Red October, by Tom Clancy

The Joy Luck Club, by Amy Tan

Kindred, by Octavia Butler

A Lesson Before Dying, by Ernest Gaines

The Lion, the Witch, and the Wardrobe, by C. S. Lewis

Lord of the Flies, by William Golding

The Lovely Bones, Alice Sebold

The Lucky One, by Nicholas Sparks

The Notebook, by Nicholas Sparks

The Other Wes Moore, by Wes Moore

The Pearl, by John Steinbeck

Point of Impact, by Stephen Hunter

The Rapture of Canaan, by Sheri Reynolds

The Reader, by Bernhard Schlink

The Secret Life of Bees, by Sue Monk Kidd

The Small Room, by May Sarton

A Thousand Splendid Suns, by Khaled Hosseini

A Time to Kill, by John Grisham

The Time Traveler's Wife, by Audrey Niffenegger

To Kill a Mockingbird, by Harper Lee

Tuesdays with Morrie, by Mitch Albom

A Walk to Remember, by Nicholas Sparks

What Looks Like Crazy on an Ordinary Day, by Pearl Cleage

Women of the Silk, by Gail Tsukiyama

A Sampling of Novels That Have Been Made into Movies

The book: *Of Mice and Men,* by John Steinbeck
The movie: *Of Mice and Men,* starring Gary Sinise and John Malkovich

The book: *Where the Heart Is,* by Billie Letts
The movie: *Where the Heart Is,* starring Natalie Portman and Ashley Judd

The book: *Like Water for Chocolate,* by Laura Esquivel

The movie: *Como Agua Para Chocolate,* starring Lumi Cavazos and Marco Leonardi

The book: *Bringing Down the House,* by Ben Mezrich

The movie: *21,* starring Jim Sturgess, Kevin Spacey, Laurence Fishburne, and Kate Bosworth

The book: *Extremely Loud and Incredibly Close,* by Jonathan Safran Foer

The movie: *Extremely Loud and Incredibly Close,* starring Thomas Horn, Tom Hanks, and Sandra Bullock

The book: *Harry Potter and the Order of the Phoenix,* by J. K. Rowling

The movie: *Harry Potter and the Order of the Phoenix,* starring Daniel Radcliffe, Rupert Grint, and Emma Watson

The book: *The Hunger Games,* by Suzanne Collins

The movie: *The Hunger Games,* starring Jennifer Lawrence, Josh Hutcherson, and Liam Hemsworth

The book: *The Help,* by Kathryn Stockett

The movie: *The Help,* starring Emma Stone, Viola Davis, and Octavia Spencer

The book: *Memoirs of a Geisha,* by Arthur Golden

The movie: *Memoirs of a Geisha,* starring Ziyi Zhang, Suzuka Ohgo, and Ken Watanabe

The book: *One for the Money,* by Janet Evanovich

The movie: *One for the Money,* starring Katherine Heigl, Jason O'Mara, and Daniel Sunjata

The book: *Sahara,* by Clive Cussler

The movie: *Sahara,* starring Matthew McConaughey, Steve Zahn, and Penelope Cruz

The book: *Sisterhood of the Traveling Pants,* by Ann Brashares

The movie: *Sisterhood of the Traveling Pants,* starring Amber Tamblyn, Alexis Bledel, America Ferrera, and Blake Lively

The book: *The Mist,* by Stephen King

The movie: *The Mist,* starring Thomas Jane, Marcia Gay Harden, Laurie Holden, and Andre Braugher

The book: *The Kite Runner,* by Khaled Hosseini

The movie: *The Kite Runner,* starring Khalid Abdalla, Homayon Ershadi, Shaun Toub, Atossa Leoni, and Said Tashimaoui

To find more books that have been made into movies, you can visit the following site: **http://www.bookreporter.com/features/books2movies.asp.**

A Few Tips for Reading the Book and Seeing the Movie

If your instructor gives you particular directions for reading a novel and seeing the movie, follow them. Otherwise, you might think about the following:

1. **Which comes first...the book or the movie?** This question has caused a great debate. Some people feel strongly that you should watch the movie first. This way, you will not be disappointed because the movie did not live up to the expectations you had for it. For example, this happened with the movie *Eragon.* Many fans of the book did not like the movie because they felt it was not as good as the book. Another reason given is that by watching the movie first, you will be better able to understand the plot and character interactions in the book. Others swear by reading the book first. They say that you then have a better perspective of the story while you are watching the movie. Sometimes a movie gives a book more depth or adds another dimension to it. You may have more insight into the story and you can enjoy the director's interpretations of a story you enjoyed. We think either one is okay. While it is more often the case that the book is better than the movie (because you are using your imagination), both media can be helpful whether you are reading for pleasure or for insight in order to write a report. Reading and viewing are both fun!

2. **Compare and contrast the book and the movie.** Whether you read the book first or watched the movie, a great way to approach the second media choice is by looking for similarities or differences between it and the first. For example, how are the characters, point of view, plot, setting, symbolism, style and tone, and theme of the author and director similar or different?

3. **Compare and contrast your interpretation of the book versus the director's interpretation.** This is similar to the previous suggestion, except you approach it from your point of view. How is the director's vision of the film different from or similar to your interpretation of the characters, point of view, plot, setting, symbolism, style and tone, and theme? If you had been the director, what would you have kept the same or done differently?

4. **Pause and take notes.** Whether you are reading first and watching second or vice-versa, stop and take notes of the similarities or differences you want to emphasize while you are in the process of reading or watching. It is much easier to take a moment and stop reading or hit pause and write down your thoughts than it is to go back and try to remember everything from beginning to end.

Good luck and enjoy!

A Guide to
Taking Tests

" *The difference between school and life? In school, you're taught a lesson and then given a test. In life, you're given a test that teaches you a lesson.* "

—TOM BODETT

Even though tests do not always accurately reflect what you know or have learned, they are an integral part of school. It's pretty safe to expect tests in most if not all of the classes you take. There is no doubt that tests equal stress. So the real trick to doing well on your tests is to create a process that can help you be better prepared. The more prepared you are, the better success you should have. Once you internalize a good preparation and test-taking process, you will trust yourself, and then you will begin to do even better. Read the following tips and strategies for guidance in becoming a skilled and confident test taker.

Preparing to Test

So, you've registered for class, bought your text, shown up, read, and taken notes…or at least listened. Guess what!? It's test time! You better get ready. So do you cram? NO! You have a plan. PROCRASTINATION IS NOT A PLAN! You must avoid procrastination. It only causes pain, suffering, and even failure. So how do you avoid procrastination and actually successfully prepare for your test? Read further for some strategies.

▶ The key to preparing for tests is to have effective study habits.

1. Be intentional with your time. Create a daily and weekly calendar so you know what you are doing and when. (See "Plan for Success" at the beginning of this book for examples.)

"I'm too busy going to college to study."

2. Set goals and reward yourself when you complete a goal. For example, if you make Friday the goal to complete a writing assignment, then your reward is to go out to the movies with friends that night. However, if you do not finish, you need to have the courage to tell yourself and your friends that you can't go because you must finish your writing assignment. Being hard but fair with yourself will cause you to grow in responsibility and ability.

3. Chunk big assignments into smaller pieces. For example, a 40-page chapter could be divided into 8 pages a day for 5 days.

4. Have a dedicated study space or time. Use the same space to study and your mind will be prepared to study in that space. If you cannot dedicate a single space, then pick consistent times each day to study.

5. Do not cram at the last minute. This is the worst possible way to study! Time management is essential. You may need to spend extra time studying before a test, but this is different from cramming. You should space out your studying in shorter, consistent blocks of time. For example, if you know you have a test next week, study 1 hour each night rather than 5–7 hours the night before!

6. Overlearn your material. Most students underprepare and assume they will remember the information they are studying after just seeing it one time. Unless you have a photographic memory, this approach will not work. One process to follow is:

   a. Read→annotate text→turn annotations into written notes→type notes→review notes→test your knowledge by writing notes from memory

   b. Another strategy is to create essay questions from the key ideas of each chapter and write and rewrite your answers until you know the information by heart.

▶ Make studying interesting.

1. Adjust your attitude. Learning is more successful if it is fun, or at least pleasant.

2. Set a goal, take action toward it, and complete it.

3. Role-play. For example, in biology class, think of yourself as a biologist trying to discover something; in history class, think of yourself as a historian who goes back in time.

4. Remember your long-term goal. The goal of getting an A or graduating is built upon doing small tasks each day, each week, and each semester to reach the bigger goal. So keep your end in sight.

General Tips for Taking Tests

In college, the most common way to check your comprehension of an individual concept, a broad subject, or specific material is by testing. Because you will probably take tests in most of your classes, you should use strategies that help you approach tests in a clear, logical, and precise manner. The following list can help you lay a firm foundation for successful testing.

Before the Test

Survey the entire test before you begin.

- How many questions are there?
- How many points is each question worth?
- How much time do you have to complete each item?
- Read and pay attention to ALL directions.

During the Test

Start with what you already know. Work from what you know to what you don't know.

- Read each question carefully.
- Make sure you understand key words.
- Decide exactly what the question is asking for before you answer it.
- Read all the possible answers carefully before you choose one.
- Eliminate answers that you know are wrong first.
- Double-check the answer you think is correct.
- If you are unsure of an answer, mark the choice you think might be correct and then return to that question after you complete the test if there is time.
- Change your answer if you have a good reason to believe that a different answer would be better. In other words, only change an answer based on reflection, NOT fear or uncertainty.

After the Test

When you get the test back, you can evaluate your strategies based on the results.

- If you have done well, celebrate! Repeat those strategies for the next test.
- If you have done poorly, ask questions to find out why.
- Evaluate what you missed and ask yourself how you could have done better.
- Set a time to meet with your instructor for suggestions about how you could do better on the next test.
- Ask students who did well on the test how they studied and if they would be willing to help you prepare for the next test.

Specific Strategies for Different Types of Tests

Objective Tests

Objective tests include multiple-choice and true/false questions.

▶ On multiple-choice tests, you need to understand the question. Look for key words to understand what task you are being asked to do.

▶ Evaluate ALL the answers to find the one that best answers the question. Also use key words to choose the best answer.

▶ Eliminate any answers you are certain are wrong.

▶ If an answer is only partially correct, then eliminate it. An answer has to be 100% correct to be the best answer.

▶ Carefully evaluate answers with "all or nothing" words (*all, never*) or superlatives (*best, worst*), as these answers tend to be wrong. Be suspicious, however; if the passage has proof to support an answer with one of these words, it is okay to pick it!

▶ If two answers are the same, then they are probably both wrong.

▶ Carefully look at similar answers. Determine how they differ, and then choose the one that is best supported.

▶ Verify correct answers based on your studying or by using the details of the test.

▶ Look for clues in the answers of other questions. This might not always happen, but it does sometimes.

▶ Answer all items. If you are unsure about an item, still answer it, mark it in some way, and then return to look at it later. Otherwise, it is possible that you will run out of time and turn in a blank answer, which is guaranteed to be wrong.

▶ It's okay to change your answer if you have reflected on the answers and determined the correct one. Do not change an answer based on doubt.

Essay Tests

An essay test requires writing. To do well on these types of tests, you must be able to organize your thoughts and develop your ideas.

▶ Read the question carefully. Look for key words to understand the depth of the task being asked of you. Critical thinking levels are often reflected by the key words or verbs used.

▶ **Level 1:** *remember, identify, list, reproduce, define*
▶ **Level 2:** *understand, paraphrase, conclude, match, exemplify*
▶ **Level 3:** *apply, diagram, demonstrate, solve, illustrate*
▶ **Level 4:** *analyze, compare, examine, explain, investigate*
▶ **Level 5:** *evaluate, assess, rank, critique, justify*
▶ **Level 6:** *create, develop, design, adapt, imagine*

▶ Make sure you answer the question completely. If you answer only one part of a two-part question, then you will only receive half credit or even no credit.

▶ Be direct and support your answers sufficiently. Keep in mind that you need to create a topic sentence, including the topic and main idea, and then give clear and relevant supporting details.

  ▶ You can often restate the question as a statement to create your topic sentence.

Short-Answer Tests

Short-answer tests often include defining terms, filling in the blank, or listing information.

▶ OVERSTUDY!

▶ Make flash cards of terms and key concepts.

▶ Create mnemonics for lists (such as PIE for an author's three main purposes; see Chapter 2).

▶ Use visual strategies. Use as many of your senses as you can to experience a concept.

▶ Self-test or have a family member, friend, or classmate test you.

▶ Use context clues if you can.

Tips for Taking Reading Tests

Questions on reading tests often cover specific skills. These include understanding the main idea and supporting details; skills related to inference—vocabulary in context, literal versus figurative meaning, purpose, tone, or drawing conclusions; relationships between ideas; skills related to critical reasoning—point of view, assumptions, implied main idea, fact and opinion; and skills related to organization—understanding an outline or a summary or interpreting a table, chart, or graph.

Main Idea

▶ The main idea is the point that the author is making about the topic.

▶ You need to understand the relationship between the topic, main idea, and supporting details to effectively answer a main idea question.

▶ On multiple-choice reading tests, the possible answers to main idea questions generally fall into three categories:

  1. Too broad—the topic or an idea falls outside the scope of the passage.

  2. Too narrow—these are often the supporting details of the passage. A too-narrow answer will actually support the correct answer choice.

3. Just right—this is an answer that both supports the topic and is supported by the details.

▶ Eliminate any answers that are too broad or too narrow.
▶ Double-check your chosen answer. Do this by turning the answer into a question. If it is the main idea, the details of the passage should answer the question.

Supporting Details

▶ Look carefully through the passage for the answer. Don't rush or lose patience.
▶ Pay attention to synonyms used. The answer is usually stated differently than the information in the passage, but the answer means the same thing.
▶ Be cautious of answers in which two items from the text are put together—but in an incorrect relationship.
▶ Be aware of "all or nothing" words (*all, never, always, none*). Make sure the statements they are in have specific support in the passage.
▶ Make sure the detail in the answer isn't broader than what is supported by the text.
▶ When dealing with numbers or percentages, look carefully at the numbers stated.

1. The reading passage may say "75 percent will not," but the test answer might say "25 percent will."

2. The reading passage may say the words "twenty-five percent," but the test answer might say "25%."

3. The reading passage may say "one-third," but the test answer says "33%."

Skills Related to Inference

▶ **Vocabulary in Context.** Always look for signal words and relationships between ideas.

1. Examples—look for words like *for instance, such as,* and *for example,* but understand that even without a signal word, an author can still give an example.

2. Antonyms—look for opposite relationships (*however, but, although, not*).

3. Synonyms—look for similar relationships (*also, similarly, and, that is*).

4. Your Logic and Prior Knowledge—focus on what you know and understand to help you figure out what you are not sure about.

▶ **Literal Versus Figurative Meaning.** Apply your understanding of denotative meaning (the literal, dictionary definition) and connotative meaning (the figurative, emotional definition). Do the answers contain any of the following?

1. Metaphor—a direct comparison (The sun is a big yellow ball.)

2. Simile—an indirect comparison using *like* or *as* (The sun is *like* a big yellow ball.)

3. Personification—the giving of human characteristics to non-human objects (The cool summer rain *kissed* my face.)

4. Hyperbole—an exaggeration (My teacher gives a *ton* of homework.)

▶ **Purpose.** Remember PIE. The author's main purpose is often supported by the details, just as the main idea is.

1. Persuade—the author wants you to change your mind or behavior and gives you reasons to support his or her opinion or claim.

2. Inform—the author is giving you objective information about something that you can verify. This type of answer may include words like *describe, list,* or *explain* to show what kind of information the author gave or how the author organized his or her information.

3. Express—the author is trying to pull an emotion from you—laughter, fear, sympathy, dread, suspense, and so on. This is often done through stories.

▶ **Tone.** What emotion is the author using in his or her writing? Once you decide the general tone, you can drill down to the specific word that best describes the tone.

1. Positive—the tone words are positive, showing the author likes or is in favor of something.

2. Negative—the tone words are negative, showing the author does not like or is against something.

3. Neutral—the tone words are objective, factual, and informative.

▶ **Drawing Conclusions.** The answer chosen must have proof in the passage.

1. Pay attention to key words used.

2. Turn your answer into a question.

3. Verify the proof with details from the passage.

Relationships Between Ideas

Pay attention to relationships between ideas by asking questions and looking for signal words.

▶ **Time Order.** When did this happen? Look for information that takes place in a particular order of time.

▶ **Space Order.** Where are things located? Look for description and location.

▶ **Definitions.** What does this mean? Look for a key term, followed by a definition and examples explaining the term.

▶ **Examples.** What are the examples of this general idea? Look for multiple examples of the same general idea.

▶ **Cause and Effect.** Why? What made this happen? What does this lead to? Look for a direct relationship between a reason and the result.

▶ **Comparison and Contrast.** How are these the same? How do they differ? Look for two or more items being talked about in terms of similarities or differences.

▶ **Classification.** What kinds are there? Look for groupings of items into categories or types.

Skills Related to Critical Reasoning

▶ **Point of View and Assumptions.** Both can be proven by details from the reading, paying special attention to tone.

1. Decide what point of view the author is using, and whether that makes the selection seem more positive, negative, or neutral. Ask yourself, "How does the passage make me feel?" The author chooses a tone to make a certain impression on readers. So take that impression into account.

2. Look for subjective words (some reading tests call such words "biased") that indicate the author's attitude or opinion about the topic. In other words, look for words with positive or negative connotations. If there are several, think about what attitude they all add up to. If you don't find any, the author's point of view might be objective.

3. Look for any suggestions that the author is being figurative rather than literal. Do the words seem appropriate for the situation?

▶ **Implied Main Idea.** Use the topic and the details to determine the missing main idea.

1. Look for the topic of the passage by noticing repeated words, phrases, and ideas.

2. Find the details. Pay attention to how they are organized (the pattern of organization).

3. Think about what all the details have in common.

4. Create a sentence around this idea.

5. See if one of the answers closely matches the answer you came up with.

6. Turn the answer you chose into a question to see if the details of the passage support it.

▶ **Fact and Opinion.** Facts can be proven; opinions cannot be verified.

1. Double-check for words that are suspicious, such as *all, none, most beautiful, smartest, best,* and so on.

2. ALWAYS ask, "Can this be proven? How?" Just because something is stated in the passage, that does not make it a fact. Can this be proven by observation, looked up, duplicated, or found?

Skills Related to Organization

▶ **Understanding an Outline.** Each point of the correct answer must be directly supported by the text and follow the same order as it appeared in the text. Be patient with this type of question, and go point by point. Ask the following questions:

1. Are the points of the outline too broad, too narrow, or just right?

2. Do they have direct support in the reading?

3. Do the points of the outline match the order of the reading?

4. Do the answers match the same pattern of organization as is in the passage?

5. If any one point is wrong, then the entire answer is wrong.

▶ **Proving Which Is the Best Summary.** A summary usually needs the following:

1. The topic (a must);

2. The main idea (a must); and

3. The major supporting details (usually required but not absolutely necessary).

If two answers are similar, look for something that is mentioned in one answer that is not in the other answer. If that "something" is a key detail, then that will probably be the best answer. If it is a minor or irrelevant detail, then choose the other answer.

*A note about minor details: including these often (not always) makes the answer wrong because it focuses on unimportant information. However, you will have to take each answer case by case and evaluate it within the context of the passage and compare it with the other answers to see which one is the most complete summary.

▶ **Interpreting a Table, Chart, or Graph.** Depending on what type of visual is presented, you will need to follow steps similar to these:

1. Read the title of the table, chart, or graph carefully. (Know the main idea.)

2. Read the captions, categories or headings of rows and columns, or the labels on x- and y-axes carefully. (Understand how the information is organized.)

3. Notice the meaning of each color used. (Understand what the colors represent.)

4. Think critically about the implications of the headings, the numbers, and the way the information is presented.

5. Double-check that your chosen answer is supported by the details of the table, chart, or graph.

INDEX